The Complete Art of Cooking

1,000 Techniques and Recipes

© 2004 COPYRIGHT SA, 12, Villa de Loucine – 75014 Paris, France
© 2006 Rebo International b.v.

This edition reprinted in 2009.

Text: Stéphane Lagorce
Photographs: Michel Barberousse
Chief editor: Sylvie Girard
Editors: Sophie Bouet, Pierre Gourdé, Priscilla Haddak, Gwenaël Le Cossec, Andréa Le Naour, Jacqueline Leymarie,
Nicole Leymarie, Jean-Claude Marguerite, Gildaz Mazurié de Keroualin, Jeanne Pothier, Isabelle Raimond, Julie Rochette,
Audrey Toudic, Dominique Trépeau, Edith Walter.
Concept: Copyright
Layout: Copyright SA, Jacques Hennaux
Cover design: Irène de Moucheron
Typesetting and pre-press services: A. R. Garamond, Prague, Czech Republic
Translators: Judith Phillips, Matthew Clarke, Vivien Groves and Jennifer Forbes for
First Edition Translations, Cambridge, UK
Editor: Sally Heavens for First Edition Translations, Cambridge, UK
Proofreading: Sarah Dunham

Printed exclusively for MJF Media.

ISBN: 978 90 366 1947 9

The Complete Art of Cooking

1,000 Techniques and Recipes

Sylvie Girard

Text: Stéphane Lagorce
Photographs: Michel Barberousse

Cooking in any context

Foreword

A beautiful cookery book is a collection of recipes illustrated with mouthwatering photographs, but also a repository of know-how from the simplest to the most technical. Once you have done your shopping and prepared your ingredients, then the real adventure begins: transforming these carefully selected foodstuffs into appetizing dishes. A complete guide to cookery in general and French "savoir faire en cuisine" in particular is here placed at your fingertips. There are innumerable recipes that need a trick or two to bring to fruition—from fried eggs to terrines, from gratins to roasts, from papillotes to grills, from tarts to soufflés, without forgetting sauces and creams. Precision is indispensable in cooking: this can be learned, and once you have mastered it, you will be ready to tackle all kinds of processes. This practical guide aims to respond to any context that may arise, from the most traditional to the most modern: cooking pasta correctly or preparing an Asian stir-fry in a wok; making your own doughnuts or jam; cooking chili con carne, fish soup, or Tandoori chicken. Here is a quick preview: Eggs and cheeses: all the different ways of cooking an egg, but also omelets, fondues, soufflés, gratins, pizzas, and quiches. Rice, pasta, and cereals: risotto, paella, and Cantonese rice; rice and semolina puddings; sauces for pasta, couscous, and salt-cured pork with lentils; meals based on crêpes. Summer and winter vegetables: soups, ratatouilles, gratins and purées; braised, fried, and sautéed vegetables. Fish and seafood: poaching and court-bouillon; papillotes and kebabs; steaming and sauces. Poultry and game: fricassées and civets; ballottines and rillettes; stuffing and roasting. Lamb and mutton: mixed-grill and navarin; mutton stew, leg of lamb, cassoulet, Irish stew, and curry. Beef and veal: fondue and stew; roasting and sautéing; pot-au-feu and blanquette; beef bourguignon with coarse salt; ribs and barbecue cuts. Pork and charcuterie: grills and sauerkraut; pâtés and potées; sausages and terrines. Fruit and candies: crumbles and pies; clafoutis and compotes; marmalades and jellies; chutneys and doughnuts. Desserts and cakes: biscuits and pancakes. Passing on the tricks of the trade, revealing all the various stages of a recipe, right up to its final presentation: these are the aims of this book, which promises to be your constant companion in the kitchen.

Sylvie Girard

Contents

Summer vegetables

pages 12 through 69

Winter vegetables

pages 70 through 127

Rice, pasta, and cereals

pages 128 through 185

Beef and veal

pages 186 through 243

Contents

Lamb and mutton

pages 244 through 301

Pork

pages 302 through 359

Poultry and game

pages 360 through 417

Fish and crustaceans

pages 418 through 475

Contents

Eggs and cheese

pages 478 through 533

Desserts and candies

pages 534 through 591

Fruit

pages 592 through 649

Know-how

Recipes

Pastries

pages 650 through 707

Know-how

Recipes

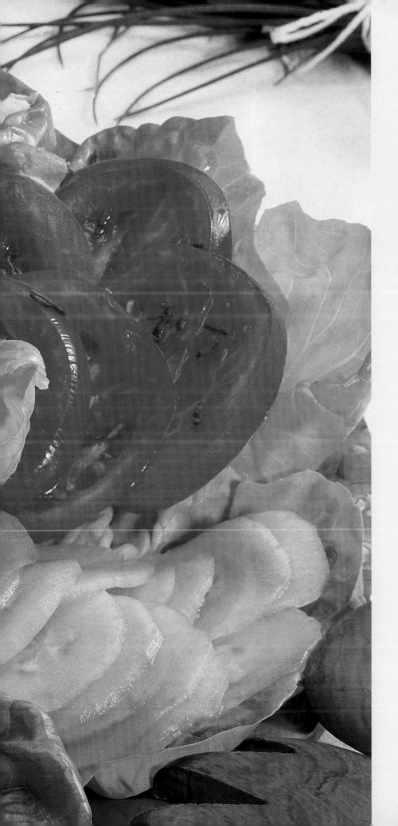

Summer vegetables

The principle of boiling

Boiling is the most common method applied to green vegetables. It requires careful attention, however, as the cooking time must be exact.

Boiling broccoli

For $2^1/4$ lb (1 kg) broccoli, pour 2 quarts (2 liters) water into a large pot and bring to the boil. Add salt and trimmed broccoli into the boiling water, making sure that the florets are the same size, so that they cook evenly. You could also add 2 cloves of peeled and crushed garlic to the cooking water. The broccoli will be ready in 25-30 minutes; they should be tender but remain intact. Drain them carefully, without crushing them, as the florets are delicate. The peeled broccoli stems should ideally be cooked apart, for a slightly longer time.

Boiling green beans and mange-tout

Bring plenty of water to the boil—the volume must be at least five times greater than that of the vegetables to be cooked. Add $1^1/2$ tsp (8 g) salt per quart (liter) of water. Plunge the green beans or mange-tout into iced water for a few minutes, then drain them quickly. Add the vegetables to the water when it starts to boil fiercely. Bring the water back to the boil and keep it bubbling vigorously over a high heat. Do not cover. Cook for 3–8 minutes, to taste. Check their progress by putting a bean into the iced water at regular intervals and biting it to assess its consistency. If the beans are to be eaten hot or warm, drain them and place them on a serving dish with butter. If they are to be used in a salad, plunge them into the iced water to cut short the cooking process.

Blanching spinach

Bring to the boil a large amount of water. Reckon on 5 quarts (5 liters) water for $2^1/4$ lb (1 kg) spinach. Add $1^1/2$ tsp (8g) salt for every quart (liter) of water. When the water is boiling fiercely, add the spinach (having previously washed it thoroughly). Bring back to the boil over high heat, stirring continuously. Do not cover. Drain the blanched spinach immediately in a large colander, pressing down gently to squeeze out as much water as possible. If the spinach is to be eaten hot, drain, then put it in a serving dish with butter. If it is to be used in a cold dish (terrine, ramekin, etc.), leave to cool in the colander, then refresh it immediately by sprinkling with cold water and stirring. Leave to drain for a few minutes, then pick up the spinach in handfuls and squeeze out the remaining liquid.

Boiling asparagus

Bring to the boil a large amount of water. Add 1$\frac{1}{2}$ tsp (8g) salt for every quart (liter) of water. Put the asparagus shoots into the liquid, making sure that there is enough room in the saucepan to keep them separate from each other. Bring back to the boil, then keep the temperature moderate but constant. Put a clean, white dishcloth over the asparagus to make sure the temperature is even in the pan. Cook for 15–25 minutes, depending on their thickness. Check their progress by piercing the center of a shoot with the tip of a knife. If the asparagus is to be eaten hot or warm, drain and then place them on a serving dish. If, by contrast, they are part of a cold recipe, plunge them into water with ice cubes to cool them quickly. Drain and then serve with a good herb vinaigrette.

Boiling petits pois

This method, known to the French as "à l'anglaise," simply involves cooking them in a large amount of salted boiling water. They will be ready after about 20 minutes. You can flavor the cooking water by adding a sprig of fresh fennel. Petits pois "à l'anglaise" are served on their own, with butter.

Steaming artichokes

Pour water into the lower part of a steamer and the artichokes in the top, removing any black or broken leaves; bring to the boil and cover. Cook for 30–40 minutes, depending on their size. Serve the artichokes hot with a vinaigrette, or leave to cool if you prefer to eat them cold. Cooking vegetables in this way has the benefit of not "leaching" them and so conserves their nutritional value to the maximum. Avoid using a pressure cooker, however, as this alters their taste and texture.

Hints

At the height of summer, iced vegetable soups are a real treat; furthermore, they are very easy to make. Always choose the best vegetables, of supreme freshness and preferably of small dimensions (these are the tastiest). Prepare these soups a few hours before eating—this makes them even tastier, as the flavors will be more thoroughly blended. You can also put them briefly into the freezer, in order to serve them extremely chilled. Andalusian gazpacho is the most well-known cold soup, but there are plenty more, especially in the South of France and other hot regions.

Iced cucumber soup

This soup is very easy to prepare, provided you have a blender available. It involves making a cucumber pulp seasoned with lemon and dill. To serve 4, peel and seed 3 cucumbers. Peel 2 new, white onions. Put the cucumber flesh and the onions in the blender. When the mixture is uniform and thoroughly blended, pour it into a salad bowl. Add 2 tbsp chopped dill, the juice of 1 lemon, and $^2/_3$ cup (15 cl) mineral water (without gas). Add salt and pepper, then leave in the refrigerator for at least 2 hours. You can also add a generous glass of liquid cream to this recipe—in this case, omit the mineral water.

Cold tomato soup

To serve 4, put 3 cups (75 cl) tomato juice in the refrigerator before starting to prepare this chilled soup. Peel 1 clove garlic, chop finely, and crush with 1 tbsp olive oil. Peel 2–3 red, but firm, tomatoes over a soup dish (to collect the juice), seed them, and cut the pulp into small pieces. Mix the tomato juice with the garlic mixture, the tomatoes, and their juice; add 2 pinches of sugar, celery salt, and pepper to taste, a little chopped fennel leaf, and a small bunch of chervil. Put everything in the blender to obtain a uniform liquid. Chill until just before serving and garnish with sprigs of chervil.

Iced cucumber soup

Gazpacho for 6–8

Antillean acassan

This cold soup from the Caribbean has a highly distinctive flavor. Traditionally, the grains of corn are soaked for 24 hours, but if you are in a hurry, you can simply scald them briefly. Grind them in a mortar until you obtain a paste: reckon on 10½ oz (300 g) grains to serve 4. Thin the paste with water, removing any impurities that rise to the surface. Pass the resulting purée through a sieve. Leave the liquid you collect to rest, then pour it into a saucepan and heat gently. When it starts to boil, gradually pour in 4 cups (1 liter) milk, stirring with a wooden spoon to stop lumps forming. Add salt and 1–2 pinches cinnamon, 2 tbsp cane syrup, and a touch of Cayenne pepper. Leave to cool thoroughly. Serve cold or iced.

1 Gazpacho originally came from Seville, but it is now found in numerous varieties. This cold soup based on tomato, cucumber, onion, bell pepper, and bread with no crust is traditionally prepared in a large pottery tureen, which gives it a special flavor. Peel 3 lb 5 oz (1.5 kg) plump ripe tomatoes, keeping aside one or two firmer ones.

2 Wash 1 green bell pepper, cut it in two and remove all the seeds and white partitions; cut into strips. Put roughly half to one side. Peel and slice 1 cucumber; put aside one third. Peel and thinly slice 2 onions and 3 cloves of garlic. Put everything in the blender, add 2 tbsp vinegar and 1 glass olive oil.

3 Add 9 oz (250 g) stale bread without its crust and, if necessary, a little water. Pour the mixture into a bowl and chill. Taste just before serving and add salt, along with a few ice cubes and cold water, depending on whether you want the gazpacho thick or runny. Serve the reserved vegetables, cut into small dice, allowing guests to garnish the soup to their taste.

Sautéed carrots, chives, and new onions for 4

1 Prepare the vegetables. Peel 1 lb (450 g) carrots and cut them julienne style into thin sticks; set aside. Peel 9 oz (250 g) new onions; cut each into 6 pieces of roughly equal size. Untie a bunch of chives; wash thoroughly, then drain, discarding any black or broken stems. Cut into pieces 2 in (5 cm) long. Pat dry all the vegetables with paper towels.

2 Cook the vegetables. Heat 3 tbsp sunflower oil in the wok; when it is very hot, add all the vegetables in one go. They must not take up more than one third of the volume available in the wok—otherwise they will cook too slowly. Add salt and pepper. Sauté over very high heat for 3 minutes, stirring continuously with a spatula or long-handled spoon.

3 Add about 3½ tbsp (5 cl) water, still over high heat. Taste the vegetables from time to time, and stop cooking when the desired texture is reached. Put them in a serving dish. They can be eaten alone, with just salt and pepper, or with a dash of soy sauce or a few drops of sesame oil.

4 Serve immediately. This delicious recipe is an excellent accompaniment to roast pork or grilled chicken. It can also be the highlight of a vegetarian menu, along with brown rice. In this case, you can do as the Chinese, and sprinkle a few crushed cashew nuts on top.

Hints

Vegetables sautéed Chinese style are colorful, deliciously crispy, and packed with vitamins and flavor. This fast cooking method shows up any defects in the ingredients, so it is essential to acquire the best produce available. The first step, however, is to buy a good wok from an Asian store. The cooking process with a wok usually involves two phases: in the first, the vegetables are sautéed intensely, with or without meat, to bring out their color slightly; after that, a small amount of liquid (bouillon, water, soy sauce) is added to obtain a full-bodied juice. A wide range of vegetables can be cooked in this way: carrots, onions, broccoli, green beans, mange-tout, zucchini, bell peppers. When meat is required, opt for thin slices of pork loin or chicken. Be aware that this cooking technique is not suited to small vegetables or small pieces. We present two recipes for mixed vegetables sautéed in a wok, which you can modify to taste, by incorporating alternative ingredients such as sliced fennel, strips of cabbage, or bean sprouts.

Choosing a wok

Ken Hom, born in the United States of America of Cantonese parents, is the author of several Chinese cookbooks that staunchly propound the use of the wok, even in Western cooking. He maintains that "the authentic flavors of China are only achieved by means of the appropriate techniques and equipment. In this respect, the wok is by far the most useful tool. In my personal experience, I find that the wok most suited to the West is one with a 13^1/$_2$-in (35-cm) handle and a slightly flattened bottom, which gives it stability on a European-style cooker. Although this formula may appear to be a contradiction of the traditional, round-bottomed wok, which concentrates all the heat in the center of the pan, it is a necessary adaptation. A wok must be quite heavy, if possible made of sheet steel rather than aluminum or stainless steel, as these materials do not stand up well to the high temperatures demanded by some recipes. I do not like woks with a non-stick finish: not only are they more expensive, but also they cannot become impregnated with oils or aromas in the same way as an ordinary wok, which adds flavor to the food you are going to cook in it."

Sautéed mange-tout, green beans, and diced ham for 4

1 Trim 12^1/$_2$ oz (350 g) green beans and 12^1/$_2$ oz (350 g) mange-tout. Wash and pat them dry with paper towels. Cut the mange-tout into thick strips and slice the green beans lengthwise. Cut 7 oz (200 g) cooked ham into slices ^{3}/$_{16}$ in (5 mm) thick, then slice into strips with a knife or pair of scissors. (Uncooked ham, such as Bayonne or Parma ham, can also be used). Cut the white part of a leek into thin strips.

2 Heat 3 tbsp sunflower oil in a wok. When the oil is hot, add the vegetables in one go. Add salt and pepper. Sauté over very high heat for 3 minutes, stirring continuously with a long-handled spoon or chopsticks. Add about 3^1/$_2$ tbsp (5 cl) water, along with the ham and 3^1/$_2$ tbsp (5 cl) soy sauce. Cook over high heat for another minute, still stirring continuously, until the vegetables are crispy.

3 Having checked that they are sufficiently cooked, put them into a serving dish or porcelain bowls. Sprinkle with a finely chopped bunch of fresh cilantro or chervil. This recipe is ideal with cooked cereals, such as semolina or bulgur wheat, but you can also combine it with plain white rice.

Glazed baby onions for 4

1 Prepare 1 lb 2 oz (500 g) new onions. Peel them one by one in a bowl of water, to prevent them from stinging your eyes. Choose baby onions, known as "grelots," either white or yellow, with a round bulb. Cut the roots from the bottom and the stem from the top. (The onions can be prepared in advance and kept in plastic wrap in the lower part of the refrigerator.)

2 Strain the onions and put them in a saucepan with $1/4$ cup (60 g) sugar, 3 pinches salt, $1\,1/2$ oz (40 g) butter, and $1\,2/3$ cups (40 cl) water. Bring to the boil over medium heat and cook for around 15 minutes. Check the progress of the onions by piercing them gently with the tip of a knife. When they are cooked, but still firm, scoop them out of the saucepan with a slotted spoon. Take care not to squash them.

3 Boil the cooking water; when it turns slightly syrupy, plunge the cooked onions back into it, stirring with a wooden spatula to make sure that they are thoroughly coated. Make sure they are not crushed against the sides of the pan. They should be shiny and slightly colored.

4 Serve glazed onions piping hot with meat, such as a rib of beef, a sirloin steak, or veal cutlets. To obtain a brown glazing, continue cooking over a fairly high heat and allow the mixture to caramelize, stirring continuously and ensuring that it does not burn, as this will give the onions an acrid taste.

General points

When cooked slowly in salted water with sugar and butter, vegetables acquire an enticingly shiny glaze. There are two types of glazing. In the first, known as white glazing, the vegetables gleam and conserve their natural colors, while in the second—brown glazing—the sugar is caramelized and stains the dish a mouthwatering dark color. The vegetables used for glazing must be small: new carrots and onions are therefore ideal. If they are bigger, they must be cut with a knife into oblong shapes the size of a walnut. Zucchini and turnips can be prepared in this way. Both white and brown glazed vegetables usually accompany roast or broiled meat, such as ribs of beef or leg of lamb. They are often served in an assortment, making their bright colors stand out even more on a table. Glazed white vegetables, particularly onions, are traditionally used to garnish dishes with a white sauce, such as blanquettes, while brown ones accompany recipes in a brown sauce, such as matelote or sautéed dishes.

glazed vegetables

Assortment of glazed vegetables for 4

1 Peel 5¹/₂ oz (150 g) small, new turnips and 5¹/₂ oz (150 g) new carrots; chop 5¹/₂ oz (150 g) zucchini. To allow the vegetables to cook evenly, cut them into similar sizes. Use the small new turnips as a guide for cutting the carrots and zucchini.

2 To achieve a more decorative presentation, cut the pieces of carrot and zucchini into "cloves" or "olives" with a small knife: trim the ends to round them off and scrape the sides to eliminate any irregularities..

3 Once the vegetables are all prepared, put them into a large saucepan, add ¹/₄ cup (60 g) sugar, 3 pinches salt, and 1¹/₂–1³⁄4 oz (40–50 g) butter; pour in 1 ²/₃ cups (40 cl) water and bring to the boil over medium heat. Cook for 15–20 minutes without covering the saucepan.

4 Check the progress of the vegetables by piercing them with the tip of a knife. When they are cooked, but still somewhat firm, take them out of the saucepan with slotted spoon and put them on a plate. Keep boiling the broth. As soon as it turns slightly syrupy, put the assorted vegetables back in and stir them, so that they are thoroughly coated. Serve piping hot with, for example, a braised white meat, such as a leg or shoulder of veal.

Ratatouille for 6-8

1 Ratatouille is a vegetable stew originating from the Nice area in France, although it is now characteristic of the cuisine throughout Provence. It is simmered with olive oil and spices and served alongside poultry, meat, and fish. It is also delicious cold, with a dash of lemon juice or vinegar. The principle consists of precooking the different vegetables separately, before bringing them together to be braised.

2 Prepare the vegetables. Wash and wipe dry 1 lb 2 oz (500 g) eggplant, 1 lb 2 oz (500 g) zucchini, 1 lb 2 oz (500 g) red bell peppers, and 1 lb 2 oz (500 g) tomatoes. Cut the eggplants and zucchini into slices $3/8$ in (1 cm) thick. It is useless to peel the tomatoes; choose ripe, aromatic specimens at the height of the season, with plenty of flesh. Dry the slices of eggplant and zucchini with paper towels if they are still very wet.

3 Cut the bell peppers into two, remove the seeds and inner membranes, then chop the remainder into big squares (not thin strips). Remove the peduncle from the tomatoes, then cut them into four roughly equal pieces. There is no need to seed the tomatoes. Once all these vegetables have been prepared, keep them separate, without mixing, as they will be cooked individually at first.

4 Peel 4 onions and slice thinly. Peel and chop 4 cloves garlic. Add salt and pepper to the eggplant, then brown them in a skillet with 3 tbsp olive oil. Remove from the skillet and set aside. Next, sauté the zucchini in the skillet, adding a little more olive oil. Remove and set aside; repeat the procedure with the bell peppers.

5 Heat 3 tbsp olive oil in a cast-iron saucepan, then sauté the onions for 5 minutes, stirring continuously, until they are slightly golden. Add the tomatoes and cook for a further 5 minutes, then add all the other previously sautéed vegetables. Mix, add a sprig of thyme, a bay leaf, salt, and pepper.

6 Cover the saucepan, lower the heat, and cook gently for about 30 minutes, stirring occasionally. Add the chopped garlic and cook for a further 5 minutes; taste and adjust the seasoning, remove the thyme and bay leaf, then serve immediately.

ratatouille and braised vegetables

Braised fennel with black olives for 4

1 Fennel is distinguished by a flavor slightly reminiscent of aniseed. It is used to accompany poultry and baked fish, such as sea bream, as well as bass grilled with olive oil. Braised fennel is also appreciated as a main dish by vegetarians, served with a starchy accompaniment like potatoes or pilaf rice. The secret is to brown the fennel initially and then cook it slowly with condiments, in a covered pan.

2 Prepare 4–6 fennel. Remove the first two hard leaves on the outside, along with the stems on the top. Peel them to remove any fibers and woody parts. Put aside the fine green foliage at the tips of the stems; these can be kept in the refrigerator and used later as a herb, in the same way as dill and chervil, with raw vegetables or in a soup.

3 Then cut the fennel into two or four pieces, depending on their size. Place the pieces face down in a saucepan with 4 tbsp olive oil, over fairly high heat. At the start of the cooking process, press down on the pieces of fennel with a spatula for a few seconds to seal them.

Tip

Fennel seeds are prized for their distinctive aroma, and they were once considered a symbol of strength. They can be mixed with dill and caraway seeds and chewed to refresh the breath. Fennel reseeds itself in a garden and multiplies very quickly.

4 Leave to cook for 10 minutes, then turn the pieces over and cook them for a further 5 minutes. Pour in 1 2/3 cups (40 cl) chicken stock bouillon (or water), until the fennel is just covered. (You can also use lemon juice diluted with water or the cooking juices of roast meat or chicken, thinned with water and with the fat removed.)

5 Add salt, pepper, and a sprig of thyme, along with 5 1/2 oz (150 g) drained black olives. Bring to the boil. Cover and cook for 30 minutes over medium heat; the cooking juice will be sufficiently reduced to form a pale, slightly syrupy sauce. Coat the fennel with this sauce, sprinkle with 2 tbsp chopped flat parsley, and serve very hot.

Macedoine of vegetables with mayonnaise for 4

1 Prepare the vegetables. Peel 9 oz (250 g) carrots and 5¹/₂ oz (150 g) turnips. Wash, drain, and cut with a sharp, fairly long knife into four pieces ³/₁₆ in (5 mm) thick. Cut these pieces into sticks of the same size, then dice. Set aside on a plate. Line up 3¹/₂ oz (100 g) green beans, then dice to the same size as the carrot and turnip. Wash thoroughly and set aside.

2 Shell 3¹/₂ oz (100 g) petits pois into a dish. Boil in plenty of salted water. Cook the vegetables separately. Boil the water fiercely and add the green beans, cooking them uncovered for 2–3 minutes. Cool them immediately in a bowl of iced water. Drain and set aside. Follow the same procedure for each of the other vegetables. They will all require a different cooking time, so test them by tasting.

3 Prepare a stiff mayonnaise. Place an egg yolk in a bowl with 1 tbsp mustard and beat. Leave to rest for 1 minute. Gradually add 1 scant cup (20 cl) oil, mixing briskly with a small beater. Add salt and pepper, then set aside. Put the vegetables (thoroughly drained) into a salad bowl. Add the mayonnaise and mix.

4 Season to taste with salt and pepper. Pour the mixture onto a serving platter. Even out the top surface and decorate with twirls of mayonnaise (use a glazing bag), a tomato cut in the form of a rose, and a few quarters of hard-boiled egg. This dish does not keep well and should be eaten within 24 hours.

General points

A macedoine is made up of vegetables in small pieces (sliced green beans, diced carrots, and turnips) and petits pois. Some recipes also add dwarf kidney beans and potatoes, but these make the preparation unnecessarily burdensome. When made at home, this dish requires a certain amount of time, but it is a tasty recipe that cannot be compared to any canned substitute. It can be used to garnish meat and poultry, in combination with butter, oven cooking juices, crème fraîche, and herbs. When served cold with mayonnaise, macedoine can provide a stuffing for tomatoes or a filling for pie-crust pastries, or it can be set in aspic. It can also be served as a cold starter, accompanied by hardboiled eggs or cold fish. The Sicilian caponata is another form of macedoine, with distinctive ingredients, and there is no limit to the number of colorful alternatives on offer.

Tip

Macedoine sauce is an original complement for leftover meat: it is a reduction of shallots in vinegar, combined with a brown roux with slices of cooked carrot, chopped gherkins, crumbled hard-boiled eggs, capers, and mashed anchovies.

Caponata
for 6

1 This Sicilian specialty based on vegetables simmered in olive oil, accompanied by capers, olives, pine nuts, and, occasionally, anchovy fillets, is always served cold. It is characterized by its slightly acid taste. It can be served as an appetizer, often in the company of sliced, hard-boiled eggs, a salad of baby octopus, sardines in oil or strips of poutargue, pieces of lemon, and chopped parsley.

2 Wash and wipe 2 eggplants; cut off the peduncle and chop them into small dice ($3/16$ in/5–6 mm wide); peel and dice 2 onions; put 2 stalks celery side by side and chop them finely; wash and wipe 3 red bell peppers, remove the seeds and inner membranes, then cut them into small dice, in the same way as the eggplants. Peel, seed, and dice 3 plump tomatoes.

3 Heat 2–3 tbsp olive oil in a large frying pan. Braise the vegetables, apart from the tomatoes, in the oil for 20 minutes. Add the cubes of tomato, 1 tbsp tomato concentrate, $1/3$ cup + $1^1/2$ tbsp (10 cl) white wine, and 20 chopped green olives, then cook over fairly high heat for around 10 minutes. Stir regularly with a wooden spoon to make sure that the ingredients are cooked evenly.

4 Add salt, pepper, $1^3/4$ oz (50 g) capers, 4 tbsp vinegar, and $1^3/4$ oz (50 g) pine nuts. Adjust seasoning to taste. Put the caponata in a vegetable dish and allow to cool thoroughly before serving. It is advisable to prepare the caponata well in advance (even the day before serving); keep it in the refrigerator.

Petits pois "bonne femme" for 4

1 This is a classic recipe that deserves to be rediscovered. The peas are slowly simmered with onions and diced bacon slices. Do not forget to blanch the bacon, to avoid giving the dish an excessively smoky flavor. Cut 4$\frac{1}{2}$ oz (125 g) smoked bacon slices into small dice and swiftly blanch in boiling water; drain and pat dry with paper towels.

2 Peel around twenty small new onions. Melt 1 oz (30 g) butter over medium heat in a saucepan or deep skillet. Add the peeled onions and blanched bacon and season with salt and pepper. Simmer over low heat for 5 minutes, then remove the onions and diced bacon with a slotted spoon. Mix in 1 tsp flour and cook for 1 minute, stirring continuously; put the onions and the bacon back in the pan.

Petits pois "à l'anglaise"

In this recipe, the peas are simply boiled in water. Bring to the boil plenty of water (the volume should be at least five times greater than that of the vegetables to be cooked). Add 1$\frac{1}{2}$ tsp (8 g) salt per quart (liter) of water. To serve 4, plunge 1 lb (450 g) shelled petits pois into iced water for a few minutes, then roughly drain them. When the water is boiling fiercely, add the peas. Bring back to the boil, maintaining a high, constant temperature. Do not cover. Cook for 2–3 minutes, according to taste. Monitor the cooking process at regular intervals by plunging a petit pois into the iced water then tasting it to test the consistency. Next, drain the petits pois and put them into a dish with 3$\frac{1}{2}$ oz (100 g) butter (in dabs); season with salt and pepper and serve.

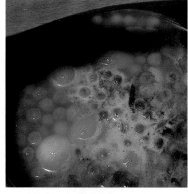

3 Add 1$\frac{1}{4}$ cups (30 cl) piping hot chicken bouillon and 1 lb 2 oz (500 g) shelled petits pois; mix, add a bouquet garni and cook, covered and boiling gently, for 25 minutes. Next, take out the bouquet garni, check the seasoning and serve in a soup dish. Petits pois "bonne femme" are an ideal accompaniment for roast meat and poultry, as well as magret of duck.

Petits pois "à la française" for 4

1 In this dish with a subtle, slightly sweet taste, the petits pois are also simmered slowly in cooking juices. The inclusion of lettuce adds a delightful aroma. Wash a lettuce heart and chop roughly. Peel 15 small new onions, removing the base and roots.

2 Put the lettuce and onions in a saucepan with 1 lb 2 oz (500 g) petits pois. Add a bouquet garni, 1 oz (30 g) butter, 1 tsp sugar, and season with salt and pepper. Pour in $2/3$ cup (15 cl) cold water. Bring to the boil, stirring gently. Cover and cook over low heat for 25 minutes.

3 Remove the bouquet garni, check the seasoning, and add a bunch of chopped chervil. Serve in a soup plate. Petits pois à la française are an ideal accompaniment for delicate meats like veal, lamb, and pigeon, and most particularly for veal olives.

Variant

Southwest France offers another way of cooking petits pois, providing a superb garnish for duck magret and confit. To serve 4, peel 12 small onions, without removing the base (so that they remain whole); melt 3 tbsp goose fat in a large saucepan; brown the onions, being careful not to burn them; add $1^3/_4$ lb (800 g) shelled petits pois and $5^1/_2$ oz (150 g) cooked ham, diced small; moisten with a little warm water, then add 2 lettuce hearts and season with salt and pepper. Cook gently for 30 minutes, adding a little warm water halfway through, if required. Adjust seasoning to taste and serve.

General points

Among the countless specialties from southeastern France, the small stuffed vegetables from Nice are in a class of their own, forming a range of summer dishes that are not only delicious, but also highly colorful and decorative. These recipes are based on tomatoes, eggplants, and zucchini, hollowed out and filled with a range of stuffings, such as rice, bread and garlic, or meat. The results can be served piping hot, warm, or chilled, according to the occasion. Ideally, reckon on one tomato, one eggplant, one zucchini, and one pepper per person. The choice of vegetables is vital because, for the best visual effect, you must select slightly round, but not overly plump, specimens; fortunately, the new varieties of zucchini and eggplants now available are perfectly suited to this dish, although it is also possible to prepare this recipe successfully with normal-size vegetables, cut to your requirements.

Tip

Some French provinces boast a culinary tradition dominated by meat, charcuterie, or dairy produce, particularly to the north. On the Riviera, however, the opposite is the case, as the basis of the diet is vegetables and herbs, with fragrant aromas and flavors nurtured by the sun and set off perfectly by olive oil.

1 To serve 4, you need the following ingredients: 2 small eggplants, 2 zucchini, 2 red and 2 green bell peppers, 2 onions, 4 tomatoes, 1 clove garlic, 4 slices Mozzarella, 2 eggs, 7 oz (200 g) minced meat, 1¹/₄ cups (250 g) white rice, breadcrumbs, olive oil, 2 sprigs thyme, 1 small bunch parsley, 1 sprig basil, salt, and pepper.

2 Start by preparing the bell peppers: cut them into two, crossways, to obtain eight shells ready to be stuffed. Carefully remove all the seeds and white inner membranes. Pass them quickly under cold, running water, wipe dry with paper towels, then set aside.

3 Wash and wipe the zucchini. Cut each one into pieces 2–2¹/₂ in (5–6 cm) long. To hollow out the flesh of the zucchini conveniently and uniformly, use an apple corer. Meanwhile, cook the rice in the water, then drain and allow it to cool. Mash the pulp of 1 tomato.

4 Cut the eggplants into large pieces, then incise a cross in the flesh with a sharp knife. Arrange them in a baking pan (previously coated with a thin layer of oil), with the incised part facing upward. Cook at 350 °F (180 °C) for about 30 minutes, then remove from the oven. Allow to cool slightly before removing the cooked flesh, which should now come away easily. Set both the flesh and the hollowed shells aside.

5 Fill a large saucepan with water, bring to the boil, plunge in the pieces of zucchini, and blanch for a few minutes. Drain and pat dry with paper towels. Set aside on a dishcloth. Bring the water back to the boil, add the emptied bell peppers, and blanch them in the same way. Remove and dry them thoroughly, as before.

6 Prepare the stuffings for the vegetables. For the bell peppers: cook a sliced onion in a little olive oil, mix it with the cooked rice, the tomato pulp, a sprig of thyme, and half the chopped parsley, and season with salt and pepper. For the eggplants: brown a chopped onion in a little oil, add the eggplant flesh (chopped), a few breadcrumbs, chopped garlic, the remaining thyme, salt, and pepper.

7 Stuff the hollowed eggplants with the onion mixture and place a slice of Mozzarella on top. For the zucchini: break the eggs into a shallow bowl, mix in the minced meat, then add the basil and the rest of the chopped parsley. Stuff the zucchini pieces with this mixture, preferably using a fairly large glazing bag.

8 Fill the hollowed bell peppers with the rice stuffing. If any stuffing mix is left over, spread it over the bottom of an oven dish and set the petits farcis on top. Sprinkle with oil. Put the dish halfway up the oven and cook for 20–25 minutes at 350 °F (180 °C). Serve as a garnish to dishes such as lamb cutlets, ribs of veal, or grilled entrecote.

Artichokes "à la barigoule" for 4

1 In the Provençal language, the word "barigoulo" means both a wide-rimmed felt hat, traditionally worn by peasants, and a mushroom that is eaten broiled or stuffed. It also refers to a technique for cooking artichokes, either stuffed with ham and mushrooms or braised (as in this case)—perhaps because the results slightly resemble fricasséed mushrooms.

2 Prepare 8 small artichokes. Cut off their woody stems and use scissors to chop the leaves to a third of their height. Hollow out the center and extract the heart and choke with a spoon. Cut a lemon into two, then rub over all the exposed areas of the artichokes to prevent them from turning black. Wash 3 tomatoes, remove their peduncles, and cut them into quarters. Peel and chop 2 cloves garlic and 2 onions.

3 Blanch 5^1/$_2$ oz (150 g) diced, sliced, rindless bacon in a saucepan of boiling water; drain and pat dry with paper towels, then set aside. Pour some olive oil into a large, shallow skillet. Add the bacon and brown, stirring continuously, for 5 minutes. Add the finely chopped onion and garlic, then mix thoroughly with the bacon and continue cooking for 5 minutes, still stirring.

4 Add the tomatoes. Season with salt and pepper and cook for a further 5 minutes over medium heat. Heat 4 tbsp olive oil in a saucepan and brown the artichokes for 10 minutes over medium heat. Pour on ^{2}/$_3$ cup (15 cl) white wine, add salt and pepper, and cook for 5 minutes. Add the tomato mixture and a little thyme, then simmer, covered, for 20-25 minutes.

5 Complete the dish by adding a chopped bunch of basil and adjust seasoning to taste. Artichokes "à la barigoule" are served hot with grilled meat (lamb, veal, beef) or chilled as an appetizer and served in soup plates. The accompanying sauce can be enhanced with lemon juice and fresh, chopped herbs.

General points

Artichokes are eaten boiled, served with vinaigrette, or braised in a sauce. Artichokes "à la barigoule," a dish usually prepared at the height of summer, provides perhaps the best example of the latter option. Look for small, tender artichokes with a violet tinge for this recipe; if they are really small, they will not have developed a choke and so can be eaten whole. In this case, double the quantity of artichokes.

Artichokes "à la barigoule" and tomato confit

Other produce based on tomatoes

Specialist Italian groceries sell sun-dried tomatoes. These are generally small specimens, cut into two, seeded, and dried naturally in the sun. They can be eaten whole or incorporated into sauces or pasta dishes. Also on the market are petals of tomato confit. Here, the fruits are peeled, seeded, and cut into quarters; these are salted, slowly baked in olive oil and, finally, dried. The petals are generally $1\frac{1}{2}$–2 in (4–5 cm) long and their pulp is soft. They can be eaten alone or as part of an hors d'oeuvre, or as an enrichment for a salad or plain rice.

1 Select $2\frac{1}{4}$ lb (1 kg) ripe tomatoes with firm flesh. Wash, remove the peduncles, and cut into quarters. Peel and thinly slice 7 oz (200 g) onions and 2 cloves garlic. The best tomatoes for this recipe are the plump, round, and ribbed varieties that ripen in August and September.

Tomato confit (makes 2 jars)

2 Put all these ingredients into a saucepan. Add 1 sprig thyme, 1 bay leaf, and 1 chopped bunch of basil. Season with salt and pepper. Bring slowly to the boil, skim, and simmer very gently for 35 minutes. Stir regularly to prevent the mixture from sticking.

Dried tomatoes

3 Soak two jars in boiling water, then turn them upside down to drain thoroughly. Use a ladle to transfer the piping hot tomatoes to the jars. Pour a $\frac{1}{2}$-in/2-cm layer of olive oil over the top of the tomato mixture and close the jars tightly. Leave them to cool, then refrigerate. Tomato confit can be kept for 2 months in a refrigerator. Use it for garnishes, sauces, and stuffings, and particularly with fresh pasta.

Vegetable kebabs (makes 8)

1 Vegetable kebabs and grilled vegetables are the ideal accompaniment to grilled meat. Peel and chop 2 new onions and 2 cloves garlic. Wash and wipe 10^1/$_2$ oz (300 g) zucchini, 10^1/$_2$ oz (300 g) red and green bell peppers, and 10^1/$_2$ oz (300 g) carrots. Trim the ends of the zucchini and carrots, then cut them into slices ^{3}/$_4$ in (2 cm) thick. Peel and wash 10^1/$_2$ oz (300 g) of mushrooms and cut 3 slices bacon into pieces ^{3}/$_4$ in/2 cm wide.

2 Remove the peduncle, seeds, and white membranes from the bell peppers, then cut them into pieces roughly ^{3}/$_4$ in (2 cm) square. Put all these vegetables into a bowl with a few pinches of thyme, the chopped onions and garlic, a bunch of basil (finely chopped), and ^{1}/$_3$ cup + 1^1/$_2$ tbsp (10 cl) olive oil. Season with salt and pepper. Mix by hand to distribute the spices evenly through the vegetables, then leave to marinate for 2–3 hours.

3 Place the vegetable pieces at regular intervals on fairly long metal skewers with a ring on the end, so that you can turn them. Keep the leftover marinade (you could add some sprigs of thyme), as this can be used to baste the kebabs during the cooking process. Put the kebabs side by side on a barbecue grill, previously coated with a thin layer of oil. The contact with the grill caramelizes the vegetables slightly, while the proximity of the embers gives them a unique smoky taste.

4 Make sure that you leave a little space between each skewer. Cook them for 5–8 minutes, sprinkling occasionally with the marinade, then turn the skewers (wearing gloves) and cook for 5 minutes more. Check progress by piercing the vegetables with the tip of a knife.

Grilled vegetables for 8

1 Wash and wipe 10$^1/_2$ oz (300 g) zucchini, 10$^1/_2$ oz (300 g) eggplants, 10$^1/_2$ oz (300 g) red or yellow bell peppers, and 10$^1/_2$ oz (300 g) tomatoes. Trim the ends of the zucchini and eggplants, then cut them into slices $^3/_8$ in/1 cm thick. Chop the tomatoes in the same way, without peeling (but wash and wipe them first).

2 Remove the peduncle, seeds, and white membranes from the bell peppers and cut them in two. Set aside. Peel 2 onions and chop them roughly. Arrange the vegetables alternately on the bottom of a reversible grill pan. Sprinkle them with a few drops of olive oil, add salt and pepper, and dust with dried thyme.

3 Close the grill and place it 4 in (10 cm) from the red-hot embers of the barbeque. Cook for 10–15 minutes, then turn and continue cooking for 8–10 minutes on the other side. Open the grill away from the fire and slide the cooked vegetables into a serving dish.

N.B.

Vegetables used for grilling must be firm and thickly sliced otherwise they risk being burnt over a particularly intense heat. As a general rule, a thickness of $^5/_{16}$ in (8 mm) to $^3/_8$ in (1 cm) is recommended. Also make sure that that the vegetables are sliced uniformly, to ensure that they cook evenly.

Tip

Eggplants, zucchini, bell peppers, and mushrooms are most readily associated with grilling, but chicory hearts provide another option; in Italy, they are traditionally prepared in this way, accompanied by a lemon vinaigrette.

Greek-style mushrooms for 4

1 Wash around 1 lb 2 oz (500 g) small, cultivated mushrooms (they should be very firm and white). Cut them into thick strips or two pieces, depending on their size. Put them in a terrine and sprinkle with the juice of half a lemon. Add 12 coriander seeds and 1 clove garlic, peeled and finely chopped. Meanwhile, peel 7 oz (200 g) small new onions (or substitute chopped carrot, if preferred).

2 Peel 1 big onion (or 2–3 smaller ones). Slice, then cut into the smallest dice possible. Heat 4 tbsp olive oil, supplemented by 2 tbsp corn oil, in a pan. Add the chopped onion, then the whole, new onions (or chopped carrot). When these are golden, pour in 2 tbsp white wine and season with salt and pepper.

3 Put the mushrooms into the pan, along with a bouquet garni containing fresh thyme. At this point, you could also add 2 tomatoes, peeled and roughly mashed, along with a little more white wine. Cook gently, uncovered, for around 20 minutes, allowing the sauce to reduce gradually.

General points

When cooked "Greek style," summer vegetables make delicious and refreshing appetizers. The secret is to simmer the various vegetables in a slightly acid sauce, then allow them to marinate for a few days, thereby giving the flavors and spices time to soak in. Greek-style vegetables are served well chilled.

Tip

The designation "Greek" does not necessarily mean that a recipe is inspired by Greek cooking or prepared that way in Greece. It simply refers to vegetables cooked in a spicy, acid sauce that are chilled before serving. Cultivated mushrooms are often used like this.

4 Stir from time to time, to ensure the ingredients and spices are mixed thoroughly. Remove from the heat and leave to cool slightly before removing the bouquet garni. Now add 2 tbsp best-quality olive oil. Adjust seasoning to taste. Sprinkle with 2–3 tbsp finely chopped flat parsley and a dash of lemon juice. Leave to cool thoroughly.

Greek-style vegetables and bell peppers in oil

Bell peppers in oil (makes 2 large jars)

1 Even more than in the case of Greek style, vegetables conserved in oil are prepared well in advance and make ideal accompaniments to an hors d'oeuvre or appetizer of Mediterranean inspiration, as well as to pasta and rice dishes. The most common vegetables for this method are bell peppers, small artichokes, and some types of mushrooms.

2 Prepare 4$^1/_2$ lb (2 kg) bell peppers. It is vital to peel them: wash and wipe, before putting them in an oil-free baking pan in the middle of the oven. Cook for 3–4 minutes at 400 °F (200 °C). Remove from the oven and place in plastic bags. Wait a few minutes, then take them out of the bags: they will now be easy to peel.

3 Cut them into two and remove the seeds and inner membranes, leaving only the flesh: cut them into wide strips and distribute between two jars, adding 2 cloves garlic (peeled and finely chopped), crushed thyme, and a few peppercorns to each jar. Mix the ingredients with chopsticks.

4 Pour best-quality olive oil over the bell peppers and their condiments, until they are completely covered. Store them in a dry place, preferably in the dark. Serve as an hors d'oeuvre with anchovies and olives. You can also use them in thin strips, to enrich a tomato sauce: for example, for pasta.

Broccoli purée for 4

1 Prepare 1 lb 11 oz (750 g) broccoli. Divide into florets, removing the hard ends and retaining only the blooms. Discard any that are discolored or yellowing. Boil plenty of salted water. Add the broccoli and simmer for 20-25 minutes.

2 Check their progress by tasting from time to time—the broccoli should have a fairly soft consistency. Drain, then place in a blender or vegetable mill. Reduce the broccoli to a thin purée, adding 2 tbsp of the cooking water and mixing several times.

3 If the purée is to be served as an accompaniment to fried escalopes or broiled rib of lamb, add 3¹/₂ oz (100 g) butter and season with salt and pepper to taste. It can also be served in the form of molded domes, by using small, lightly buttered ramekins. Combine three different purées.

Tip

Broccoli purée is by nature fairly soft. To stiffen it, add 1–2 potatoes when you cook the broccoli and put everything into the blender. Another possibility is to add a handful of cooked rice.

Ramekins of carrot for 8

1 Peel and wash 1 lb 5 oz (600 g) carrots and 10¹/₂ oz (300 g) potatoes. Cut the former into slices ¹/₂–1 in (2–3 cm) long, the latter into cubes. Boil plenty of salted water. Add the carrots and potatoes and cook for 25–30 minutes. Check their progress by tasting from time to time—the vegetables should be soft. Drain and transfer to a blender or a vegetable mill.

2 Reduce the vegetables to a fine purée. Leave to cool thoroughly. Melt 1¹/₂ oz (40 g) butter and brush 8 ramekins with it. Put the purée, 3¹/₂ oz (100 g) crème fraîche, 3 whole eggs, and a pinch of grated nutmeg into a bowl, and season with salt and pepper. Mix everything together with a wooden spoon. Adjust seasoning to taste. Use a large tablespoon to fill the ramekins, leaving a space of ³/₈ in (1 cm) at the top.

3 Place them in a bain-marie or baking pan of water. Cover with buttered aluminum foil, and cook for 25 minutes in an oven preheated to 350 °F (180 °C). Place the ramekins on a serving platter. They can be served as an appetizer, accompanied by a tomato sauce, or as a garnish to fish fillets, whether poached or baked in the oven with white wine. You can also use celery root or green beans as a substitute for carrots in this recipe.

Eggplant caviar for 4

1 Wash and wipe 4 eggplants; remove their peduncles, and place them whole in an oven preheated to 350 °F (180 °C) for 25–30 minutes. Take them out of the oven and leave to cool. Cut them into two and remove the pulp with a spoon.

2 Place this pulp in a bowl and add 1 chopped clove garlic, juice of 1 lemon, 5 tbsp olive oil, and 1 bunch chopped, fresh cilantro. Add salt and pepper to taste. Place in the refrigerator for 1 hour.

3 Serve the eggplant caviar thoroughly chilled as an appetizer, with slices of toast. For an original variant, you can also serve this dish with slithers of poutargue, dried tomatoes, and slices of lemon.

General points

There are several ways of preparing purées, depending on the vegetables used. In all cases, it is essential to soften them by thorough cooking, providing a delicate accompaniment for meat, game, or poultry, or a basis for the creation of ramekins, soufflés, or terrines. A wide range of utensils appropriate for making purées can be found on the market. The most common is the vegetable mill, but you can also use a potato masher, a strainer, a sieve, or an electric blender. To make a purée smoother, add a little crème fraîche. A purée must always be generously seasoned.

Zucchini terrine with ricotta

for 6–8

1 Separate the leaves of a lettuce, blanch, and set aside. Wash 3 lb 5 oz (1.5 kg) zucchini. Cut off the ends and chop the zucchini into 3/8-in (1-cm) slices. Have the other ingredients ready and waiting: eggs, crème fraîche, breadcrumbs, chives, and, above all, ricotta, a soft Italian cheese resembling cottage cheese.

2 Boil plenty of salted water. Add the zucchini and cook for around 20 minutes. Check the progress from time to time—they should be quite soft. Drain the cooked zucchini as thoroughly as possible—otherwise, the terrine may turn out too moist.

3 Put the zucchini in a blender and reduce to a fine purée. Leave to cool thoroughly. Butter a terrine mold and put the zucchini purée, 1 scant cup (20 cl) crème fraîche, 1 3/4 oz (50 g) breadcrumbs, 10 1/2 oz (300 g) ricotta, 4 eggs, 1 bunch chives (chopped), and 1 pinch grated nutmeg into a bowl. Season with salt and pepper.

4 Mix the ingredients with a wooden spoon. Adjust seasoning to taste. Set aside. Line the mold with lettuce leaves, then fill it to within 3/8 in (1 cm) of the top with a spoon. Press down hard on each layer of the mixture with the back of the spoon to ensure it is well compacted and uniform in consistency.

5 Place the mold in a bain-marie or baking pan of water, cover with a sheet of buttered aluminum foil, and cook in an oven preheated to 350 °F (180 °C) for 45 minutes. Check progress by pricking the terrine with a skewer: this should be hot to the touch. Leave to cool, then put in the refrigerator for 24 hours. Serve in slices with a spoonful of crème fraîche mixed with finely chopped chives.

General points

Vegetable terrines always make an impact on account of their bright colors and springtime flavors. Many are made up of one or several different vegetables, reduced to a purée then mixed with whole eggs and breadcrumbs. Slow cooking in a bain-marie allows the egg to bind the terrine, thereby making it easier to slice once it is chilled. Terrines are often enriched by the addition of an extra ingredient, such as cheese, shrimp tails, or small dices of ham. The top surface can be glazed with a thin layer of aspic.

vegetable terrines

Tricolor terrine for 6–8

1 Prepare 1 lb 2 oz (500 g) zucchini, 1 lb 2 oz (500 g) carrots, and 1 lb 2 oz (500 g) spinach. Trim the zucchini and chop them into 3/8-in (1-cm) slices. Peel the carrots and cut them into small pieces. Remove the stalks from the spinach, then thoroughly wash and drain it. Bring plenty of salted water to the boil.

2 Add the carrots and cook them for around 20 minutes. Check the progress—they should be soft. Refresh the carrots under running water then drain them thoroughly. Prepare the zucchini and spinach in the same way, cooking the latter for 2–3 minutes longer.

3 Blend each of the cooked vegetables in turn, reducing them to a thin purée. Leave to cool thoroughly. Butter a mold for the terrine—ideally a Pyrex or non-stick cake mold (the latter still needs to be oiled, but very lightly).

4 Put the carrot purée, 1/3 cup + 1 1/2 tbsp (10 cl) crème fraîche, 3 tbsp breadcrumbs, 2 eggs, 1 tbsp chopped chives, and 1 pinch nutmeg into a bowl; add salt and pepper. Mix everything together with a wooden spoon. Adjust seasoning to taste. Prepare the zucchini and the spinach in the same way (with the same proportions of crème fraîche, breadcrumbs, eggs, and condiments).

5 Put a layer of the zucchini mixture into the mold, followed by the carrot purée and, finally, the spinach mixture. Proceed with great care to prevent the different layers from merging into each other. Put the mold in a bain-marie or baking pan of water, cover with buttered aluminum foil, and place in an oven preheated to 350 °F (180 °C) for 45 minutes. Check progress by pricking the terrine with a skewer: this should be hot to the touch.

6 Leave to cool, then put in the refrigerator for 24 hours. Serve in slices with a coulis of fresh tomatoes garnished with chopped fresh basil. Using the same method, you can replace the zucchini with artichoke hearts. Another option is to slip a few strips of truffles—4 or 5 will be sufficient—between the layers of vegetables; this will give your terrine an exquisite aroma.

Asparagus puff pastry with York ham

Of all the culinary treasures of summer, asparagus occupies pride of place, especially as it is only available for a relatively short period. Green or purplish asparagus, with an earthier, more full-bodied taste than the white varieties, is an authentic treat, to be enjoyed between April and May. Obviously, asparagus can be eaten with just vinaigrette, mousseline sauce, or orange butter, but it can also be used to make a more sophisticated appetizer, in crusty puff pastry with top-quality ham, rounded off with a cream sauce and chives. If you come across any fresh morels, take the opportunity to add them to the sauce. This hot appetizer can be washed down with a Meursault or pink champagne; follow it with poached salmon and round off the meal with a strawberry tart.

Serves 6
Preparation: 40 minutes
Cooking: 30 minutes

Ingredients

2$^1/_4$ lb (1 kg) asparagus
2 cups (50 cl) chicken bouillon
1$^1/_2$ oz (40 g) butter
$^1/_2$ cup (60 g) flour
14 oz (400 g) puff-pastry dough
6 slices York ham
1 bunch chives
1 egg yolk
$^1/_3$ cup + 1$^1/_2$ tbsp (10 cl) crème fraîche
Salt and pepper

1 Prepare the asparagus. Lay them out on the worktop to check that they are all fresh and firm. Working with care to ensure that you do not cause any bruising, cut off their base with a knife. Peel off a thin layer of skin near the tip and a thicker one near the woodier base. Plunge the asparagus into cold water. Divide them into groups of 15, held together loosely with string.

2 Cook the asparagus in plenty of salted water, over medium heat. Drain, then remove the string and keep the asparagus warm under a moist dishcloth. Heat the chicken bouillon. Meanwhile, melt the butter, without allowing it to become discolored; add 1/3 cup (40 g) flour and stir with a wooden spoon for 2 minutes.

3 Pour the hot bouillon onto this mixture and continue stirring. Cook for 10–12 minutes, making sure, above all, that the sauce does not boil (otherwise it will acquire a gluey taste); add salt and pepper, then keep warm by placing it in a bain-marie or double boiler. Roll the puff-pastry dough on a floured worktop until it forms a large rectangle 3/16 in (5 mm) thick.

4 Remove the rind and fat from the ham, then cut into long, fairly thin strips. Cut the asparagus, keeping only the tips. Bake the dough in the oven until it has puffed up and turned a golden color. Take it out of the oven and carefully cut out a lengthwise section from the top; hollow out the inside.

5 Wash the chives and gently pat dry in a dishcloth. Complete the white sauce by adding the egg yolk and the crème fraîche. Adjust seasoning to taste, then add the chives (finely chopped) and beat. Put the pastry back into the oven (complete with its cut-out section) to heat it up.

6 Pour a little of the white chives sauce into the hollowed-out interior of the pastry, then make an even layer of ham and cover this with a bed of asparagus tips. Pour the rest of the sauce on top. Replace the cutout section of puff pastry and serve immediately on warm plates.

Salt

Kitchen salt, known as sodium chloride to chemists, is obtained from the evaporation of seawater from salt marshes or extracted from mines. It is the only mineral condiment introduced directly into foodstuffs. It is indispensable to life, as salt deficiency causes severe physiological disorders. Apart from the flavor it gives to food, salt also acts as both a taste enhancer and a means of

Chicken with coarse salt

Stuffed leg of lamb with kidneys

conservation, depending on the amount used. There are various types of kitchen salt. Fine salt is used in cooking to adjust the seasoning. We can distinguish here between refined salt, which is white and flows freely, and "gray" salt, often fairly moist, but with higher iodine content. Coarse salt is classified in the same way—it only differs in the size of the grains. It is used to salt cooking water and bouillons, as well as serving to "cook" food under a crust of salt. Its crunchy texture is appealing on broiled meat, or with a stew or calf's head. It also sets off fresh foie gras very effectively.

Salmon with pepper

Pepper

Only the grains of Piper nigrum have the legal right to the title of "pepper." Freshly ground pepper is always better than the powdered pepper sold in stores. The subtle flavor of white pepper adds a pleasant touch to sauces, pasta, vinaigrettes, charcuterie, and fish. Black pepper, in contrast, is hotter and more aromatic; when coarsely ground, it is a perfect complement to broiled red meat. Green pepper, harvested before it is fully ripe, is sold dried or in brine; its aroma is somewhat fruity. Gray pepper is simply a mixture of black and white pepper. Red pepper comes from the berries of an exotic tree: it is both aromatic and decorative. As for Cayenne pepper, this is in fact chili, ground into a fine powder.

Peppered pavé

Duck with green pepper

Garlic vinegar

The subtle flavors of spring and summer vegetables often deserve to be highlighted by an accompaniment. Vinaigrette is the most obvious option. It can be prepared very simply with oil, salt, pepper, and vinegar. It is a delicious foil to green salads and green beans served cold, but a similar effect can be achieved accompanied solely by garlic-flavored vinegar or thinly sliced new garlic.

Cider vinegars

Flavored vinegar always offers many possibilities: vinegar with shallots or tarragon, for example, add zest to boiled vegetables. Experiment with altering standard recipes by incorporating oils and vinegars of your choice, thereby discovering the combinations that suit you best. Try the following blends, for instance: olive oil and lemon juice; walnut oil and wine vinegar; peanut oil and cider vinegar; or olive oil and balsamic vinegar.

Rose vinegar

Rose vinegar is easy to make with fragrant rose petals (3$^{1}/_{2}$ oz/100 g for 1 bottle) and is particularly delicious when prepared with cider vinegar: leave the petals to marinate for ten days before filtering and combining it with grapeseed oil to season a salad of cucumbers, zucchini, or tomatoes.

Vinaigre au fenouil

Parsley and shallot vinaigrette

To prepare the basic vinaigrette, dissolve 3 pinches salt in 2 tbsp vinegar by stirring, then add 6 tbsp oil. Beat, and add pepper. This vinaigrette can be enhanced by various ingredients: chopped shallots, chopped parsley, fresh garlic, chives, mustard, and even crushed Espelette chili.

Yogurt vinaigrette

Consider sauces with yogurt or white cheese to accompany raw vegetables (cucumber, radish, fennel). Mix the yogurt with lemon juice, herbs, mustard, salt, and pepper. Serve in a bowl, allowing your guests to help themselves.

Green sauce

Green sauce is an enticing variation of the standard vinaigrette. It is particularly suited to fleshy artichoke hearts: prepare a basic vinaigrette and add a generous amount of finely chopped green herbs (parsley, tarragon, chives) and a spoonful of mustard.

Recommended drinks

Rosé de Provence
Coteaux-d'Aix
Tavel

Menu suggestions

1. Serve these artichokes as an appetizer, followed by lamb (cutlets or grilled kebabs), accompanied by green beans sprinkled with parsley.

2. You can also offer this appetizer from the Italian repertoire with a pasta dish complemented by tomato sauce and grilled vegetables.

Artichokes alla romana

An Italian dish

Serves 4
Preparation: 15 minutes
Cooking: 20 minutes

Ingredients

4 artichokes
1 lemon
4¹/₂ oz (125 g) stale bread
(without crust)
1 glass olive oil
Garlic
4 tbsp wine vinegar
Parsley
Fresh mint
Fennel seeds

1 large glass fruity white wine
1 large glass veal or chicken
bouillon
Black olives
Salt and pepper

1. Prepare the artichokes by cutting off the leaves and stalks.

2. Blanch for 15 minutes in salted, boiling water with lemon juice. Drain them head down, then remove the choke and immediately sprinkle with lemon juice to prevent them from turning black.

3. Break up the bread roughly and fry gently in olive oil with 1–2 cloves peeled and crushed garlic. As soon as the bread starts to turn a golden color, add the vinegar and simmer gently.

4. Stir salt, pepper, chopped parsley and mint, and a few fennel seeds into the bread mixture. Place the artichoke hearts face down in a casserole and garnish with the mixture. Skim the fat off the liquid in the frying pan and add equal parts of wine and stock (2 cups/50 cl in all). Pour this liquid between the artichokes; it should rise to one third of their height.

5. Seal the artichokes by placing a sheet of aluminum foil over the artichokes, before putting the lid on the casserole and simmering in an oven preheated to 400 °F (200 °C) for 1 hour.

6. Serve the artichokes thoroughly chilled, cut into two lengthwise, accompanied by black olives and fresh mint leaves.

Eggplants with coulis

A family dish

> Serves 4
> Preparation: 10 minutes
> Waiting: 2 hours
> Cooking: 45 minutes

Ingredients

2¼ lb (1 kg) long eggplants
1 lb 2 oz (500 g) ripe tomatoes
(or 1 jar of coulis)
2 cloves garlic
1 small sprig thyme
1 small bay leaf
Few sprigs parsley
1 onion
1 glass of olive oil
3 eggs

2 cups (50 cl) milk
A few black olives
Salt and pepper

1. Wipe the eggplants (only peel them if they are very plump); cut into thin strips; place in a soup dish, sprinkle with fine salt, and leave to "sweat" for 1–2 hours.

2. Meanwhile, cut the tomatoes into two horizontally, put them in a thick-bottomed saucepan with ¹/₂ glass water, the garlic (peeled and crushed), thyme, bay leaf, parsley, and onion (peeled and thinly sliced). Cook over low heat for 30 minutes. Add 1 tbsp oil and plenty of salt and pepper; simmer, stirring occasionally, until you obtain a fairly thick coulis.

3. Drain the eggplants and wipe them on paper towels, then sauté them gently in a covered saucepan for about 15 minutes; they should be barely browned, but very tender. Add pepper when they are cooked.

4. Oil a cake mold and arrange the strips of eggplant in several layers, first in one direction, then in the other; add the eggs, previously beaten with the milk.

5. Place the mold in a large baking pan, pour hot water all around it to make a bain-marie, and cook for about 25 minutes.

6. Turn the eggplant onto a warm serving platter, top with coulis and garnish with parsley and black olives.

Recommended drinks

Côtes-du-Roussillon
Bergerac Rouge
Côtes-du-Rhône

Menu suggestions

1. These eggplants with coulis make a good main course for a family dinner, preceded by a salad of curly endive and diced ham and followed by a seasonal cheeseboard.

2. You can also serve this dish after a fish soup with garlic croûtons.

Recommended drinks

Coteaux-d'Aix
Gamay
Coteaux Varois

Menu suggestions

1. These eggplant fans make a good summer appetizer, preceding a baked fish dish with green salad and followed by lavender ice cream or iced nougat.

2. This dish can also be served as a garnish for leg of lamb, preceded by melon and followed by small goat's cheeses with oil.

Eggplant fans

A regional dish

Serves 4
Preparation: 20 minutes
Cooking: 1 hr 30 minutes

Ingredients

4 long, medium-sized eggplants
Coarse salt
2–3 onions
Olive oil
3–4 cloves garlic
4–5 tomatoes (not too ripe)
Parsley
Thyme
Bay leaves

A few black olives
Salt and pepper

1. Wash the eggplants and wipe them. Put them on a cutting board and take a sharp knife. Remove the peduncle by chopping off the base, then cut the eggplants lengthwise into thin pieces, without slicing them right to the end. Sprinkle with coarse salt and leave them on a plate to "sweat."

2. Peel the onions. Slice them and then sauté, barely allowing them to brown, in a skillet with plenty of olive oil. Peel and slice the garlic. Add the garlic to the frying pan when the onions become transparent. Add salt and pepper and continue cooking for a few minutes more.

3. Wash and wipe the tomatoes, but do not peel them. Cut them from top to bottom into slices $3/16$ in (5 mm) thick. Spread half the contents of the skillet on the bottom of an oiled casserole. Wipe the eggplant "fans" and place them on this bed.

4. Garnish the fans by inserting pieces of tomato between strands of eggplant. Add a little salt and plenty of pepper to each layer of tomato before going on to the next. Once they are garnished, the eggplant fans must fit snugly into the dish, neither too tight nor too loose, because either way they risk losing their shape. Preheat the oven to 445 °F (230 °C). Chop and mix a generous amount of parsley, thyme, and bay leaves. Spread the rest of the onions and garlic on top of the eggplants.

5. Dust with the chopped herbs and season with salt and pepper. Cover with aluminum foil or wax paper. Bake in the oven for 15 minutes, lower the oven temperature to 350 °F (180 °C), and bake for a further 1 hr 15 minutes.

Charlotte Nantaise

A party dish

Serves 5
Preparation: 15 minutes
First cooking: 45 minutes
Second cooking: 45 minutes

Ingredients

2¼ lb (1 kg) carrots (not too big)
5½ oz (150 g) minced meat
1 slice Paris ham
5½ oz (150 g) veal
Stale bread
1 glass milk
2 eggs
Parsley½ glass very fruity white wine
Butter
1 pinch potato flour

1 glass bouillon
Salt and pepper

1. Peel the carrots very carefully, cutting the thickest ones in two lengthwise and removing their heart. Cook them for 45 minutes in boiling, salted water.

2. Prepare the stuffing: mix the minced meat with the ham and chopped veal; add a generous handful of stale bread (previously soaked in milk and gently pressed), the whole eggs, salt, pepper, chopped parsley—reserving a few bunches—and a little white wine.

3. Butter a charlotte mold well and add the carrots, cut lengthwise on the bottom and into smaller sticks and slices on the sides, with the convex part of the carrots turned inward.

4. Put some of the stuffing in the mold, spread a layer of carrots on top, and top with the rest of the stuffing, dabbing it with butter and covering with a disk of buttered wax paper.

5. Cook in an oven preheated to 375 °F (190 °C) for 45 minutes.

6. Shortly before the end of cooking, prepare a sauce by thickening the hot bouillon with the potato flour and boiling for a few minutes in a small saucepan, beating continuously. Adjust seasoning to taste. Turn out the charlotte onto a serving platter. Pour the thickened stock around its base, garnish with small bunches of parsley, and serve.

Recommended drinks

Saumur-Champigny
Coteaux-d'Ancenis
Anjou

Menu suggestions

1. Served as an appetizer, this exquisite charlotte can be followed by pike in white butter and followed by almond tart.

2. If you prefer meat, consider following the charlotte with roast veal and small new vegetables, with a brioche with caramelized fruit for dessert.

51

Crown of zucchini

A light dish

> Serves 6
> Preparation: 20 minutes
> Cooking: 40 minutes

Ingredients

3 lb 5 oz (1.5 kg) small, very fresh zucchini
Olive oil
1 oz (30 g) butter
$1/3$ cup + $1^1/2$ tbsp (10 cl) crème fraîche
4 eggs
1 sprig basil
4 leaves gelatin
Salt and pepper

1. Cut the ends off the zucchini and peel them lightly, so that some of the skin remains visible. Poach in boiling, salted water for around 5 minutes. Drain. Cut the most regular ones into thin slices and the rest into larger pieces.

2. Brown the zucchini briefly in a mixture of oil and butter. Set aside the thin slices and make a purée of the rest, with a blender if possible. Stir in the crème fraîche beaten with the eggs and basil leaves (finely chopped at the last moment). Season to taste with salt and pepper. Complete the mixture by adding the gelatin leaves dissolved in a little warm water.

3. Butter a ring-shaped mold and arrange the reserved slices of zucchini and a few basil leaves on the bottom and sides. Pour the mixture into the mold, making sure you do not dislodge the zucchini slices.

4. Place the mold in a bain-marie or baking pan of water and cook for 40 minutes, in an oven preheated to 400 °F (200 °C).

5. Take the mold out of the bain-marie and leave to cool. Place a serving platter face down on top of the mold and turn everything upside down in one brisk movement. Gently remove the mold to reveal the crown. The selection of the zucchini is important in this recipe: choose firm, fairly small ones, with a smooth skin, so that they will not lose too much water and thus retain their delicate flavor. The decorative effect is achieved by forming stripes with the peeled and unpeeled zucchini.

Recommended drinks

Water
Tomato juice
Vegetable cocktail

Menu suggestions

1. This crown of zucchini constitutes a light, but balanced, meal when served with a slice of steamed fish sprinkled with lemon juice and followed by fromage frais.

2. You can also serve this crown as a main course with a slice of braised ham, followed by fresh fruit salad.

Cream of green beans with sage

An easy dish

Serves 4
Preparation: 15 minutes
Cooking: 35 minutes

Ingredients

1 lb 2 oz (500 g) green beans
1 oz (30 g) butter
1 large onion
1 white part of a leek
Fresh sage
1 egg
1 small pot crème fraîche
Salt and pepper

1. Trim the green beans, wash them, and pat dry with paper towels. As they are going to be boiled and put through a vegetable mill, the beans do not need to be especially thin: buy the cheapest available, provided they are totally fresh, firm, velvety, and brittle, with a strong, uniform coloring. You can even use lima beans, but in this case the soup will not turn out green!

2. Melt the butter in a fairly big, heavy-bottomed saucepan. Peel the onion, wash the leek, slice them both thinly, and brown in butter. Add the green beans.

3. Pour on 6 cups (1.5 liters) water; bring to the boil, and simmer gently for 30 minutes. Add salt and pepper halfway through.

4. When the beans are cooked, put the mixture through a vegetable mill and then through a fine sieve. Put the soup back in the saucepan, add finely chopped fresh sage, and cook over very low heat for a further 5 minutes.

5. Just before serving, mix in an egg yolk beaten with a few spoonfuls of crème fraîche and adjust seasoning to taste. Sprinkle a little finely chopped sage into each dish when serving the soup.

Recommended drinks

Water
Arbois Blanc
Tavel

Menu suggestions

1. For a summer dinner, serve this soup as an appetizer then prepare papillotes (parcels) of fish and finish off with a light touch, such as melon "en surprise."

2. You can also complement this cream of green beans with a simple herb omelet, followed by lavender ice cream with almond macaroons.

Spinach barbouillade

A regional dish

Serves 4
Preparation: 10 minutes
Cooking: 40 minutes

Ingredients

2¼ lb (1 kg) spinach
1 large onion
4 tbsp olive oil
1 lb 2 oz (500 g) potatoes
saffron
1 bunch fennel
Garlic
4 eggs

Sliced bread, toasted
Salt and pepper

1. Wash and pick over the spinach, removing the stalks, and then blanch in boiling, salted water for a few minutes. Peel and roughly chop the onion, then fry lightly in oil in a large casserole until transparent.

2. Add the spinach, having first wrung it dry; stir a few times with a spatula, then add the potatoes, peeled and cut into fairly thin slices. Season with a little salt, pepper, and saffron, before adding sliced fennel and 1–2 cloves garlic, peeled and crushed. Add 4 cups (1 liter) boiling water, cover, and reduce gently over low heat, simmering for 40 minutes.

3. When the potatoes are cooked, break the eggs and poach them in the spinach broth. Serve in the casserole with slices of toast.

This Provençal recipe is also known as spinach bouillabaisse. When buying the potatoes, it is advisable to choose fairly small, yellow ones with firm flesh. Saffron is always better in the form of threads, rather than powder: only a tiny amount is required. As for the fennel, if the green stalks are not sufficiently fresh, slice the bulb very finely. Before serving, put two slices of bread in each dish and pour the soup over them with a ladle, without breaking the eggs, which should be only lightly poached.

Recommended drinks

Côtes-du-Rhône
Ajaccio
Bandol

Menu suggestions

1. This barbouillade can serve as a hot appetizer for a family dinner. Follow with a ground meat and potato pie, with crème caramel for dessert.

2. You can also serve it as a main course, following a pissaladière. Finish the meal with fresh figs and small cookies with honey.

Puff pastry with eggplant caviar

A party dish

Serves 4
Preparation: 15 minutes
Waiting: 1–2 hours
Cooking: 1 hour

Ingrediënten

4 medium-size eggplants
2 cloves garlic
Olive oil
Puff-pastry dough
4 small tomatoes
4 baby eggplants
Fresh rosemary
Salt and pepper

1. Bake the eggplants in their skin in an oven preheated to 330 °F (165 °C), until they are soft to the touch—reckon on about 1 hour. The flesh should be tender. Leave to cool for a while before peeling, cutting them lengthwise into four pieces, and seeding.

2. Crush the pulp of the eggplants with a fork until you obtain a thick purée; add salt, pepper, crushed and thinly chopped garlic, and a dash of olive oil. To save time, you can make the eggplant caviar in a microwave oven: cook the eggplants on high, wrapped in paper towels, for 5 minutes, turning once. Leave to rest for 5 minutes, then take them out and cut lengthwise into two to remove the pulp; put this in a terrine and season with oil, chopped garlic, salt, and pepper.

3. Prepare the pastry shells with puff-pastry dough, partially baked beforehand on its own. Coat with the eggplant purée and slices of tomato, seasoned with salt and pepper and garnished with chopped garlic. Put a baby eggplant cut into two in the center of each patty; cover with the eggplant purée and top with an arrangement of sliced garlic. Sprinkle on a little olive oil and finish baking in the oven for about another 20 minutes.

4. Serve these pastries hot, preferably with a small sprig of fresh rosemary planted in the center as adornment. You can also serve them warm or cold, with one or two leaves of basil.

Recommended drinks

Tavel
Côtes-de-Provence
Lirac

Menu suggestions

1. This original appetizer can precede a beef stew with olives, followed by apricot gratin for dessert.

2. If you prefer to serve fish, stay in southern climes with a stuffed sea bream followed, after a few goat's cheeses, by pine-nut tart.

Recommended drinks

Muscadet
Arbois
Cloudy cider

Menu suggestions

1. This carrot flan is perfect for a light family dinner, accompanied by a good green salad enlivened by slices of hard-boiled eggs, with baked apples for dessert.

2. You could also serve it after watercress soup, followed by a cheeseboard, green salad, and seasonal fruit.

Carrot flan

A family dish

Serves 6
Preparation and first cooking:
20 minutes
Second cooking: 20 minutes

Ingredients

2 cups (250 g) flour
1 tbsp oil
$5^1/_2$ oz (150 g) butter
2 lb 11 oz (1.2 kg) small carrots
1 tbsp superfine sugar
1 scant cup (20 cl) thick crème fraîche
Parsley
Salt and pepper

1. Make a well in the flour and insert the oil, a pinch of salt, and $3^1/_2$ oz (100 g) butter, divided into small pieces. Gently, but quickly, blend all these ingredients together using your fingertips. Gradually moisten with sufficient water to obtain a sturdy dough. Roll it into a ball and leave to rest in a cool place. If you want to make the carrot flan more quickly, you can also use a base of piecrust pastry ready to roll out. If you prepare the pastry yourself, do not forget to leave it to rest in a cool place for at least 30 minutes.

2. Scrape the carrots, then wash and cut them into thin slices. Set aside one quarter and simmer the rest in a pan containing a pinch of salt, a pinch of sugar, $1/_2$ glass water, and 1 tbsp butter. Cover and cook very gently. The carrots should be tender when the water is totally reduced.

3. Meanwhile, blanch the reserved slices of carrot in boiling, salted water.

4. Reduce the simmered carrots to a purée, then mix them with the remaining butter and the crème fraîche.

5. Roll out the pastry and place in a buttered pie dish; fill with the carrot purée, garnish with the blanched carrot slices, dust with sugar, and cook in an oven preheated to 435 °F (225 °C) for 20 minutes.

6. Just before serving, garnish with parsley leaves.

Fricassée of artichoke hearts

An easy dish

> Serves 4
> Preparation: 10 minutes
> Cooking: 40 minutes

Ingredients

5$^1/_2$ oz (150 g) sliced bacon
1 tbsp oil
12 small onions
10$^1/_2$ oz (300 g) small potatoes
1 bouquet garni
4–6 cooked artichoke hearts (or a can of artichoke hearts with no dressing)
1 lemon
Salt and pepper

1. Remove the rind from the bacon and dice. Heat the oil in a large, heavy-bottomed skillet, add the bacon, and sauté gently, turning continuously with a wooden spoon. Pour away any excess fat. Remove from the heat.

2. Peel the onions. Peel and wash the potatoes (choose the Charlotte or Ratte varieties, with firm flesh); pat dry with a dishcloth. Return the skillet to the heat and add the onions, stirring continuously, until they start to change color.

3. Put the potatoes in the skillet, add the bouquet garni, cover, and sauté gently for 15 minutes.

4. Cut the artichoke hearts into thick pieces and put them into the skillet; add salt and pepper and cover. Sauté gently for some twenty minutes. The dish is ready when the potatoes are cooked. Sprinkle with lemon juice and serve piping hot.

This very easy, but extremely tasty, recipe is far better with fresh artichoke hearts prepared especially for the occasion. If you use canned artichoke hearts, be sure to drain them very thoroughly and pat them dry with paper towels. You can also use frozen artichoke hearts.

Recommended drinks

Rosé de Provence
Beaujolais
Lirac

Menu suggestions

1. This fricassée can be served as a garnish for red meat, such as grilled entrecote or beef kebabs, with a salad appetizer and ice cream sundae for dessert.

2. This dish constitutes a full meal with a herb omelet, followed by orange salad.

Green beans with almonds

A regional dish

> Serves 4
> Preparation: 10 minutes
> Cooking: 10 minutes

Ingredients

3$^1/_2$ oz (100 g) slivered almonds
1 lb 2 oz (500 g) green beans
2–3 small, fresh white onions
2 tbsp olive oil
1 bouquet fresh savory
2–3 tbsp crème fraîche
Salt and pepper

1. Broil the almonds, either spread out on a baking sheet or in a heavy-bottomed skillet (with no oil). Meanwhile, trim the green beans, then wash and drain them. Extra-thin beans, supremely fresh and intensely green, are best suited to this typical recipe of the Aix-en-Provence region, which is also renowned for its apricots and figs. Take care when choosing the slivered almonds: they tend to go off when sold in bulk. Pine nuts can also be used for this recipe.

2. Add the green beans to a large pan of simmering, salted water and cook uncovered for around 10 minutes. Plunge them immediately into very cold water; they should still be crisp.

3. Peel the onions, cut them into slices, separate into rings, and sauté in a little oil. Add the beans when the onions start to turn golden, followed by half the almonds. Sprinkle with savory leaves, then add salt and pepper. Savory is extremely aromatic: it is picked in the early summer, dried, and conserved away from sunlight. It is traditionally used to flavor goat's cheese, but also combines very well with vegetables, particularly potatoes and beans.

4. Leave to simmer while mixing the olive oil, crème fraîche, salt, pepper, and remaining broiled almonds in a small saucepan. Heat this sauce, without boiling, and serve separately.

Recommended drinks

Cassis
Coteaux-d'Aix
Côtes-de-Provence

Menu suggestions

1. Green beans prepared in this way make an original garnish for rabbit or roast chicken. Accompany with tomato and basil salad as an appetizer and floating islands for dessert.

2. These beans make a good appetizer for a vegetarian meal; follow them with pasta and pesto, and a dessert of lemon sorbet served in the shell of the fruit.

Piquillos stuffed with salt-cod brandade

A foreign dish

Serves 4
Preparation: 10 minutes
Cooking: 40 minutes

Ingredients

8 large bell peppers
$10^1/_2$ oz (300 g) brandade
1–2 cloves garlic
Parsley
2 glasses bouillon
Tomato coulis
1 tbsp cornstarch
Oregano
Grated nutmeg
1 small pot heavy cream
Salt and pepper

1. Cut a hole around the peduncle of the bell peppers; empty them, then rinse and drain.

2. Preheat the oven to 400 °F (200 °C). Pour the brandade into a bowl. Peel and thinly chop the garlic, then add to the brandade. Finely chop 2–3 tbsp parsley and add this as well, mixing thoroughly. Adjust seasoning to taste. You can find "natural" brandade (made solely of cod reduced to a purée with milk and olive oil) in supermarkets, either fresh in a jar or canned; brandade can also be found in a more compact and less aromatic form, made with mashed potatoes, but this is less desirable.

3. Fill the bell peppers with the brandade. Place them in a baking pan, add a little bouillon, and cook in the oven for 20–25 minutes, regularly sprinkling with a little bouillon.

4. Mix the tomato coulis and cornstarch in a small saucepan; beat in a little bouillon, then add the oregano and nutmeg. Bring to the boil, stirring continuously, then simmer for 2 minutes. Add the cream to the sauce and pour into a dish. Once the stuffed piquillos are cooked, place them in the sauce and keep them hot in the oven (switched off). Sprinkle a little chopped fresh parsley on each piquillo.

Recommended drinks

Beer
Irouléguy
Madiran

Menu suggestions

1. When this Basque specialty is served as an appetizer, follow with broiled tuna and then ewe's cheese with black cherry jam.

2. These piquillos can constitute a main course, after piperade with scrambled eggs. Basque gateau makes an appropriate dessert.

59

Chilled soup with garden herbs

A light dish

Serves 4
Preparation: 15 minutes
Cooking: 20 minutes

Ingredients

1 bunch parsley
1 small bunch chives
1 small bunch basil (around 20 leaves if small; just 4–5 if large)
2 generous handfuls sorrel
1 bunch chervil
2 tbsp butter
4 cups (1 liter) chicken bouillon
2 eggs
Salt and pepper

1. Wash all the herbs, having set aside a few leaves of chervil; drain, chop roughly, and sauté gently in butter in a deep skillet. Stir continuously with a wooden spoon, making sure they do not change color. Use a variety of parsley with large, flat leaves. Traditionally, herb soups also contain dandelion and nettle leaves. Basil comes in all kinds of varieties, some more aromatic than others: the most common is a fine-leaved variety sold in France under the name of Marseillais.

2. Add the hot bouillon when the herbs are on the verge of absorbing all the butter. Bring to the boil and simmer gently, but evenly, for 10 minutes.

3. Put the yolks of the eggs in a bowl; thin them with a little bouillon then pour this mixture into the soup, away from the heat, stirring continuously. Return the soup to the heat, stirring all the time, until it starts to bubble. Adjust seasoning to taste with salt and pepper.

4. Leave the soup to cool thoroughly. Cover and put in the bottom of the refrigerator until just before serving in bowls or soup plates. Wash, drain, and finely chop the rest of the chervil and sprinkle on each helping. This soup can also be served hot, as soon as it has finished cooking.

Recommended drinks

Water
Apple juice
Vegetable cocktail

Menu suggestions

1. Served as an appetizer, this light, aromatic soup can be followed by poached chicken breasts accompanied by leaf spinach, with grapefruit salad for dessert.

2. If you prefer fish, prepare whiting with mushrooms and lemon "en papillote" for the main course, and apple compote for dessert.

Fresh cilantro salad

An exotic dish

Serves 4
Preparation: 40 minutes
Cooking: 20 minutes

Ingredients

1 white cabbage heart
1 handful Chinese vermicelli
A little bread (without the crust)
A little bouillon or milk
4$^{1}/_{2}$ oz (125 g) minced steak
1 egg
1 bunch fresh cilantro
oil
4$^{1}/_{2}$ oz (125 g) cultivated mushrooms
1 lemon

2 carrots
9 oz (250 g) petits pois
1 small bunch spinach
3$^{1}/_{2}$ oz (100 g) shelled shrimps
Vinegar
Salt and pepper

1. Trim the cabbage, removing its stalk and outer leaves. Cut into two lengthwise and blanch in boiling, salted water for 15 minutes. Rinse the shelled shrimps. Soak the Chinese vermicelli for 20 minutes in the cabbage water.

2. Meanwhile, prepare some small meatballs. Soak 1–2 pieces bread in a little bouillon or milk, drain, and wring dry with your hands; place in a bowl, add the minced steak, and the lightly beaten whole egg. Mix thoroughly, adding salt and pepper to taste and a little finely chopped cilantro. When the mixture is uniform, roll it firmly into small balls with your hands. Heat a little oil in a skillet and add the meatballs, turning them several times to brown evenly. Keep them hot.

3. Trim the mushrooms and cut into slices; set aside in a little water mixed with lemon juice. Scrape and grate the carrots. Shell the petits pois and blanch them in boiling, salted water for 15 minutes. Sort the spinach while washing it; if it is not soft, blanch briefly in boiling, salted water.

4. Put everything in a dish; the meatballs should be hot, the cabbage still a little warm, and the rest cold. Sprinkle with cilantro (chopped and whole).

5. Serve with vinaigrette flavored with ground coriander.

Recommended drinks

Light beer
Tavel
Saumur-Champigny

Menu suggestions

1. This Asian dish can form a main course, preceded by a soup of asparagus tips and shrimp tails and followed by lychees in syrup for dessert.

2. You can also serve it as a side-salad, with chicken consommé as an appetizer, baked monkfish as the main dish, and green apple sorbet for dessert.

Recommended drinks

Bergerac
Cahors
Côtes-du-Rhône

Menu suggestions

1. This salad, a delightful combination of extremely varied ingredients, can be followed by tournedos on a bed of potatoes and then a Saint-Honoré.

2. If you like seafood, you can follow this salad with scallops and parsley, and finish with succès praliné.

Salad of magret, arugula, and lettuce sprouts

A party dish

Serves 4
Preparation: 20 minutes
Cooking: 10 minutes

Ingredients

8 quail's eggs
7 oz (200 g) green beans
1 avocado
1 lemon
A few small white onions
1 bunch radish
Young lettuce and arugula sprouts
A few bunches chives and tarragon
2 peaches
4 apricots

8 slices smoked magret
 (duck breast)
Oil
Vinegar
Salt and pepper

1. Harden the quail's eggs in boiling water for 4 minutes. Leave to cool, remove their shells, and cut them into two. Quail's eggs can also be bought hard-boiled, in small jars, in specialist groceries. If you cannot find them, use small chicken's eggs and cook them until they are hard (i.e., for about 8 minutes).

2. Trim the green beans and cook them in boiling, salted water, making sure they remain crispy (no more than 5 minutes).

3. Cut the avocado in half and remove the pit with the tip of a knife. Remove the skin and cut the flesh into uniform strips. Sprinkle with a little lemon juice to prevent it turning black.

4. Peel the onions and cut them into very thin slices. Wash and trim the radishes. Cut some into the form of flowers, the rest into thin slices.

5. Sort the young sprouts of lettuce and arugula. Finely chop a little chives and tarragon.

6. Peel the peaches (if need be, after blanching for a moment in boiling water). Open the apricots and cut them into small quarters, removing the pit. Do the same with the peaches. Keep the smallest slices of magret as they are, and cut the others into two or three pieces. Put all the ingredients in a salad bowl, add a generous dusting of pepper, and finish with a light vinaigrette.

Vegetable tartare

A light dish

Serves 6
Preparation: 20 minutes
Cooking: 1 hr 45 minutes
Marinade: overnight

Ingredients

2 red bell peppers
$10^1/2$ oz (300 g) tomatoes
1 bunch new onions
Olive oil
2–3 small artichokes
1–2 small zucchini
1–2 carrots
1–2 turnips
$5^1/2$ oz (150 g) green beans
1 lemon
Balsamic or Modène vinegar

Mustard
Tomato coulis
Herbs (chives, parsley, chervil,
sage, thyme, etc., according to
taste and season)
A few nasturtium flowers
Salt and pepper

1. Put the bell peppers in the oven until their skin starts to blister. Wrap them individually in moist paper towels and leave to cool. You will now be able to peel them easily. Open them, remove the fibers and seeds, then chop into small pieces. Peel the tomatoes, having first plunged them briefly into boiling water. Cut them into two and seed, squeezing slightly. Cut the flesh into small pieces. Peel and chop the onions, then let them sweat with olive oil in a casserole over low heat. Wait until they start to change color before adding the bell peppers and tomatoes. Add salt, pepper, and thyme. Cover and bake in an oven preheated to 350 °F (180 °C) for 30 minutes. Leave to cool.

2. Peel the other vegetables and cut into small dice. Cook individually in salted water: reckon on $1^1/2$ minutes for the artichokes, carrots, and turnips, and 30 seconds for the green beans and zucchini. Drain immediately and then plunge into ice water. Place the drained, diced vegetables in a salad bowl, mix gently with the lemon juice, and leave to marinate overnight in a cool place.

3. Prepare a mustard vinaigrette and spicy tomato coulis; these will be served separately, allowing guests to help themselves according to taste. Just before serving, add the herbs, finely chopped, to the vinaigrette. Serve the vegetables in the salad bowl, after mixing them one last time. Garnish with nasturtium flowers and a sprig of green thyme. Serve chilled, but not ice cold.

Recommended drinks

Chianti
Anjou
Rosé de Provence

Menu suggestions

1. This original recipe makes an ideal accompaniment to fresh pasta with basil. Serve it following melon as an appetizer, with a sorbet for dessert.

2. You can also serve this dish as an appetizer, followed by a bouillabaisse. Consider an orange mousse or fresh cheese for dessert.

Roquefort and cherry tomato pie

A party dish

Serves 4
Preparation and first cooking: 15 minutes
Second cooking: 15 minutes

Ingredients

9 oz (250 g) piecrust dough, ready to bake
$^3/_4$ oz (20 g) butter
1 egg yolk
4$^1/_2$ oz (125 g) Roquefort or Auvergne blue cheese
1 small pot crème fraîche
Strong prepared mustard
1 whole egg
1 bunch chives
12$^1/_2$ oz (350 g) cherry tomatoes
Salt and pepper

1. Line a lightly buttered mold with the pastry dough, leaving a small protruding edge; trim with a pastry knife and baste with egg yolk, using a brush. Place a disk of wax paper on top of the dough and then a weight to hold it down (dried beans, pits, baking beans, etc). Bake for 15 minutes in an oven preheated to 365 °F (185 °C). You can also make individual patties, especially for a buffet. In this case, bake the pastry for just 8–10 minutes.

2. Break down the cheese with a fork, then mix it in a bowl with roughly the same quantity of crème fraîche, 1 tbsp mustard, and the whole egg. Sprinkle finely chopped chives on top.

3. Remove the weights and wax paper from the pastry and spread the cheese mixture over it. Preheat the oven to 400–435 °F (205–225 °C). Remove the peduncles from the tomatoes before arranging them on the cheese mixture. Trace concentric circles and try to keep them tightly together as they will tend to sink into the cream during the cooking process. Bake in the oven for 15 minutes. This Roquefort pie can either be served hot, straight from the oven, or warm, after resting for 15 minutes. You can also prepare it in advance and freeze it; heat in a very hot oven for about 10 minutes before serving.

Recommended drinks

Madiran
Graves
Palette

Menu suggestions

1. As a hot appetizer, this pie makes an ideal prelude to a summer menu of lamb kebabs with bell peppers and mushrooms, followed by vacherin with raspberries.

2. Another option after this pie is leg of lamb with garlic and rosemary, garnished with eggplant purée, with orange tart for dessert.

Pascale pie with spinach

A regional dish

Serves 6
Preparation: 20 minutes
Cooking: 45 minutes

Ingredients

8 eggs
1 lb 5 oz (600 g) spinach
1 clove garlic
2 shallots
14 oz (400 g) pork loin
10 1/2 oz (300 g) cushion of veal
Nutmeg
Sweet white wine or port
1 3/4 oz (50 g) butter
14 oz (400 g) piecrust pastry dough, ready to bake

1 small pot crème fraîche
Salt and pepper

1. Cook 5 eggs in boiling water for 10 minutes. Meanwhile, cut the stalks off the spinach, then wash and drain it. Peel the garlic and the shallots, then chop them finely.

2. Finely grind the pork (ham can be used as a substitute). Repeat the process with the cushion of veal, then mix the two meats together in a bowl; add the chopped garlic and shallots, salt, pepper, and a pinch of grated nutmeg. Finally, add 1–2 tbsp white wine or port to obtain a malleable stuffing that is not too compact. Adjust seasoning to taste.

3. Preheat the oven to 350 °F (180 °C). Melt a little butter in a deep skillet and simmer the spinach. When it has given off most of its moisture, wring it dry, a little at a time. Shell the eggs.

4. Roll the pastry on a floured worktop until it is 1/8 in (3 mm) thick. Butter a mold and add the dough. Spread the spinach in the bottom, and then the stuffing; bury the hard-boiled eggs in the stuffing.

5. Beat together 1 whole egg, two yolks, and 5–6 tbsp crème fraîche in a bowl. Add salt, pepper, and nutmeg, then cover the top of the pie with this mixture.

6. Put the pie in the middle of the oven and bake for about 45 minutes. Remove it, leave for a few minutes, then turn it out (while still warm) onto a serving platter.

Recommended drinks

Cider
Mercurey
Sancerre

Menu suggestions

1. Serve this specialty from central France as a hot appetizer, before plates of veal with watercress fondue and followed by goat's cheese with baked apples.

2. This pie can also act as the main dish for a dinner, with sorrel soup as an appetizer. Finish the meal with goat's cheese and salad.

Broccoli terrine

A family dish

Serves 10
Preparation: 20 minutes
Cooking: 50 minutes

Ingredients

1 celeriac
9 oz (250 g) potatoes
3 lb 5 oz (1.5 kg) broccoli
Olive oil
1 oz (30 g) butter
1¼ cups (30 cl) crème fraîche
6 eggs
8 leaves gelatin
Salt and pepper

Sauce:
2 cups (50 cl) bouillon
Butter
Flour
Powdered aspic

1. Trim and wash the celeriac, then cut into fairly thin slices. Put these into a pan, cover with cold water, add salt, and boil. Peel the potatoes and put them in the pan, after the water has been simmering for 30 minutes. Cook until the prongs of a fork penetrate the slices of celeriac and the potatoes are just done.

2. Trim the broccoli and blanch in boiling, salted water. Make sure it remains fairly firm. Brown all these ingredients in a mixture of oil and butter. Set aside some small florets of broccoli and reduce the rest to a purée, using a blender if possible.

3. Similarly, reduce the celeriac and potatoes to a purée, which must then be dried out a little in a deep skillet over high heat. Divide the crème fraîche, beaten with the eggs, salt, and pepper, between the purées and likewise the gelatin leaves, dissolved in a little warm water.

4. Bring to the boil 2 cups (50 cl) bouillon. Make a roux with butter and flour, thinned with the hot bouillon. Stir over low heat for 5 minutes. Add a little cream and powdered aspic thinned in 1 glass water. Cook for 5 minutes, stirring continuously, and then leave to cool.

5. Butter a terrine and fill with alternate layers of celeriac and broccoli purée. Bake in a bain-marie or baking pan of water for 50 minutes in an oven preheated to 400 °F (200 °C). Leave to cool, then add a layer of sauce and thin slices of broccoli florets.

Recommended drinks

Chianti
Entre-deux-mers
Arbois Blanc

Menu suggestions

1. This original and tasty broccoli terrine can precede the delicious Italian specialty of veal and tuna, followed by lemon tart.

2. This terrine is equally suitable as an appetizer, before papillotes of mullet with fennel and tiramisu for dessert.

Terrine of green beans

An economical dish

Serves 6–8
First preparation: 15 minutes
Marinade: 12 hours
Second preparation: 30 minutes
Cooking: 50 minutes

Ingredients

10¹/₂ oz (300 g) best-quality, trimmed
pork loin
7 oz (200 g) chicken breast
1–2 carrots
Celery
Butter
2 shallots
1 clove garlic
2 glasses chicken bouillon
1 scant cup (20 cl) Madeira

1 sprig rosemary
Bay leaf
1 sprig cilantro
5¹/₂ oz (150 g) cow's liver
9 oz (250 g) lard
2 eggs
12¹/₂ oz (350 g) very fresh green
beans
Thin strips of pork fat
Salt and peppercorns

1. Cut the pork and chicken breast into strips, removing the nerves. Dust them with salt and pepper, then set aside.

2. Trim the carrots and celery. Cut them into small dice and brown in butter with the chopped shallots and garlic. Add the bouillon and Madeira. Simmer for 15 minutes and leave to cool, before pouring over the meat. Marinate all these ingredients for 12 hours with the rosemary, bay leaf, and cilantro. Remove the meat and strain the marinade, before heating and reducing it to 1 glass. Leave to cool.

3. Cut the liver into strips and chop it very thinly, with the meat. Also chop the lard, having previously cut it into strips. Work this stuffing together by placing the meat in a terrine set in a basin of crushed ice, and gradually folding in the chopped lard.

4. Add 1 egg yolk and the reduced marinade. Adjust seasoning to taste. Meanwhile, cook the green beans until they are al dente. Refresh them in ice water. Divide into small bundles and roll them in the thin strips of fat, along with the stuffing.

5. Line the terrine with further strips of fat, then add a layer of stuffing. Put the bundles of beans in the terrine and fill the remaining space with the stuffing. Smooth the surface and cover with strips of fat. Pack this down tightly, then cover the terrine and cook in the oven in a bain-marie or baking pan of water for 50 minutes, at 175 °F (80 °C). Turn out the terrine and serve it thoroughly chilled on lettuce leaves, with a garnish of cherry tomatoes.

Recommended drinks

Quincy
Gamay
Anjou Rouge

Menu suggestions

1. This terrine is appropriate for a buffet, accompanied by Italian charcuterie and small vegetables marinated in olive oil; for dessert, serve an assortment of ice creams and sorbets.

2. In a more classical setting, this terrine can serve as an appetizer before roast chicken with petits pois and strawberry tart for dessert.

Vegetarian cooking

A vegetarian diet is a lifestyle that attracts many devoted followers. It is by no means incompatible with refined cooking or healthy living, provided it includes eggs, milk, and cheese (to avoid any risk of nutritional deficiencies). Summer, with its abundance of fresh fruit and green vegetables, is the perfect time to discover the benefits and delights of vegetable dishes, in all their delicious variety.

Tip

Do not confuse vegetarianism and veganism: the latter excludes all animal derivatives (sometimes even including a product like honey). It can be dangerous if it leads to deficiencies of proteins, calcium, iron, and vitamins.

Vegetable stuffing with dried fruit

Ingredients for 4
1¼ cups (250 g) white rice
2 onions
2 tomatoes
1 tbsp sugar
1 pinch thyme
1¾ oz (50 g) raisins
1 bunch cilantro
Salt and pepper

1. Wash the rice in the water, then drain. Gently brown the chopped onions for 5 minutes in a saucepan over medium heat. Add the tomatoes (mashed), sugar, thyme, salt, and pepper.

2. Cook, stirring occasionally, for 5 minutes. Add the rice and then enough cold water to just cover all the ingredients. Simmer for 20–25 minutes, until the water has completely evaporated.

3. Remove from the heat, cover, and leave to cool for 20 minutes. Put the mixture into a bowl, add the raisins and chopped cilantro, and adjust seasoning to taste. Use to stuff peppers, pieces of zucchini, or hollowed-out eggplants.

Mixed vegetarian salad

Ingredients for 4
1 cup (200 g) rice
2 bell peppers
2 zucchini
2 carrots
2 tomatoes
5½ oz (150 g) canned corn
2 lemons
8 tbsp olive oil
1 bunch basil
Salt and pepper

1. Boil good white rice or, even better, brown rice in salted water. Leave to cool, then drain. Broil then peel a mixture of red, green, and yellow bell peppers.

2. Wash and wipe the zucchini and carrots and cut into thin, uniform strips. Blanch and drain. Peel the tomatoes, then seed and crush them. Drain the corn.

3. Prepare a vinaigrette: squeeze the juice from the lemons, add salt and pepper, then beat in olive oil. Wash and chop the basil, then add it to the vinaigrette. Mix all the ingredients with the vinaigrette. Serve thoroughly chilled.

Bohémienne of vegetables

Ingredients for 4
1 lb 2 oz (500 g) sliced eggplants
Olive oil
1 lb 2 oz (500 g) sliced zucchini
1 lb 2 oz (500 g) sliced bell
peppers
4 sliced onions
1 lb 2 oz (500 g) quartered
tomatoes
Thyme
Bay leaf
4 chopped cloves garlic
2 lemons
Salt and pepper

1. Sprinkle the eggplants with salt
and pepper, then brown them in 3 tbsp
oil. Remove from the heat and set
aside. Sauté the zucchini in the skillet,
adding a little oil. Remove from the
heat and follow the same procedure
with the bell peppers.

2. Heat 3 tbsp oil in a pan and then
brown the onions for 5 minutes. Add
the tomatoes and cook for a further 5
minutes. Add the other browned
vegetables. Mix everything together,
then add the thyme, bay leaf, garlic,
salt, and pepper. Cover, lower the heat,
and cook for 40 minutes, then leave to
cool. Add the lemon juice and 5 tbsp
oil. Adjust seasoning to taste and serve.

Peperonata

Ingredients for 4
6 red and green bell peppers
9 oz (250 g) onions
1 lb 2 oz (500 g) tomatoes
2 cloves garlic
Olive oil
2 bay leaves
Salt and pepper

1. Cut the bell peppers in half, then
remove the stalks, seeds, and
membranes. Pass them under cold,
running water and cut into strips.
Peel the onions and cut them into
thin slices. Peel the tomatoes and
cut them into quarters. Roughly
chop the garlic cloves.

2. Heat the oil and briefly sauté the
onions, garlic, and bay leaves,
without allowing them to change
color. Add the bell peppers, stir,
cover, and simmer gently for a good
10 minutes. Add the tomatoes, salt,
and pepper and cook for 30 minutes,
uncovered, until the liquid from the
vegetables has evaporated and the
peperonata is cooked, but still
crispy.

3. Leave to cool and serve as an
appetizer or salad, or as an
accompaniment to cold meat or
chicken.

Assortment of vegetables for pasta

Ingredients for 4
3 tomatoes
2 bell peppers
1 zucchini
1 carrot
1 bunch basil
1 clove garlic
8 tbsp olive oil
Salt and pepper

1. Peel, seed, and crush the
tomatoes. Broil the bell peppers,
then peel and dice them.

2. Wash and wipe the zucchini. Peel
the carrot. Cut the two vegetables
into small dice, in the same way as
the bell peppers, then cook them in
boiling salted water. Drain.

3. Cook your fresh pasta as normal;
drain and place in a large bowl.

4. Add the tomatoes, diced
vegetables, basil leaves (finely
chopped), and garlic (also chopped),
along with the olive oil. Season with
salt and pepper. Mix quickly and
serve immediately.

Winter vegetables

General points

The main advantage of steaming is that it is extremely healthy, as no fat is required at all. Furthermore, it faithfully preserves both the taste and aromas of vegetables.

Root vegetables

These can be boiled or steamed. When boiling, reckon on 1½ tsp (8 g) coarse salt per quart/liter of water. There is no need to bring the water to the boil before adding the vegetables; just put them in cold, salted water and then start cooking. There is one exception to this rule, however: leeks. If you want to conserve their splendid, green color, it is vital to put them into boiling water. For steaming vegetables, several utensils are equally effective: a couscous-maker; a wicker basket (typical of Asian cooking) placed over a saucepan of boiling water; or a specially designed steamer. The vegetables can be cooked whole or in pieces.

Leek and potato soup

This simple, but tasty dish can be enjoyed throughout the winter. For 1 quart (1 liter) of soup, peel and wash 4 large potatoes and 4 leeks. Thinly slice the leeks, then sauté gently in 3½ oz (100 g) butter for 15 minutes, stirring

Guide to steaming vegetables		
VEGETABLES	**WHOLE**	**IN PIECES**
Potato	50 minutes	40 minutes
Carrot	45 minutes	30 minutes
Celeriac	60 minutes	45 minutes
Turnip	50 minutes	40 minutes
Parsnip	50 minutes	40 minutes
Rutabaga	50 minutes	40 minutes

Guide boiling vegetables		
VEGETABLES	**WHOLE**	**IN PIECES**
Potato	55 minutes	30 minutes
Carrot	45 minutes	20 minutes
Celeriac	55 minutes	40 minutes
Turnip	35 minutes	25 minutes
Parsnip	40 minutes	25 minutes
Rutabaga	40 minutes	30 minutes

Leek and potato soup

Green cabbage soup

frequently to ensure they do not change color. Add the potatoes, also sliced fairly thinly. Cover and continue cooking over a low heat for 10 minutes. Pour in 8 cups (2 liters) cold water and bring to the boil with a small bouquet garni, salt, and pepper. Cook the soup uncovered, over low heat, for about 1 hour. Remove from the heat and reduce the vegetables to a fine purée with a hand beater. Adjust the seasoning and serve piping hot. This dish can be complemented by chopped parsley and 1 small tbsp crème fraîche per person.

Cabbage soup

This warming and nourishing dish is ideal for cold winter days. For about 6 cups (1.5 liters) soup, peel 2 carrots and 2 onions, then slice them thinly. Discard the outer leaves of 1 green cabbage, cut the remainder into four pieces, and separate the leaves. Blanch them quickly. Heat 3 tbsp duck fat in a saucepan and add the onions and carrots, along with 7 oz (200 g) thickly sliced bacon, cut into chunks. Simmer for 15 minutes, stirring occasionally. Add the blanched cabbage leaves (roughly chopped), 8 cups (2 liters) water, 7 oz (200 g) dried navy beans (previously soaked in water), 5^1/$_2$ oz (150 g) suet, 1 bouquet garni, salt, and pepper. Cook for 1 hour 30 minutes. Remove the bouquet garni, adjust seasoning to taste, and serve piping hot.

Vichy carrots

This an ideal garnish for braised veal and beef. Wash and peel 1^3/$_4$ lb (800 g) carrots, then slice thinly. Place them in a saucepan with 1^3/$_4$ oz (50 g) butter, salt, pepper, and just enough cold water to cover them.

Bring to the boil, reduce the heat, and simmer gently for 35 minutes. Garnish with 1 tbsp chopped parsley.

Steamed celeriac

For 6 people, peel 2 heads celeriac and cut them into slices around ^{1}/$_4$ in (5 mm) thick. Rub these with half a lemon. Place them in the top of a steamer and cook for 40 minutes. Serve with melted butter and chopped chives.

Tip

When boiling vegetables, do not forget to salt the water—otherwise they will turn out very dull. Furthermore, boiled vegetables must not be left in water longer than necessary, as they will swell and quickly lose their flavor.

Steamed celery root

General points

When simmered in a sauce made with bouillon or cream, winter vegetables soften quickly to acquire a deliciously tender consistency. This method is used to cook vegetables with firm flesh, such as carrots, oyster plants, Jerusalem artichokes, and cardoons.

Glazed carrots

These make a wonderful accompaniment to roast pork. Peel about 10 carrots and cut them into slices around $1/8$ in (3 mm) thick. Put them in a saucepan of cold water. Bring to the boil, cook for 3 minutes, and drain. Brown a sliced onion with $1^1/2$ oz (40 g) butter in another saucepan, then add the blanched carrots, a small sprig of thyme, $1/3$ cup + $1^1/2$ tbsp (10 cl) water, and all the cooking juices (with some of the fat skimmed off) from a piece of pork. Cook over medium heat for about 30 minutes. After this time, the cooking juices should be reduced and thickened, leaving the carrots bathed in a delicious sauce. Remove the sprig of thyme, adjust the seasoning, and serve very hot. You can also prepare turnips and parsnips in this way, or a mixture of the two.

Oyster plants with béchamel sauce

These are easy to prepare and go particularly well with roast veal. To serve 6, peel $2^1/4$ lb (1 kg) oyster plants. Wash then boil them for 50 minutes in a mixture of 7 pints (3.5 liters) water, $5/8$ cup (70 g) flour, and the juice of 2 lemons. Meanwhile, prepare a béchamel sauce. Add the cooked and drained oyster plants to this sauce then simmer slowly, stirring frequently, for 15 minutes. Adjust the seasoning and serve very hot. You can also cook the final mixture in the oven, "au gratin," with grated cheese sprinkled on top.

Vegetable blanquette for 6

1 Vegetable blanquette is an original and tasty recipe for winter vegetables. Peel and wash 4 carrots, 3 onions, 3 turnips, 3 leeks, 2 parsnips, and 3 potatoes. Cut them into slices and then into sticks, no more than $3/8$ in (1 cm) wide. Cook them separately in salted, boiling water, making sure that they remain a little crispy.

2 Meanwhile, prepare the white sauce: bring to the boil 3 cups (80 cl) chicken bouillon in a saucepan and keep it bubbling constantly. At the same time, heat $3/8$ cup (50 g) flour and 2 oz (65 g) butter, stirring frequently. Pour this mixture, piping hot, into the bouillon, beating vigorously. Bring to the boil very slowly and cook for 5 minutes.

3 Add about $3^1/2$ oz (100 g) crème fraîche, along with salt and pepper, then mix in the precooked vegetables. Simmer over low heat for 20 minutes. Add $1/2$ bunch chopped parsley before serving. This blanquette makes an excellent garnish for boiled poultry, plates of veal, or a fleshy poached fish. The parsley can be replaced by chervil.

vegetables cooked with cream and bouillon

Turnips with cream for 6

1 Peel 8 medium-size turnips. Cut them into slices around $1/4$ in (6 mm) thick; add these to a saucepan of salted, boiling water for 15 minutes, then drain. Pat them dry carefully with a dishtowel and set aside. If the turnips are very fresh and tender, you can skip this step.

2 Simmer 2 sliced shallots with $1^3/4$ oz (50 g) butter in another saucepan, then add the slices of precooked turnip, stirring to coat them thoroughly in the butter. You can add a few peeled small onions ("grelots.") Use salted butter to enhance the other ingredients. The shallots must be sliced as thinly as possible.

3 Add salt, pepper, and $1^2/3$ cups (40 cl) light cream. Cover and cook over low heat for 25 minutes. Just before serving, add 1 bunch chopped chives and adjust seasoning to taste. These turnips make a succulent accompaniment to roast chicken. Be sure to use the youngest vegetables you can find.

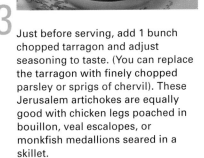

Jerusalem artichokes with cream for 6

1 Peel 1 lb 11 oz (750 g) medium-size Jerusalem artichokes. Cut them into slices around $1/4$ in (6 mm) thick, add to a saucepan of salted, boiling water for 15 minutes, then drain. If you find the taste of Jerusalem artichokes a little strong, you can mix them with a few slices of firm potato.

2 Brown 2 sliced onions in another saucepan with $1^3/4$ oz (50 g) butter, then add the precooked vegetable slices. Add salt, pepper, and $1^2/3$ cups (40 cl) light cream. Cover and cook over low heat for 25 minutes. Check from time to time, to see if the vegetables are tender. You can also add a little crème fraîche.

3 Just before serving, add 1 bunch chopped tarragon and adjust seasoning to taste. (You can replace the tarragon with finely chopped parsley or sprigs of chervil). These Jerusalem artichokes are equally good with chicken legs poached in bouillon, veal escalopes, or monkfish medallions seared in a skillet.

Potatoes "à la sarladaise"

To serve 6, peel and wash 2¼ lb (1 kg) potatoes. Cut them into slices about ⅛ in (2–3 mm) thick. Wash them again, rinse thoroughly, then drain and wipe. Heat 5 tbsp goose or duck fat over high heat in a large, iron skillet. Add the potatoes, seasoned with salt and pepper. Brown for 5 minutes, then turn them over, and repeat this operation for around 35 minutes. You should obtain a fairly compact "cake." Reduce the heat then add 4 chopped cloves garlic and 3 sliced and precooked boletus mushrooms. Mix well and cook, until the potatoes are golden (about 20 minutes). Finish the dish with

½ bunch chopped parsley. Serve these potatoes very hot, with roast beef, veal, or chicken.

Small fried potatoes

To serve 6, peel 2 lb 11 oz (1.2 kg) small, round potatoes. Place them in a large saucepan of cold water, bring to the boil, and drain immediately. Wipe the blanched potatoes carefully. Heat 5 tbsp clarified butter in a large skillet. Add the potatoes and fry them over medium heat, turning frequently, for about 40 minutes. Serve them hot, with chopped fresh parsley.

Grilled vegetables

Vegetables sautéed in a wok for 6

1 Peel 4 carrots and 4 turnips, then cut them into medium-size julienne strips. Wash and drain 7 oz (200 g) bean sprouts. Trim and thoroughly wash a few small leeks, then cut them into uniform segments. The aim is to obtain pieces roughly the same length and thickness. Pat dry with paper towels.

2 Peel and slice 1 onion. Heat the wok with 4 tbsp peanut oil over very high heat. Add the onion and fry, stirring continuously for about 3 minutes. Add the strips of turnips and carrots, along with the bean sprouts. Sauté these vegetables, still over a very high heat, for about 5 minutes, stirring regularly.

3 Add a mixture of ⅓ cup + 1½ tbsp (10 cl) soy sauce, 2 tbsp (3 cl) vinegar, 1 tbsp sugar, and 10 drops sesame oil. Cook for 1 minute, then serve immediately. Do not cook the vegetables more than necessary as they will quickly become soft and lose their taste. These vegetables can be served as a vegetarian dish or a garnish for poultry.

Sautéed pumpkin with rosemary for 6

1 Sautéed pumpkin with rosemary is a succulent specialty that can be prepared from early September onwards, when pumpkins come on the market. Peel and seed a pumpkin until you have 1³/₄ lb (800 g) flesh. Peel with a very sharp, wide knife. Be sure to remove the fibers surrounding the seeds, so that the pumpkin is thoroughly cleaned.

2 Cut into slices about ⁵/₁₆ in (8 mm) thick. Add salt, pepper, and around 10 fresh rosemary leaves. Rosemary is an herb with a spicy flavor and fairly strong smell, so usually only a small quantity is required to enrich an entire dish. It is particularly distinctive in combination with pumpkin. If rosemary is unavailable, replace it with fresh thyme.

3 Heat 4 tbsp virgin olive oil in a large, iron skillet and add the pumpkin, chopped and seasoned. Brown the pumpkin over medium heat then turn the pieces over. Continue in this way for about 20 minutes, stirring occasionally to ensure that all the pieces are browned, with a slightly reddish tinge on the sides.

4 Taste the pumpkin: serve it as soon as it is tender, adding, at the last moment, a dash of olive oil flavored with garlic or basil. This dish makes an ideal accompaniment to roast lamb or poultry. You can also include it in a vegetarian menu, accompanied by bulgur wheat, brown rice, or spicy semolina.

General points

Vegetables melt in the mouth and soak up flavors after simmering slowly in their cooking juices. It is important to cook them at a constant, low temperature. Braised endives must be cooked with lemon juice, to prevent them turning black. Melt 2³/₄ oz (80 g) butter in a casserole and add the endives, along with ¹/₃ cup + 1¹/₂ tbsp (10 cl) chicken bouillon, salt, pepper, 3 tsp sugar, and the juice of 1 lemon. When the liquid comes to the boil, cover the casserole and place it in the oven. Bake at 350 °F (180 °C) for about 35 minutes then remove the endives from the casserole. Reduce the cooking juices for 1 minute then pour them over the vegetables. If you would like these endives a pretty orangey-red color, add 2 tsp powdered paprika to the liquid. Endives can sometimes be tasteless; liven them up with the addition of 2 tsp curry powder at the start of the cooking process. "Sweating" is a very common method for cooking vegetables. It consists of gently sautéing onions, shallots, leeks, or garlic with a tiny amount of fat, in order to eliminate, through evaporation, some or all of the water contained in the vegetables. This evaporation brings out the aromas of a vegetable, in conjunction with the heat. Sweating also gives vegetables more taste, thereby making them ideal for an aromatic garnish.

Chicken with braised endives

Endive fondue for 4

1 Endive fondue can be made in a moment and is equally appropriate for big occasions and everyday meals.Remove any damaged outer leaves from 6 endives

2 Thinly slice the vegetables with a stainless-steel knife. Wash them quickly and drain, then add to a large skillet with the juice of 1 lemon, a generous ¹/₈ cup (40 g) sugar, 2³/₄ oz (80 g) butter, salt, and pepper.

3 Bring to the boil and cook fairly quickly, for 4 minutes, stirring continuously. Serve immediately with fillets of fish, braised white meat, or even a very rare roast beef.

Leek fondue with scallops for 4

1 Leek fondue with cream is a delicious garnish that is ideal for fish or scallops. It is also an excellent way of appreciating the delicate flavor of leeks. Peel 5 very fresh leeks and wash them carefully. Cut off the root and three quarters of the green part. Choose medium-size leeks that are not thick. Keep the green part for an aromatic garnish or soup.

2 Cut the leeks into two, lengthwise, and slice them thinly. Wash and drain. In order to wash leeks thoroughly, hold them vertically under a jet of cold water, allowing it to penetrate between the tightly packed leaves as grit can be trapped in the white part. Pat dry thoroughly, using a dishtowel.

3 Melt 3½ oz (100 g) butter over low heat in a large skillet. Add the leeks, salt, and pepper. Simmer slowly, covered, for 5 minutes, stirring from time to time with a wooden spoon. The leeks will lose much of their volume. If they give off too much water, simmer them uncovered for a little longer.

4 Add 1 scant cup (20 cl) crème fraîche. Bring to the boil and cook over medium heat for 20 minutes. Adjust the seasoning—do not be afraid to add a generous amount of freshly ground pepper—and serve piping hot. If you want, you can also add, at the last moment, a sprinkling of chopped chives or a few sprigs of chervil. Opt for fairly thick crème fraîche.

General points

Stuffed vegetables are always a treat, and winter produce is particularly suited to this way of serving.

Cabbage paupiettes

These are prepared with curly green cabbage, preferably of a substantial size, as its leaves will be larger and easier to stuff. To serve 6, trim 1 large green cabbage, removing the stalk and outer leaves. Take off the leaves one by one and remove any overly large ribs with a knife. Boil plenty of salted water and add the cabbage leaves. Refresh and drain the leaves. Meanwhile, prepare a stuffing. Put 1 lb 5 oz (600 g) minced meat, 2 eggs, 3^1/$_2$ oz (100 g) chopped cured

Cabbage paupiettes

Stuffed chayote

ham, 3 chopped chicken livers, 3^1/$_2$ oz (100 g) bread soaked in milk, 2 shallots, and ^{1}/$_2$ bunch chopped parsley in a bowl. Add salt and pepper then mix thoroughly with a wooden spoon. Place 2 cabbage leaves on the worktop, put 2 generous tbsp stuffing on top of each one, fold the leaves to form a "parcel," and tie with string to close it tight. Heat 3 tbsp peanut oil in a saucepan, add the cabbage parcels, and brown them over a medium heat for 15 minutes. Add a small aromatic garnish (onion, carrot, leek) and sweat for 10 minutes. Then add 1 scant cup (20 cl) beef bouillon, 2 sliced tomatoes, 1 bouquet garni, salt, and pepper. Cover and cook slowly for 1 hour 30 minutes. Serve very hot, with steamed potatoes.

Whole stuffed cabbage

Stuffed chayote

These are very fine and delicate, especially when small. To serve 6, open 3 chayote lengthways and remove the pits. Bake in an oven preheated to 350 °F (180 °C) for 35 minutes, then use a small spoon to remove the flesh; set aside both this and the shells. Prepare the stuffing by mixing the chayote flesh with 1 cup (300 g) boiled rice, 2 eggs, and 2 finely chopped onions. Season the mixture with the juice of 1 lime, salt, pepper, 1 tbsp sugar, 1 tsp curry powder, and 1 pinch Cayenne pepper. Fill the chayote shells with the stuffing, then cook them in the oven at 350 °F/180 °C for 50 minutes.

Stuffed onions

These are prepared in the same way as stuffed tomatoes. To

Stuffed onions

serve 6, peel 6 large onions and cut them in half, vertically. Hollow out the onion halves to create enough space for a stuffing. Boil some salted water in a saucepan and plunge the hollowed onions into it for 10 seconds. Drain. Prepare the stuffing. Put 7 oz (200 g) bread (without the crust) soaked in milk, 2 chopped garlic cloves, 1/2 bunch chopped parsley, 1 tbsp flour, 1 lb 5 oz (600 g) minced meat, and 1 egg in a bowl. Mix these ingredients

Stuffed celeriac

together and fill the hollowed onion halves, using a tablespoon. Put them in a baking pan and cook at 350 °F (180 °C) for 40 minutes. Serve the stuffed onions with white rice and a tomato sauce.

Stuffed potatoes

Large potatoes must be used for this dish (ideally, each one should be large enough for a single helping). To serve 6, peel and wash 6 large potatoes. Cut them lengthwise and make a deep hollow in each piece with a small spoon. Boil the extracted potato flesh in salted water and keep the remainder in cold water. Prepare the stuffing. Put the cooked potato, 1 lb 5 oz (600 g) minced meat, 2 3/4 oz (80 g) breadcrumbs, 1 chopped onion, 1 bunch chopped chives, 2 eggs, 1 chopped clove garlic, salt, pepper, and some fresh thyme in a bowl. Mix these ingredients with a wooden spoon for 3 minutes. Fill the potatoes with the stuffing, creating a dome

shape, and cook for 1 hour in an oven preheated to 350 °F (180 °C). A lighter alternative is a stuffing of onion and mushrooms, instead of the minced meat.

Stuffed potatoes

General points

Deep-frying with hot, clean oil is an ideal method for cooking a number of winter vegetables. The most obvious example is potato, but celeriac and sweet potato can also be fried in the same way. Use peanut or sunflower oil.

French fries

This recipe never fails to please. Select firm, white potatoes, large enough to cut into long, elegant strips. The success of fries depends on their being cooked twice, at two different temperatures. The first stage cooks the potato inside, while the second gives it its color. To serve 6, peel then wash 2 lb 11 oz (1.2 kg) potatoes. Using a knife or mandolin, cut them into slices around 1/4 in (7 mm) thick,

then into sticks of identical width. Wash these strips in a colander under cold running water, to eliminate any excess starch. Drain and wipe dry with a large, clean dishtowel. Pour 10 cups (2.5 liters) sunflower oil into a deep-fat fryer and heat to a temperature of about 265–285 °F (130–140 °C). Place the potatoes in the wire basket, lower into the oil, and fry for about 10 minutes, shaking the basket periodically. Check progress by squeezing one of the fries with a pair of tongs: it should be easy to crush, but without being brown. Drain the precooked fries and raise the temperature of the oil to 365 °F (185 °C). Insert the potatoes once again, making sure that none of the oil splashes. Cook for 2–3 minutes, then drain. Pat the potatoes dry with absorbent paper towels, season generously with salt, and serve immediately.

Puffed potatoes

To serve 6, choose 1 lb 5 oz (600 g) fairly large potatoes and, using a very sharp knife, peel and trim them to obtain a cylinder (as regular as possible). With another knife or mandolin, cut the potato cylinders into slices 1/16 in (2.5 mm) thick. Plunge them into cold water, stir briefly, drain, and wipe with a clean dishtowel. Heat 8 cups (2 liters) oil to

Puffed potatoes

265–275 °F (130–135 °C) (the temperature is vital, so you will need a thermometer). Add the potatoes and cook, stirring from time to time, for 7–8 minutes. The potato slices must remain white, while being cooked inside. Drain and leave to cool for a few minutes. Just before serving, heat the oil to 350–365 °F (180–185 °C) and add the precooked potato slices; these will quickly puff up. Take them out of the fryer when they are browned to your taste. Add salt and serve.

French fries

Sweet-potato fries

These are an excellent accompaniment to dishes from the Caribbean. To serve 4, peel 1 lb 5 oz (600 g) sweet potatoes. Remove any dark patches with the tip of a knife. Using a mandolin or thick knife, slice the sweet potatoes into fairly thin strips, around $^1/_{16}$ in (2 mm) thick. Wash and drain, then thoroughly wipe them with a dishtowel. Pour 8 cups (2 liters) sunflower oil into a deep-fat fryer and bring to a temperature of 345–350 °F (175–180 °C). Put the sweet-potato strips in the basket and immerse them in the oil. Stir frequently, to prevent the slices from sticking to each other. Cook for 6–8 minutes, then drain. The fries should be thoroughly browned. Add salt and serve immediately.

Breaded celery slices

This tasty and original vegetable is excellent with roast game or other meat. To serve 6, wash and trim 2 bunches celery and cut into slices around $^1/_4$ in (8 mm) thick. Steam for 25 minutes to soften, then leave to cool. Season with salt and pepper then dip the slices successively into flour, beaten egg, and white breadcrumbs. In a large skillet, heat 3$^1/_2$ oz (100 g) butter until it bubbles, then color and sauté the breaded

Breaded and fried celery

celery slices over low heat, for 8 minutes on each side.

Potato pancakes

These never fail to please. They are easy to make and offer a simple, but original, variation on everyday fare. To serve 4, peel 1 lb 9 oz (700 g) large, white potatoes. Use a vegetable mill or mandolin to shred them like grated carrots. Work quickly as, once the potatoes are cut, they will turn dark very quickly. Do not wash them. Add salt and pepper. Heat 3 tbsp peanut oil in a medium-size

Sweet potato fries

skillet. Add the grated potatoes and, using a tablespoon, make a pancake mixture about 1 in (2.5 cm) thick that exactly fits the skillet. Cook over medium heat for about 10 minutes then turn it over. Continue cooking for another 15 minutes. Both sides should be golden. When the pancake is cooked, cut it into four equal portions and serve immediately.

Potato paillasson

Duck with duchesse potatoes

General points

When potatoes are mashed, made into little balls, and then deep-fried, they acquire an unusual taste and appearance. To achieve maximum succulence and a perfect texture, these dishes must be prepared just before serving.

Duchesse potatoes

This dish has fallen out of fashion, although it can still be found and is useful to know. It is based on mashed potatoes, which can be served both as a vegetable, along the lines of dauphine potatoes, and as a garnish for other dishes.

Choose firm, white potatoes with smooth, unblemished skins. To serve 6, peel and wash 2¼ lb (1 kg) potatoes. Cook them in salted boiling water for 40 minutes. Drain and leave to cool. Scrape them roughly, then place them in an oven preheated to 250 °F (120 °C) for 30 minutes, to dry them out. Mash the potatoes in a pan with 2¾ oz (80 g) butter, salt, pepper, and grated nutmeg and stir with a wooden spoon, over low heat, for 2 minutes. Leave to cool for a few moments then add 1 whole egg and 2 yolks. Mix thoroughly. Heat 8 cups (2 liters) oil to 345 °F (175 °C) in a saucepan. Put the mixture into a glazing bag with a plain nozzle about 5/8 in (2 cm) in diameter, and squeeze pieces 1 in (2.5 cm) long into the oil. Brown the potato mixture, then drain, pat dry, and add salt. To use duchesse potatoes to garnish a dish, place the mixture in a glazing bag with a grooved nozzle and trace your designs onto the edges of a baking dish. Place this in an oven preheated to 350 °F (180 °C) and cook for 20 minutes. Duchesse potatoes also serve to make breaded, fried croquettes: two recipes in particular transform simple croquettes into classic dishes. In the first, the potato mixture is added to a peeled, finely chopped truffle and the croquettes are coated in slivered almonds before being fried; the second involves enhancing the mixture with chopped ham (either cured or boiled).

Pojarski veal ribs with duchesse potatoes

duchesse and dauphine potatoes

1 Dauphine potatoes are prepared by mixing mashed potatoes with choux pastry mix. Choose firm, white, smooth-skinned potatoes. Peel and wash 1^3/$_4$ lb (800 g) potatoes and cook in salted, boiling water for 40 minutes, until they are very tender. Drain and leave to cool.

2 To make the pastry mix, put 1 generous cup (25 cl) milk and 2 oz (60 g) butter in a pan then add 1 tsp sugar and 2 pinches salt. Bring to the boil then remove from the heat. Add 5^1/$_2$oz (150 g) sieved flour in one go and stir for 1 minute, using a wooden spatula.

3 As it absorbs the liquid, the flour will form a compact mass. Put the saucepan over gentle heat and continue working the flour into the milk for another minute. Cool the pan by briefly plunging the base into cold water. Add 4 eggs one by one, beating hard all the while.

Tip

It is easy to invent personal variations on dauphine potatoes. At the last moment, just before cooking, you could add grated Parmesan, chopped chives, small cubes of bacon streaked with fat, or paprika to the mixture.

4 Put the boiled potatoes in a vegetable mill. Finish the dauphine mixture by combining the mashed potatoes with the pastry mix. Add salt, pepper, and a pinch of ground, fresh nutmeg. Without waiting for the mixture to cool, heat 8 cups (2 liters) oil in a saucepan to 345 °F (175 °C).

5 Put the mixture into a glazing bag and squeeze pieces about ^{5}/$_8$ in (2 cm) into the hot oil. When they are puffed and golden, drain them, then dry on paper towels or a very clean dishtowel. Add salt and serve immediately with roast beef or veal. You can also use a spoon to make balls with the mixture, coated with a thin layer of flour.

Picardy leek pie

General points

When winter vegetables are baked on a bed of piecrust or puff pastry, they provide the basis for delicious pies and tarts. The most common vegetables for these are spinach, leek, potatoes, oyster plants, and mushrooms. They should always be cooked before being laid on the pastry.

Onion tart

To serve 6, prepare 14 oz (400 g) piecrust pastry dough. Roll it out and use it to line a buttered and floured circular mold 10 in (25 cm) in diameter. Meanwhile, peel and finely slice 6 large onions. Sweat them before sautéing very gently in a fairly large skillet until they start to turn transparent. Season with salt and pepper and add a few sprigs of thyme before baking. Leave the cooked onions to cool, then arrange them on the dough. Combine 1 generous cup (25 cl) light cream, 2 eggs, salt, pepper, and grated nutmeg in a small bowl. Pour this liquid over the onions. Add a few dabs of butter to the tart and bake it in an oven preheated to 375 °F (190 °C) for about 35 minutes. Leave to cool for 15 minutes before cutting into slices.

Pumpkin tart

To serve 6, prepare 14 oz (400 g) piecrust pastry dough. Roll it out and use it to line a buttered and floured circular mold 10 in (25 cm) in diameter. Meanwhile, peel and finely slice 1 3/4 lb (800 g) pumpkin flesh. Add this to 1/4 cup (50 g) rice and cook the mixture in milk with 1 sliced onion, salt, and pepper for about 1 hour. Drain thoroughly and leave to cool. Place in a vegetable shredder or blender to obtain a very fine pulp. Add 3 whole eggs, 2 tbsp crème fraîche, 1 pinch Cayenne pepper, and 3 pinches curry powder. Adjust seasoning to taste then spread the mixture on the dough. Dab with butter and bake in an oven preheated to 375 °F (190 °C) for about 40 minutes. Leave to cool for 15 minutes before cutting.

Flamiche

To serve 6, prepare 14 oz (400 g) puff-pastry dough. Roll and then use it to line a buttered and floured circular mold 10 in (25 cm) in diameter. Wash, peel, and finely slice 6 large leeks, discarding the green parts of the leaves. Sweat them very slowly in butter, in a fairly large skillet. This can take as long as 40 minutes. Add salt and pepper. Leave the cooked leeks to cool then arrange them on the dough. Mix 1 generous cup (25 cl) heavy cream, 3 eggs, salt, pepper, and grated nutmeg in a small bowl. Pour over the onions, spreading it evenly. Dab with butter and bake in an oven preheated to 375 °F (190 °C) for 40 minutes. Leave to cool for a few minutes. Serve hot.

Berrichon pastry

Berrichon pastry

To serve 6, prepare 1³/₄ lb (800 g) piecrust pastry dough and use it to line a mold 10 in (25 cm) in diameter. Peel 1³/₄ lb (800 g) potatoes and wash them. Cut them into slices about ¹/₄ in (8 mm) thick, rinse in cold water, and drain. Put the potatoes, 8 cups (2 liters) milk, 1 sliced onion, salt, pepper, and a pinch of grated nutmeg in a saucepan. Bring to the boil then cook very slowly for about 40 minutes. The potatoes should be cooked, but still intact. Drain them carefully then spread over the dough. Sprinkle with chopped parsley and chives. Add 4 tbsp crème fraîche then cover everything with another layer of dough, sealing it tightly with the lower one. Make a small chimney so the steam can escape. Brush the pastry with beaten egg and cook in an oven preheated to 400 °F (200 °C) for 1 hour 20 minutes.

1 This can be made with cultivated or, when available, wild mushrooms. Prepare 1³/₄ lb (800 g) piecrust dough and roll it to a thickness of about ³/₁₆ in (5 mm). Use just over half of it to line a buttered and floured circular mold 10 in (25 cm) in diameter, leaving the edge protruding. Cut off any excess, but leave a substantial margin.

3 Melt 3¹/₂ oz (100 g) butter in a skillet and brown the boiled mushrooms over medium heat. Add salt and pepper, 3 cloves garlic, and 1 small bunch chopped parsley. Cook for 5 minutes, then finish by adding 1 scant cup (20 cl) thick crème fraîche. Adjust seasoning to taste and leave to cool. You could also add 1 small, finely chopped bunch of chives to the dish.

Mushroom pie

for 6

2 Peel, wash, and slice 1 lb 2 oz (500 g) cultivated mushrooms, 7 oz (200 g) black trumpets, 5¹/₂ oz (150 g) chanterelles, and 5¹/₂ oz (150 g) hedgehog mushrooms. Place the mushrooms in a saucepan with 1 scant cup (20 cl) cold water and 3 pinches coarse salt, then cook them over medium heat for 15 minutes. Drain them in a colander and pat dry with paper towels.

4 Lay the mushrooms on the bed of dough then cover with the rest of it, sealing the two layers tightly together. Make a chimney so the steam can escape. Brush the pastry with a thin layer of beaten egg and cook in an oven preheated to 400 °F (200 °C) for about 1 hour 10 minutes. Pour a little hot cream through the chimney before serving.

General points

The gratin is a cooking technique ideally suited to many winter vegetables, such as potatoes, endives, and carrots. These recipes are also very convenient, as they can be prepared in advance and browned shortly before the meal.

Carrot gratin

This dish, rounded off with Parmesan, is easy to make and offers an original way to present

carrots. To serve 6, peel, wash, and slice fairly thinly 2¼ lb (1 kg) carrots and 1 onion. Fry the onion gently in a casserole for 5 minutes until transparent, then add the carrots and braise over low heat for 15 minutes, stirring occasionally. Add ⅔ cup (15 cl) chicken bouillon and ⅔ cup (15 cl) heavy cream. Cook very slowly, covered, for 25 minutes. Check the progress of the carrots: they should be supple, but remain intact. Pour the whole mixture, including the liquid, into a buttered baking pan. Add some dabs of butter and sprinkle with grated Parmesan and Gruyère. Brown at 430 °F (220 °C) for about 15 minutes.

Endive gratin with ham

To serve 6, remove the stalks from 12 endives. Boil 3 quarts (3 liters) water in a saucepan, with the juice of 2 lemons and ⅓ cup + 1½ tbsp (10 cl) white wine. Add the endives to the boiling liquid and cook over low heat for 10 minutes. Drain, then leave to cool for a few minutes. Roll each

Dauphinois gratin

endive in 1 slice cooked ham. Line up the endives in a buttered baking pan, then add 8 tbsp crème fraîche and a dusting of grated Gruyère. Bake for 15 minutes in an oven preheated to 410 °F (210 °C).

Dauphinois gratin

This is one of the few potato dishes that can be reheated successfully, so feel free to make a large amount. Use firm, white potatoes. To serve 6, peel 2 cloves garlic and rub them vigorously over the surface of a baking pan, then add a layer of butter. Peel 2 lb 11 oz (1.2 kg) large potatoes and cut them into slices about ⅛ in (3 mm) thick; wash and drain. Wipe the potatoes carefully with a large, clean dishtowel then arrange them in the baking pan. The top

Endive gratin

Savoyard gratin

layer should be about 3/16 in (5 mm) from the rim. Put 3 eggs, 1¼ cups (30 cl) milk, 1¼ cups (30 cl) light cream, salt, pepper, and 3 pinches ground, fresh nutmeg in a bowl. Whisk to obtain a uniform mixture then pour over the potatoes. Add a few small dabs of butter (3½ oz/100 g). Cook in an oven preheated to 410 °F (210 °C) for 50 minutes.

Savoyard gratin

This is similar to Dauphinois gratin, but is richer because it is prepared with cheese. To serve 6, peel 2 cloves garlic and rub them vigorously over the surface of a baking pan, then add a layer of butter. Peel 2 lb 11 oz (1.2 kg) large potatoes and cut them into slices about ⅛ in (3 mm) thick; wash and drain. Wipe the

potatoes carefully with a large, clean dishtowel then lay them in a bed ¾ in (2 cm) thick in the baking pan. Dust with grated Gruyère (you can also use Comté or Beaufort), then add another layer of potatoes. Repeat the process until the dish is almost full. Put 2 eggs, 1 generous cup (25 cl) milk, 1 generous cup (25 cl) light cream, salt, pepper, and 3 pinches ground, fresh nutmeg in a bowl. Whisk to obtain a uniform mixture then pour it over the potatoes. Add a few small dabs of butter (3½ oz/100 g). Cook for 50 minutes in an oven preheated to 410 °F (210 °C).

Pumpkin gratin

Pumpkin is delicious with béchamel sauce. To serve 6, you will need 2¼ lb (1 kg) pumpkin flesh, without seeds or skin. Cut it into medium-size dice. Heat 2 oz (60 g) butter in a saucepan. Add the pumpkin dice, 1 chopped onion, salt, pepper, and grated nutmeg. Sweat, stirring occasionally, for 20 minutes. Add 1 scant cup (20 cl) chicken bouillon and cook for 15 minutes. Pour the mixture into a buttered casserole and cover with 2 cups (50 cl) béchamel sauce. Sprinkle with grated Gruyère and dab with butter. Cook for 20 minutes in an oven preheated to 410 °F (210 °C).

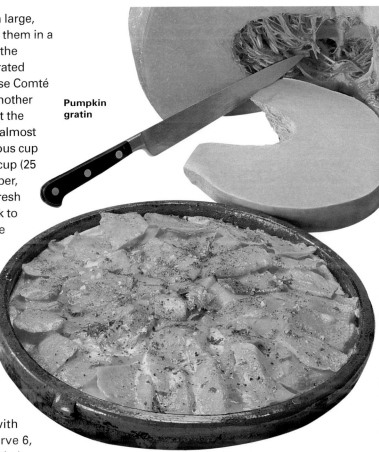

Pumpkin gratin

General points

Winter vegetables melt in the mouth when they are reduced to thin purées and enriched with butter and cream. Vegetable purées can also be turned into soups, terrines, and flans. Here are a few ideas.

Carrot purée

Pumpkin soup

Choose fairly large vegetables, with a strong color, to enhance the visual impact. To serve 6, wash and peel 2 lb 11 oz (1.2 kg) carrots. Cut them into fairly thin slices. Put them in a saucepan with ½ sliced onion, salt, pepper, and 2 cups (50 cl) chicken bouillon (or water). Cook very gently, covered, for about 40 minutes. Drain the cooked carrots, place them in a blender, and reduce to a purée. Add 4½ oz (120 g) butter and 2 tbsp thick crème fraîche. Stir and adjust seasoning to taste.

Pumpkin soup

To make a soup from purée, you must add some of the cooking liquid, in the quantity appropriate for the consistency you require. Choose fairly large and strongly colored vegetables. To serve 6, cut 2 lb 11 oz (1.2 kg) pumpkin flesh into thin slices. Place in a saucepan with ½ sliced onion, salt, pepper, and 2½ cups (60 cl) chicken bouillon (or milk). Cook gently, covered, for about 40 minutes. The pumpkin should be completely soft. Transfer to a blender, reserving the cooking liquid, and reduce to the thinnest possible purée. Put the purée in a saucepan to keep it hot. Add 7 oz (200 g) thick crème fraîche and half the cooking liquid. Mix and adjust the seasoning to taste. Serve hot.

Small ramekins of carrot

Small vegetable flans

To serve 6, wash and peel 2 lb 11 oz (1.2 kg) carrots. Cut into fairly thin slices. Cook them in plenty of salted water. The carrots should be thoroughly softened. Drain for several minutes. When they are cool, put the cooked carrots in a blender and reduce them to the thinnest purée possible. Add 7 oz (200 g) crème fraîche, 3 eggs, and 1 tbsp breadcrumbs. Add salt, pepper, and a pinch of grated nutmeg. Mix thoroughly. Fill some buttered molds with this mixture and cook in a bain-marie or baking pan of water at 350 °F (180 °C) for 40 minutes. The carrot can be replaced by celery or pumpkin.

Split-pea purée with chipolatas

Split-pea purée

To serve 6, boil 1 lb 2 oz (500 g) split peas in plenty of salted water. Drain the peas, put them in a blender, and reduce to a uniform purée. Add 3 tbsp crème fraîche and 4$^1/_2$ oz (120 g) butter. Season with salt and pepper. Reserve the split-pea purée in the bain-marie until just before serving.

Spicy sweet-potato purée

To serve 6, peel and wash 2 lb 11 oz (1.2 kg) sweet potatoes. Put them in plenty of cold water, bring to the boil, and cook for about 40 minutes. Drain the sweet potatoes and purée with a vegetable mill. Mix them with $^2/_3$ cup (15 cl) boiled light cream, 3$^1/_2$ oz (100 g) butter, salt, pepper, 5 pinches ground cinnamon, and 2 pinches nutmeg.

Potato purée with olive oil

To serve 6, peel and wash 2 lb 11 oz (1.2 kg) potatoes and 4 cloves garlic. Put them in plenty of cold water, bring to the boil, and cook for 50 minutes. Drain, then purée with a vegetable mill. Mix together with $^2/_3$ cup (15 cl) boiled light cream, $^2/_3$ cup (15 cl) virgin olive oil, salt, and pepper. The result should be a very soft, white, aromatic purée.

Multicolored terrine

To serve 6–8, peel 1 lb 5 oz (600 g) celeriac and cut it into slices $^3/_8$ in (1 cm) thick. Peel 1 lb 5 oz (600 g) carrots and cut them into small pieces. Peel 1 lb 5 oz (600 g) pumpkin and cut the flesh into cubes. Boil plenty of salted water and cook the carrots in it for 40 minutes. Refresh them under a jet of water, then drain. Prepare the celery and the pumpkin in the same way. Put the cooked vegetables into a blender, separately, and reduce each one to a purée. Leave to cool. Butter a terrine. Mix the carrot purée, 3$^1/_2$ oz (100 g) crème fraîche, 2 tbsp breadcrumbs, 2 eggs, 1 pinch nutmeg, salt, and pepper in a bowl. Prepare the other vegetables in the same way. Put the pumpkin purée in the terrine, followed by the celeriac and then the carrots. Put the terrine in a bain-marie or baking pan of water, cover with buttered aluminum foil, and cook for 45 minutes in an oven preheated to 350 °F (180 °C). Leave to cool, then put into the refrigerator for 24 hours.

Baked potatoes with olive oil

Grilled pumpkin slices

cook them at relatively low temperatures, to prevent them from drying out or burning.

Baked potatoes with olive oil

Small and medium-size potatoes are most appropriate here; make sure that their dimensions are similar, so that they will all be ready at the same time. To serve 6, peel 2 lb 11 oz (1.2 kg) firm, white potatoes. Put them on a baking sheet, season with coarse salt, pepper, 2 chopped cloves garlic, 3 chopped marjoram leaves, a few thyme sprigs, and 2/3 cup (15 cl) olive oil. Cook for about 35 minutes in an oven preheated to 345 °F (175 °C), turning them occasionally. Serve piping hot with roast pork or lamb.

Baked pumpkin slices

This dish is easy to make and has a distinctive flavor. Use small pumpkins. To serve 6, remove the skin and seeds from 6 slices of pumpkin. Prick both sides of the slices with a fork. Add salt, pepper, and fresh thyme, then glaze each side with high-quality virgin olive oil. Preheat the oven to 400 °F (200 °C). Put the pumpkin slices on a wire rack, so that the heat can reach both sides at the same time. Bake for 25–30 minutes. Check progress: the pumpkin flesh should be soft and succulent. Serve with roast poultry or grilled fish.

For children

To prepare a potato "hedgehog," peel the potatoes, then cut them into slices lengthwise with a knife, stopping around 3/8 in (1 cm) from the end and making sure not to detach the strips. Add salt and a little pepper. Put the potatoes on a baking sheet and baste them with a little peanut oil. Cook for 35 minutes in an oven preheated to 350 °F (180 °C). The heat causes the slices to separate from each other, like the quills of a hedgehog rolled up in a ball.

General points

Baking vegetables in an oven concentrates and conserves their flavor. The cooking process is slow, and particularly suited to root vegetables. It is important to

Potatoes in a salt crust for 6

1 This recipe deserves to be prepared with the very best potatoes. The substantial coating of salt protects the vegetables without imbuing them with its flavor. Wash and scrub 3 lb 5 oz (1.5 kg) firm, white potatoes with smooth, unblemished skins. This recipe is especially suited to potatoes from the Île de Ré or Noirmoutier, two places famous for their salt marshes.

Tip
For this recipe, the ingredients must be top quality, as any undesirable impurity will be trapped inside the crust. Wash the potatoes thoroughly to eliminate all traces of soil and use coarse, gray sea salt with plenty of iodide.

2 The idea is to cook the potatoes in a jacket of salt seasoned with herbs. Mix in a bowl 9 lb (4 kg) coarse salt (ideally Guérande salt) with 5 pinches ground pepper, 4 crushed bay leaves, and 5 sprigs thyme. Pour a layer of this salt (about 1 in/3 cm thick) in a fairly deep baking dish.

3 Arrange the potatoes on the salt, without allowing them to touch each other. It is advisable to use potatoes that are not too small, but it is particularly important that they are roughly the same size. The dish should be large enough to hold 8–10 potatoes. Make sure that their skin is not broken.

4 Cover the potatoes with the remaining salt, completely submerging them. Cook for 2 hours in an oven preheated to 375 °F (190 °C). During the course of the cooking process, the salt will harden and form a solid crust: break it open with a small hammer and serve the potatoes immediately. This dish is a perfect accompaniment to roast chicken or fish baked whole in the oven, garnished with a green salad.

Fricassée of mousserons

General points

Mushrooms are delicate ingredients that need to be treated with special care. They are generally cooked in two phases: they are first softened slowly in a covered pan then seared in a skillet, with oil or butter.

Fried mushrooms

To serve 6, sort and trim (removing any mold) 10¹/₂ oz (300 g) chanterelles, 10¹/₂ oz (300 g) hedgehog mushrooms, 10¹/₂ oz (300 g) gray chanterelles, and 10¹/₂ oz (300 g) pleurotes. Leave the smaller mushrooms whole and cut the larger ones into pieces. Wash carefully in plenty of cold water and drain them. Put all the washed mushrooms into a large stewpot with 1 scant cup (20 cl) cold water and 4 generous pinches coarse salt. Cover and bring to the boil over medium heat, stirring occasionally. Cook for about 12 minutes and leave to drain for about 10. Fifteen minutes before serving, heat 6 tbsp peanut oil in a large skillet (9 in/24 cm in diameter) and add the cooked mushrooms. Season with salt and pepper then brown the mushrooms over medium heat for about 8 minutes, making sure that they do not dry out. Add 1 bunch chopped chives at the last moment. Serve very hot with roast meat.

Sautéed chanterelles with parsley vinaigrette

This tasty dish requires small, orangey chanterelles. As a vegetable for 6, sort 2¹/₄ lb (1 kg) chanterelles and cut off the earthy tips. Wash them carefully in plenty of cold water and drain for a few minutes. Put the chanterelles in a large skillet then add salt and pepper. Cover the skillet and set at low to medium heat. The mushrooms should cook slowly for about 15 minutes; stir them occasionally with a wooden spoon. When the chanterelles are cooked, drain them in a colander for 10 minutes. Meanwhile, peel 3 cloves garlic. Wash and thin out the leaves of 1 bunch parsley. Finely pare these ingredients with a knife or vegetable mill. A few minutes before serving, heat 2³/₄ oz (80 g) butter with 1 tbsp sunflower oil in the skillet over medium heat. Add the chanterelles and brown them for 10 minutes, shaking the

Fricassée of chanterelles

skillet from time to time, and pour in some parsley vinaigrette. Mix and cook for 5 minutes. Serve very hot.

Pleurotes with Parmesan and chili

Pleurotes

These are particularly delicate mushrooms. Be sure to preserve their slightly crispy consistency in the cooking process; this means buying them very fresh (with a uniform gray color and supple, gleaming heads). Cut the bottoms off the stalks with a small knife and, if necessary, cut the heads into two. If the pleurotes are very fresh, there is no need to wash them in water, but remove any woody parts. Put the washed mushrooms in a large stewpot with 1 scant cup (20 cl) cold water and 4 generous pinches coarse salt. Cover the pot and bring to the boil over medium heat. Cook for about 10 minutes, stirring occasionally. Check the progress of the mushrooms: they should be cooked, but still slightly firm. Drain them for a few minutes. Fifteen minutes before serving, heat $2^3/_4$ oz (80 g) butter in a large skillet (9 in/24 cm in diameter) over very low heat and add the cooked mushrooms. Season with salt and pepper, then braise over medium heat for about 8 minutes. Add 2 thinly chopped shallots and 1 tbsp chopped parsley. Cook, shaking the skillet occasionally, for a further 5 minutes. Serve very hot.

Ceps "à la bordelaise"

As a side dish for 6, sort $2^1/_4$ lb (1 kg) ceps and cut off the earthy tips. Chop the heads and the bases. Put them in a large skillet, add a small glass of cold water, then season with salt and pepper. Cover the skillet and place over a low to medium heat. The mushrooms should cook slowly for about 15 minutes; stir occasionally with a wooden spoon. When the ceps are cooked, drain them in a colander for 10 minutes. Meanwhile, peel 3 cloves garlic. Wash and separate some parsley leaves. Pare these ingredients finely with a knife or a vegetable mill. A few minutes before serving, heat $2^3/_4$ oz (80 g) butter with 1 tbsp sunflower oil in the skillet, over medium heat. Add the ceps and brown them for 10 minutes, shaking the skillet occasionally. Then add freshly made parsley vinaigrette. Stir it in and cook the mixture for 5 minutes, before serving very hot.

Ceps "à la bordelaise"

Lentil salad "à la dijonnaise"

General points

There are numerous dried legumes or pulses on the market, each with a host of specific recipes, giving you a particularly wide range of dishes to choose from.

Lentils

Lentils are often eaten hot, as a main course, but they can also be used to make delicious salads. To serve 6, boil plenty of salted water, then add 10 1/2 oz (300 g) green lentils. Cook for about 35 minutes. Check progress by tasting the lentils: they should be soft, but still remain intact. Drain and cover, to keep them hot. Put 1 finely chopped onion, 1 bunch chopped chives, 2 tbsp prepared mustard, 2 tbsp wine vinegar, and 8 tbsp virgin olive oil in a bowl. Mix thoroughly to obtain a full-bodied vinaigrette. Add salt, pepper, and, finally, the hot lentils. Mix and adjust seasoning to taste. You can serve this salad on its own or enliven it with diced smoked haddock, herring, or other fish, according to your fancy.

Navy beans

These can be cooked fairly simply, complemented by pesto. The ideal variety is the Lingot bean. This dish is even better when it is reheated, so it is worth making a large amount. To serve 6–8, soak 1 lb 5 oz (600 g) dried navy beans in 4 quarts (4 liters) cold water for about 8 hours, then put them into a saucepan with plenty of cold water and bring to the boil. Cook over medium heat for 30 minutes. Drain the beans. Heat 1/3 cup + 1 1/2 tbsp (10 cl) olive oil in a saucepan, over medium heat, and add 3 chopped onions. Fry them until they are transparent, stirring occasionally. Add 3 tomatoes cut into slices, 1 tbsp tomato paste, 8 cups (2 liters) chicken bouillon, then the blanched beans, salt, pepper, 1 sprig thyme, and 1 bouquet garni. Bring to the boil and cook slowly, covered, for about 2 hours. Check the progress of the beans: they should be

Fresh beans with basil

tender, but still intact. Add 1 bunch chopped basil and 4 chopped cloves garlic to the sauce. Mix thoroughly and cook for 2 more minutes. Adjust seasoning to taste. Serve piping hot.

Dhal

Dhal is prepared in India with all types of pulses and beans. To serve 8, soak 1 lb 5 oz (600 g) dried beans in 4 quarts (4 liters) cold water for about 10 hours. Put them in a saucepan with plenty of cold water and bring to the boil. Cook over medium heat for 30 minutes. Drain the beans. Heat 1/3 cup + 1 1/2 tbsp (10 cl) sunflower oil in a saucepan, over medium heat. Add 3 sliced onions and 4 chopped cloves garlic and fry until they are transparent, stirring occasionally. Add 3 sliced tomatoes, 1 tsp turmeric, 1/2 tsp powdered ginger, and 3 pinches Cayenne pepper. Pour in 8 cups (2 liters) water and the blanched beans. Add salt, pepper, 1 sprig thyme, and 1 bouquet garni. Bring to the boil then cook slowly, covered, for 3 hours. Check the progress of the beans: they must be thoroughly cooked, to the point where they start to lose their shape. Add water during the cooking process if the beans are too dry. Adjust the seasoning: dhal should be fairly spicy. Add 1 bunch of chopped cilantro to the sauce. Stir it in and cook for a further 2 minutes.

Chickpea casserole with chorizo

To serve 6–8, soak 1 lb 5 oz (600 g) chickpeas in 4 quarts

Assortment of dhal

(4 liters) cold water for about 8 hours. Put them in a saucepan with plenty of cold water and bring to the boil. Cook over medium heat for 30 minutes, then drain. Heat 1/3 cup + 1 1/2 tbsp (10 cl) peanut oil in a saucepan over medium heat and add 2 onions, 1 chopped leek, and 3 chopped garlic cloves. Fry these ingredients until they are transparent, stirring occasionally. Add 3 sliced tomatoes, 1 tbsp tomato paste, 8 cups (2 liters) chicken bouillon, the blanched chickpeas, salt, pepper, 1 sprig thyme, 1 bouquet garni, and 2 tbsp yellow ras al-hanout. Bring to the boil then cook, covered, for about 2 hours. Check the progress of the chickpeas: they should be tender, but remain intact. Twenty minutes before they are ready, add 20 slices strong chorizo and 1 bunch chopped cilantro to the sauce and mix well. Stir occasionally during the remainder of the cooking time.

Chickpea salad

To serve 6, cook 12 1/2 oz (350 g) chickpeas in plenty of salted water for 35 minutes. Drain

Galician chickpeas

then cook them again in fresh water for 2 hours. Put 1 finely sliced onion, 1 bunch chopped cilantro, 5 tbsp lemon juice, and 10 tbsp virgin olive oil in a bowl. Add salt, pepper, and the hot chickpeas.

Cassoulet

Cassoulet, the main specialty of the French Languedoc region, is made with navy beans simmered with a variety of meats. Its name is undoubtedly derived from the term "cassollo" (referring to the terracotta dish in which this stew was traditionally cooked), which was later corrupted to "cassoulet." It comes in three major recipes, all with a different taste and personality. The first originates from Castelnaudary: this is prepared with pork in several forms: hock, sausage, ham, and rind. The second comes from Carcassonne: its preparation is almost identical, apart from the fact that it is cooked with lamb or mutton (leg or shoulder). Finally, the cassoulet from Toulouse also boasts lamb, but complements it with Toulouse sausage and duck confit.

Serves 6
Preparation: about 1 hour
Cooking: about 4 hours

Ingredients

1³/₄ lb (800 g) navy beans
2 rolled pork rinds
7 oz (200 g) unsalted bacon
2 large bouquets garnis
5 onions
4 cloves
4 carrots
7 cloves garlic
1 shoulder of lamb
3 tbsp goose fat
3 cups (80 cl) meat bouillon
4 tomatoes
1 large sprig thyme
1 hock slightly salted pork
Salt and pepper

1 Put the navy beans into a large saucepan and cover them with cold water. Bring to the boil then drain the beans. Put them in a large saucepan and cover them once again with cold water. Add the rolled rinds, unsalted bacon, 1 bouquet garni, 2 onions (each spiked with 2 cloves), 2 carrots, and 4 chopped garlic cloves. Put the saucepan over medium heat and cook for 1 hour.

2 The beans should be well cooked, but remain slightly firm. Meanwhile, take the lamb off the bone and trim it. Cut it into cubes about 1 in (3 cm) wide, then season with salt and pepper. Heat the goose fat in a skillet. Brown the meat in the hot fat for 15 minutes then stir in 2 chopped onions and 3 chopped garlic cloves.

3 Cook for 5 minutes. Pour in the meat bouillon, then add the sliced tomatoes and the thyme. Season with salt and pepper and cook for 1 hour. Put the slightly salted hock in a saucepan with plenty of water. Add 1 bouquet garni, 1 onion, and 2 carrots and simmer for about 2 hours. Set the hock aside on a dish.

4 Put a generous layer of the cooked navy beans in a large ovenproof dish. Add a layer of lamb, with its juice, then another layer of beans. Repeat the process with the cooked hock of pork and the rinds and add, if necessary, 1–2 ladlefuls of the lamb's cooking juice. Fill the dish to ³/₈ in (1 cm) from the rim.

5 Put it in the oven, preheated to 350 °F (180 °C). Cook for about 1 hour. When a golden crust forms, use a spoon to push this down into the mixture and allow a new crust to form. Repeat this operation two or three times. Serve the cassoulet straight from the dish, using a large spoon. It combines well with a full-bodied red wine like Tursan or Vin de Cahors.

6 It is advisable to start preparing a cassoulet in the morning if you are going to serve it for dinner. The success of this dish depends not only on the quality of its ingredients, but also on the cooking process, which should be fairly long and requires regular monitoring. Once the crust takes on its color, it needs to be pushed down into the beans: when repeated two or three times, this is the trick that gives a cassoulet its special flavor.

Glass of fresh milk

by refrigeration and will not keep for more than two days: it is therefore vital to boil it to kill any microorganisms that it might contain. This highly aromatic milk is the favorite of connoisseurs.

Pasteurized milk

This has been brought to a temperature just under 212 °F (100 °C) for a few moments, then immediately cooled so that it can conserved. It must be kept in the refrigerator, as bacteria are not totally destroyed by this process.

Sterilized UHT milk

This product can be kept for months at room temperature, as all its natural microorganisms have been killed by a brief exposure—just a few seconds—to an intense

Concentrated milk

heat (about 285 °F/140 °C). This procedure has the advantage of being very safe, without altering the flavor of the milk too radically.All these forms of milk are sold in "homogenized" form: i.e., they are stirred mechanically with immense force to fix the lipids in the liquid and prevent them rising to the surface. Nowadays milk is available that has been enriched with trace elements and vitamins.

General points

Milk is a complete foodstuff and an important dietary staple. The most widespread type is cow's milk, which is available in a number of forms, thanks to the variety of treatments to which it is subjected.

Fresh untreated milk

This type of milk is only found in the country or close to livestock. It can be conserved only

Sterilized UHT milk

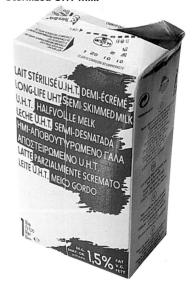

Concentrated milk

This is available in cans, tubes, and cartons. It is concentrated in a vacuum through evaporation, and the resulting low water content allows it to be conserved. This highly nourishing product is often sold sweetened and sometimes flavored for children.

Powdered milk

In this case, the milk has lost virtually all its water content. It is very easy to use, as it is designed to be "instant:" it dissolves in water immediately once it is stirred. It is also very easy to store, as it will last for several months in a cool, dry place. Whole milk contains about $1\frac{1}{4}$ oz (36 g) fat per quart/liter; semi-skimmed $\frac{1}{2}$ oz (15 g); and skimmed milk less than 0.1 oz (3 g). Milk is a complete foodstuff because it contains calcium, phosphorus, potassium, and magnesium; when whole or semi-skimmed, it is also a substantial source of fat-soluble vitamins (A, B2). Milk contains a sugar—lactose—that causes allergy in some people. Never forget that milk is inherently fragile and alters

Powdered milk

Preparing milk for custard

quickly: once it has been opened, it must be drunk within two days and always kept cold.

Milk at breakfast time

101

Savory
Parsley

Dried legumes are delicious when they are cooked with savory; this herb also enhances the digestion of beans and lentils.

Oyster plant (salsify) is first boiled and then sautéed in butter in a skillet. To bring out its exquisite flavor, add 1 tbsp chopped, fresh parsley just before it is ready.

Sage

Winter soups often combine carrots, potatoes, leeks, and sometimes also dried beans. To enhance their flavor, add 3 or 4 whole sage leaves at the start of the cooking process.

Thyme

large number of dishes. Try adding a pinch of fresh thyme to potatoes sautéed in goose fat, as soon as they are ready: the effect is immediate and mouthwatering.

Chervil

Grated carrots can be made into something more than a mere garnish: season them with hazelnut oil and chopped chervil to transform them into a succulent starter, with a few drops of lemon juice to round off this delicious recipe.

Tarragon

Jerusalem artichoke can be excellent if prepared imaginatively: braise it in butter then simmer with crème fraîche and a few tarragon leaves to create a delicious and surprising dish.

Marjoram

Chickpeas are often served with couscous, but they can also be cooked alone as an accompaniment to roast meat. Enhance their flavor exquisitely by adding a few whole marjoram leaves while cooking. Remember to remove them just before serving.

Recommended drinks

Pomerol
Saint-julien
Saint-émilion

Menu suggestions

1. Serve these fritters in fall as an appetizer, followed by jugged hare and an orange meringue tart.

2. These fritters make an excellent accompaniment to fried fillets of sander (pike-perch), after an appetizer of hare terrine with hazelnuts and before a dessert of chocolate gateau.

Boletus fritters

A party dish

Serves 4
Preparation: 15 minutes
Cooking: 20 + 5 minutes

Ingredients

9 boletus mushrooms
1³/₄ oz (50 g) butter
3¹/₂ oz (100 g) chopped veal
1 small bunch parsley
Grated Parmesan
1 tbsp cream
Flour
1 egg
Breadcrumbs
Oil

1–2 lemons
Salt and pepper

1. Try to find medium-size boletus that are firm and, if possible, roughly the same size. Separate the heads from the stalks and remove the tubes with a small knife, without breaking them. Chop the tubes and stalks, then fry them in butter for about 20 minutes with salt and pepper.

2. Fry the chopped meat separately in butter for about 10 minutes. Add the cooked mushrooms, a little chopped parsley, 1 tbsp grated Parmesan, and the cream. Mix all these ingredients thoroughly.

3. Fill the hollow in the mushroom heads with the fried mixture. Divide eight of the heads into pairs, pushing them together slightly so that they stick. Roll them in flour, then beaten egg and, finally, breadcrumbs.

4. Reserve the prepared mushrooms in the refrigerator for a moment, while you prepare the oil. Pour 8 cups (2 liters) sunflower or corn oil into a large saucepan and heat. Throw in a small piece of bread: it should start sizzling immediately. Take the boletus out of the refrigerator and cook them.

5. Fry the mushrooms in oil that is not too hot, until they are thoroughly golden. Cut the ninth boletus head into thin slices, sauté in butter, season with salt and pepper, then use them to garnish your plates. Serve with chopped parsley and lemon quarters.

Carrot bread

An economical dish

Serves 4–6
Preparation: 15 minutes
Resting: 2 hours
Cooking: 45–50 minutes

Ingredients

4 $^1/_2$ cups (500 g)
flour
1 oz (30 g) yeast
1 generous cup (25 cl) milk
1 large dab butter
10$^1/_2$ oz (300 g) carrots
1 tsp sugar
Oil
Salt

1. Pour the flour and salt into a bowl, then mix together. Crumble the yeast and thin it in a little warm milk; pour this mixture into the flour and stir, before adding the melted butter and the rest of the milk. Knead vigorously to obtain a uniform dough.

2. Scrub and grate the carrots, then add them to the contents of the bowl, kneading all the while. Cover this mixture and allow it to double in volume in a warm place, away from any drafts.

3. Start kneading again and pour the mixture into a lightly oiled loaf pan. Allow it to rise slightly again while preheating the oven to 400 °F (205 °C). Bake the cake for 45–50 minutes (a skewer stuck into the center should come out clean). Leave to cool before turning out of the pan.

N.B. To serve this bread with a green salad, prepare a little sauce made with fromage blanc beaten with pepper, a dab of mustard, and finely chopped chives. You can also accompany it with black or green olive purée, or a sauce combining fromage blanc and Roquefort. If you serve the bread as a tidbit, cut it into cubes and stick these onto small wooden toothpicks with an olive or cube of cheese.

Recommended drinks

Muscat de l'Alsace
Sancerre
Mâcon Blanc

Menu suggestions

1. This cake makes a good cold appetizer, accompanied by a green salad. Follow it with roast pork with small potatoes and a dessert of fromage blanc with poached fruits.

2. You can also serve this cake in small portions as a tidbit, before cabbage hotpot and an apple pie.

Stuffed mushrooms "à la nîmoise"

A regional dish

Serves 4
Preparation: 10 minutes
Cooking: 25 minutes + 25 minutes

Ingredients

12 large cultivated mushrooms
Butter
Vinegar
Flour
1 glass milk
9 oz (250 g) brandade (salt fish cooked
with olive oil, garlic, and cream)

1 small pot crème fraîche
1 egg
Salt and pepper

1. Remove the stalks from the mushrooms (keep them for another recipe),
wipe the heads carefully, and put them in a saucepan.

2. Add 1 tbsp butter, a dash of vinegar, and a pinch of salt. Cover and cook
the mushrooms for 25 minutes over low heat. Season with pepper when
cooked.

3. Meanwhile, prepare a little white sauce: melt a dab of butter in a saucepan,
add 1 heaped tbsp flour, and stir vigorously, making sure that the mixture
does not become discolored.

4. Thin with the milk, bring to the boil, and cook for 5 minutes over low heat,
stirring continuously with a wooden spoon. Season to taste with salt and
pepper.

5. Leave the mushrooms and white sauce to cool. Arrange the mushrooms in
a buttered baking dish, then fill each one with 1 tbsp brandade thinned with
crème fraîche.

6. Add 1 egg yolk to the white sauce, along with the stiffly beaten egg white
and a little crème fraîche. Cover the mushrooms with this mixture and brown
for 20 minutes in a medium oven preheated to 350 °F (180 °C), then for a
further 5 minutes in a hot oven (480 °F/250 °C).

Recommended drinks

Côtes-de-Provence Rosé
Hermitage
BlancCostières-de-Nîmes

Menu suggestions

1. These mushrooms stuffed with brandade make a
hot appetizer, perfectly complemented by beef stew
with olives and a crème brûlée for dessert.

2. If your guests are fish lovers, follow these
mushrooms with monkfish stew with aioli or a
lobster stew, and cinnamon tart for dessert.

Basque fricassee of ceps

A regional dish

Serves 4
Preparation: 10 minutes
Cooking: 15 minutes

Ingredients

1 lb 2 oz (500 g) ceps
2–3 cloves garlic
1 bunch parsley
$1/2$ glass oil
Green bell peppers
Salt and pepper

1. Trim and clean the ceps, remove the stalks, and cut the heads into pieces. Prepare a parsley vinaigrette complete with chopped garlic.

2. Heat some of the oil in a skillet. Add a little of the vinaigrette and then the mushrooms; cook them over medium heat at first. Turn the ceps over. Turn up the heat as soon as the mushrooms start to sweat, as the moisture needs to be evaporated fairly quickly. Finish eliminating this water over low heat, before adding salt, pepper, and the rest of the vinaigrette. Turn up the heat to complete the cooking process.

3. Meanwhile, wipe the bell peppers, split them into two, seed, and sauté in oil in another skillet. Serve the mushrooms piping hot, separately from the bell peppers. It is the contrast between the different flavors that makes this way of preparing ceps so special.

N.B. If you use bottled ceps, put them in a bowl of hot (not boiling) water to remove their sticky coat. Drain, then pat them dry thoroughly with paper towels. Treat them in the same way as fresh ceps, but cook for less time.

Recommended drinks

Ilrouléguy Rouge
Madiran
Pécharmant

Menu suggestions

1. To continue the regional theme, serve this fricassee as an appetizer, followed by a Basque-style sautéed chicken, ewe's cheese with cherry jelly, and a crème caramel.

2. This fricassee can serve as an accompaniment to roast chicken, with navy-bean soup as an appetizer and Basque gateau and custard sauce for dessert.

Curried cabbage and peanut gratin

An exotic dish

Serves 4
Preparation: 10 minutes
Cooking: 30 minutes

Ingredients

1 cabbage about 2¹/₄ lb (1 kg)
in weight
4 cups (1 liter) bouillon
1 clove garlic
2 medium onions
2 cloves
1 bay leaf
3¹/₂ oz (100 g) butter
3 tbsp flour
1 pot crème fraîche

Curry powder
2³/₄ oz (75 g) salted peanuts
1 oz (30 g) breadcrumbs
Salt and pepper

1. Boil the bouillon in a large saucepan. Separate the leaves of the cabbage, discarding the large outer ones, and cut them into strips. Add them to the bouillon together with the peeled garlic clove, the onions (each spiked with a clove), and bay leaf.

2. Bring the bouillon back to the boil and cook for about 10 minutes. Drain the contents of the saucepan. Discard the onions, crush the garlic, and mix it with the cabbage.

3. Layer the cabbage in a buttered baking dish. Add salt and pepper. Set aside. Prepare a little roux in a saucepan with the rest of the butter and the flour; season with salt and pepper.

4. Barely allow the sauce to take on any color before pouring in the crème fraîche and a little of the cabbage bouillon. Simmer until the sauce is smooth.

5. Add a generous amount of curry powder (at least 1 heaped tbsp) then pour the sauce onto the cabbage. Sprinkle with the salted peanuts and breadcrumbs. Place in an oven preheated to 430 °F (220 °C) until the top starts to brown slightly.

Recommended drinks

Vin Jaune
Gewurztraminer
Riesling

Menu suggestions

1. This gratin can serve as the main course of an Indian-style vegetarian meal, with small vegetable fritters as an appetizer and rice pudding for dessert.

2. You can also incorporate this dish into a Western menu as a garnish for fried sausages, with corn and beet salad to start and orange sorbet in its skin to finish.

Irish potato gratin

A foreign dish

Serves 5
Preparation: 30 minutes
Cooking: 1 hour

Ingredients

4–5 potatoes
1 glass of milk
5$\frac{1}{2}$ oz (150 g) grated cheddar (or Dutch cheese, or Gruyère)
Worcester sauce
1 heaped tbsp flour
3$\frac{1}{2}$ oz (100 g) butter
9 oz (250 g) onions
2 heaped tbsp breadcrumbs
Salt and pepper

1. Wash and peel the potatoes; cut them into thin, uniform slices.

2. Put the milk and the grated cheese into a small, heavy-bottomed saucepan and heat them over very low heat or, even better, in a double boiler, stirring until the cheese has melted and is thoroughly mixed with the milk. Remove from the heat and season with 1 tsp Worcester sauce.

3. Put the flour in a bowl and stir in a generous pinch of salt and a little pepper.

4. Butter a baking dish, very lightly, and lay a bed of potatoes on the bottom: dust with a little seasoned flour then add a few dabs of butter.

5. Add a layer of peeled and finely sliced onions, then a second layer of potatoes; dust with flour, then add a few more dabs of butter and sliced onions. Cover with the cheese sauce, then sprinkle on the breadcrumbs.

6. Bake and brown in an oven preheated to 350 °F (180 °C) for about 1 hour.

Recommended drinks

Light beer
Bordeaux Blanc
Sancerre

Menu suggestions

1. To maintain the Irish touch, serve smoked salmon and toast as an appetizer, followed by this gratin with lamb chops, and, finally, an Irish coffee.

2. These potatoes can serve as an accompaniment to leg of lamb. Provide an endive, orange, and beet salad to start, and chocolate mousse for dessert.

111

Recommended drinks

Mercurey
Givry
Morgon

Menu suggestions

1. For an authentic Burgundy menu, start with snails in garlic butter, then serve these beans with pig-feet ragoût and finish with a blackcurrant flan.

2. More simply, serve these beans with braised ham, preceded by a dandelion salad and rounded off with a fruit compote.

Navy beans "à la bourguignonne"

A regional dish

Serves 6
Soaking: 12 hours
Preparation: 10 minutes
Cooking: 1 hour 45 minutes

Ingredients

1 lb 2 oz (500 g) dried navy beans
Rosemary
4$\frac{1}{2}$ oz (125 g) bacon streaked with fat
2 shallots
Bay leaf
Tomato coulis
Olive oil
1 glass red wine

Parsley
Chervil
Salt and pepper

1. Put the beans in a bowl, cover them with cold water, and soak overnight.

2. Drain and put the navy beans in a saucepan. Add 3 cups (75 cl) water and the rosemary. Slowly bring to the boil and simmer for 30 minutes.

3. Meanwhile, cut the bacon into small dice (having previously removed the rind). Peel the shallots and chop them finely. After 30 minutes of cooking the beans, add the shallots to the saucepan with 1–2 bay leaves and a few tbsp tomato coulis. Mix, cover, and continue cooking over low heat until the beans are tender.

4. Heat a little olive oil in a large saucepan and brown the diced bacon. Add the wine and the beans, while removing the rosemary and the bay leaf. Season with salt and pepper, then finish cooking the beans (about 10 minutes).

5. Before serving, add the herbs, finely chopped, and allow enough time for their aroma to permeate the beans.

Morel pastries

A party dish

Serves 4
Preparation: 15 minutes
Cooking: 15 minutes

Ingredients

10¹/₂ oz (300 g) ready-prepared puff-pastry dough
2 eggs
1 lb 5 oz (600 g) morels
1³/₄ oz (50 g) butter
1 pot thick crème fraîche
Parsley
Salt and pepper

1. Prepare the pastry: roll the dough to a thickness of ³/₁₆ in (5 mm), then cut it into rectangles measuring 2 x 3¹/₂ in (5 x 9 cm). Use the tip of a knife to cut out a groove around each rectangle, ³/₈ in (1 cm) from the perimeter, and score it lightly; these rectangles will serve as lids. Brush the pastry with beaten egg yolk. Cook for about 10 minutes in a very hot oven.

2. Wash the morels thoroughly, drain and put them in a deep-sided skillet with the butter, and sauté over low heat for 5 minutes. Once they are cooked, take them out of the pan, drain, and set aside, keeping them hot.

3. Reduce slightly the water exuded by the morels. Add the crème fraîche; heat and reduce it for 5 minutes over low heat. Put the morels in the sauce and bring it to the boil again. Taste and adjust the seasoning, if necessary. Remove the sauce from the heat and thicken with 1 egg yolk, previously mixed with a little sauce. Sprinkle with finely chopped parsley. Set aside, keeping hot.

4. Take the lids off the pastries; hollow them out slightly and fill them with the morel mixture. Replace the lid and serve immediately.

N.B. Never eat morels raw, as they can be toxic, and discard any that are overly ripe, as they will be tough and indigestible. Wash morels meticulously, particularly in their cavities, which usually contain soil and small insects. The best plan is to soak them in salted water.

Recommended drinks

Meursault
Graves Blanc
Arbois

Menu suggestions

1. Serve these pastries as a hot appetizer, followed by poached salmon accompanied by steamed potatoes and horseradish cream sauce, with a blueberry vacherin for dessert.

2. If your guests like poultry, follow these pastries with a fattened chicken served with béchamel sauce and rice and, as a dessert, floating islands.

113

Sweet onions stuffed with spinach

A light dish

Serves 4
Preparation: 20 minutes
Cooking: 20 minutes

Ingredients

1 lb 2 oz (500 g) spinach
4 sweet onions
2 large dabs of butter
1 small pot crème fraîche (1 scant cup/20 cl)
2 eggs
1³/₄ oz (50 g) grated Gruyère
16 fresh bay leaves
A little well-seasoned tomato coulis

Parsley (as optional garnish)
Salt and pepper

1. Sort the spinach while washing it, then blanch it for 3–4 minutes in salted boiling water. Drain the spinach in a colander and squeeze, as it must be extremely dry when you come to use it.

2. Peel the onions. Chop off the top third. Hollow them out slightly in order to make a hole for the spinach. Set aside the upper section of the onions, along with the surplus from the hollowed cavities.

3. Heat a little butter in a skillet. Braise the onions, covered, turning them occasionally, until they start to take on some color.

4. Meanwhile, chop the upper sections and the other surplus onion, then sauté them in butter in a second skillet until they are very transparent.

5. Mix the thoroughly drained spinach in a large bowl with the crème fraîche—maybe not the whole pot, depending on how dry the spinach is—the sautéed chopped onions, beaten eggs, and grated cheese, along with salt and pepper.

6. Fill the onions with the stuffing until it protrudes from the top. Meanwhile, blanch the bay leaves in salted, boiling water.

7. Loosely tie the bay leaves to the onions with string. Cook the onions in an oven preheated to 435 °F (225 °C) for 20 minutes. Untie the string to remove the bay leaves and dab the onions with coulis 2 minutes before they are cooked. Garnish with parsley, if desired.

Recommended drinks

Water
Tea
Bergerac Rosé

Menu suggestions

1. After these sweet onions, serve papillotes of coalfish (a type of cod) with mushrooms as a main course and lime sorbet for dessert.

2. If you prefer poultry, follow this appetizer with poached chicken breasts and a spinach salad, then fromage frais with cinnamon.

Cabbage Parmentier

A family dish

Serves 4
Preparation: 20 minutes
Cooking: 25 minutes

Ingredients

1 lb 2oz (500 g) potatoes
2 cups (50 cl) milk
Butter
Nutmeg
1 small cabbage
2 shallots
4¹/₂ oz (125 g) cultivated mushrooms
Oil
2 eggs
1 bunch chervil

2 slices cooked ham
1³/₄ oz (50 g) grated cheese
(Cantal or Gruyère)
1 small pot crème fraîche
1 bunch of chives
Salt and pepper

1. Cook the potatoes and prepare a light purée with the milk, a little butter, salt, pepper, and grated nutmeg.

2. Trim the cabbage and discard the outer leaves. Separate the others and blanch them for a few minutes in salted, boiling water; drain and set aside, flattened down, on a dishtowel.

3. Peel and chop the shallots; trim and chop the mushrooms. Gently brown these ingredients in a little oil and butter.

4. Beat the eggs into an omelet mixture with salt, pepper, and grated nutmeg, all the while incorporating the thinned-out chervil, chopped ham, and two-thirds of the grated cheese. Combine the mushroom and shallot mixture with the beaten eggs then stir all this into the potato purée.

5. Butter a mold then spread the cabbage leaves on the bottom and sides (in several layers, if necessary), making sure they protrude well over the edges. Fill the mold with the purée and fold the cabbage leaves into the center; sprinkle on the rest of the grated cheese and dab with butter.

6. Put the mold in a baking pan of water in an oven preheated to 400 °F (200 °C) for 25 minutes. Serve the cream apart—hot, seasoned with salt and pepper, and flavored with the chives.

Recommended drinks

Sancerre
Bourgogne Rouge
Saumur Champigny

Menu suggestions

1. For a family dinner, serve this cabbage Parmentier as the main course, preceded by celery remoulade and followed by a pear tart.

2. You can also serve it simply with a green salad, before a good cheeseboard and crêpes with jelly.

Endive paupiettes

An economical dish

Serves 4
Preparation: 15 minutes
Cooking: 25 minutes

Ingredients

4 fairly large endives
1 lemon
1 onion
Butter
5$\frac{1}{2}$ oz (150 g) chopped pork

1 egg
Nutmeg
Parsley
Breadcrumbs

1 glass white wine
1 glass bouillon
8–12 fine slices smoked bacon
Tomato coulis
Salt and pepper

1. Wash and wipe the endives, discarding their outer leaves. Cut out the stalks with a small, pointed, and very sharp knife. Cut them lengthwise into two. Remove the small leaves in the heart of each half. Sprinkle with lemon juice and add salt.

2. Peel the onion and chop it very thinly. Melt the butter in a saucepan and fry the onion gently until it is transparent. Add the small leaves from the chopped endives. Cook for about 2 minutes.

3. Preheat the oven to 400 °F (200 °C). Mix the onion and endive leaves with the chopped pork, egg, salt, pepper, grated nutmeg, chopped parsley, and a few breadcrumbs. Distribute this mixture between one half of each endive, allowing it to protrude, then form the paupiettes by placing the other half on top. Close them securely by wrapping round 2 or 3 thin slices of bacon (without the rind). When each one is ready, lay it in a buttered baking dish, with the tips of the bacon underneath.

4. Pour the white wine into the bouillon. Put the dish in the oven and wait for 5 minutes, then sprinkle it with the bouillon. Cook for 25 minutes, sprinkling frequently and, if necessary, adding a little of the bouillon to the dish. Meanwhile, prepare a small tomato coulis, as an enticing complement to these endive paupiettes.

N.B. If the endives are particularly large, you can blanch them for a few minutes in salted, boiling water before using them. If the endives are medium-sized and extremely fresh, frequent sprinkling while they are cooking in the oven will be enough to make them tender.

Recommended drinks

Light Beer
Riesling
Muscadet

Menu suggestions

1. When served as an appetizer, these endive paupiettes can be followed by quiche Lorraine and then a coffee cream.

2. You can also present these endives as an accompaniment to broiled magrets of duck, preceded by eggs cocotte with chives and followed by mango sorbet for dessert.

Small stuffed turnips

A party dish

Serves 4
Preparation: 20 minutes
Cooking: 25 minutes, in two phases

Ingredients

2$^1/_4$ lb (1 kg) very fresh, small, round turnips
4$^1/_2$ oz (125 g) butter
1 lb 2 oz (500 g) cultivated mushrooms
3 shallots
1 bunch parsley
Salt and pepper

1. Peel the turnips, turning them to obtain a uniform shape, then trim them so that they are all more or less the same size. Put them in a saucepan and cover with cold, salted water; bring to the boil and blanch them for about 10 minutes.

2. When the turnips are half-cooked (soft to the touch, but still a little firm), remove them from the pan with a slotted spoon. Hollow them out with the tip of a paring knife, taking care not to pierce the sides or bottoms.

3. To cook the turnips, put them in a buttered baking dish covered with a sheet of aluminum foil and place in an oven preheated to 445 °F (230 °C) for 15–20 minutes. Prepare a finely chopped mixture of mushrooms and shallots, add salt and pepper, and sauté in a skillet for a few minutes. Fill the turnips with this mixture, then put a dab of butter on each.

4. To cook the turnips, put them in a buttered baking dish covered with a sheet of aluminum foil and place in an oven preheated to 445 °F (230 °C) for 15–20 minutes.

Recommended drinks

Riesling
Cassis Blanc
Sancerre

Menu suggestions

1. Serve these stuffed turnips as an appetizer with fresh foie gras of duck, followed by a fillet of beef "en croûte" and, finally, nougat glacé.

2. You can also present these small turnips as an accompaniment to fried salmon steak. Serve a mixed salad with foie gras as an appetizer and ice soufflé for dessert.

Chickpeas with bacon

An economical dish

Serves 5
Preparation: 20 minutes
Cooking: 45 minutes

Ingredients

2$\frac{1}{4}$ lb (1 kg) chickpeas
10$\frac{1}{2}$ oz (300 g) carrots
1 bunch celery
2–3 leeks
2 onions
2 thick slices bacon, streaked with fat
Oregano
1oz (30 g) lard
13⁄4 oz (50 g) butter
Salt and pepper

1. The night before the meal, soak the chickpeas in a bowl of salted, cold water. Pick them over and wash under cold, running water.

2. Scrape the carrots and chop them roughly; trim the celery, then line up the stalks and chop them equally; trim and wash the leeks, then cut them into slices (use all the white part and about 2 in/5 cm of the green); peel and chop 1 onion.

3. Boil 6 cups (1.5 liters) water in a heavy-bottomed saucepan, casserole, or terracotta dish. Add the chickpeas, bacon, carrots, celery, leeks, chopped onion, and a little oregano. Cover about three-quarters of the pan and simmer until the chickpeas are tender and the water has reduced substantially.

4. Remove the bacon, then drain it and pat dry with paper towels. Put the chickpeas and vegetables through a vegetable mill and make a thick purée (using the cooking liquid as required). Taste and add salt if necessary; season generously with pepper.

5. Put the purée in a baking dish. Cut the bacon into small dice. Melt the lard in a skillet and brown the bacon. Meanwhile, peel the second onion and cut it into thin rings. Remove the bacon from the skillet and brown the onion rings. Put the bacon and the onion on top of the purée, add the melted butter, then heat and slightly brown in the oven a few minutes before serving. Serve straight from the oven.

Recommended drinks

Madiran
Bergerac
Cahors

Menu suggestions

1. These chickpeas can be served as a main course, preceded by an assortment of raw vegetables and followed by a lemon tart.

2. You can also use them as an accompaniment to chorizo and strips of cured ham. Try curly salad as an appetizer and honey ice cream for dessert.

Stuffed potatoes

A family dish

Serves 4
Preparation: 20 minutes
Cooking: 1 hour 15 minutes

Ingredients

8 large, firm potatoes, all the same size
1 medium onion
1 clove garlic
A little stale bread with no crust
1 glass milk
$5^{1}/_{2}$ oz (150 g) minced meat
Thyme or other herbs, to taste
A few sprigs parsley
8 small slices bacon, smoked or unsmoked (to taste)
Butter
Salt and pepper

1. Peel the potatoes, giving them a regular shape. Wash them, then cut off a little bit of one side so that they will lie flat. Cut off the opposite side a third of the way down; set these tops aside. Hollow them out as deeply as possible, taking care not to pierce them. Use a special serrated spoon any small spoon with a slightly sharp edge to scoop out the flesh.

2. Prepare the stuffing: peel and chop the onion and garlic; break up the bread, soak it in the milk, and then wring out the moisture. Mix these ingredients with the minced meat, then add salt, pepper, and herbs to taste, along with the chopped parsley.

3. Fill the potatoes with the stuffing, without packing it too tightly. Make sure that the stuffing protrudes above the potato because a band should be visible when the top is in place. Put the reserved tops on the stuffing, ensuring that they fit securely. Do not press down, as this will pack the stuffing in too tightly. The tops will stay in place better if they are slightly hollowed out.

4. Cut the rind off the bacon. Wrap each potato with a slice of the bacon then place in a generously buttered baking pan. Cook in an oven preheated to 400 °F (200 °C) for 1 hour 15 minutes. The bacon, but not the potatoes, should be brown.

N.B. You can serve these stuffed potatoes with a simple green salad in rustic style, with escarole or Webb lettuce, for example. This will provide an unfussy, but tasty, dinner that is made easier as the potatoes do not need to be served immediately.

Recommended drinks

Pauillac
Pomerol
Saint-joseph Rouge

Menu suggestions

1. These stuffed potatoes constitute an excellent main course, preceded by a vegetable soup and followed by apples bonne femme.

2. Another idea, still with the potatoes as the main dish: eggs cocotte as an appetizer and pears poached in wine for dessert.

Pumpkin soup

A regional dish

Serves 6–8
Preparation: 15 minutes
Cooking: 2 hours

Ingredients

1 small, round, thick pumpkin
1 large pot crème fraîche
4 cups (1 liter) milk
1 bunch parsley
A little grated Gruyère
Salt and pepper

1. Carefully clean the skin of the pumpkin and cut its stalk down to a length of 3/4–1 in (2–3 cm). Cut a circle all round this stalk in order to remove the top of your future soup tureen. Make a fairly deep, conical incision.

2. Remove all the fibers and seeds from inside the pumpkin and then dislodge a little of its flesh with a sharp-edged spoon, allowing it to fall to the bottom.

3. Add salt and pepper to this dislodged flesh and cover it with all the crème fraîche; pour on the milk.

4. Finely chop the parsley and sprinkle it onto the milk. Reckon on about 1 level tbsp per person

5. Put the cover back in place and cook the pumpkin in an oven preheated to 330 °F (165 °C) for 1 hour 30 minutes.

6. Remove the pumpkin from the oven, take off its top, and add the grated cheese, making sure that it stays on the surface. Put the pumpkin back in the oven, without its top, for about 30 minutes; the cheese should be slightly browned. Serve, adding a little of the pumpkin flesh still attached to the top.

Recommended drinks

Bergerac
Graves Rouge
Pinot Noir

Menu suggestions

1. As pumpkin soup is traditional in some parts of Europe, you can decide to continue along similar lines—either apple pie "à la Solognote," with quails plus chanterelles and tarte Tatin, or …

2. Flemish style: with a main course of broiled blood sausage with apple compote, followed by rhubarb meringue tart.

Lentil salad with bacon lardoons

An economical dish

Serves 4
Preparation: 30 minutes
Cooking: 30 minutes

Ingredients

9 oz (250 g) lentils
2–3 small onions
1 carrot
1 bouquet garni
7 oz (200 g) bacon, streaked with fat
2–3 shallots
Vinegar
Oil
Salt and pepper

1. The night before the meal, leave the lentils to soak in warm water.

2. Drain them, cover with cold water, and cook very gently with 1–2 onions, the carrot (scraped and sliced), and the bouquet garni. Add salt and pepper when they are half done.

3. Just before serving, trim the rind from the bacon and dice the meat. Peel the shallots and chop them roughly. Prepare the vinaigrette as follows:

4. To achieve a tasty vinaigrette, first pour 1 generous tbsp red wine vinegar into a bowl, add a few pinches of salt, mixing thoroughly to dissolve it; then pour on 5 tbsp corn or sunflower oil and add plenty of pepper. Beat these ingredients vigorously. You can obtain a more original flavor if you combine equal amounts of two different oils (corn and walnut oil, for example). You can also add a dash of balsamic vinegar.

5. Drain the lentils thoroughly and transfer them to a soup dish. Sauté the bacon so that it is crispy and gives off some of its fat. Sprinkle the shallots on the lentils, the vinaigrette sauce on the shallots, and, finally, the lardoons of bacon and their cooking juices on top of the whole dish.

Recommended drinks

Beaujolais
Sancerre Rouge
Saumur-Champigny

Menu suggestions

1. As a hot appetizer, this lentil salad can be followed by trout meunière accompanied by celery purée. For dessert, serve apple fritters.

2. For a quick meal, serve these lentils with an endive and braised ham salad, followed by pear compote with cinnamon.

Oyster plant with ham and cream

A family dish

Serves 4
Preparation: 15 minutes
Cooking: 30 minutes

Ingredients

2¹/₄ lb (1 kg) oyster plants
(1 lb 5 oz/600 g when peeled)
1 lemon
1 onion
3 slices cooked ham (7 oz/200 g)
Oil
A little bouillon (made from a cube)
1 glass white wine
1 small pot crème fraîche

1 bunch parsley
Salt and pepper

1. Brush the oyster plants under cold, running water and peel them. As soon as they are ready, put them into water flavored with lemon juice, in order to preserve their white color.

2. Peel and chop the onion. Cut the ham into strips. Heat 2 tbsp oil in a casserole and fry the chopped onion until it is transparent, then lightly brown the strips of ham.

3. Cut the oyster plants into pieces 1¹/₂ in (4 cm) long. Put these in the casserole then cover with bouillon and the white wine. Season with salt and pepper then simmer over medium heat for 20 minutes.

4. Add the crème fraîche and continue to simmer, over very gentle heat this time, for about 10 minutes. When the oyster plants are cooked, sprinkle them with chopped parsley, after adjusting seasoning to taste.

N.B. Avoid buying large oyster plants, as they are often hollow inside; smaller ones are generally better. They can be bought fresh only in winter (but you can also prepare this recipe with frozen ones, thereby saving yourself the fiddly preliminaries). Fresh oyster
plants must be very firm. Try to find straight ones, too, as they will be easier to peel; this process is also easier if they are left to soak in a basin of cold water for at least an hour. Use a vegetable peeler and be sure to wear gloves, as oyster plants will stain your fingers.

Recommended drinks

Muscat de l'Alsace
Pouilly-Fumé
Chinon Rouge

Menu suggestions

1. Serve these oyster plants as a main dish for a family dinner, with an appetizer of roll mops accompanied by beet salad and sugared waffles for dessert.

2. You can also try this dish as an accompaniment to roast chicken, after a salad of cultivated mushrooms. For dessert, serve plum clafoutis.

Country soup with bacon

A family dish

Serves 4
Preparation: 10 minutes
Cooking: 1 h 20 minutes

Ingredients

10½ oz (300 g) carrots
7 oz (200 g) turnips
2 onions
2–3 leeks
1 oz (30 g) butter
2 firm potatoes
4½ oz (125 g) bacon, streaked with fat
1 bouquet garni (parsley, thyme, bay leaf)
Salt and pepper

1. Peel the carrots, turnips, and onions, then cut them into uniform slices. Trim the leeks by cutting off the roots and most of the green ends, then wash them in plenty of water, spreading the leaves, and cut them into slices.

2. Melt the butter in a large saucepan. Add the vegetables and coat them in the melted butter. Over medium heat, cover and braise for about 20 minutes.

3. Pour 4 cups (1 liter) water (or, preferably, vegetable or chicken bouillon, if available) onto the vegetables. Bring it to the boil slowly then add salt and pepper. Cover once again and leave to simmer gently for 30 minutes.

4. Peel the potatoes, then wash and wipe them, before cutting them into uniform cubes (not too small). Slice the rind off the bacon with a sharp knife, then cut the meat into small strips, removing the cartilage if necessary.

5. When the vegetable soup has cooked for 30 minutes, add the diced potato, bacon, and bouquet garni.

6. Cover once again and simmer for a further 30 minutes, until the potatoes are cooked. Adjust seasoning to taste. Serve piping hot in a soup tureen, possibly with small garlic croûtons or thin strips of slightly stale farmhouse bread.

Recommended drinks

Pessac-léognan
Chanturgues
Cahors

Menu suggestions

1. This traditional appetizer for winter meals in the French countryside can be followed by poultry with sautéed potatoes. Serve a vanilla cream with waffles for dessert.

2. Another idea: breaded pig's feet with fries. For dessert, serve blueberry pie.

123

Potato pie with bacon

A regional dish

Serves 4
Preparation: 15 minutes
Cooking: 1 hour 30 minutes

Ingredients

2¹/₄ lb (1 kg) firm potatoes
6 thin slices bacon, streaked with fat
2 cloves garlic
2 shallots
Parsley
Thyme
Chives
1 dab butter
12¹/₂ oz (350 g) piecrust dough

1 egg
1 small pot crème fraîche
Salt and pepper

1. Peel the potatoes, then wash and wipe them, before cutting them into thin slices. Slice the rind off the bacon and cut it into very small dice. Peel the garlic and shallots, then chop them finely, along with the herbs.

2. Butter a round pie dish. Divide the piecrust dough into two parts, then roll the larger one on a floured worktop, lay it in the pie dish, and extend it up the sides.

3. Spread a layer of potatoes over the dough then add salt and pepper. Cover the potatoes with a layer of bacon mixed with the chopped herbs. Continue this process, with successive layers of potatoes and bacon plus herbs, until there are no ingredients left. Add salt—in moderation, on account of the bacon—and plenty of pepper.

4. Roll the rest of the dough to form the top of the pie and put it into place. Seal the edges of the dough by moistening it slightly and then pinching the two layers tightly together all the way round. Brush the top and sides with beaten egg. Preheat the oven to 435 °F (225°C) and bake the pie for 1 hour 15 minutes.

5. Take the pie out of the oven and carefully cut round its edges to remove the top. Pour the crème fraîche inside and swivel the pie so that it is evenly distributed. Put the top back in place and leave the pie to rest in the oven (with the heat turned off) for a further 15 minutes.

Recommended drinks

Macon Rouge
Pessac-léognan
Brouilly

Menu suggestions

1. For a rustic meal in fall, serve a fricassée of ceps, then this pie with a game terrine, and finally a fruit salad.

2. You can also serve this pie as an appetizer, followed by duck with olives and, as a dessert, pears Belle Hélène or chocolate profiteroles.

Cream of split pea soup

A family dish

Serves 5
Preparation: 15 minutes
Cooking: 1 hour 15 minutes

Ingredients

1 lb 2 oz (500 g) soaked split peas
2 onions
2 leeks
1³/₄ oz (50 g) butter
2–3 tbsp crème fraîche
1 sugar lump
Chives
Salt and pepper

1. Drain the split peas (having soaked them for 24 hours), put them in a large saucepan, add water until they are completely covered, and bring to the boil. Cover the saucepan and simmer for 10 minutes.

2. Peel and finely slice the onions. Trim the leeks, discarding the roots and all the green parts. Wash them carefully, separating the leaves. Cut them into thin slices. Add the onions and leeks to the saucepan. Cover and cook for about 1 hour, over medium heat. Add salt and pepper once the vegetables are cooked.

3. Pass the contents of the saucepan through a vegetable mill (in several batches, if necessary). Put the resulting purée in a clean saucepan, add the butter (in dabs), and thin with sufficient hot water to obtain a creamy consistency.

4. Mix thoroughly until the butter has completely melted, then adjust seasoning to taste. Continue heating the purée, stirring occasionally, without letting it boil. If you want a slightly sweeter soup, you can add a sugar lump and then stir the mixture thoroughly.

5. Stir in the crème fraîche at the last moment, then pour the soup into a hot tureen. As a final touch, garnish with a few finely chopped sprigs of chives just before serving.

Recommended drinks

Riesling
Bergerac Blanc
Sancerre Blanc

Menu suggestions

1. Serve this creamy soup as an appetizer, followed by pork roast with garlic and ratatouille, and a dessert of crème caramel.

2. For a family dinner, follow this split pea soup with a garnished sauerkraut, rounded off by a green-apple sorbet.

125

Potato salad

Serves 4
1 lb 11 oz (750 g) boiled
potatoes
3 eggs
3 small, fresh onions
1 jar pickled capers
1 bunch chives
Oil
Vinegar
Salt and pepper

1. Peel the potatoes, then cut them
into slices $^3/_{16}$–$^5/_{16}$ in (5–8 mm)
thick. Arrange them in a dish.

2. Meanwhile, boil the eggs until
they are hard and remove their
shells. Cut them into slices.

3. Peel the onions and cut them
into slices, then separate the rings.
Prepare the vinaigrette.

4. Place the eggs and onions on the
potatoes. Add some capers (you
should serve most of them
separately). Add the chives and toss
with the vinaigrette.

Gratin of boiled vegetables

Serves 4
2$^1/_4$ lb (1 kg) boiled
Brussels sprouts
2 slices ham
1 small pot crème fraîche
Grated Comté cheese
1 dab butter
Salt and pepper

1. Butter an oven dish and add the
Brussels sprouts.

2. Cut the ham into small strips and
arrange them on the cabbage.

3. Cover with crème fraîche,
sprinkle with the grated Comté, and
cook for 10–15 minutes in an oven
preheated to 435 °F (225 °C).

Pumpkin gratin

Serves 4
1 lb 5 oz (600 g) cooked pumpkin
flesh
2 oz (55 g) flour
2$^1/_2$ oz (70 g) butter
3 cups (60 cl) milk
$^1/_2$ sliced onion
Grated Gruyère
Salt and pepper

1. Dice the cold pumpkin flesh and
put it in a bowl. Add salt and pepper.
Heat the flour and butter slowly for 4
minutes. Set aside.

2. Boil the milk with the sliced onion,
salt, and pepper in another saucepan,
and allow it to infuse for 10 minutes.
Take out the onion, then, away from
the heat, add the butter and flour
mixture.

3. Simmer the sauce over low heat
for 3 minutes. Butter an oven dish and
arrange the pumpkin in it. Cover with
the sauce and sprinkle with grated
Gruyère. Brown in the oven at 375 °F
(190 °C) for 40 minutes.

Cream of navy bean soup

Serves 4
1 lb 2 oz (500 g) navy beans
2/3 cup (15 cl) crème fraîche
1/4 cup + 1 1/2 tbsp (10 cl) bouillon
1 dab butter
Salt and pepper

This simple recipe offers a delicious way to use up leftover, cooked navy beans.

1. Put the cooked beans in a blender, without any liquid. Reduce them to a very fine purée with no lumps.

2. Put the bean purée in a saucepan then add the crème fraîche, bouillon, salt, pepper, and butter.

3. Bring to the boil, adjust seasoning to taste, and serve very hot. If there are any lumps after the beans have been blended, put the soup through a very fine sieve.

Cream of mushroom soup

Serves 4
1 lb 2 oz (500 g) cooked mushrooms
2 3/4 oz (80 g) butter
2 shallots
Light cream
1 scant cup (20 cl) bouillon
Salt and pepper

You can use any type of mushroom for this recipe.

1. Blend the cooked mushrooms and set aside.

2. Melt the butter in a saucepan, add the finely chopped shallots, and simmer over low heat for 2 minutes. Add the cream, bouillon, and mushroom purée, along with salt and pepper.

3. Bring to the boil and cook very slowly for 2 minutes. Serve piping hot.

Tomatoes with mushroom stuffing

Serves 4
2 finely chopped onions
5 tbsp olive oil
A few cultivated mushrooms
Juice of 1 lemon
2 peeled and seeded tomatoes
3 cloves garlic
1 bunch parsley
5 1/2 oz (150 g) minced meat
Salt and pepper

1. Braise the onions in olive oil in a saucepan. Add the mushrooms, roughly chopped, seasoned with salt and pepper, and cook with the lemon juice for 10 minutes.

2. Cut the tomatoes in half, then add them to the mushrooms along with the chopped garlic, chopped parsley, and minced meat. Cook for 5 minutes then remove the saucepan from the heat.

3. Hollow out the tomatoes and fill them with the stuffing. Place them in a baking dish. Sprinkle with grated cheese and brown in the oven at 350 °F (180 °C) for 25 minutes.

127

Rice, pasta, and cereals

Rice cooked in plentiful water for 4

1 Fill a large saucepan with water. Add salt and bring to the boil. Put 1¹/₄ cups (250 g) rice in a metal sieve and rinse it with cold water to eliminate the starch, then add it to boiling water. Stir with a long-handled spoon to distribute the grains evenly. Making sure that the water keeps boiling constantly, but moderately, cook the rice without covering the saucepan, tasting from time to time.

2 Drain in a large sieve then add a generous dab of fresh or semi-salted butter and adjust the seasoning. Rice normally takes 15–20 minutes to cook in this way. A similar technique, known as the Italian method, consists of cooking the rice in boiling water for 10 minutes, rinsing and draining it, then putting it in an oven, preheated to a low temperature, for another 10 minutes.

N.B.

There are three basic ways of cooking rice, so choose the one most appropriate for the recipe that you are preparing. Cooking in plentiful water is recommended for plain rice served with a cold salad or simply seasoned with a little butter. When rice is cooked with a limited amount of water, the aromas become concentrated and the grains soften. This technique is used in countless recipes, such as Creole and pilaf rice, risotto, and paella. Steamed rice is less common and mainly associated with Asia, particularly when sticky rice is used.

Steamed rice for 4

1 This technique is especially suited to sticky varieties of rice. Soak 1¹/₄ cups (250 g) round-grained rice for 30 minutes in cold water then place it in a clean, white dishtowel. Steaming is also appropriate for long-grained rice, previously rinsed in cold water; in this case, the rice is sometimes blanched for a few minutes before being put in the top of the steamer.

2 Fill the bottom of the steamer, or just an ordinary saucepan, with water and bring to the boil. You can also use a couscous-maker. If you use a bamboo steaming basket, choose a saucepan whose diameter corresponds as exactly as possible with it, in order to avoid any loss of steam.

3 Place the dishtowel containing the rice into the steamer and cover with the lid. Cook for 25–30 minutes, until you achieve the desired texture. If this rice is intended for making sushi, put it in a dish as soon as it is cooked and season it immediately; mix thoroughly, then leave to cool at room temperature.

Variations

There are countless variations. You can replace the water with bouillon or season it with a mixture of spices especially blended for this purpose. A wide range of spices can be used: saffron adds both fragrance and a wonderful orangey color, while curry powder not only flavors a dish, but also turns it bright yellow. You can also use paprika or turmeric. Do not forget that pilaf rice denotes a general

Pilaf rice with mussels

approach to a dish rather than any fixed recipe. You can replace the onions with shallots or a leek. You can also add sliced cultivated mushrooms. Brown the ingredients in olive oil or the juices of a roast chicken. The cooking time varies according to the type of rice used: never forget to taste it before taking it off the heat.

Pilaf rice for 4

1 Melt a generous dab of butter in a fairly large saucepan. Add a chopped onion and sauté it for 5 minutes, then add 1^1/$_4$ cups (250 g) unwashed rice and cook over low heat for a further 4 minutes. The grains of rice should gradually become opaque when they are stirred with a wooden spoon and start to sizzle in the fat.

2 Cover the rice with boiling water (2 parts water to 1 part rice). Add salt and stir for 1 minute, to prevent the rice sticking to the bottom of the saucepan. Cover and cook over low heat without stirring. When all the liquid is absorbed, after about 20 minutes, stir in 3/4 oz (20 g) butter. Adjust the seasoning.

Tip

When cooking white rice in a limited amount of water to accompany a Chinese or Asian meal, use an automatic rice cooker: you only have to add the indicated amounts of rice and water, and the machine does the rest, guaranteeing a constant cooking process with perfect results every time.

Creole rice for 4

1 Boil some water (1 part rice to 2 parts water), then add 1^1/$_4$ cups (250 g) unwashed rice in one go.

2 Cover and cook over a low heat until the liquid has been completely absorbed (15–20) minutes.

Guide to cooking rice

Type of rice	Cooking time (pilau)	rice:water
White rice	15–20 minutes	1:2
Brown rice	30–45 minutes	1:2
Wild rice	35–50 minutes	1:2–2^1/$_2$

A warming dish

Countries with a tradition of growing rice have come up with numerous specialties: paella in Spain, Cantonese rice in China, nasi goreng in Indonesia. In Italy, risotto is the typical rice dish. This very popular recipe can form the basis of a simple family meal or be converted into a sophisticated treat, depending on the accompaniment chosen. The underlying principle of risotto is always the same. The rice is cooked in bouillon, along with various ingredients and condiments. It is a complete dish that includes starch,

Eggplant risotto

vegetables, and meat or fish. Less commonly, it can be served as an accompaniment to meat, in which case the recipe is lightened and simplified. Several spices can be used to enhance it: for example, pepper, saffron, or paprika. A risotto should boast an outstanding personality, and so Parmesan cheese features among its ingredients. The rice itself should have round grains; choose high-quality varieties from Italy or the Camargue. Risotto is also characterized by its cooking method and the distinctive consistency of the rice. The sauce should be thick, but fairly fluid, while the grains should be soft and swollen with liquid.

Indonesian risotto

Indonesian risotto

To serve 4, wash thoroughly 1 1/2 cups (300 g) long-grained rice and leave it to drain in a sieve for about 30 minutes. Heat 2–3 tbsp oil and use it to lightly brown 2 sliced cloves garlic and 1 sliced onion. Add the rice in one go and sauté for 2 minutes. Add, little by little, 3 cups (75 cl) milk. Season with salt and powdered turmeric then bring to the boil, stirring constantly. Cover the saucepan as soon as the milk starts bubbling and simmer over very low heat for 20 minutes. When the rice is cooked, take off the saucepan lid and stir gently with a fork to incorporate the milk that has not yet been absorbed. Sauté 1/2 chicken, cut into small pieces, in oil. Cover the rice once again and cook it for a few more minutes, then take it off the heat and season it with a few pinches of curry powder. Arrange the rice in a dome on a warm dish. Garnish with 1 red and 1 green bell pepper, 1 cucumber scratched with a fork then cut into slices, 2 hard-boiled eggs, and the chicken pieces. Finally, sprinkle on a little paprika and serve.

Seafood risotto

for 4

1 To cook an authentic Italian risotto, you need a special variety of rice, such as Arborio, Carnaroli, or Vialone Nano. Their short, thick grains have a high level of starch and, if the dish is cooked properly, without over-boiling the rice, its distinctive character is assured. Risotto should be creamy but not sticky, with every grain very tender.

2 Over low heat, brown 1 sliced onion and 2 chopped cloves garlic with virgin olive oil in a fairly large, thick-bottomed skillet. Add 1¼ cups (250 g) rice and sauté it for 5 minutes, stirring with a wooden spoon until the grains are entirely coated with oil and turn opaque. Meanwhile, heat 3 cups (75 cl) chicken bouillon in another saucepan.

3 Then add ⅓ cup + 1½ tbsp (10 cl) dry white wine and half the chicken bouillon, followed by paprika, a pinch of ground pepper, and a pinch of saffron. Cook the rice over very low heat for 10 minutes, until the liquid has been absorbed, then gently pour in the rest of the bouillon.

Tip

A good risotto requires slow, gradual cooking. To achieve this, it is vital to have the appropriate equipment. Prepare this recipe in a thick-bottomed, stainless steel skillet with deep sides, 10–12 in (25–30 cm) in diameter.

4 Add 3½ oz (100 g) cockles, 5½ oz (150 g) blanched almonds, 7 oz (200 g) mussels, and 1 lb 2 oz (500 g) thoroughly washed, raw langoustines to the rice. You can replace the langoustines with shrimp. To vary this recipe with meat, you can substitute the seafood with finely diced ham, browned ground meat, and slices of smoked sausage.

5 Continue cooking for a further 10 minutes, checking that the rice does not thicken too quickly: add stock if necessary. Risotto must never be allowed to dry up—it should be creamy when it is served. Risotto is not dusted with cheese if it is cooked with seafood. Adjust the seasoning and serve immediately: even a short wait will turn the seafood rubbery.

Paella valenciana for 6

Preparing the meat: cut a large chicken into pieces and brown these in oil. Add 1 chopped onion, 3 cloves garlic, and 4 sliced tomatoes. Sauté for 10 minutes then add 4 cups (1 liter) bouillon. Simmer for 30 minutes over very low heat and set aside. Cut 20 slices of chorizo, then set aside. Preparing the vegetables: boil and chop $5^1/_2$ oz (150 g) green beans. Peel and cook 3 artichokes. Set aside the hearts.

Preparing the shellfish: wash 7 oz (200 g) each of cockles, clams, and mussels in plenty of water, scrubbing them vigorously. Wash and gut 4 squid, sauté them in olive oil in a skillet, and set aside. Sauté a dozen langoustines.

Preparing the paella: heat 2–3 tbsp olive oil and put 2 cups (400 g) unwashed rice in a paella pan. Braise for 5 minutes, then add 2 pinches of saffron, salt, pepper, the chicken stew, and the chorizo. Cook over fairly high heat at first, then a gentler one toward the end.

When the rice is cooked, but still firm, add the squid, the seafood, and the vegetables. Then cover the pan with aluminum foil and cook some more, so that the shellfish open. Discard any unopened shellfish, sprinkle the paella with chopped parsley, and serve from the pan, garnished with langoustines.

Spanish rice

Paella is a sumptuous dish in which, unlike risotto, the abundance of seafood and meat upstages the rice; the latter remains absolutely essential, however, for, without it, the various ingredients would have no cohesion; furthermore, its soothing, sweet taste tempers the impact of the spices and the richness of the garnish. Paella is cooked in a black, wrought iron pan with two handles that is specially designed for this dish. It has no lid, as paella is usually cooked "open," fairly fast.

Ingredients

A wide range of ingredients is used in paella: rabbit, chicken, pork, sausages, chorizo, various vegetables, fish, and shellfish. To achieve perfect results, this diversity demands that the ingredients that take a longish time to cook (chicken, artichokes, and squids) are cooked separately, at least partially. Mussels and other shellfish can be added raw, as they only need a few minutes to cook. Opt for a round, slightly sticky French or Spanish rice. The grains absorb the aromas given off by the meat and turn the dish into an exquisite delicacy. Paellas with long-grained rice can also be successful, provided they are not cooked too much, as they quickly become too soft. This is a fairly simple dish to prepare,

Chicken paella

provided you follow strictly the various steps involved.

Variants

You can make other paellas by changing the ingredients. Replace the chicken with pork or rabbit and sprinkle some slivered almonds on top, or substitute the langoustines with shrimp or king prawns. Paella can dispense with meat entirely, in favor of fish: combine bass, mullet, or dory with squid and sea almonds: the result is surprising, but delicious. The cooking process must be monitored carefully, however, to ensure that the fish are not overcooked.

Tip

Saffron is the most important spice in paella. Buy only saffron of the highest quality from a specialist grocer. Powdered saffron has the advantage of being easy to dose, but its coloring is often stronger. All types of saffron keep longer when stored in a tightly closed, opaque container.

Rabbit paella

Ingredients for fried rice with cockles

General points

Fried rice, incorrectly translated from Chinese as "Cantonese rice," is undoubtedly the most widespread staple in Southeast Asia. It is found virtually everywhere in China, where it has been adapted to suit local customs and produce; the northern regions, not traditionally rice producers, are perhaps now its main consumers. Fried rice was originally a pauper's dish, but it has grown into a highly prized specialty. It is often made with very light, long-grained varieties, and sometimes even scented rice. Whatever the end result, the principle is always the same: white rice is boiled and then set aside; ingredients of varying richness and complexity—fish, meat, or just vegetables—are prepared and then sautéed with spices; and the rice is added to these ingredients toward the end of cooking.

Variants

Several distinctive versions of the basic recipe are often found.

Five-spice rice

To serve 4, cook 1¼ cups (250 g) rice and prepared the other ingredients, following the instructions overleaf. When you add the rice, season it with 3 generous pinches of a mixture of five powdered spices (star anise, clove, fennel, cinnamon, and pepper). Apart from that, the basic recipe is the same.

Fried rice with shrimp

To serve 4 people, cook 1¼ cups (250 g) white rice and set aside. Chop 1 onion and 1 tbsp fresh ginger. Soak, blanch, and chop 2 aromatic mushrooms. Sauté the onion, ginger, and mushrooms, then add the cooked rice, 5½ oz (150 g) of cooked, shelled shrimp tails, salt, pepper, and a dash of sesame oil. Cook for 10 minutes then serve.

Fried rice with black mushrooms and chives.

To serve 4, cook 1¼ cups/250 g white rice and set aside. Chop 1 onion and 1 tbsp fresh ginger. Soak, blanch, and chop 10 black mushrooms. Sauté the onion, ginger, and mushrooms then add the cooked rice, 3 tbsp chopped chives, salt, pepper, and a pinch of chili powder. Cook all these ingredients over medium heat for 10 minutes, then serve.

Cantonese rice with cockles and shrimp

Cantonese rice

1 Cook 1¼ cups (250 g) white rice in an automatic rice-cooker or covered saucepan, in a limited amount of water. The Chinese normally wash their rice before cooking it, but this serves no purpose with the rice on the market in the West. Choose long-grained rice—including aromatic Thai and Basmati varieties—but above all avoid brown rice, which is unheard of in Chinese cooking.

Tip

In this recipe, successful results depend on the quality of the rice and the boiling process. Choose a Thai or Basmati variety with fine grains. Use an automatic, electric rice-cooker, adding slightly less water than recommended. This will allow the grains to separate from each other far more easily. Do not prolong the boiling phase unnecessarily.

2 Peel and finely chop 1 piece fresh ginger; peel and slice 1 onion; wash the white of 1 leek and cut it into thin slivers. Set aside. Break 4 eggs in a bowl and beat. Make a flat omelet in a non-stick skillet and leave to cool. Mix 1 tbsp of soy sauce and a handful of shrimp tails in a small bowl.

3 Cut the omelet into strips 1/16–3/16 in (3–5 mm) thick. Cut 4 slices ham in the same way. Blanch 3½ oz (100 g) petits pois and set aside. Heat a little peanut oil in a wok, over medium heat, and add the ginger, onion, and leek. Sauté these ingredients for about 5 minutes, without allowing them to change color.

4 Add the omelet, ham, and petits pois, then continue cooking for another 5 minutes. Finally, add the rice, along with the shrimp tails (seasoned with salt and pepper) and cook for a maximum 10–15 minutes. Adjust the seasoning. This fried rice can be served as either a side dish or main course.

Andalusian salad

Rice salad with squid

Drugstore salad

N.B.

Rice salads are ideal for fine weather. As they are fresh, attractive, and simple to prepare, they are guaranteed to go down well with all the family. Do not cook the rice more than 6 hours

before assembling your dish: this will make it firmer and plumper. Cold rice always has a tendency to become gluey and pasty, so only use "non-stick" varieties whose grains remain completely separate. It is important to cool the rice quickly once it has been cooked. Do

not leave it in the saucepan; instead, rinse it in a sieve under cold, running water, as this will reduce its temperature faster. Then, drain it. There is a wide choice of ingredients: tuna, chicken, ham, shrimp, crab, tomatoes, olives. Give your imagination full rein. As for the seasoning, lemon and olive oil are indispensable along with fresh herbs, particularly tarragon, basil, and fresh thyme. Rice salads can sometimes be rather dull, either through lack of seasoning or because the vinaigrette has not been mixed with the rice for sufficient time. So, prepare the following recipes 5 or 6 hours in advance, to bring out the flavors. The ideal dishware for serving a rice salad is colorful Provencal or Moroccan-style soup bowls, but you can also consider a hollowed-out marrow, watermelon, or squash.

Stuffed squash

Veracruz salad

Select 4 young, tender corncobs. Boil 4 quarts (4 liters) water with 4 cups (1 liter) milk. Add salt and cook the corn, uncovered, in fast boiling water for 30 minutes. Drain the corncobs and leave them to cool. Cut the tops off 4 yellow bell peppers. Seed then poach the bell peppers for 10 minutes in salted, boiling water. Meanwhile, cook 1 glass rice in salted, boiling water. Prepare a mayonnaise; divide it in two, then season one half with paprika. Drain the rice, then mix it with another yellow bell pepper (raw), 1 raw green bell pepper, and ham (all previously diced). Stuff the poached yellow bell peppers with the rice mixture. Arrange them on a plate, surrounded by a bed of sliced green bell pepper; then add some diced green bell pepper and the corn. Garnish with a bunch of watercress and serve with the mayonnaise in two small bowls.

Dauphinois salad

Bring to the boil 2 glasses apple juice with 3 glasses water and a $3/4$ cup (150 g) rice and cook until the liquid has been completely absorbed. Add a pinch of saffron and leave to cool. Prepare a vinaigrette. Trim and chop a few celery stalks. Wipe 2 green apples and cut them into a mixture of thin slices and small chunks. Put them in a bowl and sprinkle them with the juice of 1 lemon. Mix the boiled rice with the vinaigrette, shelled walnuts (in pieces), the apple chunks, and the celery. Garnish with the apple slices, some whole walnuts, and a sprig of celery. To turn this salad into a main course, add strips of chicken, cubes of ham, or broiled lardoons.

Rice salad with chicken

Boil $1^1/4$ cups (250 g) non-stick rice in a large amount of cold water. Put the cooked rice in a sieve and refresh it under cold, running water. Leave to drain for 15 minutes, pressing down on it slightly to squeeze out as much water as possible. Cut $10^1/2$ oz (300 g) cold chicken into small strips. Prepare a vinaigrette with 10 tbsp peanut oil, 3 tbsp wine vinegar, 1 tsp of mustard, salt, and pepper. Put the rice, chicken, 1 diced red bell pepper, 1 diced tomato, the vinaigrette, and a chopped bunch of chives in a bowl. Toss the salad, without squashing the rice. Leave in the refrigerator, inside a tightly closed container, for about 6 hours. Take the salad out of the refrigerator, toss it once again, check the seasoning, and serve very cold.

Rice and red kidney bean salad

Oriental rice salad

Camargue salad

Grandmother's rice

Empress rice with chocolate

Apt-style rice pudding

Rice as dessert

When rice is boiled in whole milk, it swells up to form a sticky cream. If it is left to cool, it can be turned out of a mold like a pudding: this is a time-honored dessert, appreciated by children and adults alike.

Stuffed pears with rice and milk

The choice of rice is decisive here. In order to achieve an agreeable texture with soft but unbroken grains, select round-grained rice with a fairly high starch content, to give the dish bulk and consistency: rice from the Camargue or Italy is perfect. Use high-quality, pasteurized, whole milk. The rice is cooked slowly in milk until it turns into a fairly thick cream. It is then sweetened and poured into a mold.

Variants

Plain rice pudding is often complemented by candied fruit, caramel, or spices and chocolate. Treat it like an empty canvas and allow your imagination to fill in the details.

Rice cake with caramel

To serve 4, put 1 ⅓ cups (300 g) sugar in a saucepan, then melt and caramelize it over low heat, stirring constantly with a wooden spatula. Pour the boiling caramel in the bottom of a mold, then leave to cool until it is completely solid. Cook some

fairly firm rice with milk and pour it into the mold once it is ready. Leave to cool then place overnight in the refrigerator. This rice pudding can sometimes be difficult to turn out of the mold on account of the caramel; if so, simply leave the mold in hot water for a little while.

Rice cake with candied fruit.

Boil 4 cups (1 liter) milk with 1 vanilla bean. Cook 1¼ cups (250 g) rice, then add 2 egg yolks and ½ cup (120 g) sugar. Dice 5½ oz (150 g) assorted candied fruit, angelica, melon, orange, and lemon, and add them to the cooked rice. Stir thoroughly then pour the mixture into a fairly deep mold (along the lines of a Charlotte mold). Leave to cool then place overnight in the refrigerator. Turn the cake out on a serving dish and garnish with pieces of angelica.

N.B.

A rice pudding can be served on its own or with a sweet sauce. Custard milk is the most common accompaniment, but a fresh fruit coulis is also satisfying: a coulis of strawberries or raspberries, for example, adds a deliciously fresh touch. You can also try a caramel or dark chocolate sauce. Another good complement for rice pudding is fruit of any kind: fresh or poached, candied or dried. The rice and milk mixture is traditionally poured into a mold containing caramelized sugar. Another approach involves placing the mixture in a pastry shell, combined with candied fruit.

Rice pudding with pears for 4

1 Open a vanilla bean lengthwise and scrape out its contents into a saucepan containing 4 cups (1 liter) milk; bring the milk to the boil, beating all the time, then remove from the heat. Briefly rinse 1¹/₄ cups (250 g) rice with cold water then add it to the hot milk. Bring to the boil, stirring constantly, then cook over very low heat for 20–25 minutes.

2 The milk should be almost totally absorbed and the grains of rice soft and plump. Prolong the cooking time, if necessary, to achieve a thick, sticky consistency. Remove from the heat and add 2 egg yolks, stirring all the while: the mixture will thicken and turn an attractive, pale yellow.

3 Stir in ¹/₂ cup (120 g) sugar and pour the mixture into a mold. Leave to cool at room temperature for 2–3 hours then place overnight in the refrigerator. Put the mold in hot water for 3–4 minutes. Separate the rice mixture from the edges of the mold with the tip of a knife then turn the mold upside down over a dish.

141

Lasagna

1 Boil plenty of salted water over high heat. Lay the fresh pasta on a worktop and disentangle the pieces by shaking, without breaking, them. Eliminate any surplus flour, if necessary. This process is the same for tagliatelle, fettucini, and lasagna. Add salt (preferably coarse).

2 When the water boils, plunge in the fresh pasta (two by two in the case of lasagna) and stir with a spoon in circular movements, until the water starts boiling again. Turn down the heat so that the water bubbles constantly. Monitor the cooking process carefully, as its time will vary according to the volume of water.

3 Take a piece of the pasta out of the water. Plunge it into a little cold water and taste it. Note that only dried pasta is cooked "al dente" (slightly firm). This term has become the benchmark for cooking all types of pasta, but fresh pasta is naturally soft and should remain so; it is never hard before cooking and becomes supple in boiling water.

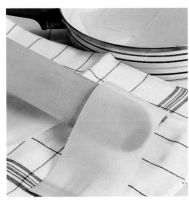

4 The pasta sample should be a uniform color, with no pale patches. Once the pasta is cooked, pour it into a sieve, making sure you do not scald yourself. Shake the sieve to drain the water more quickly. In the case of lasagna, remove from the water with a skimmer and place on a dishtowel to drain.

Lasagna with strawberries

Woven sole and pappardelle

Morels with fresh noodles

Tagliatelle with diced salmon

N.B.

The best-quality fresh pasta accompanied by the tastiest sauce imaginable can still prove unappetizing if the pasta has not been cooked properly. Pasta basically consists of starch, which is highly sensitive to heat and humidity.

Cooking

If the cooking process is too short, pasta turns out insipid and indigestible; if it is too cold, the pasta becomes soft and swollen with water; if it is too long, it loses all its flavor. You have to find the right balance. Select a stewpot or saucepan with a capacity of 3–5 quarts (3–5 liters). Use the hottest burner on your stove: the critical point for cooking pasta comes when it is plunged into the water, on account of the drop in the water temperature—this should be as brief as possible. Afterwards, use a sieve with large holes so that the water can drain quickly.

Serving

Have your complements (sauce or condiments) ready and hot, so that you can add them immediately to the steaming pasta. Mix them together in a large bowl, to have sufficient room for maneuver and avoid any hot splashes. The cooking procedure for ravioli, tortellini, and other stuffed pasta follows the same rules, but you must take special care not to tear them.

Cooking ravioli

Boil plenty of salted water over high heat. Lay the raw ravioli on a worktop and eliminate any residual flour, if necessary. When the water comes to the boil, plunge in the stuffed pasta and stir gently with a spoon in circular movements, making sure not to break the ravioli. Continue stirring until the water starts to boil again. Turn down the heat so that the water bubbles at a constant level.

Remove a piece of ravioli from the water; plunge it into a little cold water, and taste. It should be firm, but not hard. Drain the ravioli, add your sauce, and serve.

Ravioli and barigoule

Spaghetti

1 Boil plenty of salted water over high heat. The volume of water should be five times greater than that of the pasta you are going to cook. The suitable dose of salt is 2 tsp (10 g) per quart (liter), but if the planned sauce is intrinsically salty (anchovies, olives), this proportion can obviously be reduced.

2 When the water reaches boiling point, plunge in the dried pasta and stir with a long-handled wooden spoon in circular movements until the water starts to boil again. Cook quickly, with the water bubbling intensely, while making sure that none is spilt. The manufacturer's recommended cooking time is only an indication—it is advisable to check the pasta is cooked to your personal taste.

3 Take a piece of pasta out of the water. Plunge it in a little cold water and taste it. The consistency should be firm and slightly resistant to your teeth, but not hard. Cut the pasta sample—it should be a uniform color, with no pale patches when soft; when cooked "al dente," the pasta will reveal a thin white area in the middle—this is the least cooked part of the dough.

Tip

Only dried pasta can be cooked "al dente." Fresh pasta cooks uniformly; it is also very moist and softens quickly. Dried pasta is cooked more slowly, from the edges to the center; when it is only slightly cooked, and so remains firm and resists the teeth, it can be described as "al dente."

4 The pasta is ready: pour it into a sieve, taking care not to scald yourself. Shake the sieve to drain the water more quickly. At the same time, finish off your sauce and heat it up in a saucepan. Put the cooked pasta in a bowl and mix in the sauce by lifting up the pasta. Serve immediately.

Pasta shells with bacon

N.B.

As its name suggests, dried pasta has been dehydrated before being put on sale. This desiccation results in a longer cooking time: fresh tagliatelle cooks five or six times faster than dried tagliatelle of the same thickness. As dried pasta has little moisture content, it has a marked tendency to absorb the liquids into which it is plunged, whether water, bouillon, or milk. Dried pasta left in a saucepan of hot water can absorb eight times its volume in water and turn into an insipid, unappetizing mass. This is why dried pasta must be cooked dry in fiercely boiling water and never left standing in its cooking water. The cooking process must be fast, to avoid absorption of the water. The smaller the pasta, the quicker they swell up, so take special care when you are preparing pasta shells, penne, or butterflies. Once pasta has been drained,

Small Royan ravioli with ham

it sticks together very quickly to form a compact block. If it is going to be eaten hot, mix it straight away with its sauce or condiments; if it is intended for a salad, refresh it immediately under cold, running water. Drain it again,

Magret of duckling with penne

then mix it with a trickle of oil to prevent it from sticking together.

Tip

Thin your pesto with the cooking water: this will make it easier to mix it evenly into the pasta. Only a small amount of water should be added, however, to avoid rendering the dish tasteless. Reckon on 1 part water to 5 parts pesto. Do not forget to adjust the seasoning.

145

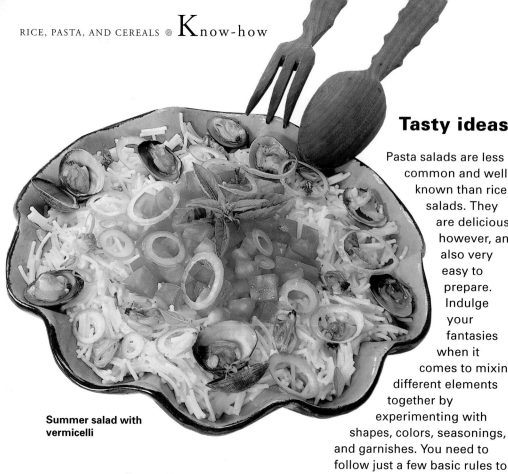

Summer salad with vermicelli

Penne salad with zucchini

Tasty ideas

Pasta salads are less common and well known than rice salads. They are delicious, however, and also very easy to prepare. Indulge your fantasies when it comes to mixing different elements together by experimenting with shapes, colors, seasonings, and garnishes. You need to follow just a few basic rules to guarantee success.

only a little and thereby avoid any risk of the salad drowning in its sauce, as is all too often the case. Finally, choose colorful garnishes, as these will enliven your dish.

Rotelle salad with dry ham

To serve 4, cook 9 oz (250 g) rotelle "al dente" in a large quantity of salted, boiling water. Pour the pasta into a sieve and refresh it with plenty of water. Leave it to drain for 15 minutes. Beat together 3 tbsp wine vinegar, salt, pepper, 10 tbsp peanut oil, and 1 tbsp grain mustard. Mix the drained pasta in a bowl with the vinaigrette and dried ham cut into strips, without breaking the rotelle. Adjust the seasoning and serve thoroughly chilled. You can replace the rotelle with fusilli and complement the vinaigrette with chopped tarragon.

Ingredients

Use small, thin pasta, as this will remain firmer in a salad. Use only dried pasta, as its texture is more suitable. Cook the pasta slightly "al dente," for any overcooking will lead to an excessively soft and unappealing mixture. Make your vinaigrette fairly concentrated, so that you need

Spaghetti salad with olives and feta

Spaghetti salad with lemon and black olives

Cook 9 oz (250 g) spaghetti "al dente" in plenty of salted, boiling water. Pour the pasta into a sieve and refresh it under cold, running water. Leave to drain for 15 minutes. Shake the sieve to drain as much water as possible. Squeeze out the juice of 1 lemon, along with a pinch of its grated zest. Beat these ingredients with 6 tbsp olive oil, 12 pitted and chopped black olives, salt, and pepper. Mix the pasta and the vinaigrette in a bowl and serve thoroughly chilled.

Penne salad with basil and bell peppers

Cook 9 oz (250 g) penne "al dente" in plenty of salted, boiling water. Pour the pasta into a sieve and refresh under cold, running water. Leave to drain for 15 minutes. Shake the sieve to drain as much water as possible. Roast 4 red bell peppers in the oven, then seed and dice. Squeeze the juice of 1 lemon and chop 1/2 bunch fresh basil and 2 cloves garlic. Beat these ingredients together with 10 tbsp olive oil, salt, and pepper. Mix the pasta, vinaigrette, and bell peppers in a bowl. Mix and serve chilled.

Vermicelli salad

Blanch 1 head of broccoli in plenty of salted, boiling water for 2–3 minutes. Wash 2 tomatoes, then wipe and thickly slice. Prepare a vinaigrette. Cook 9 oz (250 g) vermicelli in plenty of salted water for 3 minutes, then drain. Garnish a plate with lettuce leaves. Spread a thin layer of vermicelli on top of these, then the slices of tomato, the broccoli (cut into small florets), 4 hard-boiled eggs cut into quarters, a can of anchovy fillets in oil, and a few black olives. Arrange the rest of the vermicelli in a dome in the center of the plate. Season to taste.

Ligurian salad with spaghetti

Beet with pasta ruffs

Salad of pasta butterflies and tuna

Chives

Shallots, tarragon, and parsley

A classic

Of all the many accompaniments to pasta, Bolognese sauce is in a class of its own, as it is the most widespread and the most popular. Originally from the Bologna region in Italy, it has traveled around the world, adapting itself to local circumstances. For years, this recipe has been inspiring the food industry to turn it into an everyday staple, with varying degrees of success. Bolognese sauce is traditionally prepared in summer with fresh tomatoes, but it can also be made with canned tomatoes without altering its essential character; whichever you use, it is essential they have a low acidity level and plump flesh. The meat is also of crucial importance: choose best-quality beef, chopped into medium-size pieces in front of you. You can also use leftover cooked meat, but this could detract from the end result. There is some controversy on this subject: purists insist that only beef is acceptable, but some recipes list pork or ham. Try both versions and decide for yourself, but be sure to extend the cooking time when using pork. Prepare this sauce in a thick-bottomed saucepan.

wine. The most common spices are pepper and thyme, but fresh sage, rosemary, and savory are also used. It is possible to set off tomato sauces with a pinch of chili: the dosage must be exact, to prevent the chili from drowning the taste of the broiled meat. A dash of olive oil rounds off a sauce, by adding aroma and moisture. To achieve an unusual effect, mix a pinch of curry powder into the sauce a few minutes before serving. Chopped fresh herbs are often used: basil, naturally, but also chives, mint, and flat parsley.

Variants

Pasta can also be accompanied by meat sauces without tomatoes, as in the case of civet sauce, with its strong taste of

Basil

Bolognese sauce for 4

1 Chop 1 onion finely. Ask your butcher to chop 9 oz (250 g) beef, or cut it into small pieces yourself with a knife. Peel 1 carrot and cut it into tiny dice. Trim and chop 2 stalks celery. Wash 5–6 tomatoes. This recipe offers a good way of using chopped frozen steaks: there is no need to thaw them beforehand.

2 Place a saucepan over medium heat and heat 5 tbsp olive oil. Add the meat and brown it for a good 2 minutes, stirring all the while. Add the chopped onion and diced carrot, then sauté for 5 minutes, still over medium heat. Deglaze with $^1/_3$ cup + 1 $^1/_2$ tbsp (10 cl) red wine and reduce for 2 minutes. Chop a few basil leaves.

3 Add 6 tomatoes (previously peeled, seeded, and diced), 1 bouquet garni, the celery, and the basil; season with salt and pepper. Mix thoroughly and, if necessary, add a little wine (or vegetable bouillon) if the mixture seems too dry or compact. Put a lid on the saucepan.

4 Lower the heat and simmer for about 30 minutes, stirring frequently. Adjust the seasoning and add, as required, a little tomato coulis to thin the sauce, which is now ready to crown a pasta dish. You can prepare this sauce in large amounts and freeze it in containers for future use.

Oriental relish (makes 5 jars)

1 Cut 2 lemons into quarters. Seed then reduce them to a fine purée, using a blender if possible. You can also grate the zest and chop the white skin and flesh very finely.

2 Plunge 4^1/$_2$ lb (2 kg) tomatoes momentarily into salted, boiling water, then peel them. Cut them into two, seed by squeezing gently, and chop them roughly. Put the tomatoes and lemons in a large saucepan. Mix all the ingredients together with a long-handled wooden spoon.

3 Add 10 apples (peeled, seeded, and roughly chopped just before using), ginger, and allspice. Break the apples down over high heat. Add 4^1/$_2$ cups (1 kg) white sugar and 2 cups (450 g) brown sugar, stirring constantly. Simmer for 2–2^1/$_2$ hours, stirring occasionally with the wooden spoon. Put the relish into jars.

Spaghetti Reggiana

Tip

As its recipe does not include vinegar, this relish will keep for less time than other chutneys. Make sure that the jars are closed tightly, and that they are kept in a cool, dark place.

Sauces and coulis

As tomato sauces are light and aromatic, they prove ideal accompaniments for pasta. Furthermore, they are easier to make than Bolognese sauce as they contain no meat. They are prepared with whole tomatoes (preferably peeled and seeded beforehand) that must be supremely fresh. In winter, you can use canned tomatoes; they sometimes have a more acid taste, however, although a pinch of sugar will be enough to compensate for this. The basic recipe is always the same: only the pulp of the tomatoes is used; this is broken down into a thick juice, which is then cooked, with or without spices and herbs. Tomato coulis can be kept for a long time in sterilized jars. Ideally, it should be prepared at the height of the season, in July, when tomatoes are at their sweetest and fleshiest. It merely needs to be reheated when pasta is served.

Variants

Tomato coulis with anchovies. Prepare a tomato coulis. Set aside. Grind 2 fresh cloves garlic, 1^3/$_4$ oz (50 g) anchovies, 4 tbsp olive oil, and a pinch of paprika. Mix the resulting paste with the coulis and heat, without boiling. Serve with small pasta.

Tomato coulis with olives. Prepare a tomato coulis and set aside. Grind 1 onion, 3^1/$_2$ oz (100 g) pitted black and green olives, and 5 tbsp olive oil. Mix the resulting paste with the coulis and heat, without boiling. Serve with tagliatelle.

fresh tomato sauces

1 Boil plenty of water in a saucepan. Remove the green peduncle from 12 tomatoes and make an incision in their tops with a small knife. Plunge them into fast boiling water for about 15 seconds. Remove the tomatoes with a skimmer and place them in a basin of cold water. Leave them to cool for 1 minute, then drain and peel them.

2 Cut the tomatoes in half. Squeeze them to seed then put their flesh into vegetable mill. Alternatively, you can simply pass it through a fine sieve placed over a bowl. Peel and thinly slice 2 cloves garlic.

3 Put the tomato pulp into a saucepan and cook it slowly for 1 hour with salt, pepper, 1 bouquet garni, the sliced garlic, and 2 tbsp tomato paste. Stir from time to time.

Tip

In season, prepare your coulis with plum tomatoes. These are cheap and very fleshy, as well as being easy to peel, and they give a sauce plenty of body.

4 Strain the tomato mixture once it is cooked and adjust seasoning to taste. Round off the coulis with a dash of virgin olive oil just before serving. Have no qualms about preparing this coulis in large amounts; sterilize some jars (1 hr 15 minutes) to store it over the winter—it will keep for eight months in this way.

151

General points

Noodles and pasta are ubiquitous in Asian cooking. Round and flat noodles can be based on rice flour (vermicelli and angel-hair pasta) or wheat, and be made with or without eggs; in China, soy vermicelli are particularly popular. Whatever type of Asian pasta you use, it must be soaked in cold water before cooking. All these products are generally sold in bundles that correspond to one or several portions. They can be added to soups, or pastries like spring rolls, as well

Sautéed vermicelli with black mushrooms

Vermicelli with shrimp

as to boiled and sautéed main dishes. There are countless recipes for sautéed noodles and vermicelli that can be enjoyed at any time of the day, either as a main dish or snack. Vegetables and meat are sautéed with spices and herbs,

then the pasta is added, either precooked or soaked. All the ingredients are cooked together for a few minutes and then served piping hot. In

traditional restaurants, it is not unusual for these dishes to be highly spiced, but you can always moderate this when preparing them at home.

Cabbage soup with vermicelli

Tip

Using a wok instead of a skillet makes a real difference with these recipes. The stronger and more evenly distributed heat enhances the cooking process. Furthermore, the special shape of a wok makes it possible to cook various ingredients at the same time. Buy your wok in a specialist grocery.

Asian cooking: noodles and vermicelli

1 Cut 14 oz (400 g) pork loin into thin strips. Place them in a bowl and marinate in salt, pepper, 1 tbsp vinegar, 1 tbsp sugar, and 2 tbsp soy sauce for about 1 hour. You can replace the pork loin with steak, chicken breast, or even magret or aiguillettes of duck.

2 Soak $1^1/_2$ cups (300 g) rice or soy vermicelli in cold water for 5 minutes. Blanch them quickly in boiling water, then refresh in cold, running water. Drain and set aside. Chinese vermicelli come in various forms, from very thin angel-hair pasta to wider, flatter noodles. Take your pick, but always soak and blanch them before using.

3 Cut 1 clove garlic, 1 onion, 1 white part of a leek, and 1 red bell pepper into fairly thin slices. Drain the vermicelli and set aside. Heat a dash of peanut oil over high heat in a skillet or, even better, a Chinese wok. Brown all the vegetables for 5 minutes, stirring them constantly with a wooden spatula to ensure they retain their color and crispness.

4 Add the strips of meat, with its marinade. Continue cooking, still over high heat. Prepare a complementary sauce by mixing thoroughly in a bowl 2 tbsp sesame paste, 2 tbsp water, 1 tbsp soy sauce, a dash of chili paste, and a few drops of sesame oil.

5 Add the vermicelli, shaking the skillet or wok to distribute the meat and vegetables evenly. Cook for about 5 minutes then transfer to a serving dish. Round off the dish by sprinkling it with chopped, fresh cilantro. Trickle on a few drops of sesame oil at the last moment. Serve the sauce in small china bowls.

Macaroni timbale with ham and broccoli for 4

1 A timbale is a dish that is cooked in a mold (generally round), but served out of the mold. By arranging cooked macaroni in a buttered mold, you can obtain an unusual wrapping for a wide array of stuffings and sauces: sweetbreads and mushroom in cream sauce, chicken with oregano, or, as in this case, ham and vegetables.

2 Cut the rind off 6 slices of boiled ham and chop them very thinly. Grate 4$^{1}/_{2}$ oz (125 g) Beaufort or Gruyère and put in a bowl with the ham. Separate 1 lb 11 oz (750 g) broccoli into small florets and blanch for 10 minutes in highly salted, boiling water. Melt 4$^{1}/_{2}$ oz (125 g) butter and pour this over the ham and cheese. Mix gently, adding a little salt and pepper to taste.

3 Cook 9 oz (250 g) macaroni in a large saucepan with 4 cups (1 liter) each of milk and water, brought to the boil and seasoned with a handful of coarse salt. The pasta will be ready in 8–9 minutes. Drain carefully. Preheat the oven to 400 °F (200 °C). You can also prepare timbales in individual molds: these take longer to prepare, but cook more quickly.

4 Break 4 eggs. Set aside the whites, but add the yolks to the ham and cheese in the bowl. Stir them in before adding half the broccoli florets; stir these in as well, with great care, as they are delicate and must remain intact. Beat the egg whites and add them to the bowl, taking care not to break up the other ingredients.

5 Butter the mold and place a layer of macaroni in it, then a layer of the stuffing, another of macaroni, another of stuffing, etc. Finish off with a layer of the pasta. Cook in the oven for 45 minutes in a bain-marie or baking pan of water. Turn the dish onto a warm plate, cut the macaroni timbale into portions, and serve with the rest of the broccoli.

macaroni timbale

1 Heat plenty of salted water. When it is bubbling, add $10^{1}/_{2}$ oz (300 g) macaroni. Add a generous trickle of olive oil and cook for 5–6 minutes over high heat. The macaroni must be "al dente," otherwise the dish will be too soft and lack flavor. Drain the pasta thoroughly and set aside, after sprinkling with olive oil.

Tip
Monitor the seasoning of the sauce or stuffing carefully, because you will not be able to adjust it once it is in the mold. If there is not enough stuffing, add a few pieces of cooked macaroni.

2 Melt $1^{1}/_{2}$ oz (40 g) butter in a thick-bottomed saucepan; add $^{1}/_{3}$ cup (40 g) flour in one go. Cook for a few moments, without allowing the mixture to change color. Add $1^{2}/_{3}$ cups (40 cl) milk, salt, and pepper. Simmer this sauce gently for about 10 minutes, without allowing it to come to the boil. For a simple white sauce, replace the milk with bouillon.

3 Peel and chop 1 medium-size onion, then sauté it in butter, gradually adding $10^{1}/_{2}$ oz (300 g) mushrooms, scraped and thinly sliced. Season to taste with salt and pepper, cover, and sauté for 10 minutes over very gentle heat. If you have a handful of chanterelles available, do not hesitate to add them, to enhance the flavor of your timbale.

4 Butter a timbale or soufflé dish. Fill it with the thoroughly drained macaroni, mixed with the mushrooms and onion. Drizzle with the butter from the saucepan. Cover with the béchamel sauce and sprinkle on $1^{3}/_{4}$ oz (50 g) grated cheese. Brown the dish in an oven preheated to 400 °F (200 °C). You can enliven your béchamel sauce with a pinch of grated nutmeg.

A complete dish

Bouillon, spicy meat and vegetables, meticulously prepared semolina—these are the ingredients of the most famous dish from North Africa: couscous. Its recipe varies greatly from region to region, depending on local customs. It can be served with just vegetables and chickpeas, or accompanied by merguez sausage, meatballs and kebabs. Mutton is the most commonly used meat, with the neck and ribs serving to make bouillon; when lamb is on the menu, it acts as the basis for kebabs, meatballs, and merguez. Chicken is cooked in pieces in the stock or grilled.

The grain

This must be chosen with care. Never buy the fast-cooking brands available on the market; opt instead for couscous sold in a specialist grocery, taking the advice of the staff. The choice of small or medium grains depends on you. The former cook faster, but stick together more readily; they give couscous an unexpected touch of sophistication. Before cooking, make sure that the holes in your couscous-maker are small enough to accommodate the fine grains. Medium grains are easier to prepare and are typical of traditional recipes.

The bouillon

This must be richer in vegetables than in meat. Some contain tomatoes, others do not; again, the decision as to whether or not to include tomatoes depends on your personal preferences. The bouillon must not be too fatty. Its aroma is derived from ras al-hanout, a mixture of spices largely made up of cinnamon and coriander.

Couscous with fish balls

Variants

You can try fish couscous: to serve 4, cook 1 piece conger eel and 2 gurnards in the bouillon, then grill 2 bass, a few cuttlefish, and 4 mullet (to be served separately). Another subtle delight is vegetarian couscous: leave out the meat and replace it with the corresponding amount of zucchini, turnips, onions, and cubes of pumpkin.

Couscous salad

Couscous with fava beans and turnips

Couscous for 4

1 Preparation of the bouillon: heat 2–3 tbsp oil in the bottom of a couscous-maker and brown 1 lb 2 oz (500 g) pieces of neck and 1 chicken cut into pieces. Cook for 35 minutes. Whatever meat you use, you will achieve better results if you marinate it in advance with salt, pepper, ras al-hanout, oil, and herbs.

2 Remove the cooking fat then add 2 cloves garlic, 1 onion, and the following vegetables, cut into pieces: 3 carrots, 2 tomatoes, 2 zucchini, 2 eggplants, 4 turnips. Add enough cold water to just cover them. Bring to the boil, skim off any fat, and then cook gently for 1 hr 30 minutes. Add 5^1/$_2$ oz (150 g) cooked chickpeas and check the seasoning. Prepare a side dish of condiment by diluting some harissa with the bouillon. Serve piping hot with the couscous grains.

3 Preparation of the grains: spread 1 lb 2 oz (500 g) couscous on a worktop in a layer about 3/8 in (1 cm) thick. Sprinkle the grains with water with your fingertips, to moisten. Leave the couscous to swell for 10 minutes then aerate it by kneading gently with your fingers. Moisten again and repeat the whole process.

4 Roll the grains between your fingers to eliminate any small, sticky lumps then pass them through a thick-meshed sieve. The grain should now have increased in size and become extremely swollen. Put the couscous in the steam chamber of your couscous-maker then place it above the bouillon (already in the process of being cooked) and steam for 30 minutes. Pour the couscous into a large bowl and aerate it. Put it back in the couscous-maker and cook for a second time, for 20 minutes. Serve the couscous after stirring it with a fork.

Empress strawberries

Timbale of semolina with cherries

Crown of semolina with fruits

Semolina as a dessert

Semolina can be eaten with meat in savory dishes, but it can also be the basis of excellent desserts—the most famous being semolina pudding. The grains are cooked in a saucepan, not in an oven. Use the finest durum wheat semolina you can find, along with pasteurized whole milk and extremely fresh eggs. There are countless variations, but the basic principle is always the same. Pour the semolina straight into the milk (when it is very hot), mix it in, and cook it slowly over low heat. This will result in soft, cooked semolina, to which you can now add various ingredients: sugar, vanilla, raisins, chocolate, rum. Pour the semolina into a mold and allow it to cool for several hours. Once it has solidified, turn it out of the mold.

Semolina pudding with raisins for 4

1 Pour 4 cups (1 liter) whole milk into a saucepan, bring to the boil, and set aside. Weigh exactly 1^1/$_2$ cups (270 g) semolina and pour it into hot milk, stirring constantly. Put the saucepan over gentle heat once again and allow the mixture to thicken and cook for a good 5 minutes.

2 Vigorously stir in 4 egg yolks then take the semolina off the heat. Add ^{2}/$_3$ cup (150 g) sugar and 3^1/$_2$ oz (100 g) butter, mix again, and check the consistency. At this point, you can add raisins. Pour the cooked semolina into molds, to cool for at least 1 hour.

3 Then, place the molds in the refrigerator for 4–8 hours, depending on their size (4–6 hours for small molds, 8 hours for bigger ones). The puddings should be soft, but also solid enough to be turned out intact from the molds.

Variants

Let your imagination be your guide: semolina is suited to all kinds of combinations.

Semolina pudding with vanilla. Proceed as indicated in the recipe for the plain pudding, but infuse 1 vanilla bean (cut open lengthwise) in the milk, which should also be enriched with vanilla sugar.

Semolina pudding with rum, raisins, and cinnamon. Soak 3$^1/_2$ oz (100 g) currants and sultanas in good white rum. Cook 1$^1/_2$ cups (270 g) semolina in 4 cups (1 liter) milk, then add $^2/_3$ cup (150 g) sugar, 1$^3/_4$ oz (50 g) butter, 1 pinch powdered cinnamon, and the rum-raisin mixture. Pour the pudding into individual molds and leave to cool overnight.

Semolina pudding with dark chocolate. Finely grate 3$^1/_2$ oz (100 g) dark chocolate. Cook 1$^1/_2$ cups (270 g) semolina in 4 cups (1 liter) milk and add 3$^1/_2$ oz (100 g) butter and $^2/_3$ cup (150 g) sugar. Round off the mixture

Semolina pudding with Agen prunes

with 2$^3/_4$ oz (80 g) of the chocolate, allowing it to melt completely. Pour the pudding into a mold and leave overnight in the refrigerator. Sprinkle with the remaining grated chocolate before serving.

Praline semolina pudding. Heat 4 cups (1 liter) milk with 5$^1/_2$ oz (150 g) praline. When the latter has totally dissolved, add 1$^3/_4$ cups (300 g) semolina and cook until it has thickened thoroughly. Add $^1/_2$ cup (100 g) sugar and 1$^3/_4$ oz (50 g) butter then pour the pudding into a mold and leave to cool for 8

Apricots in fragrant mousse

hours in the refrigerator. Once a semolina pudding has been turned out of its mold, it can be garnished with fresh, poached, or caramelized fruit, or whipped cream.

Ramekin of semolina with cherries

Black and white dream

Fresh pasta makes an exquisite complement to exceptional ingredients. Black and white truffles are culinary treasures, and it is not always easy to take full advantage of them when mixed together in the same dish: fresh pasta allows these small gastronomic miracles to be combined to the satisfaction of even the most fastidious connoisseur. Serve pasta in this way as a hot appetizer or as an accompaniment to meat such as ribs of beef or roast poultry. Black truffles can be found bottled all year round, or fresh from December through March—the latter are most suitable for cooking, as they are far more aromatic. They are mainly found in the Vaucluse, Lot, and Périgord regions of France. The black truffle is distinguished by its dark, wrinkled skin and white pulp with prominent veins and a strong smell. The white truffles from Piedmont are the easiest to find in bottled form. Their more subtle aroma is well worth discovering, and their robust, crispy texture offers a pleasant surprise. The ideal wine accompaniment would be a Pomerol.

Serves 4
Preparation: 10 minutes
Cooking: 6 minutes

Ingredients

1 black truffle
1 white truffle
3¹/₂ tbsp (5 cl) Armagnac
14 oz (400 g) fresh pasta
Butter
2 tbsp crème fraîche
Parmesan
Salt and pepper

1 Prepare the ingredients near the cooker, as the success of this recipe is dependent on its swift execution: avoid having to look for anything at the last moment. Also, do not forget to thoroughly heat both the bowl intended for the end result and the serving plates themselves. Start to heat water in advance in a big stewpot.

2 Cut 1 black truffle into slices $1/16$ in (3 mm) thick. When you buy a fresh truffle, make sure that it is very dense and check carefully that there are no wormholes that could contain pieces of soil. Gently brush it to remove any soil. To slice, place it on a chopping board. You can also cut it into dice or small sticks.

3 Place the slices in a small saucepan. If you have peeled your truffle, keep the peel, either to chop it to flavor a sauce or to add flavor to fresh eggs (by enclosing them in the same jar). Take care when cleaning white truffles: they are more fragile than the black ones and are easily damaged. There is a special utensil available for slicing them, in the form of a twin-bladed razor.

4 Sprinkle with $3^1/2$ tbsp (5 cl) Armagnac, a dash of water, then add salt and pepper and simmer, covered, over very gentle heat, for about 5 minutes. You can also marinate the slices of black truffle in Armagnac for 1 hour in advance then heat them in a dab of butter. Pay particular attention to the seasoning, which should be fairly strong.

5 Prepare fresh, uncolored fettucini or tagliatelle. Boil plenty of salted water and plunge the pasta into it. Cook for about 1 minute, in fast boiling water, then check the progress of the pasta by tasting a sample; drain in a sieve once it is soft and supple, but not too limp.

6 Place the pasta in a bowl, season with salt and pepper, and add 1 generous dab of butter, 2 tbsp crème fraîche, a few flakes of Parmesan, the simmered strips of black truffle and their juices, and the thinly sliced white truffles. Mix everything together thoroughly, arrange in a dome on a warm serving platter, and serve immediately.

Spaghetti with garlic sauce

An easy dish

Serves 4
Preparation: 5 minutes
Cooking: 12 minutes

Ingredients

10^1/$_2$ oz (300 g) spaghetti
^{2}/$_3$ cup (15 cl) olive oil
2 cloves garlic
1 small red chili
1 large red bell pepper
1 bunch parsley
Salt

1. Pour 3 quarts (3 liters) water into a large saucepan, then add 1 tbsp coarse salt and bring to the boil. Add the spaghetti, pour on 1 tbsp olive oil, and cook in bubbling water for some ten minutes (check the cooking time recommended by the manufacturer).

2. Meanwhile, peel and finely chop the garlic; cut the chili in two, remove the seeds and peduncle, then chop it finely. If you are using dried chili, break it into pieces. Cut the bell pepper in half, remove the seeds and membranes, and chop the flesh into even strips.

3. Heat ^{1}/$_3$ cup + 1 ^{1}/$_2$ tbsp (10 cl) olive oil in a deep-sided skillet, then add the garlic, chili, and bell pepper. Cook for 5–6 minutes, without allowing the ingredients to brown too much. Remove from the heat. Wash the parsley and pat it dry with paper towels, then finely chop the leaves and stir them into the mixture; set aside.

4. Test the spaghetti to see whether it is "al dente." Drain it thoroughly and transfer immediately to a bowl containing a few tbsp oil. Mix quickly, add the garlic and pepper sauce, and serve immediately, as hot as possible.

5. Accompany the dish with a side dish of freshly grated Parmesan and a flagon of olive oil flavored with chili.

One variation typical of Rome involves sprinkling over the dish, at the very last moment, a few handfuls of breadcrumbs fried in very hot olive oil.

Recommended drinks

Chianti Classico
Beaujolais-Villages
Côtes-du-Rhône

Menu suggestions

1. This spaghetti dish makes an ideal evening meal with small artichokes marinated in oil, black olives, and anchovy fillets, followed by a sorbet of oranges served in their skins.

2. This is an ideal dish for whipping up in a few minutes when you arrive home from the movies!

Stuffed rice balls

An international dish

Serves 4
Preparation: 5 minutes
Resting: 2 hours
Cooking: 45 minutes

Ingredients

1½ cups (300 g) round-grained rice
2 onions
1 bunch chives
1 clove garlic
16 leaves fresh mint
7 oz (200 g) chopped beef
7 oz (200 g) chopped pork
Stale bread, with the crust removed

1 egg
Salt and pepper

1. Soak the rice in cold water for 2 hours, then drain it. Spread a large dishtowel on the worktop, put the rice on it, and smooth it out to form a uniform layer.

2. Peel the onions and slice them finely. Wash the chives, pat them dry, and cut into small pieces with a pair of kitchen scissors. Peel and chop the garlic. Chop the mint leaves.

3. Mix the chopped beef and pork in a bowl (you can use frozen steak; make sure the pork is lean). Add the onions, chives, garlic, and mint. Mix these ingredients together for a few minutes with a wooden spoon then add a generous handful of the stale bread, broken down into small crumbs. Add salt and pepper.

4. Finally, add the egg, to bind all the ingredients together. Separate this stuffing into portions, rolling them between your palms (previously moistened with water) to form balls ¾–1 in (2–3 cm) in diameter. Then roll these balls on the rice, applying a little pressure so that the grains become encrusted in the meat, penetrating inside and sticking securely to the surface.

5. Line the bottom of a steamer with wax paper and put the balls on top. Leave a certain amount of space between them, as they will swell up when cooked. Put the lid on the steamer, before setting it on top of a saucepan full of boiling water. Cook for 45 minutes. Serve these rice balls with small dishes of soy sauce.

Recommended drinks

Jasmine tea
Chinees beer
Rosé de Provence

Menu suggestions

1. In a Chinese meal, this hot dish can follow a cold appetizer such as bean sprout salad and precede a small asparagus-tip soup, with Chinese nougat for dessert.

2. In a Western meal, these rice balls can constitute a main course, after avocado with shrimp. Finish with fresh pineapple.

Cannelloni au gratin

A family dish

Serves 4
Preparation: 25 minutes
Resting: at least 1 hour
Second preparation: 25 minutes

Ingredients

13 oz (375 g) flour
2 eggs
1 slice cooked veal
4¹/₂ oz (125 g) cooked ham
1 onion
Mixed herbs
Olive oil
2³/₄ oz (75 g) grated Parmesan
1 oz (30 g) butter
Tomato sauce

Salt and pepper

1. Put the flour in a bowl, then form a well with it; put the eggs in the center, whole, with a generous pinch of salt. Mix the these ingredients together with a fork, gradually incorporating the eggs into the flour and moistening it with water, until you obtain a soft dough that is firm enough to hold together in the form of a ball.

2. Flour a worktop, put the ball on it, and knead with the palm of your hand for about 15 minutes. Divide this dough into 3 or 4 equal parts, rolling them out as thinly as possible. Cut into rectangles measuring 2³/₄ x 3¹/₂ in (7 x 9 cm). Leave them to dry for at least 1 hour.

3. Plunge them into salted boiling water to poach for 5 minutes (without letting the water come back to the boil). Put them under cold water as soon as you remove them from the saucepan then spread them out on a clean, dry dishtowel.

4. Chop the veal, ham, onion, and mixed herbs, then mix them together, with salt and pepper; brown this mixture in olive oil, until the onion is cooked, then leave to cool.

5. Add 2–3 tsp grated Parmesan. Spread the stuffing on the pieces of dough and roll them up. As soon as each one is ready, put it in a buttered baking dish; cover with plenty of pre-prepared tomato sauce and sprinkle on grated Parmesan; heat and slightly brown the cannelloni in an oven preheated to 365 °F (185 °C) for 25 minutes. Serve immediately.

Recommended drinks

Chianti Classico
Bourgueil
Bergerac Rouge

Menu suggestions

1. This dish is ideally suited to an evening meal, along with a good salad sprinkled with garlic croûtons. Finish with a fruit salad.

2. You can also prepare these cannelloni in the morning and brown them quickly at night for a fast meal, accompanied by fromage blanc.

Stuffed zucchini

An exotic dish

Serves 4
Preparation: 15 minutes
Cooking: 20 minutes

Ingredients

1¼ cups (250 g) rice
5½ oz (150 g) golden raisins
1 cup of tea
8 small, round zucchini
2–3 tomatoes
5½ oz (150 g) pine nuts
Olive oil
Salt and pepper

1. Cook the rice in salted boiling water; the grains should remain slightly firm. Drain the rice and put it in a large bowl. Put the raisins in a bowl, pour the warm tea over them, and set aside while you prepare the vegetables.

2. Fill a large saucepan with water, add salt, and bring to the boil; add the zucchini and blanch them for about 10 minutes. Take them out of the water with a skimmer and drain them thoroughly in a sieve. Plunge the tomatoes into the same saucepan of water, still boiling; take them out after a few seconds, then drain and peel them. Cut in half, seed by squeezing them slightly, then cut the pulp into small dice. Preheat the oven to 400 °F (200°C).

3. Drain the raisins (which will now be very swollen) and add them to the rice. Also add the tomatoes (having mashed them), the pine nuts, salt, and pepper. Trickle a little olive oil over the stuffing to bind it. Adjust seasoning to taste.

4. Cut off about one third of the zucchini (from the end with the peduncle) to serve as a lid then gently hollow them out, chopping the extracted flesh. Add to the rice mixture and fill the hollowed zucchini, allowing the stuffing to protrude from the top. Replace the "lids," slightly hollowed out to ensure a snug fit.

5. Arrange the stuffed zucchini in an oiled baking pan and put them in the oven for around 20 minutes, making sure they do not brown. You can replace the pine nuts with slivered almonds and add a small bunch of finely chopped mint leaves to the stuffing.

Recommended drinks

Mint tea
Rosé de Provence
Rioja

Menu suggestions

1. When served as an appetizer, these stuffed zucchini can be followed by broiled lamb cutlets and an Oriental dessert, such as baklava or khab el ghzal (gazelle horns).

2. These zucchini stuffed with rice are perfect for a vegetarian meal, complemented by a salad of raw vegetables and fig tart.

Couscous with vegetables and mint

An economical dish

Serves 4
Preparation: 20 minutes
Cooking: 40 minutes

Ingredients

9 oz (250 g) carrots
9 oz (250 g) turnips
4 cups (1 liter) chicken bouillon
1 bouquet garni
1 lb 2 oz (500 g) petits pois
1 bunch fresh mint
1 lb 11 oz (750 g) couscous (medium grains)
Harissa (a spicy paste)
4¹/₂ oz (125 g) butter

Salt and pepper

1. Peel the carrots and turnips. Put them in the bottom of a couscous maker then add salt and pepper. Pour the chicken bouillon over them and add the bouquet garni. Heat gently. Shell the petits pois and set aside. Wash the bunch of mint, pat it dry, and separate it into sprigs.

2. Pour the couscous into a large bowl, sprinkle a few spoonfuls of cold water over it, and leave to swell up for a few minutes, kneading with your hands to prevent the grains from sticking together. Repeat this operation several times.

3. Once the grain has swollen considerably, put it in the couscous maker, on top of the bouillon and vegetables. Bring to the boil, cover, and cook gently for 30–40 minutes.

4. Meanwhile, cook the petits pois apart in a saucepan of salted water with a small bunch of mint. Drain them thoroughly once they are cooked and add the mint. Melt the butter in a small saucepan over low heat.

5. Put the couscous in a bowl, then add the petits pois and melted butter. Mix thoroughly and transfer to a serving platter, arranging the semolina in the form of a dome. Place the drained carrots and turnips around it, complemented by a few sprigs of fresh mint.

6. Put some of the bouillon in a bowl and add 2 or 3 tsp of harissa; stir it vigorously into the sauce and serve separately.

Recommended drinks

Coteaux-d'Ajaccio
Corbières
Rouge Cahors

Menu suggestions

1. If you serve this couscous as a vegetarian main course, consider crêpes filled with cheese for an appetizer and chocolate gateau for dessert.

2. This vegetable couscous makes a good accompaniment to leg of lamb, with asparagus for an appetizer and sorbet for dessert.

Polenta fritters with salami

A family dish

Serves 4
Preparation: 30 minutes
Cooking: 10 minutes

Ingredients

$^2/_3$ cup (100 g) polenta
8 thin slices cheese
8 slices salami
2 eggs
$^2/_3$ cup (80 g) flour
$3^1/_2$ oz (100 g) breadcrumbs
Oil for frying
Salt and pepper

1. Add the polenta to 2 cups (50 cl) boiling, salted water and stir it continuously.

2. Spread the cooked polenta on a worktop, in a layer $^1/_4$–$^5/_{16}$ in (7–8 mm) thick. Leave to cool, then cut into 16 disks with a glass. Use the same glass and a sharp, small knife to cut out 8 disks of cheese and 8 disks of salami. It is vital that all these disks are exactly the same size.

3. Assemble the fritters by putting (from top to bottom) 1 disk of polenta, 1 of cheese, and 1 of salami on top of each other, making sure they are superimposed precisely. Finish the fritter with another disk of polenta.

4. Beat the eggs with a fork, add salt, and put them aside in a soup dish. Dip the fritters in the flour (spread out on a plate) and then the beaten eggs. Finally, roll them in the breadcrumbs.

5. Heat the oil in a deep-fat fryer until it is burning, but not smoking (around 345 °F/175 °C). Gently add the fritters, one after the other, with the help of a skimmer. Monitor the fritters closely, especially when they start to rise to the surface, as this means that they have been browned underneath. Turn the fritters with a spatula then brown the other side. Serve hot. To check the temperature of the oil, throw in a few pieces of polenta and see how they react and brown. Do not forget to remove these pieces from the oil; otherwise, they will blacken and could spoil the taste of your fritters.

Recommended drinks

Barolo
Bergerac Rouge
Côtes-de-Provence

Menu suggestions

1. When served as a hot appetizer, these fritters can be followed by broiled meat and Provencal tomatoes.

2. For a quick meal, accompany these fritters with an assortment of Italian cooked pork meats and follow with a tiramisu.

Macaroni pudding with walnuts

An Italian dish

Serves 4
Preparation: 20 minutes
Cooking: 10-11 minutes
Resting: 2 hours

Ingredients

4^1/$_2$ oz (125 g) macaroni
2 eggs
1 glass milk
1 sachet vanilla sugar
1 oz (30 g) butter
10^1/$_2$ oz (300 g) walnuts
Runny honey
Salt

1. Fill a saucepan with water, then add 1 tbsp coarse salt and bring to the boil. When the water starts to bubble vigorously, add the macaroni in one go and cook for around 15 minutes. Drain thoroughly.

2. Break the eggs in a bowl, then add the milk, first stirring and then beating the mixture to obtain a smooth liquid. Add the vanilla sugar. Butter a cake pan and put in the macaroni; slowly pour the egg mixture on top, making sure that it penetrates to the bottom of the mold. Preheat the oven to 300 °F (150 °C).

3. Place the cake pan in a larger baking dish, half-filled with water, and bake the pudding in this bain-marie for about 1 hour.

4. Take the bain-marie out of the oven, remove the cake pan, and cover it. Allow it to cool completely—if necessary, put it in the refrigerator for 30 minutes once it is almost cold. Meanwhile, roughly chop the walnuts, put them in a bowl, and pour over 3–4 tsp honey. Stir the walnuts into the honey and set aside.

5. Turn the pudding onto a long dish and cut into thick slices. Transfer these to dessert bowls and cover with honey, before garnishing the top with the walnut and honey mixture. If you so wish, you can reheat the dish at this point by popping the dishes back in the oven—this can only make them more delicious. You can also spice up the egg and milk mixture by adding, along with the vanilla sugar, a few pinches of powdered cinnamon or grated nutmeg.

Recommended drinks

Barsac
Monbazillac
Red Port

Menu suggestions

1. This original dessert can be appropriate for a winter menu, after a hearty stew served without an appetizer.

2. Serve this dessert from the Italian Piedmont region at a family meal, after osso buco preceded by an artichoke salad with olive oil.

Red kidney beans with rice

A family dish

Serves 4
Preparation: 5 minutes
Resting: overnight
Cooking: 1 hr 45 minutes

Ingredients

10 1/2 oz (300 g) red kidney beans
4 onions
4 cloves
1 bunch thyme
5 1/2 oz (150 g) butter
1 1/2 cups (300 g) rice
6 slices bacon
Salt and black pepper

1. Put the red kidney beans in a bowl, cover them with cold water, and leave them to soak overnight. The next day, drain them and pour away the water. Put the beans in a large saucepan. Peel the onions, leaving them whole if they are not too big; otherwise, cut them into halves or quarters. Spike them with the cloves.

2. Add the onions to the saucepan, along with the bunch of thyme. Season with pepper but not, above all, with salt (this would harden the skin of the beans). Cover with cold water and bring to the boil. Put the lid on the saucepan, regulate the heat so that the water bubbles constantly, and cook for 1 hr 30 minutes; the beans should be tender. Remove the thyme, along with the cloves from the onions.

3. Drain the beans with the onions and put aside them in a bowl; reserve the cooking water. Heat 1 oz (25 g) butter in a large, thick-bottomed saucepan and add the rice, stirring to ensure that the grains are thoroughly coated with the butter. Pour in the reserved cooking water and cook the rice, covered, over very low heat.

4. About 10 minutes before the rice is cooked, complement it with the rest of the butter, in dabs, along with the beans and the onions. Mix them with the rice then add the sliced bacon. Season with just a little salt (on account of the bacon). Serve very hot in a soup tureen. This dish plays a leading role in the Creole culinary repertoire of the French Caribbean, where it is used to accompany dishes with sauce and stews. The bacon can be streaked with fat, according to taste, and the beans can be cooked with a small chili.

Recommended drinks

Very cold light beer
Rosé de Provence
Madiran

Menu suggestions

1. This bean dish can serve as a main course, preceded by tomato soup with basil and followed by pineapple flambé.

2. With an appetizer of avocado and lemon, this bean hotpot can accompany a beef stew. Round off the meal with fresh pineapple.

Provençal penne

A regional dish

Serves 4
Preparation: 20 minutes
Cooking: 15 minutes

Ingredients

14 oz (400 g) small zucchini
1 bunch basil
Olive oil
1 red bell pepper
1 yellow bell pepper
14 oz (400 g) penne
1 picodon (goat's cheese)
Salt and pepper

1. Wash and wipe the zucchini, without peeling them. Cut into thin slices over a bowl. Add salt, pepper, and finely chopped basil leaves. Pour 2 tbsp olive oil into a skillet and add a glass of water. Bring to the boil then add the zucchini. Sauté over very high heat for 5 minutes, turning from time to time. All the cooking water should evaporate and the zucchini should still be a little crispy. Remove from the heat and set the zucchini aside.

2. Wash and wipe the bell peppers, then pass them quickly over a flame on all sides until their skin starts to blister; peel them with a sharp knife; split into two, remove the seeds and membranes, then cut them into uniform strips. Put these into a large bowl, sprinkle with 2 tbsp olive oil, and season with salt and pepper.

3. Fill a large saucepan with water, add 1 tbsp salt, and heat. Once the water is bubbling, add the pasta and cook for 15 minutes. Meanwhile, mash the picodon on a small plate.

4. Drain the pasta and transfer it immediately to a large serving platter drizzled with 2 tbsp oil and some chopped basil leaves. Season with salt and pepper then mix all the ingredients together. Add the zucchini slices, the strips of bell pepper, a few more basil leaves, and the mashed picodon. Mix again and serve immediately. You can replace the picodon with banon or even small cubes of Greek feta and also add a handful of small black olives, pitted and roughly chopped.

Recommended drinks

Coteaux-d'Aix
Bandol
Côtes-du-Rhône

Menu suggestions

1. To complement this summer dish, serve after a salad of mullet fillets and fennel and before a pine-nut tart.

2. You can also accompany this recipe with a mixed green salad, goat's cheese, and a selection of Provençal tidbits: caramelized fruit, calissons, and biscotins.

Cabbage leaves stuffed with rice

An economical dish

Serves 4
Preparation: 20 minutes
Cooking: 1 hr 30 minutes
Resting: 24 hours
Reheating: 30 minutes

Ingredients

2 onions
2 tbsp lard
3 tbsp rice
4 cups (1 liter) bouillon
1 lb 2 oz (500 g) cooked meat
(from a stew or roast)
1 cabbage
Stale bread
Parsley

Paprika
2 carrots
1 leek
Pork fat
1 tbsp tomato paste
Salt and pepper

1. The night before serving the dish, peel and slice the onions. Sauté for a few minutes in the lard. Half cook the rice in a little bouillon. Chop all the meat. Separate the leaves of the cabbage one by one, cutting off any large ribs, then blanch for 3–4 minutes in salted, boiling water.

2. Prepare a stuffing with the chopped meat, onions, a little stale bread (soaked in cold bouillon with the crust removed and then squeezed dry), the rice, a little chopped parsley, salt, pepper, and paprika.

3. Drain the cabbage leaves thoroughly and spread them out on a dishtowel; season with salt and paprika, spread the stuffing on top, and close the leaves to form large balls.

4. Scrape, wash, and slice the carrots and leek. Smear the bottom of a casserole with the pork fat, arrange the vegetables on top, then add the cabbage balls.

5. Brown these ingredients over medium heat then cover them with the rest of the bouillon (complemented by the tomato paste). Cover the dish with wax paper and cook in an oven preheated to 435 °F (225 °C) for 1 hr 30 minutes. Cover and leave to cool then place in the refrigerator overnight.

6. The next day, sprinkle the cabbage balls with their own juice. Warm them for 30 minutes in an oven preheated to 365 °F (185 °C) uncovering them in the final stages to allow the top of the balls to dry a little.

Recommended drinks

Saumur-Champigny
Beaujolais-Villages
Bergerac Rouge

Menu suggestions

1. These stuffed cabbage leaves make a satisfying family meal, with an appetizer of vegetable soup and crème caramel for dessert.

2. You can also accompany them with curly endive and diced bacon; round off the meal with baked apples.

173

Greek stuffed bell peppers

A Greek dish

Serves 4
Preparation: 25 minutes
Cooking: 1 hour

Ingredients

1 oz (30 g) butter
$1/2$ cup (100 g) rice
2 glasses bouillon
$10^1/2$ oz (300 g) cooked meat
2 onions
4 tbsp finely chopped flat parsley
4 tbsp chopped mint
$1^3/4$ oz (50 g) raisins
$1^3/4$ oz (50 g) pine nuts

4 tbsp tomato coulis
4 bell peppers, regular in shape and
not too long
Oil
Salt and pepper

1. Melt the butter in a heavy-bottomed saucepan, then add the rice, stirring with a wooden spoon for 2 minutes until the grains are thoroughly coated. Meanwhile, heat the bouillon. When it is very hot, add the rice and continue cooking, keeping the water bubbling, until the grains are ready (they should be completely detached from each other). Remove the rice from the heat and set aside.

2. Chop the meat into small pieces and place in a bowl. Peel the onions and chop them finely. Heat a little oil in a skillet, then brown the onions before adding them to the bowl along with the parsley, mint, raisins, and pine nuts.

3. Add the rice to this mixture, season with salt and pepper, then add the tomato coulis to bind the ingredients together. Wash and wipe the bell peppers. Cut a lid out of each pepper, from the end with the peduncle. Remove the seeds and membranes then wash the insides.

4. Boil some water in a large saucepan then plunge in the bell peppers and their lids; blanch for 1 minute to tenderize, then drain and pat them dry in a dishtowel. Oil a baking dish. Stuff the bell peppers with the mixture, arrange them in the dish, and replace the lids. Pour a little bouillon or water into the dish then cover with aluminum foil.

5. Cook the stuffed bell peppers in an oven preheated to 400 °F (200 °C) for around 20 minutes, then lower the heat to 340 °F (170 °C) and continue cooking for 40 minutes. Serve in the oven dish.

Recommended drinks

Cassis Blanc
Muscadet
Pouilly-Fumé

Menu suggestions

1. When served as a hot appetizer, these stuffed bell peppers can be followed by grilled sardines and then chilled melon.

2. If you are serving this as a main dish, start the meal with a salad of cucumber, yogurt, and mint, then finish with a cheesecake and caramelized fruit.

Black plums stuffed with rice

A family dish

Serves 5
Preparation: 15 minutes
Cooking: 30 minutes

Ingredients

Oil
3/4 cup (150 g) rice
5 plump black plums
1–2 tomatoes, ripe but firm
8 slices smoked bacon, sliced very thinly
Flat parsley
Salt and pepper

1. Heat 2 tbsp oil in a heavy-bottomed saucepan; when it is very hot, add the rice and stir the grains immediately with a wooden spoon, to coat them thoroughly with the butter. Once they are very hot, sprinkle them with twice their volume of hot water (or light bouillon) and season with salt and pepper. Cover and cook over gentle heat until all the water has been absorbed (about 12 minutes). The grains must not stick together.

2. Wash and wipe the plums, cut them in half, and pit. Scald the tomatoes, then drain and peel before cutting them in half and seeding. Cut the tomato pulp into small dice.

3. Heat a skillet (without any fat). Make several notches in the rind of the smoked bacon slices, then put them in the heated skillet and sauté until crispy and curly.

4. Preheat the oven to 375 °F (190 °C). Put the cooked rice in a bowl then add the tomatoes and 2–3 bacon slices, chopped into small pieces. Add a little salt and pepper. Mix these ingredients thoroughly with a wooden spoon.

5. Fill the hollowed plums with this rice stuffing, allowing it to protrude from the top in the form of a small dome. Arrange the stuffed plums in a lightly oiled baking dish; put this into the oven for 10 minutes. Meanwhile, keep the unused bacon slices hot.

6. Just before serving, garnish the dish with the rest of the broiled bacon slices and a few sprigs of parsley.

Recommended drinks

Madiran
Pécharmant
Gewurztraminer

Menu suggestions

1. This is an original appetizer for an informal meal: follow with roast beef "en croûte" and a tutti-frutti ice cream.

2. For a more rustic feel, prepare a leg of lamb as the main course and Armagnac pie for dessert.

175

Fennel ravioli and artichoke barigoule

A party dish

Serves 4
Preparation: 25 minutes
Cooking: 30–40 minutes
Resting: 2 hours

Ingredients

For the barigoule:
8 medium artichoke hearts
2 large carrots
20 cloves garlic
20 small onions
7 oz (200 g) salt pork
Olive oil
1 glass Provencal white wine
Parmesan
Thyme and rosemary

Salt

For the stuffing:
$2^{1}/_{4}$ lb (1 kg) fennel bulbs
A few anchovy fillets in oil

For the pastry:
1 lb 2 oz (500 g) flour
5 eggs
Liquid chlorophyll or concentrated
spinach juice

1. Knead the flour with 3 whole eggs plus 2 yolks, a few drops of liquid chlorophyll, and enough water to obtain soft dough that still keeps its shape. Roll in a ball and leave to rest.

2. Trim the artichoke hearts. Cut them into two or four pieces, according to size; slice the carrots, peel the cloves of garlic and the onions, and cut the salt pork into pieces. Brown all these ingredients in a few spoonfuls of olive oil in a casserole. Deglaze with the white wine when everything has taken on some color, then reduce the liquid over high heat until its volume has halved. Add 1 glass olive oil and simmer very gently for around 15 minutes, so that the ingredients become impregnated with the liquid. Season to taste with salt. Set aside at room temperature.

3. Trim the fennel then dice into pieces 1/16 in (2 mm) wide. Heat some olive oil in a saucepan, add the fennel, and cook, covered, until all the water it exudes has evaporated. Bind the fennel with $3^{1}/_{2}$ oz (100 g) puréed anchovy fillets. Set aside in the refrigerator.

4. Role the ravioli dough very thinly. Cut it into disks $2-2^{1}/_{2}$ in (5–6 cm) in diameter. Add 1 tbsp stuffing to each disk, then moisten the circumference and stick the edges together by folding the dough over the stuffing. Poach the ravioli for 10 minutes in salted water.

5. Heat the artichoke barigoule and serve on warm plates, along with 1 piping hot ravioli. Sprinkle with olive oil and a few slivers of Parmesan, and garnish each piece of artichoke with thyme and rosemary.

Recommended drinks

Bandol
Coteaux-d'Aix
Costières-de-Nîmes

Menu suggestions

1. After this colorful, sophisticated appetizer, serve bass with fennel then nougat glacé with biscotins.

2. If you prefer a meat dish, leg of lamb is perfect, followed by goat's cheese and a lavender ice cream.

Seafood rice

A family dish

Serves 4
Preparation: 15 minutes
Cooking: 20 minutes

Ingredients

1 cup (200 g) rice
1–2 red bell peppers
1 onion
2 cloves garlic
Olive oil
4 cups (1 liter) mussels
4 cups (1 liter) cockles
9 oz (250 g) prawns
1 bunch mixed herbs
Chili powder or Cayenne pepper

Saffron
Salt and pepper

1. Cook the rice in salted water over a medium heat (exactly two and a half measures of water for one of rice). The rice is ready when it has completely absorbed the water and the grains are separate from each other.

2. Meanwhile, peel the bell pepper (after toasting it over a flame) and set it aside for a few minutes, wrapped in damp paper towels; cut it open, seed, and chop into small pieces. Peel and slice the onion. Peel the cloves of garlic, crush them, and heat with a little oil in a casserole. Add the pepper, onion, and garlic, and sauté gently.

3. Clean the mussels and cockles by scrubbing or washing them several times with cold water. Open by heating them in water over high heat; discard any that remain closed and shell some of the opened ones, while keeping the most attractive (opened) shells intact. Similarly, shell the prawns, while leaving the best-looking ones whole.

4. Add the rice to the mixture of peppers, onion, and garlic, then add the shelled crustaceans and prawns. Chop the mixed herbs and gently stir them in. Season with saffron and pepper, together with chili powder or Cayenne pepper.

5. Garnish with the reserved shells and prawns, cover, and reheat very gently.

Recommended drinks

Vouvray
Muscadet
Cassis Blanc

Menu suggestions

1. Accompany this seafood rice with an appetizer of tomato and Mozzarella salad and a dessert of ripe apricots.

2. If you serve this dish for dinner, precede it with a fish soup and follow with a fruit salad.

Spicy rice with prawns and pineapple

An exotic dish

Serves 4
Preparation: 20 minutes
Cooking: 20 minutes

Ingredients

1½ cups (300 g) long-grained rice
9 oz (250 g) prawns
1 onion
3 cloves garlic
1 small chili
1 small piece fresh ginger
2¾ oz (75 g) butter
2 tbsp oil
Curry powder
1 pineapple

1 bunch fresh cilantro or parsley
Salt

1. Put the rice in a sieve, then rinse under cold, running water. Drain thoroughly. Shell the prawns, while leaving about 15 whole for the final garnish. Rinse the shelled prawn tails and put them in a bowl with some freshly ground pepper.

2. Peel the onion and chop it finely. Peel the cloves of garlic and chop them in the same way. Cut the chili in half and seed, then cut it into small pieces. Peel and grate the ginger.

3. Heat half the butter and oil in a cast-iron casserole. Add the prawn tails and brown them quickly. When they take on a slight color, take them out of the casserole with a skimmer and set aside. In their place, add the chopped onion and garlic, chili, and grated ginger. When the onion starts to brown, add the drained rice, and mix then brown it stirring for 2 minutes; add salt, 1 level tsp curry powder and mix thoroughly. Pour in water (twice the volume of the rice).

4. Bring the water to the boil slowly, then cover and cook gently for about 20 minutes. Meanwhile, peel the pineapple and cut it into slices, then chop into chunks. Heat the remaining butter and add the pineapple, browning it gently.

5. When the rice is cooked, put the contents of the casserole in a lightly oiled, circular mold, packing them tightly. Put a round plate on top, upside down, and turn the mold over to release the crown of spicy rice. Arrange the sautéed pineapple pieces, green cilantro leaves, prawn tails, and cooked whole prawns in the center and the rest of the ingredients around it.

Recommended drinks

Bandol Rosé
Pouilly-Fumé
Meursault

Menu suggestions

1. Serve avocadoes stuffed with crab to precede this hot dish, and round it off with a coconut custard tart.

2. In a slightly less exotic menu, you can serve this crown of rice after curried tomato soup and before a dessert of pear and almond tart.

Rice and tuna salad

An easy dish

Serves 10
Preparation: 20 minutes
Resting: 4–5 hours
Cooking: 12 minutes

Ingredients

3 lb 5 oz (1.5 kg) fish (preferably white tuna)
3 lemons
3 limes
2 cups (400 g) rice
1–2 bell peppers
1 large can anchovy fillets in oil
10 eggs
Parsley, thyme, chives

Oil
Salt and pepper

1. Cut the tuna into small cubes, removing any bones, skin, and black patches. Set aside 1 lemon and squeeze the juice from the remaining lemons, and the limes, over the fish. Mix the juice in thoroughly, then cover the fish and place it for 4–5 hours in the refrigerator (not the freezer compartment). Turn the fish pieces over once an hour. At the end of this marinating period, the pieces of tuna should be opaque and firm.

2. While the tuna is marinating, cook the rice in salted, boiling water, refresh it under cold water, drain, and set aside.

3. After searing the pepper over a flame, peel and cut it into strips, then dice. Open the can of anchovy fillets; set aside the best-looking ones, and cut the others into small pieces.

4. Prepare a vinaigrette. Boil the eggs until they are hard then shell them. Place a layer of tuna, impregnated with the citric juices, on a large serving platter. Cover with the rice, mixed with the small pieces of anchovy and some of the diced bell pepper.

5. Put the rest of the tuna in the center of the rice, then sprinkle it with the remaining juice and garnish with the whole anchovy fillets, each rolled around a piece of bell pepper. Scatter the herbs and remaining diced peppers over the tuna.

6. Serve with slices of lemon and quartered hard-boiled eggs, and the vinaigrette in a separate dispenser. You can prepare this dish with small cubes of bass or fillets of sea bream instead of the tuna. Before using the anchovy fillets, rinse them with hot, previously boiled water.

Recommended drinks

Chilled light beer
Lemonade with lime
Muscadet

Menu suggestions

1. Consider preceding this summer dish with hors d'oeuvre, including raw vegetables with fromage-blanc sauce. Finish with sorbets.

2. You can serve this dish at the beginning of the meal and follow it with a cheese-board, green salad, and fresh fruit.

Recommended drinks

Smoked tea
Mulled wine with cinnamon
Sweet white wine

Menu suggestions

1. As the sole complement to this soup, you can serve an aioli (cod poached with vegetables, accompanied by a garlic mayonnaise).

2. You can also present this somewhat rich dessert after trout "en papillote" and a salad of cultivated mushrooms.

Rice and almond soup

A family dish

Serves 4
Preparation: 15 minutes
Cooking: 20 minutes

Ingredients

$1/2$ cup (100 g) rice
$3/4$ oz (20 g) butter
2 oz (60 g) raisins
$51/2$ oz (150 g) sweet almonds
5 bitter almonds
5 cups (1.25 liters) milk
1 tbsp sugar
Nutmeg
Cinnamon
Salt

1. Cook the rice Creole style, in plenty of slightly salted water, making sure that the grains remain separate from each other. Consider using basmati or camarguais rice with short, thin grains.

2. Drain the rice and put the butter in a large saucepan. Over gentle heat, add the rice and stir until the butter melts, then cover the saucepan and set aside from the heat. Meanwhile, put the raisins in a bowl, cover with boiling water, and leave to swell.

3. Put the almonds in a large bowl, sprinkle them with boiling water, and wait a few seconds before draining them. Then remove their skins and chop them fairly finely or cut them into strips. Meanwhile, heat the milk.

4. Put the almonds in a saucepan, add the boiling milk, and cook gently, stirring for a few minutes. Add a few pinches of grated nutmeg and 1 pinch powdered cinnamon. Stir.

5. Add the sugar, mix it in, and add the rice. Stir once again then add the raisins, now thoroughly drained. You can also add 1–2 tbsp caramelized fruit diced small. Heat very gently, stirring occasionally, up until you serve the dish, but making sure, above all, that it does not boil. This sweet soup used to be served in some parts of France, particularly the southeast, on Christmas Eve, just before midnight Mass.

Spelt-wheat soup

A regional dish

Serves 4
Preparation: 20 minutes
Cooking: 1 hour

Ingredients

2$^1/_4$ lb (1 kg) mutton pieces, with the bones
1 onion
2 cloves
1 clove garlic
2–3 small leeks
1–2 sticks celery
2–3 carrots
1 cup (200 g) spelt wheat

1. Put the mutton pieces in a large saucepan; choose shoulder or leg, with the bones, but above all make sure it is mutton and not lamb. The total weight should be about 2$^1/_4$ lb (1 kg). Pour 3 quarts (3 liters) cold water on top and heat gently. When the water comes to the boil, skim it carefully several times.

2. Meanwhile, prepare the vegetables: peel the onion and spike it with the cloves; leave the clove of garlic whole, in its skin; wash the leeks, cut off the green ends, and tie them together in a bundle; remove any filaments from the celery stalks, and peel the carrots.

3. Once the water is bubbling, add the vegetables (you can also add a few turnips and a bouquet garni). Mix, then add the spelt. This is a variety of wheat whose husks stick to the small, brown grains, in contrast to other types; once they have been husked, these grains are cooked like rice or serve to enrich soups.

4. Cook very gently, covered, for 45 minutes to 1 hour, until the soup is thick.

5. To serve, pour the sticky, aromatic bouillon and spelt grains into a soup tureen and arrange the meat and vegetables separately on a serving platter. In Sault, in the Vaucluse region of Provence, this soup forms part of the tradition at the start of Lent, when it is served with a large andouille (cold sausage). In other parts of Provence, spelt soup constitutes a winter staple, with a variety of vegetables and sausages.

Recommended drinks

Coteaux-d'Aix
Gigondas
Côtes-de-Provence

Menu suggestions

1. Serve this soup as an appetizer to a Provencal meal, before a salad of celery and anchovy and followed by goat's cheeses marinated in olive oil and dried fruit compote with Beaumes-de-Venise.

2. You could also start the meal with artichoke barigoule and finish with orange gateau.

Pumpkin soup with wheat germ

A light dish

Serves 4
Preparation: 10 minutes
Cooking: 45–60 minutes

Ingredients

2¼ lb (1 kg) pumpkin
4 cups (1 liter) milk or bouillon
1 oz (25 g) ground wheat germ
1 large dab butter
Chives
1 oz (25 g) whole wheat germ
Salt and pepper

1. Peel the pumpkin and remove its fibers and seeds. Cut the flesh into small, uniform pieces.

2. Cook the pumpkin pieces in salted, boiling water in a saucepan until supple to the touch. Remove from the water with a skimmer and drain.

3. Place in a large bowl and mash with a fork, then pour on, spoonful by spoonful, the milk or hot bouillon.

4. Transfer the pumpkin mixture to a saucepan and gently simmer until a creamy liquid is obtained; add salt and pepper halfway through this second cooking period.

5. Mix in the ground wheat germ, then pour the soup into a tureen containing the dab of butter. Mix again, until the butter melts. Adjust seasoning to taste.

6. Serve in individual bowls, sprinkling the soup with a few chopped sprigs of chives and placing a large pinch of wheat germ in the center.

The ground wheat germ contributes a hint of hazelnut; you can also enrich this soup with tomato or zucchini.

Recommended drinks

Weak tea
Sparkling water
Rosé de Provence

Menu suggestions

1. Serve this soup as an appetizer, followed by papillotes of fish with lemon and fromage blanc with mixed herbs for dessert.

2. You could also opt to follow this soup with a spinach salad and chicken breasts, with a dessert of crème caramel.

Spaghetti "alla marinara"

An Italian dish

Serves 4
Preparation: 20 minutes
Cooking: 15 minutes

Ingredients

8 cups (2 liters) mussels
1 carrot
A few sprigs parsley
1 lb 2 oz (500 g) striped Venus clams
1 lb 2 oz (500 g) littleneck clams
8 langoustines
1 clove garlic
2 shallots or 1 onion
Olive oil

3 tomatoes (or $1/2$ can peeled tomatoes, with no juice)
9 oz (250 g) spaghetti
1 dab butter
Salt and pepper

1. Scrape the mussels and scrub them under the cold, running water; put them in a large saucepan with the carrot (grated and cut into little sticks), a little chopped parsley, and pepper. Sauté for a few minutes over high heat until the mussels are fully open. Take them out of their shells and set them aside in their cooking water (previously sieved through very fine muslin).

2. Put the clams in a saucepan over medium heat and allow them to open; take them out of their shells and set them aside them in their cooking water (previously sieved through very fine muslin).

3. Poach the langoustines in a little salted water, flavored with the parsley.

4. Peel the garlic and the shallots, then sauté them in a skillet with a little olive oil. Wait until they start to brown, before adding the peeled tomatoes (chopped into pieces); moisten with the mussel bouillon when the tomatoes reabsorb their water, then season with salt and pepper.

5. Cook the spaghetti in salted, boiling water with 1 tbsp olive oil; make sure that they remain a little firm ("al dente.") Drain.

6. Shell the langoustines, cut the flesh of their tails into pieces, and add them to the sauce, along with the mussels and clams. Reheat, without bringing to the boil.

7. Stir the sauce into the spaghetti and transfer to a warmed serving dish.

Recommended drinks

Valpolicella
Coteaux-d'Aix
Irouléguy Rouge

Menu suggestions

1. Start a meal with this pasta dish, then serve Gorgonzola and Mascarpone followed by coffee granita for dessert.

2. For a more substantial meal, follow the pasta with stuffed sardines and a Sicilian cassata.

Chicken and corn tidbits

N.B.

Most bread becomes hard and barely edible if left in the open air for more than 48 hours. Traditionally baked farmhouse bread grows stale very slowly, however, and, rather than throwing it away, you can cook it and rediscover some almost forgotten dishes. These recipes are suitable not only for bread that is still fairly supple (whether sliced or unsliced), but also for hard crusts.

Breadcrumbs

These appear in countless recipes (in breaded dishes, for example, as a binding for stuffings and some cold sauces, or as a complement to cheese in gratins). There are two kinds of breadcrumbs.

White breadcrumbs

White breadcrumbs

Remove the crust from a piece of bread with a knife and cut the remainder into large pieces, then put them into a food mill to obtain fine crumbs. Sieve to eliminate any lumps. Spread the breadcrumbs on a baking sheet and dry them for 20 minutes in an oven preheated to 230 °F (110 °C). You can keep these breadcrumbs in a tightly sealed container for up to a month.

Golden breadcrumbs

Cut the stale bread into big pieces, keeping the crust, and spread them out on a baking sheet. Heat them in an oven preheated to 340 °F (170 °C) for 10 minutes. Leave to cool then put them into a food mill. Sieve and store in a tightly sealed container.

Tapioca pudding with cherries

Bread pudding

Serves 4
  4–6 slices of bread with no crust
  3 cups (75 cl) milk
  1 vanilla bean
  Zest of $1/2$ lemon or orange (chopped)
  4 eggs
  $5/8$ cup (140 g) sugar

1. Cut the bread into soldiers the size of your little finger and place them in mold.

2. Boil the milk with the vanilla and zest of lemon or orange.

3. Beat together the eggs and sugar, add the milk, and pour the resulting mixture over the bread.

4. Leave the bread to swell with the liquid for 10 minutes, then cook in an oven preheated to 310 °F (155 °C) for 40 minutes.

French toast with apples

Guinea fowl with fresh noodles

Tomato canapé

French toast

Serves 4
4 eggs
3 sachets vanilla sugar
2 tbsp flour
3 cups (75 cl) milk
6–8 slices bread
Butter

1. Whip the eggs with the vanilla sugar, the flour, and then the milk in a bowl, as if you were preparing dough for crêpes.

2. Leave to rest for about 5 minutes, then plunge the slices of bread into the mixture and leave them to soak.

3. Brown the slices on both sides in a foaming dab of butter. Serve hot with jam, sugar, or maple syrup. Easy and quick to make, French toast is ideal for children's meals.

Bread stuffing

For one chicken
$2^3/_4$ oz (70 g) stale bread
Milk
9 oz (250 g) ground meat
$3^1/_2$ oz (100 g) chopped chicken's liver
2 cloves garlic
$1/_2$ bunch parsley
$1^3/_4$ oz (50 g) dry ham
2 eggs
Salt and pepper

1. Cut the bread, with its crust, into dice 3/8 in (1 cm) wide; sprinkle with cold milk, and leave to swell for a few minutes.

2. Mix the ground meat, livers, garlic and parsley (both chopped), ham (chopped into dice), eggs, salt, and pepper in a bowl, along with the bread (now squeezed dry).

3. Mix the stuffing thoroughly to obtain a uniform mass. Stuff and cook the chicken.

Bruschetta

Serves 4
8 slices farmhouse bread
4 tomatoes
1 clove garlic
Olive oil
Fresh thyme
Salt and pepper

1. Rub the slices of bread with the garlic.

2. Lay some thin slices of tomato on the bread, then sprinkle with olive oil, salt, pepper, and a little fresh thyme.

3. Put the bread into an oven preheated to 340 °F (170 °C) for 10 about minutes. Serve piping hot.

You can vary the recipe by adding black and green olives, anchovies, tuna, Mozzarella, or Fontina.

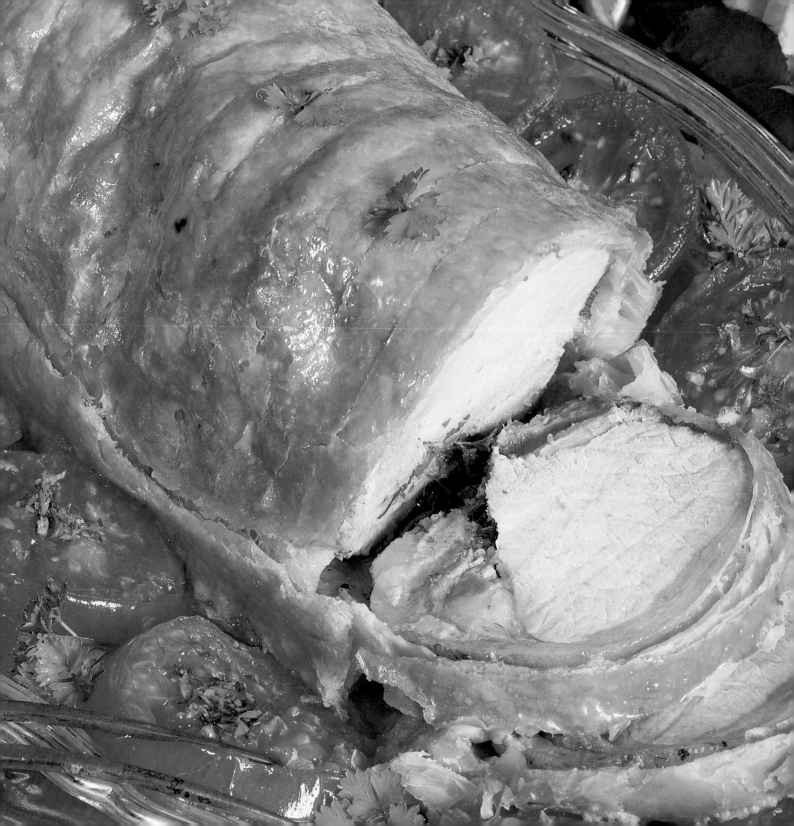

Beef
and veal

General points

Frying is a simple method that is perfect for cooking tender cuts like round, short loin, and sirloin. Meat can be fried in a mixture of peanut oil and butter (do not use butter on its own, as it cannot tolerate high temperatures and becomes indigestible) or in just a pinch of coarse salt, sprinkled in a skillet and heated. The cooking time depends on the nature and thickness of the meat and the temperature in the skillet. Its progress can be monitored by

Blue, medium rare, and well-done meat

applying slight pressure to the meat: it becomes less supple the more it is cooked. There are five main ways of frying and broiling red meat.

The quickest way is to cook it **"blue,"** merely searing the meat and turning it over. It takes on a reddish-blue tinge and, when pressed, has more or less the same consistency as raw meat; in fact, the inside is virtually raw, as it is barely warmed and very rare. This technique is popular with devoted carnivores and best suited to tenderloin steaks such as filet Mignon, fillet, and Chateaubriand.

Cooking meat **"rare"** also takes little time, as each side is fried for about 45 seconds only. The meat should be very supple when pressed. The interior is reddish blue and the cooked surfaces slightly brown. The best steaks for this method are tenderloin, sirloin, and round tip.

The most common way of cooking meat, however, is **"medium rare."** This results in meat that is hot, but scarcely cooked, red on the inside, and markedly brown on the outside. When pressed, the meat is supple, but slightly resistant. All the cuts mentioned above are also suited to this cooking method.

"Well-done" meat is cooked for much longer—up to 7 or 8

Pepper steak

minutes per side. The interior is still fairly red, but looks dry, while the outer surface is dark brown. When pressure is applied, the meat resists noticeably. Very thin steaks like round tip should not be well done, as they will turn out dry.

The most prolonged process of all produces meat that is **"very well-done."** The meat is totally cooked and strongly resists any pressure. When cut open, the interior is uniformly brown; unfortunately, even the best meat can end up dry when cooked like this.

Steaks mimosa

Charbroiled rib steak

Fried steak

Put the steak on the worktop and leave it at room temperature for 20 minutes. Season the steak with salt and pepper to taste (broiled meat is succulent with coarse salt) on both sides. Place 1 dab of butter with 1 tbsp peanut or sunflower oil in a skillet. When the oil is very hot (but not yet smoking) gently lay the steak in it. The oil must be sizzling and the meat seared quickly. Turn the steak over and cook on the other side in the same way, then put on a warmed platter and serve immediately. Reckon on 6¹/₂ oz (180 g) meat per person. For this dish to be successful, it is vital that at least one-third of the skillet is left free; otherwise, the meat will not be browned.

Charbroiled rib

Nothing is more delicious than a thick rib of beef broiled over a log fire. To serve 3–4, light a fire, if possible with vine shoots or oak wood, as the embers will be more intense. Leave the meat at room temperature for 30 minutes then season it on both sides. Put it on a grill and put this in the fireplace, 8 in (20 cm) above the fire. Broil for about 5 minutes, according to the thickness of the meat, then turn it over and cook for a further 4 minutes. Put the rib on a wooden chopping board, then cut it into three or four pieces and serve immediately, as hot as possible. Accompany this delicacy with baked potatoes and coarse salt.

Broiled rib of beef

Roast beef

for 6

1 Preheat the oven for 20 minutes to 445 °F (230 °C). Put a 3 lb-5 oz (1.5-kg) piece of beef in an oiled roasting pan. Baste the meat with peanut oil then season with salt, pepper, and a little thyme. For a stronger flavor, tie 10 cloves of garlic around the meat. Roast the beef for 15 minutes then lower the heat to 350 °F (180 °C), without opening the door of the oven.

2 Cook for 12–15 minutes per 1 lb (0.5 kg) to obtain medium-rare meat. This cooking time will vary according to your personal taste and the characteristics of the meat (thickness, whether it is on or off the bone, etc.) Take the dish out of the oven, then remove the meat and place it in a dish, covering it with aluminum foil to prevent it from drying out.

3 Deglaze the roasting pan with 2 glasses beef or veal bouillon and 1/2 tomato cut into thin slices. Boil this mixture for 5 minutes. Add salt and pepper then remove from the heat. Stir in 2 dabs of butter. Keep this gravy hot, with the garlic cloves floating on the surface. To serve, place the roast meat on a chopping board.

4 Untie any strings or layers of fat that you may have put around it. Cut the meat into slices about 3/8 in (1 cm) thick. Reckon on 3 slices for 2 people. Arrange these slices on a flameproof serving platter, overlapping them slightly. Add salt and pepper, pop the platter into a hot oven for about 30 seconds, and serve immediately, with the gravy separate.

Fillet of beef

General points

Roasting is suited to choice cuts of beef, both off the bone (tenderloin or sirloin steak) or on it (ribs). Before cooking, the meat must stand for at least 1 1/2 hours at room temperature, to allow it to warm through and therefore cook more uniformly. You can roast beef with or without aromatic garnishes like garlic or onions, but their presence will enhance the flavor of the gravy.

Tip

You can roast your beef to perfection by using a thermometer. Reckon on 122–131 °F (50–55 °C) for medium-rare meat, 140–149 °F (60–65 °C) for well done, and over 158 °F (70 °C) for very well done.

Yorkshire pudding

for 6

1 There is an accompaniment to roast beef that is particularly appreciated in England: Yorkshire pudding, served piping hot. It is very easy to make. Preheat the oven to 430 °F (220 °C). Beat 3 eggs and 9 oz (250 g) flour together in a bowl for 3 minutes to obtain a uniform consistency, then add 1³/₄ cups (45 cl) milk, 3¹/₂ oz (100 g) melted butter, and 3¹/₂ tbsp (5 cl) beef bouillon, beating all the while.

2 Season to taste with salt, pepper, and grated nutmeg. Using a brush, grease a round mold (such as a cake pan) with melted butter, then pour the batter into it. Put it into the oven and bake for about 35 minutes. Serve the pudding immediately, straight from the mold, dividing it into portions with a tablespoon.

N.B.

It is very important to allow roast beef to "rest" for a few minutes after cooking, because the heat makes all the blood flow to the center of the meat and it will spill out if it is carved straight away. Leaving it to stand for a moment, covered in two layers of aluminum foil, will enable the blood to spread throughout the meat, making it more juicy and tender. This principle applies to all roast meat.

Hungarian roast beef

Hungarian veal medallions

Escalope in a "wallet"

Grilled veal chops

General points

Frying is appropriate for veal in thin or medium cuts (up to 1 in/3 cm): escalopes, chops (1–5 ribs, loin), piccatas, paillardes, and grenadins. Whereas beef is seared over high heat, veal needs less heat, but applied over a longer period, as it is always eaten well done and never rare.

Calf's liver Norman style

Plain escalopes

To serve 6, put 6 escalopes weighing 6 oz (170 g) on a worktop and leave them at room temperature for 30 minutes. Season both sides with salt and pepper. Set a skillet over medium heat and melt 3¹/₂ oz (100 g) butter. When it starts to foam, lay the escalopes gently in the skillet. Cook one side for 3 minutes and the other for 2 minutes. Shift the meat slightly in the skillet with a fork to stop it sticking. Place the cooked escalopes in a serving dish and serve them very hot with pilau rice. As the cooking temperature is not very high, you can use farmhouse butter, which gives a delightful hint of hazelnut to the meat. Veal comes from a young animal and dries up fairly quickly, so it must not be fried for too long.

Escalopes with cream

To serve 6, put 6 escalopes on the worktop. Leave them at room temperature for 30 minutes. Season both sides with salt and pepper. Set a skillet over medium heat and melt 1 dab of butter; when this is frothy, add the escalopes. Cook one side for 3 minutes and the other for 2 minutes. Shift the meat in the skillet with a fork, to prevent if from sticking. Place the cooked escalopes in a serving dish and keep them hot. Add 2 finely chopped shallots to the skillet and sauté them for 2 minutes. Add ¹/₄ cup (6 cl) of white wine and reduce for 3 minutes. Add 1 scant cup (20 cl) crème fraîche. Bring to the boil then remove from the heat. Add salt and pepper, then pour the sauce on the escalopes and serve immediately.

Périgourdine veal chop

Vendangeuse calf's liver

Calf's liver Nantes style

Escalopes with Marsala

To serve 6, leave 6 escalopes at room temperature for 30 minutes. Season both sides with salt and pepper. Set a skillet over medium heat and melt 1 dab of butter in it; when it is frothy, add the escalopes. Cook on the first side for 3 minutes and the second for 2 minutes. Nudge the meat with a fork to prevent it from sticking. Place the cooked escalopes on a dish and keep them hot. Add 2 finely chopped shallots to the skillet and sauté them for 2 minutes. Pour on a scant $1/2$ cup (10 cl) Marsala and reduce for 3 minutes. Add $2/3$ cup (15 cl) crème fraîche and $1/3$ cup (8 cl) veal bouillon. Bring to the boil, cook for 3 minutes, then remove from the heat. Stir in salt, pepper, and 1 dab of butter, then pour the sauce on the escalopes and serve immediately.

Veal chops with cream

To serve 6, season 6 veal chops with salt and pepper. Heat a generous dab of butter in a skillet until it is frothy, then add the chops. Sauté them over medium heat for 5 minutes, turn them over, and continue cooking on the other side for 3 more minutes. Keep the chops hot while you prepare the sauce. Place 1 finely chopped white onion in a skillet and sauté for 2 minutes. Deglaze with $1/3$ cup (8 cl) port and boil for 2 minutes. Add $2/3$ cup (15 cl) crème fraîche and $1/3$ cup (8 cl) veal bouillon, then cook over gentle heat for 3 minutes. Stir in 1 dab of butter then add salt and pepper. Bathe the chops in the sauce and serve immediately. If you want the chops to be well done, increase the cooking time by 3 minutes per side.

Calf's liver

To serve 6, season 6 slices of calf's liver ($5^1/_2$ oz/150 g each) with salt and pepper. Melt 1 generous dab of butter in a large skillet and add 2 tbsp peanut oil. When the mixture starts to foam, add the slices of liver and cook them over medium heat. The liver colors rapidly and does not require much heat. Turn the slices after cooking for 4 minutes then continue for a further 2 minutes on the other side, before transferring the slices to a serving platter. To make Venetian calf's liver, sauté the sliced liver with chopped onions in butter, then, after quickly deglazing the skillet with white wine and cognac, sprinkle this over the liver with some lemon juice and serve piping hot.

**Roast veal with
small onions**

Flavors

Veal is at its tastiest when it is roasted whole, preferably on the bone. It is important to take the trouble to allow the meat to rest at room temperature before putting it in the oven; this makes the meat a great deal easier to cook, as well as helping it to retain more of its juices and turn out much more tender. Veal needs to be roasted at higher heat, and for longer, than beef, but beware of taking this to extremes. Ideally, the meat should turn out somewhere between "pink" and "medium rare"; to achieve this, roast the veal at a fairly sustained temperature, then take it out of the oven before its core is completely cooked. For a perfect

Roast veal Saint-Gilles

result, leave the meat to stand for 30 minutes, wrapped in three or four layers of aluminum foil. This allows all the heat stored in the edges of the meat to gradually spread into the middle. This technique, known as "cooking by inertia," can be applied to all white meat and large specimens of poultry.

N.B.

Should meat be salted before it is roasted? This question is often posed, but it can receive contradictory answers. The response is … preferably, yes. Apart from seasoning meat, kitchen salt also has the capacity to slightly intensify its taste by acting on its component proteins. Salt should only be added a few minutes before cooking the meat, not too far in advance, otherwise it will cause it to lose some of its juices.

Roast veal Dijon style

Roast veal with spinach

Farmhouse roast veal

Roast veal stuffed with green olives

Roast veal

Preheat the oven for 20 minutes to 445 °F (230 °C). To serve 6–8, put a joint of veal weighing 3 lb 5 oz (1.5 kg) (standing rump, shoulder, cushion) in a lightly oiled roasting pan. Baste the meat with peanut oil, then season it with salt, pepper, and a little thyme; scatter 2 onions, chopped into large dice, around the meat. Put the pan in the oven and cook for 10–15 minutes per pound (half kilo). If the meat starts changing color too quickly, open the oven door for 2 seconds and lower the temperature to 410 °F (210 °C). Take the pan from the oven, remove the meat, put it on another dish, and wrap it in four layers of aluminum paper. Leave to rest for 30 minutes in a place that is not excessively cool. Deglaze the roasting pan with 2 glasses beef or veal bouillon and $1/2$ tomato cut into thin slices. Boil this mixture for 5 minutes. Add salt and pepper, then take the pan off the heat

and stir in 2 dabs of butter. Keep warm, with the onions floating on the surface. Before serving, recover any juice that may have flowed out of the aluminum foil, then unwrap the meat and place it on a chopping board. Untie any strings or layers of fat that you may have tied around the joint; if this is a standing rump or haunch, bone it with a small knife, trying not to break up the meat (this operation is in fact fairly easy). Carve the veal into slices roughly 1 cm thick . Reckon on

3 slices for 2 people. Arrange these slices on a flameproof serving platter, overlapping them slightly. Add salt and pepper. Put the dish into the hot oven for about 30 seconds, then serve immediately, with the gravy separately.

Roast veal Agen style

195

General points

Fondue bourguignonne is a very convivial dish that involves guests searing the meat themselves in boiling oil. The meat is cooked on the table itself, in a casserole heated by a flame. The meat must be very fresh, with no nerves, tendons, or fat. The most appropriate steaks are top loin, tenderloin, and round. This dish must always be accompanied by at least four fairly thick sauces, either hot or cold. You could consider Béarnaise, barbecue, tartare, and tomato sauces, as well as aēoli. Do not forget mustard, pickles, and small onions in vinegar.

Fondue bourguignonne

To serve 6, put 3 lb 5 oz (1.5 kg) meat on the worktop and trim it to remove the nerves and fat. Cut into uniform cubes ³/₄ in (2 cm) wide and place these in an attractive serving dish. Serve the sauces and condiments in small bowls. Peel 1 clove garlic and rub the insides of a small casserole or fondue pot with it. Heat 2 quarts (2 liters) peanut or sunflower oil in a saucepan, then pour it into the casserole; place this over the burner (making sure that it is absolutely stable) and keep the oil at a temperature of 340 °F (170 °C) (a thermometer is useful here). The guests spear the cubes of meat with long skewers and cook them to their taste, turning them once or twice in the oil: just a few seconds for very rare meat, up to 1 minute for well done. You can improve this recipe by marinating the meat overnight in a mixture of spices or herbs (such as thyme, bay leaves, oregano, or sage).

Beef kebabs

These are not only delicious, but can also be prepared very quickly. They are ideal for a log fire in summer, but you can cook them all the year round in a skillet. Prepare the meat the night before the meal. The most suitable cuts are tenderloin, boneless top loin, and round steak. Reckon on 3 lb 5 oz (1.5 kg) to serve 6. Place the meat on a worktop and trim it carefully to remove the nerves and the fat, before chopping it into uniform cubes 3/4 in (2 cm) wide.

Beef kebabs

for 6

1 Peel and seed 2 red bell peppers. Peel 3 white onions then cut them into pieces the size of a walnut. Finely chop 2 shallots. Put the cubes of meat and vegetables in a bowl, along with 1/3 cup + 1 1/2 tbsp (10 cl) olive oil, 1 pinch fresh thyme, 1 pinch dried oregano, and 2 tbsp chopped basil. Cover the bowl with plastic wrap, then put it in the refrigerator and leave to marinate overnight.

2 The following day, prepare the kebabs by skewering the chunks of marinated meat, alternating each cube with a piece of vegetable (pepper or onion). Use long, flat skewers. Light a fire, ideally with vine shoots or oak logs. When the embers are glowing red, add salt and pepper then put the kebabs on a grill, set 8 in (20 cm) above the fire.

3 Cook the meat very quickly, as it should be fairly rare: reckon on 2–3 minutes per side. Wear gloves to turn the skewers, as the metal heats up rapidly. Beware! Prolonged cooking dries up the meat. Serve the kebabs immediately with a green salad and a Béarnaise or barbeque sauce. Guests can slide the hot ingredients from each skewer on to their own plates.

Sautéed veal Marengo

for 6

1 Place 3 lb (1.3 kg) meat on the worktop and cut it into pieces around 1 in (2–3 cm) wide. Season them with salt and pepper. Peel 2 onions and chop them finely. Peel 4 cloves garlic and chop these finely as well. Plunge 4 fresh tomatoes into boiling water, seed, and cut into small dice. Peel 14 oz (400 g) asparagus, cook, then set aside the tips. Peel 9 oz (250 g) cultivated mushrooms, discarding the stalks if they are too hard. Fry the mushrooms in butter for 5–6 minutes then set them aside.

2 Heat 2 tbsp peanut oil in a casserole. Brown the pieces of meat on all sides for 20 minutes. Add the chopped onions and cook for a further 5 minutes, then add ¹/₂ cup (60 g) flour. Cook for 5 minutes, stirring all the while. Pour 3 cups (70 cl) hot beef or veal bouillon, 3 tbsp tomato paste, 1 bouquet garni, the fresh tomatoes, and the chopped garlic. Bring to the boil, add salt and pepper, and cook over very gentle heat for about 1 hour 30 minutes. Taste the meat.

3 Once it is cooked to your requirements, drain it and put it in a dish. Add 1 glass beef or veal bouillon to the sauce and bring slowly to the boil. Skim the fat off the top of the sauce with a ladle and take out the bouquet garni. If the sauce is too liquid, thicken it with a little flour, mixed into a paste with butter. Adjust seasoning to taste. Fifteen minutes before serving, put the cooked meat, mushrooms, asparagus, and 1 bunch of chopped chives in the sauce. Simmer to heat up the sauce and serve in a hot dish with steamed potatoes.

Sautéed veal

There are many recipes for sautéed veal, but they all follow the same principle. Look for best-quality meat in the following cuts: neck, cushion, flank, shoulder, or brisket. There is no need to trim the meat very much, as the nerves take on a delicious consistency. If you use a non-stick pan, you can reduce the amount of fat.

sautéed veal and blanquette

Blanquette of veal
for 6

1 Put 3 lb (1.3 kg) meat on the worktop and cut it into pieces around 1 in (2–3 cm) wide. Place them in a casserole and cover them with cold water. Bring to the boil, skim off the fat, then cook slowly for 15 minutes. Meanwhile, peel 3 carrots and cut them into two. Peel 3 onions and cut these into two as well, then spike them with 2 cloves. Wash 2 leeks. Prepare 1 bouquet garni. Wrap a dozen peppercorns in a small piece of muslin and tie a knot to hold them in.

2 Put the vegetables, peppercorns, herbs, and 1 level tbsp coarse salt into the casserole with the veal. Cook over low heat, but making sure that it boils constantly, for 1 hour 30 minutes. Meanwhile, peel 9 oz (250 g) mushrooms and 7 oz (200 g) baby onions. Put them in a saucepan containing water, 1/8 cup (30 g) sugar, the juice of 1 lemon, 1 oz (30 g) butter, and salt. Simmer gently for 20 minutes. Once the meat is cooked, drain it. Remove the vegetables and peppercorns from the bouillon. Keep the carrots and leeks for future use in another dish.

3 Cook 5/8 cup (70 g) flour and 3 1/2 oz (100 g) butter for 5 minutes over a low heat. Add this mixture to the piping-hot bouillon, beating vigorously. Add 1 scant cup (20 cl) crème fraîche, beaten with 1 egg yolk. Adjust seasoning to taste, then add the cooked meat, onions, mushrooms, and 1/2 bunch chopped parsley. Simmer, without bringing to the boil, and serve very hot with plain white rice.

Blanquette

This is one of the most famous recipes for veal. You can make it with neck, cushion, flank, shoulder, or brisket, although the best results are obtained by mixing several different cuts. Blanquette can be reheated successfully, so have no qualms about making it in large quantities. As its name suggests, a blanquette is white: it is traditional to squeeze on a little lemon juice when adjusting the seasoning.

199

Braised beef Nantes style

Braised beef Gascony style

Beef stew

General points

Braised dishes are cooked in two phases—the first involves browning the meat and the second cooking it slowly in a sauce. Braising requires cuts suited to slow cooking: chuck, shoulder, or blade.

Provençal stew

To serve 6, cut 3 lb 2 oz (1.4 kg) meat into cubes $3/4$ in (2 cm) wide. Season them with salt and pepper. Heat 2 tbsp oil in a casserole then brown all the meat over medium-high heat for 20 minutes. Meanwhile, prepare the vegetables. Seed 2 red and 2 green bell peppers and chop them into big pieces. Peel 1 onion then cut it into medium-size dice. Peel and chop 5 cloves garlic. Wash 4 tomatoes and remove the peduncle; wash 1 eggplant and cut it into fairly thin slices. When the meat is crispy, place it in a dish. Brown the onion and the peppers for 5 minutes then add the eggplant. Cook for 5 minutes

then add the tomatoes, 3 tbsp tomato paste, the meat and its juices, 1 scant cup (20 cl) rosé wine, the chopped garlic, and 5 cups (1.2 liters) veal bouillon. Add 1 bouquet garni, bring to the boil then cook slowly, covered, for 2 hours. Taste the meat. When it is cooked, drain and set it aside in a dish. Add 1 glass beef or veal bouillon to the sauce and boil slowly. Skim the fat off the sauce with a ladle and remove the bouquet garni. Purée $3^{1}/_{2}$ oz (100 g) green olives in a blender then add them to the mixture. If the sauce is too liquid, thicken it with a little flour mixed into a

paste with butter. Adjust seasoning to taste. The sauce is now ready. Fifteen minutes before serving, put the cooked meat in the sauce and add $5^{1}/_{2}$ oz (150 g) whole black olives and 10 chopped basil leaves. Simmer to heat up the ingredients and serve with fresh pasta.

Mon Moulin stew

Herdsman's stew

Bœuf bourguignon

for 6

1 Cut 3 lb 2 oz (1.4 kg) meat into cubes 3/4 in (2 cm) thick. Peel 3 onions and 4 carrots. Cut the first into small cubes and the second into pieces around 1 1/2 in (3–4 cm) long. Prepare 1 bouquet garni. Place all these ingredients in a bowl and mix them with 5 1/2 cups (1.4 liters) red wine. Cover the bowl with plastic wrap then place in the refrigerator for 24 hours. When you come to prepare the dish, leave the ingredients to drain for 30 minutes.

2 Separate the meat from the vegetables and set the marinade aside. Heat 2 tbsp peanut oil in a casserole then sauté the vegetables over medium heat for 10 minutes. Meanwhile, sauté the pieces of meat in a skillet over high heat, until they are all browned. Add them to the vegetables being cooked, skim the fat off the casserole, and sprinkle over 5/8 cup (70 g) flour.

3 Cook over medium heat for 5 minutes, stirring constantly. Pour the marinade into the skillet that you used to sauté the meat and boil for 30 minutes, skimming off the fat at regular intervals. Pour this boiling red wine over the meat and the vegetables, add the bouquet garni, 1 2/3 cups (40 cl) beef or veal bouillon, salt, and pepper, then cook very slowly, covered, for about 2 hours. Taste the meat.

4 When it is cooked to your requirements, drain and set it aside in a dish. Add 1 glass beef or veal bouillon to the sauce and boil it slowly for 10 minutes. Skim the fat off the sauce with a small ladle and take out the bouquet garni. Cook 7 oz (200 g) baby onions and set them aside. Blanch 3 1/2 oz (100 g) bacon lardoons.

5 Add the bacon and onions to the sauce. If it is too liquid, thicken it with a little flour mixed into a paste with butter. Adjust seasoning to taste and your sauce is ready. If you wish, you can complement the sauce with a handful of small, cultivated mushrooms, sliced and cooked in butter, then thoroughly drained.

6 Fifteen minutes before serving, simmer the cooked meat in the sauce. Serve in a hot dish with boiled potatoes. Accompany it with the same, full-bodied wine that you used in the recipe: red Burgundy is obviously suitable, but so are Chairs or Madigan.

Stuffed oxtail

Oxtail

This long piece of meat is mouth-watering. It is often boiled, but it is also succulent when braised with red wine.

Oxtail braised in red wine

To serve 6, ask your butcher to cut the oxtail in 1-in (3-cm) pieces. Peel 3 onions and 3 carrots then cut them into small cubes. Prepare 1 bouquet garni. Put all these ingredients in a large bowl and pour in 4 cups (1 liter) red wine. Cover the bowl with plastic wrap then marinate the contents in the refrigerator for 24 hours. When it is time to prepare the dish, remove the ingredients from the wine and leave them to drain for 1 hour, then separate the meat from the vegetables and put the marinade aside. Heat 2 tbsp peanut oil in a casserole, then sauté the vegetables for 10 minutes over medium heat. Meanwhile, sauté the oxtail in a skillet over high heat, until all the pieces are thoroughly browned. Add them

Oxtail with wine

to the vegetables that you are cooking, then skim off the fat from the casserole, sprinkle in $5/8$ cup (70 g) flour, and cook the meat and vegetables over medium heat for 5 minutes, stirring continuously. Pour the marinade into the skillet that you used to sauté the oxtail and boil vigorously for 30 minutes. Skim regularly, then pour this boiling red wine onto the meat and the vegetables: add the bouquet garni, 2 cups (50 cl) beef or veal bouillon, salt, and pepper, then cook very slowly for about 3 hours. Taste the meat. When it is cooked to your requirements, strain and set it aside in a dish. Add 1 glass beef or veal bouillon to the sauce and boil slowly for 10 minutes. Skim the fat off the sauce with a small ladle and take out the bouquet garni. If it is too liquid, thicken it with a little flour mixed into a paste with butter. Adjust

Chili con carne

seasoning to taste then your sauce is ready. A few minutes before serving, put the cooked meat back in the sauce to reheat it. Serve in a hot serving dish with fresh pasta or steamed potatoes as an accompaniment. The sauce for this recipe can be deliciously complemented by 2–3 tbsp fresh parsley vinaigrette a few minutes before serving.

Chili con carne

This is a dish typical of Tex-Mex cuisine, originally from Mexico and the state of Texas. Its name means "hot pepper with meat:" it is always very spicy and goes down well with chilled beer.

braised beef: oxtail and chili con carne

1 Soak 10½ oz (300 g) red kidney beans in cold water for 24 hours. Drain and place them in a saucepan, covering them once again with cold water. Bring to the boil and cook for 1 minute, then drain the beans. Repeat this operation then set the beans aside. Prepare the vegetables: plunge 4 tomatoes into boiling water, then peel and seed them.

Chili con carne

for 6

2 Cut the tomatoes into quarters. Peel 5 cloves garlic and 2 onions, then slice them. Wash 1 red and 1 green bell pepper. Take off their peduncles, seed, then cut the flesh into small dice. Put 2 lb 11 oz (1.2 kg) meat on the worktop (boned shoulder is perfect for this recipe); eliminate the nerves and chop the meat into small dice. Season to taste with salt and pepper.

3 Heat 2 tbsp peanut oil in a casserole and brown the meat for 10 minutes, then place it in a dish. Brown the onions, garlic, and peppers in the same casserole for 10 minutes. Stirring continuously, add the fresh tomatoes, 2 tbsp tomato paste, the cooked meat, 2 cups (50 cl) beef or veal bouillon, and the blanched beans.

4 Add salt, pepper, 1 tsp ground cumin, ⅛ cup (30 g) sugar, and 4 pinches ground chili powder. Bring to the boil and simmer for about 2 hours 30 minutes. Adjust seasoning to taste. Serve on a large platter with a sprinkling of chopped, fresh cilantro. Accompany this dish with chopped onion and Tabasco®.

Pot-au-feu and beef with coarse salt

The pot-au-feu is one of classic dishes of the French culinary repertoire. This delicacy is made by slowly boiling, at the same time, meat and an assortment of winter vegetables. The choice of meat is very important—the best results are achieved by mixing various cuts. Some enrich the flavor of the broth (brisket, shank, tail), while others, more fleshy and gelatinous, provide tasty meat (blade, shoulder, chuck). Traditionally, there are two main techniques for cooking pot-au-feu. The first consists of putting the meat in cold water then cooking it. This produces an intensely aromatic broth, but rather plain meat. The second method is to cook the meat directly in boiling water; this allows the meat to retain its full flavor, but leaves little for the broth. There is also an intermediary recipe, given below, that allows you to achieve meat and broth that are equally satisfying.

Tip

Stringed beef is a quick and delicious way of preparing meat. Short loin is the most commonly used cut in this case. The meat is briefly poached in a vegetable bouillon, but, unlike other recipes for boiled beef, this dish can be prepared in a very short time.

Pot-au-feu

To serve 6–8, place 1 chopped oxtail and 1¾ lb (800 g) brisket tied with string in a large saucepan. Cover with at least 3 quarts (3 liters) cold water, set the saucepan over high heat, and bring to the boil. When the meat starts to cook, it will coagulate and produce a great deal of foam. Use a small ladle to remove this, along with the fat floating on the surface of the water. Lower the heat so that the water boils slowly, but constantly. Cook for 30 minutes then add 2¼ lb (1 kg) blade, 4 marrowbones, 1¾ lb (800 g) shank, and 1¾ lb (800 g) shoulder. Skim the stock once again and cook for 30 minutes. Meanwhile, prepare the vegetables. Peel 4 onions and 6 carrots, then cut them into two; spike the onions with 5 cloves. Peel 5 cloves garlic, leaving them whole. Wash 3 leeks and tie them into a bunch with string. Peel 4 turnips and cut them in half. Wash 3 celery stalks. Prepare 1 bouquet garni with 1 bunch flat parsley, fresh thyme, and bay leaves. Wrap 20 black peppercorns in muslin, to prevent them from being dispersed in the liquid while allowing their aroma to infuse in the broth. Add all the vegetables, the bouquet garni, pepper, and 2 tbsp coarse salt in the bouillon. Bring back to the boil then keep the water boiling at a slow, regular rhythm. Skim the fat off the stock every 20 minutes with a small ladle. After cooking for 1 hour 30 minutes, drain the vegetables and keep them hot in a dish. Cook the meat for a further 30 minutes. By then, the various meats and vegetables should be cooked to perfection.

Hotpot

Pot-au-feu

Brisket in a Parisian pot

boiled beef: pot-au-feu and beef with coarse salt

Scarlet blade

Whole stringed beef

Chopped stringed beef

Beef with coarse salt

To serve 6–8, fill a large saucepan with 3 quarts (3 liters) water, set it over high heat, and bring to the boil. Add 5 lb 9 oz (2.5 kg) shank and blade. Skim off any foam or fat. Lower the heat until the water is boiling slowly, but constantly. Cook for 30 minutes then add 6 marrowbones. Skim the bouillon again and cook for 30 minutes. Meanwhile, prepare the vegetables. Peel 4 cloves garlic, 3 onions, and 5 carrots. Spike the onions with 5 cloves. Leave the cloves of garlic whole. Wash 4 leeks and tie them into a bunch. Peel 4 turnips and cut them in half. Wash 4 celery stalks. Prepare 1 bouquet garni with 1 bunch of flat parsley, fresh thyme, and bay leaves. Wrap 20 black peppercorns in muslin, to prevent them from being dispersed in the liquid while allowing their aroma to infuse in the bouillon. Add all the vegetables, the bouquet garni, the pepper, and 2 tbsp coarse salt to the stock. Bring back to the boil then keep the water boiling at a slow, regular rhythm for 1 hr 30 minutes, skimming the fat off the stock every 20 minutes with a small ladle. Remove the vegetables and the meat and drain them, then put them straight into a dish. Remove the bouquet garni and the pepper, and untie the string around the leeks. Cut the meat into slices about 3/8 in (1 cm) thick. Place them in the middle of the dish and sprinkle them with a few ladlefuls of the hot bouillon. Arrange the marrowbones and the vegetables around the meat. Accompany the dish with coarse, gray sea salt, mustard, and pickles in small bowls.

Stringed beef

To serve 6, peel and chop 3 carrots. Wash 2 leeks and 2 celery stalks and tie them together in a bundle with string. Peel 3 onions then cut them in half. Wrap 10 peppercorns and 3 cloves in a piece of muslin. Put all these ingredients in a saucepan with 2 1/2 quarts (2.5 liters) water and 2 tbsp coarse salt. Bring to the boil then simmer gently for 50 minutes. Ask your butcher to trim 2 lb 11 oz (1.2 kg) beef fillet. Tie one of its ends securely with string and plunge it into the bubbling (but not boiling) bouillon. Reckon on 20 minutes to obtain pink meat. Remove the vegetables and arrange them in a hot dish. Take the fillet out of the saucepan and remove the string. Cut it into slices 3/8 in (1 cm) thick and serve immediately with pickles.

Flemish carbonade

for 4

1 Cut 1 lb 11 oz (750 g) beef into pieces about 1 in (3 cm) wide, removing the skin and nerves. Trim the rind of 3¹/₂ oz (100 g) bacon streaked with fat and dice the meat. Sauté in a big dab of piping hot lard. The most suitable cuts of meat are skirt or shoulder. You can cut the meat into thin slices rather than chopping it.

2 Wait until the meat starts to become crispy before adding the diced bacon. Lower the heat and sauté the bacon, allowing it to release its fat without drying up. Take the meat and bacon out of the pan, drain them thoroughly, and put them in a terracotta casserole. Traditionally, the meat and bacon are arranged in alternate layers, along with a few sliced onions.

3 Sprinkle 2 tbsp flour on the cooking fat, sauté for a few moments, stirring all the while, before pouring on 1 generous glass of beer (opt for a slightly bitter, light beer) and a little bouillon; allow the roux to color slightly in the skillet before adding the beer. While the sauce is simmering, peel 2 cloves garlic and cut them into thin slices.

4 Peel 6 onions and cut them into thin sticks, then scatter them over the meat. Place the garlic on the onions. When the sauce thickens, adjust seasoning to taste (without overdoing the salt, on account of the bacon). Dust the garlic with 1 tsp of sugar and pour the sauce over the meat.

5 Chop 1 bunch parsley and scatter it on top, then add 2 bay leaves. Cover and cook for 2 hours in an oven preheated to 330 °F (165 °C). Transfer the mixture to a serving platter, sprinkle with a few drops of vinegar, and serve. This carbonade is accompanied by small turnips and carrots, gently sautéed at the end of the cooking process.

braised beef: carbonade

Carbonada criolla

Carbonada criolla

1 Cut 1 lb 11 oz (750 g) lean beef into cubes the size of a walnut. Peel 2 carrots and cut them into slices. Trim and wash 1 leek, then cut it into thin slices. Plunge 4 tomatoes briefly into boiling water, then peel them. Cut open 2 bell peppers, remove the fibers and seeds, then slice them into strips. Peel 1 clove garlic and 2 onions, then chop them very finely.

2 Sauté the meat with 1 dab of butter and a little oil in a casserole. Add the garlic and onion and wait until they begin to color before adding the vegetables. Sauté them for a few minutes, then add 1 glass of white wine, the juice of a small can of pineapple (without syrup), and enough water to cover them. Add salt, pepper, a bay leaf, oregano, and thyme.

3 Cover and put into an oven preheated to 400 °F (200 °C). Cut out a large lid from 1 pumpkin. Remove its seeds and fibers, then take out its flesh with a spoon designed to turn potatoes or any small spoon with a cutting edge. Add this flesh to the casserole, after it has been cooking for 45 minutes.

4 Continue cooking for another 15–17 minutes before adding 2 apples cut into thin slices, a small can of sweetcorn, and the slices from the can of pineapple, cut into small pieces. Adjust seasoning to taste. Pour the carbonade into the hollowed pumpkin, then sprinkle it with finely chopped parsley.

207

Braised calf's leg

Valois fricandeau

Veal braised in milk

General points

Calf's leg is a magnificent cut of meat that is only enhanced by prolonged braising. Ask your butcher to cut it from the cushion, without trimming it, as it will turn out better if you retain the fat (negligible anyway in this case). A fricandeau is a thick piece of veal cut from the cushion, shoulder, or standing rump. It takes a fairly long time to cook, so it is ideally suited to braising. To make the meat even tenderer, you can spike it with strips of fresh lard. This operation is also delicate, but your butcher can do it for you.

Braised calf's leg

To serve 6, put 2 lb 14 oz (1.3 kg) veal leg on the worktop and leave it at room temperature for 1 hour. Cut the stalks off 14 oz (400 g) mushrooms and peel the heads. Cut them into four. Peel 3 shallots and chop them finely. Heat 2 tbsp peanut oil in a thick-bottomed casserole. Season both sides of the meat with salt and pepper. Brown it on both sides for 15 minutes. Add the mushrooms and chopped shallots, distributing them evenly in the casserole. Cover and cook over a medium heat for about 30 minutes, then add $^1/_3$ cup + $1^1/_2$ tbsp (10 cl) dry white wine, bring to the boil for 10 minutes, and pour in $1^1/_4$ cups (30 cl) fond de veau and 1 scant cup (20 cl) cream. Cook for a further 10 minutes, then take out the meat and put it, while still hot, in a dish. Season the sauce with salt and pepper, add $3^1/_2$ tbsp (5 cl) Armagnac mixed with $^1/_4$ cup (30 g) potato flour, beating vigorously, then $2^1/_2$ oz (70 g) butter and $^1/_2$ bunch chives, thinly chopped. Put the meat back in its sauce to heat it up, then transfer it to a large serving dish and cut it at the table. Serve this calf's leg with steamed potatoes and a selection of small, glazed vegetables.

**Fricandeau
with sorrel**

for 6

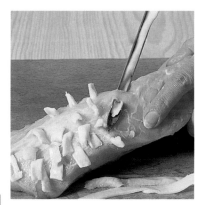

1 Ask your butcher to cut a 3 lb 2 oz (1.4-kg) piece of veal from the standing rump and then lard it. Heat 2 tbsp peanut oil in a thick-bottomed casserole. Season both sides of the fricandeau with salt and pepper. If you are going to lard the fricandeau yourself, use very cold strips of lard and sew them into the meat at close intervals with a larding needle.

2 Brown it for 15 minutes on each side, then add 3 sliced onions and continue cooking over medium heat for 30 minutes, stirring from time to time to prevent the meat from sticking. Then, add 2 bunches washed sorrel, $1/3$ cup + $1^1/2$ tbsp (10 cl) white wine, and $1^1/4$ cups (30 cl) of veal bouillon. Choose robust, shiny sorrel leaves and chop them roughly after removing the stalks.

3 Cover the casserole and cook over low heat for 1 hour, then remove the meat and stir in $2/3$ cup (15 cl) cream. Adjust seasoning to taste.
To ensure that this fricandeau cooks slowly and uniformly, you can lay a sheet of wax paper on the surface, buttered on the side in contact with the meat. The sorrel leaves should dissolve in the gravy. Do not add too much salt.

4 Put the fricandeau on the worktop and cut it into slices $3/3$ in (1 cm) thick; arrange the slices in a serving dish and cover them with very hot sauce. Serve immediately. You can garnish the edges of the dish with triangles of garlic bread, fried in a little hot butter, and accompany it with a fondue of creamed sorrel.

General points

"Osso buco" literally means "bone with a hole" because this Italian recipe is prepared with veal shanks cut into slices 3/4–1 in (2–3 cm) thick. Every part of this cut is delicious: the meat is gelatinous and mouthwatering, the marrow is spread on toast, and the bone flavors the sauce. This delicacy is a stew in which the meat is braised at length in white wine, tomatoes, and herbs.

Osso buco for 6

1 Put 3 lb 9 oz (1.6 kg) veal on the worktop and leave it at room temperature for 1 hour. Incise any membranes that may cover the meat, to avoid the pieces losing their shape while they are cooking. Add salt and pepper. Cover the bottom of a casserole with peanut oil and place over high heat. Brown the pieces of meat for about 15 minutes on each side. Meanwhile, prepare the vegetables: peel 3 onions, 2 celery stalks, and 3 carrots, then cut them into small cubes around 1/16 in (1 mm) wide with a sharp knife.

2 Lower the heat, remove the veal, and set aside, replacing them in the casserole with the vegetables. Sauté for 10 minutes, stirring occasionally. Add 1/3 cup + 1 1/2 tbsp (10 cl) white wine and boil for 5 minutes. Meanwhile, peel and seed 3 tomatoes then cut the flesh into large cubes. Add them to the casserole, along with the meat, 1 scant cup (20 cl) veal bouillon, 2 chopped cloves garlic, 1 bouquet garni, salt, and pepper. Cover and cook over gentle heat for about 1 hour 30 minutes. Skim the fat off the broth from time to time with a small ladle.

3 When the veal is cooked, keep the stew hot, but without letting the broth boil. Adjust seasoning to taste. To round off the recipe, you must prepare the "gremolata." Finely chop 3 cloves garlic and 1 bunch parsley. Grate the zests of 1 lemon and 1 orange, taking care not to include any of the bitter white skin, until you obtain a total of 1 tbsp. Mix all these ingredients together. A few minutes before serving the osso buco, remove the bouquet garni, and make sure the broth is bubbling and free of fat. Sir in the gremolata thoroughly so that it is evenly distributed throughout the broth. Serve immediately.

Basket of fresh tomatoes

Tip

For this recipe, ask your butcher for veal knuckle from the thigh and not from the shoulder. This cut of meat is plumper and, above all, its central bone is rounder and endowed with far more marrowbone.

Milanese osso buco

N.B.

Tomato is the other important ingredient in osso buco. Opt for bright red specimens that are fresh and plump. Out of season, you can use canned tomatoes with tomato paste. You can also vary the recipe by adding dried or fresh herbs: oregano or thyme would be perfect. Osso buco is generally accompanied by fresh pasta, white rice, or saffron risotto.

211

Veal shank with carrots

Veal-shank hotpot

Tasty pot-au-feu

One of the most satisfying veal recipes is pot-au-feu made with shanks. This is cooked like a pot-au-feu, but for slightly less time. Always choose the rear shanks of the animal, as these are more fleshy and succulent than the front ones.

Basic recipe

Fond de veau is a base that allows you to make a large number of sauces, as it can replace water and enhance a dish's flavor. It is fairly easy to prepare and far superior to any dehydrated industrial equivalents. You can prepare fond de veau in advance and keep it until you need it.

Fond de veau

Ask your butcher to crush 6¾ lb (3 kg) veal bones. Place these bones on a baking sheet and roast them in an oven preheated to 400 °F (200 °C) for about 1 hour, turning them from

time to time so that they take on the same color all over. Place them in a saucepan. Peel 4 onions and 3 carrots, then chop them roughly. Put them on the same baking sheet with 1 head of garlic, unpeeled and cut into two. Brown these ingredients in the oven for 20 minutes, then add them to the bones. Wash and tie together 2 leeks and 2 stalks of celery. Prepare 1 bouquet garni,

then put all these ingredients in the saucepan with 1 tbsp coarse salt, 3 tbsp tomato paste, 1 tsp pepper, and 2 cloves, then cover them with cold water. Bring to the boil then cook very slowly for 4 hours, skimming the fat off occasionally with a small ladle. Sieve the liquid then leave it to cool. Fond de veau can be kept for 5 days in a refrigerator, but you can also ensure that it is always at hand by freezing it in plastic ice-cube trays. This method is extremely convenient as it allows you to use the fond de veau according to your needs.

Ingredients for fond de veau

Pot-au-feu with veal shanks and fond de veau

Pot-au-feu with veal shanks

for 6

1 Place 5 lb 9 oz (2.5 kg) veal shanks in a large saucepan. Cover with about 3 quarts (3 liters) cold water. Place the saucepan over high heat and bring to the boil; this will produce a large amount of foam on the surface of the water, so remove it with a small ladle. Lower the heat so that the water boils gently but constantly. Cook for 20 minutes.

2 Meanwhile, prepare the vegetables. Peel 5 cloves garlic, then 4 carrots and 8 onions. Leave the cloves of garlic whole, but cut the other vegetables in half; spike each piece of onion with 3 cloves. Wash 3 leeks and tie them into a bunch. Peel 4 turnips and cut them into two, then wash 2 stalks of celery. Prepare 1 bouquet garni with 1 bunch of flat parsley, fresh thyme, and bay leaves.

3 Wrap 10 black peppercorns in a muslin bag. Add all the vegetables, the bouquet garni, and peppercorns to the bouillon, then season it with salt. Bring back to the boil then cook slowly and steadily for 1 hour 30 minutes. Skim the fat off the bouillon every 20 minutes with a small ladle. Remove the bouquet garni, the bag of peppercorns, and the string around the leeks.

4 Strain the meat and place it in the center of a serving platter, garnished with the cooked vegetables. Pour on a few ladlefuls of hot bouillon and sprinkle with chopped chives. Accompany this delicious recipe with mustard, pickles, coarse sea salt, or a vinaigrette sauce enriched with mixed herbs and a chopped, hard-boiled egg.

213

Fillet of beef "en croûte"

When beef fillet is protected by a thin covering of pastry it retains all its succulence—as well as making a splendid sight and giving your table a festive touch. The best time to prepare this recipe is in winter, in the fresh truffle season. Truffles provide an ideal complement to the garnish and sauce of this exceptional dish. Fillet of beef "en croûte" is a dish with a long tradition in France. It does not go so far back in England, but is nevertheless very popular there. The story goes that the Duke of Wellington, the hero of the Battle of Waterloo, was particularly partial to this dish and introduced it to his compatriots. So it was that "beef Wellington" became a standard feature of official banquets in early 19th-century Britain.

Serves 6
Preparation: 40 minutes
Cooking: 35 minutes

Ingredients

2 lb 11 oz (1.2 kg) fillet of beef
1 truffle
$1/2$ cup + $1^1/2$ tbsp (10 cl) port
$1/3$ cup + $1^1/2$ tbsp (10 cl)
Armagnac
2 tbsp oil
$1^2/3$ cups (40 cl) fond de veau
1 lb 2 oz (500 g) puff-pastry
dough
1 egg
$5^3/4$ oz (160 g) butter
$1/3$ cup (40 g) flour
Salt and pepper

1 Ask your butcher to prepare the meat. For this recipe, you need to remove the tip of the fillet so that you are left with only the thickest part. Season the meat with salt and pepper. Wash the truffle in cold water, pat it dry with a dishtowel, and chop it with a knife. Put the chopped truffle, port, and Armagnac in a small saucepan. Cover and boil gently for 6 minutes.

2 Pour oil into a large skillet and heat until it is piping hot. Brown the fillet for about 5 minutes, so that its surface is completely colored. Place it in a dish and leave it to cool thoroughly. Meanwhile, pour the fond de veau in a saucepan and reduce it to a third of its volume, then add the truffle. Simmer for about 20 minutes, stirring occasionally.

3 Roll the puff-pastry dough into a rectangle $5/16$ in (8 mm) thick, 6 in (15 cm) wide, and slightly longer than the fillet. Beat the egg and use a pastry brush to coat the dough with it. Gently melt $1^1/2$ oz (40 g) butter in another saucepan without allowing it to change color, then add the flour and mix it in. Cook for 2 minutes, stirring continuously, then remove from the heat.

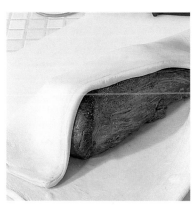

4 Once the meat is thoroughly cooled, put it on top of the dough and wrap the latter all round it, sealing the edges by pressing with your fingertips. Put it on a previously buttered metal baking sheet. Hide the seam of the dough by putting it underneath the meat. Beat the roux into the sauce, then beat in the rest of the butter, divided into dabs.

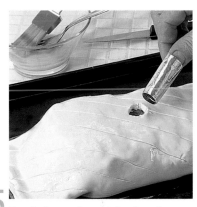

5 Brush the surface of the dough once again with the beaten egg. Make grooves $1/16$ in (1 mm) deep with the tip of a knife. Cut out a circle $3/8$ in (1 cm) in diameter in the center of the dough. Make a small tubular chimney with aluminum foil and put it in the hole. Preheat the oven to 410 °F (210 °C) then put in the fillet of beef and bake for 30 minutes.

6 Take it out of the oven, remove the aluminum foil, and place the pastry parcel on a serving dish. Pour the Périgueux sauce into a hot sauceboat. Cut the meat at the table and leave your guests to help themselves to the sauce. Accompany this recipe with sautéed potatoes, possibly with a garnish of a few strips of truffle. Round off the dish with small sautéed tomatoes.

Assortment of salads

Parsley and shallot vinaigrette

crunchy purslane, spicy rocket, or bitter dandelion greens. Whatever you choose, opt for specimens with fresh, firm, and gleaming foliage. Eat them as soon as possible; if you have to keep them in the refrigerator (for a maximum of 3 days), dry the leaves thoroughly and wrap them in a clean dishtowel.

General points

Green salads can play an important role in the composition or presentation of a meal, whether as hors-d'œuvre or garnish. Lettuce immediately springs to mind when we hear the term "green salad," but there are other possibilities beside plump butter lettuce, or green varieties with a yellow heart; you can also use romaine lettuce with stiff leaves or batavia (either green or red), or again oak-leaf garnet, with its slightly peppery taste, or lollo rossa, with its curly leaves. Furthermore, endive and chicory, escarole and curly endive, lambs' lettuce and raddichio all provide crispy freshness, even in winter, while a wide range of other leaves allow you to play with flavors in your salads: delicate watercress,

Mixed green salad

Viennese escalope with lambs' lettuce

Salad niçoise

Salad with citrus fruit

Seasoning

Green salad only comes into its own when it is seasoned. The magic of the seasoning means that a simple vinaigrette can be varied in countless ways, with respect to either the basic ingredients (oil—sunflower, olive, walnut, or hazelnut—and vinegar—wine, cider, or balsamic) or the complementary garnishes: garlic or shallot, mustard or mixed herbs, hard-boiled egg or blue cheese, etc.

Serving

When presented in an olive-wood, glass, or china bowl, a green salad served as an hors-d'œuvre stimulates the appetite; when presented in individual side dishes, it can accompany meat or fish. It is also often the ideal comple-ment to a cheeseboard. If a green salad is enriched with ingredients like small cubes of cheese, or slices of tomato, dried fruit, or garlic croutons, it can be a sufficient vegetable for roast beef or chicken, or a plate of assorted cold meats.

Tip

According to one old saying, four people are needed to prepare a good green salad: a miser to pour on the vinegar, a spendthrift to add the oil, a sage to season it with salt and pepper, and finally a madman to toss it...

Endive salad

For beef

The taste of beef or veal is often set off by a complementary flavor. Buy best-quality vegetables and make sure that they are not seasoned too strongly. These accompaniments can be served on the same plate as the meat, or in a separate dish of their own (previously warmed). As beef has a stronger taste than veal, the vegetables that accompany it must likewise have a strong character.

French fries

These are the perfect accompaniment to beef. When golden, crispy, and mouth-watering, they appeal to young and old alike. Prepare them with firm, white potatoes and deep-fry them in fresh, clear sunflower oil.

French fries

Beef ragoût with green beans

Green beans

When boiled in salted water, then quickly sautéed in parsley vinaigrette, green beans are an ideal match for broiled or braised meat. Try them with bœuf bourguignon or rib steak with shallots. Choose extra-thin beans and avoid overcooking them. You can also cook them "al dente," drain them thoroughly, and season them while still warm with vinaigrette (made with shallots or mustard) to accompany a roast meat, or mix them with slices of tomato and a little garlic.

Gratin dauphinois

This is a dish in its own right, but it can also serve as an excellent garnish to several beef recipes: broiled rib steaks, kebabs, roast sirloin, stews, and sautés. Do not forget to dust it with a few pinches of fresh nutmeg.

Sliced beef with tomatoes

Provencal tomatoes

When Provencal tomatoes are rounded off with a little fresh garlic, they make an attractive garnish for your serving dish and complement numerous beef dishes, such as Provencal beef stew or beef with olives. They are also extremely appropriate accompaniments to plain broiled meat or a whole fillet. Cut them in half and seed, begin cooking by frying them in a skillet with olive oil, flesh face downward, then turn them over, and, finally, glaze them in the oven with garlic and parsley by dusting them with a little sugar.

Celery

Celery makes a delicious purée when it is boiled and then blended. Its striking white color and distinctive taste enhances dishes based on broiled or fried beef.

Paupiettes of veal with carrots

Crown of veal with sorrel

Roast veal with fennel

With veal

The delicate flavor of veal deserves to be highlighted by fresh, colorful accompaniments. These will taste even better if prepared at the last moment.

Petits pois

Petits pois never go amiss. Select very small ones and braise them with a lettuce heart: the combination is sweet and mouthwatering.

Watercress

This is served in two ways. It can either be sautéed for a few minutes in butter or added to a salad, provided the vinaigrette is not too acid. In the latter case, it must be supremely fresh.

Mushrooms

Cultivated mushrooms, ceps, or morels make a superb foil to veal. Cook them with Madeira and crème fraîche. Reckon on about $5^1/_2$ oz (150 g) raw mushrooms per person.

Fennel

Braised fennel is a first-rate garnish for roast veal (standing rump or shoulder).

The juice of cooked fennel, slightly reminiscent of aniseed, subtly emphasizes the aroma of the meat. Reckon on 1 or 2 fennel per person.

Lemon

Lemon can help you produce exquisite sauces. Its acidity and enticing aroma are a perfect foil for small, fried pieces of veal, such as medallions and escalopes.

Celery purée

Milanese escalopes with lemon

Beef with onions

An economical dish

Serves 6
Preparation: 20 minutes
Cooking: about 1 hour 30 minutes

Ingredients

2³/₄ lb (1.25 kg) onions
2 rounded tbsp lard
2¹/₄ lb (1 kg) lean beef, sliced fairly thin
1 small bunch thyme
1 tbsp chopped celery
1 clove garlic
1 lemon
2 tbsp tomato paste
1 tsp Tabasco®
4 tomatoes
1 lb 2 oz (500 g) pasta
Salt and pepper

1. Peel the onions, cut them into thin rings, and sauté them in a casserole containing the lard over high heat. Wait until they start to brown, then add the slices of meat and brown them as well, on both sides. Add salt and pepper, along with the thyme, celery, and the garlic (peeled and chopped). Squeeze out the juice of the lemon, grate half its zest, and add to the mixture.

2. Sauté these ingredients for a few seconds, stirring continuously with a wooden spoon, then pour on 1 large glass of water. When it starts to boil, add 2 tbsp tomato paste and the Tabasco (this dish should be quite spicy).

3. Cover and simmer until the beef is very tender (50–70 minutes, depending on the quality of the meat).

4. Cook for a few minutes longer, before adding the tomatoes (peeled, seeded, and roughly cut into four).

5. A few minutes before the meat is ready, cook the pasta in salted, boiling water and then arrange it, with a well in the middle, in a large serving dish; pour the meat and its sauce into the well. Serve piping hot.

This dish should ideally be cooked in a cast-iron or terracotta casserole with a tightly fitting lid that prevents the liquid from evaporating. If necessary, you can place a heat diffuser between the burner and the casserole.

Recommended drinks

Bordeaux Supérieur
Madiran
Pécharmant

Menu suggestions

1. Start the meal with a cultivated mushroom salad with lemon and chives and finish off with a green salad and cheese, followed by crème caramel.

2. You can also serve a selection of seasonal raw vegetables as an appetizer and a dessert of thin apple tart.

Meatballs with stuffed olives

A family dish

Serves 4
Preparation: 20 minutes
Resting: 30 minutes
Cooking: 20 minutes

Ingredients

For the meatballs
12$\frac{1}{2}$ oz (350 g) ground beef
1$\frac{1}{2}$ oz (40 g) breadcrumbs
1 egg
15 stuffed olives
A few sprigs of fresh oregano

For the tomato sauce
2$\frac{1}{4}$ lb (1 kg) tomatoes
2 cloves garlic
1 bunch thyme and parsley
2 bay leaves
1 onion
1 small glass olive oil
Salt and pepper

1. Peel the tomatoes, having first plunged them for a moment into boiling water. Cut them into pieces and put them in a saucepan. Add the cloves of garlic, peeled and slightly crushed.

2. Pour on 1 glass of water and add the thyme, parsley, and bay leaves. Peel and finely slice the onion, then add it to the water. Bring to the boil, then keep it bubbling gently but regularly, stirring from time to time. Thicken the liquid with olive oil in the final stages, then season with salt and pepper.

3. Mix the ground meat, breadcrumbs, egg, salt, and pepper. Make balls from this mixture, then flatten them in the form of a disk. Put 1 stuffed olive on each disk and wrap the meat around the olive to recover the ball shape. Put these balls into the refrigerator for 30 minutes to allow the stuffing to harden.

4. Preheat the oven to 350 °F (180 °C). Put the meatballs on a barely oiled baking sheet and cook for 20 minutes, turning them at least once during that time.

5. Pour the tomato sauce (which should be much reduced and not too liquid) in the bottom of a large soup tureen. Put the meatballs on top, piping hot, and garnish with a few sprigs of fresh oregano (or, alternatively, some basil leaves).

Recommended drinks

Côtes-du-Rhône
Côtes-du-Roussillon
Châteauneuf-du-Pape

Menu suggestions

1. Serve zucchini flan with mixed herbs as an appetizer, followed by these meatballs with plain rice and peach soup for dessert.

2. To add a more Provencal touch, start with tomatoes and mozzarella, then serve eggplant gratin as an accompaniment to the meatballs and nougat glacé for dessert.

Sweetbread kebabs

A party dish

Serves 4
Preparation: 25 minutes
Waiting: 1 hour
Cooking: 25 about minutes

Ingredients

1³/4 lb (800 g) sweetbreads
4 cups (1 liter) bouillon (from a cube)
1 tbsp oil
1 bunch parsley
10¹/2 oz (300 g) sliced bacon streaked with fat
4 slices stale bread

1. If your sweetbreads have not been pre-prepared, you will have to soak them in cold water for several hours; generally, however, they are sold ready to cook.

2. Put the sweetbreads in a cooled, light bouillon. Bring gently to the boil and simmer for 5 minutes. Remove the skin and cartilage, then wrap the sweetbreads in a cloth and put them under a weight of about 4¹/2 lb (2 kg) for 1 hour.

3. Cut the sweetbreads into pieces 3/8 in (1 cm) thick, 3/8 in (1 cm) wide, and ³/4 in (2 cm) long. Sprinkle them with oil and finely chopped parsley. Cut the bacon into rectangles measuring ³/4 in x 1 in (2 x 2.5 cm). Cut the crust off the bread and put it briefly into a blender to grind it finely.

4. Thread the meat onto the skewers alternating sweetbread with bacon, baste with a little melted butter, and roll in the breadcrumbs. Bake them low down in the oven, so that the cooking process is slow and regular; it should take 15–18 minutes, and you will need to turn the sweetbreads over several times. Season with salt and pepper.

5. Meanwhile, prepare a little rice and add some butter blended with chopped parsley and lemon juice. Serve piping hot with a few lettuce leaves.

Recommended drinks

Mersault
Mercurey Blanc
Saint-Véran

Menu suggestions

1. Start with a foie gras au torchon (poached in a cloth) and toast, then serve these sweetbreads with plain rice and a celery purée, and finish with a raspberry vacherin.

2. Start off with a gratin of pike dumplings. For the main course, use plain rice once again as an accompaniment, then serve a pear-and-caramel Charlotte for dessert.

Chateaubriand with Roquefort butter

A regional dish

Serves 4
Preparation: 5 minutes
Cooking: 6–10 minutes

Ingredients

2 tbsp oil
4 Chateaubriands
Pepper
1 bunch chives
3½ oz (100 g) butter
3½ oz (100 g) Roquefort
1 tbsp cognac

1. Prepare a bed of burning embers a good 30 minutes before serving the pieces of meat. If no fireplace or barbecue is available, use an electric grill, heating it up in advance. Coat the barbecue grill or the heating surface of the electric grill with a thin layer of oil.

2. Rub a little oil into both sides of the Chateaubriands; grind pepper over them, but do not season them with salt. Leave them to rest at room temperature while you prepare the Roquefort butter.

3. Briefly rinse the bunch of chives and pat dry before chopping them finely over a bowl with a pair of scissors. Put the butter in another bowl (it needs to be soft, so has to be taken out of the refrigerator well beforehand) together with the Roquefort, roughly crumbled into pieces.

4. Stir these two ingredients with a fork until you obtain a uniform consistency. Add the cognac and pepper to taste (there is no need to add salt, due to the Roquefort). Finally, add the chopped chives and mix thoroughly.

5. When the embers are ready, put the Chateaubriands on the grill and cook them on one side for 5 minutes (or a little less, if you like rare meat), then turn them over quickly and cover them with the Roquefort butter. Grill them for a further 3 minutes and serve immediately. You can of course substitute another type of soft, blue-veined cheese, if you prefer.

Recommended drinks

Côte Roannaise
Beaujolais-Villages
Brouilly

Menu suggestions

1. If you like farmhouse cooking, serve a green salad with gizzards preserved in fat as an appetizer, potato gratin as an accompaniment to the Chateaubriand, and a rhubarb meringue tart for dessert.

2. Try Roquefort pastries as an appetizer, then accompany the meat with sautéed potatoes, and finish with clafoutis.

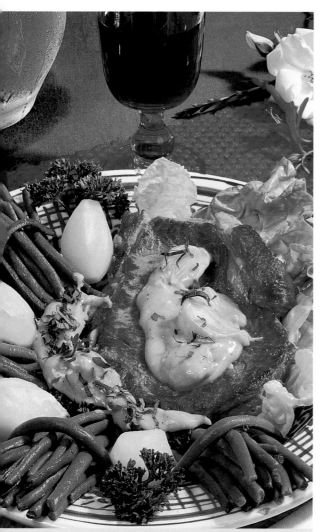

Sirloin with garlic butter

A family dish

Serves 4
Preparation: 10 minutes
Cooking: 10–12 minutes

Ingredients

4³/₄ oz (130 g) butter
1 sirloin steak about 1 lb 11 oz (750 g)
6 large cloves garlic
¹/₂ glass vinegar
2–3 sprigs fresh tarragon
2 sprigs thyme
A few sprigs of parsley and chervil
Salt and peppercorns

1. 1. Season the steak with salt and pepper, then brown it in a skillet with 1 heaped tbsp butter. Reckon on 5–6 minutes each side for rare meat.

2. Meanwhile, cut the rest of the butter into small pieces (to bring it quickly down to room temperature) and warm the serving dish and plates.

3. Put the meat in the heated dish as soon as it is cooked, then cook the cloves of garlic (previously peeled) in the cooking juices until it turns golden. Add the vinegar, tarragon leaves (roughly chopped), thyme, salt, and peppercorns (roughly crushed).

4. Reduce this sauce over high heat until only 1 tsp liquid remains. Take the skillet off the heat, then add to its contents the small pieces of butter, one after the other, beating them all the while to obtain a thick cream.

5. Cover the sirloin with sauce and transfer any surplus to a sauceboat. Sprinkle on the parsley and chervil.

6. Serve with green beans and potatoes, prepared in advance to avoid any delay in serving the meat.

Recommended drinks

Mercurey
Côte-de-Nuits-Villages
Pécharmant

Menu suggestions

1. Begin with grapefruit stuffed with shrimp, assemble a cheese board, and finish off with floating islands.

2. For a summer meal, you can start with a tomato salad with mixed herbs, then follow the meat with a green salad with Cabécous and a dessert of strawberry tart.

Coufidou rouergat

A regional dish

Serves 4
Preparation: 15 minutes
Cooking: 3 hours 30 minutes

Ingredients

3 lb 5 oz (1.5 kg) beef (half neck, half brisket)
1 tbsp lard
2 onions
1 tbsp flour
1 bottle Cahors
2 tbsp thick seasoned tomato coulis
(or 1 tbsp tomato paste)
1 bouquet garni with plenty of bay leaves
2 cloves garlic
4 slices cured ham
Salt and pepper

1. Cut the meat into pieces and brown it on all sides in a casserole, with a little lard. Peel the onions, then slice and sauté them in a saucepan with the lard; they should become slightly transparent.

2. Once the pieces of meat are browned, dust them with flour then brown them again, before adding enough wine to cover them.

3. Add the onions, tomato coulis, bouquet garni, and cloves of garlic (peeled and crushed). When the water starts to bubble, cover the ingredients with a layer of sliced ham; add salt (with caution, on account of the ham) and plenty of pepper.

4. Cover the casserole as tightly as possible and cook for 3 hours 30 minutes over very gentle heat. Check the progress of the sauce—it should be very thick by the time the dish is ready; if necessary, either add a few tbsp hot water or leave it uncovered in the final stages.

To accompany your coufidou, you can prepare potatoes, either plain boiled or baked in their skins. You can also try sautéed potatoes with ceps in parsley vinaigrette. Coufidou, or beef stew with red wine and onion, can also include fried diced bacon among its ingredients.

Recommended drinks

Cahors
Madiran
Beaujolais

Menu suggestions

1. For a winter meal, serve farmhouse pâté as an appetizer with a green salad dressed with walnut oil, and finish the meal with a pumpkin tart.

2. Soup lovers will appreciate an appetizer of onion soup. For dessert, serve apples bonne femme with honey.

Mexican entrecote

An international dish

Serves 4
Preparation: 10 minutes
Resting: 12 hours
First cooking phase: 1 hour 30 minutes
Grilling: 7–8 minutes

Ingredients

4$\frac{1}{2}$ oz (125 g) red kidney beans
1 tbsp oil
1 oz (30 g) diced salt pork
1 tsp finely chopped garlic
2 tbsp finely chopped green bell pepper
1 finely chopped onion
1 glass rice
1 rib steak about 1$\frac{3}{4}$ lb (800 g)
A few sprigs of parsley
Salt and pepper

1. Soak the beans overnight in a bowl of cold water. Drain, put them in a saucepan of cold water, and cook until they are soft (about 1 hour 30 minutes). Drain and set aside.

2. Heat a little oil in a skillet and brown the diced pork until it is crispy, then remove from the pan and set aside. Replace the pork in the skillet with the garlic, bell pepper, and onion; lightly sauté these ingredients for 5 minutes, without letting them turn brown, then add the beans and the fried pork; sauté gently for a further 5 minutes, uncovered.

3. Pour the contents of the skillet into a saucepan and add the rice, 1 generous pinch salt, and 2 glasses hot water. Bring to the boil, cover, and simmer gently until the rice is cooked and has absorbed all the liquid.

4. The entrecote is cooked at the same time as the rice; the intensity of the heat depends on the thickness of the meat (reckon on 1 minute per 3$\frac{1}{2}$ oz/ 100 g). Lightly baste the entrecote with oil, put it on a very hot grill and turn it over after two-thirds of the anticipated cooking time, adding salt and pepper at the same time.

5. Sprinkle a little chopped parsley on the meat and serve it piping hot, along with the kidney beans. You can accompany this dish with small green pineapples cooked in their skins or sweet-potato gratin.

Recommended drinks

Côtes-du-Roussillon
Light beer
Madiran

Menu suggestions

1. To continue the Mexican theme, serve an appetizer of guacamole with corn chips and a dessert of dark chocolate tart.

2. Another idea: empanadas (small pastries with ground meat) to start and an assortment of exotic sorbets to finish: mango, passion fruit, and coconut.

Braised veal with orange

A light dish

Serves 4
Preparation: 15 minutes
Cooking: 1 hour 15 minutes

Ingredients

2¹/₄ lb (1 kg) veal (brisket or hindquarter flank)
1 dab butter
2 shallots
1 tbsp green peppercorns
2 glasses dry white wine
1³/₄ oz (50 g) currants
2–3 oranges
1 small pot crème fraîche
¹/₂ tsp potato flour
Salt and pepper

1. Put the veal on a chopping board and cut it into uniform, fairly sizeable pieces with a very sharp knife. Add salt and pepper.

2. Heat the butter in a cast-iron casserole. Before it starts to take on any color, add the pieces of veal and brown them, turning them several times. Take the casserole off the heat.

3. Peel the shallots and chop them finely. Crush the green peppercorns roughly. Put the casserole back on the burner, add the shallots and the green peppercorns, then mix them together and pour on the white wine. Cover and simmer for 40 minutes.

4. Rinse the currants in warm water, pat them dry, and add to the casserole. Cover with the lid and continue cooking for a further 35 minutes.

5. About 8 minutes before serving the dish, peel the oranges and divide them into four; conserve any juice that results in a bowl. Mix the crème fraîche into the potato flour and pour this combination into the bowl containing the orange juice.

6. Mix these ingredients thoroughly and add them to the casserole. Stir gently, then add the orange quarters. Finish cooking the meat, making sure that the sauce does not boil. Adjust seasoning to taste before serving in a warmed soup tureen.

Recommended drinks

Côtes de Provence
Rioja
Bandol Rouge

Menu suggestions

1. Try starting with an endive salad with lemon, then accompany the veal with celery purée and finish with lemon granita for dessert.

2. More simply, serve an appetizer of half a grapefruit, lightly broiled, a side dish of celery or broccoli purée, and a dessert of fromage blanc with orange zest.

Recommended drinks

Meursault
Morgon
Graves

Menu suggestions

1. This subtle and original dish makes an excellent appetizer. Follow it with poached salmon steaks accompanied by mushrooms, then a Saint-Honoré.

2. If you serve the calf's liver as the main course, precede it with vol-au-vents and finish the meal with a savarin.

Roast calf's liver and green-leaf salad

A party dish

Serves 5
Preparation: 15 minutes
Cooking: 1 hour

Ingredients

2$^1/_4$ lb (1 kg) calf's liver
  1 pork caul, wide enough to wrap the liver
  1 lb 2 oz (500 g) potatoes
  1 small celeriac
  1 hard-boiled egg
  1 small pot crème fraîche
  1 fresh egg
  1 glass oil
  1 lemon
  2–3 endives
  1 small bunch watercress
Salt and pepper

1. A whole calf's liver is a delicacy that should be ordered from your butcher in advance; ask him to trim it carefully. Soak the pork caul in warm water then drain it gently and spread it flat on the worktop.

2. Season the liver on every side with salt and pepper. Place it in the middle of the caul and wrap it up by bringing up the sides of the caul to cover it completely. Put this package in a casserole, cover, and cook in an oven preheated to 350 °F (180 °C) for 1 hour. Leave it to cool in its cooking juices, then unwrap the liver.

3. Peel the potatoes and cook them in salted, boiling water until they are easily pierced by the prongs of a fork. Wash and peel the celery, removing any fibers, then cut it into large cubes and cook these in the same way as the potatoes.

4. Put the potatoes, celery, and hard-boiled egg through a food mill, then season with pepper and adjust the salt. Mix this purée with the crème fraîche. Leave to cool.

5. Prepare a mayonnaise with the fresh egg, oil, salt, pepper, and lemon juice. Put the cold purée in the center of a large serving platter. Plant the endive leaves in it and then cover it with mayonnaise; arrange the cold liver in thin slices around the edge and garnish with watercress.

Keftedes with zucchini

An international dish

Serves 4
Preparation: 30 minutes
Cooking: 20 minutes

Ingredients

1³/₄ oz (50 g) stale bread with no crust
  Bouillon (2–3 cubes)
  1 onion
  2¹/₂ oz (65 g) butter
  12¹/₂ oz (350 g) ground beef
  3¹/₂ oz (100 g) fatty, ground pork
  1 egg
  ¹/₃ cup (40 g) flour
  1 small pot thick crème fraîche
  2–3 large zucchini
  A few sprigs parsley
  Salt and pepper

1. Break up the bread in a bowl and pour the bouillon over it; leave it to swell up, then squash it with a fork to obtain an appealing, uniform paste. Peel the onion and slice it finely.

2. Heat 1 oz (25 g) butter in a small saucepan, add the onion, and brown it, stirring until it turns transparent. Remove from the heat and leave to cool.

3. Put the ground beef in a terrine and add the pork, mixing thoroughly with a wooden spoon; stir in first the bread soaked in bouillon and then the sliced onion. Mix all these ingredients together for 3 minutes.

4. Add the egg and 5 tsp (25 g) flour, then season with salt and pepper. Finally, thin the mixture with a little crème fraîche—just enough to obtain a mass that is fairly supple, but still retains its shape. Cover and place in the refrigerator.

5. Peel the zucchini. Cut their flesh into dice and poach them in a little bouillon seasoned with chopped parsley.

6. When the zucchini are almost ready, roll the meat mixture into balls, and flour then brown them in a skillet with plenty of butter or oil, in several batches. Shake the skillet continuously to turn the balls without breaking them. Season well and keep them hot. Serve on a warm platter garnished with parsley leaves.

Recommended drinks

Bergerac
Côtes-du-Roussillon
Costières-de-Nîmes

Menu suggestions

1. For a summer dinner, serve an appetizer of Moroccan salad of oranges, olives, and raw onions, and a dessert of cinnamon ice cream with almond biscuits.

2. Maintaining the Oriental flavor: stuffed vine leaves and eggplant caviar as an appetizer and an assortment of Arab pastries for dessert.

231

Recommended drinks

Beaujolais-Villages
Saumur-Champigny
Brouilly

Menu suggestions

1. For a family lunch, serve baked goat's milk cheese on salad for an appetizer and an omelet soufflé with jelly for dessert.

2. For a dinner, consider starting with a potato and leek soup and finishing with a fruit salad.

Matelote of veal with lovage

An economical dish

Serves 4
Preparation: 20 minutes
Cooking: 1 hr 30 minutes

Ingredients

$2^1/_4$ lb (1 kg) of brisket or plate of veal
$2^3/_4$ oz (75 g) butter
1 heaped tbsp flour
1 large glass white wine
12 baby onions
9 oz/250 g of carrots
1 bouquet garni
1 bunch lovage
4 slices of bread with no crust
Salt and pepper

1. Cut the meat into small pieces and put them into boiling water for 5 minutes; drain, refresh under the cold faucet, and drain once again. Put these pieces aside.

2. Melt 1 large dab of butter in a casserole, then pour in the flour; cook for a few moments, stirring with a wooden spoon, then add the wine.

3. Peel the onions and put them in this sauce, along with the carrots (scraped, washed, and sliced), veal, bouquet garni, lovage, salt, and pepper. Cover and cook for 1 hour 30 minutes over low heat.

4. Monitor the water level; it must be neither too high nor too low; if necessary, add 1 or 2 tbsp of hot water or uncover in the final stages (this basically depends on the quality of the veal).

5. Cut the bread into small pieces and sauté them in butter to make croutons, then serve them with the matelote (after adjusting the seasoning at the last moment). Garnish with the chopped lovage.

Lovage is an aromatic plant sometimes known as "mountain celery" on account of its scent. It is little used in France, but its fresh leaves serve as a wonderful complement to salads, soups, and meat dishes, in just the same way as parsley.

Veal medallions with pineapple

An international dish

Serves 4
Preparation: 15 minutes
Cooking: 12 minutes

Ingredients

1 pineapple (not too ripe)
1 large dab of butter
8 medallions of veal
1 tbsp oil
1 tbsp dark rum
4 very thin slices of bacon
1 pinch Cayenne pepper
4 sprigs parsley
4 cherry tomatoes
Salt and pepper

1. Peel the pineapple, eliminating all traces of its skin. Cut it into slices about 3/8 in (1 cm) thick, trimming them to ensure that they are all the same size. These steps should be carried out over a bowl, in order to catch the juice. Put the pineapple in a skillet with some butter and brown them slightly. Put them aside.

2. Trim the medallions to make them as uniform as possible, and roughly the same size as the slices of pineapple. Sauté them in the skillet over high heat, in a mixture of equal quantities of butter and oil, for 1–2 minutes on each side. Sprinkle them with the rum and flambé them.

3. Brown the slices of bacon in the same skillet. Spear them with wooden skewers. Place the medallions on a hot dish, two by two, with a slice of pineapple in between. Put these on the skewers and keep them warm in the oven.

4. Deglaze the skillet with the pineapple juice from the bowl, then add salt, pepper, and Cayenne pepper, and boil for a few moments. Cover the kebabs with this sauce and stick 1 sprig of parsley and 1 cherry tomato on the end of each one.

As garnish—apart from rice, which is obligatory for many Caribbean dishes—you can also prepare a papaya gratin or spicy sweet potatoes.

Recommended drinks

Moulin-à-vent
Brouilly
Saint-Émilion

Menu suggestions

1. To develop the Caribbean theme, you can serve an appetizer of stuffed crabs and a dessert of upside-down pineapple tart or coconut flan.

2. You can also integrate these stylish kebabs into a more classical menu: cheese soufflé to start and dark-chocolate Charlotte to finish.

Beaujolais papillotes

A regional dish

Serves 4
Preparation: 35 minutes
Cooking: 30 minutes

Ingredients

1 onion
1 small leek
1 celery stalk
2 carrots
1 clove of garlic
1 bouquet garni
4 thin slices of beef
1 bottle of Beaujolais
4 very thin slices of cured ham
Salt and pepper

1. Peel and slice the onion. Peel and wash the other vegetables, then cut them into pieces. Put them in a terrine, along with the bouquet garni.

2. Carefully trim any fat and nerves from the slices of beef, then place them on top of the vegetables. Season generously with salt and pepper and pour on some wine (with similar generosity). Marinate overnight, turning from time to time.

3. Heat some charcoal in a barbecue. Cut the rind off the slices of ham. Trim the slices of meat to make them slightly smaller than the slices of ham, then put each one on top of a slice of ham.

4. Put these paired slices on four sheets of buttered wax paper. Pour a little of the marinade and its vegetables on top of each one, then wrap the meat in the paper.

5. Cook them for 30 about minutes, fairly high above a lively fire. Turn them over two-thirds of the way through the cooking process. Meanwhile, heat and reduce the marinade, then strain it and add a little butter. Use it to accompany and enhance the flavor of the meat.

Recommended drinks

Chénas
Chiroubles
Juliénas

Menu suggestions

1. For a typically Beaujolais meal, serve a snail omelet to start and a blackcurrant tart for dessert.

2. Another idea: a curly endive with diced bacon to start, a mushroom fricassée with the papillotes, then pears poached in red wine.

Calf's kidneys with two mustards

A family dish

Serves 4
Preparation: 10 minutes
Cooking: 20 minutes

Ingredients

3 calf's kidneys
1 tbsp oil
6$^{1}/_{2}$ oz (180 g) butter
1 glass Armagnac
2 glasses Madeira
1 tbsp hot mustard
1 tbsp aromatic mustard
Salt and pepper

1. Carefully trim the kidneys with a sharp knife, cutting off some of their fat, and then season them with salt and pepper. Cook them for 10–15 minutes in a saucepan with just a little oil and butter (this cooking method is known as "à la coque.")

2. Drain the kidneys, remove all the cooking fat from the saucepan, then put the kidneys back in and flambé them with the Armagnac (which should be young and of high quality). Drain the kidneys and transfer them to a plate. Add the Madeira to the saucepan, then reduce it to half its volume.

3. Cut the kidneys into thin strips and keep them warm by putting them in a warm dish and covering them with another (these dishes should not be too hot, as the kidneys do not need to cook any more). Mix 5$^{1}/_{2}$ oz (150 g) butter with the two mustards.

4. Pour the kidney juices into the reduced sauce and bring fiercely to the boil; add the kidneys and keep the sauce hot, but without boiling. Take the saucepan off the heat and stir in the butter mixture, little by little. The sauce should become thick and creamy.

5. Serve as hot as possible. You can garnish this dish with browned small potatoes or cultivated mushrooms sautéed in butter. As regards the choice of mustards, although the hot mustard is necessarily white (such as Dijon mustard), the aromatic mustard can be grain mustard or flavored with tarragon or basil, or even purple Brive mustard, enriched with marc brandy.

Recommended drinks

Rully
Mâcon-Villages
Passe-Tout-Grain

Menu suggestions

1. For a family dinner, serve an appetizer of tomato and vermicelli soup, then a walnut gateau for dessert.

2. For a more sophisticated meal, try starting with scallop gratin and finishing off with a chocolate mousse.

Roast veal "en croûte"

A party dish

Serves 6
Preparation and first cooking phase: 45 minutes
Resting: 2 or 3 hours
Second cooking phase: 40 minutes

Ingredients

1 bunch parsley
1 small bunch fresh thyme
2 onions
1 tbsp breadcrumbs
2 eggs
3¹/₂ oz (100 g) butter
3 lb 5 oz (1.5 kg) loin or cushion of veal
12¹/₂ oz (350 g) puff-pastry dough
3 or 4 tomatoes
Salt and pepper

1. Break the leaves off the parsley and the thyme; slice the onions, then chop them finely with the herbs and mix in the breadcrumbs and 1 egg yolk. Blend in 1³/₄ oz (50 g) butter and season with salt and pepper. Cut a deep groove all the way down the meat and garnish it with the mixture. Loosely tie up the meat with string.

2. Heat 1 large dab of butter in a casserole large enough to comfortably hold the meat; watch the butter carefully to make sure that it does not turn brown. Put the meat in the casserole.

3. Gently brown the meat on all sides. Add salt and pepper, then lower the heat and simmer for about 30 minutes. Take the meat out of the casserole and put it in a dish. Leave to cool. Roll the puff-pastry dough into a rectangle on the worktop.

4. Allow the veal to cool completely, before wrapping it in a layer of dough. Brush the dough with 1 egg yolk thinned with a trickle of water, then put it in the refrigerator while you preheat the oven to 435 °F (225 °C). Bake the veal in the oven for 40 minutes.

5. Meanwhile, cut the tomatoes into two, then sauté them in a skillet with salt, pepper, and a little parsley. Transfer the meat to a warm dish, garnish it with the tomatoes, and decorate it with parsley and a few lettuce leaves.

Recommended drinks

Chablis
Meursault
Aloxe-Corton

Menu suggestions

1. For a sophisticated lunch, start with a seafood platter and finish off with a coffee Bavarois.

2. If you do not fancy shellfish, another option is a salmon terrine to start and a soufflé Grand Marnier for dessert.

Sauté of veal with leeks

A light dish

Serves 4
Preparation: 25 minutes
Cooking: 1 hour 15 minutes

Ingredients

2¼ lb (1 kg) small, very fresh leeks
1¾ lb (800 g) veal
1 tbsp olive oil
1½ oz (40 g) butter
1 glass very dry white wine
2 glasses milk1 bunch parsley
1 sprig thyme
2 lemons
Salt and pepper

1. Wash the leeks meticulously, cutting off some of the green part, and then cut the remainder into small strips. Cut the veal into pieces. Heat the oil and half the butter in a casserole, wait until it starts to smoke very slightly, and then brown the veal. Turn over the pieces of meat several times and season them with salt and pepper while they are cooking.

2. Take the meat out of the casserole and reduce the heat. Add the rest of the butter and sweat the leeks gently for 5 minutes, covered.

3. Pour the white wine into the casserole and deglaze by scraping its bottom with a wooden spoon; put the pieces of veal back in the casserole and add the milk, parsley, and thyme. Cover and continue cooking for 45 minutes, over low heat.

4. Around 20 minutes before serving, squeeze the juice of 1 lemon into the casserole and taste to adjust the seasoning. Just before serving, cut the second lemon into very thin slices, carefully removing the seeds, and add the slices to the casserole. Choose moist lemons with a thin skin (they must be heavy for their size). If you use a non-stick casserole, you can reduce the fat required to merely 1 tbsp oil.

Recommended drinks

Sparkling water
Tea with no milk
Grapefruit juice

Menu suggestions

1. Try a salad of grated carrots and chervil with hazelnut oil as an appetizer, then a fruit soup as dessert.

2. You can also serve a gazpacho to start and a dessert of natural yogurt with 1 tbsp of honey.

Saltimbocca with Parmesan

An international dish

Serves 4
Preparation: 30 minutes
Cooking: 1 hour

Ingredients

A few stalks of celery
  3 or 4 carrots
  1 or 2 onions
  2 cloves garlic
  4 very thin escalopes of veal,
  cut from the cushion,
  standing rump, or loin
  2 tbsp hot mustard
  4 thin slices of Parma ham
  3$\frac{1}{2}$ oz (100 g) smoked bacon

1 tbsp olive oil
1 large dab of butter
1 glass dry white wine
Salt and pepper

1. Trim the celery, wash it carefully, and then cut it into small dice. Blanch it for about 10 minutes in salted water, then drain, rinse in cold water, and drain once again. Peel the carrots and grate them into long strips. Peel the onion and chop them very finely. Peel the cloves of garlic and crush them with the blade of a knife.

2. Spread out the escalopes on paper towels and pat them dry before seasoning them on both sides with salt and pepper. Smear their upper face with the hot mustard and place 1 slice of ham on each escalope. Trim both the meats into a regular shape; these will be the basis of the saltimbocca, which will resemble small punnets.

3. Cut the bacon into small dice and sauté these in a skillet until they start to brown. Mix them with the vegetables and spread this mixture on the ham, in a layer no more than a fraction of an inch (few millimetres) thick. Put aside any remaining mixture. Roll up the escalopes and tie them loosely, leaving space for the filling to swell when it is cooked.

4. Heat some oil in the skillet and brown the escalopes. Remove them from the pan, discard the oil, and replace it with butter. Add the rest of the vegetable and bacon mixture, season with salt and pepper and then sauté over low heat. Add one or two squirts of white wine. Put the saltimbocca back in the skillet, then cover and cook gently for up to 1 hour, adding a dash of wine if required. Serve a leek gratin with Parmesan as an accompaniment.

Recommended drinks

Valpolicella
Barbera
Barbaresco

Menu suggestions

1. For an Italian dinner, accompany this dish with an appetizer of fresh ravioli stuffed with Ricotta and basil and a dessert of pear and chocolate tart.

2. For a more informal lunch, serve a green bean salad with olive oil and lemon to start and finish off with almond tarts.

Pepper steaks

A family dish

Serves 4
Preparation: 10–15 minutes
Cooking: 15 minutes

Ingredients

3/4–1 oz (50–60 g) peppercorns (black or white)
4 steaks about 6 oz (175 g), cut from the tenderloin or sirloin
8 potatoes
A little watercress
2 large dabs of butter
1 or 2 tbsp oil
1 glass cognac, Armagnac, or whisky
2 or 3 tbsp crème fraîche
Salt

1. Put the peppercorns in a mortar and grind them coarsely until they are reduced to small pieces the size of a pinhead. Spread the peppercorns out and place the steaks on top of them, first on one side and then on the other, pressing hard with the palm of your hand so that the pepper becomes incrusted.

2. While leaving the steaks to soak up the flavor of the pepper, boil the potatoes and wash and drain the watercress.
Heat equal amounts of butter and oil in a skillet then sear the steaks and sauté them for 2–4 minutes per side, depending on how rare you like your meat.

3. Put the steaks on a dish that has been heated in the oven or on top of a saucepan of boiling water. Deglaze the skillet with 1 small glass of cognac, Armagnac, or whisky. Scrape the bottom of the skillet thoroughly to release all the juices, heating all the while, then flambé the mixture. Add salt.

4. Add the crème fraîche, bring to the boil, and reduce the cream a little. Taste and adjust the salt. Pour the sauce onto plates then put 1 steak on each. Add the potatoes and watercress, then serve immediately.

It is vital not to add any salt to your steaks in advance, as this would draw out the blood and make it difficult to sear them. The best time to salt the meat is during the frying stage, just after you have turned the steak over. Sprinkle plenty of salt on the cooked side, and repeat the process on the other side once it is ready.

Recommended drinks

Saumur-Champigny
Bourgueil
Médoc

Menu suggestions

1. For a classic family lunch, start the meal with two half melons accompanied by Bayonne ham and end with a coffee mousse.

2. For a dinner, start with onion gratin and serve a dessert of Tarte Tatin accompanied by vanilla ice cream.

Plates of veal with red wine

A family dish

Serves 4
Preparation: 30 minutes
Cooking: 1 hour 30 minutes

Ingredients

1³/₄–2 lb (800–900 g) plates of veal
12 baby onions (fresh, if possible)
4 or 5 carrots
2 tbsp butter
1 level tbsp flour
1 bottle red Burgundy
2 sprigs thyme
1 bay leaf
4 sprigs parsley
Salt and pepper

1. Cut the plates of veal into large, uniform pieces, trimming the fat and the skin. Peel the onions and carrots, then cut them into thickish slices.

2. Put the pieces of plate in a deep-sided skillet, cover them with cold water, and bring to the boil over high heat. Remove the pieces of meat immediately, then drain and pat them completely dry with paper towels.

3. Heat the butter in a casserole and brown the pieces of veal gently for about 10minutes. Dust them with flour, sauté them briefly, and then pour on the entire bottle of red Burgundy.

4. Now add the carrots, onions, thyme, bay leaf, salt, and pepper. Cover and simmer over a very low heat for at least 1 hour 30 minutes. Just before serving, sprinkle on a little chopped parsley.

As a complementary side dish, you can prepare a pumpkin gratin while the meat is cooking. Plate of veal is a thick, fairly well larded piece of meat cut from the belly, with one part lean and the other fatty. It becomes especially so. when cooked. You can also cook this dish with the hindquarter flank, shoulder, or upper ribs.

Recommended drinks

Rully
Vosne-Romanée
Savigny-lès-Beaune

Menu suggestions

1. Serve an appetizer of eggs in red wine sauce and, after a cheese board, a dessert of fruit compote with honey biscuits.

2. More simply, begin the meal with headcheese and finish off with poached bush peaches and fromage blanc.

Sweet and sour veal

A regional dish

Serves 4
Preparation: 30 minutes
Cooking: 1 hour 30 minutes

Ingredients

2$^1/_4$ lb (1 kg) veal (cushion, under-cushion,
or standing rump) cut into pieces
1$^3/_4$ oz (50 g) butter
1 tbsp olive oil
3 or 4 onions
1 lb 2 oz (500 g) carrots
9 oz (250 g) prunes
1$^3/_4$ oz (50 g) raisins
1 generous cup (25 cl) light beer
2 or 3 tbsp honey
Salt and pepper

1. Cut the meat into regular, but not too small, pieces. Add salt and pepper.
Heat the butter in a cast-iron casserole,
adding a dash of oil to stop it burning. Add the pieces of veal in several
batches, so that they all have room to brown without any overlapping.

2. Sauté the pieces of meat, turning them several times to ensure that they
are thoroughly browned on all sides. Take the casserole off the heat. Peel the
onions and slice them very finely. Peel and slice the carrots.

3. Put the casserole back on the heat and heat its contents once again. Add
the onions and carrots, mixing them in with a wooden spoon. Add the prunes
and raisins, then pour on the beer. Add a moderate amount of salt and plenty
of pepper.

4. Cover the casserole and cook gently for 1 hour 30 minutes over gentle
heat. Check from time to time that there is sufficient liquid; the level should
be low, but without any risk of the meat sticking to the bottom. When it is
cooked, stir in the honey very thoroughly.

5. You should have no qualms about serving this dish straight from the
casserole, but another alternative is a hot serving dish. The seasoning should
have a marked presence of pepper. As regards the accompaniment, plain
boiled potatoes or fresh pasta are good options.

Recommended drinks

Bière du Nord
Chablis
Riesling

Menu suggestions

1. Serve a mussel salad to start and, after a
selection of northern French cheeses, a dessert of
apple and cinnamon tart.

2. Another idea: shrimp soup to begin and, as a
dessert (apart from the same cheese board),
apples baked in pastry.

241

Slices of cold tenderloin

General points

There is nothing simpler than using the leftovers of roast, sautéed, or boiled meat to create tasty dishes. There follow a few suggestions. One of the most obvious strategies is to use them to prepare a salad, sandwich, or cold meal, accompanied by mustard, mayonnaise, or tartare sauce.

Hachis Parmentier

To serve 4
2¼ lb (1 kg) potatoes
⅓ cup + 1½ tbsp (10 cl) milk
⅔ cup (15 cl) cream
6½ oz (180 g) butter
Grated nutmeg
1 lb 9 oz (700 g) leftovers from a pot-au-feu
2 onions
2 shallots
⅓ cup + 1½ tbsp (10 cl) fond de veau
3 tbsp chopped parsley
Grated cheese
Salt and pepper

Hachis Parmentier

1. Peel the potatoes and cut them into large pieces. Cook them in salted boiling water and then drain them. Put them through a potato masher and add to a saucepan. Boil the cream and add it to the potato, along with the milk and 4½ oz (120 g) butter; sprinkle on nutmeg, salt, and pepper, then mix all the ingredients with a wooden spoon to obtain a uniform purée.

2. Separate the leftovers of the pot-au-feu into slivers of meat. Melt some butter in a skillet and add the onions and shallots, finely chopped.

3. Sauté for a few minutes, then add the meat. Add salt, pepper, the fond de veau, and the parsley; cook slowly for 5 minutes, then put aside.

4. Butter a large baking dish and pour in half the purée. Spread it out in a uniform layer and add first the meat and then the rest of the purée.

5. Sprinkle on some grated cheese and dab with butter. Brown at 375 °F (190 °C) for about 30 minutes.

Veal-shank salad

Veal-shank salad

To serve 4
1¾ lb (800 g) potatoes
2 shallots
3½ oz (100 g) pickles
½ bunch chives
1 tbsp parsley
5 tbsp mustard
4 tbsp vinegar
10 tbsp oil
14 oz (400 g)
veal shank cut into cubes
Salt and pepper

1. Peel the potatoes and boil them in water; drain them and then leave them to cool.

2. Prepare the vinaigrette. Peel the shallots, then cut them into dice. Slice the pickles and chop the chives and parsley. Mix the mustard, vinegar, salt, and pepper in a bowl. Add the oil, then the pickles, shallot, and herbs.

3. Add the potatoes, cut into slices, and the cubes of cooked veal to the vinaigrette. Serve chilled.

Empanadas

Empanadas

To serve 4
1 lb 2 oz (500 g) flour
1 scant cup (20 cl) + 2 tbsp olive oil
2 eggs
3 fresh tomatoes
3 onions
3 cloves garlic
1 lb 5 oz (600 g) cold roast meat
4 pinches cumin
3 tbsp breadcrumbs
Flour
Salt and pepper

1. Make a well with the flour on the worktop and mix in 2 pinches of salt, 1 scant cup (20 cl) olive oil, and 1 egg, without kneading excessively. Leave the dough to rest for 1 hour.

2. Meanwhile, prepare the stuffing. Peel, seed, and cut the tomatoes into small dice. Chop the onions finely and cut up the cloves of garlic and the meat.

3. Brown the onions for 5 minutes in olive oil in a skillet, over medium heat, then add the meat, garlic, and tomatoes. Add salt, pepper, and cumin. Cook all these ingredients over low heat for 25 minutes.

4. Mix in the breadcrumbs, adjust seasoning to taste, then leave to cool.

5. Cut the dough into 16 equal parts. On a floured worktop, roll each of these into the form of a pancake. Spread each pancake with cold stuffing, then fold over half the dough to form a turnover.

6. Join the edges of the dough by pressing them firmly together. Baste the turnovers with 1 beaten egg, then cook them in an oven preheated to 375 °F (190 °C) for about 25 minutes.

Tip

In France, leftover meat was traditionally known as "desserte." In olden times, the remains of royal meals were collected by the butlers of the court, who were allowed to put them on the market and so sold them to caterers and restaurant owners.

Tongue salad

Tongue salad

To serve 4
1 very thick slice of tongue in jelly
2 bunches radish
4 hard-boiled eggs
Pickles and small onions in vinegar
Oil
Vinegar
Salt and pepper

1. Cut all the jelly off the tongue, then cut it into slices and small dice. Wash the radish, then wipe and slice them. Shell the hard-boiled eggs. Cut them into two or four.

2. Take a few attractive radish leaves and arrange them in the form of a crown at one end of a dish. Put the radish slices on this dish, partially overlapping the leaves; at the other end, lay out the sliced and diced tongue, then set the hard-boiled eggs in the middle.

3. Garnish with a few of the pickles and small onions. Accompany this salad with vinaigrette, along with side dishes of pickles and small onions that everybody can take according to their fancy.

Lamb and mutton

General points

A mixed grill is particularly popular in English-speaking countries, but its appeal is now almost worldwide. It consists of meat and vegetables grilled over charcoal or on a griddle pan or grilling stone, accompanied by strong sauces. There should be a wide-ranging selection of meat: a mixed grill worthy of its name includes lamb cutlets, pork chops or spare ribs, chipolatas or flat sausages, lamb's kidneys, and slices of lean bacon. In addition, it is not unusual to find offal or marinated kebabs.

Complementary vegetables must also be included: peppers, mushrooms, tomatoes, and onions are grilled and then added to kebabs or served in slices. The secret of a successful mixed grill lies in timing the cooking phases correctly, as the ingredients must be seared quickly. Along with the cooked vegetables, you can also serve a green salad and white rice, simply dressed with 1 or 2 tbsp of virgin olive oil. To accompany the meat, there is nothing better than the American barbecue sauce sold commercially, but you can also

Lamb kebabs with cumin and paprika

prepare your own sauce with mashed, peeled tomatoes, simmered in olive oil with 1 chopped shallot and 1 sliced sweet onion, set off by thyme, oregano, and basil.

Mixed grill

Barbecue sauce

Mixed grill

Mixed grill for 6

1 Ask your butcher to cut you 6 rib chops and bone 1 lb 2 oz (500 g) shoulder of lamb. Trim 6 small kidneys and remove any fat. Discard the fat from the shoulder as well, and cut its meat into cubes the size of a large walnut. Place this meat in a bowl and add 5 tbsp of olive oil, a few pinches of thyme and rosemary, and 1 chopped onion, then season with salt and pepper. Marinate for 1–2 hours.

Tip

A mixed grill represents above all a concept for the presentation of grilled meat and vegetables, so it can easily be varied: for example, you could prepare a mixture of meats (pork, beef, and veal) or poultry (chicken, duck, turkey, and guinea-fowl). In all cases, be aware that the result will be more enticing if you take the trouble to marinate the meat beforehand.

2 Stick the pieces of meat onto skewers. Remove the skin from a 10-oz (300-g) piece of lean bacon with a big knife, then cut it into slices $3/16$ in (5 mm) thick. Stab 6 sausages with a fork so that they do not burst when cooked. Prepare the vegetables. Cut 3 tomatoes into equal halves.

3 Peel 4 onions and also cut them into halves. Cut the ends off 2 eggplants and then slice them lengthwise into strips $3/16$ in (5 mm) thick. Remove the stalks from 12 oz (350 g) of large cultivated mushrooms, then peel and wash their heads. Meanwhile, light the barbecue and prepare a bed of glowing red embers (do not make it too deep).

4 Season all the vegetables and put them on one half of the grill. Turn them all over—apart from the tomatoes—after about 10 minutes. Season the various pieces of meat with salt and pepper, then lay them on the grill. Cook them for 5 minutes on each side. Leave the sausages on the grill for longer, as they need a little more time.

247

Pie with sage flowers

Ground-meat pie

Pézenas pastries

Any description of pies and pastry dishes based on lamb should also mention the pastries from Pézenas, typical of the French Languedoc region, but also found in Béziers. They contain a mixture of ground lamb and kidney fat, set off by brown sugar and lemon zest, in a small, round pastry. These are served hot, either as an appetizer or as a dessert.

General points

In the United Kingdom, lamb is also cooked under mashed potato, where it acquires an exquisite flavor during the cooking process and is known as "shepherd's pie." The principle of a meat pie is always the same: the meat is first cooked in an aromatic bouillon, flavored with vegetables and herbs, then placed in a mold sealed by piecrust pastry (or mashed potato) and, finally, baked in the oven. Whatever pie recipe you use with lamb, always make sure to choose meat from the shoulder. Resist any temptation to replace the lamb with mutton, as the end result will have a far stronger taste. Shepherd's pie was originally conceived as an appetizing way of using up leftovers; when made with ground beef, it goes under the name of cottage pie. It can often be seen in the food section in pubs. Pies go back a long way, to the Elizabethan era, when they were made with sugar and spice.

Pézenas pastries

1 Prepare the dough for the piecrust. Mix 9 oz (250 g) flour with 2 pinches of salt in a terrine, then add 7 oz (200 g) butter and 1 whole egg; knead for 2–3 minutes to obtain a uniform mixture. Leave the dough to rest for 30 minutes in a cool place, covered with a dishtowel. Peel and slice 1¹/₂ lb (800 g) onions; wash and finely chop 2 bunches of parsley. Bone and trim 2¹/₂ lb (1 kg) shoulder of lamb.

2 Cut this meat into cubes the size of a large walnut. Heat a little oil in a deep-sided skillet. Add salt and pepper, then brown the meat for 15 minutes. Add 1 chopped onion and cook for a further 5 minutes. Pour on 3 scant cups (60 cl) water or bouillon and boil, covered, for about 25 minutes. Drain the cooked meat and let it rest in a dish.

3 Thicken the gravy by vigorously beating in a paste made from ¹/₃ cup (40 g) flour mixed with 5 Tbsp (70 g) butter. Boil slowly and skim off any fat with a spoon. Adjust the seasoning and remove from the heat. Place a layer of the lamb pieces in a pie dish, followed by a layer of onions, and one of chopped flat parsley.

4 Continue alternating the ingredients in this way until the top level is 3/8 in (1 cm) from the edge of the dish. Pour in the thick gravy until it reaches the same height. Roll the dough and put it on top of the pie filling, sticking it to the outer edges of the dish. Make a hole ³/₈ in (1 cm) in diameter in the middle of the dough and insert a chimney so that the steam can escape.

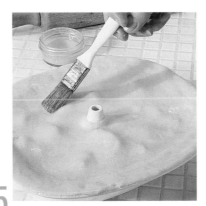

5 Brush the dough with 1 egg yolk. Cook the pie in an oven preheated to 375 °F (190 °C) for 40 minutes, then serve it piping hot with crème fraîche and plain white rice. In one variation on this recipe, a layer of mashed potatoes is placed between the meat and the lid of pastry, which should be golden-brown.

General points

Poaching in a vegetable broth with spices is a particularly good way to preserve the delicate flavor of lamb. The meat cooks slowly, without browning, and is in no danger of being dried out by the heat, as is sometimes the case when it is cooked in the oven. The poaching time depends on the piece of meat; the more gelatinous the meat, the longer the cooking time. The best cut for poaching is the leg, with tender, lean meat that lends itself admirably to this method of preparation. It is important for the success of this dish to keep the broth at simmering point when the meat is plunged into it and to ensure it never reaches boiling point. The cooking broth should contain a variety of vegetables, which are served with the meat.

Cumberland sauce

Mint sauce

Accompanying sauces

White sauce with capers

Bring 1 2/3 cups (40 cl) bouillon to the boil and skim off the fat. Mix together 1/4 cup (35 g) flour and 5 Tbsp (70 g) butter in a small bowl. Add this mixture to the bouillon, beating vigorously. The sauce should have the consistency of custard. Then add 1/3 cup + 11/2 tbsp (10 cl) crème fraîche mixed with 1 egg yolk. Mix well and finish the sauce with 2 3/4 oz (80 g) capers and 1/2 bunch parsley, finely chopped. Season with salt and pepper and add the juice of 1 lemon. Heat to simmering point and serve in a sauceboat.

Mint sauce

Wash 1 bunch mint and remove the leaves. Chop the leaves finely and set aside. Heat 1/2 cup + 11/2 tbsp (10 cl) of the broth in which the leg of lamb was cooked, 1/3 cup + 11/2 tbsp (10 cl) wine vinegar, 2 tbsp brown sugar and a pinch of salt in a saucepan. Bring this mixture to the boil and pour it over the mint. Cover and leave to infuse for 30 minutes. Reheat this sauce gently and pour into a sauceboat.

Cumberland sauce

Peel 2 shallots and chop finely. Place in a saucepan with the juice of 2 oranges and 1 lemon and 5 tbsp gooseberry jelly and bring to the boil over a very low heat. Then add 2/3 cup (15 cl) port, the grated zest of 1 lemon, 1 tsp hot mustard, 1 pinch Cayenne pepper, and 1 tsp chopped fresh ginger. Cook for 2 minutes, then add 1 oz (30 g) unsalted butter, stirring constantly. Leave to cool and serve at room temperature.

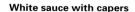

White sauce with capers

poached lamb

1 Ask your butcher to prepare a leg of lamb and remove the saddle bone. If necessary, remove the fat. This recipe, which is typical of Normandy—and Britain—truly comes into its own if you choose salt-marsh lamb, reared and fattened up in the grasslands near the coast, impregnated with the salt and iodine that give the meat its characteristic flavor. Above all, do not flavor the meat with garlic—this would be heresy.

Tip

To give your guests a pleasant surprise, do not be afraid to serve the poached leg of lamb with three different sauces. Reserve the cooking broth; you can serve it as a soup with vermicelli.

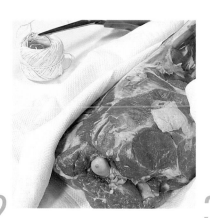

2 Spread out a large white dishtowel on the worktop and place the leg of lamb on it. Wrap it up by winding string around it three or four times. Peel 1 lb 2 oz (500 g) carrots, 4 leeks, and 4 turnips. Peel 2 onions. Place all the ingredients in a stewpot with 4 stalks parsley and 1 sprig thyme. Cover with 4 quarts (4 liters) cold water.

3 Bring to the boil and cook over low heat for 1 hour. Then add $2^{1}/_{4}$ lb (1 kg) potatoes and continue cooking for a further 40 minutes. Drain and set aside the cooked potatoes in a warm place. Poach the leg of lamb in the simmering broth for 30 to 40 minutes. Remove the meat, cut the string, and transfer to the worktop.

4 Cut the leg of lamb into slices and arrange on a serving platter. Strain the cooked vegetables and arrange around the slices of meat. Serve the potatoes separately. Poached leg of lamb cools down very quickly, so serve immediately with capers, gherkins, and an accompanying sauce, chosen from the selection suggested on the page opposite.

General points

Shoulder of lamb is at its most tender when it is braised. Browned on all sides first, then covered and cooked slowly in its own juices, its flavor has universal appeal. You can prepare it just as it is, simply seasoned with salt, pepper, and spices, or better still stuff it with a mixture of meat and vegetables flavored with garlic. Do not be afraid to vary the ingredients of the stuffing. Although mixtures of herbs, spices, and mushrooms are traditional, stuffings based on dried fruit and semolina are equally successful. Consider using offal meat (livers or kidneys), too. Avoid cooking stuffed shoulder of lamb for too long; after a certain stage, it becomes dry and stringy and loses its flavor. If you like braised meat dishes that are well cooked, prepare this recipe in exactly the same way, but replace the shoulder of lamb with neck of lamb, which tolerates, or indeed demands, much longer cooking times of between 2 and 3 hours. You can enrich the braising juices by adding black and green olives, dried figs, or even sweet bell peppers halfway through the cooking time. You can also finish this sauce with fresh chopped chives or basil.

1 Ask your butcher to prepare a shoulder of lamb, then bone it completely. Trim the meat, removing any remnants of skin and connective tissue. Prepare all the ingredients required for the recipe—the minced or chopped stuffing ingredients, the weighed breadcrumbs, the broken egg, and a little white wine to moisten the stuffing if it is too dry.

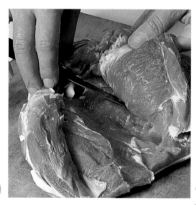

2 Remove the fat from the meat using a small knife, taking great care not to pierce the flesh so that the stuffing does not escape during cooking. Follow the instructions on page 39 carefully to bone the shoulder of lamb properly. If you are worried about this, you can ask your butcher to do it for you.

3 Prepare the stuffing. Assemble the following finely chopped ingredients in a large bowl: 1 onion, 2 cloves garlic, 4 white button mushrooms, 14 oz (400 g lamb), 1 bunch chives and 1 bunch parsley. Add 2 tbsp breadcrumbs and 1 egg. Mix thoroughly using a wooden spoon. The stuffing is now ready; it should be used immediately.

Stuffed and braised shoulder of lamb

4 Open out the boned shoulder of lamb and flatten it, then season with salt and pepper. Spread the herb stuffing on the seasoned shoulder in an even layer of uniform thickness. The stuffing should have a homogeneous, malleable consistency, neither too dense nor too soft. Before using it, cook a spoonful in a skillet and taste to see whether you need to adjust the seasoning.

5 Then roll the shoulder, folding the edges towards the middle and supporting it with one hand. Tie a piece of string around one of the ends of the shoulder and wind the string around the roll at intervals of 1¹/₂ in (4 cm) in order to keep the shoulder in as regular a cylindrical shape as possible. Do not pull the string too tight or the stuffing might escape. Secure the string with a knot.

6 Heat 8 tbsp of peanut oil in a stewpot. Season the stuffed shoulder of lamb with salt and pepper and brown it on all sides for 25 minutes. Add 3 diced onions and continue cooking. Pour in ¹/₃ cup + 1¹/₂ tbsp (10 cl) white wine and bring to the boil for 2 minutes, then add 1¹/₄ cups (30 cl) chicken bouillon, 1 sliced tomato, and 1 clove of garlic.

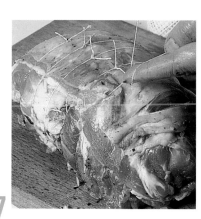

7 Lower the heat, cover, and simmer slowly for about 1 hour 30 minutes, turning occasionally and skimming the fat off the cooking liquid with a ladle. Transfer the lamb to a dish and leave to cool for 10 minutes. Keep the cooking liquid hot. Slice the shoulder of lamb with a well-sharpened knife and spoon some of the cooking juices over the slices.

General points

The recipes for stewed lamb are delicious and very varied. They are found in every region of France and in every country, as is demonstrated by navarin of lamb, Irish stew, and tagine dishes. The principle of these recipes is always the same: the meat is boned and cut into pieces of whatever size, which are then sealed over high heat and browned on all sides. They

Mutton stew

Stew d'ouessant

then continue cooking in a sauce, generally tomato, sometimes thickened with flour. For all these recipes, choose meat that has a fairly long cooking time (neck with the bones, or breast). If necessary, shoulder can also be used. The most original recipes for lamb or mutton stew include carbonade of breast of mutton with raw ham, which originates from Gascony; a hot pot from the Berry region (pot-au-feu berrichon), which

combines beef, knuckle of veal, and shoulder of mutton with vegetables of all kinds; Lancashire hot pot, a typically English mixture of neck of lamb cooked with onions, potatoes, and a few oysters; Georgian chanakhi, which combines pieces of boned lamb simmered with tomatoes, potatoes, green beans, and eggplant; and Turkish kapama, in which pieces of lamb are cooked in a casserole, layered with salad leaves and spring onions, and sprinkled with lemon juice.

Mutton stew "à la croix haute"

Tip

Spices play an important role in the cuisine of the Middle East. Coriander seeds are often used, as is fresh cilantro, cumin, and also ras al-hanout, a mixture of several spices that is absolutely essential for couscous, but is equally good with tagine dishes.

Stewed Lamb

1 This typically Irish recipe is usually cooked with mutton, but lamb, with its more delicate flavor, is perfectly suitable. Trim and remove the fat from 3³/₄ lb (1.7 kg) cubed breast and neck of lamb on the bone. Pour 2 tbsp oil into a skillet and skillet and place this over high heat. Brown the meat on all sides for 10–15 minutes.

2 Set aside the meat in a large bowl. Peel and chop 1 lb 2 oz (500 g) onions. Peel 2¹/₄ lb (1 kg) potatoes and cut into slices ¹/₁₆–¹/₈ in (3–4 mm) thick. Layer three-quarters of the onions, half the potatoes, the browned meat, and the remaining potatoes in a fairly large casserole.Season each layer well with salt and pepper.

3 Pour 2 generous cups (55 cl) meat bouillon over the ingredients, sprinkle with ¹/₂ bunch chopped parsley and two stems of snipped tarragon, and bring to the boil. Adjust the heat so the stew is boiling very gently, cover with a tight-fitting lid, and simmer for about 2 hours. Serve very hot from the casserole. This stew was originally prepared with young goat. It is usually served with pickled red cabbage.

Tagine of lamb with artichokes for 6

1 Cut 3 lb 5 oz (1.5 kg) boned shoulder of lamb into pieces, then peel and chop 3 onions. Heat 2 tbsp olive oil in a casserole and add the pieces of lamb, seasoned with salt, cumin, and pepper, together with the onions. Cook for about 15 minutes until golden brown. Peel 4 potatoes and cut into pieces. Wash and slice 4 tomatoes.

2 Put the tomatoes, potatoes, and browned meat in a casserole. Add 7 oz (200 g) shelled fava beans, 4 halved artichoke hearts, 1 scant cup (20 cl) water, and 1 tsp coriander seeds. Cook in the oven at 350 °F (180 °C) for a good hour. Take the casserole out of the oven, transfer the contents to an earthenware tagine dish and finish cooking in the oven (20 minutes).

3 Just before serving, sprinkle the top with ¹/₂ bunch fresh cilantro, chopped. Serve the lamb tagine semolina. If you wish, you can add dried fruit to this recipe. It is important to brown the meat well it to retain its full flavor. If using neck of lamb, add about 30 minutes to the cooking time.

Lamb with fennel

Lamb with prunes

Lamb à la grecque

General points

Contrary to what the name suggests, haricot of mutton does not necessarily contain haricot (navy) beans. The name of this very old recipe actually comes from the old French word "halicoter," which meant to "cut into small pieces." Note that this dish was already widespread before navy beans were known in Europe. The famous 14th-century French cook Taillevent himself gives a recipe for haricot of mutton, indicating that the meat should be cut into small pieces and cooked with onions, verjuice (acid juice extracted from large, unripened grapes), and beef bouillon. Today, haricot of mutton is a meat dish in a sauce seasoned more or less strongly according to taste and accompanied by potatoes and turnips. Like all sauté dishes and dished cooked in sauce, haricot of mutton is highly nutritious and is generally served in winter. If you do not like the rather strong flavor of

mutton, you can substitute lamb, in which case the cooking time will of course be shorter. Haricot of mutton is a magnificent main course and should be served after a fairly light appetizer, for example a soup or a plate of crudités; follow it with a selection of

cheeses and a dessert based on fruit or alternatively a sorbet. Choose a really full-bodied red wine such as a Cahors or a Bergerac. According to experts studying the history of cuisine, this is a traditional dish from the Orléans region.

Haricot of mutton

1 Ask your butcher to cut 3 lb 5 oz (1.5 kg) breast or neck of mutton into small pieces. Season with salt and pepper. You can marinate the meat for several hours with a little white wine, 1 bay leaf, some fresh thyme, and some crushed black peppercorns. You can prepare this stew in large quantities; like all dishes cooked in sauce, it can be frozen.

Tip

If you have a large casserole, you can cook the meat and vegetables together. Follow the recipe as indicated, but add the potatoes and turnips halfway through the cooking time. You can also add chopped fresh parsley to this dish.

2 Heat a little oil in a casserole, then brown the meat on both sides for about 15 minutes. Drain the pieces of meat and set aside in a large bowl. Finely chop 4 onions and arrange in a layer in the bottom of the casserole, followed by the browned meat; then add 3 chopped carrots and 1 bouquet garni.

3 Add enough beef bouillon, from which the fat has been skimmed, to cover the ingredients. Season with salt and pepper. Set the casserole over moderate heat, bring to the boil, and cook over gentle heat for about 1 hour 30 minutes. Peel 1 lb 2 oz (500 g) potatoes and boil until cooked. Peel 1 lb 2 oz (500 g) turnips, cut into four, and cook in salted water with a little butter and sugar.

4 Keep hot. Remove the cooked meat from the casserole and transfer to a serving dish. Bring the cooking liquid to the boil and skim off the fat with a small ladle. Reduce for several minutes, then adjust the seasoning. Drain the potatoes and turnips and transfer to the serving dish with the meat. Spoon over the cooking juices.

General points

Lamb and mutton offal meat provide some of the greatest gastronomic delights. Usually, red offal meat (heart, liver, kidneys) is cooked in a skillet and seasoned with parsley, or grilled on skewers on the barbecue. White offal meat (trotters, tripe, tongue, sweetbread) needs longer cooking times and acquires a delicious flavor when simmered slowly.

Tripe Rouergue style

This recipe for tripe, variations of which are found all over the Auvergne, uses the sheep's stomach, which is shaped and tied up into small parcels stuffed with a filling of diced bacon or meat. To serve 6, ask your butcher to clean a single 3 lb 5 oz (1.5 kg) piece of sheep's stomach. Cut this into triangles (with sides measuring approximately 3 in/8 cm). Prepare the stuffing. Chop the off cuts of tripe and mix with 1 onion, 2 cloves of garlic, 10 1/2 oz (300 g) lamb, 1 bunch chives, and 1 bunch parsley, all finely chopped. Then add 2 tbsp breadcrumbs and 1 egg. Season with salt and pepper and mix well using a wooden spoon. Place spoonfuls of stuffing in the middle of the triangles of tripe and then roll up to enclose the stuffing completely, securing the parcels with string or wooden cocktail sticks. In a casserole, brown 2 onions and 1 finely chopped carrot with 3 1/2 oz (100 g) unsmoked fat bacon, cut into strips, then add the tripe and 1 1/4 cups (30 cl) white wine. Boil for 10 minutes, then add 1 tbsp tomato paste, 1 sliced fresh tomato, 1 and 2 1/2 cups (60 cl) skimmed chicken bouillon.

Bring to the boil, then reduce the heat, cover, and cook for 4 to 5 hours, stirring occasionally so that the tripe does not stick to the pan. Remove the tripe parcels from the casserole, discard the bouquet garni , bring the cooking liquid to the boil and carefully remove the fat. Reduce this stock for about 30 minutes, then adjust the seasoning with salt and pepper. Return the tripe parcels to the cooking liquid to reheat them thoroughly. Serve piping hot with steamed potatoes.

Trotters and tripe "à la marseillaise"

This recipe, which combines sheep's trotters with tripe, was created in the suburbs of Marseilles. To serve 6, ask your butcher to clean a 2 1/4 lb (1 kg) piece of sheep's stomach and 6 sheep's trotters. Cut the tripe into triangles (with sides measuring approximately 3 in/8 cm). Plunge the trotters into cold water and blanch them. Set aside. Prepare the stuffing. Chop the off cuts of tripe and mix with 1 onion, 2 cloves of garlic, 10 1/2 oz (300 g) diced bacon, 5 1/2 oz (150 g) sausage meat and 1 bunch parsley, all finely chopped.
Add 1 tbsp breadcrumbs and 1 egg. Season with salt and pepper and mix thoroughly with a wooden spoon. Place spoonfuls of stuffing in the middle of the triangles of tripe and then roll up to enclose the stuffing completely, securing

Tripe

Offal specialties

so that the tripe and trotters do not stick to the pan. Remove the offal meat from the casserole, discard the bouquet garni, bring the cooking liquid to the boil, and carefully remove the fat. Reduce this broth for about 30 minutes, then adjust the seasoning with salt and pepper. Return the offal meat to the cooking liquid to reheat it thoroughly. Serve piping hot with steamed potatoes or pasta with butter.

Trotters and tripe "à la marseillaise"

the parcels with string or wooden cocktail sticks. In a casserole, brown 2 onions, 1 carrot, and 1 leek, all finely chopped, with 3^1/$_2$ oz (100 g) bacon lardoons. Then add the tripe, the blanched trotters, and 1^1/$_4$ cups (30 cl) white wine. Boil for 10 minutes, then add 1 tbsp concentrated tomato purée, 4 sliced fresh tomatoes, 1 bouquet garni, and 2^1/$_2$ cups (60 cl) skimmed bouillon, 1 large sprig of thyme, 1 sprig of rosemary, and 4 sage leaves. Bring to the boil, then reduce the heat, cover, and cook for 4 to 5 hours, stirring occasionally

Nest of lamb's kidneys

General points

Traditionally, "navarin" is the term for a mutton stew, usually featuring shoulder, neck, or breast of lamb. The meat is browned in oil, then simmered in a tomato sauce with vegetables, in particular turnips ("navet" in French, hence the name). When spring vegetables are used (small onions, new potatoes, carrots, and turnips) the dish is called spring navarin ("navarin printanier"). In addition to lamb, the name "navarin" has been applied by extension to poultry and even fish and crustaceans. Spring is

the best season for cooking navarin, because that is when the best new vegetables are available. You can of course add asparagus tips, artichoke hearts, peas, or fava beans; they will only serve to make the recipe more appetizing and colorful. The secret of success with this recipe is to take great care to observe the cooking times—long for the meat and the sauce, short for the vegetables.

A good menu

Although it is certainly a nutritious meal in itself, this

Lamb with fresh figs

dish is fairly light, especially if you have carefully skimmed the fat from the broth. Serve with a chilled, light red wine, for instance a Chinon or Bourgueil. As an appetizer, serve a seasonal dish such as tomatoes marinated with basil or even a well-chilled Andalusian gazpacho. For dessert, choose a recipe worthy of your navarin— a frozen raspberry mousse, an assortment of sorbets, or, better still, a vacherin (a dessert made with meringue and cream or ice cream).

Braised lamb Angoulême style

N.B.
The success of your navarin will depend on the quality both of the meat and the vegetables. Choose the best available ingredients and do not hesitate to discard a vegetable you do not think is fresh enough or a piece of meat that does not look as good, or you will have to adapt your cooking time.

Navarin of lamb

Spring navarin of lamb for 6

1 Cut 3 lb 5 oz (1.5 kg) boned shoulder of lamb, trimmed and with the fat removed, into cubes the size of a large walnut. Season with salt and pepper and brown, a few pieces at a time, in a casserole for about 10 minutes. When they are all brown, transfer them all to the casserole and add 1 heaped tbsp flour, then cook over a moderate heat for 5 minutes, stirring constantly.

2 Next, add 1 scant cup (20 cl) dry white wine and cook for a further 5 minutes. Then incorporate 4 ripe tomatoes, seeded and cut into cubes, 3 crushed cloves of garlic, 1 bouquet garni, and 1 ^{2}/$_3$ cups (40 cl) bouillon from which the fat has been skimmed. Bring to the boil, skim again, cover, and cook over a low heat for about 45 minutes. When the meat is cooked, remove from the broth and set aside. Skim the fat off the broth.

3 Return the meat to the broth and set aside in the casserole, off the heat. Meanwhile, peel 3 ^{1}/$_2$ oz (100 g) small onions, 7 oz (200 g) baby carrots and 7 oz (200 g) baby turnips. Cook these vegetables in boiling water until they are just done, but retain a slightly crunchy texture. Shell 7 oz (200 g) peas and blanch them. If the broth is too liquid, thicken with 1^3/$_4$ oz (50 g) creamed butter.

4 Scrape 10^1/$_2$ oz (300 g) new potatoes and boil or steam them. Peel and cook 15 stalks of asparagus, then remove the tips. Add all the cooked vegetables, carefully drained, directly to the broth containing the meat together with ^{1}/$_2$ bunch chopped chives. Set over high heat and boil for exactly 2 minutes. Serve immediately.

261

General points

Potatoes with a floury consistency on the inside are the accompaniment of choice for roast lamb. During cooking, they absorb the juices, and their moisture prevents the meat drying out. Choose either small potatoes and leave them whole after scraping them, or large, firm, white ones, which should be peeled and cut into fairly thin slices. When in season, you could also choose varieties with yellow flesh.

Tip

For this recipe, choose loin chops finely marbled with fat, as they will remain succulent in spite of the long cooking time.

Leg of lamb boulangère

Like leg of lamb with flageolet beans, this recipe is one of the great classic ways to prepare leg of lamb. You can also use shoulder or saddle of lamb.

Lamb chops Champvallon

This delicious recipe involves cooking lamb loin chops in the oven with sliced potatoes and onions. It dates back to the time of Louis XIV and is said to have been named after one of his mistresses, who cooked it to indulge his gluttony.

Lamb chops Champvallon

Lamb chops Champvallon for 6

1 Ask your butcher to prepare 12 lamb loin chops, finely marbled with fat. Heat 2 tbsp peanut oil over high heat in a skillet and brown the chops on both sides after seasoning them with salt and pepper. Then arrange them in a circle in a large earthenware casserole, facing outwards. Set aside.

2 Melt 3½ oz (100 g) butter in a saucepan and add ⅜ cup (50 g) flour. Cook for 5 minutes, stirring constantly, then add 4 cups (1 liter) boiling bouillon from which the fat has been skimmed. Beat and leave to cook slowly for 5 minutes. Set aside. Peel 5 white onions. Peel, wash, drain, and slice 2¼ lb (1 kg) potatoes.

3 Spread the chopped onions over the browned chops, then add the potatoes and 1 bouquet garni and pour in the thickened bouillon. Place the casserole in a pre-heated oven at 375 °F (190 °C) for 1 hour 15 minutes. At the end of the cooking time, brown the top of the potatoes, placing the dish in a hot broiler for 2 to 3 minutes. Serve immediately in the casserole.

Lamb and potatoes

Leg of lamb boulangère for 8

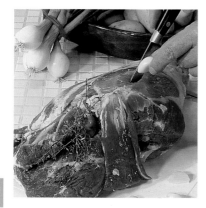

1 Ask your butcher to prepare a leg of lamb weighing about 6³/₄ lb (3 kg). Remove the bone from the saddle. You can also bone the leg completely, which will enable you to carve the cooked meat more easily. Peel 6 cloves of garlic, cut them in half, and remove the green shoot. Make 6 incisions in the leg of lamb and insert the half cloves of garlic. Peel 3 lb 5 oz (1.5 kg) potatoes.

2 Cut the potatoes into slices ¹/₁₆–¹/₈ in (3–4 mm) thick and wash under plenty of running water. Drain and set aside. Peel and finely chop 5 white onions and place in a large bowl with the potatoes, some salt and pepper, 4 Tbsp (60 g) melted butter, and 1 sprig of thyme. Mix all the ingredients thoroughly and then spread the potatoes and onions in a roasting pan or in the bottom of a large, deep, baking dish.

3 Place the leg of lamb on the bed of potatoes and onions. Heat the oven to 410 °F (210 °C), then roast for 30–35 minutes. Take out the leg of lamb and wrap it a large piece of aluminum foil, then keep it hot before carving. As this is a large joint of meat, it will need to rest for 10 minutes for the juices to permeate the muscles.

4 Pour 1 generous cup (25 cl) hot bouillon from which the fat has been skimmed over the potatoes and cook for a further 10 minutes. Arrange the cooked potatoes on a large serving platter with slices of lamb on top. Season with salt and pepper and serve very hot. The sliced lamb is also very good eaten cold the next day with a salad flavored with garlic.

General points

The delicate meat of lamb lends itself admirably to the spiced subtleties of Indian cuisine. The cuts most often used are boned shoulder of lamb or breast. To cook these recipes successfully, buy good quality spices. Choose them in an Asian food store, where you will find a good choice of cumin, coriander, and curry powder, offering a wide range of colors and flavors.

Lamb tandoori

One of the typical accessories of Indian cuisine is the tandoor, a conical terracotta stove that is placed directly in the hearth and in which the food cooks in the moisture it contains, without the addition of fat. In the West, you can substitute a simple casserole. The tandoor has given its name to a specialty in which pieces of chicken or lamb are marinated in a yogurt-based sauce with red-colored spices and then broiled—the famous tandoori, or tandouri.

Lamb curry

Lamb curry (the word is also written "cari") is one of the seminal recipes of Indian cuisine. It is more or less highly spiced, depending on the mixture of spices used, which give the recipe its name. Serve with basmati rice and chapatis, which are thin pancakes made of brown flour, cooked in a skillet and served very hot. Do not forget, either, to offer mango chutney in small dishes. If the curry is very highly spiced, slices of banana and pineapple cubes are served at the same time. Other traditional curry flavorings include raisins, blanched almonds, grated coconut, and tomato paste flavored with pimentos. In the absence of coconut milk, the preferred choice of drink to accompany curry is hot tea, without sugar.

Lamb tandoori for 6

1 Ask your butcher to bone a 3 lb 5 oz (1.5 kg) shoulder of lamb and remove the fat using a small knife. Cut into approximately 1 in (3 cm) cubes and place in a large earthenware pot. Mix together some salt, 1 tsp powdered cumin, and the juice of 1 lemon. Pour this mixture over the cubes of meat, stir, and set aside.

2 In a large bowl, combine 1 2/3 cups (40 cl) natural yogurt, 1 tbsp chopped fresh ginger, 1 tbsp chopped fresh cilantro, 1 tsp turmeric, 1 tsp powdered paprika, 3 chopped cloves of garlic, and 1 pinch Cayenne pepper. Mix and add the pieces of lamb. Leave to marinade in the refrigerator for at least 4 hours, but preferably overnight.

3 Pre-heat your oven to 410 °F (210 °C). Place the marinated pieces of meat on a rack, season with salt and pepper, drizzle with a little melted butter, and cook for 20 to 25 minutes. Remove the meat from the oven and arrange on lettuce leaves with slices of lemon and tomato. Serve with a cucumber salad with yogurt and basmati rice with raisins.

Lamb and Indian cooking

1 Ask your butcher to bone a 3 lb 5 oz (1.5 kg) shoulder of lamb and remove the fat using a small knife. Cut into approximately 1 in (3 cm) cubes. Season with salt and pepper and brown in a casserole with a little oil for 10 minutes. Remove the pieces of meat with a skimming ladle and transfer to a sieve; allow the juices to drain off for 5 minutes.

2 Peel and chop 3 onions and place in a saucepan over a moderate heat after draining off nearly all the oil in which the meat was cooked. Braise for about 8 minutes, stirring constantly. If you are using spring onions in bunches, take some of the crunchy green shoots and chop finely to mix with the spices.

3 Add 1 tbsp flour and 2 heaped tbsp curry powder. Continue cooking over moderate heat. Meanwhile, plunge 4 tomatoes into boiling water and leave to cool. Skin the tomatoes and seed. Then cut into cubes. Peel and chop 3 cloves of garlic, then transfer all these ingredients to a saucepan with a chopped piece of ginger and 1 scant cup (20 cl) water.

4 Leave to cook for a few minutes, then add the browned meat, 1 mashed banana, and 1 apple, peeled and cut into very thin slices. Mix well, cover, and leave to cook very slowly, shaking the pan from time to time, for 1 hour 15 minutes. Skim the fat off the sauce, adjust seasoning to taste, and add the juice of $1/2$ lemon. Serve very hot.

Sauté of lamb with fava beans and tomatoes for 6

1 Peel and finely chop 3 onions and 4 cloves of garlic. Choose 4 large, well-ripened tomatoes, plunge them into boiling water and leave to cool in order to remove the skins, then seed and crush them. Shell 10 1/2 oz (300 g) fava beans. Bring some salted water to the boil, add the fava beans and cook for 2 minutes, then remove them from the water and cool immediately. Remove the coarse outer skins, leaving only the bright green beans inside.

2 Heat a little sunflower oil in a large casserole over high heat. Brown in turn 1 lb 2 oz (500 g) neck of lamb, 1 lb 2 oz (500 g) breast of lamb, and 1 lb 5 oz (600 g) boned shoulder of lamb. Place the meat in a dish and set aside. In the same casserole, brown the chopped onions and garlic over moderate heat for 5 minutes. Add 1 tbsp flour and continue cooking for 3 minutes, stirring.

3 Add 2/3 cup (15 cl) white wine, previously heated in a saucepan. Continue cooking for 2 minutes, then add the tomatoes together with 1 2/3 cups (40 cl) meat bouillon from which the fat has been skimmed, 2 tbsp tomato paste, 1 tbsp paprika, 1 stem of rosemary, and 1 bouquet garni. Bring to the boil, skim off the fat, then cover and cook slowly for 1 hour 20 minutes, stirring occasionally.

4 When the meat is cooked, drain it in a dish. Discard the bouquet garni and remove the fat from the sauce carefully using a small ladle. Then add 1 crushed tomato, 1/2 bunch chopped parsley, the blanched fava beans, and the meat. Reheat slowly and serve with steamed potatoes. As an accompanying wine, choose Côtes-du-Rhône rouge, Hermitage, or Châteauneuf-du-Pape.

Sauté and blanquette of lamb

1 Cut 3 lb 5 oz (1.5 kg) boned shoulder of lamb from which the fat has been removed into approximately 1 in (3 cm) cubes. Place these cubes in a casserole and add enough cold water to cover the meat by $3/8$ in (1 cm). Set the casserole over high heat and bring to the boil. Then turn down the heat and adjust the heat so that the meat cooks slowly and evenly. Carefully remove the scum and fat with a small ladle.

2 Add 3 carrots, 7 oz (200 g) white button mushrooms, 3 turnips, cut into pieces, 2 peeled and quartered onions, and 2 leeks, carefully washed and with the outside leaves removed. Then add 1 tbsp coarse salt, 10 peppercorns,

3 Discard the bouquet garni and strain the cooking broth. Boil for 15 minutes, skimming off the fat from time to time using a spoon. Melt $3^1/4$ oz (100 g) butter in another saucepan, add 2 oz (60 g) flour and cook, stirring constantly. Then pour this roux into the boiling broth, beating vigorously.

4 Add 1 generous cup (25 cl) crème fraîche mixed with 2 egg yolks. Make sure that the sauce does not boil again. Adjust the seasoning, then add 1/2 bunch chopped chives, the vegetables, and the meat, and reheat without boiling. Serve immediately in a deep dish that has been kept very hot, accompanied by white rice.

Traditions and flavors

Of all the recipes for white offal meat, lamb's feet with poulette sauce is one of the most delicious. They are prepared in much the same way as a blanquette. Traditionally, the sauce served with this famous traditional dish was a chicken ("poulet" in French) fricassee, hence the name. Lamb's feet in poulette sauce should be served very hot, as the sauce has a tendency to congeal rapidly as it cools. Ideally it should be served in a stainless steel or silver-plated metal dish on a hot plate heated with an alcohol burner.

1 Ask your butcher to prepare 10 lamb's feet. Inspect them yourself to make sure that all the hairs have been removed. If not, singe them, then scrape off any remaining small black marks. Put the thoroughly cleaned feet in a casserole and cover them with plenty of cold water. Bring slowly to the boil, then remove the scum and skim off the fat regularly using a small ladle.

2 Meanwhile, peel 4 carrots, 3 onions, 2 stalks celery, and 2 leeks. Add these vegetables to the lamb's feet with 1 tbsp coarse salt, 10 peppercorns, 1 clove, and 1 bouquet garni. Bring to a gentle boil and cook for about 3 hours. When the feet are cooked, remove them with a skimmer ladle and leave to cool.

3 Prepare the sauce. Carefully remove the fat from the stock, strain, and then boil slowly for 1 hour, skimming off the fat from time to time. Melt 3 oz (100 g) butter in a saucepan, add $5/8$ cup (70 g) flour, and cook the mixture while stirring. Then add this roux to 4 cups (1 liter) boiling bouillon, beating very vigorously.

Lamb's feet with poulette sauce

4 Combine 1 generous cup (25 cl) crème fraîche, 2 egg yolks, and 1/2 bunch parsley in a bowl. Beat this mixture, then add to the sauce, stirring constantly. Do not allow the sauce to boil and keep it warm. As when making other sauces thickened with egg yolk, it is essential that this sauce is not allowed to boil; when it is ready, keep it warm in a bain-marie or double boiler.

Tip

In this recipe, it is possible to substitute calf's feet for lamb's feet; the cooking time will just be a little longer.

5 To prepare the accompaniment, wash and remove the stalks from 1 lb 2 oz (500 g) white button mushrooms. If they are large, cut them up. Put them in a large saucepan, adding 1/3 cup + 1 tbsp (10 cl) water, the juice of 1 lemon, 1 tbsp (20 g) butter, 1 pinch salt, and some pepper. Cover and bring to the boil. Cook for 15 minutes. Drain the mushrooms.

6 Take the cooled feet, one by one, and remove the bones, using your hands. Do not overlook the tiny bones, of which there are a great many. In addition, try not to damage the feet too much during this operation, keeping them whole if possible. Transfer them to a casserole and add the button mushrooms.

7 Place the casserole over moderate heat and simmer, without boiling, for 10 minutes, stirring from time to time so that the lamb's feet absorb all the flavor of the sauce. Adjust the seasoning if necessary, add 1/2 bunch chopped chives, and serve immediately with white rice, steamed potatoes, or fresh bread.

269

General points

Cassoulet is a stew of navy beans and various meats originating from the Cathar region in the southwest of France. Its name is derived from "cassolo," the term for the terracotta dish in which this stew is traditionally cooked. There are three major recipes for cassoulet. According to the famous dictum of Prosper Montagné: "Cassoulet is the god of Languedoc cuisine, a god in three persons: the Father, who is the cassoulet of Castelnaudary, the Son, who is the cassoulet of Carcassonne, and of course the Holy Spirit, who is the cassoulet of Toulouse." The first of these is prepared with pork as the main ingredient (knuckle, uncooked sausage, ham, and rind). The second is prepared with the addition of lamb or mutton (leg or shoulder).

Finally, in the Toulouse cassoulet, Toulouse sausage and preserved duck are added to the same meat.

Cassoulet Carcassonne style

This superb recipe is fairly easy to cook, but is prepared in several stages. Given the amount of time necessary for its preparation, it is advisable

Cassoulet with fresh navy beans

to start in the morning if you wish to serve the dish that evening. As in all cassoulets, the choice of bean is crucial: use lingots, white coco beans, or soissons from Pamiers. The important thing to remember is that, when a golden crust

Cassoulet with preserved goose

forms, it must be broken and pushed down with a spoon and allowed to form again. Repeat two or three times. Serve in the dish in which it has been cooked, using a large spoon.

Cassoulet with Toulouse sausage

Tip

You can enrich this recipe with Toulouse sausage or with 1 or 2 quarters of preserved duck ("confit de canard"). Cassoulet reheats very well. When simmered several times it acquires more flavor and becomes more succulent, as the beans gradually absorb more juice. Do not be afraid to prepare this dish in large quantities.

Cassoulet

Cassoulet Carcassonne style for 6

1 Pour 1¹/₂ lb (800 g) navy beans into a cooking pot. Cover with cold water. Bring to the boil, then drain. Transfer to a saucepan and cover with cold water. Add 14 oz (400 g) lean bacon lardoons, 7 oz (200 g) unsmoked bacon fat, 1 large bouquet garni, 2 onions stuck with 2 cloves, 2 carrots, and 4 chopped cloves of garlic. Set over moderate heat and leave the navy beans to cook for 1 hour.

2 The beans should be fairly well cooked, but still slightly firm. Bone and trim a shoulder of lamb and cut into cubes measuring around 1 in/3 cm. Season with salt and pepper. Heat 3 tbsp goose fat in a skillet. Brown the meat in the hot fat for 15 minutes. Then add 2 onions and 3 chopped cloves of garlic and cook for 5 minutes.

3 Pour in 6 cups (80 cl) meat bouillon and add 4 slices tomatoes and 1 good stem of thyme. Season with salt and pepper and cook for 1 hour. In another saucepan, plunge 1 knuckle of pork, slightly salted, into some water with 1 bouquet garni, 1 onion, and 2 carrots. Cook the knuckle for about 2 hours and then drain on a plate.

4 Pour a generous layer of cooked navy beans into the bottom of a large flameproof dish, then add a layer of lamb with its juices, then another layer of navy beans. In addition, incorporate the cooked knuckle of pork and diced bacon. If necessary, add 1 or 2 ladles of the liquid in which the lamb was cooked. Fill the dish in this manner until the ingredients are ³/₈ in (1 cm) below the rim and transfer to an oven heated to 350 °F (180 °C) for 1 hour.

271

Leg of lamb with 40 cloves of garlic

Leg of lamb with 40 cloves of garlic is an unusual recipe that is nevertheless quite simple to cook, provided you choose the best ingredients. Order a really fresh, best-quality leg of lamb weighing about 7 lb (3 kg). Ask your butcher to trim it and remove the fat very carefully. Find 2 or 3 heads of pink garlic that are very fresh and not sprouting. In season, choose new garlic, which is even better for this recipe. Contrary to popular belief, garlic prepared in this way is not strong and is easily digested. It is simply very important to choose a good quality pink garlic, as fresh as possible, and especially garlic that has not sprouted. As an accompaniment to this dish, serve a plate of potatoes boulangère and a good red Bordeaux, preferably a Saint-Émilion or a Pomerol. As an appetizer, serve asparagus with a mousseline sauce, and for dessert vanilla crème brûlée.

Serves 8
Preparation: 30 minutes
Cooking: 45 minutes

Ingredients

1 leg of lamb, weighing about 7 lb (3 kg)
A few sprigs of thyme
2 or 3 heads pink garlic
Salt and pepper

1 Place the leg of lamb on the roasting pan of your oven. Oil it lightly, season with salt and pepper, and sprinkle over some sprigs of fresh thyme. A pastry brush will help you brush the oil over the meat, but you can also use a stem of thyme or even basil with plenty of leaves on, as they do in Provence. Make sure the meat is well moistened on all sides.

2 The best thyme grows on pebbly, arid soils in hot sunshine; when it starts flowering it is particularly rich in active substances and aromatics. If you cannot gather delicious, flowering thyme in the scrubland of Provence, use garden thyme, provided that its roots are growing in dry soil in full sun.

3 Crush the garlic heads gently using the palm of your hand to release all the cloves. Count exactly 40 of them. Set them aside without peeling them. New garlic, harvested at the end of spring, is ideal in this recipe, as it does not contain the small green shoot that eventually develops in older cloves and makes them less digestible.

4 Heat your oven to 410 °F (210 °C). Arrange the unpeeled cloves of garlic around the leg of lamb and cook everything for between 40 and 45 minutes, depending on how well cooked you like it. As soon as the cooking time is finished, wrap the leg of lamb in a double layer of aluminum foil and leave to stand for 10 minutes.

5 Meanwhile, retrieve the cooked garlic cloves and collect the juice, keeping everything really hot. When it is time to serve, unwrap the leg of lamb and carve into slices. Arrange the slices in the dish, season with a little salt and pepper, then scatter the garlic cloves on top. Serve immediately, as once it is carved the lamb will go cold quickly.

6 For best results from this recipe, take a fork and remove one of the cloves of garlic from the plate. Then press it with the blade of a knife to extract the pulp. Spread this aromatic white paste over the slices of lamb, spoon over some of the juice and taste. Serve with gratin dauphinois to complement this dish.

White wine marinade

Marinated haunch of venison

Deglazing

This means pouring wine or spirits into a pan in which meat, fish, or vegetables have been browned. All the concentrated flavors in the residues that have formed during cooking dissolve in the liquid and are thus

Deglazing with white wine

General points

Wine and spirits are frequently used in cooking because of the incomparable flavor they give to the ingredients with which they are combined. Red wine, for instance, is responsible for the quintessential flavor of beef bourguignon, the fish stew with onions and herbs known as matelote, and coq au vin, while white wine is used to flavor marinades and bouillons for cooking fish. Because of their strong flavor, spirits are always used in small quantities, while red and white wines can be incorporated less sparingly.

Techniques

Marinating

Marinating is essentially a technique applied to meat, firstly to flavor it and secondly to tenderize it. This is why game animals are often prepared in this way. However, fish are also marinated prior to grilling, as are the ingredients for pâtés, terrines, or small pieces of meat for broiling.

Marinated lamb with sauce paloise

incorporated in a sauce, while the wine loses its acidity during the cooking process. It is helpful to scrape the walls and the bottom of the container with a wooden spatula to loosen the caramelized deposits and dissolve them in the wine.

Flaming

Flambé dishes are flamed (spirits or liqueurs are poured on the food and set alight) either in the kitchen or at the table; only at the table is this witnessed by the guests. The aim of both procedures is to add flavor to various dishes while avoiding giving them the strong, unpleasant taste of pure alcohol. When it is set alight, the alcohol evaporates, leaving only the aromatic constituents. The technique is not without risk. For maximum safety, heat your alcohol prior to setting it alight with the kind of long matches used to light cigars.

Deglazing with cognac

Red wines with a high tannin content

These wines are suitable for marinades for meat and game. Reserve softer red wines for beef and poultry recipes, or for poaching pears. For deglazing to make sauce or for fish recipes, choose Gros Plant Nantais. Use rum or cognac to flame crêpes and kirsch or Armagnac for Norwegian omelets. Armagnac is also very good for game.

Tapenade

There are numerous variations on this Provençal recipe based on olive oil, garlic, and anchovies. The black paste can be used instead of mustard, to great advantage in the case of lamb. Remember to remove it from the refrigerator 1 hour before serving so that it reaches room temperature. You can serve tapenade with noisettes of lamb and broiled chops, for example. To serve 6, you will need: 4 oz (125 g) pitted olives, 1 clove of garlic, 2 oz (80 g) anchovies, 3 oz (100 g) tuna flakes, 5 tbsp olive oil. Purée all the ingredients in a blender.

Thyme

Thyme is used to flavor roast or braised cuts of meat and is sprinkled over the raw meat before cooking. It is very strong, especially when fresh, so be careful about the quantity you use: 1 pinch for each side is sufficient.

Pink garlic

This is the ideal companion for all roast cuts (leg, saddle, shoulder). The unpeeled cloves are added to the dish during cooking and are served together with the sliced meat; the cooked pulp inside each clove is truly delicious. Choose a good head of pink garlic, or new garlic when in season.

Mint sauce

This English specialty with its individual, unexpected taste is traditionally served with poached leg of lamb, but also with roast lamb.

Breadcrumb and herb coating

This mixture of fresh herbs, chopped garlic, and breadcrumbs is spread over loin of lamb before roasting. To serve 6, you will need: 3 oz (100 g) chopped parsley and snipped chives, 3 oz (100 g) garlic, peeled and chopped, and 7 oz (200g) breadcrumbs.

Maître d'hôtel butter

This is a mixture of chopped parsley, chopped garlic, and unsalted butter, seasoned with salt and pepper. Place a dab of maître d'hôtel butter on slices of leg of lamb cooked in the skillet: the result is delicious. To serve 6, you will need: 7 oz (200 g) butter, 5 oz (150 g) parsley, 3 oz (100 g) garlic, and salt and pepper.

Lamb "à la chilindron"

A regional dish

Serves 4
Preparation: 15 minutes
Cooking: 30 minutes

Ingredients

2¹/₄ lb (1 kg) neck of lamb, cut into pieces
4 cloves of garlic
Oil
3" oz (100 g) raw cured ham
1 onion
3 red bell peppers
1 lb 2 oz (500 g) tomatoes
Salt and pepper

1. Carefully trim and remove the fat from the pieces of neck of lamb and season on both sides with salt and pepper. Set aside in a cool place.

2. In a skillet, sauté 2 cloves of coarsely chopped garlic in some oil. When the garlic has just turned golden, add the lamb.

3. After a few moments, add the ham cut into small pieces, the chopped onion and the remaining cloves of garlic, finely chopped. Stir gently. When the onion begins to brown, add the bell peppers, peeled and cut into thin strips.

4. Cook for a few more minutes before adding the tomatoes, peeled, seeded, and cut into large pieces.

5. Simmer until the lamb is cooked and the tomatoes are transformed into a rich sauce.

In order to make this recipe easier, it is a good idea to prepare all the ingredients in advance: peel the onion and the cloves of garlic; blanch the tomatoes and then skin them before seeding and cutting them into pieces. In addition, if you are worried that you might find the bell peppers rather indigestible, you can cut them in half, seed them, cut them into thin strips, and soak them in lukewarm water for 1 hour before using. To accompany this typically Basque lamb specialty, you can serve either plain rice or cornmeal porridge (polenta).

Recommended drinks

Red Irouléguy
Rioja
Madiran

Menu suggestions

1. Add a Basque flavor by serving an appetizer of marinated anchovies and sweet bell peppers stuffed with cod, with a crème caramel for dessert.

2. You can also opt for a tomato salad with mild onions and bell peppers as an appetizer, and follow the main dish with thin slices of ewe's milk cheese with black cherry jelly.

Blanquette of lamb Paris style

A family dish

Serves 4
Preparation: 15 minutes
Cooking: 1 hour

Ingredients

2 carrots
12 small onions
2 cloves
2 walnut-size pieces of butter
2¼ lb (1 kg) boned lamb,
  cut into pieces
1 bouquet garni
1 tbsp flour
²/₃ cup (125 g) rice
4 eggs

4 tbsp crème fraîche
2 lemons
Salt and pepper

1. Peel the carrots and cut into small pieces. Peel the small onions and stick two of them with the cloves. Melt 1 dab of butter in a casserole. Sauté the meat on all sides without allowing it to brown. Add the carrots, the onions, and the bouquet garni. Add enough cold water to cover, season with salt and pepper, and heat gently. Cook for 1 hour from the point at which the contents of the casserole start to simmer.

2. Melt the remaining butter in an enameled saucepan over a gentle heat. Add the flour and mix with a hand whisk until it begins to foam gently, without allowing it to brown; then pour in 2 cups (50 cl) cooking liquid. Simmer until this sauce coats the back of a spoon. Adjust seasoning to taste.

3. Meanwhile, carefully wash the rice, placing it in a fine sieve. Drain and cook for 15–20 minutes (depending on the quality of the rice) in plenty of boiling, salted water.

4. Mix 4 egg yolks in a bowl with 4 tbsp crème fraîche and the juice of 1 lemon, then pour this into the sauce, beating with a hand whisk. Do not allow to boil.

5. Drain the pieces of lamb, the carrots, and the onions. Place them in a deep dish and spoon a little of the sauce over them. Drain the rice and transfer to a vegetable dish. Pour the remaining sauce into a hot sauceboat and serve immediately, accompanied by lemon quarters. Make sure that you have enough sauce, not only for the blanquette, but for the rice as well.

Recommended drinks

White Auxey-Duresses
Red Volnay
Côtes-de-Beaune-Villages

Menu suggestions

1. For a family lunch, serve a variety of seasonal crudités or half an avocado with vinaigrette dressing as an appetizer and pineapple surprise for dessert.

2. For a more sophisticated dinner, serve eggs in aspic with smoked salmon as an appetizer, with cheese after the main course followed by an apple charlotte.

Lamb kebabs Nauplia style

A foreign dish

Serves 4
Preparation time: 20 minutes
Cooking time: 10 minutes

Ingredients

2 medium onions
3 tomatoes, not too ripe
4 cultivated mushrooms
14 oz (400 g) lamb's liver
4 thin slices smoked fat bacon
3^1/$_2$ Tbsp (50 g) butter
Salt and pepper

1. Peel the onions, cut them into quarters, and quarter the tomatoes. Remove the stalks from the mushrooms and wipe them with a cloth.

2. Cut the liver into even-sized pieces. Remove the rind from the bacon slices and roll them up.

3. Assemble your kebabs by threading a quarter tomato, a roll of bacon, a piece of liver, a quarter onion, another quarter tomato, and another piece of liver on a skewer; finish with a mushroom.

4. Melt the butter and drizzle over the kebabs. Season them with sparingly with salt and pepper.

5. Place on the grill rack over a drip pan or dish in your broiler, pre-heated to high. The kebabs will cook in about ten minutes; turn them two-thirds of the way through the cooking time.

6. Serve on a platter of saffron rice decorated with watercress leaves.

7. If you want to prepare these kebabs in really authentic Nauplia style, substitute olive oil for the butter.

Recommended drinks

Patrimonio
Gigondas
Red Chilean wine

Menu suggestions

1. In keeping with the Greek theme, serve a salad of marinated bell peppers, tarama, and tzatziki as an appetizer before these kebabs, with a fig tart for dessert.

2. For an "al fresco" barbecue, serve tabbouleh flavored with plenty of herbs as an appetizer and iced nougat for dessert.

Lamb's brains "à la grenobloise"

A light dish

Serves 4
Preparation: 5 minutes
Cooking: 15 minutes

Ingredients

8 lamb's brains
Wine vinegar
2 cups (50 cl) dry white wine
1 carrot
1 onion
1 bouquet garni
2 lemons
1 small pot crãme fraîche
1 bottle capers in vinegar

Parsley
Salt and pepper

1. Soak the brains for a few hours in fresh water to which you have added a little vinegar.

2. Pour 2 cups (50 cl) wine and the same quantity of water into a saucepan. Add the peeled and chopped carrot and onion, the bouquet garni, and the juice of 1 lemon. Season with salt and pepper. Boil for about 30 minutes.

3. Clean the brains. Plunge into the bouillon and leave to simmer for 15 minutes.

4. Mix a little of the cooking liquid with the crãme fraîche. Pour a little of the sauce onto individual heated plates, and arrange the brains, well drained, on top, spooning over a little more sauce. Add the capers and decorate with thin slices of lemon and a little finely snipped parsley.

5. Serve immediately.

Fish cooked "à la meunière," i.e., lightly floured and cooked in butter in the skillet, then garnished with capers and small pieces of lemon, is traditionally referred to as having been cooked "à la grenobloise." The capers and the lemon are indeed two of the ingredients found in this recipe for lamb's brains. For successful results, it is essential to wash the brains under running water, to remove the membranes and blood vessels, to soak them, and then to wash them again. They should be cooked in the cooking liquor over a very low heat. However, you can also use deep-frozen brains in this recipe, once they have been defrosted.

Recommended drinks

White Côtes-du-Jura
White Vin de Savoie
Sparkling water

Menu suggestions

1. After a salad of cucumber with mint, serve this dish of lamb's brains as the main course, followed by a bowl of fromage frais with red fruits.

2. You can also serve lamb's brains as a hot appetizer, followed by a light gratin of carrots with herbs and a sorbet.

Stuffed crown of lamb

A party dish

Serves 6
Preparation: 30 minutes
Cooking: about 1 hour

Ingredients

2 onions
9 Tbsp (125 g) butter
9 oz (250 g) seedless raisins (Smyrna)
9 oz (250 g) juicy dried apricots
Stale bread
1 glass poultry bouillon
1 egg
1 bunch parsley
1 crown of lamb consisting of 12 loin chops
prepared by your butcher

3 lb 5 oz (1.5 kg) firm-fleshed potatoes
3 lb 5 oz (1.5 kg) green beans
Powdered cinnamon
Salt and pepper

1. Set the oven to 350 °F (180 °C) and, while it is heating, peel and chop the onions, then sauté them in a little butter. Transfer to a basin as soon as they start to turn brown and make the stuffing by adding the raisins, the coarsely chopped apricots, the stale bread previously dipped into bouillon (or milk) then squeezed and coarsely chopped, a whole egg, and the chopped parsley. Season with salt and pepper and add cinnamon to taste. Knead all the ingredients well until you have a homogeneous, slightly crumbly stuffing.

2. Season the inside and the outside of the crown of lamb with salt and pepper. Place in a roasting pan and fill with the stuffing. Transfer to the oven and cook for 30 minutes per pound, including the stuffing.

3. Meanwhile boil the potatoes, then the green beans.

4. Place a few curls of butter on top of the stuffing half way through the cooking time.

5. Transfer to a warmed serving platter and drizzle some melted butter over both meat and vegetables.

Instead of green beans and boiled potatoes, you could serve a more unusual choice of vegetables, depending on the season. In autumn, for example, you could serve a fricassee of wild mushrooms and Jerusalem artichokes seasoned with parsley; in summer, a gratin of tomatoes; and, in winter, pumpkin gratin.

Recommended drinks

Cornas
Chambertin
Vougeot

Menu suggestions

1. For a classic, stylish meal, serve smoked salmon soufflé as an appetizer and a Saint-Honoré gâteau or rum baba for dessert.

2. As an appetizer, you could also serve a salad of green beans with a slice of foie gras, and for dessert a lemon meringue tart.

Couscous with fresh fava beans

A foreign dish

Serves 4
Preparation time: 10 minutes
Cooking time: 1 hour 15 minutes

Ingredients

1 lb 2 oz (500 g) couscous
1 lb 2 oz (500 g) boned shoulder of mutton
Olive oil
SaffronOil
1 onion
1 lb 2 oz (500 g) fresh fava beans, shelled
Butter
Ginger
1 bouquet garni
Harissa
Salt and pepper

1. Moisten the couscous and leave for about ten minutes without draining so that it hardens, then spread out in a dish with the fingertips to dry.

2. Brown the meat in the bottom of the couscous pan with the saffron, oil, onion, a pinch of salt, and some pepper. When the meat is a golden color, cover with plenty of water and cook over moderate heat for a good hour.

3. After you have made sure that the grains of couscous have not stuck together, transfer the couscous to the top part of the couscous pan to cook in the steam from the meat for about 20 minutes. Then remove the couscous, making sure that the grains do not stick, as they will swell again during further cooking.

4. As soon as the meat is cooked, take it out, then add the vegetables and the fava beans to the bouillon. Return the couscous to the top part of the steamer and cook for another 20 minutes in the steam from the bouillon, checking the water level in the lower part of the couscous pan during the cooking time.

5. Return the meat to the bouillon with the vegetables and cook the couscous for a further five minutes in the steam.

6. Then stir a large dab of butter into the couscous and serve separately. The broth is served in a small basin. Mix the harissa with a little of the broth.

Recommended drinks

Mint tea
Grapefruit juice
Provence rosé

Menu suggestions

1. This couscous dish is a meal in itself. Serve an appetizer of fresh radishes with a yogurt sauce and for dessert a selection of fruits in season.

2. As a pleasant accompaniment to this dish, you can also serve grapefruit halves, simply sprinkled with brown sugar and caramelized.

Recommended drinks

Côtes du Rhône
Saint-Joseph
A good Bordeaux

Menu suggestions

1. For an informal meal with friends, serve a plate of smoked fish as an appetizer and an apple tart flambé for dessert.

2. Alternatively, you could serve pumpkin soup as an appetizer and baked apples with jelly for dessert.

Shoulder of lamb with spicy sauce

An economical dish

Serves 6
Preparation: 15 minutes
Waiting: 12 hours
Cooking: 2 hours

Ingredients

1 boned shoulder of lamb (ask your butcher to remove the skin and fat) with the bone cut into pieces
Hot mustard
Paprika
2 carrots
2 onions
2 cloves
1 bouquet garni (parsley, thyme, bay leaves, celery)
1 large dab lard or butter

2 tsp cornstarch
1 large glass red wine, fairly full-bodied
Salt and pepper

1. Flatten the shoulder of lamb on a board and spread with mustard, then sprinkle with salt and paprika. Roll up in the direction of the fibers in the meat and secure with a few loops of kitchen string (without pulling them too tight). Spread with mustard and sprinkle with salt and pepper again. Place on a dish and leave in a cool place overnight.

2. Prepare a bouillon with the bone from the shoulder and 6 cups (1.5 liters) water; bring to the boil over high heat. Skim, then add the quartered carrots, 1 onion stuck with the cloves, and the bouquet garni. Cover about three-quarters of the pan with the lid and simmer over gentle heat for 2 hours. Strain, pressing well to retain all the concentrated flavors, then turn up the heat and reduce until only 3 cups (75 cl) liquid remains. Melt the lard in a casserole and brown the meat.

3. Pre-heat the oven to 350 °F (180 °C). When the joint is nicely browned, keep it hot in a roasting pan, and add the second onion, sliced horizontally, to the casserole. Pour in the bouillon, which has previously been passed through a fine strainer, and bring to the boil. Return the shoulder of lamb to the casserole and cook in the oven for 1 hour 45 minutes, basting on four occasions during the cooking time, then keep the meat hot. Strain the cooking liquid and thicken with a little cornstarch mixed with 1–2 tbsp water. Simmer for 2 minutes over gentle heat, then add the red wine; return to the boil, then simmer for 5 minutes. Adjust seasoning to taste. Spoon a little of the sauce onto a hot plate, carve the meat into slices, and arrange on the sauce. Serve boiled potatoes as an accompaniment, and the sauce separately in a hot sauceboat.

Fillet of lamb with potatoes and pumpkin mousse

A party dish

Serves 4
Preparation: 25 minutes
Cooking: 12 minutes

Ingredients

1 lamb fillet with belly flap
(piece of fat and muscle from saddle of lamb)
9 oz (250 g) potatoes
1 lb 2 oz (500 g) pumpkin
Rosemary
Butter
Salt and pepper

1. Carefully remove the fat from the fillet and the belly flap, making the latter as thin as possible.

2. Peel and wash the potatoes and cut them into thin slices, $1/16$–$1/8$ in (2–3 mm) thick. Blanch in boiling, salted water. Sponge them thoroughly then cover the belly flap with them. Add a little rosemary, season with salt and pepper, and roll the fillet in the seasoned belly flap. Secure without pulling too tightly. Place the fillet in a roasting pan, surrounded with the crushed lamb bones. Roast for 10–12 minutes in the pre-heated oven with the heat turned up to 435 °F (225 °C). Leave to rest for 10 minutes after it has finished cooking.

3. Meanwhile, prepare the pumpkin mousse.

4. Deglaze the cooking juices with some bouillon or water. Strain the juices through a sieve and thicken with butter, off the heat.

5. Slice the fillet and arrange with the pumpkin mousse in the center. Serve on hot plates decorated with a few sprigs of rosemary.

To make the pumpkin mousse, remove the skin from the pumpkin and cut the flesh into large pieces. Place in a thick-bottomed saucepan, season with salt and pepper, and add a few small dabs of butter. Trickle some water on top, cover the saucepan with a lid, and heat gently, checking from time to time. When the pumpkin is very soft, purée in a blender.

Recommended drinks

Côtes-du-Rhône-Villages
Vacqueyras
Côtes-du-Roussillon

Menu suggestions

1. As an appetizer, serve a salad of finely chopped fennel with a tapenade sauce and pineapple fritters for dessert.

2. For a slightly more elaborate menu, serve Roquefort pastries as an appetizer and a chocolate mousse with candied orange peel for dessert.

287

Fillet of lamb with dried apricots

A family dish

Serves 4
Preparation: 15 minutes
Waiting: 3 hours
Cooking: 20 minutes

Ingredients

4 boneless lamb chops 1–2 in (4–5 cm) thick
(cut from the fillet and with the bib)
12 very succulent dried apricots
Green rosemary
Olive oil
1 lb 11 oz (750 g) small potatoes
1 large dab of butter
Salt and pepper

1. Remove the skin and the fat that is usually found between the bib and eye of a chop, as well as that partly covering the fillet and bib. Roll the bib around the fillet, place 2 apricots in the middle, and keep everything in place by piercing almost all the way through with two small wooden skewers. Place in a dish, drizzle with olive oil, and flavor with finely chopped rosemary. Cover and leave to marinate for 3 hours, basting with the marinade as frequently as possible.

2. Heat your broiler and brown both sides of each fillet and its surrounding bib at high heat. Then lower the heat and finish cooking for about 10 minutes. As the first step at high temperature takes 10 minutes, the total cooking time is about 20 minutes. Season with salt and pepper halfway through the cooking time.

3. Serve straight from the broiler with boiled potatoes prepared in advance and kept hot; a few apricots served in addition will enhance this dish.

Alternatively, you can serve these fillets with sautéed grains: boil 7 oz (200 g) pre-cooked whole-wheat in water for 15 minutes, then drain and brown immediately in a skillet with some butter and 3 small white onions, peeled and finely chopped. Season with salt and pepper. Just before serving, scatter a few sprigs of chervil or some flat-leaved parsley on top.

Recommended drinks

Fitou
Cornas
Gewurztraminer

Menu suggestions

1. As an appetizer on a summer's evening, serve a tomato and basil soup or a gazpacho, with an orange mousse or stewed peaches for dessert.

2. For an autumn or winter menu, serve cream of mushroom soup as an appetizer, with apple fritters or crystallized oranges for dessert.

Lamb's liver with Provençal herbs

An easy dish

Serves 4
Preparation: 10 minutes
Cooking: 15 minutes

Ingredients

7 oz (200 g) pasta
1 lb 5 oz (600 g) lamb's liver
7 Tbsp (100 g) butter
Fresh thyme
Fresh rosemary
1 stem fresh basil
1 bunch tarragon
1 bunch flat-leaved parsley
Salt and pepper

1. Cook the pasta in plenty of boiling, salted water and keep hot until needed. Cut the liver in pieces and sauté in the skillet in 1 tbsp butter. As soon as they are golden brown on one side, turn them over. Season with salt and pepper and flavor them with thyme, a little rosemary chopped into very small pieces, and a few basil leaves.

2. Meanwhile, heat the rest of the butter in a saucepan and add plenty of tarragon leaves, parsley, and basil, very coarsely chopped. Leave to infuse for several minutes in the hot butter, then season with salt and pepper.

3. Arrange the well-drained pasta on a hot dish, place the lamb's liver in the center, and pour the contents of the saucepan over the meat just before serving.

The choice, freshness, and aroma of the herbs are fundamental to the success of this recipe. Do not substitute dried thyme for fresh thyme, as the aroma is spicier and more aggressive. The same applies to the rosemary: if no fresh rosemary is available, do not use dried rosemary, but opt instead for a few mint leaves. You can replace the flat-leaved parsley with sorrel. The basil, however, is absolutely irreplaceable.

Recommended drinks

Faugères
Fitou
Côtes-du-Roussillon-Villages

Menu suggestions

1. As an appetizer, serve a Provençal-style salad of squid or octopus, and for dessert baked figs with lavender honey.

2. For a really quick meal, serve a salad of mushrooms with herbs as an appetizer and finish with strawberries steeped in red wine.

Recommended drinks

Moulis
A good Graves
Pauillac

Menu suggestions

1. Begin this celebratory meal with sun-dried tomato and basil tartlets and finish with an orange tart.

2. An equally elegant solution: fresh melon with Parma ham and, for dessert, ice nougat accompanied by a raspberry coulis.

Leg of lamb with two beans

A party dish

Serves 4
Preparation: 5 minutes the day before; 15 minutes on the day
Cooking: 30–40 minutes, depending on the weight of the leg of lamb

Ingredients

1 lb 2 oz (500 g) small navy beans
1 lb 11 oz (750 g) green beans
1 fine leg of salt-marsh lamb
2 cloves garlic
1 tbsp lard
Parsley
Salt and pepper

1. Put the navy beans to soak the day before; you will then be able to simmer them very gently while the leg of lamb is cooking. Remove the strings from the green beans and wrap in a damp dishtowel ready to be cooked in boiling, salted water 15 minutes before the leg of lamb has finished cooking. Ideally the leg of lamb should be short and plump, with a thin knuckle and very white fat. You should not insert cloves of garlic under the skin, although this is common practice. To cook the leg of lamb, make some shallow cuts in the surrounding fat, rub in a little lard, transfer to a roasting pan, and slide into a very hot oven at 535 °F (280 °C). Cook for 15 minutes per pound, reducing the heat considerably (to 400 °F/200 °C) as soon as the meat is well browned on all sides. Do not baste it during cooking. Season with salt and pepper 5–10 minutes before the end of the cooking time.

2. To serve, pour the navy beans onto a serving platter, then arrange the green beans in small bundles over them, with the leg of lamb in the center. Decorate with a few parsley leaves and serve with the juices from the meat after skimming off the fat.

Choose dried navy beans less than a year old, as they cook better than older beans. Nevertheless, to save time you can cook your beans in a pressure cooker, which will take 30 minutes from the point at which it comes up to pressure. Another solution is to use canned or bottled navy beans, thoroughly drained, remembering to check them for seasoning. If possible, choose ones cooked in goose fat. Finally, you can make the beans even more colorful by using a mixture of red kidney and navy beans.

Leg of lamb with walnuts

A regional dish

Serves 6
Preparation: 15 minutes
Waiting: 48 hours
Cooking: 30–45 minutes, according to the weight of the leg of lamb

Ingredients

1 leg of lamb, on the bone
Walnut oil
A few lamb bones
2 carrots
2 onions
1 bunch of aromatic herbs
2 glasses white wine
10 walnuts
Salt and black pepper

1. Remove the fat and the tendons from the leg of lamb, then place it in a large pot and drizzle generously with walnut oil. Cover and refrigerate for 48 hours. Baste and turn the meat several times during this period.

2. Place the bones in a large saucepan and cook over high heat until they brown. Add the peeled and chopped carrots, peeled and chopped onions, and the bunch of herbs. Cook for a further 10 minutes or so. Pour in 1 glass of wine, bring to the boil, then pour some lukewarm water over the bones and simmer for 1 hour. Transfer the cooking liquid to another saucepan and reduce slowly until it has a gleaming appearance reminiscent of varnish. Leave to cool and remove the fat.

3. Remove the leg of lamb from its marinade and place in a roasting pan. Brown over high heat, then transfer to an oven pre-heated to 400 °F (200 °C) for about 30 minutes until the meat is cooked, but still pink in the middle. Turn it and keep it hot.

4. Pour the second glass of wine into the dish and bring to the boil again, stirring and scraping the bottom of the saucepan thoroughly. Add the sauce and chopped nuts and simmer for 2 minutes. Season with salt and pepper. Serve the leg of lamb garnished with green walnut halves. Spoon a little of the sauce over the meat, but serve most of it separately, in a hot sauceboat.

Recommended drinks

Bergerac
Madiran
Cahors

Menu suggestions

1. Serve duck rillettes to start this meal from the southwest of France and stewed strawberries with rolled waffles for dessert.

2. If it is a fall menu, start with a fricassee of wild mushrooms and finish with a marron glacé ice cream.

291

Leg of lamb with garlic cream

An easy dish

Serves 6
Preparation: 10 minutes
Cooking: 25–30 minutes, according to the weight of the leg of lamb

Ingredients

1 leg of lamb

1 dab butter

3 heads of garlic

Thyme

Bay leaves

1¹/₄ cups (30 cl) crème fraîche

Salt and pepper

1. Set the oven to 520 °F (270 °C).

2. Do not insert the usual cloves of garlic in the skin of the leg of lamb. Simply cut slits in the fatty parts and rub with a little butter. Place in a roasting pan. Open out the heads of garlic, arrange the cloves around the leg of lamb without peeling them, add the thyme and the bay leaves, and pour 1 glass water over the ingredients.

3. Cook in the oven for 15 minutes for the first pound and 10 minutes per pound thereafter. Baste from time to time with the juices, and season fairly generously with salt and pepper at the end of the cooking time.

4. Keep the leg of lamb hot. Peel the cloves of garlic and reduce their pulp to a purée. Transfer this to a small saucepan with the crème fraîche and heat without bringing to the boil. Season with salt and pepper.

5. Serve with green beans that you have cooked in the meantime, or with another vegetable of your choice.

Instead of cooking the cloves of garlic in their skins around the leg of lamb, you can make the garlic cream separately: peel 6 cloves garlic, blanch in boiling water, drain and crush them, and place in a bowl with 1 egg yolk, a little mustard, and some salt and pepper. Beat with an electric whisk and incorporate 1 scant cup (20 cl) olive oil, one drop at a time, then in a steady trickle, beating as when making mayonnaise.

Recommended drinks

Tursan
Red Gaillac
Gigondas

Menu suggestions

1. As an appetizer, and when in season, serve small artichokes raw with salt and a vinaigrette highly seasoned with pepper, with apricot tart for dessert.

2. For a more "general purpose" menu, serve tomato and mozzarella salad as an appetizer and finish with a mango sorbet.

Leg of lamb Provence style

A regional dish

Serves 6
Preparation: 15 minutes
Cooking: 50 minutes

Ingredients

1 leg of grass-fed lamb weighing about 4″ lb (2 kg)
2 cloves garlic
1 generous tbsp lard
1 good bunch fresh thyme
7 lb (3 kg) navy beans, soaked
Olive oil
1 bunch savory
Salt and pepper

1. A good leg of grass-fed lamb should be short and plump, with a fine shin and very white fat. Insert garlic cloves at equal intervals down the length of the leg.

2. Prepare a very hot wood fire, with glowing embers at the bottom and a good, clear flame. Make some shallow cuts in the fat surrounding the leg of lamb, smear with lard, and place on the spit, passing this first through the knuckle then spearing the joint near the top of the leg. Place a drip pan underneath. Turn the meat, initially over a very hot flame, then over moderate heat once the meat is golden brown. Then add a large collar of fresh thyme, held in place with string. Cook for 15 minutes per pound. Do not season with salt and pepper until the last moment.

3. Meanwhile, cook the previously soaked navy beans in boiling, salted water with a dash of olive oil and flavored with 1–2 cloves garlic and 1 bunch savory, if you have any. The beans will be just cooked after boiling slowly for 45 minutes. Drain and transfer them to the drip pan under the roasting lamb, where they will finish cooking while absorbing the meat juices.

4. With a wild salad, this mountain lamb is truly a dish fit for a king.

Recommended drinks

Corbières
Red Bandol
Red Palette

Menu suggestions

1. For a summer meal, serve arugula salad with parmesan shavings as an appetizer and Saint-Tropez tart for dessert.

2. For a winter meal, serve celery stalks with a tapenade sauce as an appetizer and, for dessert, a honey mousse with almond croquant.

Recommended drinks

Tea (without milk or sugar)
Pale ale
Saumur-Champigny

Menu suggestions

1. As an appetizer, serve plain grated carrot with hazelnut oil, with apple fritters to finish.

2. For a TV dinner, arrange some corn chips and guacamole around the burgers, and serve vanilla ice cream for dessert.

Lamb burgers with bulgur wheat

A family dish

Serves 4
Preparation: 15 minutes
Waiting: 2 or 3 hours
Cooking: 10 minutes

Ingredients

5 oz (150 g) bulgur wheat
1 lb 2 oz–1 lb 5 oz (500–600 g) lamb, yielding 14 oz (400 g) lean chopped meat after the fat and connective tissue have been removed
1 red onion
1 tomato
A few sprigs of parsley
Mint or lemon grass
2 cloves of garlic
1 lime
1 tbsp brown sugar
4 small round poppy seed or sesame seed rolls
A few salad leaves
4 tsp yogurt or crème fraîche
Oil
Butter
Salt and pepper

1. Place the bulgur wheat in a large salad bowl and pour on plenty of boiling water. Leave to swell for 2–3 hours.

2. Meanwhile, remove the connective tissue and fat and carefully trim the lamb, then chop into pieces. Peel and finely chop the red onion. Skin the tomato after plunging it into boiling water for a moment; seed and chop. Chop the parsley and lemon grass (or mint); peel and crush the cloves of garlic. Grate the zest of the lime and squeeze the fruit to extract the juice.

3. Take a large handful of bulgur wheat and squeeze between the palms to remove excess water, mix with the chopped lamb, lime juice and zest, half the parsley, onion, cloves of garlic, and lemon grass. Season generously with salt and pepper. Divide into four and shape into burgers.

4. Mix together the remaining onion, garlic cloves, parsley, lemon grass, tomato, a little brown sugar, salt, and pepper in a basin. Heat the oil in a skillet and cook the burgers for 4 or 5 minutes on each side until they are nicely golden and nearly brown. Cut the rolls in half and heat in the broiler for a few minutes to crisp them.

5. Fill each roll with a few salad leaves, a little dressing, and a burger. Add a little yogurt or crâme fraîche and serve while they are still really hot. Serve with the reheated bulgur wheat, drained and seasoned with salt and pepper and some butter.

Lamb stew with navy beans

An easy dish

Serves 6
Preparation: 15 minutes
Cooking: 1 hour 15 minutes

Ingredients

4$^{1}/_{2}$ lb (2 kg) fresh navy beans, or
1 lb 2 oz (500 g) dried navy beans
3 onions
1 clove
4 carrots
2 cloves of garlic
A little oil
2$^{1}/_{4}$ lb (1 kg) boned shoulder of lamb,
 rolled into a roasting joint and secured with string
1 large dab of butter

1 bouquet garni
Salt and pepper

1. Start cooking the soaked beans with 1 onion stuck with the clove, 1 peeled carrot, cut julienne style, the peeled garlic cloves, salt, and pepper. Cover with boiling water; add a drop of oil, cover, and simmer gently.

2. Brown the meat in a casserole with the butter and the oil. Add 3 carrots, scraped and quartered, 2 peeled onions, and the bouquet garni; season with salt and pepper. Add a little of the liquid in which the navy beans have been cooked, cover, and braise for 30 minutes.

3. Cut the meat into pieces and place the navy beans, their juice, and accompanying flavorings in the casserole. Cover and finish cooking over very low heat until the beans are very soft, which will take 45 minutes.

4. After this time, the liquid in which the beans have been cooked should have disappeared completely. If necessary, add a little hot water and butter.

To complement this dish, you can serve some small glazed onions. Peel, blanch, and refresh 10 oz (300 g) small round onions and arrange in a single layer in a saucepan. Add 2 Tbsp (30 g) butter in small pieces, some salt, pepper, and a few pinches of sugar; barely cover with water and simmer gently for 50 minutes, until the onions are nicely golden and covered with a coating of caramel.

Recommended drinks

Cahors
Irouléguy
Pécharmant

Menu suggestions

1. As an appetizer, serve a good green salad with the addition of green walnuts and small bacon lardoons, with a simple pistachio ice cream for dessert.

2. You could also serve sardine rillettes as an hors-d'oeuvres and an exotic fruit salad for dessert.

Lamb stew with artichokes

A regional dish

Serves 4
Preparation: 20 minutes
Cooking: 2 hours

Ingredients

1 lb 11 oz (750 g) breast and neck of mutton
1 tbsp lard or 2 tbsp olive oil
6 onions
1 tsp flour
2 glasses white wine
2 glasses bouillon (optional)
2 cloves of garlic
1 large tomato
1 bouquet garni

12 small artichokes
Salt and pepper

1. Brown the meat in the lard, together with the coarsely diced onions. Allow them to color, then sprinkle with flour. Make a roux, then slowly add the white wine and the same quantity of water or bouillon. Season with salt and pepper, then add the peeled crushed garlic, the quartered tomato, and the bouquet garni, all at once.

2. Wait until the liquid starts to boil before adding the artichokes, cut into 4–6 pieces, after carefully removing the outer leaves, all the tips, and the choke.

3. Cover and cook over low heat for about 2 hours. Check the water level and if necessary add a little hot water during the cooking time.

Serve creamed eggplant and garlic to accompany this stew. Wash 3 eggplants and cut in half lengthwise. Make cuts in the flesh at right angles and sprinkle with salt. Line a baking sheet with aluminum foil and arrange the eggplants on top. Leave to stand for 30 minutes, pat dry with paper towels, and then slide the baking sheet into the oven, halfway up (having previously pre-heated the oven for 10 minutes to 410 °F/210 °C). Cook for about 20 minutes. Peel and finely chop 2 small cloves of garlic; wash, pat dry, and snip 1 small bunch of flat-leaved parsley. Remove all the flesh from the eggplants and place in a blender, mixing the resulting purée with the garlic and parsley. Reheat gently, incorporating 2 tbsp crème fraîche. Season with salt and pepper.

Recommended drinks

Saint-Joseph
Collioure
Corbières

Menu suggestions

1. As an appetizer, serve baked goat's cheese on toast, and for dessert lavender ice cream.

2. As an appetizer for this recipe from the Drôme region in southeast France you can also serve little turnovers with tapenade, with small melons for dessert.

Kidneys bolognese

A foreign dish

Serves 4
Preparation: 15 minutes
Cooking: 20 minutes

Ingredients

8 lamb's kidneys
1 clove of garlic
2 onions
Olive oil
4 tbsp vinegar
2 Tbsp (50 g) butter
1 bunch parsley
1 glass beef bouillon (or extract)
Salt and pepper

1. Trim the kidneys, removing all traces of fat and connective tissue. Cut into thin slices. Peel the garlic and onions. Chop one onion finely and slice the other into fairly thin rings.

2. Heat the oil in a saucepan and brown the onions for 4–5 minutes over gentle heat. Add half the vinegar, stir, and cook for a further 2 minutes. Drain the kidneys and keep hot.

3. Heat the butter in another saucepan and brown the onions, the finely chopped garlic, and the snipped parsley. Remove the garlic and place the kidneys over the onions and parsley. Turn up the heat and stir for 2 minutes. Add 3–4 tbsp bouillon and the rest of the vinegar, and let the liquid evaporate over high heat. Season with salt and pepper and serve immediately.

Pay close attention to the cooking time of the kidneys—even if slightly overcooked, they have a tendency to be rubbery. Instead of cutting them into thin slices, you can ask your butcher just to cut them in half, removing the white bits in the center and the thin skin on the outside. The choice of vinegar is crucial in this recipe: opt for red wine vinegar flavored with shallots or sherry vinegar. To accompany this dish you can serve fresh pasta mixed with a little crème fraîche, potato purée, or a mild onion compote with white rice.

Recommended drinks

Barolo
Chianti Classico
Gigondas

Menu suggestions

1. To start this Italian menu, serve prosciutto with fresh figs, with a tiramisu to finish.

2. As an appetizer, you can also serve a carpaccio of finely chopped boletus with olive oil and an almond and pine nut tart for dessert.

Recommended drinks

Chinon
Saint-Nicolas-de-Bourgueil
Saint-Emilion

Menu suggestions

1. You can serve moules mariniāre as an appetizer and peaches in syrup with a tourteau fromager—a cheesecake made with goatÅfs cheese, which is a specialty of the Poitou region—for dessert.

2. For a really quick meal, serve terrine of rabbit with hazelnuts as an appetizer and fromage frais with herbs to finish.

Lamb's kidneys with cream

A regional dish

Serves 4
Preparation: 25 minutes
Cooking: 10 minutes

Ingredients

9 oz (250 g) mushrooms
2 Tbsp (50 g) butter
1 lemon
8 lamb's kidneys
2 cloves of garlic
Parsley
A little cognac
1 large pot thick crème fraîche
Salt and pepper

1. Clean the mushrooms, remove the stalks, and wipe them. Cut in half or into quarters, depending on their size, and fry with a little butter, the juice of half a lemon mixed with 2–3 tbsp water, and some salt and pepper.

2. Wash the kidneys, cut them in half, and remove the tubes and connective tissue inside. Sauté them quickly in butter, cut side first, turning them after 3 minutes and browning the other side. Add the chopped garlic and parsley to the skillet soon after turning the kidneys, pour in the hot cognac, and flambé.

3. Keep the kidneys warm on a serving platter. Place the mushrooms in the skillet, deglaze and thicken with the crème fraîche, adjust seasoning to taste, and pour over the kidneys.

4. Serve very hot.

To accompany this specialty from the Angouême region, delicately flavored with cognac, do not be afraid to serve a rustic dish that is also typical of the region—potato cake with herbs. The potatoes are first cooked and puréed, then mixed with a generous quantity of parsley, garlic, basil, a little mint, and some nutmeg, formed into a large cake, and finally cooked in a skillet with a little oil.

Sauté of mutton Crécy style

A family dish

Serves 4
Preparation: 20 minutes
Cooking: 1 hour 30 minutes

Ingredients

2¹/₂ pounds (1 kg) mutton
(shoulder, breast, or neck)
9 oz (250 g) carrots
4 oz (125 g) onions
4 tbsp oil
2 Tbsp (50 g) butter
2 Tbsp (30 g) flour
1 large glass white wine
3–4 cloves garlic
1 bouquet garni

4 cups (1 liter) bouillon
Salt and pepper

1. Cut the lamb into chunks. Season with salt and pepper. Peel the carrots and cut into rings. Peel and chop the onions. Heat the oil and the butter in a casserole, add the mutton and vegetables, and brown well.

2. Remove the pieces of meat, making sure you drain them thoroughly. In the casserole, sprinkle the vegetables with flour and brown them, stirring vigorously with a wooden spoon. Deglaze with the white wine then add the chopped garlic and the bouquet garni.

3. Return the meat to the casserole, then cover with the bouillon.

4. Cover and cook for at least 1 hour 30 minutes over low heat.

All the dishes with "Crécy" in their name traditionally contain carrots, either as a purée or sliced in rings. The name derives from produce from the market gardens in the Crécy region, but it is not known whether the place in question is Crécy-la-Chapelle, in Seine-et-Marne, or Crécy-en-Ponthieu, on the Somme. Other dishes bearing the same name include fillets of sole Crécy, with a cream sauce and accompanied by baby carrots, consommé Crécy, the basic ingredient of which is finely diced carrot, or fried eggs Crécy, served on a bed of creamed carrots. To accompany this sauté of mutton, choose carrots from Nantes, long or medium-sized, and very fresh and crunchy (from May through September).

Recommended drinks

Pale ale
Alsace
Chinon

Menu suggestions

1. As an appetizer, serve celeriac with a rémoulade dressing and black olives, with warm apple turnovers for dessert.

2. Alternatively, you could serve vegetable soup as an appetizer and brioche with jelly for dessert.

Croquettes of lamb au gratin

Minced lamb au gratin

Stuffed vegetables

General points

Using leftovers of cooked lamb in other recipes is very easy; all you need is a little time and imagination. Keep the leg and saddle meat to serve cold, thinly slices, or to make sandwiches. Use the shoulder meat or neck for stuffings, minced meat, and meatballs. Serve cold leg of lamb with garlic mayonnaise and assorted raw vegetables—cauliflower florets, carrot rings, slices of fennel, and stalks of celery. Cold, thinly sliced leg of lamb is also excellent in a salad; arrange on a mound of spinach leaves, seasoned with a vinaigrette made with sherry vinegar.

Minced lamb

Ingredients for 4
1 large, finely chopped onion
Olive oil
2 finely chopped cloves of garlic
1 lb 2 oz (500 g) minced lamb
3 tomatoes, skinned and seeded
7 oz (200 g) chopped mushrooms
Chopped parsley
A little bouillon made from a cube
Flour
2–3 eggplants, cut into rings
Grated parmesan
Breadcrumbs
Salt and pepper

1. Brown the onion in the oil. Add the garlic and the meat and cook until golden brown. Incorporate the tomatoes, cut into pieces, the mushrooms, parsley, salt, and pepper. Add the bouillon and simmer for 15 minutes. Coat the eggplants in flour and cook in oil in a skillet until golden.

2. Spread the minced lamb in the base of an oiled gratin dish, then add the eggplants, parmesan, and breadcrumbs. Brown the top in the oven for 10 minutes.

Vegetable stuffing

Ingredients for 6
1 lb 5 oz (600 g) cooked lamb
$3^1/_2$ oz (100 g) sausage meat
3 chopped onions
2 chopped cloves garlic
4 tbsp olive oil
$^1/_2$ bunch parsley, chopped
3 shallots, chopped
1 egg
4 tbsp breadcrumbs
Salt and pepper

1. Mince the cooked lamb finely. Add the sausage meat.

2. Cook the onions and garlic in the olive oil for 10 minutes

3. Mix the parsley, the cooked onions and garlic, the shallots, egg, breadcrumbs, and salt and pepper.

This stuffing is suitable for vegetables such as zucchini or tomatoes, which should be cooked in the oven at 350 °F (180 °C) for 25–30 minutes.

Leg of lamb Paris style

Pasta twists with chasseur sauce

Leg of lamb sandwich

Using up leftover cold sliced leg of lamb

To make the garlic mayonnaise
6 cloves garlic
1 egg yolk
1$^1/_2$ cups (30 cl) virgin olive oil
Salt and pepperr

1. Peel and chop the cloves of garlic very finely; place in a large bowl with the egg yolk and season with salt and pepper.

2. Slowly add the olive oil, beating very vigorously.

Pasta twists with chasseur sauce

Ingredients for 4
1 finely chopped onion
1 carrot, finely diced
1 stalk of celery cut julienne style
Butter
1 slice cooked ham
7 oz (200 g) cooked mutton
1 tbsp flour
2 cups (50 cl) bouillon
10 oz (300 g) skinned tomatoes
9 oz (250 g) pasta twists
Salt and pepper

1. Sauté the onion, carrot, and celery in a saucepan with some butter. Add the ham and the minced meat, season with salt and pepper. Cook until golden, sprinkle with flour, and brown over low heat.

2. Add the bouillon and crushed tomatoes and simmer for 30 minutes over low heat.

3. Cook the pasta "al dente" in boiling, salted water. There should be plenty of fairly thick sauce.

Leg of lamb sandwich

Ingredients per person
A few salad leaves
1 crusty whole-wheat roll
1 thin slice cold leg of lamb
or 5 oz (150 g) chopped lamb
1 tsp Meaux mustard
2 gherkins

1. Sort the small salad leaves, wash, and drain carefully.

2. Cut the roll open, without completely separating the two halves, and place the slice of meat or chopped lamb inside.

3. Add one or two salad leaves and serve with some Meaux mustard and gherkins.

Pork

Three cooking methods over high heat

Frying, deep-frying, and sautéing are terms used to describe the rapid cooking over high heat of thin pieces of tender meat. To sauté and fry meat, it is best to use a heavy-bottomed skillet that diffuses the heat better. For deep-frying, there should be enough oil for the meat to be completely immersed. The cuts of pork that can be cooked in this manner are loin chops, pork steaks, medallions cut from the loin, filets mignons (cut from the end of the fillet), and kidneys. For a successful result, remove the meat from the refrigerator 1 hour before cooking and season with salt and pepper.

Pork chops with apple sauce

Pickwick Club pork chops

Pork chops Normandy style

To serve 6, season 6 pork chops with salt and pepper. Melt a large dab of butter in a skillet and then add the seasoned chops. Cook for a good 5 minutes over medium heat, turn, and cook on the other side for 3 minutes. Keep hot while you prepare the sauce. Place 1 chopped white onion in the skillet and braise for 2 minutes. Deglaze with 3 1/2 tbsp (5 cl) calvados and boil for 2 minutes. Add 2/3 cup (15 cl) crème fraîche, 1/3 cup (8 cl) veal bouillon, and 3 tbsp apple compote. Cook over low heat for 3 minutes. Add 1 dab of butter while stirring the sauce, season with salt and pepper, spoon over the cooked pork chops, and serve immediately.

Basque pork chops

To serve 6, peel 2 onions, 3 red bell peppers, and 3 cloves of garlic. Heat some olive oil and braise the onions in it, followed by the bell peppers cut into small strips. Next, add 4 tomatoes, skinned and seeded, the chopped garlic, and 1 pinch Espelette (Basque chili) pepper, cover, and cook for 30 minutes. Season with salt and pepper, then keep hot. Place 6 pork chops on the worktop and leave them to reach room temperature for 30 minutes. Season with salt and pepper on both sides. Heat a skillet with some oil in the bottom over medium heat and cook the chops for 5 minutes on each side. Arrange the cooked chops on a serving dish and spoon over the bell pepper sauce. Serve immediately.

Pork chops with anchovies

To serve 6, peel and finely chop 2 onions. Heat some olive oil and braise the onions. Then add 4 skinned, seeded tomatoes, 1 tsp tomato paste, and 2 crushed cloves of garlic, cover and cook for 30 minutes. Then add to the sauce 1³/₄ oz (50 g) anchovy fillets puréed in a blender, some salt, pepper, and a dash of olive oil. Season with salt and pepper and keep hot. Place 6 pork chops on the worktop and season with salt and pepper on both sides. Heat some oil in the bottom of a skillet over medium heat and cook the chops for 5 minutes on each side. Arrange the cooked chops on a serving dish and spoon over the anchovy sauce.

Barbecued pork chops

Pork chops Corbigny

Fried bacon and eggs

Fried bacon slices

These should be cooked with a little oil over moderate heat to prevent them drying out. Grease a skillet with a little groundnut oil and put the bacon in the pan. Set over medium heat and brown for 2 minutes each side, watching them carefully. Drain on paper towels to soak up excess fat.

Pork chops with apples

To serve 6, peel 3 apples, seed, and cut into quarters. Cook the apples in butter in a skillet over low heat, with a little sugar and ground cinnamon. Meanwhile, season 6 pork chops with salt and pepper. Sauté in a very hot skillet for 5 minutes on each side, moving them around the pan occasionally so they do not stick to the bottom. Arrange the cooked chops on a serving dish. Pour the remaining oil into the skillet and deglaze with half a glass of water. Reduce, season with salt and pepper and add 1 small dab of butter. Spoon the juices over the chops and arrange the cooked apples on the dish.

Pork chops with apples

305

Pork kebabs with onion for 6

1 Meat, offal meat, and vegetables can be combined in numerous ways in this recipe. Use a tender meat such as shoulder or boned loin. Cut 2¼ lb (1 kg) shoulder of pork into medium-sized pieces. Season with salt and pepper and flavor the meat with 1 bunch chopped fresh basil and 3½ tbsp (5 cl) olive oil.

2 Mix all the ingredients well. Cut the smoked breast of pork into small rectangles 3/16 in (5 mm) thick, having first removed the rind and the cartilage, and blanch. Cut 4 onions into cubes. Prepare the kebabs by threading the meat, diced bacon, and onions alternately onto the skewers. You can add a bay leaf or two and a quarter tomato here and there.

3 This recipe can be varied by using pig's kidneys, mushrooms, bell peppers, or slices of baby leek. Cook the kebabs for about 15 minutes, 8 in (20 cm) from the charcoal. Turn them regularly, holding the skewers with a cloth, so that they cook evenly.

N.B.

When grilling over charcoal, the food is not in direct contact with the heat source, but is suspended above it, generally on a rack that is perforated to a greater or lesser degree. This is therefore a healthy way of cooking meat, as the fat usually needed to stop the meat sticking to the cooking receptacle is no longer required. Despite this, the meat can be flavored with a drizzle of olive oil. The smoke produced during cooking flavors the pork, which is why it is always best to cook over a good bed of charcoal. It is of course possible to use an electric grill, but the result is far less appetizing. The best cuts of meat for cooking on a charcoal grill are chine, chops, steaks, kidneys, and also andouillettes and sausages.

Pork kebabs Camargue style

Spare ribs with cherries

Pork chops Valencia style

Grilled pork chops with sage

Spare ribs

To serve 6, cut 3 lb (1.4 kg) ribs into the pieces the size of a finger. Place in a large bowl and mix with 2 tbsp paprika, 10 tbsp sugar, some salt, $1/3$ cup + $1^1/_2$ tbsp (10 cl) lemon juice, 3 tbsp tomato paste, 1 chopped onion, 6 tbsp Worcestershire sauce, and 1 tsp tabasco. Leave to marinate in the refrigerator overnight. Cook over a fairly hot charcoal grill so that the meat can cook without browning too much. You can serve this recipe with white rice and prepared barbecue sauce.

Glazed spare ribs

For this Chinese recipe, you will need some of the "five spice" mixture found in Oriental grocery stores. For 6 people, cut 3 lb (1.4 kg) pork spare rib into pieces lengthwise. Place the meat in a large bowl and mix with 10 tbsp honey, 2 chopped cloves of garlic, 3 tbsp chopped fresh ginger, 1 tbsp five-spice mixture, 10 tbsp soy sauce, and 10 tbsp sesame oil. Leave to marinate in the refrigerator overnight. Cook these spare ribs fairly slowly over the grill, turning frequently, and serve with a dish of plain rice.

Grilled pork chops with herbs

These are as delicious as they are simple to prepare. The day before, season 6 good loin or spare rib pork chops with salt and pepper and sprinkle them with oregano, thyme, and dried rosemary. Add a dash of olive oil, mix, and refrigerate overnight. Prepare a good charcoal fire; brush the grill rack and wipe with a cloth to clean. Heat the rack 8 in (20 cm) above the charcoal for 5 minutes, then place the pork chops on the rack. Cook for approximately 6 minutes on each side. Serve very hot with mustard and baked potatoes cooked in foil.

General points

When cooked in the direct heat of the oven, pork browns rapidly and develops succulent flavors. In order for the meat to brown, it is important to brush the surface of the meat with oil. The flavor of roast pork also depends on the seasoning, which should be added prior to cooking. Salt, pepper, and thyme are generally used, but this may include other seasonings and spices.

Crown of roast pork

To serve 6–8, ask your butcher to cut 3 lb 5 oz (1.5 kg) loin of pork and form it into a crown.

Prepare the stuffing by washing and chopping 2 stalks parsley. Peel and chop 6 cloves of garlic and 3 onions. Braise the chopped onions until they are pale golden and set aside. Place 3½ oz (100 g) breadcrumbs, 10½ oz (300 g) sausage meat, 7 oz (200 g) cooked spinach, the chopped parsley, the cooked onions, the garlic, and 4 pinches fresh thyme and 4 chopped sage leaves in a large bowl. Stir everything together well until you have a homogeneous mixture. Line a roasting pan with aluminum foil, place the loin of pork in the pan, season, and fill the center with the stuffing. Protect the stuffing and the ends of the bones by covering them with aluminum foil. Cook in the oven at 400 °F (200 °C) for 30 minutes, then at 350 °F (180 °C) for 1 hour, basting several times during cooking. Leave to stand for a few minutes before carving. Serve quickly, carved into equal-sized portions of meat and stuffing.

Loin of pork with apples and cider for 6

1 Heat 4 tbsp lard in a large casserole and add 4 finely chopped onions. Stir and cook over medium heat for 15 minutes. Then add 2 or 3 large firm-fleshed apples that have been peeled, sprinkled with lemon juice, cored, and cut into even-sized rings. Pour in 2 cups (50 cl) cider.

2 Cover and cook slowly for 15 minutes before adding 1 lb 2 oz (500 g) smoked breast of pork cut into small cubes. Meanwhile, season a loin of pork with salt and pepper and cook in the oven at 410 °F (210 °C) for 35 minutes per 2¼ lb (1 kg). Baste several times during cooking until the juice runs clear when you pierce the meat with a fork.

3 Remove the pork loin from the oven and place on top of the apples. Cover and cook for a further 30 minutes. Serve in a large dish that has been heated in the oven. Cut the loin into individual chops and arrange on top of the apples. As an alternative, you can substitute sauerkraut for the apples and white wine for the cider, and serve with mustard.

Roast ham cooked in its rind

1 Brush a 3 lb 5 oz (1.5 kg) loin of pork with oil and season. Cook in the oven at 410 °F (210 °C) for 30 minutes. Meanwhile, peel 7 oz (200 g) onions and 1³/₄ lb (800 g) potatoes. Cut the vegetables into fairly thick slices.

2 Wash the potatoes, then season them with some salt, pepper, and thyme. When the loin of pork is well browned, place the potatoes and the onions in the roasting pan and continue cooking at 350 °F (180 °C) for 50 minutes. Carve and serve very hot.

Roast ham cooked in its rind

Use a small ham for this recipe. The skin caramelizes and protects the meat underneath. To serve 15, ask your butcher to remove the bone from the chump end of a ham weighing about 11¹/₄ lb (5 kg). Using a very sharp knife, make incisions in the rind without cutting the meat. Make an initial longitudinal incision and several more down the sides. Place the ham in a roasting pan and season with salt and pepper. Brush with groundnut oil. Cook the meat in the oven at 350 °F (180 °C), basting frequently as soon as it begins to color, for about 4 hours. When the meat is cooked, remove it from the oven and leave to stand for a few minutes. Remove the skin in a single piece, uncovering the meat beneath. Cut into slices, not too thinly, and serve with the cooking juices from which the fat has been skimmed.

Poaching

This is a slow, even method of cooking, in which the meat is cooked in barely boiling or simmering water or bouillon.

Salt pork with marrowfat peas

To serve 6, soak $4^1/_2$ lb (2 kg) salt pork in cold water the day before cooking to remove the salt. When ready to cook, place in a cooking pot with 4 quarts (4 liters) water. Bring to the boil, skim, and add 3 carrots, 2 onions, 3 leeks, 1 bouquet garni, 10 peppercorns, and 1 clove. Cook slowly for 2 hours. Meanwhile, blanch 1 lb 2 oz (500 g) marrowfat peas, then cook them in 3 quarts (3 liters) water with 1 large bouquet garni for 1 hour. Drain the peas, then reduce them to a fine purée in a blender. Add $3^1/_2$ oz (100 g) butter and 2 tbsp crème fraîche. Season with salt and pepper and set aside. Once the meat is cooked, drain, slice, and serve it with the vegetables and the very hot marrowfat pea purée.

Salt pork with marrowfat peas

Knuckle of pork with vegetables

Pork knuckle with vegetables

To serve 6–8, place 2 unsalted pork knuckles in a large stewpot, cover with 4 quarts (4 liters) cold water, and bring to the boil. Skim. Adjust the heat until the contents of the pan are simmering very gently and evenly. Cook for 1 hour. Peel 5 cloves of garlic and leave them whole. Cut 6 carrots in half and stick 4 onions with 4 cloves. Wash 3 leeks and tie with string. Tie 20 black peppercorns in a muslin bag. Add all the vegetables, 1 bouquet garni, 2 tbsp coarse salt, and the peppercorns to the bouillon. Bring back to the boil and adjust the heat so the bubbles just break the surface regularly. Skim off the fat every 15 minutes using a small ladle. At the end of the 1 hour 30 minutes' cooking time, drain the vegetables and keep them hot in a dish. Discard the bouquet garni, the muslin bag of peppercorns, and the string around the leeks. Reheat the vegetables in the broth from the stewpot and set aside. Drain the knuckles and cut into

Cocido

slices, not too thinly. Spoon over a few ladles of boiling hot broth. Serve the vegetables in a separate dish, with mustard and coarse salt.

Cocido

To serve 6, soak $3^1/_2$ oz (100 g) chickpeas in some cold water the day before. Peel 6 cloves of garlic, and peel and finely chop 2 onions and 2 carrots. Place $4^1/_2$ lb (2 kg) pork chine in a stewpot with 4 quarts (4 liters) water. Bring to the boil, skim, and cook for 1 hour. Then add 1 large bouquet garni, 1 tbsp paprika (to add color), 1 tbsp coarse salt, and the vegetables, and cook slowly for 2 hours. Wash and peel $2^1/_4$ lb (1 kg) potatoes and cut into fairly thick slices. Add to the pot and cook for 35 minutes. Finish by adding 20 rings of chorizo sausage. Carve the meat into slices and serve with the vegetables and broth.

Casseroling

This method of cooking produces succulent meat full of flavor and delicious cooking juices. The meat is always browned first in oil over high heat, and is then covered and cooked fairly slowly with seasonings and spices. For these recipes, use a heavy cast iron or enameled casserole.

Roast pork with milk

To serve 5–6, season with salt and pepper and brown a 3 lb 5 oz (1.5 kg) pork roasting joint cut from the loin or the chine. When the meat is golden brown on all sides, add 1 large chopped onion and cook until pale golden for 10 minutes, then add 2 cups (50 cl) full-fat milk, cover, and cook slowly for 1 hour 30 minutes, stirring from time to time. Remove the cooked meat and, if necessary, reduce the milk further for several minutes. Adjust the seasoning, carve the meat into slices, and spoon over the milk sauce.

Roast pork with milk

1 Soak 1 slightly salted shoulder of pork weighing about 2¹/₄ lb (1 kg) in cold water for 3 hours to remove the salt, discarding the water at least once during this time. Then place the pork shoulder in a stewpot, cover with cold water, and bring gently to the boil. Simmer for 5 minutes, then drain. Peel and chop 2 onions. Peel 6 carrots and cut into small sticks.

3 Drain the pork shoulder. Strain the broth and allow to cool a little. Place 14 oz (400 g) green Puy lentils in a saucepan with 2 cloves of garlic and 1 bouquet garni. Cover with the broth and if necessary top up with a little cold water. Season with salt and pepper and bring to the boil, then leave to simmer for 10 minutes. Place the shoulder in the pan with the lentils and cover. Continue simmering very gently for 10 minutes.

Shoulder of pork with lentils for 4

2 Heat 2 tbsp goose fat in a saucepan. Add the carrots and the onions and brown for a few moments, but do not allow them to brown. Add 1 bouquet garni and then place the shoulder on the bed of vegetables. Cover with cold water and bring slowly to the boil. Lower the heat, cover, and simmer for 2 hours 30 minutes.

4 After completing these two steps, add 4 sausages to the lentils and cook them around the pork shoulder, pushing them down slightly into the lentils. Replace the lid and cook for a further 20 minutes or so. Heat the serving dish before pouring the lentils into it and arranging the sausages and sliced pork shoulder on top. Serve on very hot plates with an assortment of flavored mustards.

311

General points

Braised dishes are cooked in two stages. The meat is first browned in oil over high heat and then cooked slowly in a sauce. Practically all cuts of pork are suitable for braising: shoulder, chine, knuckle, loin, and breast.

Flemish carbonade

Braised pork vintner style

To serve 6, cut 3 lb (1.4 kg) meat (chine or shoulder) into $3/4$ in (2 cm) cubes. Peel 3 onions and 4 carrots. Cut the onions into small cubes and the carrots into sticks 1–$1^1/2$ in (3–4 cm) long. Prepare 1 bouquet garni. Place all these ingredients in a large bowl and mix with 6 cups

(1.4 liters) red wine. Cover with plastic wrap and refrigerate for 24 hours. The next day, drain all the ingredients for 30 minutes. Then separate the meat from the vegetables and reserve the marinade. Heat some groundnut oil in a casserole over medium heat and brown the vegetables for 10 minutes. Meanwhile, brown the pieces of meat in a very hot skillet. All the pieces should be well browned all over. Add them to the pan in which you are cooking the vegetables, remove the fat from the casserole, sprinkle in $5/8$ cup (70 g) flour and cook over medium heat for 5 minutes, stirring constantly. Pour the marinade into the skillet in which you browned the meat and boil very rapidly for 30 minutes, skimming regularly. Then pour this red wine sauce over the meat and vegetables, add the bouquet garni, 1 $2/3$ cups (40 cl) beef or veal bouillon, season with salt and pepper, cover, and cook very slowly for about 2 hours. Taste the meat. If it is cooked to your liking, drain and set aside in a dish. Add 1 glass beef or veal bouillon to the sauce and boil slowly for 10 minutes. Skim the fat off the sauce using a small ladle and discard the bouquet garni. Blanch $3^1/2$ oz (100 g) bacon lardoons and add to the sauce. If it is too liquid, thicken with a little flour mixed with butter. Finish the sauce by adjusting the seasoning. Fifteen minutes before serving, place

the cooked meat in the sauce, bring to simmering point, and serve in a very hot serving dish with boiled potatoes as an accompaniment.

Chine of pork with Chinon

To serve 5–6, season with salt and pepper brown a 3 lb 5 oz (1.5 kg) roasting joint of pork cut from the loin or the chine. When the meat is golden on all sides, add a good-sized onion, 2 shallots, and 2 carrots, all chopped. Braise for 10 minutes, then add $1^1/4$ cups (30 cl) Chinon wine. Cover and cook slowly for 30 minutes before adding $1^1/4$ cups (30 cl) bouillon. Cook for 1 hour, stirring from time to time. Remove the cooked meat and reduce the sauce for a few minutes. Adjust the seasoning and thicken with 1 oz (30 g) cornstarch mixed with 2 cups (50 cl) red wine. Carve the roast meat into slices and spoon over the Chinon sauce.

Baeckeoffe

Baeckeoffe

This recipe from Alsace is cooked in a terrine, tightly sealed. To serve 6, cut a generous 2¼ lb (1 kg) of pork into cubes and leave them to marinate overnight in 4 cups (1 liter) white wine, some salt, 3 chopped cloves of garlic, some pepper, and three finely chopped onions. Butter a terracotta terrine and place a layer of sliced potato in the bottom, followed by the meat and the finely chopped onions. Cover with a layer of potatoes. Pour in the marinade, season with salt and pepper, and add 1 bouquet garni. Knead 2 cups (250 g) flour and ⅓ cup + 1½ tbsp (10 cl) water in a large bowl to form a soft dough. Put the lid on the terrine and seal with the dough. Cook in the oven at 340 °F (170 °C) for at least 3 hours.

Pork braised in red wine with eggplants for 6–8

1 Cut 3 lb (1.4 kg) pork into ¾ in (2 cm) cubes. Season with salt and pepper. Heat some oil in a casserole and brown the meat over high heat for 20 minutes. Prepare the vegetables. Seed 1 red and 1 green bell pepper and cut into large pieces. Peel 1 onion and cut into medium-sized pieces. Peel and chop 5 cloves of garlic. Wash 4 tomatoes and remove the stalks; wash 4 eggplants and slice fairly thinly.

2 When the meat is well browned, place in a dish. Then brown the onions and peppers for 5 minutes before adding the eggplants. Cook for 5 minutes and add the tomatoes, 3 tbsp tomato paste, the browned meat and the meat juices, 1 scant cup (20 cl) rosé wine, the chopped garlic, and 5 cups (1.2 liters) veal bouillon. Add 1 bouquet garni, bring to the boil, then cover and cook very slowly for 2 hours. Taste the meat.

3 When it is cooked to your liking, drain and set aside in a dish. Add 1 glass of beef or veal bouillon to the sauce and boil slowly. Remove the fat from the sauce using a small ladle and discard the bouquet garni. If the sauce is too liquid, thicken with a little flour mixed with some butter.

4 Adjust seasoning to taste. The sauce is now ready. Fifteen minutes before serving, return the cooked meat to the sauce. Bring it back to simmering point for the last time, before transferring to a very hot serving dish. Serve this dish with steamed potatoes as an accompaniment.

sauerkraut can be prepared with monkfish, salmon, and haddock. The method is identical, but the cooking time is shorter. There are also recipes in which sauerkraut is served with roast pork and preserved duck thighs. You can also vary the flavor by using different white wines (Riesling, Sylvaner, Edelzwicker) or substituting (either in full or in part) good quality pale ale.

Alsatian sauerkraut

N.B.

Sauerkraut is a dish in which cold meats and white cabbage, chopped, salted and fermented, have pride of place. There are numerous regional variations. Commercial sauerkraut is generally already cooked, and all that is required is to simmer it with the white wine and the meat. If you are using raw cabbage, the cooking time will be much longer. The quality of the cold meats is of crucial importance. Choose best-quality products (with a quality label or of known origin) from a specialist butcher. You can vary the recipe by using different specialties such as smoked ham, Frankfurter or Montbéliard sausages, and semi-salted rind or breast. Similarly, fish

Tip

Contrary to popular belief, sauerkraut is light and easily digested, provided it is not cooked with too much fat. It does not contain any lipids at the start of the cooking time. It is therefore recommended that you choose good cooked meats in order to avoid making the dish heavy.

Polish sauerkraut

1 Soak 1 knuckle of slightly salted pork overnight. When you are ready to cook, blanch the soaked knuckle and then boil in water with 1 large bouquet garni, 1 chopped carrot, and 1 onion stuck with cloves. Heat 4 tbsp lard in a large casserole and add 4 finely chopped onions. Stir and cook over medium heat for 15 minutes, without browning.

2 Add 3 lb 5 oz (1.5 kg) sauerkraut and 6 juniper berries. Break up the cabbage with a fork, lifting it from time to time. Add 2 cups (50 cl) dry white Alsace wine. Cover and cook slowly for 30 minutes. Then add the cooked knuckle, 1 lb 2 oz (500 g) smoked breast of pork cut into thin slices, 4 smoked sausages (Morteau sausages), and 4 Strasbourg sausages.

3 Slowly pour in $1^{1}/_{4}$ cups (30 cl) dry white wine. Season with salt and pepper, cover, and continue to cook over low heat for 30 minutes. Meanwhile, peel $2^{1}/_{4}$ lb (1 kg) potatoes and boil or steam them. Adjust the seasoning of the sauerkraut to taste. It should be aromatic, not too wet, slightly acidic, and should have absorbed the flavors of the smoked meats.

4 Transfer the cabbage to a large serving platter and arrange the sausages, the breast of pork slices, and the sliced pork knuckle over it. Pour over the cooking juices and serve the potatoes separately. Do not forget the hot mustard or the horseradish. It is also essential to serve and enjoy sauerkraut while it is still very hot; serve on heated plates with a plate warmer on the table.

Gratin of leeks rolled in ham for 4

1 Cut off the roots of 16 small leeks. Remove the outer leaves and cut off part of the green section. Cut the leeks into four, starting from the base, and wash thoroughly. Cook in boiling salted water for 25–30 minutes. Drain, then leave to cool for a few minutes. Roll a bundle of 4 leeks in 1 slice of cooked ham. Arrange in a buttered gratin dish.

2 Heat and then slowly boil 1³/₄ oz (50 g) butter and 1 tbsp flour in a small saucepan for 4 minutes. Set aside. Boil and then infuse 2 cups (50 cl) milk in another saucepan with ¹/₂ finely chopped onion, some salt, pepper, and grated nutmeg for 10 minutes. Discard the onions, then add the butter and flour mixture off the heat, beating with a fork, until the mixture has a smooth consistency.

3 Return the sauce to the burner and boil over very low heat for 3 minutes, stirring slowly. Adjust seasoning to taste. If a few lumps have formed, do not beat the sauce too much or it may curdle. Strain through a fine sieve. Then spoon the béchamel sauce over the leeks, sprinkle the surface with grated cheese, add some small dabs of butter, and brown the top in the oven for 15 minutes at 475 °F (245 °C).

Toad in the hole

Toad in the hole

This is an English specialty for which you should use small English sausages. To serve 6, you will need 18 sausages. Prick them with a fork and brown over a brisk heat for 5 minutes. Combine 3 eggs, 1³/₄ cups (200 g) flour, 3 pinches salt, 1 pinch sugar, some pepper, some mustard, and 2 cups (50 cl) milk in a large bowl. Beat well and strain through a fine sieve. Butter a gratin dish, arrange the browned sausages in the bottom, and pour the liquid over them. Cook in the oven at 400 °F (200 °C) for 35 minutes and serve piping hot.

Pork escalopes with tapenade sauce

To serve 6, score 6 escalopes in squares using a small knife. Combine 125 olives, 1 clove of garlic, 2³/4 oz (80 g) anchovies, 3¹/₂ oz (100 g) flaked tuna, 5 tbsp olive oil, and some salt and pepper in a bowl then blend to a fine purée. Spread both sides of the escalopes, then dip them in the beaten egg followed by the breadcrumbs. Melt a large dab of butter in a skillet and cook the escalopes over gentle heat for 10 minutes on each side. Turn them gently so as not to dislodge the tapenade.

Gratins, breadcrumbs, and pasta

1 Make the brioche dough the day before. Heat a scant $^1/_2$ cup (10 cl) milk until lukewarm, then mix in $^1/_8$ cup (30 g) sugar, 3 tsp salt, and 4 tsp (20 g) dried yeast. Take 12$^1/_2$ oz (350 g) butter out of the refrigerator and cut into small cubes. Set aside until they have reached room temperature. Combine 4 $^1/_3$ cups (500 g) flour, the milk mixture, and 6 eggs in the bowl of a dough mixer and knead all the ingredients on a high speed setting for 5 minutes. Stop the machine.

2 Use a rubber spatula to scrape any flour and egg from around the top of the bowl into the mixture. Mix again, this time on a medium speed setting, for 5 minutes. The dough will gradually become firmer. Knead at a slightly higher speed for another 5 minutes. The dough will come away from the sides of the bowl and stick to the dough hook. Add the small pieces of butter and mix on a medium setting for 2 minutes to incorporate.

3 The dough is ready when the butter has completely disappeared. Remove from the bowl, dust with flour, and roll into a ball. Place in a covered bowl and leave to rest in the refrigerator overnight. Next day, choose a large sausage and poach in bouillon for 1 hour 30 minutes, ensuring that the liquid never boils. Drain the sausage and leave to cool for a few moments.

Chipolatas in pastry

Prick the chipolatas with a fork, season with salt and pepper, and brown in a skillet for 5 minutes. Leave to cool. Roll out some puff pastry and cut into rectangles slightly longer than the sausages and 1$^1/_2$ in (4 cm) wide. Place the sausages on the pastry rectangles and roll them up. Seal the base and top of the turnovers, glaze with beaten egg, and cook in the oven at 375 °F (190 °C) for 20 minutes. Serve very hot with a curly endive salad flavored with mustard vinaigrette.

4 Cut open the skin and discard it. Roll out the brioche dough fairly thickly and wrap the sausage in it so it is completely sealed, then transfer to a rectangular, buttered mold. Glaze the surface with milk or beaten egg and make a chimney out of aluminum foil to allow the steam to escape during cooking. This dish can either be served very hot with Madeira sauce or cold with lamb's lettuce.

General points

Cooking sausages is straightforward and only requires a few elementary precautions. There is always a risk that the sausages will burst during cooking. This is why raw sausages are pricked, to allow the steam to escape freely. Most sausages are grilled, broiled, or fried in a skillet, whereby they brown and acquire a subtle flavor. Others are poached slowly in seasoned broth.

Merguez West Indian style

Grilled sausages

Merguez and chipolatas can be cooked over a bed of charcoal. First, spread the sausages on the worktop and prick them with a fork along their whole length. Season with salt and pepper and place on the grill, about 8 in (20 cm) above the charcoal. Turn as soon as they are brown. Dripping fat can make the charcoal flare; extinguish the flames with a sprinkling of coarse salt.

Chipolatas with polenta

Boudins noir and boudin blanc

These are also sold ready cooked. Their skin is very fragile and they can easily burst if they are reheated too quickly. Never pierce them. Place in a skillet with 1 large dab of butter and reheat very gently for about 20 minutes. Turn frequently so that they turn pale golden brown all over.

Boudin with onions

Grilled andouillette

Andouillettes

These are cooked products that are reheated in the skillet or grilled. It is not necessary to prick them. Season them with salt and pepper and place on the grill, about 8 in (20 cm) above the charcoal. Turn them when they are brown. Serve very hot.

Small pork sausages and flat sausages

These are served with oysters in the Bordeaux region and are cooked on a charcoal grill or in a skillet. Spread out the sausages on the worktop and prick with a fork along their whole length. Season with salt and pepper. Place on the grill about 8 in (20 cm) above the charcoal. Turn them when they are brown. Serve very hot.

Savoy cabbage sausages

Toulouse stew

Toulouse sausage

Toulouse sausage can be grilled or cooked in a skillet. Place on the worktop and prick with a fork. Season, then roll the sausage around itself and pierce with two long fine metal skewers to keep in shape. Heat 4 tbsp peanut oil in a large skillet. Place the rolled sausage in it and cook over high heat for about 8 minutes on each side. When the sausage is cooked, remove it from the skillet and leave to rest for a few moments. Remove the skewers, then unroll the sausage and cut it into fairly large pieces. Always serve very hot with mustard and sautéed potatoes.

Uncooked sausages

As the name suggests, these sausages are sold raw and it is essential to cook them in broth. You should start cooking them in cold or lukewarm water so that the skin does not harden too quickly. Place one cooking sausage, 1 onion stuck with cloves, 2 carrots, 2 leeks, 1 large bouquet garni, some salt, some pepper, and some cold water in a saucepan. Bring slowly to the boil and cook in water that is just simmering, skimming regularly. Cooking times vary widely and depend on the diameter of the sausage. Take 30–40 minutes per pound as a guide. When the sausage is cooked, drain carefully and leave to cool for several minutes. Cut the sausage into slices and serve immediately.

Strasbourg and Frankfurter Sausages

Sold already cooked, these only need to be reheated. Cook in a pan containing water heated to about 195 °F (90 °C) (simmering) for 10 minutes. Never allow the water to boil as the sausages would burst immediately and would no longer be fit to serve. As an extra precaution, turn down the heat and cover during cooking. Do not leave any longer than necessary in the hot water as they will rapidly lose their flavor. Only poach for as long as is necessary to reheat them.

Strasbourg and Frankfurter sausages

319

Sweet and sour glazed pork

pepper. Mix. Heat 6 tbsp groundnut oil in a very large skillet (or, better still, a wok). When the oil begins to smoke, cook the meat in it with the vegetables and spices. Stir from time to time to ensure all the meat is properly cooked. Cook over very high heat for about 5 minutes, add a few drops of sesame oil, and serve immediately.

General points

Pork occupies a prominent place in Chinese cuisine, and the numerous recipes for pork show the regional influences of this vast country. Use tender cuts such as shoulder or boned chine.

Chopped pork with bell peppers

To serve 6, cut 2¹/₄ lb (1 kg) pork into thin strips. Make the meat easier to cut by placing it in the freezer for 1 hour. Place the pork strips in a large bowl. Add 3 red bell peppers, cut into thin strips, 3 cloves garlic, 2 white onions, and 1 piece of chopped, fresh ginger. Mix all these ingredients and then add some salt, 3 tbsp sugar, 3 tbsp soy sauce, and 2 pinches Cayenne

Braised breast of pork

To serve 6, remove the rind from a fresh piece of breast of pork weighing 3 lb 5 oz (1.5 kg) and season with salt and pepper. Cut into 12 pieces. Brown the meat over high heat in a casserole until it is a nice, golden color. Drain off the excess fat from the casserole and add 8 blanched seasoned mushrooms, 2 fresh bamboo shoots, each cut into four, 4 finely chopped white onions, 1 stick cinnamon, 1 piece of fresh ginger (grated), 3 star anise, 1 scant cup (20 cl) bouillon, and ¹/₃ cup + 1¹/₂ tbsp (10 cl) soy sauce. Bring to the boil, then cover and cook very gently for 1 hour, skimming the fat off the sauce frequently. Serve very hot with white rice.

Pork with peanuts

To serve 6 people, cut 2¹/₄ lb (1 kg) shoulder of pork into small cubes. Place this meat in a large bowl and mix with 1 tbsp sugar, 3 dashes soy sauce, 1 level tsp cornstarch, 3 pinches "five spice" mixture and 9 oz (250 g) raw peanuts, without their skins. Heat 6 tbsp peanut oil in a very large skillet (or, better still, a wok). When the oil begins to smoke, cook the meat mixed with the vegetables and spices. Stir from time to time to ensure all the meat is properly cooked. Cook over very high heat for about 5 minutes, add a few drops of sesame oil, and serve immediately.

Chinese pork noodles

Pork with vermicelli

Pork with mushrooms

To serve 6, slice 2$\frac{1}{4}$ lb (1 kg) boned shoulder of pork very finely. To make it easier to slice, place the meat in the freezer for 1 hour. Soak 4 shitake mushrooms and 5 black mushrooms for several hours, then wash and blanch them. Place the sliced pork in a large bowl. Add the drained mushrooms, cut into pieces, 3 cloves garlic, 2 white onions, 1 piece fresh ginger (grated), and the white part of 1 leek, cut into juliennes. Mix all these ingredients and then add some salt, 3 tbsp sugar, 4 tbsp soy sauce, 2$\frac{1}{2}$ tbsp (4 cl) Chinese vinegar, and 2 pinches Cayenne pepper. Mix. Heat 6 tbsp peanut oil in a very large skillet (or, better still, a wok). When the oil begins to smoke, cook the meat mixed with the vege-tables and spices. Stir from time to time to ensure all the meat is properly cooked. Cook over very high heat for about 5 minutes, add a few drops of sesame oil, and serve immedia-tely.

Imperial pancake rolls for 4

1 Soak 3$\frac{1}{2}$ oz (100 g) dried black mushrooms in lukewarm water. Heat 1 tbsp oil in a skillet and sauté 9 oz (250 g) chopped pork in this. Sprinkle with 1 tsp cornstarch and deglaze with 1 tbsp Chinese wine. Peel 1 carrot and 1 onion and cut into juliennes. Heat 1 tbsp oil and cook the mushrooms slowly in it, adding the carrot and the onion once the water from the mushrooms has been absorbed.

2 Add 3$\frac{1}{2}$ oz (100 g) peeled shrimp and 5$\frac{1}{2}$ oz (150 g) soybeans. Place the pancakes (they can be bought in packets from Asian food stores) on a board. Brush the top of each with lukewarm water and spread them out side-by-side, dry side down. Allow them to absorb the water and soften, which will take 3–4 minutes.

3 Mix the pork and the contents of the skillet in a basin. Taste and season with salt and pepper. Add a little soy sauce. Place 2 tbsp of this stuffing in one of the pancakes, keeping it well away from the edges. Fold the two sides of the pancake over the stuffing, then fold over the end nearest you and roll it away from you.

4 Make sure you do not press too hard as it might tear. Turn, with the last fold facing downwards. Heat some oil in a skillet and sauté your pancake rolls in it until they are crunchy and golden. Transfer to a hot plate. Garnish with lemon grass, coriander, or mint. Serve with soy sauce and Tabasco®.

General points

"Potée" is the term for a stew of vegetables and meats cooked together in an earthenware cooking pot, usually turnips, cabbage, and pork. There are numerous regional variations on this hearty, rustic, winter dish.

Potée from the Col de la Lauter

Maria Paradis potée

Potée from the Auvergne

To serve 6–8, place 1 joint of slightly salted blade of pork, 1 lb 2 oz (500 g) slightly salted breast of pork, and ¹/₂ a pig's head (thoroughly cleaned) in a stewpot. Cover with cold water and bring to the boil. Remove the scum and fat and cook over low heat for 1 hour 30 minutes. Then add 2 onions stuck with 2 cloves, 3 carrots, and 3 leeks tied together. Remove the outer leaves of 1 large head of kale. Remove the stalk and pull off all the leaves. Add the kale and 1 uncooked sausage to the bouillon and continue to simmer very gently for 1 hour 30 minutes. Remove some of the bouillon and boil 2¹/₄ lb (1 kg) peeled potatoes in it. Drain the meat, slice, and serve very hot with the cooked vegetables and some bouillon.

Potée from southwest France

To serve 6–8, place 1 joint of slightly salted blade of pork, 1 lb 2 oz (500 g) slightly salted breast of pork, 2 trotters, and 2 rolls of rind in a stewpot. Cover with cold water and bring to the boil. Remove the scum and fat and leave to cook over low heat for 1 hour 30 minutes. Then add 2 onions stuck with 2 cloves, 3 carrots, 3 leeks tied together, 1 large bouquet garni, 10 black peppercorns, and some sprigs of fresh thyme. Remove the outer leaves of 1 large head of kale. Remove the stalk, cut into four, and pull off all the leaves. Peel 1 kohlrabi and cut into large pieces. Add to the bouillon and cook over very low heat for 1 hour 30 minutes. Thirty minutes before the end of the cooking time, brown 4 pieces of preserved duck in the fat and then add to the bouillon. Remove some of the bouillon and boil 2¹/₄ lb (1 kg) peeled potatoes in it. Drain the meat, slice, and serve everything very hot with the cooked vegetables and some bouillon.

Potée Vosges style

Potée from Franche-Comté

To serve 6–8, place 2¼ lb (1 kg) rib of beef, 1 lb 2 oz (500 g) of slightly salted brisket, and 1 lb 2 oz (500 g) shoulder of lamb with the bones in a cooking pot. Cover with cold water and bring to the boil. Remove the scum and fat and cook over a low heat for 1 hour 30 minutes. Then add 2 onions stuck with 2 cloves, 3 carrots, and 4 turnips. Remove the outer leaves from a large head of kale. Remove the stalk, cut into four, and pull off all the leaves. Add the kale and 3 Morteau sausages to the bouillon and simmer very slowly for 1 hour 30 minutes. Drain the meat and the vegetables and serve very hot with mustard.

Potée from Britanny

This is a lighter recipe than the previous one. It is prepared using firm-fleshed fish. To serve 6–8, place 1 lb 2 oz (500 g) slightly salted breast of pork in a stewpot. Cover with 3 quarts (3 liters) cold water and bring to the boil. Remove the scum and fat and cook over low heat for 1 hour. Then add 3 onions stuck with 2 cloves, 4 carrots, 3 leeks tied together, 4 peeled turnips, and some salt and pepper. Remove the outer leaves from a large head of kale. Remove the stalk, cut into four, and pull off all the leaves. Add the kale to the bouillon and simmer very slowly for 30 minutes. Then add 2¼ lb (1 kg) conger eel portions and continue cooking for 35 minutes before adding 1 lb 2 oz (500 g) monkfish for the last 10 minutes of cooking time. Serve the meat and fish in one dish and the vegetables and bouillon in another.

Tip

The term "potée" originally signified a dish cooked in an earthenware pot. Although it was subsequently applied more widely, there are still regions in which the dish is still cooked in earthenware vessels, in particular in the Auvergne.

Light potée with knuckle of ham

Parisian potée

Buttered cabbage

General points

Cooked ham is almost always eaten cold. However, when reheated with the addition of spices, flavorings, or sauces, it is a succulent treat. Only use best quality ham for these recipes. If the recipe calls for slices of ham, make sure they are thick (about $3/8$ in/1 cm).

Glamorgan ham

adding 1 scant cup (20 cl) thickened veal bouillon, 7 oz (200 g) white button mushrooms, and 1 bouquet garni. Cover and cook all the ingredients over low heat for 30 minutes. Remove the meat and keep hot. Reduce the sauce for 5 minutes and skim off the fat. Adjust the seasoning and spoon the sauce over the ham. Serve this delicious recipe, which you can also prepare with a whole ham, with fried green cabbage.

Ham with Madeira

York ham braised with Madeira

To serve 6, ask your pork butcher for a joint of cooked ham with rind weighing 3 lb 5 oz (1.5 kg). Season the meat with pepper and brown over moderate heat in a little peanut oil in a casserole. Then add 2 finely chopped onions and cook them gently with the ham for 5 minutes, stirring from time to time. Pour in $1/3$ cup + $1^1/2$ tbsp (10 cl) Madeira, then cover and cook for 10 minutes before

Saupiquet Morvan style

In medieval cookery, "saupiquet" was the term for an acidic, spicy sauce served with roast meat. To serve 6, place 6 large slices of ham on the worktop and season them with pepper. Heat a large dab of butter in a skillet until it is foaming and reheat the slices of ham for 2 minutes on each side. Remove them from the skillet, transfer to a dish, cover, and keep warm. Discard the butter in the skillet then add 2 finely chopped shallots, followed by 5 peppercorns, 1 juniper berry, and $1/3$ cup (8 cl) wine vinegar. Reduce for 2 minutes, then add 1 generous cup (25 cl) veal bouillon, 15 chopped tarragon leaves, and some salt. Cook for 3 minutes, adjust the seasoning, and thicken the sauce with 1 tbsp cornstarch mixed with 4 tbsp red wine. Finish with 1 dab of butter and 2 tbsp crème fraîche. Shake the pan and pour the sauce over the very hot slices of ham.

Serve this dish with spinach leaves browned in butter.

Sliced ham Vendée style

To serve 6, cut 6 x 6$1/2$ oz (180 g) slices of raw Vendée ham. This recipe has been devised specifically for this type of ham, which has the most delightful, delicate, smoked flavor. Season the ham slices with pepper and heat a mixture of butter and oil in a skillet over medium heat. Fry the slices for 1 minute on each side so that they brown without drying out. Serve immediately with mustard and accompanied by potato purée with butter.

Ham soufflé

To serve 6, prepare a thick béchamel sauce with 1 $2/3$ cups (40 cl) milk, $2/3$ cup (80 g) flour, and 3$1/2$ oz (100 g) butter. Season the sauce with salt and pepper, and do not forget to add a little grated nutmeg.

Finely chop 9 oz (250 g) cooked ham. Combine the béchamel sauce, 3¹/₂ oz (100 g) grated gruyère cheese, the chopped ham, and 3 egg yolks in a large bowl. Beat 3 egg whites in another bowl until they form snowy peaks. Fold the ham sauce gently into the egg whites. Butter a soufflé dish and pour in the mixture. Cook in the oven at 400 °F (200 °C) for 30 minutes. Serve without delay, because the ham soufflé will collapse very quickly.

Sliced ham with cider

To serve 6, place 6 large slices of ham on the worktop and season with pepper. Heat a large dab of butter in a skillet until it is foaming and reheat the slices of ham for 2 minutes on each side. Remove them from the skillet, transfer to a serving dish, cover, and keep warm. Discard the butter in the skillet and deglaze with 1 small glass of calvados. Reduce, then add ¹/₃ cup + 1¹/₂ tbsp (10 cl) sweet cider and ¹/₃ cup + 1¹/₂ tbsp (10 cl) thickened veal bouillon. Season with salt and pepper and cook for 2 minutes. Taste the sauce and spoon it over the ham slices.

Cooked ham

Everglades roast ham for 15

1 Dissolve 6³/₄ lb (3 kg) coarse salt in some water. Immerse 1 raw ham, weighing about 11¹/₄ lb (5 kg), in this brine and leave for 6 days, covered with a cloth, so it impregnates the meat, turning the ham frequently. Wash the ham, wipe it, and place in a very large stewpot, cover with cold water, and then add 1 lb 2 oz (500 g) carrots cut into large rounds, 3 or 4 onions (having stuck 2 or 3 of these with cloves), and 5 or 6 peppercorns.

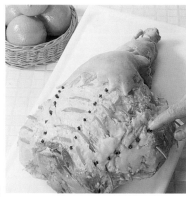

2 Heat and maintain the cooking temperature between 140 and 150 °F (60 and 65 °C) for 12 hours. Allow to cool in the cooking liquid. Remove almost all the rind from the ham, leaving only the rind on the knuckle, and score with a sharp knife. Stick with cloves at regular intervals and "lard" with juliennes of zest from 2 oranges.

Tip
To avoid having to wait for 6 days, you can find hams that have already been soaked in brine or have been prepared ready for cooking by your pork butcher, who will have pierced them in several places so the brine can penetrate the meat.

3 Wipe the ham again so that the mustard will stick to it easily. Place in a roasting pan and spread 1 pot of mustard over it using a rubber spatula. Sprinkle generously with 4 cups (1 kg) brown sugar, then caramelize in an oven set to 480 °F (250 °C). Serve hot with a vegetable accompaniment (usually spinach), or cold; in the latter case, leave to cool in the roasting pan before slicing.

Ragoût of pork with onions and beer for 6

1 Cut 2³/₄ lb (1.3 kg) pork chine into ³/₄–1 in (2–3 cm) cubes. Season with salt and pepper. Peel 8 onions and chop fairly finely. You will undoubtedly think this quantity excessive, but onions shrink by three-quarters during cooking. Peel 9 oz (250 g) white button mushrooms, discarding the stalks if they are too hard.

2 Cut in thick slices, sauté in a skillet, and set aside. Prepare the ragoût. Heat some peanut oil in a casserole and brown the seasoned pork cubes on all sides for 20 minutes. Add the chopped onions and cook over medium heat for 30 minutes.

General points

There are numerous recipes for ragoût of pork, but all of them are prepared on the same basic principle. Above all, it is important to choose good quality meat. Use cuts such as shoulder, chine, or breast. It is not necessary to trim the meat excessively; any connective tissue will soften during cooking to a delicious consistency. The meat should be cut into pieces the size of a large walnut, browned in fat over high heat, then covered and cooked gently with vegetables, spices, and a sauce. Fruit, such as quartered apples, prunes, or raisins, are sometimes added.

3 Add 1 pinch dried thyme, followed by 3 cups (75 cl) beer with ¹/₃ cup + 1¹/₂ tbsp (10 cl) beef or veal bouillon and 1 bouquet garni. Bring to the boil, season with salt and pepper, and cook over very low heat for about 1 hour 30 minutes. Taste the meat. When it is cooked to your satisfaction, drain and set aside in a dish. Add 1 glass of beef or veal bouillon to the sauce and bring to a slow boil. Skim off the fat with a small ladle and remove the bouquet garni.

4 If the sauce is too liquid, thicken with a little flour mixed to a paste with some butter. Finish the sauce by adjusting the seasoning. Fifteen minutes before serving, add the mushrooms and ¹/₂ bunch chopped chives. Heat until simmering and serve in a very hot serving dish with steamed potatoes or a fairly stiff celery purée.

Ragoût of pork with chanterelles

Ragoût of pork jardinière

Ragoût of pork with navy beans

Ragoût of pork with apples

This is a recipe in which you should use slightly acidic apples such as pippins. To serve 6–8, cut 2³/₄ lb (1.3 kg) shoulder or chine of pork into pieces the size of a large walnut and season them with salt, pepper, and 1 level tsp ground cinnamon. Pour a little oil into the bottom of a casserole and sauté the pieces of pork in it over fairly high heat. Only brown a few pieces of meat at a time to allow the meat to color well; if you put too many in at once they will boil rather than brown. Meanwhile, peel, core, and quarter 3 apples and sauté in a skillet with some butter and sugar for about 10 minutes until they turn golden. Set aside. Add 4 chopped shallots to the meat and cook for 10 minutes, stirring. Then incorporate the apples, 3¹/₂ tbsp (5 cl) cognac, 1 tbsp superfine sugar, 1 scant cup (20 cl) sweet cider, and 1 generous cup (25 cl) thickened veal, or

other, bouillon. Cover the casserole and leave to cook very slowly for about 1 hour. When the meat is cooked, drain it with the apples and keep hot in a dish. Add 1 small glass of bouillon to the sauce and bring to a slow boil. Remove the fat carefully using a small ladle, adjust the seasoning, and, if the sauce is too liquid, thicken it with 1 tbsp flour mixed with 2 oz (60 g) butter. Return the apples and the meat to the sauce, bring to simmering point, and serve immediately with a dish of plain white rice.

Ragoût of pork with navy beans

To serve 6–8, soak 10¹/₂ oz (300 g) dried navy beans in plenty of cold water the day before. When you are ready to cook, blanch the beans, cook them in water for 1 hour 30 minutes, then drain. Ask your butcher to

cut 2³/₄ lb (1.3 kg) shoulder of pork into pieces. Season them with salt and pepper. Heat a little oil in a casserole and brown the pieces of meat on all sides for about 15 minutes. Drain and transfer to a large bowl. Finely chop 4 onions and place in the bottom of the casserole. Lay the pieces of browned meat on top, then add 3 chopped carrots, 1 bouquet garni, 3 chopped tomatoes, the navy beans, and 2 bay leaves. Cover all the ingredients with beef bouillon from which the fat has been skimmed. Season with salt and pepper. Place the casserole over moderate heat, bring to the boil, then cover and cook over low heat for about 1 hour 30 minutes. When the meat is cooked, adjust the seasoning and skim the fat off the cooking liquid.

Barbecue sauce

General points

Pork can be flavored and seasoned in many different ways, and in particular with sauces. Some are acidic, some are hot, while others are mild or spicy. To prepare them, an intermediate stage—preparing a veal stock—is often necessary, but a simple beef or chicken bouillon can sometimes be substituted. As sauces do not keep very well, especially at room temperature, they should be used quickly or refrigerated.

Sage sauce

For 2 cups (50 cl) sauce, peel and finely chop 2 onions. Fry them in a little unsalted butter until golden. Then add 1 tsp crushed sage leaves, 1 small bouquet garni, and 1 scant cup (20 cl) dry white wine. Bring to the boil and reduce the liquid for about 10 minutes. Then add 1 2/3 cups (40 cl) veal bouillon and 1 tsp tomato paste. Cook the sauce over low heat so that it is barely bubbling for 15 minutes, skimming off the fat with a small ladle. In another saucepan, cook 1/4 cup (30 g) flour with 2 oz (60 g) butter for 2 minutes. Then pour this mixture into the boiling sauce, beating vigorously. Strain the sauce into another saucepan and add 2 peeled, seeded, crushed tomatoes, 1 tbsp chopped parsley, and 5 chopped sage leaves. Adjust the seasoning with salt and pepper. Serve the sage sauce very hot with pork chops, roast pork, or broiled pork steaks.

Piquant sauce

For 2 cups (50 cl) sauce, peel and finely chop 4 large shallots and place in a saucepan with 1/2 tsp crushed peppercorns, 1 small bouquet garni, 1/3 cup + 1 1/2 tbsp (10 cl) vinegar and 1 scant cup (20 cl) dry white wine. Bring to the boil and reduce everything for 10 minutes. Then add 1 2/3 cups (40 cl) veal bouillon and 1 tsp tomato paste. Simmer the sauce very slowly for 15 minutes, skimming the fat off with a small ladle. Cook 1/4 cup (30 g) flour and 2 oz (60 g) butter in another saucepan for 2 minutes. Then pour this mixture into the sauce, beating vigorously. Strain the sauce into another pan and add 10 chopped gherkins, 1 dab of butter, and 1 tbsp chopped parsley. Adjust the seasoning with salt and pepper and serve the piquant sauce very hot with broiled or fried pork chops.

Rosemary jelly

Piquant sauce

Sauce Robert (makes 2 cups/50 cl)

1 Peel and finely chop 1 onion and brown in 1 tbsp unsalted butter for 5 minutes. Then add a scant $^{1}/_{2}$ cup (10 cl) wine vinegar and 1 scant cup (20 cl) dry white wine. Boil, then reduce this liquid to two-thirds of its original volume. The alcohol in the wine should have evaporated.

2 Add 2 cups (50 cl) veal or other bouillon and 1 tsp tomato paste. Season with salt and pepper and cook very slowly for about 30 minutes. Skim off the fat from time to time using a small ladle. In another saucepan, cook $^{1}/_{4}$ cup (30 g) flour with 4 tbsp (60 g) butter for 2 minutes.

3 Pour this mixture into the boiling sauce, beating vigorously. Finish by adding 1 tbsp hot mustard, 1 dab of butter, and some salt and pepper. Mix well and serve very hot. Sauce Robert was already in existence at the time of Rabelais, who recommended serving it with rabbit.

Apple sauce

For $1^{1}/_{4}$ cups (30 cl) sauce, peel 1 onion. Peel and core 3 sharp apples (e.g., pippins). Chop them finely and cook in some butter in a covered pan for 30 minutes. Then add $1^{1}/_{4}$ cups (30 cl) veal bouillon, 1 tbsp honey, $3^{1}/_{2}$ tbsp (5 cl) lemon juice, salt, pepper, and 4 pinches of ground cinnamon. Cook for 20 minutes then blend. Adjust the seasoning and stir in a dab of butter. If the sauce is too thick, add a little bouillon. Serve very hot with roast pork, which complements the bittersweet flavors very well.

Sauce Robert

Christmas ham

Christmas menus give pride of place to fine cuts of meat. Usually, it is poultry, capon, and goose that take center stage, but it is possible to vary the tradition by drawing inspiration from more exotic cuisines. In the West Indies, there are many highly original and tasty recipes that are suitable for such occasions. Glazed ham with pineapple is one of these, prepared with cooked ham bought from the pork butcher. Only use fresh pineapple in this recipe, ripened to perfection, not the canned variety. Keep this recipe for special occasions, because you should have at least 20 guests for a ham weighing 11^1/$_4$–13^1/$_2$ lb (5–6 kg). Ask your pork butcher for a good quality cooked ham on the bone, without the rind but with a layer of fat to protect the meat.

Serves 20
Preparation: 40 minutes
Marinating: 24 hours
Cooking: 2 hours

Ingredients

1 cooked ham weighing
11^1/$_4$–13^1/$_2$ lb (5–6 kg)
Oil
3 onions
^{3}/$_4$ oz (20 g) fresh ginger
3 pineapples
Cloves
2 cups (50 cl) orange juice
1 tsp ground cinnamon
Pepper
3^1/$_2$ tbsp (5 cl) vinegar
3^1/$_2$ tbsp (5 cl) rum
Honey

1 Make a series of $3/8$ in (1 cm) cuts in the ham with a knife at right angles in order to score the surface in a fairly dense lattice pattern, ensuring that you do not cut into the flesh itself. Then brush the ham all over with a little oil and leave to stand in a roasting pan at room temperature while you prepare the marinade.

2 To prepare la marinade, assemble the chopped onions, chopped fresh ginger, flesh of 1 chopped pineapple, 10 cloves, the orange juice, ground cinnamon, pepper, vinegar, rum, and honey in a large casserole or other non-metallic pot. Place the scored ham in the marinade and leave in a cold place for 24 hours, turning from time to time.

3 Preheat the oven to 265 °F (130 °C). Drain the ham and put it in the oven in a baking pan containing some of the marinade. Cook for about 2 hours, basting frequently. If the ham browns too quickly, cover it with aluminum foil and lower the oven temperature slightly.

4 While the ham is cooking, peel the remaining pineapples and cut into even-sized rings, not too thick. Do not remove the core. Set aside some of the rings to cover the ham. An hour before the end of the cooking time, place slices of pineapple on the ham and secure with cloves, overlapping the rings so they cover the ham completely and making sure they stay firmly in position.

5 Brush with some of the marinade and some honey and caramelize, increasing the oven temperature if necessary. Remove the ham from the oven and wait for 5 minutes. Remove the pineapple rings and discard the cloves. Cover the ham with a double layer of aluminum foil and set aside. Return all the pineapple rings to a saucepan with a few spoonfuls of juice and heat gently.

6 Carve this ham at the table in front of your guests and serve the heated marinade as a sauce, with white rice as an accompaniment and the pineapple rings in a separate dish. This dish is traditional Christmas fare in the West Indies, preceded by creole boudin or small "pork pasties" stuffed with pork and lime. As a wine to accompany this dish, choose a red Médoc or a Madiran.

Mustard

Mustard is a plant whose culinary value was recognized a long time ago, having been used by the Greeks when preserving fish in brine. Mustard as we know it seems to have appeared in recipes from the fourth century onwards and subsequently became widely used in Burgundy. It was also held in high esteem for its medicinal properties and was used to treat lung diseases. Today, mustard is a very fashionable condiment, and can be divided into three distinct categories.

"Hot" or "white" mustard. This is the most popular kind. Its composition is strictly regulated and it may contain preservatives. Hot mustard takes the form of a yellow paste, very fine, acidic, and very strong. Traditional mustard. This product is very different in appearance; the grains are left whole, with the husk still on, and are clearly visible in the paste. This mustard is less hot and slightly more acidic than white mustard.

Flavored mustards. These are generally prepared using hot mustard as a base, mixed with a wide variety of flavorings and spices—green bell pepper, herbs, paprika, Provençal herbs, anchovies, horseradish, or shallots.

Preparation

Hot mustards are prepared in a very simple manner. The grains of mustard are sorted, cleaned, and then soaked until a softer consistency is obtained; they are then milled to a fine purée and the husks are discarded. The resulting paste is then refined and mixed with water, vinegar, salt, and preservatives. Dijon mustard is the best-known variety. It is fine, very strong, and pale yellow in color. It is eaten just as it is with cold or hot meat, pickled pork, sausages, and ham. It is also incorporated into sauces and is a basic ingredient in most vinaigrettes. Orléans mustard has a distinctive, refined flavor. The high quality of the vinegars used accounts for the extremely characteristic taste of this mustard, which is found in specialist grocery stores. Meaux mustard is instantly recognizable by its rustic, grainy appearance. It is served with meat and used to prepare delicious sauces and vinaigrettes. Brive mustard owes its distinctive violet color to the addition of grape must. It is fairly mild and provides a delicious accompaniment to all meats and cold cuts.

Storage

Mustard is kept in sealed pots in the refrigerator. To ring the changes, have a number of different kinds, varying in flavor, color, and appearance.

Seven delicious specialties

Pork is an easy meat to cook and is appreciated in a large number of countries, almost all of which have their own specialties.

Pork confit

This is a preserved pork product which is eaten in slices. The meat (fillet or chine) is first macerated overnight with some salt, pepper, thyme, and garlic, and is then sealed in lard, canned, and sterilized. Unopened, it will keep for several months.

Sweet and sour pork

This is one of the classic dishes in Chinese cuisine, originally from the southern part of the country. The pieces of meat are coated in a light batter made from rice flour and deep-fried to make crunchy fritters. They are then cooked for a few minutes with pineapples, bell peppers, and a tomato sauce sweetened with sugar.

Shoulder of pork with five spices

This recipe is from South-East Asia. The rind is removed from the shoulder of pork and macerated with a mixture of fennel, aniseed, cinnamon, pepper, cloves, salt, sugar, and soy sauce. The meat is then braised slowly in a small casserole. Shoulder of pork with five spices is served with plain white rice.

Barbecued spare ribs

These pork ribs are cut into small pieces, the thickness of a finger. They are then marinated in "barbecue" sauce with tomatoes, sugar, and spices. The spare ribs are then cooked on a grill over very hot charcoal. This is a dish typically eaten "al fresco" at family gatherings or with friends, as an alternative to hamburgers..

Sweet and sour pork

Barbecued spare ribs

Pork confit

Berliner Eisbein

This is a superb German dish in which a whole knuckle of slightly salted pork (sometimes also lightly smoked) is served on a bed of sauerkraut stewed in white wine.

Pörkölt

In this Hungarian recipe, the meat (chine or blade) is cut into fairly large cubes and browned with onions and paprika. The sauce is a lovely red color with a delicate flavor. Note that pörkölt can also be made with veal, duck, or carp. The condiment that gives pörkölt its authentic taste is none other than paprika, which is derived from the sweet peppers native to South America; thanks to the climate of Hungary and the expertise of its peasant farmers, however, the paprika industry has thrived there, its popularity being reflected in the local cuisine.

Hungarian pörkölt

Berliner Eisbein

Arista "à la Fiorentina"

This delicious Italian recipe is served in thin slices. A good quality pork loin is seasoned with salt, pepper, rosemary, and chopped fresh garlic. The meat is then roasted and afterwards braised gently. The meat should melt in the mouth, with a delicious flavor from the spices used.

Arista "à la Fiorentina"

Andouillettes with leeks and Pouilly

An easy dish

Serves 4
Preparation: 15 minutes
Cooking: 30 minutes

Ingredients

3 lb 5 oz (1.5 kg) young leeks
1 tbsp butter
1 tbsp oil
4 andouillettes
3 shallots
1 large glass
Pouilly
1 bunch parsley
Salt and pepper

1. Remove the outer leaves from the leeks and wash them thoroughly. Cut into 2–2½ in (5–6 cm) lengths and blanch for 3 minutes in simmering, salted water. Drain.

2. Melt the butter in a casserole. Add the leeks, season with salt and pepper, cover, and simmer over low heat for 10 minutes.

3. Heat the oil in a saucepan. Prick the andouillettes to stop them bursting and brown them, turning several times.

4. Discard any excess fat. Add the chopped shallots and, when they have just started to turn color, pour in the wine. Simmer for 10 minutes.

5. Place the andouillettes and shallots on top of the leeks and pour over the juices. Leave to stand for a few minutes in a warm place, add a little snipped parsley, and serve.

N.B. Pouilly-fumé, a white wine from the Loire valley, and Pouilly-fuissé, a white wine from southern Burgundy, are often confused. Both are dry wines; the first is made from the sauvignon grape, and is light, round, crisp, pleasant and refreshing; the second is made from the chardonnay grape, and is light and very dry, full of finesse and elegance. For cooking, it is recommended that you use a simple Pouilly from the Loire made from the chasselas grape, dry, but less refined, while serving a Pouilly-fuissé with the dish. Excellent andouillettes can be found in Brittany, in Troyes, Lyon, and Rouen.

Recommended drinks

Pouilly-Fuissé
Mâcon-Villages
Beaujolais

Menu suggestions

1. As an appetizer, serve a curly endive salad garnished with garlic croûtons and small bacon lardoons; serve a celery purée or potatoes to accompany the dish, with a selection of sorbets for dessert.

2. For a very simple meal, serve a green salad with croûtons with the andouillettes, followed by an apple tart.

Flemish carbonade

A regional dish

Serves 4
Preparation: 30 minutes
Cooking: 2 hours

Ingredients

1 lb 11 oz (750 g) pork chine
31/2 oz (100 g) smoked bacon
1 tbsp lard
2 tbsp flour
1 large glass beer
A little bouillon
2 cloves of garlic
6 onions
1 tsp sugar
1 handful parsley
2 bay leaves
1 sprig thyme

Vinegar
Salt and pepper

1. Cut the meat into approximately 1 in (3 cm) pieces, removing the skin and connective tissue. Remove the rind from the bacon and cut into small dice. Sauté the meat in the very hot lard.

2. Wait until the meat is browned in places before adding the diced bacon. Reduce the heat a little and sauté the bacon so that the fat runs, without drying out.

3. Remove the meat and bacon from the pan, drain well, and transfer to an earthenware cooking pot. Sprinkle the flour into the cooking fat, cook for a few minutes, stirring constantly, before pouring in the beer and the bouillon.

4. While the sauce is simmering, peel the cloves of garlic and chop them into thin slices. Peel the onions, cut them into thin, short sticks, and place on the meat. Place the garlic on top of the onions.

5. When the sauce is rich and creamy, adjust seasoning to taste, adding salt sparingly because of the bacon. Sprinkle the garlic with sugar and pour the sauce over the top.

6. Chop the parsley and sprinkle on top together with the bay leaves and the thyme. Cover and cook in the oven at 330 °F (165 °C) for 2 hours. Arrange in a dish, add a few dashes of vinegar, and serve.

N.B. To accompany this carbonade, serve baby turnips and carrots gently sautéed at the end of the cooking time.

Recommended drinks

Pale ale
Brown ale
White Moselle wine

Menu suggestions

1. To continue the regional theme, serve marinated herring fillets as an appetizer and waffles with coffee ice cream for dessert.

2. For a lighter menu, serve an endive salad with beet and, for dessert, baked apples with cinnamon.

339

Loin of pork with peaches

A party dish

Serves 4
Preparation: 15 minutes
Cooking: 1 hour 45 minutes

Ingredients

1 loin of pork, on the bone
(at least 4 chops)
Ground ginger
5 cloves
3 1/2 oz (100 g) butter
Tabasco®
1 glass good quality cider vinegar
or white wine vinegar
2 bay leaves
2 sprigs thyme
2 sage leaves
2 cinnamon sticks

Superfine sugar
2 1/4 lb (1 kg) peaches, not too ripe
Salt and pepper

1. Sprinkle the pork loin with ginger and place on a rack over a drip pan in an oven pre-heated to 435 °F (225 °C). Cook for 30 minutes so that the fat runs.

2. Pour off the excess fat, stick the pork loin with 3 cloves, and then place in a roasting pan. Spread with butter, season with salt and pepper, add a little Tabasco, and return to the oven.

3. Boil the vinegar with 2 cloves, the bay leaves, the sprigs of thyme, the sage leaves, the cinnamon sticks, and 3 tsp sugar. Strain the vinegar and add 3–4 tbsp to the pan in which the pork is cooking.

4. Cook in the oven for a further 1 hour 15 minutes, but lower the temperature to 365 °F (185 °C) and baste from time to time with the vinegary juices.

5. Peel and halve the peaches. Melt a little butter and, when it starts to color, gently add the peaches. Season with pepper, pour over the remaining flavored vinegar, and reduce.

6. Serve the pork and the peaches with all the cooking juices mixed together.

N.B. When choosing the peaches, look for yellow ones with fairly firm flesh. Bring a large saucepan of water to the boil and immerse the peaches, poach them for no more than 30 seconds, drain with a slotted spoon, and plunge immediately into cold water. The skin will then be very easy to remove: just pierce it with the point of a small knife and pull.

Recommended drinks

Crozes-Hermitage
Jurançon sec
Saint-Chinian

Menu suggestions

1. For this festive menu, serve salmon tartare with dill as an appetizer, green beans and noisette potatoes as an accompaniment, and for dessert a lemon meringue pie.

2. For an alternative festive menu, serve a salad of scallops with herbs as an appetizer, the same accompaniments as above, and an upside-down pineapple tart for dessert.

Pork chops with Ardennes ham

A regional dish

Serves 2
Preparation: 10 minutes
Cooking: 25–30 minutes

Ingredients

1 lb 5 oz (600 g) small potatoes
10 button onions
3½ oz (100 g) Ardennes ham, sliced not too thickly
2 tbsp butter
2 pork chops
1/2 glass white wine
5 or 6 juniper berries
A few lettuce leaves
Salt and pepper

1. Peel and wipe the potatoes. Peel the button onions. Cut the ham into small squares. Brown all the ingredients in butter until the onions and potatoes are nearly cooked. Be careful; they should cook very gently.

2. Then season the pork chops and cook them in butter for 7 to 10 minutes on each side, depending on their thickness. When they are well browned and cooked to perfection, remove them and place on top of the potatoes and onions; keep warm.

3. Deglaze the pan with the white wine, add a few juniper berries, and reduce for a few moments.

4. Serve the chops, potatoes, onions, and ham on a hot dish garnished with a few salad leaves. Spoon over a little of the reduced cooking juices and serve the remainder in a hot sauceboat.

N.B. You can also use country ham in this recipe, but the results will not be exactly the same because Ardennes ham, smoked with herbs, has a highly individual flavor that gives this recipe its unique character. For the pork chops, you have a choice between chops cut from the loin or the middle of the fillet, which have the advantage of being fairly lean, but are slightly dry; chops cut from the end of the fillet, which are at the same time plumper, larger, and above all more tender and succulent; and finally chops cut from the chine, which are distinctly more fatty and rather thick, but nevertheless full of flavor.

Recommended drinks

White Moselle
White Côtes-de-Toul
White Coteaux-Champenois

Menu suggestions

1. For a winter menu, start with a French onion soup and serve baked apples in pastry or brioche with raisins and custard for dessert.

2. For a springtime menu, serve dandelion salad as an appetizer and champagne zabaglione for dessert.

Pork chops with cider

A family dish

Serves 4
Preparation: 20 minutes
Cooking: 45 minutes

Ingredients

1 celery heart
7 oz (200 g) mushrooms
3 or 4 onions
2 or 3 firm apples
1 1/2 oz (40 g) butter
1 tbsp oil
4 small pork chops
Flour
1 bottle cider
Thyme

Bay leaf
Parsley
Salt and pepper

1. Peel, wash, and chop the celery heart and the mushrooms.

2. Peel the onions and cut into even-sized rings. Peel and quarter the apples, remove the core and pips, and cut each quarter in two.

3. Heat the butter and oil in a casserole. Add the onions and brown gently, followed by the pork chops. As soon as they start to turn golden, add the vegetables and then the quartered apples.

4. Sauté for 4 minutes, stirring. Sprinkle with flour and cook for another 2 minutes. Then add enough cider to cover the ingredients, plus a little extra. Season with salt, pepper, thyme, bay, and parsley.

5. Cover and cook in the oven at 400 °F (200 °C) for 45 minutes.

6. To serve, take the casserole out of the oven and remove the lid. If you can, discard the thyme and bay leaf (which is easier to do if you have taken the precaution of wrapping them in a little muslin bag).

N.B. Your pork chops will be even more succulent if you choose those cut from the chine. The best apples to use are the variety Belle de Boskoop or Canadian Reinettes Grises, not too ripe; they will hold their shape well during cooking.

Recommended drinks

Champagne cider
Muscadet sur lie
Pouilly-fuissé

Menu suggestions

1. As an appetizer, serve a selection of crudités or garnished avocados, and for dessert an île flottante or individual pots of crème caramel.

2. A more manageable alternative would be to serve grated carrot as an appetizer and then a cheeseboard with green salad and seasonal fruits.

Crépinettes with chestnuts

An economical dish

Serves 4
Preparation: 20 minutes
Cooking: 25 minutes

Ingredients

1 lb 11 oz (750 g) chestnuts
Butter
2 bay leaves
4 flat sausages (crépinettes)
Parsley
Salt and pepper

1. Pierce the chestnut shells on the convex side, not too deeply. Place in a baking dish and add enough water to come a third of the way up them, then transfer to a very hot oven for about 10 minutes.

2. Peel the chestnuts while they are still lukewarm. Butter a saucepan, place the chestnuts in it, and cover with water. Season with salt and bay, bring rapidly to the boil, cover, and cook for 25 minutes over medium heat.

3. Place the flat sausages in a skillet with a little butter and sauté gently. Turn two or three times so that they are well browned on all sides. Add the chestnuts when the sausages are half cooked. They should dry and the surface should harden slightly in the fat from the sausages. Garnish with a little parsley and serve from the skillet itself or in a hot dish.

N.B. Crépinettes are small, flat sausages made with sausage meat flavored with parsley and wrapped in caul. They should be pricked in several places before they are fried. They cook quite quickly, but you need to keep an eye on them and turn them several times. You can make this same recipe using chipolatas or even Toulouse sausages, or you could make your own flat sausages with sausage meat and herbs, adding a few shavings of truffle. Prepare 4$^1/_2$ oz (125 g) portions and wrap in squares of caul soaked in cold water and sponged thoroughly. To save time, on the other hand, you can use bought chestnuts, whole and ready peeled, which you will just need to reheat in the cooking juices from the crépinettes.

Recommended drinks

Saint-Emilion
Fitou
Côtes-de-Duras

Menu suggestions

1. Having started the meal with a terrine of chicken livers, serve the crépinettes with a green salad, and for dessert a fruit salad.

2. If you have time the day before, make a vegetable terrine for the appetizer and a tarte tatin for dessert.

Pork curry with pineapple

An exotic dish

Serves 5–6
Preparation: 15 minutes
Cooking: 1 hour 15 minutes

Ingredints

2 1/4 lb (1 kg) pork cut from
   the chine
Oil
2 onions
2 or 3 tomatoes
1 pepper
1 fresh pineapple
3 or 4 cloves of garlic
1 piece root ginger

Curry powder
Salt and pepper

1. Cut the pork into pieces the size of a large walnut. Heat 2–3 tbsp oil and sauté the peeled and coarsely chopped onions and the peeled and chopped garlic.

2. Add the meat when the onions and garlic are just starting to brown. Continue to sauté until all the pieces of pork are well browned.

3. Add the tomatoes, peeled and cut into chunks. Add the pepper, cut into thin rings (be careful not to include any seeds). Season with salt and pepper, cover, and leave to simmer.

4. Meanwhile, peel the pineapple and collect the juice. Cut some of the pineapple into thin rings and some into pieces, then add to the pan. Pour in the pineapple juice.

5. Simmer until the meat is thoroughly tender (for about 45 minutes). Remove from the saucepan and keep hot. Strain the cooking juices and add some grated ginger and curry powder. Cook for a few more moments.

6. Serve very hot with white rice. There should be plenty of sauce to moisten the rice.

Recommended drinks

Provençal rosé
Côtes-du-Roussillon
Fitou

Menu suggestions

1. To transform this curry into a celebration meal, serve an appetizer of stuffed crabs au gratin with a coconut flan and pineapple fritters for dessert.

2. For a simpler menu, start with celeriac salad with a rémoulade sauce and finish with a selection of Oriental pastries.

Cabbage sausages

A regional dish

Serves 6
Preparation time: 1 hour
Cooking time: 40 minutes

Ingredients

1 Savoy cabbage
14 oz (400 g) bacon
2 or 3 cloves of garlic
Grated nutmeg
Ground cloves
Salt and peppercorns
Sausage skins

1. Trim the cabbage and blanch in boiling water for 10 minutes from the moment at which the water comes back to the boil. Drain, pressing with a cloth, and chop. You will need about 2 1/4 lb (1 kg) for this recipe.

2. Add the bacon cut into small pieces, mix with the chopped cabbage, season with the chopped garlic, nutmeg, cloves, salt, and crushed peppercorns, and stuff the sausage skins with this mixture. Do not fill them too full, or they may burst during cooking. Form into sausages the size of large andouillettes and tie at each end.

3. Not long before you are ready to eat, prick your sausages and poach them. Start by immersing them completely for 1–2 minutes in boiling water and then continue to cook for a good 30 minutes more in barely simmering water.

4. Serve hot with braised cabbage or boiled potatoes. If you have prepared a few too many, do not worry, as these "diots de chou" are equally good eaten cold the next day with a green salad flavored with chopped garlic.

Recommended drinks

Saint-Pourçain
Crépy
Mondeuse

Menu suggestions

1. As this is a recipe from Savoy, continue the regional theme by serving a gratin of lobster tails or trout in white wine as an appetizer and for dessert a blueberry crumble.

2. As an alternative, serve morel mushrooms on fried bread as an appetizer with a vacherin for dessert, not forgetting a plate of cheeses.

345

Marinated roast shoulder of pork

A family dish

Serves 4
Preparation: 1 hour 30 minutes
Marinade: 12 hours at least
Cooking: 1 hour 30 minutes

Ingredients

2 carrots
2 onions
1 bunch parsley
1 sprig thyme
2 bay leaves
2 cloves of garlic
1 stalk celery
4 tbsp (60 g) butter
2 glasses vinegar
Cloves
Grated nutmeg

1 boneless shoulder of pork weighing 2¾ lb (1.25 kg)
1 lb 2 oz (500 g) potatoes
2 tbsp oil
2 shallots
¹/₃ cup (40 g) flour
2 glasses white wine
A little bouillon
Capers in vinegar
Salt and pepper

1. Sauté the carrots and the onions cut into rings, half of the parsley, the thyme, a bay leaf, 1 clove of garlic, and the chopped celery in 2 tbsp (30 g) butter. Add the vinegar and 2 cups (50 cl) boiling water.

2. Season with salt, pepper, cloves, and nutmeg. Simmer for 1 hour. Strain and leave to cool before adding the pork to marinate for at least 12 hours.

3. Heat the oven to 365 °F (185 °C). Drain the shoulder and roast in the same dish, without any fat, just adding 3–4 tbsp water and some salt and pepper; baste from time to time with the cooking liquid.

4. Peel the potatoes. Cook in the oven with the oil and some salt and pepper while the shoulder of pork finishes cooking.

5. Melt the rest of the butter in a saucepan and sauté the remaining clove of garlic and the chopped shallots, sprinkle with flour, and add the rest of the chopped parsley.

6. Cook for 2 minutes before thinning the mixture with the white wine and a little bouillon; add 2 glasses of the marinade, some salt, pepper, nutmeg, cloves, thyme, and a bay leaf.

7. Simmer for 40 minutes, skimming off the fat as required. Strain and add some capers; do not allow to boil again. Serve in a large hot dish, with the sauce separately.

Recommended drinks

Fronsac
Côtes-de-Bourg
A good red Bordeaux

Menu suggestions

1. For a family Sunday lunch, serve an appetizer of marinated smoked salmon with dill and for dessert a fruit salad with vanilla ice cream.

2. For a simple dinner, make a pumpkin soup as an appetizer and for dessert serve baked apples with strawberry jelly.

Braised pork

A light dish

Serves 4
Preparation: 15 minutes
Resting: 1 hour at least
Cooking: 2 hours

Ingredients

2 cloves of garlic
Paprika
Mustard
Provençal herbs
(thyme, savory, oregano, etc.)
Cayenne pepper
1 joint of pork (2 lb 14 oz/1.3 kg)
cut from the front part of the leg or the loin
6 red bell peppers
1 green bell pepper

1 small head of celery
Olive oil
1 onion
Cornstarch
Parsley
Salt and pepper

1. Peel the cloves of garlic and crush with a little salt and pepper, 1 level tsp paprika, 1 tbsp mustard, 2 large pinches of herbs, and a very small pinch of Cayenne pepper.

2. Rinse the meat quickly, sponge with paper towels, then spread the aromatic mixture all over it. Leave to stand for at least 1 hour.

3. Meanwhile, place the bell peppers in the oven until the skin blisters, wrap in damp paper towels, and wait a few minutes before peeling them.

4. Cut open the peppers and remove the fibers and the seeds inside. Cut the flesh into wide strips. Trim the celery, wash the stalks, cut into strips lengthwise, then cut into pieces about 2³/₄ in (7 cm) long.

5. Oil a casserole. Place some vegetables in the bottom, lay the meat over, and arrange the strips of green pepper, a third of the red peppers, the remaining celery, and the chopped onion around the meat. Cover and place on a fairly low shelf in a cold oven. Set the temperature to 430 °F (220 °C) and cook for no more than 2 hours.

6. Blend the remaining red bell peppers, season with salt and pepper, and bind with the olive oil. Keep cool. Make a sauce with the strained cooking juices from the meat, thickening with a little cornstarch. Reheat without boiling. Serve the joint of meat garnished with parsley, with the two sauces, one really hot, the other really cold.

Recommended drinks

Chinon
Bourgueil
Saumur-Champigny

Menu suggestions

1. To keep the menu light, serve a cucumber salad in low-fat yogurt as an appetizer and, for dessert, stewed peaches with mint.

2. As an alternative, serve tomato soup as an appetizer and a soft white cheese with slices of strawberry for dessert.

347

Fillet of pork "en chevreuil"

A regional dish

Serves 6
Preparation: 10 minutes
Marinade: 24 hours
Cooking: 2 hours 30 minutes

Ingredients

1 large glass red wine
1 large glass wine vinegar
2 onions
2 bay leaves
2 sage leaves
4 juniper berries
3 lb 5 oz (1.5 kg) pork fillet
1¹/₂ oz (45 g) lard
2 carrots
Flour

4¹/₂ lb (2 kg) apples
1 small pot cassis jelly
1 bunch watercress
Oil
Salt and peppercorns

1. Place the wine in a saucepan with the vinegar, 2 cups (50 cl) water, 1 onion peeled and cut into thin rings, the bay leaves, sage leaves, 5 peppercorns, and the juniper berries, all finely crushed. Bring to the boil. Add 1 tsp salt and simmer for 2–3 minutes. Leave to cool.

2. Place the pork fillet in a terrine and pour over the marinade with all its ingredients. Cover and leave to marinate for 24 hours, turning the meat from time to time.

3. Melt the lard in a casserole, drain the fillet, and brown it in the lard on all sides. Set aside. Reserve the equivalent of 2 tbsp lard and sauté 1 chopped onion in it together with the carrots, cut into thin rings. Cook until they start to color, add 2 tbsp flour, and continue to brown, stirring with a wooden spoon. Add 2 cups (50 cl) strained marinade and 2 glasses of water. Bring to the boil, add the meat, cover, and cook over gentle heat for 2 hours.

4. Meanwhile, peel and quarter the apples, removing the cores, and poach them in a large saucepan containing a few tablespoons of water over high heat. Stop cooking as soon as the apples become translucent.

5. When the fillet is cooked, keep it hot. Skim the cooking liquid, reduce if necessary, and thicken with 1–2 tbsp cassis jelly. Arrange the fillet in a hot dish surrounded by the apples, and dab with cassis jelly. Serve with a watercress salad and hand round a small dish of cassis jelly.

Recommended drinks

Saint-Emilion
Madiran
Red Irouléguy

Menu suggestions

1. To accompany this marinated pork fillet, serve a good fricassee of boletus mushrooms with parsley, and follow with chestnut charlotte.

2. You could also serve a vegetable and herb soup as an appetizer with pears Belle-Hélène for dessert.

Filets mignons with island fruits

An exotic dish

Serves 4
Preparation: 15 minutes
Resting: 1 hour at least
Cooking: 15 minutes

Ingredients

2 small pork fillets (filets mignons)
weighing about 400 g
1 lemon
Oil
1 or 2 shallots
1³/₄ oz (50 g) butter
1 large glass dry white wine
2 or 3 kiwi fruit
1 mango
1 rocambole (Spanish garlic)

1 small pot crème fraîche
1 bunch chervil
1 egg
Salt and pepper

1. Trim the pork fillets carefully and wipe with paper towels. Put them in a dish and pour the lemon juice and a drizzle of oil over them. Season with salt and pepper and leave to stand for at least 1 hour.

2. Peel and finely chop the shallots. Brown in some butter in a saucepan over medium heat, then cook for a few moments over low heat, stirring. Pour in the white wine and reduce, still over low heat.

3. Heat the broiler and cook the pork fillets until they are golden on all sides, turning them frequently so they are cooked all over. Reduce the heat and continue broiling for another ten minutes or so.

4. Meanwhile, peel and slice the kiwi fruit. Choose a mango that is not too ripe, make a cut in it all the way round with a sharp knife, peel, then halve it, removing the pit, before cutting the fruit into small pieces. Chop the rocambole (if you cannot find this, you can substitute 1 mild onion).

5. Finish the sauce by thickening it with the crème fraîche and seasoning well with salt and pepper. Add the snipped chervil to flavor it at the last moment. Serve on hot plates.

N.B. To give added flavor and subtlety to your sauce, while the meat is being kept hot, pour a little good bouillon into the saucepan, stir once or twice, and, instead of thickening the sauce with cream on its own, beat the crème fraîche with 1 egg yolk and a little mustard and stir in.

Recommended drinks

Tokay-Pinot-Gris
Gewurztraminer
White Hermitage

Menu suggestions

1. As an appetizer, serve large prawns, either broiled or in a salad; accompany the main course with plain rice and serve fresh mangoes or a mango sorbet for dessert.

2. You could also start with a salad of avocado with lemon and serve a selection of dried fruits stuffed with almond paste for dessert.

Fennel gratin with ham

An economical dish

Serves 4
Preparation: 5 minutes
1st cooking: 1 hour
2nd cooking: 15 minutes

Ingredients

4 very small fennels
1³/₄ oz (50 g) butter
1 tbsp flour
1 large glass milk
Nutmeg
3¹/₂ oz (100 g) grated cheese
4 slices ham
Salt and pepper

1. Trim each fennel, removing the outer leaves if necessary and cutting off the stalk. Place in a saucepan, cover with boiling salted water, and cook for about an hour.

2. Meanwhile, make a white sauce: melt half the butter in a saucepan, sprinkle in the flour, and cook for a few minutes, stirring constantly with a wooden spoon. Do not allow it to brown.

3. Boil the milk and add to the sauce a little at a time, still stirring. Simmer for 15 minutes, season with salt and pepper, and flavor with grated nutmeg. Add half the grated cheese at the last moment.

4. Butter a gratin dish. Cut the well-drained fennels in half. Roll each piece in a half slice of ham. Pour the sauce into the dish, arrange the fennel parcels over the sauce, and sprinkle with the remaining cheese.

5. Heat the oven to 365 °F (185 °C). Place the dish in the oven and cook until the top is golden in places.

N.B. This alternative to endives and ham au gratin has an original and subtle flavor; it is nevertheless essential to ensure that the fennel is completely drained before being wrapped in the ham. Choose slices of cooked ham, possibly braised, and for the cheese opt for a full-flavored Comté, Beaufort, or even an Edam or mimolette (also a Dutch cheese) matured for six months. Serve straight from the dish.

Recommended drinks

White Burgundy
Monthélie
Saint-Aubin

Menu suggestions

1. Serve this dish for dinner with a good green salad; follow with a cheese platter and then some clementines.

2. You could also start the meal with a salad of tomatoes with black olives and serve lemon or orange sorbets in their skins with wafer biscuits for dessert.

Jambalaya

An exotic dish

Serves 4
Preparation: 15 minutes
Cooking: 45 minutes

Ingredients

1 large glass rice
1 thick slice cooked ham
2 slices cooked roast pork
1 dried sausage
2 cloves of garlic
2 onions
1 bell pepper
4 tomatoes
Bouillon (made from a cube)
4 tbsp oilSalt

1. Wash the rice several times in cold water. Place in a pot with three times its volume of water and some salt. Bring to the boil and cook over gentle heat until the rice is swollen, then cook for 5 more minutes before draining.

2. Meanwhile, dice the ham and the pork, cut the sausage into rings, peel and crush the garlic, and peel the onions and cut them into rings. Place all these ingredients in a saucepan with just a little water and simmer.

3. Cut the bell pepper in half and remove the fibers and seeds, then cut the flesh into strips. Add these to the contents of the saucepan and cook for 10 minutes, stirring almost constantly.

4. Then add the tomatoes, skinned, seeded, and cut into pieces, the rice, and 1 bowl of bouillon. Cook gently until all the liquid has evaporated.

5. Finally, heat some oil in a shallow casserole or deep skillet and brown, stirring constantly so that the jambalaya does not stick. Serve straight from the cookware or in a very hot deep dish.

N.B. Jambalaya is a Cajun specialty, originally from New Orleans, inspired in fact by Spanish paella. You can also add leftover cooked chicken or large cooked and shelled prawns to the ingredients.

Recommended drinks

Chardonnay
Pale ale
Riesling

Menu suggestions

1. Prepare a prawn cocktail with some large broiled prawns for an appetizer and a chocolate and pecan nut tart for dessert.

2. As an appetizer, you could also serve a salad of marinated white cabbage with mayonnaise, and for dessert a chocolate mousse flavored with whisky.

Shoulder of pork with cherries

A party dish

Serves 5
Preparation: 15 minutes
Marinade: between 1 and 3 hours
Cooking: 1 hour 30 minutes

Ingredients

1 shoulder slightly salted pork, weighing about 2¼ lb (1 kg)
1 sprig fresh rosemary
½ glass oil
4½ lb (2 kg) cherries
Salt and pepper

1. Soak the pork, following the advice of your pork butcher; depending on how highly salted it is, you will need either to rinse it for several hours in cold, running water or plunge it in water for a few minutes and then wipe it.

2. Stick a few rosemary leaves into the meat and then leave to marinate for at least 1 hour, but no longer than 3 hours, in a well-oiled dish containing plenty of rosemary and some pepper.

3. Heat the oven to 435 °F (225 °C), waiting until it is hot before putting the shoulder of pork in the oven in its dish of marinade. Cook for 1 hour 30 minutes, but baste frequently with the juices and reduce the heat 400 °F (200 °C) when the meat starts to brown well.

4. Meanwhile, pit the cherries and place in the cooking dish 15 minutes before serving.

5. The fruit should poach gently and its juice be transformed into a delicious sauce; adjust seasoning to taste before serving, adding salt and pepper if necessary.

N.B. This recipe comes originally from the Apt region, famous for its fruit, which is used to make jellies and preserves. In this particular case, choose fairly plump, slightly firm bigarreau cherries with some bite—varieties such as Burlat, Reverchon, or Coeur-de-pigeon.

Recommended drinks

Côtes-de-Castillon
Pécharmant
Irouléguy

Menu suggestions

1. For a fine celebration meal, start with lobster halves in a morel sauce, accompany the main course with small, whole potatoes, and serve an ice raspberry charlotte for dessert.

2. For an equally festive menu, serve scallops with tartare sauce as an appetizer, keep the same accompaniment for the main course, and finish with strawberry tart.

Sweet and sour paupiettes of pork

A family dish

Serves 6
Preparation: 15 minutes
Cooking: 30 minutes

Ingredients

About 30 pre-cooked prunes
2¼ lb (1 kg) carrots
1 large glass bouillon
1¾ oz (50 g) butter
1 small pot crème fraîche
12 thin slices pork fillet
1 small glass calvados

1 bouquet garni (parsley, thyme, bay)
Salt and pepper

1. If you are not using pre-cooked prunes, soak them beforehand in a little lukewarm bouillon for at least an hour.

2. Prepare some carrot purée, choosing long carrots of the Nantaise variety. Peel the carrots, cut them into sticks, and cook in water until they are tender. Purée them, adding a little bouillon, 1 tbsp butter, and 1–2 tbsp crème fraîche. The purée should be of a fairly soft consistency.

3. Pit the prunes, place them on the slices of pork fillet (1–2 per slice), roll up, and tie with string.

4. Heat the remaining butter in a deep skillet; add the olives to brown them, and season with salt and pepper. When they are a deep golden color, pour over the calvados and set it alight, then quench with hot bouillon. Flavor with the bouquet garni, cover, and simmer for 25 minutes

5. A few minutes before the end of the cooking time, add the remaining prunes to the contents of the skillet. Finish cooking uncovered.

6. Place the olives in a hot serving dish and boil the juices vigorously to reduce while you remove the string. Garnish with the prunes and a few parsley leaves.

7. Take the reduced cooking liquid off the heat and thicken by adding the crème fraîche; serve separately in a hot sauceboat.

Recommended drinks

Cahors
Collioure
Red Bergerac

Menu suggestions

1. Serve mushrooms in a velouté sauce as an appetizer, with a celery purée to accompany the main course and hot brioche with custard for dessert.

2. You could also serve a salad of chopped mushrooms with chives and lemon, keeping the same accompaniment for the main course and serving pots of fromage frais with raspberries for dessert.

353

Recommended drinks

Gris de Toul
Pale ale
White Moselle

Menu suggestions

1. For a quick, balanced meal, serve this quiche with a green salad and follow with a halved grapefruit, sprinkled with sugar and broiled.

2. You could also serve this quiche as an appetizer, followed by poached cod fillets with broccoli and crème caramel for dessert.

Quiche Lorraine

An economical dish

Serves 4–6
Preparation: 15 minutes
Resting: 1–2 hours
Cooking: 30 minutes

Ingredients

3 cups (350 g) flour
Oil
3¹/₂ oz (100 g) butter
9 oz (250 g) smoked bacon
5 eggs
5¹/₂ oz (150 g) crème fraîche
1³/₄ oz (50 g) grated gruyère cheese
1 glass milk
Nutmeg

Endive
Salt and pepper

1. Place the flour in a mound in a basin, add 2 tbsp oil, the butter, cut in pieces, and 1 pinch salt. Knead everything together quickly, taking the butter in one hand and working it well into the flour. Add as much cold water as is needed to make dough that is soft, yet keeps its shape. Rest for 1–2 hours in the refrigerator.

2. Meanwhile, dice the bacon finely, having first removed the rind. Prepare the cream by breaking the eggs into a basin, adding the crème fraîche, the grated cheese, and the milk. Add some pepper, but no salt because of the bacon; flavor with a little grated nutmeg and beat until you have a foaming, creamy mixture.

3. Roll out the pastry to a thickness of 1/8–3/16 in (4–5 mm). Line a shallow pie dish; there is no need to oil it. Trim off any excess pastry. Scatter the diced bacon over the pastry and bake in the oven at 400 °F (200 °C) for 10 minutes.

4. Pour the filling over the diced bacon and bake for a further 20 minutes at the same temperature. Serve the quiche hot or lukewarm, with an accompaniment of salad, preferably curly endive.

N.B. Instead of smoked bacon, you can also use slightly salted bacon (previously blanched in boiling water and well drained), diced cooked ham, leftover roast pork cut into small cubes, or sliced bacon cut into thin strips. You can bake the pastry shell blind and then add the diced bacon and filling at the same time.

Roast pork with lemon

A light dish

Serves 4
Preparation: 10 minutes
Cooking: 50 minutes

Ingredients

1 roasting joint of pork weighing about 2$^{1}/_{4}$ lb (1 kg)
1 bunch rosemary
2 tbsp oil
1 large glass dry, but fruity, white wine
7/8 cup (100 g) superfine sugar
3 or 4 lemons
1 small glass cognac
Salt and pepper

1. Set the oven to 465 °F (240 °C) and, while it is heating, season the joint of pork with salt and pepper, then make cuts in the direction of the grain and insert a few rosemary leaves.

2. Oil a roasting pan, place the joint of pork in it, pour over the wine, and sprinkle with a few rosemary leaves. Turn it two or three times in this liquid.

3. Place on a rack over the roasting pan and cook for 15 minutes at 465 °F (240 °C), then lower the temperature to 320 °F (160 °C), baste with the juices in the pan, and cook for another 15 minutes.

4. Meanwhile, dissolve the superfine sugar in the juice of 2 lemons, add the cognac, and baste the pork with a little of this syrup. Repeat the operation at 5-minute intervals. A few minutes before the end of the cooking time—which should be 50 minutes in all—place some thin lemon rings in the pan.

5. Remove the string and serve the joint on the lemon rings in the pan in which you have cooked it, having wiped the pan thoroughly.

N.B The lemons used in this recipe must be untreated; if they are waxed, brush them well under warm, running water. Cut 1 or 2 lemons into thin rings and discard the pips. You can also use bitter oranges or blood oranges in this recipe. The pork joint should preferably be cut from the chine rather than the fillet, as it will be far more succulent. For the cooking wine, choose a chardonnay (white Burgundy or a white wine from the Languedoc).

Recommended drinks

Bordeaux rosé
Coteaux d'Aix
Côtes-du-Luberon

Menu suggestions

1. Serve an appetizer of leeks with vinaigrette or a beet salad, and for dessert a lemon sorbet served in the fruit skin or yogurt flavored with cinnamon.

2. Another suggestion for an equally light meal would be to serve a salad of oranges with mild onion as an appetizer and for dessert an apple sorbet.

Recommended drinks

Saint-Pourçain
Côte Roannaise
Beaujolais

Menu suggestions

1. For a summer meal, serve a salad of green beans with garlic as an appetizer and an apricot tart for dessert.

2. For a fall meal, serve an appetizer of roast goat's cheese on toast and for dessert a pear and almond tart.

Roast pork with buttered cabbage and button onions

A family dish

Serves 6
Preparation: 15 minutes
Cooking: 1 hour

Ingredients

1 roasting joint of pork weighing about 2¼ lb (1 kg) cut from the fillet or the chine
1 tbsp lard
24 small button onions
1 large green cabbage (or 2 small ones)
2 bay leaves
2 medium onions
2 shallots

3½ oz (100 g) butter
Salt and pepper

1. When the joint of pork has been trimmed, secured with string, and seasoned with salt and pepper, heat the lard in a casserole and cook the pork on all sides until it is golden (but do not allow to brown). Cover and cook for about 1 hour over low heat.

2. Peel the button onions and place around the meat 30 minutes before the end of the cooking time.

3. Trim the cabbage, discarding the outer leaves, the stalk, and the thick veins. Cut into quarters and cook in a large saucepan of boiling, salted water with a few bay leaves for about 20 minutes. Drain and chop coarsely.

4. Peel and chop the medium onions and the shallots. Sweat gently in a heavy-bottomed saucepan with plenty of butter. When they are transparent, add the chopped cabbage. Dry out over low heat, stirring with a wooden spoon. Adjust the seasoning by adding salt and pepper as required. Just before serving, skim the fat off the cooking juices from the meat and add 3–4 tbsp to the buttered cabbage.

5. Arrange the roast meat and button onions on a hot dish over some of the buttered cabbage, serving the remainder separately.

N.B. To add a more individual flavor to the buttered cabbage, do not be afraid to use salted butter from Guérande. The boiled cabbage should be thoroughly drained before it is cooked in the butter. Transfer it to a colander and press it with your hands, then spread it out on a large, thick dishtowel.

Ham roulades with kiwi fruit

An easy dish

Serves 4
Preparation: 10 minutes
Cooking: 15 minutes

Ingredients

1 onion
1½ oz (40 g) butter
1/8 cup (20 g) flour
1 glass dry white wine
1 bouquet garni (thyme, bay)
1 large glass Madeira

Cornstarch
12 kiwi fruit, not too ripe

4 slices cooked ham
Salt and pepper

1. Peel and coarsely chop the onion and brown it in the butter, sprinkle in the flour, and brown a little. Add the white wine and mix thoroughly, stirring to avoid lumps forming.

2. Season with salt and pepper, add the bouquet garni, and simmer uncovered for 10 minutes to allow the wine to reduce. Strain this sauce—which should be fairly thick—through a fine sieve and keep hot.

3. Add the Madeira and thicken if required with a little cornstarch previously mixed in 1 tbsp sauce.

4. Meanwhile, peel the kiwi fruit in the shape of large olives.

5. Roll up the ham slices, arrange them in a baking dish, place the kiwi fruit in between, and spoon some of the sauce over the top. Cover with a sheet of aluminum foil and cook in the oven at 300 °F (150 °C) for no more than 15 minutes. Season with plenty of pepper just before serving.

N.B. You can use various kinds of ham, as long as they are cooked. A small ham cooked in a cloth is the classic choice, but you could also used braised ham with a slightly smoky taste, York ham, Prague ham, or even Italian ham seasoned with herbs. The slices should be fairly thick. Make sure you remove the rind before rolling up the slices in the dish, but do not remove all the fat.

Recommended drinks

Red Bordeaux
Provençal rosé
Chinon

Menu suggestions

1. You could serve a gazpacho or sorrel soup as an appetizer and for dessert a seasonal fruit salad with crisp cookies.

2. For a slightly more substantial meal, serve gratin of mushrooms on toast as an appetizer and sweet omelet with jelly for dessert.

Cold roast pork

This delicious meat needs nothing more than a few sauces as an accompaniment. You could serve it with plain mayonnaise made with 1 egg yolk, 1 scant cup (20 cl) oil, 1 tbsp mustard, and some salt and pepper. This basic sauce can be flavored and enhanced in various different ways. For a fairly hot sauce, incorporate 2 tbsp traditional mustard. Chop a mixture of tarragon, fresh parsley, and shallot for a fairly fresh, very green sauce. For a more unusual flavor, add the juice of $1/2$ lemon, 1 tbsp curry powder, and a few drops of Tabasco®. A crisp salad is the best accompaniment to cold roast meat. Serve endives and chopped apples seasoned with lemon and olive oil. In season, make a salad of red and green oak-leaf lettuce leaves flavored with chopped shallots and sherry vinegar. You could also serve a salad of fresh tomatoes marinated in lemon juice, chopped basil, and olive oil.

Sliced Roast Pork in Sauce

Serves 4
$10^1/2$ oz (300 g) pork
1 lb 2 oz (500 g) soybeans
10 tbsp soy sauce
2 tbsp Chinese vinegar
2 tsp superfine sugar
1 tbsp chopped fresh ginger
20 drops sesame oil
1 bunch cilantro

1. Trim the fat off the meat and discard the string. Cut into slices and then into fairly thin strips.

2. Blanch the soybeans quickly then drain them. Transfer to the serving dish and arrange the strips of pork on top.

3. Prepare a sauce by mixing the soy sauce, Chinese vinegar, sugar, ginger, and sesame oil. Mix well and pour over the meat and soybeans. Sprinkle with chopped cilantro.

Sausage salad

Serves 4
$10^1/2$ oz (300 g) leftover, cooked sausage
$2^1/4$ lb (1 kg) potatoes
1 finely chopped onion
10 chopped gherkins
1 bunch chopped chives
2 tbsp hot mustard
2 tbsp wine vinegar
10 tbsp peanut oil
Salt and pepper

1. Cut the sausages into thin slices. Peel the potatoes and boil them. Drain and leave for 2 hours to go cold. Cut into slices $1/16$–$1/8$ in (3–4 mm) thick.

2. Mix in a large bowl with the leftover sausage, the onion, the gherkins, the chives, and a vinaigrette made from the hot mustard, the wine vinegar, the peanut oil, and some salt and pepper.

3. Stir well to distribute all these ingredients and leave the salad to macerate for 1 hour before serving.

Stuffed vegetables

To make 4 stuffed tomatoes
10½ oz (300 g) leftover cooked sausage meat
3½ oz (100 g) breadcrumbs
2 cloves garlic
1 bunch parsley
2 eggs
4 tomatoes
Salt and pepper

1. Place the sausage meat in a large bowl and add the breadcrumbs, the chopped garlic, the chopped parsley, and the eggs. Season, then mix with a wooden spoon to obtain a homogeneous stuffing.

2. Scoop out the seeds from the tomatoes and fill with the stuffing, using a tablespoon. Cook in the oven at 375 °F (190 °C) for 40 minutes.

Ham mousse

Serves 4
14 oz (400 g) offcuts of cooked ham
1 tsp Worcestershire sauce
1 tbsp catsup
1 tbsp tomato paste
2 tbsp crème fraîche
5 drops Tabasco®
1¼ cups (30 cl) light cream
Salt and pepper

1. Remove the rind and the fat from the ham. Place in a blender and reduce to a fairly coarse purée. Transfer the chopped ham to a large bowl and add the Worcestershire sauce, catsup, tomato purée, crème fraîche, salt, pepper, and Tabasco.

2. Stir vigorously with a wooden spoon. Whip the cream until it has reached the consistency of a firm mousse and fold the ham gently into it. Adjust seasoning to taste.

3. Fill some little ramekins with the ham mousse and refrigerate for 2 hours. Serve with a green salad.

Meatballs

Serves 6
1 lb 2 oz (500 g) roast pork
14 oz (400 g) sausage meat
7 oz (200 g) breadcrumbs
½ bunch chopped parsley
Grated nutmeg
Fresh thyme
2 eggs
2 chopped onions
2 cups (50 cl) tomato sauce
Salt and pepper

1. Dice the roast pork. Place the chopped meat in a large bowl and add the sausage meat, breadcrumbs, parsley, nutmeg, thyme, salt, pepper, and the eggs.

2. Mix everything well until you have a smooth paste. Roll the mixture into balls between the palms of your hands and brown in a skillet over moderate heat for 20 minutes.

3. Add the onions and tomato sauce and cook slowly for 25 minutes. Serve hot with white rice.

Poultry and game

Chicken broth

Chicken broth

Chicken broth is prepared using a chicken or the carcass of a boned chicken. You can eat it as it is, add vermicelli, or use it as a base for preparing sauces. The secret of success depends on how fresh the poultry is and on the cooking time, which should be very slow and even.

For about 6 cups (1.5 liters) broth, remove some of the fat from 2 chicken carcasses and cut each one into 3 pieces. Prepare some vegetables to cook with the bones, peeling and halving 3 onions, 3 carrots, and 2 cloves of garlic. Make 1 large bouquet garni with 2 leeks, 2 stalks celery, some thyme, and some bay leaves. Put the chicken carcasses in a saucepan, add 3 quarts (3 liters) cold water, and bring to the boil. Skim, add the vegetables, 10 peppercorns, 1/2 level tbsp coarse salt, and 4 cloves. Cook the broth for 2 hours over low heat, skimming off the fat regularly. Strain the broth, discard the vegetables

and the bones, and cool. Store in the refrigerator. The broth is also easy to freeze.

Blanquette of rabbit

This dish is always a very pleasant surprise, the lean meat going very well with a cream sauce. To serve 6, cut 1 large rabbit into 10 pieces. Place in a stewpot and cover with 3 quarts (3 liters) water. Bring to the boil, skim, and add a selection of vegetables (2 onions, 2 carrots, 1 large bouquet garni, salt, and pepper). Cook for about 1 hour 15 minutes. Drain the meat and the vegetables. Strain the broth

Steamed chicken thighs with tarragon

Blanquette of rabbit

and boil vigorously to reduce to 1 quart (1 liter). Then add a roux made from 1/2 cup (65 g) flour and 3 1/2 oz (100 g) butter, beating vigorously. Add 2/3 cup (15 cl) light cream and boil slowly for 5 minutes. Season with salt and pepper, then strain the sauce. Off the heat, add 1 egg yolk mixed with 3 1/2 tbsp (5 cl) crème fraîche. Add the meat and the cooked vegetables to the sauce, adjust seasoning to taste, and serve very hot.

Steamed chicken thighs with tarragon

To serve 6, cut 6 chicken thighs in half, place in a large bowl, season with salt and pepper, and mix with 1 bunch chopped tarragon and 2 tbsp olive oil. Transfer the seasoned chicken thighs to a steamer, add 4 sprigs tarragon to the water, put on the lid, and cook for about 35–40 minutes. Serve very hot with a few drops of lemon juice and some plain rice.

Chicken in the pot

for 8

1 This is a delicious recipe for a family meal. Make a stuffing by mixing 10$\frac{1}{2}$ oz (300 g) chopped unsalted pork breast, 3 chopped chicken livers, 2$\frac{3}{4}$ oz (70 g) chopped dried ham, 1 egg, 1 tbsp breadcrumbs, 1 tbsp Armagnac, 1 tbsp fresh parsley, and some salt, pepper, and thyme in a large bowl. Knead until the mixture is smooth.

2 Fill the cavity of the chicken from the rear end, then truss firmly. Put the chicken in a stewpot and cover with 5 quarts (5 liters) cold water. Bring to the boil, skim, then lower the heat so the chicken cooks very slowly and evenly for 30 minutes.

3 Add 3 onions, 3 carrots, 2 cloves garlic, 1 tbsp coarse salt, and 5 peppercorns. Prepare 1 large bouquet garni with 2 leeks, 2 stalks celery, some thyme, and some bay leaves, and cook for about 1 hour 30 minutes. Serve in a deep dish with the vegetables on the bottom, the carved chicken over, and the stuffing on top. Serve very hot.

Pot-cooked rabbit

This recipe is an original way of cooking this delicate meat. To serve 6, cut 1 large rabbit into about 10 pieces and place in a stewpot. Cover with 4 quarts (4 liters) water, bring to the boil, and skim. Cook for 20 minutes, then add 3 leeks, 2 stalks celery, 4 carrots, 3 onions, and 4 turnips, cut into pieces. Add 10 peppercorns, 3 pinches coarse salt, 1 bouquet garni, and 3 cloves. Leave uncovered and cook over low heat for about 1 hour 15 minutes. Serve as you would pot-cooked beef, with the broth, the vegetables, some mustard, and some coarse salt, with small steamed potatoes and mushrooms cooked in butter as an accompaniment.

Pot-cooked rabbit

Chicken in the pot

General points

Sealed and browned in oil, then cooked in a sauce, poultry acquires delicious flavors. Cook these recipes in a good cast iron or enameled cast iron casserole. So they can be easily digested, do not forget to remove the fat during the cooking time.

Chicken fricassee with mushrooms

Sauté of rabbit with herbs

Chicken from the roches de Condrieu

Chicken fricassee with mushrooms

This is a recipe in which you can either use plain white button mushrooms or field mushrooms (boletus, girolles, or trompettes-de-la-mort). To serve 6, cut 1 free-range chicken into about 10 pieces. Season with salt and pepper and brown in a saucepan for 25 minutes. Drain the oil from the pan, add 3 chopped shallots, and cook for 5 minutes. Then add 7 oz (200 g) small, peeled, white button mushrooms, 2 boletus cut into large pieces, 5½ oz (150 g)

girolles, and 5½ oz (50 g) trompettes-de-la-mort, washed thoroughly. Cook over low heat for 20 minutes, stirring gently, then add 1/3 cup + 1½ tbsp (10 cl) white wine and 2½ tbsp (4 cl) Armagnac. Boil for 5 minutes then add 2/3 cup (15 cl) veal bouillon and 2/3 cup (15 cl) crème fraîche. Season with salt and pepper, cover, and cook over very low heat for 40 minutes. Check that the chicken is cooked, adjust seasoning to taste, and serve very hot.

Provençal chicken

This recipe should be cooked in high summer when the vegetables have most flavor. To serve 6, cut 1 free-range chicken into 10 pieces. Season with salt and pepper and brown in olive oil in a saucepan for 25 minutes. Drain the oil from the pan, add 3 chopped onions,

and cook for 5 minutes. Then add 14 oz (400 g) bell peppers (red and green) cut into strips, 14 oz (400 g) sliced eggplant, and 5 chopped cloves of garlic. Cook over low heat, stirring very gently, for 20 minutes, then add 1/3 cup + 1½ tbsp (10 cl) rosé wine. Boil for 5 minutes, then add 2/3 cup (15 cl) veal bouillon, 4 sliced tomatoes, 2 stalks fresh thyme, and 1 tbsp tomato paste. Season with salt and pepper, cover, and cook over very low heat for 40 minutes. Check that the meat is cooked, adjust seasoning to taste, and serve very hot.

Tip

Cooking in a Römertopf accentuates the flavor of the ingredients. It is therefore essential to use only products of exceptional quality, otherwise the recipes may seem insipid, if not unappetizing.

Cooking in a terrine

This method allows you to cook dishes without fat that are full of flavor. The basic principle is a simple one and has numerous variations. Season a chicken on all sides and place in the terrine, surrounded by 3 onions cut into medium-sized cubes, 1 lb 5 oz (600 g) diced potatoes, 3$^1/_2$ oz (100 g) smoked bacon lardoons, and some thyme, salt, and pepper. Put the lid on and cook in the oven at 400 °F (200 °C) for about 1 hour 15 minutes. Check that the meat is cooked and serve very hot.

Chicken with apples and cream

This recipe uses pippins and crème fraîche. Sauté 10 seasoned chicken pieces and then add 4 apples, peeled, cored, and cut into quarters. Brown for 30 minutes, then deglaze with $^2/_3$ cup (15 cl) sweet cider. Boil for 2 minutes then add 1 generous cup (25 cl) crème fraîche and $^2/_3$ cup (15 cl) stock. Cook slowly for 40 minutes. Skim off any fat, adjust the seasoning, and serve.

Chicken and apple pie

1 Cut 1 rabbit into about 10 pieces. Season with salt and pepper. Brown the rabbit pieces on all sides in the oil for 20 minutes. Then add 4 chopped shallots and 14 oz (400 g) chopped white button mushrooms and cook for 10 minutes, stirring.

2 Deglaze with 1 generous cup (25 cl) dry white wine. Reduce for 10 minutes, add 3 sliced tomatoes, 1 tbsp tomato paste, and 3 chopped cloves of garlic. Add 1 generous cup (25 cl) chicken or veal bouillon. Cover and cook over low heat for 1 hour 15 minutes.

Rabbit fricassee

for 6

3 Skim any fat off the sauce with a small ladle, adjust the seasoning, add $^1/_2$ bunch chopped parsley, and serve with boiled potatoes. You can add a personal touch to this recipe by substituting a liqueur for the white wine or adding vegetables of your choice.

There is an old adage to the effect that you can become a chef, but you are born a rôtisseur— an allusion to the subtle skills required by this cooking technique. Remember that a fan-assisted oven cooks faster than an ordinary oven.

Chicken, duck and guinea fowl

It is quite easy to cook these birds successfully. For added flavor, stuff with 2 sprigs thyme and 4 whole cloves of garlic. Oil, season, and place in a pre-heated oven at 410 °F (210 °C). Cook the bird on its back for 45 minutes, basting three or four times after the first 15 minutes. Remove from the oven, cover with aluminum foil, and rest for 10 minutes before carving. In order to brown the skin on the back of the bird as well as the breast, place on a small rack in the roasting pan.

Roast capon

Pigeons with béarnaise sauce

Capon, goose and turkey

These large birds require special treatment. Place the bird on its side in a roasting pan after oiling and seasoning it and cook in the oven at 400 °F (200 °C) for about 1 hour. During this time, turn so that it cooks for 20 minutes on each side and 20 minutes on its back. Then lower the temperature to 345 °F (175 °C) (while the bird is on its back) and cook for approximately 1 hour 45 minutes more, basting every 10 minutes. Then remove from the oven, wrap in 4 layers of aluminum foil, and leave to stand in a fairly hot place for 30 minutes to allow the bird to finish cooking from the heat trapped inside the foil. Then remove the foil, collect the juices, and carve.

Duck with chestnuts

Small birds

Small birds such as pigeon should not be overcooked as this dries them out and they become unappetizing. Place the dressed, oiled, and seasoned birds in a roasting pan. They should not touch. Cook in the oven at 410 °F (210 °C) for 25 minutes, then remove and allow to cool for 10 minutes before serving.

Wood pigeon Gascony style

Haunch of venison with blueberries

Chicken "en croûte"

Haunch of venison

Like all large pieces of meat, this should first be sealed and then cooked slowly. For good results, brown the seasoned haunch on all sides in very hot oil in a skillet. Transfer to a roasting pan and roast for 15 minutes per pound at 375 °F (190 °C), basting frequently.

Cooking in a salt crust

This technique should be reserved for the best poultry and game birds. The salt crust effectively forms a barrier that concentrates the flavors, both good and bad. Oil and season a chicken. Stuff with thyme, fresh garlic, and parsley, then truss the bird. Place a thick layer of sea salt in the bottom of a deep, oval terrine and place the bird on top with 2 bay leaves, covering with coarse salt. Cook in the oven at 430 °F (220 °C) for 1 hour 45 minutes. Remove from the oven, cool for a few minutes, then break the salt shell and remove and carve the bird.

Summary

Poultry	Brown in skillet	Temperature	Cook in oven	Wrap in aluminum foil
Chicken, guinea fowl	No	410 °F (210 °C)	15 minutes/pound + 10 minutes	Yes, 10 minutes
Duck	Yes or no	410 °F (210 °C)	17 minutes/pound +7 minutes	Yes, 10 minutes
Pigeon	No	430 °F (220 °C)	20–25 minutes	No
Capon, turkey	Yes or no	400 °F (200 °C) then 345 °F (175 °C)	22 minutes/pound + 20 minutes	Yes, 30 minutes minimum
Goose	Yes or no	400 °F (200 °C) then 345 °F (175 °C)	26 minutes/pound	Yes, 30 minutes minimum
Roast turkey	Yes or no	400 °F (200 °C)	25 minutes/pound	Yes, 10 minutes

Game	Brown in frying pan	Temperature	Cook in oven	Wrap in aluminum foil
Pheasant	No	410 °F (210 °C)	15 minutes/pound + 5 minutes	Yes, 10 minutes
Duck	Yes or no	410 °F (210 °C)	15 minutes/pound + 7 minutes	Yes, 10 minutes
Partridge	No	430 °F (220 °C)	20–25 minutes	No
Saddle of hare	Yes	430 °F (220 °C)	15 minutes/pound	No
Haunch	Yes	375 °F (190 °C)	20 minutes/pound	Yes, 10 minutes minimum
Roast venison	Yes	400 °F (200 °C)	20–25 minutes/pound	Yes, 10 minutes

Fricassee of rabbit

for 5–6

1 This stew should be made with wild rabbit. Cut 1 wild rabbit into pieces, season, and brown in fairly hot oil for 15 minutes. Then add 7 oz (200 g) small onions, 5½ oz (150 g) small white button mushrooms, and 3½ oz (100 g) blanched bacon lardoons.

2 Cook over moderate heat for another 15 minutes before adding 1 tbsp flour. Mix well and continue cooking for 5 minutes. Then add 2 cups (50 cl) red wine, 1 scant cup (20 cl) stock, 2 chopped cloves of garlic, and 1 bouquet garni.

3 Cover and cook for 40 minutes. Skim the fat off the sauce, adjust the seasoning, and sprinkle with chopped fresh parsley. Serve the fricassee with sauté potatoes.

Rabbit stew

General points

Braising tenderizes tougher meats, making them succulent and tasty. Large birds (goose, turkey, and duck) and various kinds of game (venison, wild boar, hare, and wild rabbit) are cooked in this way.

Whole goose braised with apples

Ask your butcher to prepare 1 large farm-raised goose. Peel and core 3 apples (pippins) and cut them into quarters. Sprinkle the apples with superfine sugar, ground cinnamon, and 3½ tbsp (5 cl) calvados. Leave to marinate for 30 minutes. Season the cavity of the goose with salt and pepper and then stuff with the apples. Truss the bird, oil it lightly, then season with salt and pepper. Brown on all sides in a casserole over moderate heat for 1 hour, then deglaze with ⅓ cup (8 cl) calvados. Reduce for 2 minutes, then add 2 cups (50 cl) sweet cider and 1 scant cup (20 cl) bouillon. Braise over gentle heat for 1 hour 45 minutes, skimming off the fat regularly. Then remove the bird, adjust the seasoning if necessary, and reduce the sauce if it is a little thin. Carve the goose and serve with the cooked apples.

Braised shoulder of wild boar

for 8

1 Bone a shoulder of wild boar; you should have about 4¹/₂ lb (2 kg) meat. Cut into pieces and place in a large bowl with 4 cups (1 liter) red wine, 2 onions, 2 carrots, 2 shallots, and 1 stalk celery, all chopped and mixed together, 10 peppercorns, 4 cloves, 1 bouquet garni, 5 juniper berries, and ¹/₃ cup + 1¹/₂ tbsp (10 cl) cognac. Refrigerate and leave to marinate for 48 hours.

2 On the day of the meal, drain the meat and vegetables, then separate them. Brown the meat in a large skillet for 30 minutes (in several batches if necessary). Drain. Then cook the vegetables in the skillet for 20 minutes. Transfer the vegetables and meat to a stewpot, add 1 tbsp flour, and cook for 10 minutes, stirring.

3 Bring the marinade to the boil and skim, then pour into the stewpot. Cook over low heat for 30 minutes, then add 4 cups (1 liter) game bouillon and the bouquet garni. Cover and boil very slowly for 2 hours, constantly skimming the fat off the surface. Then adjust the seasoning with salt and pepper and add 3¹/₂ oz (100 g) blueberry jelly. Serve very hot.

Game broth

This is used in recipes for braising.

Place 6³/₄ lb (3 kg) game bones in a stewpot and cover with 3 quarts (3 liters) cold water and 1 quart (1 liter) red wine. Boil, skim, and add 3 carrots, 3 onions, 2 leeks, 10 peppercorns, and 2 cloves to flavor the broth. Cook over very gentle heat for 3 hours, constantly skimming off the fat. Top up with water if the level drops too low. Strain the broth and discard the bones and vegetables. The broth should be full-bodied and distinctive in flavor; it can be used either to intensify or moderate a sauce.

Braised shoulder of wild boar

General points

Grilling or frying is the best way to deal with small cuts (chops, thighs, fillets, supremes) and small game birds and animals. Here are a few suggestions.

Mississippi deep-fried chicken

American fried chicken

This dish has become an international favorite. To serve 4, prepare 4 chicken drumsticks, 4 thighs, and 8 wings. Season with salt, pepper, and Cayenne pepper, the juice of 2 lemons, 1 onion, and 2 finely chopped cloves of garlic. Marinate overnight. The next day, drain the meat. Prepare the batter by mixing $4^1/_2$ oz (125 g) flour, 1 scant cup (20 cl) beer, 2 egg yolks, and 1 pinch salt. Leave to rest for 1 hour. Dip the chicken pieces in the batter and then fry in a deep-fat fryer at about 340 °F (170 °C) for 15–20 minutes. Pat with paper towels and serve immediately.

Small birds "en brochette"

This is a delicacy reserved only for huntsmen, as such products are not licensed for sale. Pluck and draw the birds. Season the cavity and the outside. Thread 5 birds on each skewer, alternating with a fairly thick piece of blanched smoked pork breast. Grill the kebabs over high heat for 10 minutes and serve very hot.

Quail with figs

Grilled quail

Prepare the quail and truss them, then flatten well with the palm of the hand, without squashing them. Oil lightly, season with salt and pepper, and place the prepared quail, skin side down, on a very hot grill. Cook and brown for about 10 minutes, then turn and cook for a further 5 minutes. Serve the quail immediately; do not cook any longer than this or they will be rather dry. Serve 2 quail per person.

Venison chops

These can be served pinkish, or even, for those who like their meat that way, quite rare. Season with salt and pepper. Grill over high heat for 2 or 3 minutes on each side, according to the thickness of the meat. Serve immediately with a purée of celery and a pepper sauce.

Grilled venison chops

Chicken kebabs with zucchini

Barbecued chicken kebabs

Marinated chicken kebabs

These are delicious in summer, grilled on the barbecue. To serve 6, bone and remove the skin from 4 chicken thighs and 4 breasts. Cut the meat into cubes the size of a large walnut. Place these in a large bowl, season with salt and pepper, then add 3 tbsp runny honey, the juice of 2 limes, 4 tbsp olive oil, 1 tsp chopped fresh ginger, and 1 bunch chives, chopped. Mix well and leave to marinate overnight. Next day, thread the chicken pieces on skewers with strips of red bell pepper and some onions. Grill the kebabs for 10 minutes over a very hot bed of charcoal. Serve with a dish of white rice.

Papillotes

Very easy to prepare, these are always delicious. To serve 4, prepare 2 thighs and 2 saddles of rabbit. Season with salt and pepper and sprinkle with thyme and savory. Add 2 tbsp olive oil. Mix well. Wrap the seasoned pieces of meat in aluminum foil and place on the barbecue. Cook for about 30 minutes, turning very frequently. Serve the papillotes intact and let your guests unwrap them and experience their delicious aroma. You can add a personal touch to your papillotes by cooking them with different herbs (parsley, chives, basil, sage) or spices (black pepper, cinnamon, ras al-hanout, curry, cumin).

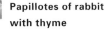

Papillotes of rabbit with thyme

Barbecued chicken portions

These take no time at all to prepare and everyone enjoys them. To serve 4, cut 4 chicken thighs in half. Cut into the flesh using a small knife and leave to marinate for 1 hour with 1 chopped onion, 1/3 cup + 1 1/2 tbsp (10 cl) soy sauce, 1 tbsp tomato paste, 1 tbsp superfine sugar, some salt and pepper, and 2 pinches Cayenne pepper. Place the seasoned portions on the barbecue, skin side down, and cook for about 12 minutes, then cook for the same length of time on the other side. Serve very hot.

General points

Pan-frying allows you to seal and brown certain kinds of game and poultry quickly. Use a cast iron skillet or one with a non-stick coating. For the cooking fat, choose peanut oil with a dab of butter, or olive oil, or goose fat.

Venison or young wild boar chops

These chops are delicious. Do not prepare them for more than 8 people, as cooking such a quantity would be difficult. To serve 6, season 12 chops with salt and pepper on both sides. Fry over high heat for about 1 minute on each side in 1 tbsp peanut oil. Place the chops in a serving dish and keep hot. Discard the fat in the skillet and add 1¹/₂ cup (35 cl) peppered vinaigrette sauce. Bring to a slow boil, then remove from the heat. Add 1 tbsp butter and 1 tbsp gooseberry jelly and adjust the seasoning. Spoon the sauce over the chops and serve at once.

Chicken breasts

These should be cooked slowly in butter to keep them succulent. Season the fillets with salt and pepper and place them skin side down in foaming butter. Cook over moderate to low heat for 12 minutes. When the skin is well browned, turn and cook for another 6 minutes over moderate heat. Serve the cooked chicken breasts with a green salad.

Venison chops Lorraine style

Chicken breasts

Turkey escalopes

These are cut from the most tender part of the turkey—the breast. Place the escalopes on the worktop. Season with salt and pepper, then dip them into some flour on a plate so they are finely coated. Sauté for about 1 minute on each side in a little, very hot oil. Arrange the escalopes on a serving platter, empty the skillet of oil, and add 2 chopped shallots. Cook for 1 minute then add 3$\frac{1}{2}$ tbsp (5 cl) white wine. Reduce for 1 minute then add 1 scant cup (20 cl) crème fraîche. Boil for 2 minutes, season with salt and pepper, and add $\frac{1}{2}$ bunch chopped chives. Spoon the sauce over the escalopes.

Duck foie gras

Cut in fairly thick slices and fried, this melts in the mouth and has the most delicious flavor.

Escalopes of foie gras with pears and grapes

To cook foie gras successfully, it should be absolutely fresh; do not entertain the idea of using liver whose freshness is suspect. Duck liver is better suited to this recipe than goose liver, as it seems to have more flavor. It is often accompanied by a slightly sweet-and-sour sauce prepared with honey, vinegar, and the juice of citrus fruit or verjuice (acidic grape juice). To serve 4, place 1 lb (450 g) duck liver on the worktop. Separate the two lobes with your hands and remove any small, red spots.

Cut the lobes into 8–10 slices, each $\frac{3}{4}$ in (2 cm) thick, using a sharp knife. Season the slices with salt and pepper. When ready to serve, place them in a skillet without any fat and set over medium heat. When the liver starts to sizzle, cook for about 1 minute on each side. During cooking, there is a danger that the skillet will fill up with duck fat; pour the fat off into a bowl from time to time to prevent the liver "deep frying," which would spoil its taste and consistency. Place the slices in a heated dish with some paper towels. Drain the fat from the skillet and add 25 peeled white grapes. Sauté gently for 30 seconds and add $\frac{1}{2}$ tsp honey and 3 tbsp wine vinegar. Reduce for about 10 seconds and add $\frac{1}{3}$ cup + 1$\frac{1}{2}$ tbsp (10 cl) stock. Bring to the boil and season with salt and pepper. Arrange the hot, fried slices of liver in a heated serving dish and spoon over the sauce. Serve immediately.

Turkey breasts with chervil

Coq au vin

Coq au vin

for 8

1 The meat of a cockerel is fairly firm and can be tenderized by marinating and braising. Ask your butcher to cut 1 cockerel into about a dozen pieces. Prepare a mixture of diced vegetables using 3 onions, 2 carrots, and 1 stalk celery. Place the vegetables and the meat in a large bowl and cover with red wine. Add 1 large bouquet garni, 10 peppercorns, and 2 cloves.

2 Refrigerate and marinade for 24 hours. Next day, drain and separate the meat from the vegetables. Brown the meat for 20 minutes in a large skillet set over high heat, followed by the vegetables. Transfer the meat and vegetables to a large saucepan, add 2 level tbsp flour, mix, turning the pieces of meat, and cook, stirring constantly, for 5 minutes.

3 Boil the marinade, skim, and pour over the cockerel with 3 cups (75 cl) bouillon and the bouquet garni. Bring to the boil, skim, remove the fat with a small ladle, season with salt and pepper, then cook over very low heat for about 1 hour 45 minutes. When the cockerel is cooked, drain and set aside. Cook the sauce for 10 minutes, carefully removing the fat. Strain and adjust the seasoning.

4 Blanch 5$\frac{1}{2}$ oz (150 g) smoked bacon lardoons and peel 7 oz (200 g) small white button mushrooms; cook for 10 minutes in $\frac{2}{3}$ cup (15 cl) water, the juice of 1 lemon and 3⁄4 oz (20 g) butter. Thirty minutes before serving, assemble the meat, sauce, mushrooms, and bacon in a saucepan and bring to simmering point; do not allow the sauce to boil. Add some chopped fresh parsley and serve very hot with steamed potatoes.

Tandoori chicken

1 This recipe is traditionally prepared in a conical clay oven called a tandoor. Cut 1 chicken into 10 pieces, remove the skin, and make cuts in the flesh. Place the meat in a large bowl and season with salt, pepper, and the juice of 2 limes.

2 Then add 4 chopped cloves of garlic, 1 tsp cumin, 1/2 root chopped fresh ginger, 1 pinch turmeric, and 4 tsp (20 g) sugar. To these spices, add 2 yogurts, 1 chopped onion, 3 pinches saffron, and 2 pinches Cayenne pepper. Mix all the ingredients well and marinate for 3–4 hours.

3 Heat the oven to 430 °F (220 °C). Thread the chicken pieces on skewers, place on a grill over a baking pan, and cook for about 10 minutes. Spoon some ghee over them, using a small ladle, and continue cooking for 15 minutes. The meat should turn a pale golden color as it cooks and should remain succulent.

4 Place the kebabs on a serving platter, pour over some lime juice, and season with pepper. Tandoori chicken is traditionally accompanied by a refreshing, slightly spicy salad, either grated cabbage with pepper and lemon juice, cucumber with yogurt and cumin, or onions and tomatoes with coriander. Hand round mango chutney in a small bowl, and serve with plain white rice.

Tip

This delicious recipe can also be prepared using other kinds of poultry or different cuts. You can for instance use cockerels cut in half or trussed, quail, or guinea fowl. Ghee is a fat used a great deal in Indian cookery, which is basically clarified butter: i.e., with the whey removed. Ghee has a unique flavor and imparts a distinctive and pleasant taste to dishes in which it is used.

375

Woodcock salmi

Woodcock salmi

for 4

1 Salmi (short for "salmigondis") is a method of preparing game birds. The meat is basically roasted, but left pink in the middle and carved; the sauce is then prepared using the bones, and the meat finishes cooking in this sauce just before serving. Woodcock, pheasant, duck, and partridge can be prepared in this way. Season 2 woodcock and roast them in the oven at 430 °F (220 °C) for 15 minutes.

2 Leave to cool for 5 minutes. Carve, reserving the breasts and the thighs. Set aside the livers and break the carcasses into 5 or 6 pieces. Heat some peanut oil in a saucepan and cook the carcasses for 10 minutes until they turn golden. Then add 4 tbsp finely shredded carrot, onion, shallot, and leek.

3 Cook, stirring constantly, for 5 minutes. Flambé with 2^1/$_2$ tbsp (4 cl) Armagnac and then add ^{1}/$_4$ cup (6 cl) white wine. Boil for 2 minutes before adding ^{2}/$_3$ cup (15 cl) veal bouillon, the juices from the carved woodcock, the chopped livers, some salt and pepper, ^{1}/$_2$ bay leaf, and 1 pinch thyme. Cover and cook over low heat for 10 minutes.

4 Strain the sauce into another saucepan, adjust the seasoning, then add 1 tbsp butter and the pieces of woodcock, skin side up. Finish cooking by heating all the ingredients very gently for 5 minutes. The sauce must not be allowed to boil. Server very hot with triangles of bread fried in butter with the crusts removed and with small white button mushrooms sautéed in butter.

Pigeons in escabèche

for 4

1 Escabèche was originally a very full-bodied, spicy marinade intended to preserve food, in particular small fish. The principle was then extended to other produce such as poultry and especially game. Game birds preserved in this way have largely fallen out of favor, but some great chefs have revived the tradition, to the great delight of gourmets.

2 Place 2 large pigeons on their backs, and use a sharp knife to remove the thighs with the breasts attached, i.e., in 2 pieces. Reserve the carcass and bones for the sauce. Brown the meat on both sides in a skillet for 10 minutes, then remove and allow to cool. Brown the bones in the same skillet for 8 minutes. Add 1 finely shredded carrot, 2 cloves of garlic, 4 shallots, and 1 onion, all chopped.

3 Sweat for 4 minutes, then deglaze with 1 scant cup (20 cl) dry white wine. Boil for 4 minutes, then add 4 sliced tomatoes, 1 tsp tomato paste, 1 generous cup (25 cl) veal bouillon, and some salt, pepper, thyme, and bay. Leave to cook over low heat for 15 minutes, removing the fat frequently. Alternatively, you can use a saucepan to avoid having to transfer the prepared food.

4 Remove the pieces of carcass and add the meat. Cook over low heat for 10 minutes, adjust the seasoning, then cool in a dish. Refrigerate and marinate for 24 hours before tasting the sauce. Serve cold after adding a little freshly ground pepper.

377

Rabbit stew

Rabbit stew with red wine

for 8

1 This stew is one of the best recipes for cooking rabbit. If the animal is fairly large, keep the saddle for roasting and make a stew with the remainder. Cut 1 rabbit into 12 portions. Finely dice and mix together 3 onions, 2 carrots, and 1 stalk celery. Place the vegetables and the meat in a large bowl and cover with 6 cups (1.5 liter) red wine.

2 Add 3½ tbsp (5 cl) cognac and 2½ tbsp (4 cl) vinegar, 1 large bouquet garni, 10 peppercorns, and 2 cloves. Refrigerate and leave to marinate for 24 hours. Next day, drain and separate the meat from the vegetables. Brown the meat in a large skillet set over high heat for 20 minutes, followed by the vegetables.

3 Transfer the meat and vegetables to a large saucepan, add 2 level tbsp flour, mix, then cook, stirring constantly, for 5 minutes. Bring the marinade to the boil, skim, and pour over the rabbit with 3 cups (75 cl) veal bouillon and the bouquet garni. Bring to the boil, skim and remove the fat with a small ladle, season with salt and pepper, then cook over very low heat for about 1 hour 45 minutes.

4 When the rabbit portions are cooked, drain and set them aside. Cook the sauce for 10 minutes, carefully removing the fat. Strain through a fine sieve and adjust the seasoning. Transfer to a saucepan. Add 3½ tbsp (5 cl) red wine and mix well, without boiling. Add 2 tbsp gooseberry jelly and 1 tbsp wine vinegar.

5 Peel 7 oz (200 g) small white button mushrooms and cook for 10 minutes in ⅔ cup (15 cl) water, the juice of 1 lemon, and ¾ oz (20 g) butter. Thirty minutes before serving, assemble the meat, sauce, and mushrooms in a casserole. Bring to simmering point (do not allow to boil), finish by adding some chopped fresh parsley, and serve very hot with fresh pasta, celery purée, or steamed potatoes.

daube of wild boar

1. The term "daube" refers to meat (and also fish) dishes that are simmered slowly in a wine sauce. The meat may or may not be marinated before cooking. The secret of success lies in the cooking, which should initially be over high heat and subsequently very slow. Cut 4½ lb (2 kg) wild boar meat, from the shoulder and collar, into pieces.

2. Season the meat with salt and pepper, add some thyme, bay, 5 crushed juniper berries, 3 chopped onions, 2 carrots cut into rings, and 2 tbsp peanut oil and mix well. Leave to stand in the refrigerator for 24 hours. When you are ready to cook, separate the meat from the vegetables. Heat some oil in a large skillet and sauté the pieces of wild boar for 25 minutes, so that they brown nicely.

3. Transfer the pieces of meat to a casserole, add the vegetables, and cook for 30 minutes. Add 2 tbsp flour. Mix well, then add 4 cups (1 liter) red wine and ⅓ cup + 1½ tbsp (10 cl) Armagnac. Boil slowly for 15 minutes, then add 3 cups (70 cl) veal bouillon, 2 tbsp tomato paste, 1 large bouquet garni, 1 tbsp superfine sugar, and some salt and pepper.

4. Bring to the boil, skim off the fat, cover and cook for about 1 hour 30 minutes. Skim the sauce, discard the bouquet garni, and adjust the seasoning. Mixing together 3 cloves of garlic and ½ bunch parsley, all finely chopped, and add to the daube 2 minutes before serving, stirring to mix. Serve the daube of wild boar with slices of rustic bread rubbed with garlic and toasted in the oven.

partridge with cabbage

Partridge with cabbage

for 4

1 The delicate flesh of partridge is a perfect partner for braised kale. Do not make this dish for more than 4, as it can be quite tricky to cook. The preparation is fairly simple and the presentation quite superb. This recipe can also be cooked with pigeon, grouse, or pheasant. Truss 2 partridge, cover with thin slices of bacon, and season. Oil lightly.

2 Roast in the oven at 430 °F (220 °C) for 20 minutes to brown them well on all sides. Remove them from the oven and leave to cool on a plate. Cut the leaves off 2 large heads of kale, remove the large veins, and blanch in plenty of salted water. Cut into strips. Heat some goose fat in a saucepan and brown 2 large carrots cut into rings and 2 onions in it for 5 minutes.

3 Add the kale. Season with salt and pepper and cook over moderate heat for 5 minutes. Add 3 juniper berries and 2/3 cup (15 cl) veal bouillon. Cover and cook for 20 minutes. Butter a soufflé dish and line with blanched kale leaves. Place a layer of cooked kale in the bottom, 2 or 2 1/2 in (5–6 cm) thick, then add the partridge (having removed the string) and cover with the remaining kale and cooking juices.

4 Stand the soufflé dish in a bain-marie or baking pan of water and cook in the oven at 375 °F (190 °C) for 1 hour. Then remove from the oven and leave to cool for 15 minutes. When ready to serve, turn out onto a serving platter and take it to the table just as it is. Serve the kale first, then the partridge, once they have been completely uncovered.

5 For an even more striking presentation, cook in individual soufflé dishes, one for each guest. You will need to cut the partridges in half before covering them in kale. Note also that blanched kale leaves can be used to make parcels, for wrapping round crépinettes or small birds such as quail or pigeon, for example.

ballottine of duck

General points

Ballottine is prepared with poultry (duck, turkey, or fattened chicken) which is boned completely, without damaging the skin. This is a particularly tricky and time-consuming operation and demands considerable expertise. The best solution is to entrust this task to your butcher, who is skilled in such matters. The bird is then stuffed, rolled up and tied, and cooked in bouillon. Ballottine is usually eaten cold, with the string removed, cut into thick slices.

Ballottine of duck

for 8–10

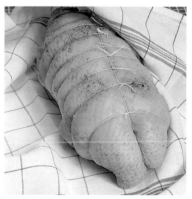

1 Bone 1 large duck. Prepare a stuffing with 10^1/$_2$ oz (300 g) duck meat, 10^1/$_2$ oz (300 g) collar and 10^1/$_2$ oz (300 g) shoulder of pork. Grind this meat through a medium plate and mix with 2 eggs, ^{3}/$_8$ cup (50 g) flour, 1 tbsp salt, 1 pinch pepper, 1 tbsp chopped parsley, 1 tbsp chopped onion, 1 pinch nutmeg, some thyme, some bay, and 2^1/$_2$ tbsp (4 cl) Armagnac. When the stuffing is thoroughly mixed, place in the freezer for an hour to become firm so that it is easier to handle.

2 Place the duck skin side down on the worktop and season the meat. Place the stuffing on top of the duck and roll into a cylinder. Keep in shape with a cloth and secure with string as you would a roasting joint. Do not pull the string too tight; you might break the skin of the duck and allow the stuffing to escape. Heat 5 quarts (5 liters) chicken bouillon and immerse the ballottine in it, protected by the cloth in which it is wrapped. Simmer (under no circumstances allow it to boil) for about 2 hours.

3 Gently remove the ballottine and leave to cool for 2 full days in the refrigerator. On the day of serving, cut the string and remove the cloth. Remove any jelly that has formed on the ballottine during cooking and at the last minute cut into slices ^{1}/$_4$–^{5}/$_{16}$ in (6–8 mm) thick. Serve as an appetizer with a salad and walnut oil dressing and with a fairly full-bodied red wine. You could refine this recipe by adding a large piece of fresh duck foie gras to the stuffing.

rabbit in sauce with fresh noodles

Rabbit in sauce with fresh noodles

for 6–8

1 Rabbit is very often cooked in a stew, but there are other recipes in which it can be cooked successfully to add variety. Wild, wood-grown mushrooms provide a particularly good accompaniment for this succulent meat. Cut 1 rabbit into 10 pieces and season with salt and pepper. Fry the pieces in a saucepan over high heat until they are well browned on all sides.

2 Discard the burned fat, add 4 chopped shallots, 7 oz (200 g) chanterelles, 7 oz (200 g) trompettes de mort, 7 oz (200 g) hedgehog mushrooms, and 3$\frac{1}{2}$ oz (100 g) small white button mushrooms. Cover and cook for about 20 minutes, stirring occasionally. Add 1 generous cup (25 cl) white wine and 3$\frac{1}{2}$ tbsp (5 cl) cognac and reduce for 10 minutes. Then pour in 3 cups (70 cl) fond de veau and season with salt and pepper.

3 Add 1 bouquet garni, $\frac{1}{2}$tbsp tomato paste, 2 chopped cloves of garlic, and 1 sprig of thyme. Bring to the boil, then skim and remove the fat with a small ladle. Cover and cook over very low heat for 1 hour 30 minutes. When the meat is cooked, remove it from the sauce. Add 3$\frac{1}{2}$ tbsp (5 cl) white wine and boil the sauce slowly for 5 minutes, again removing the fat.

4 Adjust the seasoning, discard the bouquet garni, and thicken the sauce with 2$\frac{3}{4}$ oz (80 g) softened butter. Replace the rabbit pieces in the sauce and keep hot without boiling. Cook some fresh tagliatelle in plenty of salted water, drain, and mix with 1 small dab of butter. Serve very hot with the rabbit in the sauce.

rabbit rillettes

Rabbit rillettes

(makes 5–6 pots)

1 Rabbit rillettes can be made with all the parts of a rabbit. After it has been cooked and cooled, wait 1 or 2 days before eating as it will improve greatly. Cut 1 large rabbit into 10 pieces. Season this meat with 4 tsp (20 g) fine salt, a little milled black pepper, 2 sprigs thyme, and 2 bay leaves. Refrigerate the meat overnight.

2 Melt 6³/₄ lb (3 kg) lard in a thick-bottomed saucepan and add the meat and its juices. Bring everything to the boil very slowly over moderate heat and cook for about 3 hours 30 minutes, stirring from time to time. Remove from the heat and carefully drain the cooked meat. Place on the worktop and use a fork to break the meat down until it has a fairly fine fibrous texture.

3 Transfer the meat to a large bowl and add 10¹/₂ oz (300 g) melted lard and the lean meat juices at the bottom of the cooking pan. Mix everything into a smooth paste. The fibers of the meat should still be visible. Check the seasoning and add some salt and pepper if necessary. The same dish will seem more highly seasoned and saltier when it is hot than when it is cold, so do not be afraid to add plenty of seasoning to your rillettes.

General points

Rillettes are prepared by combining cooked meat, fat, and cooking juices. You can therefore adjust the richness and the texture of your rillettes according to your taste. The more fat you add, the whiter, smoother and richer (but less highly seasoned) the finished product will be, and vice versa. Fill the pots with the rillettes while the mixture is still very hot and leave to cool completely in the refrigerator or in a very cold place. Cool the lard at the same time. When the pots have set well, cover them with ³/₈ in (1 cm) of fat, which will act as a lid to seal the rillettes.

rabbit pâté with hazelnuts

Rabbit pâté with hazelnuts

1 Prepare 2¼ lb (1 kg) rabbit meat and combine with 1 lb 2 oz (500 g) collar, 3½ oz (100 g) neck, and 3½ oz (300 g) shoulder of pork, and the rabbit's liver and kidneys. Cut all this meat into strips around 1 in (2–3 cm) wide, but leave the fillets whole. Mix and add 5 tsp (24 g) salt, 1 pinch grated nutmeg, 2 pinches pepper, 4 pinches thyme, 1 pinch powdered bay, ⅓ cup + 1½ tbsp (10 cl) white wine, 1 chopped clove of garlic, and 1 pinch Cayenne pepper.

2 Marinate overnight. Set aside the fillets. Grind the meat through a medium plate and then transfer to a large bowl. Add the marinade juices, 1 tbsp powdered milk, 1 tbsp flour, 2 eggs, 1 tbsp chopped parsley, 1 tbsp + 1 tsp (2 cl) cognac, and 5½ oz (150 g) hazelnuts. Mix again until you have a smooth stuffing. Cook 1 tbsp of the mixture in a skillet and taste.

3 Add salt, pepper, and spices if necessary. Line the sides of a mold with thin slices of bacon and fill with the stuffing. Push the rabbit fillets down into the mixture. Cover with the bacon. Sprinkle the surface with sprigs of fresh thyme and arrange 5 or 6 bay leaves on top for garnish. Instead of bacon you could use a flat sausage that completely covers the surface of the pâté completely.

4 Cook the rabbit pâté in the oven at 350 °F (180 °C) for about 1 hour 30 minutes. The surface should be golden and appetizing when it comes out of the oven. Leave to cool for 1 or 2 hours at room temperature before refrigerating. You can keep the pâté in the refrigerator for 1 week. Cut it into slices while it is still in the mold and serve with gherkins, small onions, and a green salad.

Rabbit pâté with hazelnuts

Rabbit pâté with hazelnuts is a delicious recipe. It is also one of the simplest to prepare.
You do, however, need a meat grinder and an oven. The basic requirements are totally fresh ingredients, especially the pork. To prepare this recipe, choose a good rabbit and ask your butcher to bone it for you. Rabbit pâté is cooked in an oval or rectangular mold. Some of the stuffing ingredients are chopped finely and others more coarsely so that they are more visible when the pâté is cut. The hazelnuts are left whole.

terrine of wild boar

1 Remove the bones from 2¹/₄ lb (1 kg) wild boar meat and combine with 1 lb 5 oz (600 g) collar, 3¹/₂ oz (100 g) neck, and 7 oz (200 g) shoulder of pork, and 7 oz (200 g) chicken livers. Cut all the meat into pieces. Mix and add 5 tsp (25 g) salt, 1 pinch grated nutmeg, 2 pinches pepper, 4 pinches thyme, 1 pinch powdered bay, ²/₃ cup (15 cl) red wine, 1 chopped clove of garlic, 2 pinches powdered juniper berries, and 3¹/₂ tbsp (5 cl) crème de cassis.

2 Marinate overnight. Set aside the wild boar. Grind the other meat through a medium plate and the wild boar through a coarse one. Place the meat in a large bowl. Add the marinade, 1 tbsp powdered milk, 1 tbsp flour, 1 tbsp + 1 tsp (2 cl) Armagnac, and 2 eggs. Mix again until you have a perfectly homogeneous mixture. Cook 1 tbsp of the mixture in a skillet and taste.

3 Add some salt, pepper, and spices if the stuffing seems too bland. Line a terrine mold with a caul and fill with the stuffing, pressing it down slightly as necessary. Cover with some thin slices of bacon. Sprinkle the surface with sprigs of thyme, peppercorns, and juniper berries, and garnish with a few bay leaves. Cover the terrine with two layers of aluminum foil.

4 Cook in the oven at 350 °F (180 °C) for 1 hour 30 minutes. Push a needle into the pâté: it should come out clean and very hot. Leave the pâté to cool for 1–2 hours at room temperature, then refrigerate. It will keep in the refrigerator for 1 week. Serve with rustic bread, gherkins, onion marmalade, and bilberry conserve.

Tip

The meat of wild boar is aromatic and lean and well suited to cooking in terrines. You should, however, choose the cut carefully; shoulder meat is best. You will need to add some pork collar to make the pâté more succulent. This recipe can also be made with hare, venison, and even pheasant.

Chicken giblet soup

This recipe makes a delicious broth that is very good in winter. Place 6 wings, 6 gizzards, and 6 necks in the bottom of a stewpot and cover with 3 quarts (3 liters) cold water. Bring to the boil, skim, and lower the heat so it cooks very slowly and evenly. Boil for 30 minutes, then add 3 onions, 3 carrots, 1 tbsp coarse salt, 1 clove, 5 peppercorns, and 2 cloves of garlic. Prepare 1 large bouquet garni with 2 leeks, 2 stalks celery, thyme, and bay, and cook slowly for about 1 hour 30 minutes. Remove the fat from the broth using a small ladle throughout the cooking time. Arrange the giblets with the vegetables in a large dish and serve the broth at the same time.

Giblet soup

Magret (smoked duck breast)

This has the most delicious flavor. Duck breasts are served whole or sliced thinly in little baskets. They are often served with salad as an appetizer. To serve 4, prepare a mixture of green lettuce (romaine, oak leaf, and batavia). Top and tail 7 oz (200 g) extra fine green

Magret salad with peaches and tarragon

beans and cook in plenty of salted water. Skin, seed, and crush 3 tomatoes. Season the salad with a vinaigrette made with walnut oil and arrange in a mound on a serving platter. Then add some green beans, cooked and seasoned with the same vinaigrette, followed by 8–10 slices of smoked duck breast. Sprinkle over some diced tomato and scatter with walnuts and chervil to finish. This appetizer can also be prepared with dried duck breast.

Turkey wing fricassee

To serve 6, season 8–10 turkey wings with salt and pepper. Brown in a saucepan for 20 minutes. Add 2 shallots and 1 chopped onion. Cook for 5 minutes, then add 2/3 cup (15 cl) white wine. Reduce for another 5 minutes, then add 3 sliced tomatoes, 1 tbsp tomato paste, the chopped and blanched zest of 1 orange, and 2 cups (50 cl) fond de veau. Cover and cook for 40 minutes. Skim the fat off the sauce using a small ladle, then add 1/2 bunch fresh basil blended with 2 tbsp (3 cl) olive oil and 1 clove of garlic. Mix and adjust the seasoning. Serve the fricassee with white rice.

Gizzards

Often eaten in salad, these are also excellent simmered. To serve 4, use 1 lb 5 oz (600 g) preserved duck gizzards, removing the fat and cutting each one into three. Heat 1 tbsp duck fat in a casserole and add 3 carrots, 3 onions, and 1 leek, all finely diced. Cook these vegetables, stirring frequently and without letting them brown, for 10 minutes. Then add the gizzards and 5 1/2 oz (150 g) smoked collar bacon cut into large cubes. Sweat with the vegetables for about 10 minutes, then deglaze with 2 tbsp (3 cl) armagnac. Let the alcohol evaporate, then add 1/3 cup + 1 1/2 tbsp (10 cl) red wine and 1 1/4 cups (30 cl) fond de veau. Cover and cook slowly for 20 minutes. Season with salt and pepper and add 2 tbsp fresh persillade (a mixture of finely chopped garlic and parsley). Adjust the seasoning.

Endive salad with duck gizzards

Chicken wing kebabs with peanuts

If the sauce is too thin, thicken with 1 1/2 oz (40 g) softened butter.

Chicken wings

These are succulent and often used in the cuisine of the Far East. To serve 6, blanch 18 chicken wings, then drain. Brown gently in a large skillet with a little oil, turning as necessary. Cut 3 1/2 oz (100 g) fresh ginger and the white portion of 1 leek julienne style. Add to the chicken wings and continue cooking for 10 minutes, stirring from time to time. Add 4 tbsp runny honey. Turn up the heat and bring to the boil, then caramelize without burning. Deglaze with 3 1/2 tbsp (5 cl) sherry vinegar and 3 1/2 tbsp (5 cl) de soy sauce. Boil for 10 seconds, then sprinkle with fresh cilantro. Serve very hot.

Chicken liver salad

Chicken livers

These are delicious served warm in a salad on a bed of raw young spinach leaves. To serve 6, remove any traces of green from 14 oz (400 g) chicken livers using a small knife. Sort, wash, and dry 2 1/4 lb (1 kg) young spinach leaves, and remove the stalks. Season with a vinaigrette made with sherry vinegar and arrange in a mound on a serving platter. Season the chicken livers with salt and pepper and sauté them for 3 minutes in a large skillet set over fairly high heat. Turn, then while they are still pink, transfer them to a flat plate. Discard the fat in the skillet and deglaze with little sherry vinegar. Then pour the heated vinegar over the livers. Cut in three and arrange on the spinach leaves with their vinegary juices. Garnish with crushed tomatoes and chopped fresh chives.

Hare "à la royale"

Hare "à la Royale" is a traditional recipe in the annals of French cuisine. It was prepared quite frequently during the nineteenth century in the households of the bourgeoisie, but then fell into relative obscurity. Now, however, it has been reinstated by certain chefs. It takes quite a long time to prepare, but it is an extremely fine dish and should be reserved for special occasions, accompanied by a wine such as a Mercurey.

Serves 10–12
Preparation: 1 hour
Marinade: about 12 hours
Cooking: 2 hours 30 minutes

Ingredients

1 large hare
14 oz (400 g) hare meat
10$\frac{1}{2}$ oz (300 g) unsalted pork collar
5$\frac{1}{2}$ oz (150 g) pork shoulder
3$\frac{1}{2}$ oz (100 g) chicken livers
Four-spice mixture
Thyme
6 chopped juniper berries
6 cups (1.5 liters) red wine
Cognac
1 egg
1 tbsp flour
1 lobe fresh duck foie gras
2 onions
2 carrots
2 bouquets garnis
10 peppercorns
2 tbsp (3 cl) wine vinegar
1 tsp coarse salt
3 cups (70 cl) fond de veau
Butter
Salt and pepper

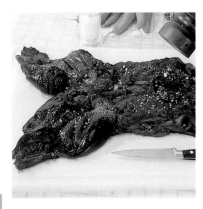

1 Ask your butcher to remove all the bones from 1 large hare, preferably one that has not been damaged too much by shot. Place on the worktop and season with salt and pepper. Cover and set aside in the refrigerator. Combine the liver, the heart of the hare, the hare meat, the collar and shoulder of pork, and the chicken livers in a large bowl.

2 Season with 1 tbsp (16 g) fine salt, 1 pinch freshly milled pepper, 1 pinch four-spice mixture, 1 pinch thyme, 2 chopped juniper berries, 3 1/2 tbsp (5 cl) red wine, and 2 tbsp (3 cl) cognac. Stand in a cool place and marinate overnight. Next day, grind all the meat through a medium plate. Mix with the marinade, the egg, and the flour.

3 When you have a homogeneous mixture, pile it on the boned hare. Press 1 lobe of foie gras, seasoned with salt, pepper, and cognac, into the stuffing. Roll up the hare to form a cylinder. Using a needle and string, sew up the hare tightly so that the stuffing cannot escape.

4 Place the hare in a large pot, with the onions and chopped carrots around it. Add 1 bouquet garni, 6 cups (1.5 liters) red wine, the peppercorns, 4 juniper berries, and the wine vinegar. Transfer to the refrigerator and marinate for 2 hours. Drain the hare, then wipe with a cloth. Season with salt and pepper and brown on all sides for 20 minutes in a large skillet. Then brown the vegetables.

5 Boil and skim the marinade, then place the hare, marinade, vegetables, coarse salt, second bouquet garni, and thickened fond de veau in a casserole. Cover and cook over low heat for 2 hours 30 minutes. Drain the hare, remove the string, and keep hot. Boil the sauce slowly, remove the fat, thicken with the softened butter, then strain. Serve very hot with steamed potatoes and sautéed slices of celeriac.

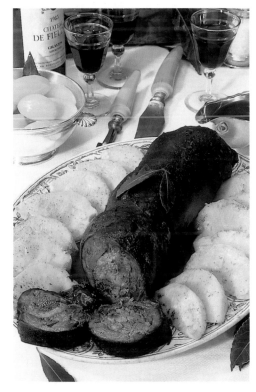

Crème fraîche

Crème fraîche is a pasteurized product and should be kept refrigerated. It can contain up to 35 percent fat. Its acidity and thickness when cold are due to lactic fermentation induced by culture, exactly as happens in yogurt. In cooking, crème fraîche is used to prepare sauces such as beurre blanc (a butter sauce based on a reduction of shallots) and blanquettes in addition to fish mousses and fillings for white boudin sausages. It is also served just as it is to accompany certain fruits, such as strawberries or raspberries. You can heat it slightly—but not too much—to give it a thick consistency, thereby imparting added richness and smoothness to sauces.

General points

Cream is the fat contained in whole milk. On the farm, it appears naturally on the surface of milk that is left to stand without being stirred by paddles. In dairies, it is obtained by centrifuging. It consists of lipids, water, proteins, and minerals. Cream is the basic raw material from which butter is produced (about 7¹/₄ lb/3.2 kg cream is needed to make 2¹/₄ lb/1 kg butter). "Fresh" cream is the term used to describe both raw and pasteurized cream; sterilized products cannot be described as fresh cream. A wide variety of cream is available on the market, either in bulk or already packaged in pots. One of these products is labeled with a certificate of origin: crème d'Isigny.

Thick cream

Crème fleurette

Crème fleurette (light cream)

This has a fat content approximately the same as that of crème fraîche. As it is not fermented, it remains liquid; its flavor is not acid, but on the contrary slightly sweet. It is sold in bottles and must be kept chilled. It is used a great deal by pastry chefs to make Chantilly cream and for glazing and ice cream. In the kitchen, its main use is for preparing sauces. It is available pasteurized, but also sterilized in the form UHT (ultra heat treated). The sterilized product can be stored at room temperature, but if it is to be whipped it is essential to refrigerate it for several hours. Once opened, it should be used very quickly. Its properties make it highly suitable for reduced sauces and it gives excellent volume.

Reduced-fat creams

These are products from which a proportion of the lipids has been removed, leaving on average only 15 percent. They are found in liquid or thickened form, pasteurized or sterilized, and are used in the same way as crème fraîche and crème fleurette. As reduced-fat cream is less rich, it allows you to follow a diet while cooking normally.

Heavy cream

This is always thick. It is enriched and undergoes a process of maturation that gives it a delicious flavor and texture. It is a pity to use it for cooking; instead reserve it for serving with strawberries in season.

Sour cream

This is a fairly acidic product with quite a high fat content, which is used a great deal in Russian cuisine: for example, added to borscht, and as an accompaniment to caviar or smoked sturgeon with blinis. It is possible to make your own sour cream simply by mixing fresh heavy cream with lemon juice.

Sour cream

Tip

Contrary to popular belief, crème fraîche does not thicken sauces, because it becomes completely liquid when it is heated; it merely adds richness to a recipe. It does thicken slightly when reduced, but then becomes very unstable and may curdle at any moment. You should therefore avoid cooking it for too long.

Whipped cream

The basis of Chantilly cream (which is sweetened), whipped cream is easily prepared by beating cold cream vigorously and thinning with a little milk if it becomes too thick. If you beat it for too long, however, there is a risk that the cream will turn into butter. Unsweetened, ready-whipped cream is commercially available and is ready to use.

Heavy cream

391

Truffles

Truffles are often associated with foie gras because the contrast of their respective colors is very appealing. The texture of truffles is also very pleasant, emphasizing the extreme smoothness of the liver with great elegance.

Orange

The combination of orange and duck has been well known for a very long time. Duck meat is fairly fatty and needs to be accompanied by a slightly acidic sauce. Orange has the advantage of being acidic and sweet at the same time.

Port

This aromatic, slightly sweetened fortified wine is ideal for cooking game birds such as partridge, pigeon, or pheasant. It is possible to use both white and red port for cooking. It is advisable not to cook it for too long, however, as port quickly loses its flavor if boiled too rapidly.

Bilberries

Game animals are frequently cooked in sauce. To soften their strong flavors, little bowls of bilberry conserve are often served as an accompaniment and the guests help themselves as they wish. The acidic flavor of bilberries makes the sauces served with game taste less strong. This is one of the very few customs from medieval cuisine to have survived to the present day.

Verjuice

This is an acidic juice extracted from unripe grapes. Its fruity flavor adds an original and pleasant flavor to roast or braised poultry.

Sage and tarragon

Fattened chicken (pullet) is a fairly fatty bird that calls for a lighter note to add emphasis; this is why it is often cooked with fresh tarragon leaves. Sage is a fairly strong herb, yet at the same time delicate: it is perfect for bringing out the subtle flavor of roast goose. If whole leaves are placed inside the bird, they flavor the flesh during cooking and make it very digestible.

Goose giblets with turnips

An economical dish

Serves 4
Preparation: 10 minutes
Cooking: 1 hour in a pressure cooker,
2 hours in a pot

Ingredients

7 oz (200 g) collar bacon

1^1/$_2$ oz (50 g) butter

2 onions

1 tbsp oil

2^1/$_4$lb (1 kg) goose giblets

1 tbsp flour

4 cups (1 liter) chicken bouillon
   (made from a cube)

1 bouquet garni

1 tomato

10 turnips

Salt and pepper

1. Cut the bacon into small pieces, blanch quickly in a saucepan of water, drain, wipe, then brown in butter in a skillet. Set aside.

2. Chop the onions and brown in the fat from the bacon.

3. Heat the oil in a pot and brown the giblets. Sprinkle with flour and when the giblets are nice and brown, pour in the hot bouillon.

4. Add the onions, diced bacon, bouquet garni, tomato cut into quarters, peeled, washed, and quartered turnips, and some salt and pepper. Cover as tightly as possible and cook for 1 hour in a pressure cooker or 2 hours in an ordinary stewpot.

5. Place the giblets on a hot serving dish, arrange the turnips around them, and spoon over the reduced juices. If you wish, you can prepare a larger quantity of turnips and cook them in the bouillon, serving them separately. You can also serve this dish with steamed potatoes or plain rice.

Recommended drinks

Beaujolais-Villages
Cabernet d'Anjou
Red Burgundy

Menu suggestions

1. For a family lunch, prepare a salad of green beans with thin slices of gizzard, then a green salad and a cheese platter, followed by a dessert of meringues.

2. For an evening meal, serve pumpkin soup with cheese as an appetizer and baked apples with gooseberry jelly for dessert.

Blanquette of chicken with leeks

A family dish

Serves 4
Preparation: 15 minutes
Cooking: 2 hours

Ingredients

2 or 3 carrots

2 turnips

3 lb 6 oz (1.5 kg) leeks

2 bags mixed chicken pieces

3 glasses chicken bouillon
(made with a cube)

1 glass white wine

1 bouquet garni with plenty
of celery

1 onion stuck with cloves

1 bunch tarragon

9 oz (250 g) mushrooms

1 tbsp butter

1 pot crème fraîche
(1 scant cup/20 cl)

2 eggs

Salt and pepper

1. 1. Peel, clean, and wash the vegetables. Chop the carrots and turnips and cut the white parts and the pale green parts of the leeks into sections around 2$^1/_2$ in (5–6) cm in length.

2. Place the chicken pieces in a pot, pour in the bouillon and wine, and add the vegetables—the turnips, carrots, some of the green part of the leeks, the bouquet garni, and the onion. Cover and cook for 1 hour 30 minutes over a low heat. Adjust seasoning to taste with salt and pepper during the cooking time.

3. When they are cooked, set aside the chicken pieces, skim the fat off the broth, and pass it through a fine sieve. Return the strained broth to the pot with the chicken pieces. Add the chunks of leek and a little chopped tarragon. Cover and simmer for 30 minutes.

4. Peel the mushrooms, cutting off the base of the stalks. Wash, dry, and cut into pieces.

5. At the end of the cooking time, sauté the mushrooms in a little butter, beat the crème fraîche with 2 egg yolks, and gradually thicken the broth with this mixture off the heat. Serve on a very hot platter garnished with a small bunch of tarragon and, if you wish, an accompaniment of white rice.

Recommended wines

Mâcon
Red Sancerre
Saumur-Champigny

Menu suggestions

1. For a Sunday meal, serve plates of smoked salmon with blinis as an appetizer, and for dessert a tarte tatin or Bourdaloue pear tart.

2. For a simpler menu, start with a selection of crudités or avocados with vinaigrette sauce, and for dessert serve sweet pancakes.

Rabbit kebabs with hazelnuts

An easy dish

Serves 4
Preparation: 15 minutes
Marinade: 1 hour
Cooking: 15 minutes

Ingredients

1 saddle of rabbit

White wine

Oil

1 bunch thyme

1 large handful hazelnuts

4 very thin slices of fat collar bacon

Starch

Salt and pepper

1. Cut the saddle of rabbit into 4 pieces. Marinate in a little white wine, a drizzle of olive oil, the bunch of thyme, and some salt and pepper for about 1 hour.

2. Meanwhile, prepare a charcoal fire on your barbecue or in your hearth.

3. Shell the hazelnuts and remove the outer skin. Remove the rabbit pieces from the marinade without draining them too much.

4. Make a cut in each piece of rabbit and insert 1 or 2 hazelnuts in each one.

5. Wrap in the collar bacon and secure each piece with two thin wooden skewers.

6. Heat the grill and cook the little parcels gently for about 15 minutes, turning at least once during the cooking time.

7. Meanwhile, strain the marinade and thicken if necessary with a little cornstarch. Heat slightly.

8. Serve on hot plates garnished with a few whole hazelnuts.

Recommended drinks

Chiroubles
Red Bordeaux
Red Buzet

Menu suggestions

1. For a summer meal "al fresco," serve these kebabs as an appetizer with a mixed salad, followed by tomato and fresh goat's cheese tart and, for dessert, an orange tart.

2. For a main course, serve the kebabs with a potato gratin after an appetizer of marinated bell peppers, with a vanilla cream for dessert.

Deviled quail in a nest of bell peppers

A party dish

Serves 4
Preparation: 15 minutes
Cooking: 40 minutes

Ingredients

7 oz (200 g) rice

4 quail

A little sliced bacon

4 tbsp olive oil

2 red bell peppers

2 green bell peppers

Parsley

Chervil

4 tomatoes

1 onion

1 clove of garlic

Thyme

Bay

Salt and pepper

1. Cook 2–3 tbsp rice in boiling salted water.

2. Trim the quail, cover loosely with the sliced bacon, and sauté in olive oil to brown.

3. Wash the bell peppers, discard the stalks, cut in half, open without separating the halves, and remove the seeds and the fibers.

4. Strip the leaves from the parsley and chervil and chop. Drain the rice, season with pepper, add the chopped herbs, and soften with a little of the oil in which the quail were cooked.

5. Remove the string and bacon from the birds. Stuff each bell pepper with rice and press a quail into each one, close up, wrap in aluminum foil or oiled wax paper, and continue cooking in the oven at 440 °F (225 °C) for 40 minutes.

6. Meanwhile, cook the remaining rice in boiling, salted water and prepare a coulis with the tomatoes, 2 tbsp oil, the onion, chopped garlic, thyme, bay, 1 sprig parsley, and some salt and pepper.

7. To serve, place the rice in the bottom of a hot dish, arrange the half-open bell peppers on the bed of rice, garnish with a little chopped parsley, and hand round the coulis separately in a hot sauceboat.

Recommended wines

Châteauneuf-du-Pape
Gigondas
Hermitage

Menu suggestions

1. Serve a slice of foie gras over lamb's lettuce salad as an appetizer. Serve a seasonal cheese and finish with poached pears and a cassis sorbet.

2. Another idea for a festive menu: as an appetizer, serve seafood in puff pastry, with a pine nut tart for dessert and seasonal cheeses to follow.

399

Recommended drinks

Riesling
Red Coteaux-d'Aix-en-Provence
Saumur-Champigny

Menu suggestions

1. Start the meal simply with a salad of grated carrot and slices of beet, and make a pineapple tart for dessert.

2. You could also serve this duckling recipe as part of a more sophisticated meal, with grapefruit and shrimp as an appetizer and coffee parfait for dessert.

Duckling with baby turnips

A family dish

Serves 4
Preparation: 15 minutes
Cooking: 30 minutes

Ingredients

1 Nantes duckling
1 thin slice bacon
3³/₄ oz (90 g) butter
24 small onions
1 lb 5 oz (600 g) baby turnips
1 tsp superfine sugar
1 level tbsp flour
¹/₂ glass dry white wine

3¹/₂ tbsp (50 cl) chicken bouillon (or cube)
1 clove of garlic
1 small bouquet garni (a few sprigs of parsley, ¹/₂ bay leaf, 1 sprig thyme)
Salt and pepper

1. Scorch any remaining feathers on the skin of the duckling, draw it, and season the cavity with salt and pepper. Truss and cover with the bacon.

2. Peel the onions (blanch in boiling water for 5 minutes unless they are new). Peel the turnips and cut into chunks and then into walnut-sized pieces.

3. Heat 1 ¹/₂ tbsp (30 g) butter in a casserole and brown the duckling in it. Cover as soon as it is golden on all sides and cook for a further 25 minutes. It is cooked to perfection when the juices run clear and are barely pink when the meat is pricked with a fork.

4. Meanwhile, heat 1¹/₄ oz (30 g) butter in a saucepan and cook the onions until they turn golden. Drain and set aside. Add the remaining butter and brown the turnips, previously blanched for 5 minutes in boiling water, and sprinkle them with the sugar as soon as they start to color. Allow to caramelize a little before sprinkling with flour, then add the white wine and just enough bouillon to cover the turnips. Return the onions to the saucepan together with the chopped garlic and the bouquet garni. Simmer, with the lid half on, until the vegetables are very tender.

5. Arrange the duckling in a hot serving dish with the onions and the turnips. Serve the broth in which the vegetables were cooked in a hot sauceboat.

Venison with capers

A party dish

Serves 4
Preparation: 25 minutes
Cooking: 45 minutes

Ingredients

3 slices unsalted bacon fat

12 oz (750 g) venison, preferably
   cut from the shoulder or the neck

1 tbsp flour

1 glass good white wine

2 glasses beef bouillon

Nutmeg

2 bay leaves

1 lemon (or a lime if possible)

2–3 tbsp capers

1. Cut some of the bacon fat into strips, roll them in salt and pepper, and use them to lard the venison using a really sharp needle. Make sure you refrigerate the bacon beforehand so it is very firm.

2. Melt the rest of the bacon fat in a casserole and brown the venison in the fat on all sides. Remove from the casserole and sprinkle the flour into the cooking juices.

3. Wait until the roux browns and then deglaze with the white wine. Return the venison to the casserole, add the hot bouillon, flavor with nutmeg and bay, and season with salt and pepper.

4. Cover with a tight-fitting lid and cook for 45 minutes. The meat should remain very slightly pink in the centrer.

5. Just before serving, add the finishing touches to the sauce, pouring in the lemon juice and adding the capers in vinegar, well drained. Place the venison in a hot dish into which you have previously spooned some sauce.

6. Decorate with alternate spoonfuls of carrot and green bean purée and a little parsley. Serve the rest of the purée separately with the sauce in a hot sauceboat.

Recommended drinks

Gevrey-Chambertin
Pauillac
Chinon

Menu suggestions

1. do justice to this celebration dish, serve small portions of salmon with tartare sauce or medallions of foie gras as an appetizer, with chocolate profiteroles or a pineapple surprise for dessert.

2. Alternatively, serve trout in aspic to begin the meal, with meringue, cream, and praline or rum baba to finish.

Rabbit crépinettes with spinach and green rosemary

Serves 4
Preparation: 30 minutes, a few hours in advance
Cooking time: 2 hours 20 minutes

Ingredients

5^1/$_2$ oz (150 g) unsalted pork
  (neck or shoulder)

9 oz (250 g) unsalted bacon fat

1 saddle of rabbit

Four-spice mixture

A few sprigs green rosemary

9 oz (250 g) spinach

Enough caul to wrap 8 balls
  the size of an egg

Parsley

1 tbsp butter

A few salad leaves

2 tomatoes

Salt and milled pepper

1. Carefully remove all the connective tissue from the pork and cut into small pieces, together with the bacon fat. Put everything through a mincer. Remove the connective tissue from the rabbit and cut into small dice. Season with plenty of salt and pepper, four-spice mixture, and finely snipped rosemary; mix well and form into a ball. Leave to rest in a cool place for several hours.

2. Sort, wash, and remove the stalks from the spinach. Poach in plenty of boiling, salted water for 5 minutes.

3. Rinse the caul in lukewarm water, drain, and cut into 8 pieces. Mix the minced meat, the diced rabbit, and the well-drained spinach together and then place a mound of the mixture on each piece of caul. Add a little coarsely chopped parsley and seal with the caul, making the sausages into the shape of a flattened egg.

4. Heat the butter in a skillet and cook the crépinettes in it for about 15 minutes. Turn them two-thirds of the way through the cooking time. They should be golden on both sides. Place 1 small bunch of rosemary on each one.

5. Serve very hot, with a simple accompaniment of a few salad leaves and some diced tomato flesh. Garnish with a sprig of rosemary.

N.B. You can also cook these crépinettes in the oven at 450 °F (230 °C).

Turkey escalopes piccata style

An easy dish

Serves 4
Preparation: 5 minutes
Resting: 2 hours
Cooking: 20 minutes

Ingredients

4 turkey escalopes
  or slices of fillet

Paprika

Olive oil

4 tomatoes

1–2 red bell peppers

2 onions

White wine

1 small pot crème fraîche

2 eggs

Nutmeg

2 tbsp butter

A little flour

Salt and pepper

1. Spread out the meat and season with paprika, salt, and pepper. Drizzle with olive oil and leave to stand for 2 hours.

2. Meanwhile, skin and seed the tomatoes, then cut open the bell peppers and remove the fibers and seeds inside. Cut the flesh firstly into strips, then into small pieces. Peel the onions and cut into thin rings.

3. Heat some oil in a large skillet or saucepan. Add the onions and cook them gently, stirring with a wooden spatula to stop them browning. Then add the bell peppers and mix with the onions, cooking until they are tender. Finally, add the tomatoes and continue cooking until their juice starts to run. Season with salt and pepper. Deglaze with a little white wine and continue cooking until the tomatoes begin to disintegrate. Mix in a few tablespoons of the crème fraîche, 2 egg yolks, and some grated nutmeg, and thicken the sauce.

4. Wipe the escalopes with paper towels. Sauté them in butter so both sides are well sealed. Place the escalopes on top of the sauce, cover, and finish cooking for a few minutes. Serve with spaghetti.

N.B. The term "piccata" in Italian cookery means a thin slice of veal that is sautéed rapidly in a skillet. Thin turkey escalopes can be treated in the same way. The reference to Italy is of course a good reason to choose spaghetti as an accompaniment, but you can also serve these escalopes with French fries or sautéed eggplants.

Recommended drinks

Beaujolais
Chianti
Rioja

Menu suggestions

1. Start this menu simply with a melon and a few slices of raw ham. For dessert, serve a seasonal fruit salad.

2. You could also serve slices of fish or vegetable terrine as an appetizer and finish the meal with a red fruit sorbet.

Chicken fricassee with olives

A regional dish

Serves 6
Preparation and first cooking: 1 hour
Second cooking: 20 minutes

Ingredients

1 chicken	Thyme
Thin slices of bacon	Bay
4^1/$_2$ oz (125 g) unsalted collar bacon	Olive oil
Parsley	Flour
Spring onion or chives	1 glass bouillon
1 small can anchovy fillets	2 glasses dry white wine
1 small jar capers in vinegar	1 orange
9 oz (250 g) green olives, pitted	Salt and pepper

1. Prepare the chicken; pluck it, singe any remaining feathers, draw, and wipe. Reserve the liver, the heart, and the gizzard. Truss, cover with thin slices of bacon, season with salt and pepper, and roast for about 1 hour until it is well cooked.

2. Remove the gall from the liver and the seeds from the gizzard. Dice the bacon finely. Wash and drain the parsley and the spring onion and chop with 4 anchovy fillets, 1 tbsp capers, two-thirds of the olives, the liver, the heart, and the gizzard.

3. Fry the diced bacon in a saucepan over low heat. When the lardoons have yielded plenty of fat, add the chopped ingredients with 1 sprig thyme and 1 bay leaf; thin with a drizzle of olive oil and allow to color a little. Sprinkle with 1 large pinch flour, pour in the bouillon and the wine, and simmer until the liquid reduces slightly.

4. As soon as the chicken is cooked, remove the string, cut through the joints, and flatten with the blade of a meat cleaver. Place in the saucepan with the remaining olives; simmer in the sauce on one side for 10 minutes, then turn over and simmer for another 10 minutes on the other side.

5. Cut up at the end of the second cooking time and place on a serving platter. Squeeze the orange and add the juice to the cooking juices from the chicken, then reheat without boiling and spoon over the chicken.

Recommended drinks

Coteaux-du-Languedoc rosé
Red Minervois
Red Bandol

Menu suggestions

1. For a meal to conjure up the hot Provence sunshine, serve a salad of tomatoes with basil and mozzarella as an appetizer and orange salad with crisp, honey-flavored cookies for dessert.

2. An alternative, equally sun-drenched suggestion is to serve octopus salad with olive oil as an appetizer and a rice cake with preserved fruits for dessert.

Huntsman's rabbit

A family dish

Serves 4–6
Preparation: 20 minutes
Cooking: 1 hour

Ingredients

1 rabbit, cut into pieces

1 tbsp butter

A few tbsp oil

4½oz (125 g) cultivated
  mushrooms

2–3 shallots

1 tbsp flour

1 small glass brandy

1 large glass dry white wine

A little bouillon

1 bouquet garni

1 clove of garlic

A little tomato paste

1 slice smoked collar bacon,
  around ½ in (1 cm) thick

A few small white onions

Chervil

Tarragon

Parsley

Salt and pepper

1. Wipe the pieces of rabbit meat and season with salt and pepper. Place them in a saucepan with a mixture of half butter and half oil and brown them. Set aside and keep hot.

2. Chop the mushrooms and peel and chop the shallots. Sauté the mushrooms in a little butter and oil in a saucepan until they just start to brown, then add the shallots and sauté for a few more minutes.

3. Sprinkle with flour and cook gently for 2 or 3 minutes, then add the brandy, flaming it first, the white wine, bouquet garni, and peeled and crushed clove of garlic, then pour in enough bouillon to cover the rabbit.

4. Color with a little tomato paste. Return to the boil and stir a few times, mixing all the ingredients well.

5. Return the rabbit pieces to the saucepan. Bring to the boil before covering and cooking in the oven at 425 °F (220 °C) for 30 minutes. Add the diced bacon and the onions and cook for a further 30 minutes.

6. Pour into a deep dish, sprinkle herbs over the top, and serve with small croûtons deep-fried in oil.

Recommended drinks

Chinon
Touraine rosé
Beaujolais-Villages

Menu suggestions

1. Serve a rustic terrine with a green salad as an appetizer before this great classic of French family cooking, and for dessert a chocolate mousse.

2. Another idea, which is equally traditional, is to serve a curly endive salad with bacon lardoons as an appetizer and a lemon meringue tart to finish.

Recommended drinks

Côte Rouennaise rouge
Mâcon rouge
Sancerre rouge

Menu suggestions

1. To keep the regional tone, stuff small puff pastries with Roquefort cheese and serve with dandelion salad as an appetizer, with blueberry tart for dessert.

2. For an even more "local" flavor, serve Cantal cheese tart as an appetizer and Murat pastry horns with fresh cream for dessert.

Stuffed rabbit Auvergne style

A regional dish

Serves 4–6
Preparation: 20 minutes
Cooking: 2 hours

Ingredients

1 rabbit
7 oz (200 g) sausage meat
Oil for frying
1 fairly thick ham steak
$5\frac{1}{2}$ oz (150 g) boiling bacon
2 onions
2 shallots
Bay
Thyme

Pepper
Cognac or Armagnac
1 egg
3 cups (75 cl) good red wine
Large bouquet garni (thyme, bay, parsley, celery)
6 tomatoes
Parsley

1. Dress and trim the rabbit and chop its liver after removing the gall bladder. Mix the chopped liver with the sausage meat and sauté in a well-oiled skillet.

2. Trim the ham and chop it coarsely with the boiling bacon. Peel the onions and shallots and fry them gently in the skillet with a little oil.

3. Finely chop a bay leaf. Add to the mixture with a little thyme and season generously with pepper. Little, if any, salt is needed because of the bacon. Add a little brandy or Armagnac and bind with the egg, beaten as for an omelet. Stuff the rabbit with the mixture and sew it up.

4. Heat a little oil in a saucepan and brown the rabbit on both sides. Add the wine and bouquet garni. Bring to the boil before transferring to an earthenware pot. Cook in the oven at 350 °F (180 °C) for 2 hours, covered with waxed paper.

5. About thirty minutes before serving, peel the tomatoes after plunging them into boiling water and arrange them around the rabbit in the dish. Split them crosswise to allow them to poach.

6. Skim the fat from the gravy and pour into a warm sauceboat. Serve the stew in a warm casserole, sprinkling the tomatoes with a little chopped parsley.

Mustard rabbit with fennel seeds

An economical dish

Serves 4
Preparation: 15 minutes
Cooking: 1 hour

Ingredients

1 rabbit
1 pot prepared mustard
3–4 tomatoes
3–4 tbsp olive oil
1 tbsp fennel seeds
1 bunch fresh basil
Salt and pepper

1. Cut the rabbit into pieces (set the liver and kidneys aside—they are not used in this recipe—and keep them in the refrigerator for use in a pâté or terrine). Rub each piece of meat thoroughly with mustard.

2. Slice the tomatoes thinly into rings. Lightly oil a soufflé dish. Lay the tomato slices in the bottom of the dish and put the pieces of rabbit on top of them.

3. Scatter the fennel seeds and the finely chopped basil over the whole dish and add salt and pepper to taste. Sprinkle generously with olive oil.

4. Cook in the oven at 435 °F (225 °C) for about an hour. Cover with waxed paper to ensure even cooking.

5. Serve very hot with potatoes boiled with a dash of olive oil.

Tip: avoid mild mustards and those flavored with herbs or spices.

Recommended drinks

Sancerre rouge
Fitou
Arbois rouge

Menu suggestions

1. If you serve this dish for lunch, offer endive salad with Roquefort as an appetizer and prune flan for dessert.

2. If this rabbit dish is the main dinner course, start with a tomato soup and serve flambéed bananas for dessert.

Chicken papillottes with honey and ginger

An exotic dish

Serves 4
Preparation: 15 minutes
Marinade: 15 minutes
Cooking: 30 minutes

Ingredients

1 glass dry white Vermouth

1 lemon

1 tbsp liquid honey

1 piece fresh ginger

4 tbsp four-spice

8 tbsp soy sauce

4 chicken breasts

Oil

1 bunch chives

1. Prepare a marinade combining the vermouth, lemon juice, honey, 4 tsp freshly grated ginger, the four-spice, and soy sauce in a bowl.

2. Slice the chicken breasts into regular, diagonal strips. Put them in the bowl, stir gently into the mixture, and leave to marinate for 15 minutes.

3. Oil 4 sheets of waxed paper about 12 in (30 cm) square. Lift their edges and divide the marinated chicken between them.

4. Sprinkle with chopped chives. Carefully close the papillottes, stitching the edges to seal them completely. Place on a baking sheet.

5. Cook the papillottes in the oven at 410 °F (210 °C) for about 30 minutes.

6. These papillottes can be served hot or cold according to your taste or the season, with or without lemon and fresh chives.

Recommended drinks

Chiroubles
Hermitage
Châteauneuf-du-Pape

Menu suggestions

1. A light summer menu, serve these chicken papillottes cold as an appetizer, accompanied by a tabbouleh with plenty of parsley and lemon. Follow with broiled fish and frosted oranges for dessert.

2. You could start with an orange and mild onion salad, follow with the papillottes and couscous, and finish with a honey ice cream.

Pigeons with wild mushrooms

A regional dish

Serves 4
Preparation: 20 minutes
Cooking: 30 minutes

Ingredients

2 pigeons

1 onion

1³/₄ oz (50 g) butter

Oil

1 glass white wine

1 small bunch parsley

1 slice stale bread (crumbed)
soaked in milk

Grated parmesan

1 egg

5 ¹/₂ tbsp (75 g) sausage meat

Salt and pepper

Sage

1 glass bouillon (made from
a cube)

9 oz (250 g) wild mushrooms

1. Gut and clean each pigeon, setting aside the livers and hearts.

2. Finely chop half the onion and gently fry in a skillet with 1 tbsp (30 g) butter and 1 tsp oil. Add the liver and heart meat. Cook for 10 minutes, gradually adding the glass of wine.

3. Remove from the heat and add the chopped parsley. Drain the milk from the breadcrumbs. Combine the breadcrumbs with a little parmesan, the whole egg, sausage meat, salt, and pepper. Mix carefully.

4. Stuff the pigeons with the mixture and sew up the openings.

5. Sauté the rest of the onion and a few sage leaves in a skillet in a mixture of hot oil and butter. Add the stuffed pigeons and brown them over high heat.

6. Add the glass of bouillon and let it evaporate before adding the sliced mushrooms. Season to taste, cover, and allow to simmer for 30 minutes over low heat.

7. This dish is eaten really hot with Sarlat-style fried potatoes with mushrooms or sautéed green beans.

Recommended drinks

Pauillac
Bergerac rouge
Cahors

Menu suggestions

1. A regional meal with a hint of southwestern France, offer potted goose or duck with green salad as an appetizer and chocolate and nut tartlets for dessert.

2. If you prefer a lighter option, serve a magret (fillet of duck breast) salad and strawberry tart for dessert.

Christmas guinea fowl with chestnuts

A family dish

Serves 4
Preparation: 15 minutes
Cooking: 1 hour 40 minutes

Ingredients

1 lb 2 oz (500 g) chestnuts

Bouillon

1 stalk celery

Sugar

1 guinea fowl

2 - 3 tbsp (20 cl) crème fraîche*

1 bouquet garni (thyme, chives, tarragon, chervil, according to taste and season)

1 tbsp butter

4 large apples

Salt and pepper

*Recipe: combine 1 cup whipping cream and 2 tbsp buttermilk in a glass container. Stir well. Cover and leave at room temperature until very thick—between 8 and 24 hours.

1. 1. Pierce the skin of each chestnut without touching the underlying membrane. This will enable the steam to penetrate beneath the skin and make the chestnuts easier to peel. Put the chestnuts in a saucepan and cover them with cold water. Bring to the boil and simmer for one minute. Remove from the heat and peel the chestnuts one by one, while they are still very hot. If you remove the chestnuts from their cooking water they will dry out and be much more difficult to peel.

2. Put the peeled chestnuts in a saucepan just big enough to contain them, cover with bouillon, and flavor with celery and 1 tsp of sugar. Bring to the boil, then continue to boil gently until the chestnuts become soft to the touch and are ready to crush. This will take about an hour. Remove them from the bouillon and keep warm until they are needed.

3. Dress and trim the guinea fowl, sprinkling the inside with 2–3 tbsp crème fraîche, salt, pepper, and 2 tsps chopped herbs. Truss and rub with a little butter, salt, and pepper. Roast in the oven at 435 °F (225 °C) for 40 minutes. Baste with a little bouillon.

4. Meanwhile, peel, core, and seed the apples, cut them into quarters, and purée in a blender.

5. Spread the purée on a warm serving platter, arrange the guinea fowl on top, and decorate with the reserved chestnuts, some whole and some chopped. Sprinkle with a little of the cooking juices.

Recommended drinks

Saint-Joseph rouge
Sancerre rouge
Meursault

Menu suggestions

1. As an appetizer for this family party meal, serve boudin (white sausage) with sautéed apples and remain traditional by offering chocolate Yule log for dessert.

2. For a lighter meal, opt for a seafood appetizer (langoustine and oyster salad) with an iced Yule log for dessert.

Guinea fowl Madagascar style

An exotic dish

Serves 4–6
Preparation: 15 minutes
Cooking: 50 minutes

Ingredients

3 lb 5 oz (1.5 kg) russet apples

4 tbsp (175 g) butter

4 vanilla beans

Salt and pepper

2 guinea fowl

10 sugar lumps

1 lemon

2 oranges

$1/3$ cup + $1^1/2$ tbsps (10 cl) rum

1. Peel, core, and seed 4 apples. Cut into rough quarters. Heat 4 tbsp (60 g) butter in a skillet, add the quartered apples, and sauté for about 5 minutes. Add 2 vanilla beans split in two lengthwise and cut into pieces. Season with salt and pepper.

2. Stuff the guinea fowl with the mixture. Truss, season, and put in a buttered baking pan. Roast in the oven at 510 °F (265 °C) for 20 minutes, basting occasionally with the cooking juices.

3. Remove the guinea fowl from the pan and put them in a saucepan with the cooking juices.

4. Meanwhile, make a caramel sauce. Put the sugar lumps in a small pan over low heat with 2 tsp of water, add the lemon and orange juice when the caramel turns lightly golden, then add warm water and flavor with the remaining vanilla beans split in half. This sauce should simmer gently for about 10 minutes.

5. Put the lid on the pan and continue cooking gently for 20 minutes.

6. Peel, core, and seed the remaining apples, cut into quarters, sauté vigorously in butter, arrange them in a warm casserole, and flambé in the rum. Put the guinea fowl on top of the apples, sprinkle with the cooking juices, and serve immediately, garnished with the remaining vanilla beans.

Recommended drinks

Tavel
Côtes-du-Roussillon rosé
Saint-Émilion

Menu suggestions

1. Start this exotic meal with cod accras (salt-cod fritters). Serve the guinea fowl with Creole rice and offer fruit salad in rum for dessert.

2. More traditionally, you could serve a smoked fish starter before this colorful dish and follow it with a coconut ice cream for dessert.

411

Chicken with fresh figs and cinnamon

A light dish

Serves 4
Preparation and first cooking: 1 hour
Second cooking: 10 minutes

Ingredients

1 clove garlic

2 medium-sized onions

2 tbsp butter

1 chicken

1 cinnamon stick

1 level tsp powdered ginger

Salt and cayenne pepper

A little light bouillon

1 lb 11 oz (750 g) figs—not too ripe

1 small bunch parsley

1. Peel the garlic and onions, chop quite finely, and sauté gently in a saucepan with the butter. Meanwhile, cut the chicken into pieces and add to the pan.

2. Add the cinnamon, ginger, a large pinch of salt, and a dash of cayenne pepper.

3. During cooking, moisten occasionally with a little of the hot bouillon. This first stage takes about 45 minutes over low heat with the pan covered.

4. Wipe the figs, cut them in two, and place them on top of everything after sprinkling the contents of the saucepan with chopped parsley.

5. Replace the lid and allow to cook for a further 10 minutes over low heat.

6. Adjust seasoning to taste and serve on a very hot platter or in a covered vegetable bowl.

7. As an accompaniment, serve sautéed carrots sprinkled with cumin, rings of steamed celeriac, or puréed broccoli.

Recommended drinks

Tavel
Bandol rosé
Côtes-du-Ventoux

Menu suggestions

1. This menu simply with a cucumber and yogurt salad and end with fromage frais and cinnamon. (NB: substitute fromage frais with 1 cup cream cheese whipped with 1/4 cup lemon juice.)

2. Another equally light suggestion: a grapefruit and crabmeat salad appetizer and pears poached in lemon juice for dessert.

Chicken pie

An English dish

Serves 6
Preparation and first cooking: 45 minutes
Second cooking: 45 minutes

Ingredients

1 chicken

1³/₄ oz (50 g) butter

2 tbsp oil

Salt and pepper

3 carrots

2 turnips

1 medium-sized onion

1 bouquet garni (thyme, parsley, bay)

3 tomatoes

18 pitted black olives

1 pack frozen pie crust, thawed

1 egg

1. Cut the chicken into pieces. Heat the butter and oil in a skillet. Add the chicken pieces and sauté. Season to taste once they have browned.

2. Scrape and slice the carrots and turnips and peel and slice the onion. When all the chicken pieces have browned, remove them from the skillet and put the vegetables in their place.

3. Reduce the heat and sweat the vegetables until they are lightly browned, then add 2 cups (50 cl) water. Season to taste and add the bouquet garni. Simmer for 45 minutes.

4. Arrange the chicken pieces in a soufflé dish, preferably made of glass. Add the wiped and quartered tomatoes, olives, and vegetables in their juices.

5. Roll out the piecrust on a floured surface. Moisten the edge of the dish with milk or water so that the crust sticks to it. Cover with the crust, making a chimney in the middle.

6. Brush the crust with egg yolk diluted with a dash of water and cook in the oven at 430 °F (220 °C) for 45 minutes.

7. This English specialty can be served with a simple green salad or buttered peas.

Recommended drinks

Beer
Pauillac
Mâcon-Villages blanc

Menu suggestions

1. This dish can be the focal point of a quick menu: serve a tomato salad as an appetizer and finish with cheese and crackers.

2. More traditionally, serve this pie as an appetizer, followed by poached salmon with cucumber salad, then gooseberry tart to finish.

413

Roast turkey with apples

A Family meal

Serves 4
Preparation: 15 minutes
Cooking: 1 hour

Ingredients

Salt

Peppercorns

1 roasting turkey,
  about 2¼ lb (1 kg) in weight

4½ oz (125 g) butter

Cider vinegar

4½ lb (2 kg) apples

2 lemons

1 cinnamon stick

¼ cup (50 g) sugar

1 tsp ground cinnamon

½ tsp powdered ginger

Cayenne pepper

1 bunch cress

1. Mix together some salt and crushed peppercorns, spread on a board, and roll the bird in the mixture, pressing down so that it is incrusted with seasoning. Transfer to a large pan and brown the bird in 3½ oz (97 g) butter, moistening with a dash of vinegar. Cover and cook for 60 minutes over medium heat, adding a dash of vinegar every 15 minutes.

2. Meanwhile, peel, core, and seed half the apples. Roll them in the lemon juice to prevent browning, paying particular attention to the empty core, then brown in butter in a skillet, turning them carefully. Moisten with a little water and vinegar. Add seasoning to taste and the cinnamon stick, cover, and simmer for 30 minutes over low heat. Remove from the heat and slice prior to serving.

3. Peel, core, seed, and chop the remaining apples. Pour the lemon juice into a saucepan and add the apple pieces. Cook with 1 oz (28 g) butter, the sugar, half a glass of vinegar, cinnamon, powdered ginger, salt, and cayenne pepper.

4. Serve the bird on warm plates, sliced and smothered in the reduced cooking juices and chopped apple mixture. Garnish with the sliced apples and decorate with cress. Serve with a sauceboat of gravy and cress salad.

Recommended drinks

Riesling
Beaujolais
Chénas

Menu suggestions

1. 1. Serve this roast for dinner, with an appetizer of sorrel soup. Finish with a selection of cheeses and seasonal fruits.

2. If serving this dish for lunch, start with a warm goat's cheese salad and offer a sharp apple tart for dessert.

Pigeon breasts with stuffed cabbage

A party dish

Serves 4
Preparation: 25 minutes
Cooking: 30 minutes

Ingredients

2 pigeons

Salt and pepper

3–4 tbsp oil

2 medium-sized onions

2 tbsp butter

2 thin slices Bayonne or other mild,
  smoked ham

2 tbsps flour

Red wine

Bouillon

1 cabbage

1. Pluck, gut, and singe the pigeons. Reserve the livers and hearts. Season the inside of the birds and brown them in oil in a skillet. Transfer to a baking sheet and roast in a hot oven for 7–8 minutes. Do not cook them for too long, as they should still be quite pink, almost red. Remove them and set aside.

2. Peel and coarsely chop the onions and sauté them in a little butter. Trim the rind from the ham, then chop and add it to the onions. Sprinkle the mixture with a little flour and allow to "stiffen" before moistening with red wine and a little bouillon.

3. Add the pigeon meat (apart from the breasts), livers, and hearts to the pan. Season to taste and simmer for 15 minutes. Strain, reserving the cooking juices.

4. Meanwhile, prepare the cabbage, removing its outer leaves, and blanch for 10 minutes in boiling, salted water. Strain, place on a board, separate the leaves, remove the heart, and replace with the strained chopped meat and onion mixture. Reshape the cabbage, tying it up with string or wrapping it in muslin, and put it in a saucepan or flameproof pot with 1 tbsp of butter and a little bouillon. Simmer for about 30 minutes.

5. Just before serving, gently reheat the pigeon breasts in the oven. In the meantime, strain the meat and onion cooking juices through a cloth and reheat. Pour this liquor into a warm serving dish, then cut the breasts into very fine slices and arrange in the dish, together with the well-drained cabbage.

Recommended drinks

Graves blanc
Meursault
Graves rouge

Menu suggestions

1. Make a splendid start to this party meal with a scallop salad, and serve an iced chocolate cake for dessert.

2. Another equally refined suggestion: gratin of stuffed crab as an appetizer and a Paris-Brest or coffee mocha cake for dessert.

General suggestions

You often have leftovers when cooking poultry. Of course you can eat them cold with mustard, but you can also use them to prepare delicious recipes. Here are a few suggestions. These recipes are suitable for all kinds of poultry.

Little turkey turnovers

These turnovers are easy to make and children love them. Cut the turkey meat into cubes or strips. Sauté them with 2 sliced onions, then add 4 tbsp crème fraîche, salt, pepper, and chopped chives. When the cream has reduced considerably, allow the mixture to cool. Roll out 7 oz (200 g) of piecrust pastry on a floured surface and cut it into circles with a diameter of 3–4 in (8–10 cm). Put some turkey filling into the middle of each circle, fold the pastry over on itself, and seal the edges. Cook the turnovers in the oven at 350 °F (180 °C) for about 20 minutes and serve at once, accompanied by French fries and a green or chopped white cabbage salad, seasoned with mayonnaise or a mustard and herb dressing.

Mexican chicken salad

Chicken salad

Serves 4
1 lettuce
1 oak leaf lettuce
1 tbsp mustard
1 tbsp sherry vinegar
4 tbsp olive oil
Salt and pepper
2 tomatoes
7 oz (200 g) extra-fine green beans
4 strips cooked chicken

1. Sort and wash the lettuces. Drain well.

2. Prepare a vinaigrette with the mustard, vinegar, olive oil, salt, and pepper.

3. Peel and seed the tomatoes and cut them into cubes. Top and tail the beans and cook them.

4. Season the salad with salt, pepper, and vinaigrette. Slice the chicken meat with a knife and arrange it in a salad bowl with the beans, tomatoes, and the remaining vinaigrette. Place this mixture on the salad and serve quite cool.

Chicken risotto

Chicken risotto

Serves 4
1/2 cold chicken
1 onion
3/4 cup (150 g) white rice
Oil
Thyme
Salt and pepper

1. Remove the chicken meat from the bones and cut into cubes.

2. Skin and chop the onion. Cook the rice in plenty of salted water and strain.

3. Sweat the onion in a little oil in a skillet over medium heat. When it starts to brown, add the cubes of chicken. Add salt, pepper, and a little thyme and cook for a further 5 minutes.

4. Add the warm, cooked rice. Sauté together. Check the seasoning and serve very hot.

416

Crépinettes

Crépinettes

Serves 4
1 lb 5 oz (600 g) cooked poultry
10$\frac{1}{2}$ oz (300 g) fresh pork
$\frac{1}{2}$ bunch parsley
2 cloves garlic
Grated nutmeg
Thyme
2$\frac{1}{2}$ tsp (12 g) salt
2 eggs
1 tbsp fine breadcrumbs
Pepper
Oil
Sausage casing

1. Grind the poultry and pork together. Place in a mixing bowl and add the parsley, garlic, nutmeg, thyme, salt, eggs, breadcrumbs, and pepper. Combine thoroughly.

2. Heat some oil in a skillet and cook a little of the mixture to check the seasoning. Adjust to taste. Cut squares of sausage casing and spread them on the work surface. Put 2–3 tbsp stuffing in the middle of each. Flatten slightly and wrap up the casing. Cook in the skillet for 10–12 minutes.

Raised chicken pie

Raised chicken pie

Serves 4
1 lb 2 oz (500 g) cooked chicken
3 shallots
14 oz (400 g) cooked salsify
1 lb 2 oz (500 g) Béchamel sauce
3 tbsp light cream
Grated nutmeg
Salt and pepper
Piecrust pastry
1 egg

1. Bone the chicken and sweat it in a skillet for 5 minutes over low heat, add the chopped shallots, and cook for 5 minutes. Add the salsify, Béchamel sauce, cream, nutmeg, salt, and pepper. Boil the mixture for 3 minutes, adjust the seasoning, and let it cool.

2. Divide the pastry into two equal portions and roll out on a floured surface. Place one layer in a buttered pie dish, allowing it to overhang the edges. Pour in the chicken mixture, then cover with a second. Seal the edges, make a chimney in the middle, and gild the surface with 1 beaten egg. Cook in the oven at 350 °F (180 °C) for about 45 minutes.

Aiguillettes of turkey with salad

Turkey salad

Serves 4
2 carrots
1 zucchini
2 stalks celery
2 tomatoes
1 egg yolk
2 tbsp mustard
1 scant cup (20 cl) oil
Turkey fillets
$\frac{1}{2}$ bunch chives
Salt and pepper

1. Cut the carrots, zucchini, and celery into small cubes and cook in salted water. Drain and reserve.

2. Seed the tomatoes and cube them.

3. Prepare a mayonnaise with the egg yolk, mustard, and oil.

4. Place the cubed turkey fillets, vegetables, and chopped chives in a salad bowl. Mix well, season with salt and pepper, and serve well chilled.

Fish and crustaceans

Trout au bleu

1 This is a very unusual recipe, as the surface color of the cooked fish is blueish-purple. To prepare this ancient recipe successfully it is essential to use freshly caught fish (less than 6 hours old).

2 Be certain not to wipe the skin, as it is the mucus that colors during cooking, when it comes into contact with the vinegar and water. Carefully gut the trout via the stomach or gills.

3 Prepare a court-bouillon with vinegar. This recipe can also be prepared with a large trout, in which case you should cook it in a fish-kettle big enough to hold the whole fish.

4 Plunge the fish into the boiling court-bouillon and cook for about 10 minutes. Drain the fish and arrange on a serving platter with slices of lemon.

Poaching

Poaching is a gentle cooking method that respects the quality and delicacy of fish and crustaceans. It can be done in salted water, court-bouillon, or milk, depending on the species.

Ray wings

These are also cooked by poaching. Prepare a court-bouillon with a generous quantity of white wine. Cut the ray wing into 2 or 3 pieces if it is too big. Allow 10 1/2 oz (300 g) of raw fish per person. Plunge the fish into the boiling liquid, lower the heat, and simmer for 15–20 minutes, depending on the thickness of the pieces. Drain. Mix the juice of 1 1/2 lemons, 3 1/2 oz (100 g) butter, 3 1/2 tbsps (50 g) capers, salt, and pepper in a saucepan. Bring this mixture to the boil and pour over the fish. Ray is also delicious served cold. Leave to cool between two plates, then place in the refrigerator for a night. Flake the fish and serve it on a salad flavored with balsamic vinegar.

Fish Blaff

This succulent specialty is prepared in Mauritius, the West Indies, and Reunion Island. To serve 4, mix together large chunks of gray mullet, bonito, hogfish, and brill. Place 5 cloves of chopped garlic, 3 shredded onions, 1 bouquet garni, 2 leek whites cut into strips, 3 cloves, salt, pepper, 20 coriander seeds, 2 pimentos, 1 fennel, 1 1/4 cups (30 cl) white wine, and 3 cups (75 cl) water in a casserole. Bring to the boil and simmer for 30 minutes. Taste the broth, adjust the seasoning if necessary, then add the fish and poach for about 30 minutes. Add the juice of 1 lemon and a 1/2 bunch of fresh, chopped cilantro. Serve the Blaff in the casserole, accompanied by a dish of Creole rice.

Haddock

for 4

1 This is one of the rare smoked fish that is cooked. Heat 4 cups (1 liter) milk and 4 cups (1 liter) water in a casserole with salt and pepper.

2 When the liquid is boiling, plunge in 4 good fillets of haddock. Cover and cook over low heat for 20 minutes.

3 Drain the fillets, arrange them on a serving platter, and coat with melted butter. You could garnish this dish with poached eggs.

Oysters

Oysters are delicious both raw and cooked. Allow 4 oysters per person and choose medium-sized specials for preference.

Oysters with herbs

Open the shells, allowing the flesh to drop into a small salad bowl. Wash the shells and keep them warm. Place the extracted oysters, their water and $\frac{1}{3}$ cup + $1\frac{1}{2}$ tbsps (10 cl) of Sauternes in a small saucepan. Boil over low heat for 45 seconds. Drain the cooked oysters and put them back into their shells. Reduce the cooking liquid by half. Add 2 tbsp crème fraîche. Allow to reduce for 1 minute. Then add $3\frac{1}{2}$ oz (100 g) fresh butter, beating all the time, salt, pepper, and 1 tbsp chopped chives. Coat the oysters with the sauce, return to the shells, and serve at once as a small appetizer. You can use a purée of very fine leeks steamed in butter instead of the chives.

Tip

The water in which fish is cooked should never be allowed to boil, because if it reaches 210 °F (100 °C) it damages the proteins and gives delicate flesh a dry, floury consistency. If you have a thermometer, the ideal cooking temperature is in the range 176–189 °F (80–87 °C).

Steamed John Dory

for 4

1 Simple preparation perfectly preserves the flavor of this remarkable fish. Gut a 3 lb (1.35 kg) John Dory or ask the fish seller to do it for you.

2 Cut off the fins. Season the inside with salt and pepper and coat the fish lightly with olive oil. Put ½ bunch fresh basil in a pan of water and bring to the boil.

3 Put the fish in a steamer or metal colander suspended above the water and cover. Steam for about 20 minutes.

4 Check that the fish is cooked by prodding the flesh with a small needle: it should be white and come away easily from the bones.

5 Prepare a vinaigrette composed of the juice of 1 lemon, salt, pepper, 2 pinches of sugar, 8 chopped basil leaves, and ⅓ cup + 1½ tbsps (10 cl) olive oil.

6 Serve the John Dory whole with the vinaigrette, garnished with basil leaves.

General points

Together with poaching, steaming is one of the best methods for preserving the delicate flavor of fish and crustaceans. It does not "launder" the fish, thus also preserving its nutritional content. Steaming can be used for whole fillets, crabs, and lobsters. The general procedure is quite simple: a quantity of liquid is set to boil and the fish to be cooked is suspended over the pan in a steamer or metal colander. Pure water or the most complex infusions can be used. To give steamed fish a subtle flavor, add thyme, basil,

Tip

Steamed fish is often accused of being bland. To avoid this, never forget to season it before cooking. You can also make small notches in the fish fillets and insert garlic cloves, fresh basil leaves, various spices, or even a slice of smoked bacon: the result is as pleasant as it is unexpected.

tarragon, oregano, or any other herb of your choice to the water. Drawn up by the steam, the flavorful substances in herbs attach themselves easily to proteins during the cooking process. The height at which the fish is hung above the boiling liquid is very important: too low and the heat will dry out the fish; too high and cooking will be difficult and uneven. About 8 in (20 cm) is a good average. The fish to cook using this principle are swordfish, red mullet, turbot fillets, sea-perch, pike, pike-perch, and John Dory. Steamed fish can be served hot or cold.

Steamed monkfish

Tip

While the fish is cooking, a delicious juice runs out and is lost in the boiling liquid below. Chinese cooks have noticed this phenomenon and so steam their fish over a deep bowl, capturing the precious juice to enjoy later with a spoon.

Steaming with seaweed

This method of cooking is very suitable for sea-perch or swordfish. To serve 4–5, scrape, gut, and rinse a 3-lb (1.35-kg) sea-perch. Season the fish. Place a 2 in (5 cm) layer of seaweed in a large pan, into which the sea-perch can comfortably fit. Put in the fish, cover it completely with seaweed, and pour in 1 1/2 cups (35 cl) water. Bring to the boil, cover with a tight-fitting lid, and cook over medium heat for 20 minutes. Add a little water during cooking if necessary. When the sea-perch is cooked, bring the pan to the table and open it in front of the diners to enable them to enjoy the delectable scent of this recipe. Remove the fish, cut into strips, and serve with melted butter, pepper, and coarse salt.

Steamed salmon

423

Mushroom sauce

for 5–6

1 This is used in the same way as Sauce Normande. Prepare it with small, very white mushrooms. Peel, rinse, and chop 10¹/₂ oz (300 g) white mushrooms.

2 Peel and slice 2 shallots. Heat 1 tbsp butter in a saucepan and add the vegetables, stirring from time to time for about 4 minutes. Add ¹/₃ cup + 1¹/₂ tbsp (10 cl) white wine.

3 Boil for 3 minutes. Pour in 1 ²/₃ cups (40 cl) fish stock and simmer over low heat for 20 minutes. Slowly cook ¹/₄ cup (30 g) flour and 1³/₄ oz (50 g) butter in another saucepan for 2 minutes.

4 Pour this roux into the hot bouillon, beating vigorously. Allow to boil for a minute and then add 4 tbsp crème fraîche, salt, and pepper. Adjust the seasoning to taste. Serve hot.

Anchovy butter

This flavorsome condiment is the perfect accompaniment to broiled fish: swordfish, red mullet, gray mullet, or sea-perch. Put 5¹/₂ oz (150 g) well-drained anchovies preserved in oil, 10¹/₂ oz (300 g) cold butter, 10 drops Tabasco®, the juice of ¹/₂ lemon, and pepper in a mixing bowl. Combine thoroughly to obtain a fine, brown paste. Transfer immediately to a small hors d'oeuvre dish and store in the refrigerator until required.

Horseradish sauce

This sauce has a strong and highly individual taste. Serve it with steamed fish. Bring 1 ²/₃ cups (40 cl) fish bouillon to the boil and cook over low heat for 15 minutes. Skim with a small ladle. Gently heat ¹/₄ cup (30 g) flour and 1³/₄ oz (50 g) butter in another saucepan for 2 minutes. Then pour this roux into the hot bouillon, beating vigorously. Boil for 1 minute, then add 4 tbsp crème fraîche and salt and pepper to taste. Add 2 tbsp horseradish and 1 tsp strong, prepared mustard. Finally, mix together 1 egg yolk and 2 tbsp cream and add to the simmering sauce. Remove from heat. Add a few drops of lemon juice and serve hot.

Nantua sauce

This is served with quenelles de brochet, but its succulent flavor can accompany many other fish dishes. Prepare a Béchamel sauce with 3 cups (80 cl) milk, ¹/₂ cup (60 g) flour, and 2³/₄ oz (80 g) butter. Set aside. Plunge 1 lb 5 oz (600 g) shrimp into 12 cups (3 liters) boiling water with 3 oz (90 g) salt, leave for 20 seconds, and drain immediately. Tail them and roughly crush the shells. Sauté in oil with 1 onion, 1 leek white, and 1 celery stalk. Cook for 15 minutes, then pour the mixture into the Béchamel sauce with 1 tbsp tomato concentrate and cook over very low heat for 1 hour. Filter the sauce, adjust the

Sauces

Sauce Normande

for 5 or 6

1 This sauce is a perfect accompaniment to poached or steamed fish such as cod or fillets of sole. Gently fry 2 chopped shallots in a little butter. Then add 1²/₃ cups (40 cl) fish bouillon and cook over low heat for 15 minutes.

2 Skim using a small ladle. Gently heat ¹/₄ cup (30 g) flour and 3 ¹/₂ tbsp (50 g) butter in another saucepan for 2 minutes. Pour this roux into the hot bouillon, beating vigorously. Boil for 1 minute.

3 Add 3 tbsp crème fraîche and seasoning to taste. Finish by mixing together 1 egg yolk and 2 tbsp cream and adding to the simmering sauce. Remove from heat. Add a few drops of lemon juice and serve hot.

Mussels with Montpellier butter

seasoning, and add the cooked and peeled shrimp tails and a dash of brandy. Coat the cooked quenelles and put them in the oven for 30 minutes.

Montpellier butter

You can serve this succulent preparation with cold poached cod. Blanch some spinach, chives, parsley, and chervil to obtain 1 tbsp of each ingredient. Chop 2 shallots and drain 2 tbsp capers. Combine all these ingredients in a blender with 7 oz (200 g) butter, 1 anchovy fillet, the yolk of one hard-cooked egg, and ¹/₄ clove garlic. Add salt and pepper and reduce the whole to a very fine paste.

425

Caldeirada
for 4

1 Soak 2 fish heads in cold water for 10 minutes. Cut 3 gurnards and 10½ oz (300 g) monkfish tails into thick slices, then wipe and flour them. Scrape and wash 2¼ lb (1 kg) mussels. Rinse 6 large prawns.

2 Slice 1 leek white, 1 carrot, and 2 small onions. Crush 2 garlic cloves. Heat 2 tbsp oil in a skillet, add the vegetables, and sauté for 2 minutes. Add the fish heads cut in two.

3 Brown the mixture for 10 minutes while stirring, pour in 3 cups (75 cl) dry white wine, and reduce for 5 minutes. Add 2 quartered tomatoes, 1 sliced pimento, 1 bouquet garni, 1 small bell pepper, and 6 cups (1.5 liters) cold water.

4 Cover and simmer for 30 minutes. Meanwhile, heat 4 tbsp oil in a large skillet. Brown the slices of fish and then add the mussels and prawns.

5 Pour the broth you have made over the fish, mussels, and prawns. Cover and simmer for 8 minutes. Adjust the seasoning to taste. Fry croutons in a little oil.

6 Serve the caldeirada hot, garnished with croutons and sprinkled with chopped parsley. To obtain a bouillon, remove the gills from the fish heads before soaking. Additional fish bones will strengthen the flavor.

General points

There are a number of recipes for fish soups, typical of all Atlantic and Mediterranean countries. They owe their flavor naturally to the variety and freshness of the species included in them. You can always cook a large amount of fish soup, as its preparation is somewhat lengthy, and it is easy to freeze in a clean, plastic bottle (provided it is well puréed). Soups of marine or freshwater fish are often served with small garlic croutons and sometimes a little grated cheese.

Frog soup

for 6–8

1 This recipe is very popular in Alsace. For 6–8 servings, slice 4 shallots and cook them in 2³/₄ oz (80 g) butter for 2 minutes.

2 Add 1 lb 9 oz (700 g) seasoned frogs' legs. Cook for 8 minutes on each side, then drain.

3 Add 2 cups (50 cl) dry white wine and 2 cups (50 cl) fish bouillon. Cook over low heat for 10 minutes.

4 Add 1 scant cup (20 cl) crème fraîche. Season, then set aside. Wash the leaves of 1 bunch cress, cook over low heat for 5 minutes, and set aside. Skin the legs.

5 Mix together 1 egg yolk and 2 tbsp cream. Add to the simmering soup and remove from heat. To finish, add the skinned legs and the cress. Serve very hot.

Tip

One of the secrets of a successful fish soup concerns the quantity and temperature of the water you add: its level must be just higher than the vegetables and fish and it must always be cold, to enable the aromas to disseminate easily.

Fish chowder (Chaudrée)

This soup is cooked in the Vendée and Saintonge regions of France. The fish in it are cut into pieces, but not mixed. For 6–8 servings, cook 3 chopped shallots, 4 chopped garlic cloves, 3 tbsp chopped tarragon, and 3 tbsp chopped parsley in 2³/₄ oz (80 g) butter. Season and pour in 2¹/₂ cups (60 cl) white wine and 2¹/₂ cups (60 cl) fish bouillon. Bring to the boil, add a generous bouquet garni, cover, and cook for 1 hour. Spread the fish on a work surface: 12¹/₂ oz (350 g) cubed conger-eel, 12¹/₂ oz (350 g) céteaux, 12¹/₂ oz (350 g) brill, 5¹/₂ oz (150 g) small prawns, and 9 oz (250 g) small cuttlefish or squid. Season with salt and pepper, then brown them in oil over high heat, species by species. Finish by plunging them into the broth. Cook over low heat for 25 minutes. Adjust the seasoning to taste, add 1³/₄ oz (50 g) butter and some chopped parsley, and serve hot in soup bowls with garlic croutons warmed in the oven.

Stuffed mussels

Mussel salad

Stuffed mussels

This dish is prepared with Spanish mussels that are quite fat and fleshy. To serve 4, open some large Spanish mussels with a small knife. Arrange them in a baking pan. Put 9 oz (250 g) butter, 8 garlic cloves, 1 bunch parsley, 1 tbsp breadcrumbs, 2 chopped shallots, juice of $1/2$ a lemon, salt, and pepper in a blender. Reduce to a very fine paste. Dab 1 tsp on each of the mussels and place in the oven at 400 °F (200 °C) for 15 minutes. Serve at once as a small, hot appetizer.

Mussels

Mussels are always quick and easy to cook. Here are some suggestions.

Moules marinières

This great classic, prepared in the twinkling of an eye, is always popular. Scrape, rinse, and trim $4^{1}/_{2}$ lb (2 kg) farmed mussels. Chop 4 shallots and cook over high heat with $3^{1}/_{2}$ oz (100 g) butter, 2 tbsp chopped parsley, thyme, and 1 bay leaf. Dilute with $1^{1}/_{4}$ cups (30 cl) white wine and the juice of 1 lemon. Add the clean, drained mussels. Cover and continue to cook until they have opened, shaking the pan frequently. Pour the mussels into the serving dish, removing the thyme and bay leaf and discarding any that have remained closed. Boil the cooking juice, add 1 tbsp butter, and pour over the mussels. Serve with fried potatoes.

Mussel salad

This dish is prepared with open mussels, scraped and chilled. To serve 4, cook $4^{1}/_{2}$ lb (2 kg) farmed mussels to expose the flesh. Discard any that remain closed. Wash 2 oak-leaf lettuces. Season the salad with a lemon vinaigrette and olive oil and arrange in a dome on a serving platter. Place the scraped and drained mussels in a bowl. Season with salt, pepper, 2 tbsp crème fraîche, 5 pinches curry powder, 4 drops Tabasco®, juice of 1 lemon, and $1/2$ bunch of chopped chives. Arrange on top of the salad and serve chilled.

Gratin of scallops

for 4

1 Prepare a Béchamel sauce with 1³/₄ oz (50 g) butter, scant ¹/₂ cup (50 g) flour, and 1³/₄ cups (450 ml) milk. Remove from heat and bind with 1 egg yolk and 1 scant cup (20 cl) crème fraîche.

2 Poach 8 scallops with their coral in a court-bouillon made from 1 generous cup (25 cl) water and 1 scant cup (20 cl) white wine, 1 chopped onion, salt, and pepper.

3 Add the cooked scallops to 9 oz (250 g) cooked white mushrooms and 2 cups (50 cl) Béchamel sauce. Mix well and adjust seasoning to taste.

4 Pour into 4 empty shells. Sprinkle with grated cheese and cook in the oven at 400 °F (200 °C) for 20 minutes.

General points

The scallop is one of the best seafood products on the market. It can be prepared in numerous ways. The essential thing is not to overcook it, as it quickly becomes rubbery.

Steamed scallops

These are succulent and easy to digest. You can present them in their shells. To serve 4, remove 20 scallops and their coral from their shells. Cut in two and place in a mixing bowl. Add the juice of 1 lime, 3¹/₂ tbsp (5 cl) olive oil, 1 bunch chopped chives, ¹/₂ tsp fresh, chopped ginger, salt, and pepper. Combine well and divide between the empty shells. Place in a steamer or metal colander and suspend over a pan of boiling water for 20–25 minutes. Serve immediately.

Scallops Provençal style

These are prepared in a skillet. To serve 4, remove 20 scallops and their coral from their shells. Season with salt and pepper, then flour them. Shake

to remove any surplus. Heat some olive oil in a skillet and brown the scallops and coral on all sides for 5 minutes. Then add 5 finely chopped garlic cloves. Cook for 1 minute. Add 1 bunch chopped parsley, 2 peeled, cubed tomatoes, salt, and pepper, and boil for 30 seconds. Add a dash of olive oil and serve immediately.

Stuffed crab

for 4

1 These are prepared from crabmeat and are served in the shell. Cook 4 small crabs in a court-bouillon and remove them from their shells.

2 Rinse and wipe the shells and set aside. Cook 3 chopped shallots in a skillet. Add a thick slice of smoked bacon cut into strips and 3 chopped garlic cloves.

3 Simmer for 5 minutes. Then add a little bread, without the crusts, soaked in milk and drained, together with the crabmeat. Add salt, pepper, and the juice of 1 lemon. Mix well together.

4 Divide the mixture between the shells. Sprinkle with breadcrumbs. Dab some butter on top and bake in the oven at 340 °F (170 °C) for 15 minutes.

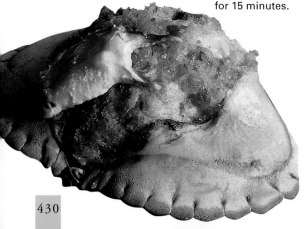
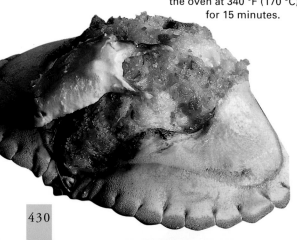

General points

There are countless recipes for cooking crustaceans: every coastal region has its specialties. Here are some delicious examples.

Shrimp sautéed in cider

You can use fresh or frozen shrimp. To serve 4, thoroughly wipe 1³/₄ lb (800 g) shrimp, season well, and sauté over high heat for 5 minutes. Keep warm. Moisten the skillet with ¹/₃ cup (8 cl) Calvados. Add 1 generous cup (25 cl) sweet cider and boil for 2 minutes, then stir in 5 tbsp crème fraîche. Simmer for 2 minutes. Add salt, pepper, and the shrimp and cook for 4 minutes. Adjust seasoning to taste and serve very hot.

Fried scampi

These are delicious, fried prawn tails. To serve 4, remove 24 prawns from their shells and season with salt and pepper. Prepare a mayonnaise and add capers, cooked egg yolk, chives, tarragon, and chervil. Mix well and season to taste. Dip the prawns in beaten egg, then in flour, and lastly in very fine white breadcrumbs. Plunge one by one into 8 cups (2 liters) peanut oil heated to 345 °F (175 °C). Cook, stirring gently, for about 3 minutes. Drain on paper towels. Serve very hot with the sauce.

Broiled crayfish

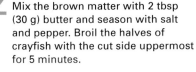

1 Split a fresh crayfish in half, remove the gut, and save the brown matter in the head. Place the halves of crayfish under the broiler.

2 Mix the brown matter with 2 tbsp (30 g) butter and season with salt and pepper. Broil the halves of crayfish with the cut side uppermost for 5 minutes.

3 Turn them over and continue broiling for 15 minutes, then turn again, spread with the mixture made as above, and complete the cooking.

Arrange the lobster on a serving platter and coat with the sauce.

Lobster Armoricaine

Use fresh lobster with the pincers and tail removed. Cut into pieces. Divide the shell in two, reserving the coral. Brown the seasoned lobster in a skillet for 5 minutes, then remove from heat. Sweat 5 sliced shallots and 4 sliced tomatoes in a pan for 5 minutes. Add 2¹/₂ tbsp (4 cl) of whiskey. Mix, then add 1 scant cup (20 cl) dry white wine and 1 scant cup (20 cl) fish bouillon. Season to taste with salt and pepper. Cook with the lobster for 25 minutes. Meanwhile, mix the coral with scant ¹/₄ cup (20 g) flour, 3 tbsp crème fraîche, 1³/₄ oz (50 g) softened butter, and 2¹/₂ tbsp (4 cl) brandy. Pass the mixture through a fine mesh strainer and add to the broth, beating all the time. Do not allow it to boil.

Crayfish salad

Cook a crayfish, let it cool, and shell it. Prepare some salad leaves (e.g., iceberg, red leaf, Boston, Romaine) then cube and blanch 1 carrot, 1 zucchini, and ¹/₂ fennel. Cube 1 peeled tomato. Arrange the salad in the bottom of the plates, season the vegetables, and sprinkle over. Cut the crayfish tail into slices and season with vinaigrette, together with the claw meat. Arrange the medallions and pieces of crayfish on top of the vegetables and sprinkle with vinaigrette.

Lobster Armoricaine

Matelote of eel

for 6

1 This fish stew can be prepared using carp, pike, eel, shad, or barbel. One type can be used alone, or in combination with others according to what is available. As a rule, the fish should be large and cut into strips 1 in (3 cm) wide. This stew is prepared in the Loire, Rhône, and Aquitaine regions of France with red wine, but sometimes also with white wine.

2 It always has sauce, smoked bacon, small onions, and mushrooms. Its name is probably derived from "sailors' stew," a flavorful fish dish very popular with seafarers. To serve 6, cut 3 lb 5 oz (1.5 kg) eel into thick slices. Boil 4 cups (1 liter) red wine in a pan for 20 minutes, then add 1¼ cups (30 cl) fish bouillon, 1 bouquet garni, salt, and pepper.

3 Simmer gently for 20 minutes. Cook scant ½ cup (50 g) flour and 2¾ oz (80 g) butter in a small pan for 1 minute. Beat the resulting roux into the wine mixture. Sauté 5½ oz (150 g) previously blanched smoked bacon, 3½ oz (100 g) small white mushrooms, and 5½ oz (150 g) small onions in a skillet for 5 minutes.

4 Place the eel, mushroom mixture, and red-wine sauce in a flameproof casserole. Bring to the boil, skim, and simmer over low heat for about 30 minutes. Add 2 tsp persillade—a paste of chopped garlic and parsley. Serve very hot with oven-baked croutons and fresh pasta. When cooking is complete, you could add 3 anchovy fillets crushed in 1 oz (30 g) butter to the sauce.

Freshwater fish

Green eels

butter in a flameproof casserole, add 2 sliced onions, and sauté for 8 minutes. Then add 7 oz (200 g) spinach, sorrel, 2 tbsp chopped parsley, tarragon, chives, and sage. Cook for a few moments. Then pour in 1 scant cup (20 cl) white wine. Cook for 5 minutes. Brown the slices of eel in a skillet and add to the casserole. Cover and cook over low heat for 35 minutes. Beat together the juice of 1 lemon and 2 egg yolks. Add this mixture to the green sauce to thicken it. Remove from heat. Adjust seasoning to taste. Brown 6 slices of bread in the oven. Serve the eel slices on the toast and coat them in the sauce. This recipe can also be served cold: put the dish in the refrigerator overnight and serve well chilled, without toast.

Freshwater fish

There is a particular way of cooking these fish, which have given rise to local specialties. They are often prepared in a ragout or stew with a red-wine sauce.

Pochouse

This is a recipe for freshwater fish: in Burgundy it used to be cooked with river burbot, a succulent fish rarely found nowadays. In the Bresse region of France, pochouse is prepared with tench, carp, and catfish. It is cooked in the same way as Matelote, but using white wine, onions, and carrots, and is served in the same way as green eels, on slices of toast that can also be rubbed with garlic cloves.

Eel

This fish has been eaten and enjoyed since Roman times. Eel is cooked in many ways: as a matelote, broiled, or pan-fried.

Green eels

This recipe has been used since the Middle Ages and has latterly become a Flemish specialty. To serve 6, skin and slice 3 lb 5 oz (1.5 kg) river eel and season with salt and pepper. Melt a generous dab of

Tip

The cooking times for all these recipes must be precise. In fact, the flesh of freshwater fish is very fragile and breaks up completely after a certain cooking time. What is more, in the specific case of these recipes, boiling for too long will impair their flavor.

General points

Oven baking has the advantage of being simple while making many fish taste succulent. All species of reasonable size can be oven baked: carp, pike, shad, pike-perch, perch, John Dory, hog-fish, cod, pollack, monkfish, and, of course, porgy or sea bream. For an attractive color, fish should be baked in the oven at a fairly high temperature (400–430 °F/ 200–220 °C). It can, however, also be baked at a lower temperature if you want to achieve a braised appearance. To prevent the flesh drying out, vegetables (tomatoes, onions, shallots) and white wine are often added at the start of the recipe. In all cases, cooking times must be as precise as possible. Fish can also be cooked "au gratin." You should then use skinned and boned fillets (fillets of sole, cod, pike, whiting), poach and coat them with a gratin sauce, then put them in the oven to color.

Cooking with salt

This unusual cooking method enables fish to retain its full flavor. It has the additional advantage of being very clean, not soiling the oven, and not giving off the smoke and odors that usually result from baking fish. Oil and season a nice sea bream weighing 3–4 lb (1.35–1.8 kg). Season then stuff with thyme, 3 cloves fresh garlic, and some parsley. Place a thick layer of coarse sea salt in a deep oval baking pan, put the fish on top with 2 bay leaves, and cover with another layer of sea salt. Bake at 430 °F (220 °C) for about

Perch in a salt crust

Sardinian Tuna

1 hour. Remove from the oven, allow to cool for a few minutes, break open the salty crust, remove the fish, and serve. For this recipe, use only the most freshly caught fish. Perch and all kinds of bream can be prepared by this method.

Monkfish

Monkfish has firm, white flesh that is very suitable for baking. It is sometimes called "gigot de mer" (leg of sea lamb). To serve 6–8, skin a nice monkfish tail weighing $4\frac{1}{2}$ lb (2 kg). Put it on the work surface, score the flesh with a sharp knife, and insert 5 or 6 blanched garlic cloves. Lay 2 or 3 slices of fairly fine-cut bacon along the sides and tie the fish up tightly with string. Put it in a baking pan. Season with salt and pepper, scatter over a few sprigs of thyme, and baste with olive oil. Slice 2 onions and scatter them over and around the monkfish. Cook in the oven at 430 °F (220 °C) for 40 minutes. When

Monkfish with herbs and garlic

Monkfish "en gigot de mer" with garlic

Oven-baked monkfish

the fish is cooked, remove the string, serve whole, and carve at the dinner table.

Baked sea bream

This succulent dish should be cooked simply with good quality ingredients. Choose a good sea bream weighing about 3 lb (1.35 kg). Gut, scale, and rinse it. Lightly oil a baking pan and arrange a thin layer of well ripened tomatoes and sliced onions in the bottom. Put the sea bream on top, season with salt and pepper, and sprinkle with thyme and rosemary. Then pour on $1/3$ cup + $1^1/_2$ tbsps (10 cl) dry white wine and bake in the oven at 430 °F (220 °C) for 35 minutes. Serve very hot with the cooking vegetables and juices. Instead of bream you can use perch, hogfish, John Dory, cod, Pollack, or tuna steak.

Baked sea bream with lemon

435

Papillottes of sardines stuffed with herbs

One-minute papillotte of salmon

Papillotte of monkfish

Papillottes

Hake "en papillotte"

A papillotte is an envelope, edible or otherwise, containing either whole or filleted fish. It protects the fish during cooking, concentrating its flavors. Non-edible papillottes are prepared using waxed paper or aluminum foil. The sheets are cut into circles or rectangles then folded around the fish. This method has the advantage of forming a reasonably hermetic seal. Without the papillotte, the fish would have no marked flavor, so it should be well seasoned and spiced and served with a flavorsome garnish: a julienne of vegetables, steamed mushrooms, or a mixture of herbs and shallots. You could also add sliced green bell peppers, small shrimps, spices, and lemon. The choice of accompaniments depends entirely on your taste and preference: anything is possible. They should, however, be cooked beforehand as the cooking time for papillottes is quite short (10–25 minutes). They can either be steamed or baked in the oven. You can prepare these papillottes with whole trout, salmon or whiting fillets, cod or tuna steaks, or mackerel. For an original recipe, butter rectangles of aluminum foil and season with salt and pepper. Put a nice 7-oz (200-g) cod steak on each sheet. Then sprinkle the fish with 2^3/$_4$ oz (80 g) of sautéed, chilled wild mushrooms and some chives. Close the papillottes and bake them in the oven at 400 °F (200 °C) for about 25 minutes. Serve immediately, allowing your guests to open the envelope

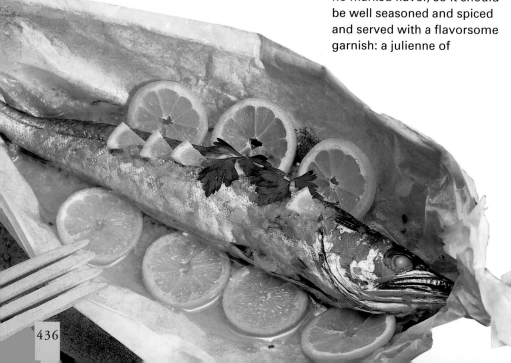

Fish "en papillotte" and "en escabèche"

themselves. Papillottes can also be made with blanched cabbage, spinach, sorrel, or lettuce leaves. These envelopes are very fragile, and should be steamed rather than baked.

Escabèche

Originally, escabèche was a strongly flavored and spicy marinade designed to preserve food, particularly small fish, for varying lengths of time. The principle was then extended to other foods such as poultry and game. Preparation in an escabèche is delicious and ideal for small fish such as mackerel, sardines, sprats, anchovies, and red mullet. Gut and scale 2¼ lb (1 kg) fish and wipe thoroughly. Season and fry in a skillet for 10 minutes, until well browned. Arrange in a deep bowl. Peel and slice 2 onions, then seed 2 pimentos and cut them into small cubes. Heat some olive oil in a pan and put in the vegetables. Simmer for 5 minutes, then add 1¼ cups (30 cl) fish bouillon, ⅔ cup (15 cl) dry white wine, 5 tbsp wine vinegar, and 10 peppercorns. Season and bring to the boil for a moment, then pour the sauce over the fish. Leave to cool, then place in the refrigerator and allow to marinate for 24 hours. Serve cold. Escabèche can be kept in the refrigerator for 1 week.

Anchovy appetizer "en escabèche"

Tip

Fish prepared in an escabèche is preserved, not only because of the cold, but also the acids in white wine and vinegar. Old escabèche recipes contained a lot of vinegar because the main aim was preservation. The recipe has been progressively modified to become what it is today—a dish in itself and not simply a pickling method.

Sardines "en escabèche"

Sole meunière

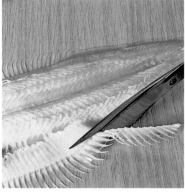

1 This can be one of the most remarkable culinary delights. Choose a fine sole weighing about 10¹/₂ oz (300 g) and skin it on both sides. Keep the roe, if any, because it is delicious.

2 Put some flour on a plate and coat both sides of the sole. Tap to remove any surplus flour, then season with salt and pepper.

3 Melt and then lightly beat 3¹/₂ oz (100 g) chilled butter in a skillet suitable to the size of the fish. Put in the sole and cook on both sides over low heat for about 8 minutes. It should be cooked slowly, the fish changing color without browning.

4 Baste regularly with the molten butter, using a spoon. The finished color should be blond. Pour over 1–2 tbsp butter and serve at once, garnished with lemon halves.

Salmon steaks

These are also cooked in a skillet. They can be dipped in flour, but this is not essential. Season the steaks with salt and pepper and place in a non-stick skillet over medium heat, without oil (the flesh of the salmon contains enough fat already). Cook for about 5 minutes to allow the flesh to color, then turn over and continue to fry on other side. The total cooking time depends on the thickness of the slices and personal taste. Salmon steaks can be served either well done or very "pink:" if pink, they gain in softness and flavor. As a rule it is best to choose thicker cuts, as thin ones dry out quickly and are often disappointing.

Pan-frying

Pan-frying is a practical, quick, and tasty way of preparing small fish dishes or thin fish fillets. It is used to cook trout, sole, red mullet, and steaks of various species such as salmon, cod, hake, pike or pike-perch. The "meunière" method is a specific way of cooking in a skillet and primarily used with sole. It is typified by a low temperature and a fairly long cooking time, using butter. The fish is usually dipped in flour first.

Tip

As a rule, when cooking fish (or other products) in butter, avoid very high temperatures: at over 275 °F (140 °C) butter breaks down into its different components, some of which are highly indigestible. At the most, cooked butter should be slightly blond in color; never brown, let alone black.

Deep-frying

Deep-frying is often used to cook fish and is good for very small fish (river fry, gudgeon, smelt), small fillets of fish with firm flesh such as sole, or larger pieces such as whiting.

Whiting in a rage

This is delicious if the fish is really fresh. Gut the fish via the gills, scale and rinse it, and wipe very thoroughly. Put the tail of the fish in its mouth and tie it to maintain its position. Dip it in milk and then flour to coat it completely. Then fry for 7–8 minutes in deep fat at a temperature of 340 °F (170 °C). Turn the fish several times using a slotted spoon so that it colors evenly.

Deep-fried smelt

Small fry

Use a sufficient quantity of very clean, very hot oil. For 2¼ lb (1 kg) smelt, allow 12 cups (3 liters) peanut oil. Gut and carefully wipe the fish and then flour in batches of about 1 lb 2 oz (500 g). Shake in a sieve to remove any surplus flour. Using a wire basket, plunge the first batch of floured smelt into

the oil, preheated to 350 °F (180 °C), shaking gently to prevent them sticking to one another. Fry for about 4 minutes, then drain on paper towels. Cook the rest of the smelt, season both batches with salt, and serve immediately.

Fish and chips

This specialty is very popular in England. It consists of battered and deep-fried fish fillets (usually plaice, haddock, cod, or rock salmon) accompanied by French fries sprinkled with vinegar. To prepare fish and chips, choose fillets of plaice, for example. Dip them successively in flour, beaten egg, and fine breadcrumbs. Then deep-fry in oil heated to 340 °F (170 °C). Serve very hot and crunchy with French fries.

Tip
A deep-fat fryer must always be very clean, as any impurities it contains after a few uses will caramelize, impairing the taste and preventing the oil from becoming hot enough. Strain the cooled oil through a fine mesh sieve after each use.

Deep-fried whiting in a rage

General points

Almost all fish can be broiled. With this cooking method they color rapidly and take on a delicious flavor. They should not cook for too long, though, as fish dries out rapidly. Oily fish are particularly suitable for this cooking method: tuna, sardines, herrings, or mackerel are broiled whole depending on their size, but can also be broiled in slices of varying thickness. Fillets can also be cooked this way, whole or cut into cubes and then spit-roasted on skewers. You can cook them just as they are, but if they are marinated overnight with spices and flavorings they will taste even more succulent. An outdoor grill heated with wood or charcoal can be used; alternatively, a metal plate, the Spanish plancha, heated simply by gas or electricity.

Monkfish kebabs

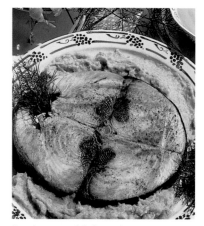

Fresh tuna with fennel

Broiling has the disadvantage of releasing a lot of rather unpleasant smoke. It is therefore advisable to broil only in the open air, particularly in the case of oily fish.

Broiled tuna steak

This family dish is easy to prepare. Cut a nice, red tuna steak 1 1/2–2 in (4–5 cm) thick. Put it on a plate, season with salt and pepper, and sprinkle with thyme, bay, 1 chopped onion, 4 chopped garlic cloves, some oregano, and a pinch of Cayenne pepper. Add a dash of olive oil and refrigerate overnight. At mealtime, put the tuna steak on the grill, about 8 in (20 cm) above the hot coals. Cook each side for 10 to 15 minutes and serve at once with rice and a green salad. You can accompany this fish with a vinaigrette of olive oil, lemon juice, salt, and pepper.

Mussel kebabs with bacon

Kebabs

Prepare 3 1b 5 oz (1.5 kg) firm-fleshed fish such as monkfish cut into medium-sized cubes. Add 1/3 cup (8 cl) olive oil, 1/2 bunch chopped chives, 1 chopped garlic clove, the juice of 1 lemon, salt, and pepper. Mix well and allow to marinate for a few hours or overnight in the refrigerator. Skewer the cubes of fish, alternating them with pieces of red pimento and onion. Broil the kebabs for about 12 minutes, turning them from time to time.

Small mackerel

These fish are very easy to broil. Allow 8 pieces per person. Scale, gut, wipe, and season the fish and arrange them on a very clean grill. Be sure to leave at least 1/2 in (1 cm) between each fish to facilitate cooking. Broil them on each side over high heat for 6–8 minutes. Serve very hot.

Hake kebabs

chopped shallots in 2 tbsp (25 g) butter, pour in 1 ²/₃ cups (40 cl) white wine, reduce, add 1 scant cup (20 cl) crème fraîche and 1 bunch chopped dill.

"One-sided" salmon

This is a Scandinavian recipe. Salmon steaks, cut from the fillet, are cooked in a skillet over low heat on one side only: the bottom is well cooked, the middle pink, and the top almost raw. This delicious recipe enables the delicacy of the wild salmon caught in the cold waters of Scandinavia to be really appreciated. One-sided salmon is served with a dill sauce, prepared either in the skillet or on the grill. Cut steaks 1¹/₂–2 in (4–5 cm) wide from the salmon, with the skin, but without bones. Season with salt and pepper and place them on the grill, not too close to the heat: cooking must be progressive, from bottom to top, as one-sided salmon is not turned. Allow the fish to cook according to taste and the size of the steaks. With prolonged grilling, the fish will be cooked through. Serve with a sauce made as follows: sweat 2

Tip

Never let fish cooking over a fire or bed of coals become too highly colored. The black marks that can appear in fact contain various aromatic compounds that have been shown to be harmful. Avoid the flames and check the color constantly during cooking.

Broiled sardines in grape leaves

Frogs' legs

Frogs' legs

There are many different and delicious ways of preparing frogs' legs. As a rule, use only very fresh frogs' legs and do not overcook them, because the flesh breaks up very rapidly.

Frogs' legs broiled or fried

These are very easy to prepare. You can cook them as they are, simply adding salt and pepper, or marinate them for a few hours with herbs and spices. They can be cooked in a skillet or on the grill. Remember to remove them from the refrigerator a few minutes before cooking and baste them with a little olive oil.

Curried frogs' legs

Frogs' leg fritters

This is a pleasure for all gourmets. Allow 6–8 legs per person. Prepare a batter with 1 generous cup (125 g) flour, 1 egg, salt, and 1 scant cup (20 cl) cold milk. Season the legs, dip in the batter, and then fry them in deep fat at 340 °F (170 °C). Allow 5–6 minutes' cooking time, stirring now and then with a slotted spoon. Drain the fried legs on paper towels and serve piping hot with a strong tartar sauce.

Frogs' leg kebabs

Frogs' legs au gratin

Prepare a white sauce using fish bouillon. Sweat 2 shallots in butter, then add 20 legs cut in two and seasoned. Cook them slowly for 1 minute, baste with 3^1/$_2$ tbsps (5 cl) white vermouth, then add 1 ^{2}/$_3$ cups (40 cl) white sauce and 9 oz (250 g) cooked white mushrooms. Mix, and adjust seasoning to taste. Add 2 egg yolks. Place the legs in a baking pan and coat them with sauce. Sprinkle grated cheese on top and cook in the oven at 400 °F (200 °C) for 20 minutes.

Frogs' leg fritters

Snails in butter

Snails

Snails are cooked in various ways and are served with or without their shells. For preference, choose Burgundy snails in their shells and petits-gris in a sauce or "en cassolette."

Snails in butter

For 4 dozen, prepare a butter garnish with 2 bunches parsley, 20 fresh garlic cloves, 2 chopped shallots, 9 oz (250 g) chilled butter, salt, pepper, and 1 tbsp breadcrumbs. Replace the cooked snails in their shells and dab them with garlic butter using a small spoon. Arrange in a baking pan and cook in the oven at 300 °F (150 °C) for about 25 minutes. The butter must not be allowed to boil.

Snails Moroccan style

Snails suçarelle style

Cook about 60 live, clean petits-gris in a strongly flavored court bouillon for 30 minutes. Brown 2 onions, 2 shallots, and 2 garlic cloves, chopped, in a casserole. Add 9 oz (250 g) sausage meat and 1 lb 2 oz (500 g) puréed tomatoes. Cook for 5 minutes and then add the pre-cooked snails. Season to taste, cover, and cook for 30 minutes.

Snails with bacon

To serve 4, allow 14 oz (400 g) Burgundy snails. Blanch 4½ oz (120 g) smoked bacon. Heat 1 tbsp butter in a pan and sweat 2 sliced shallots for 2 minutes, then add the bacon and snails. Add salt, pepper, and 3½ tbsps (4 cl) Armagnac. Cook for 1 minute, then pour on 1 scant cup (20 cl) meat bouillon. Cook slowly for 10 minutes. Adjust seasoning to taste.

Snails "en cassolette"

Allow 3½ oz (100 g) snails per person for an appetizer and 6 oz (170 g) for a main dish. Cut the in two. Wash and slice some white mush-rooms and a few chanterelles. Cook them with sliced shallots for 10 minutes. Moisten with port and then add the snails and some crème fraîche. Cook for about 20 minutes, adjust seasoning to taste, and serve in individual ramekins.

Tip

Mankind has eaten snails since the dawn of time. Quantities of broken snail shells have been found at numerous sites. During the Middle Ages, snails were considered a refined dish that was hugely enjoyed … as a dessert.

Snails suçarelle style

Crayfish

General points

Crayfish are some of the best crustaceans on the market, but are not always available: order them from your fish seller in advance.

Crayfish in garlic butter

Crayfish are often prepared this way in the Périgord region of France. Their invention is attributed to G. Galorce, the Master Chef of the famous

adding plenty of salt and pepper. Then add the garlic butter, cover, and cook for 15 minutes, stirring frequently. Serve just as it is.

Crayfish Bordeaux style

These are cooked in white wine. Sauté the seasoned crayfish over high heat with a mixture of carrots, onions, and leeks cut into small cubes. When the crayfish are good and red, add enough dry white wine

Crayfish broth

Quick to prepare, this can be eaten hot or cold. Slowly cook a mixture of carrots, celery, onions, and leeks in butter. Then add some dry white wine and fish bouillon and simmer gently for 15 minutes. Plunge the crayfish into this mixture with the juice of 1 lemon and some peppercorns. Cook for 10 minutes and then allow to rest for a further 10. To serve the dish cold, leave in the refrigerator overnight.

Crayfish au gratin

This recipe takes quite a while to prepare, but is delicious. To serve 4, braise $4^1/_2$ lb (2 kg) crayfish with 1 lb 2 oz (500 g) vegetable bouillon, then add $1^1/_4$ cups (30 cl) white wine. When cooked, remove the tails and arrange the crayfish in a buttered gratin dish. Crush the shells and prepare a fairly thick Nantua sauce with $3^1/_2$ tbsp (5 cl) brandy, $^1/_3$ cup + $1^1/_2$ tbsps (10 cl) white wine, 3 cups (70 cl) Béchamel sauce, and 2 tomatoes. Coat the crayfish tails with the sauce, dab with butter, and brown rapidly under the broiler. Serve immediately.

Crayfish broth

Duke of Abrillac. This delicious recipe is quite simple to prepare. For 80 crayfish, prepare a garlic butter garnish with 7 oz (200 g) butter, $3^1/_2$ oz (100 g) garlic cloves, and 2 bunches parsley. Sauté the crayfish in a large casserole over high heat for 15 minutes

to come halfway up the pan and cook for 10 minutes. Drain the crayfish and arrange in a dome on a serving platter. Boil the cooking liquid, adjust seasoning to taste, then beat in $3^1/_2$ tbsp (50 g) butter. Coat the crayfish with this sauce.

Squid, sea urchin, and octopus

Sea urchin chowder

1 Melt ³/₄ oz [20 g] butter in a pan, then add 3 egg yolks and 4 tbsp filtered court-bouillon. Beat over low heat or in a double boiler.

2 When the preparation has trebled in volume, stir in the coral of 6 sea urchins and some salt and pepper. This delicious sauce is served with fish cooked in a court-bouillon.

General points

Squid and octopus do not always look very attractive, but there are many refined ways of serving them.

Stuffed squid

These are prepared using very fresh pieces at least 4 in (10 cm) long and, above all, complete, neither damaged nor pierced. Remove the head and carefully clean the inside of the cylindrical body of 8 squid. Fill them with a stuffing made with 3 tomatoes, 2 onions, 9 oz (250 g) squid flesh, 3 garlic cloves, 3 tbsp breadcrumbs, and 1 egg yolk. Sew the squid up with a needle and thread to seal. Sauté in olive oil and then braise them with onions, tomato, and white wine. Serve whole with the cooking juices.

Octopus salad

This is prepared using the tentacles. Cook them in a strong court-bouillon flavored with thyme and white wine. Leave to cool. Cut the cold, cooked tentacles into fairly thin slices. Then marinate them for 24 hours in the refrigerator, in a mixture of olive oil, lemon juice, pimentos, sliced onions, salt, pepper, and chopped cilantro. Serve the octopus salad well chilled.

Octopus salad

Bouillabaisse

Bouillabaisse is a recipe from the south of France and is prepared according to tradition in Marseilles and its region. There are many variants, but it must always contain several different species of fish: girelles (also called rouquier) and hogfish to flavor the bouillon, conger eel for its consistency, and sea-perch, red mullet, and monkfish for their flesh.

The principle governing it is quite simple: first, prepare the bouillon with some of the fish, vegetables, and herbs, then cook the other, firm-fleshed fish in it. The overall taste is quite strong: fennel, saffron, and aniseed are used. This recipe must be cooked fairly quickly and served very hot. It is always served with a sauce called "rouille" (literally "rust,") which is made with garlic, olive oil, and Cayenne pepper.

Serves 6–8
Preparation: 1 hour
Cooking: 1 hour 5 minutes

Ingredients

4 onions
10 cloves garlic
1 leek white
1 2/3 cups (40 cl) olive oil
6 red mullet
2 sea-perch
1 lb 5 oz (600 g) girelles
1 edible hogfish
2 slices conger eel
6 tomatoes
2 fennels
Saffron
Cayenne pepper
14 oz (400 g) monkfish
1 egg yolk
1 baguette
Salt and pepper

The chef's recipe

1 Finely chop 2 onions, 4 garlic cloves, and the leek. Sauté in olive oil for 5 minutes. Then add the heads of 3 red mullet and 1 sea-perch (without their gills), the girelles, the hogfish cut into four, and the conger eel.

2 Season, add 2 sliced tomatoes, cover with cold water, bring to the boil, and simmer for 40 minutes. Then strain the broth, pressing the bones firmly to recover all the juice.

3 Peel the remaining tomatoes and cut them into pieces. Sauté them in a large pan with 2 tbsp olive oil. Add 2 onions, the sliced fennel, and 4 chopped garlic cloves. Sauté for 5 minutes. Then pour in the bouillon.

4 Add about ten threads saffron, 1 pinch Cayenne pepper, the monkfish, 1 sea-perch cut into pieces, and 3 red mullet. Boil over high heat for about 10 minutes. Adjust seasoning to taste. Prepare the rouille sauce. Crush two garlic cloves and put them in a salad bowl.

5 Add some Cayenne pepper and the egg yolk and beat in 1 generous cup (25 cl) olive oil. Season well. Cut the baguette into slices and toast in the oven. Serve the bouillabaisse in two large bowls: a soup bowl for the bouillon and another, slightly shallower one, for the fish.

6 Present the rouille in a ramekin. Serve your guests, giving each a fair share of the fish, vegetables, and bouillon. Accompany the bouillabaisse with a good rosé wine chilled, but not too cold. Do not offer an appetizer with bouillabaisse, but follow it with a light dessert such as fruit salad sprinkled with a few slivered almonds.

General points

For several years now, Western cuisine has opened up to ingredients customarily used in Oriental or exotic recipes. We now quite often use soy sauce, sesame seed oil, harissa, curry, cilantro, and ginger.

Tabasco®

Tabasco is manufactured by infusing chilies in vinegar. It is an extremely strong, red, acidic liquid. It also has a very pleasant smell. The liquor obtained is aged for several years in oak vats and then packed in small glass bottles. Tabasco is a condiment for use directly on various foods such as eggs, omelets, ratatouille, cold cuts, and poached fish, and also in drinks and cocktails.

Harissa

This North African condiment consists of a purée of chilies, oil, and various spices. It is used in many recipes, including tajines and couscous. It is extremely hot and often needs to be diluted before use. It is sold either in cans or tubes.

Ginger

This ancient spice has been cultivated for more than 3,000 years in Southeast Asia. Ginger is found in two forms: either fresh, as a rhizome, or dried and reduced to a very fine powder. Ginger is often used in

Tabasco®

Harissa

Asian cuisine for soups, broths, and sautéed dishes. This spice is also used in medicine, being taken, for example, to improve blood circulation and relieve cold symptoms.

Colombo

This is a mixture of spices of Indian origin with a variable composition. As a rule, it contains garlic, turmeric, coriander, cinnamon, and powdered mango. Colombo is used in stews based on fish, pork, chicken, or crustaceans.

Curry

Like Colombo, curry is a mixture of spices. Its color can range from bright yellow to orangey-green. It can be very hot or quite mild depending on its composition, which varies greatly according to its region of origin. The queen spice of Indian cookery, curry usually contains cloves, turmeric,

coriander, nutmeg, mustard, cumin, and cardamom. It is used in the preparation of vegetables, rice, and sauces for pork, chicken, lamb, and fish.

Soy sauce

This salty condiment with a characteristic taste is widely used in China, Korea, and Japan. It is prepared by mixing concentrated and fermented soya juice with salt and water and is used in numerous sautéed or slow-cooked dishes. It is also taken with sushi and sashimi. There are different qualities of soy sauce. Some are strong and quite dark, while others are light and less concentrated.

Nuoc-mam

This condiment is very popular in Vietnamese cuisine. It is prepared from fish extracts. Its flavor is quite strong and salty. It is seldom used in cooking,

Ginger

Soy sauce

Ras al-hanout

but is included in the sauce served with spring rolls, nems, and imperial pâtés. It is sold in small bottles in specialist groceries.

Ras al-hanout

This North African mixture of powdered spices is used to prepare couscous. It is made up of cloves, coriander, cinnamon, chili, and pepper. It is brown in color and its taste varies according to its region of origin.

Some fish have a subtle taste that needs to be enhanced with sauces or condiments, while others are quite strong and need to be toned down. Here are a few suggestions.

   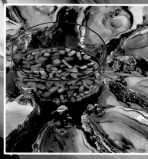

Crème fraîche and mustard

Smoked herring is very strong and cannot be eaten as it is. If its flavor is to be fully appreciated, it needs to be marinated for a few hours in a mixture of crème fraîche and strong mustard. This greatly enhances the taste.

Soy sauce

Steamed fish is excellent garnished with soy sauce. Bream, bass, cod fillet, or simple whiting can thus become a delicious dish in the twinkling of an eye. Put the hot, cooked fish on a serving platter and sprinkle lightly with soy sauce.

Mayonnaise

Cold hake is a simple and delicate dish. It should be poached whole in court-bouillon. To enhance its succulent flesh, serve a good, firm mayonnaise flavored with a few drops of lemon juice.

Vinegar, shallots

Oysters are often eaten just as they are or sprinkled with a few drops of lemon juice. They are also delicious really cold and macerated for a few minutes in their shells with a dash of wine vinegar and shallots. As a finishing touch, give each shell one turn of the pepper mill.

Tomato sauce

Broiled fish is always delicious. Bream and bass are often broiled. The flesh of these fish can sometimes dry out a little during cooking. Serve them with a lemony tomato sauce flavored with a hint of spice.

Glasswort

Poached fish, which is easy to prepare, keeps its subtle flavors intact. To accompany it, try glasswort. Buy it fresh and blanch it quickly: its iodine-rich flavor is delicious.

Lemon

Sole meunière is a great classic of French cuisine. Cooked in butter over low heat, it turns golden while developing a superb flavor. To emphasize the delicacy of this dish, sprinkle on a few drops of squeezed lemon juice. This dish is even mentioned by Proust: " ... with the zest of lemon peel, we sprinkled a few drops of gold on two soles which soon left the flourish of their bones on our plates ..." Extract from "A l'ombre des jeunes filles en fleurs."

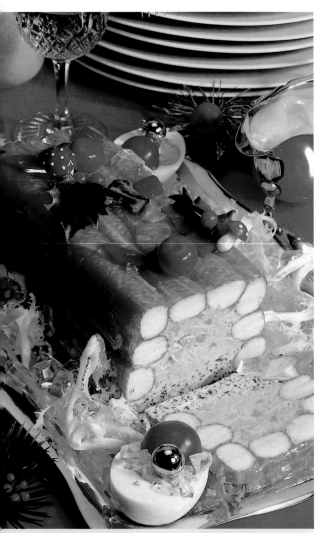

Seafood log

An economical dish

Serves 8
Preparation and cooking: 1 hour
Refrigeration: 4–5 hours

Ingredients

1 carrot

1 leek

1 onion

1 lemon

1 glass white wine

12¹/₂ oz (350 g) fish fillets

1 large pot crème fraîche

2¹/₄ lb (1 kg) surimi (frozen fish paste)

1 bunch parsley

Chervil

1 sachet powdered gelatin

Mayonnaise

Salt and pepper

1. Prepare a little court-bouillon with the carrot scraped and cut into sticks, the leek carefully washed and cut into chunks, the sliced onion, a few slices of lemon, salt, pepper, and the white wine. Boil gently for about twenty minutes, then leave to cool a little before putting in the fish. Simmer gently for 5–6 minutes. Remove the fish, drain, and purée in a blender.

2. Whip the crème fraîche until stiff and combine two-thirds with the puréed fish and a few, very small pieces of surimi. Season with salt and pepper.

3. Finely chop the parsley and chervil and mix with the remaining crème fraîche. Season.

4. Line a cake pan—bottom and sides—with long sticks of surimi. Fill with the fish mousse and then the fine herb mousse. Cover with a cutting board, place a weight on top, and leave somewhere cold for 4–5 hours.

5. Prepare a little aspic jelly according to the instructions on the bag. Remove the log from the mould and varnish with the jelly, using a pastry brush. Immediately before serving, prepare a fairly strong mayonnaise and garnish the seafood log to taste.

Recommended drinks

Muscadet
Côtes-de-Provence
Mâcon-villages blanc)

Menu suggestions

1. This recipe can be used for an appetizer that can easily be made in advance: follow it with roast chicken and green beans, a selection of cheeses, and a fruit tart.

2. The seafood log can embellish a buffet of mixed salads, cold cuts, cheese, and ice cream.

Capitaine bayou

An easy dish

Serves 4
Preparation: 20 minutes
Refrigeration: 4–5 hours
Cooking: None

Ingredients

1 lb 11 oz–2¹/₄ lb (750g–1 kg)
   fresh tuna (preferably white)

1 very fresh mackerel

2 limes

3 lemons

2–3 tomatoes

2–3 red chilies

Oregano

Olive oil

4¹/₂ oz (125 g)
   button mushrooms

1 avocado

Parsley

Salt and pepper

1. Cut the tuna into small cubes, removing the bones, skin, and black bits. Clean and gut the mackerel and remove the fins, all the bones, and the skin. Cut the fillets into strips.

2. Set 1 lime aside. Squeeze all the others and sprinkle their juice over the fish pieces placed in two different containers. Mix well. Cover and put in the coldest part of your refrigerator for 4–5 hours (not in the freezer). Turn the pieces over once an hour. After that time, the tuna pieces should be opaque and firm.

3. Cut the tomatoes into fine rounds and place in a bowl. Sprinkle over some crushed, dried chili, salt, pepper, oregano, and olive oil. Stand in a cold place for at least 15 minutes.

4. Clean and finely slice the mushrooms. Open the avocado and cut its flesh into slices, sprinkling them with lemon juice. Cut the last lime into very fine slices.

5. Arrange everything on a platter. Decorate with parsley leaves and serve chilled after seasoning and sprinkling the fish with a little of its marinade.

Recommended drinks

Sancerre blanc
Pouilly fume
Beer

Menu suggestions

1. The principle of fish marinated in lemon juice is perfect for a cold appetizer. Follow it with rare beefsteak and shallots and then fruit tartlets.

2. To retain the somewhat exotic tone, offer curried lamb or fish as a main dish and then a coconut ice cream.

Recommended drinks

Tavel
Bandol rosé
Beaujolais-villages rouge

Menu suggestions

1. In China, carp is eaten in the fall: serve mushrooms sautéed with persillade (finely chopped parsley and garlic) as an appetizer and caramelized apple tart for dessert.

2. For an authentic Chinese menu, begin with sautéed Chinese cabbage and bamboo shoots, followed by the carp and a flavored mushroom broth, and serve nougat for dessert.

Carp Chinese style

A foreign dish

Serves 4
Preparation: 20 minutes
Cooking: 40 minutes

Ingredients

1 handful black mushrooms
1 carp weighing
  2$\frac{1}{4}$ lb–2 lb 11 oz (1–1.2 kg)
2 onions
1 carrot
Bacon to cover the fish in 3 layers
5$\frac{1}{2}$ oz (150 g) chicken breast meat
1 bunch parsley
1 clove garlic
2 egg yolks (1 fresh, 1 hard-boiled)

1 handful cooked rice
6 thin slices salted bacon
4 tbsp vin jaune or white sherry
Vinegar
Soy sauce
9 oz (250 g) soy shoots
A few chives
Chili sauce
Salt and pepper

1. While the black mushrooms are soaking in warm water, scale and gut the carp. Retain the soft roe. Peel 1 onion, scrape 1 carrot, cut into rounds, and separate the onion into rings. Lay 3 slices bacon in the bottom of a baking pan. Scatter half the onion rings and carrot rounds on top.

2. Prepare the stuffing: chop the chicken breast meat, the bunch of parsley, the remaining onion, and the garlic clove. Mix the fresh and hard-cooked egg yolks, some salt and pepper, and the rice with the carp roe. Fill the carp with the stuffing and sew it up, not too tightly, with kitchen thread.

3. Lay the carp on its bed of onions and carrots. Place 3 layers of salted bacon on top and arrange a layer of onion rings and carrot rounds on the bacon. Moisten with vin jaune and flavor with 1 tbsp vinegar. Bake in the oven at 410 °F (210 °C) for 40 minutes.

4. Place the carp on a heated dish near the oven door. Strain the cooking juice, flavor with soy sauce, and coat the fish with it, as well as the black mushrooms and the soy shoots after dipping them briefly in boiling salty water: both must be al dente. Garnish with small carrot shapes and chives. Serve with the usual sauces: the bouillon from the fish, soy sauce, and chili sauce.

Scallops Moorea

A light dish

Serves 4
Preparation: 20 minutes
Cooking: 10 minutes

Ingredients

8 scallops
1 lemon
2 leeks
2 carrots
1 orange
2–3 cloves garlic
1 mango
2 kiwi fruit

Tarragon
Salt and peppercorns

1. Open the scallops and carefully wash and clean them and their coral and beards. Discard the black bits.

2. Put the beards in a pan with 8 cups (2 liters) water and the juice of 1/2 lemon. Boil, then simmer for 10 minutes. Remove the beards and make a broth with the cooking juices by adding the leek whites cut into large sections, fine carrot rounds, salt, the lemon and orange cut into rings, the peppercorns, and the garlic cloves. Boil for 20–30 minutes and leave to cool a little.

3. Poach the scallops in this broth, with their coral, for about 10 minutes (remember that "poach" means "cook without boiling.")

4. Meanwhile, peel the mango and cut into quarters. Peel the kiwi fruit and cut into fine rounds.

5. Arrange the orange and carrot slices from the broth, the coral, scallops, kiwi slices, and mango quarters in the scallop shells. Moisten with a little warm court-bouillon flavored either with lemon juice or a dash of vinegar. Add the tarragon at the last moment.

Recommended drinks

Weak tea
Grapefruit juice
Rosé de Provence

Menu suggestions

1. If you serve these scallops as an appetizer, follow them with spinach stalks and a slice of braised ham and finish with fromage frais and red berries.

2. These scallops can also be served after a seasonal vegetable soup followed by a fine puff pastry apple tart for dessert.

Breton Cotriade

A regional dish

Serves 4
Preparation: 20 minutes
Cooking: 35 minutes

Ingredients

5 onions

Butter

10 potatoes

1 bunch herbs (thyme, bay,
   marjoram, parsley, fennel)

2–3 mackerel

1 whiting

1 piece conger eel

1 sea bream

Bread

Vinaigrette

Salt and pepper

1. Chop the onions coarsely and sweat them in a casserole with 1 tbsp butter. Meanwhile, peel the potatoes. When the onions have browned nicely, add 4 cups (1 liter) water to the casserole.

2. Put the potatoes in the casserole to cook with salt, pepper, and the bunch of mixed herbs. Gut and clean the fish while the potatoes are cooking. Scale if necessary.

3. When the potatoes are almost cooked, set the cotriade to boil vigorously, throw in the fish—cut up or otherwise, depending on their size—and cook vigorously for just a few minutes, as they must not be allowed to break up.

4. Cut slices of bread, put them in a soup tureen and pour in three quarters of the broth. Keep it warm. Arrange the potatoes, onions, and fish in a warm, deep casserole. Serve, accompanied by a bowl of vinaigrette and a bowl of broth, well seasoned with salt and pepper. The fish is eaten first followed by the potatoes and ending with the broth.

N.B. Cotriade, like its Mediterranean sister bouillabaisse, is not always the same, but takes many different forms in the various fishing ports of Brittany. Its original feature is that it combines a broth and fish stew in a single dish and must be cooked very quickly. Incidentally, its name is derived from "cotret," a small bundle of dry sticks traditionally used in the fireplace to obtain a bright flame and rapid boil.

Recommended drinks

Muscadet sur lie
Bottled cider
Gros-plant

Menu suggestions

1. For a regional and seasonal menu, serve the cotriade as an appetizer, followed by duckling with green peas, and jelly pancakes for dessert.

2. For a lighter meal, serve the cotriade as the main dish, preceded by a few oysters and shrimp and followed by a strawberry salad for dessert.

Island sea bream

A foreign dish

Serves 4
Preparation: 10 minutes
Cooking: 15 minutes

Ingredients

1 lb 2 oz (500 g) tomatoes
Oil
Tabasco®
2 oz (60 g) butter
4 bananas, not too ripe
1 sea bream weighing
  1 lb 11 oz–2$^{1}/_{4}$ lb (750 g–1 kg),
  gutted and scaled

1 cup (200 g) rice
9 oz (250 g) roasted, salted peanuts
A little parsley
Salt and pepper

1. Peel the tomatoes after briefly dipping them in boiling water. Cut them in pieces, removing the seeds. Heat the oil in a casserole and gently cook the tomatoes in it with the salt, pepper, and Tabasco®.

2. Heat half the butter in a skillet and gently brown the bananas, peeled and cut in two lengthwise.

3. Heat the rest of the butter in a second skillet and put in the sea bream, split in two either side of the bone, which you will remove during this operation. Cook for 10–12 minutes and turn gently two-thirds of the way through.

4. Separately, cook the rice, either plain or Creole style.

5. To serve, lay the tomatoes on a serving platter and arrange the sea bream on top (it must not be browned). Combine the cooking juices from the bananas and the fish and vigorously sauté the peanuts in this preparation. Garnish the dish with the bananas, sprinkle half the peanuts over everything, and add a little parsley. Serve with the rice, the remainder of the sauce, and the remaining peanuts separately in an hors d'oeuvre dish.

Recommended drinks

Tavel
Côtes-de-Provence blanc
Riesling

Menu suggestions

1. As an appetizer for this island-style sea bream, serve stuffed crab au gratin and offer vanilla-flavored, sweet potato baked custard for dessert.

2. To set a less emphatically foreign tone, serve salmon tartar as an appetizer and mango sorbet for dessert.

Haddock Indian style

A foreign dish

Serves 4
Preparation: 20 minutes
Cooking: 15 minutes

Ingredients

1 carrot

1 bay leaf

1 scant cup (20 cl) white wine

1³/₄ lb (800 g) haddock in 4 pieces

1–2 apples

1 orange

1 tsp cornstarch

12 oz plain yogurt

Curry powder

Salt and pepper

1. Peel the onion and cut into quarters. Peel the carrot and cut into rounds. Put them in a skillet with the bay leaf, salt, and pepper. Add the wine and 3 cups (75 cl) water. Bring to the boil and simmer gently for about 15 minutes.

2. Meanwhile, clean and trim the pieces of fish. Plunge the fish pieces in the hot (but not boiling) court-bouillon and simmer, with the lid on, for about 15 minutes.

3. Pour 1 scant cup (20 cl) of the fish cooking juices into a small saucepan, bring to the boil, and add 1 tbsp of onion taken from the court-bouillon. Add the peeled and grated apples and the juice of 1 orange. Heat gently without boiling.

4. Mix the cornstarch and the yogurt. Strain the sauce. Bind with the yogurt preparation and re-heat, but still do not boil. Season with salt.

5. Pour the sauce into a heated casserole, put the fish pieces on top, sprinkle over a little curry powder, and garnish with parsley.

Recommended drinks

Beer
Riesling
White cassis

Menu suggestions

1. As an appetizer, serve avocado with shrimp; serve rice as an accompaniment to the fish, of course; and finish with snow eggs (oeufs à la neige) with custard for dessert.

2. Another family meal suggestion: mushroom quiche as an appetizer and, for dessert after a selection of cheeses, a coffee crème.

Fan of ray in leek and saffron broth

A party dish

Serves 4
Preparation: 10 minutes
Cooking: 45 minutes

Ingredients

1 ray wing weighing about 2¼ lb (1 kg)

8 small leeks

1 glass dry white wine

3–4 tbsp crème fraîche

Saffron threads

Salt and pepper

1. Carefully trim, wash, and wipe the ray wing. It must not retain the least trace of skin.

2. Remove the roots, outer leaves, and most of the green part of the leeks, slicing up the white part. Wash and cut them into rounds about 1/16 in (5 mm) thick.

3. Put the sliced leeks into a skillet. Season with salt and pepper and add 1 glass white wine and 1 glass water. Cook with the lid on over low heat for 30 minutes.

4. Spread the crème fraîche over the ray wing and arrange on the leeks. Scatter the saffron on top and season with salt and pepper. Cover and poach for 12–15 minutes (depending on the thickness of the wing) in the steam from the leeks.

5. Carefully flake the ray and spread it out in a fan in the broth.

Recommended drinks

Chablis
Sancerre blanc
Pouilly fumé

Menu suggestions

1. Delicate and refined, this fan of ray can be an appetizer. Follow with quails and grapes and then pears poached in red wine.

2. Fan of ray can also be served as a main course, following a terrine of liver pâté with fresh figs. For dessert, what about a dark chocolate mousse?

461

Menu suggestions

1. To accompany these whiting fillets at a family lunch, serve slices of pâté en croûte as an appetizer with salad, followed by apples "bonne femme" for dessert.

2. For a more refined dinner, serve the whiting fillets as an appetizer, followed by roast veal with mushrooms and a "floating island" (île flottante) for dessert.

Fillets of whiting Paimpol style

A regional dish

Serves 4
Preparation: 30 minutes
Cooking: 8–10 minutes

Ingredients

2 onions	Oil
3 carrots	4 scallops
Whiting heads and bones	1 bay leaf
1 bouquet garni	1 sprig thyme
1 bottle rough cider	Tomato concentrate
4 large whiting fillets or 8 small ones	1 egg yolk
2 shallots	1 scant cup (20 cl) crème fraîche
2 tbsp butter	Salt and pepper

1. Peel and chop 1 onions and 2 carrots. Put them in a saucepan with the whiting heads and bones and the bouquet garni. Pour in plenty of cider. Cook until the liquid is reduced by half. Strain and season with salt and pepper.

2. Roll the fillets into "olives," securing them not too tightly with string. Poach for 2–3 minutes in the simmering bouillon. Set aside.

3. Peel and chop the remaining onion and carrot and the shallots. Sauté them gently in butter and oil for 10 minutes. Add the well-cleaned scallops, including the coral, cut in two width-wise, the bay leaf, and the sprig of thyme. Sauté for a few moments.

4. Mix a little bouillon and tomato concentrate. Pour over the scallops and simmer for 6–7 minutes. Set aside.

5. Strain the cooking juice from the scallops, bind it with the egg yolk beaten in a little cream, and add salt and pepper. Heat without boiling.

6. Arrange everything in a baking pan and reheat very gently in the oven.

Oysters with shallot butter

A party dish

Serves 10
Preparation: 20 minutes
Cooking: 5 minutes

Ingredients

12$^1/_2$ oz (350 g) butter at room
   temperature
2–3 shallots
1 bunch mixed herbs
Breadcrumbs
3 dozen oysters
   (opened by your fish seller)
1 kg coarse salt

1. Above all, make sure your butter is at room temperature, so take it out of the refrigerator in good time.

2. Finely peel and chop the shallots. Mix the butter with the finely chopped shallots and herbs, adding some breadcrumbs.

3. Place the oysters in baking pans containing a fairly deep layer of coarse salt. Be sure to conserve all their water. Preheat the broiler.

4. Put 1 small tsp herb butter on each oyster and put under the broiler just long enough for the surface to begin to brown.

N.B. Make sure the broiler is very hot before placing the pans under it, as the oysters must heat through while their coating browns. It is important that their water does not start to boil. Contrary to popular belief, hot oysters are not an invention of modern cuisine. In centuries past, this was often the only way oysters were eaten: either in a stew or as a garnish for pies or meat dishes.

Recommended drinks

Dry champagne
Chablis
Riesling

Menu suggestions

1. These hot oysters will make an elegant and unusual appetizer. You can then serve roast partridge with fresh green peas, followed by a pear charlotte.

2. Another suggestion for seafood lovers: follow the oysters with a lobster stew and finish with a chocolate cake.

Recommended drinks

Collioure blanc
Minervois blanc
Côtes-du-Roussillon blanc

Menu suggestions

1. To retain a sunny, regional tone, serve this crayfish as an appetizer, followed by guinea fowl with banyuls and peaches poached in muscatel and cinnamon for dessert.

2. Equally regional, the following menu will take you far from home in winter: pumpkin soup, stuffed mussels, crayfish, and then cinnamon tart.

Crayfish Catalan style

A foreign dish

Serves 2
Preparation and first cooking: 20 minutes
Waiting: 1 hour
Second cooking: 15–20 minutes

Ingredients

2 small onions	2–3 tomatoes
2 carrots	Olive oil
1 stalk celery	1 glass dry white wine
Lemon	Cayenne pepper
1 small bunch parsley	Saffron
Vinegar	Salt and peppercorns
1 crayfish weighing 1 lb 2 oz–1 lb 5 oz (500–600 g)	
2 green pimentos	

1. Prepare a court-bouillon by boiling 8 cups (2 liters) water in a large stewpan with 1 chopped onion, the carrots sliced into sticks, the stalk of celery, slices of lemon, a few parsley stalks, salt, peppercorns, and a dash of vinegar. Plunge the crayfish into the court-bouillon and cook for 8–10 minutes, then allow to cool in the court-bouillon.

2. Meanwhile, peel and finely chop the second onion, split the pimentos, seed, and cut the flesh into strips. Peel, seed, and chop the tomatoes.

3. Remove the meat from the crayfish—including the claws. Cut it into large cubes. Sauté them rapidly in a skillet in hot olive oil. Keep warm.

4. Sauté the onion, pimentos, and tomatoes in the oil remaining in the skillet. After 5 minutes, add the parsley, white wine, Cayenne pepper, and saffron, followed by the crayfish pieces. Cover and simmer for 10 minutes.

5. Keep the crayfish pieces warm. Reduce the juice. Arrange them on hot plates and serve at once.

Steamed hake in piquant sauce

A light dish

Serves 2
Preparation: 15 minutes
Cooking: 15–20 minutes

Ingredients

1 hake weighing about
  1 3/4 lb (800 g)

1 onion

1 bay leaf

Vinegar

1 bunch parsley

1 bunch chervil

1 red pimento

2 3/4 oz (75 g butter)

1 lemon

Strong prepared mustard

Salt and pepper

1. Trim the well-cleaned and gutted hake. Run a trussing needle through its head and then through its tail. Knot the thread, not too tightly, to enable the fish to cook in the top of a double boiler.

2. Put the chopped onion, bay leaf, a little vinegar, and 4 cups (1 liter) water in the bottom half of the double boiler. Place the hake on a bed of parsley and chervil in the top of the boiler. Cook for 15–20 minutes with the lid on and the liquid just simmering.

3. Meanwhile, put the pimento in a very hot oven. Wait until it "blisters" before wrapping it in paper towels and sprinkling it with cold water. After a few minutes, peel and cut into strips.

4. Melt the butter in a small saucepan. When it turns golden brown, add a mixture of lemon juice, mustard, and chopped chervil. Add the pimento pieces. Mix, beating lightly. Season. Keep warm. Serve the hake fillets on a bed of sauce spread over warm plates.

Recommended drinks

Tomato juice
Iced tea
Bordeaux blanc

Menu suggestions

1. For lunch, serve a cucumber, mint, and yogurt salad before the fish and fruit kebab "en papillotte" to follow.

2. For dinner, start with a vegetable soup and vegetable terrine and serve white cheese with blueberries for dessert.

Recommended drinks

Irouléguy rosé
Tavel
Rioja rosé

Menu suggestions

1. For a summer meal on a shady terrace, serve these mussels as an appetizer, followed by an anchovy pizza and fresh apricot tart for dessert.

2. You can also serve these mussels in fall or winter as an appetizer, but followed by a cassoulet and a caramel ice cream for dessert.

Mussels Portuguese style

A foreign dish

Serves 4
Preparation: 30 minutes
Cooking: 20 minutes
Waiting: 6 hours

Ingredients

2 medium-sized onions
1 clove garlic
2 shallots
Parsley
1 glass olive oil
3 glasses white wine
3 tbsp tomato sauce
1 bunch thyme
1 bay leaf

2 level tsp crushed peppercorns
20 coriander seeds
1 lemon
8 cups (2 liters) large mussels
Salt

1. Peel the onions, garlic, and shallots. Chop so that the small pieces are not crushed. Put them in a saucepan with the chopped parsley. Add the oil. Heat, and sweat gently. Add the wine, tomato sauce, thyme, bay leaf, pepper, and coriander. Peel the lemon, cut into fine slices, seed, and add to the pan.

2. Simmer for 20 minutes over medium heat. Meanwhile, scrape and wash the mussels, put in a pan over high heat, and cover. Stir as they begin to steam.

3. Remove the mussels as and when they open. Discard any that remain closed. Save the cooking liquid and add 2 or 3 ladles of it to the contents of the saucepan, having first filtered it carefully through a fine cloth or paper towels.

4. Simmer the sauce for a further 10 minutes, removing each empty mussel shell. Arrange them in layers in a dish.

5. Adjust the seasoning of the sauce. Pour it over the mussels after removing the thyme and the bay leaf. Leave to cool before placing in the refrigerator for 6 hours. Serve on plates garnished with a few slices of tomato and parsley.

Trout mousse

A party dish

Serves 4
Preparation: 25 minutes
Cooking: 40 minutes

Ingredients

2 small trout

4 eggs

1½ cups (35 cl) crème fraîche

1 large glass milk

3½ oz (100 g) butter

1–2 onions

1–2 carrots

1 bouquet garni (parsley, thyme, bay)

1 glass dry white wine

1 bunch chives

Decorative fish-shaped pastry motifs

Salt and white pepper

1. Wash the trout fillets, reserving the bones and heads for the bouillon. Chop the fillets and sieve them. Incorporate two whole eggs plus 2 yolks and 1 generous cup (25 cl) crème fraîche, diluting with the milk. Season with salt and white pepper. Blend, or sieve once again.

2. Butter four ramekins and fill them with the mousse. Place in a bain-marie, or in a baking pan of water, and bake in the oven at 330 °F (165 °C). Cover with aluminum foil and wait 40 minutes.

3. Meanwhile, prepare the bouillon with peeled and chopped onions, scraped carrots cut into sticks, bouquet garni, trout heads and bones, white wine, the same amount of water, salt, and pepper.

4. When cooked, the bouillon should have reduced by half. Strain, purée, and beat in the butter with a hand beater. Remove the mousse from the ramekins onto hot plates, coat with the sauce, and sprinkle chopped chives on top. Garnish with fish-shaped pastry motifs.

N.B. Do not forget that the success of this recipe, as with all fish mousses, depends on two essential factors: first, the mousse must be prepared with really cold ingredients (the fish, crème fraîche, and milk). Do not remove from the refrigerator until they are needed. Second, ensure the cooking temperature is moderate: above all, avoid boiling in the bain-marie.

Recommended drinks

Mâcon
Riesling
Chablis

Menu suggestions

1. Perfect for a Sunday lunch, follow this trout mousse with roast beef and green beans, with a Paris-Brest for dessert.

2. For a family dinner party, serve quiche Lorraine as an appetizer. Follow with the mousse accompanied by a little puréed celery, with a black cherry clafoutis for dessert.

Ragout of lobster

A party dish

Serves 4
Preparation: 15 minutes
Cooking: 1 hour 40 minutes

Ingredients

2 glasses Muscadet
1 onion
1 carrot
4 shallots
2 bouquets garnis
Peppercorns
1 lb 2 oz (500 g) fish heads
and trimmings

1 fresh lobster weighing
1³/₄ lb–2¹/₄ lb (800 g–1 kg)
Butter
Olive oil
2 leeks
8–10 clams
A few langoustines (Norway lobster)

1. Start by preparing a bouillon with the Muscadet, onion, carrot, 1 chopped shallot, 1 bouquet garni, salt, and 4–5 peppercorns. Add 2–3 glasses water and simmer gently for 40 minutes. Add the fish heads and trimmings. Cook gently for a further 20 minutes. After reduction, this should yield 3 cups (75 cl) liquid.

2. Split the lobster from head to tail. Remove the pocket of grit in the head. Separate the claws from the body and cut the two pieces in half. Fry the lobster pieces in a skillet with butter and oil. They should turn red. Moisten with the bouillon. Boil over high heat for 15 minutes.

3. Add the chopped whites of leek, 3 finely chopped shallots, and 1 bouquet garni. Season with salt and pepper. Cook for 15 minutes over medium heat.

4. Add the clams and langoustines and give them the few additional minutes they need to cook. Serve, either with or without the sauce.

Recommended drinks

Dry champagne
Chablis
Meursault

Menu suggestions

1. If you are serving this lobster ragout as an appetizer, follow with an equally refined and delicious main course: veal sweetbreads in cream, and a champagne zabaglione for dessert.

2. Another suggestion: start with a plate of oysters (specials and belons) and, after the lobster, finish with an opera cake.

Red mullet broth

A party dish

Serves 3
Preparation: 10 minutes
Cooking: 45 minutes

Ingredients

2 cups (50 cl) dry, but fruity,
   white wine

2 tbsp vinegar

1 bouquet garni (thyme, bay,
   fennel, and rosemary)

1 orange

2 lemons

1 bunch tarragon

9 oz (250 g) carrots

3 turnips

4½ oz (125 g) green beans

1 fennel

1 large onion

2 oz (60 g) butter

1 pinch superfine sugar

3 red mullet weighing 9 oz (250 g)

1 pinch flour

Salt and pepper

1. Start by making the court-bouillon: put 4 cups (1 liter) water, the white wine, vinegar, bouquet garni, a few orange and lemon slices including their peel, a few tarragon leaves, salt, and pepper in a large casserole. Cover and simmer for 30 minutes.

2. Scrape the carrots and turnips and cut them into thin rounds. Trim the green beans. Peel and slice the fennel and onion. Put all the vegetables except the green beans to simmer in butter in a fairly large skillet, adding salt and pepper. Do not cover the skillet, but shake often so that the vegetables do not stick. Cook for 30 minutes, without browning.

3. Sprinkle with flour and add the green beans. Cook for 2 minutes and then add a large bowl of court-bouillon. Bring to the boil, add pepper, reduce the heat, and simmer slowly for a further 15 minutes.

4. Clean and gut the mullet, leaving the liver in. Five minutes before serving, plunge the fish into the simmering court-bouillon. Do not allow to boil, as the mullet must remain firm.

4. Put the fish on a hot serving platter garnished with orange and lemon slices and arrange the vegetables around them. Coat with the reduced cooking juices and sprinkle with a few leaves of fresh tarragon.

Recommended drinks

Tavel
Mint tea
Lemonade

Menu suggestions

1. If you serve these red mullet for lunch, start with artichokes spread with fresh goat's cheese. For dessert, serve an orange and cinnamon salad.

2. For dinner, serve a mesclun salad with parmesan shavings as an appetizer and then plain strawberries for dessert.

Recommended drinks

Chablis
Pinot gris
Pouilly fumé

Menu suggestions

1. This recipe makes an elegant appetizer. Follow with jugged hare and fresh pasta, and crème brulée for dessert.

2. As a main dish, you could also serve duck and orange, followed by a selection of cheeses and a Grand Marnier soufflé.

Sole and salmon rolls with prunes

A light dish

Serves 4
Preparation: 20 minutes
Cooking: 12 minutes

Ingredients

2 carrots

1 leek

Celery stalks

3 large dabs butter

Sole heads and bones

1 large glass dry white wine

1 bouquet garni

2 large bunches spinach
weighing 3¹/₂ oz (100 g)

4 fillets salmon or salmon trout

4 fillets sole

1 level tbsp flour

1 small pot crème fraîche

2 egg yolks

1 bag pitted prunes

Chives

Salt and pepper

1. Prepare a little fish bouillon: wash, scrape, and trim the carrots, leek, and celery (only 1 stalk). Cut them into thin sticks, julienne-style, and put them in a baking pan with a dab of butter. Cook for 5 minutes in the oven, uncovered, at 210 °F (100 °C). Stir at least twice during cooking. Add the sole heads and bones and return to the oven for 2 minutes. Lastly, add the wine, 4 cups (1 liter) water, salt, pepper, and the bouquet garni. Cover and put back in the oven for 6 minutes, then strain.

2. Meanwhile, sort and wash the spinach and remove the stalks. Wipe and season the fish fillets, then spread 3–4 spinach leaves over them. Put 1 fillet of sole on each spinach-covered salmon fillet, roll them up, and place them in buttered ramekins.

3. Put a dab of butter in a casserole and heat to 210 °F (100 °C) for 30 seconds. Drizzle in the flour, mix well, and cook again over high heat for 30 seconds. Dilute with the bouillon and return to the oven for 2 minutes. Whip the crème fraîche and egg yolks, pour in the bouillon, and beat the mixture a little. Add the prunes, cover, and return to the oven for 2 minutes. Leave to rest.

4. Meanwhile, put the ramekins in a hot oven and bake for 5 minutes. Spoon the contents of the ramekins onto hot plates coated with a little sauce. Garnish with spinach leaves, prunes, and chives.

Mussel soup

A family dish

Serves 4
Preparation: 15 minutes
Cooking: 30 minutes

Ingredients

4 cups (1 liter) mussels

2–3 carrots

1 bay leaf

Parsley

2 oz (60 g) butter

1 onion

1 egg yolk

1/3 cup + 1 1/2 tbsp (10 cl) crème fraîche

Croutons

Salt and pepper

1. Scrape and wash the mussels. Take care to remove the "byssus," the small tuft of fibers through which they attach themselves to the mussel bed. Put them in a saucepan with 1 glass water, a few, finely sliced carrot rounds, the bay leaf, a little parsley, and a pinch of pepper. Cook for 5 minutes over high heat, shaking the pan two or three times to help the mussels open.

2. Drain through a colander placed over a casserole, saving the cooking water. Discard any mussels that have not opened. Filter the water at least twice through a fine cloth placed in a sieve. It is essential to remove all the sand and grit.

3. Heat 2 tbsp (30 g) butter in a casserole and sauté the peeled and coarsely chopped onion. When turning golden, add enough cooking water from the mussels to obtain 4 bowls of soup (allowing for reduction during cooking), 2 tbsp (30 g) butter, and a dash of pepper. Simmer gently for 20 minutes.

4. Meanwhile, remove the mussels from their shells. Put them in the soup and simmer gently for 10 minutes. Adjust seasoning to taste.

5. Remove from the heat and bind with the egg yolk mixed with crème fraîche. Stir well and reheat, but do not boil. Serve accompanied by small croutons fried in butter and some chopped parsley.

Recommended drinks

Muscadet
Gros-plant
Anjou

Menu suggestions

1. If mussel soup is an appetizer, serve boiled bacon with lentils next and crème caramel for dessert.

2. For a lighter meal, follow this soup with endive au gratin with ham and a fruit purée with meringues for dessert.

Trout Savoy style

A regional dish

Serves 4
Preparation: 30 minutes
Cooking: 15–20 minutes

Ingredients

Puff pastry
2 carrots
2 celery stalks
2 leeks
9 oz (250 g) mushrooms
2³/₄ oz (80 g) butter
4 trout
3 eggs
1 onion

3 cups (75 cl) dry white wine
1 scant cup (20 cl) crème fraîche
Parsley
Salt and pepper

1. Preheat the oven to 510 °F (265 °C) and prepare a few puff pastry tidbits. Cook for 10–15 minutes and set aside.

2. Trim the carrots, celery, leeks, and two-thirds of the mushrooms. Cut them finely, julienne style, and cook with the lid on in a little butter, the mushrooms in one saucepan and the vegetables in another.

3. Clean the trout and wipe with a rough cloth. To gut, open via the spine, sliding a knife along each side of the bone, then cut off the head and tail and remove the backbone before gutting the fish.

4. When the vegetables are cooked, remove them from the heat and mix the contents of the two saucepans, bind with 1 whole egg and 2 yolks, and season with salt and pepper. Divide the stuffing between the trout then place them in a baking pan. Sprinkle with finely chopped onion, half fill each with wine, and cook in the oven at 435 °F (225 °C) for 15 minutes.

5. Sauté the remaining mushrooms in butter. Mix 1 tbsp butter with 1 large pinch flour. Keep the trout warm. Reduce their cooking liquid over high heat and bind it with the butter mixture and crème fraîche, beating all the time. Pour the sauce into a serving dish, arrange the trout on top, and garnish with the mushrooms, a little parsley, and the prepared puff pastry shapes.

Recommended drinks

Crépy
Seyssel
Vin de Savoie blanc

Menu suggestions

1. For a spring or summer lunch, serve morels on toast as an appetizer and a gratin of red fruits for dessert.

2. For an autumn or winter dinner, serve the trout as an appetizer followed by partridge with cabbage and a Vacherin cheese.

Stuffed turbot

A party dish

Serves 5–6
Preparation: 30 minutes
Cooking: 40 minutes

Ingredients

1 medium-sized onion

1 shallot

5^1/$_2$ oz (150 g) butter

Sole bones from the fish seller

1 bouquet garni (parsley,
thyme, bay)

3 glasses fruity dry white wine

1 turbot weighing about
2^1/$_4$ lb (1 kg), gutted

7 oz (200 g) mushrooms

5^1/$_2$ oz (150 g) whiting fillets

2 egg yolks

Four-spice

Stale breadcrumbs

Scant ^{1}/$_4$ cup (20 g) flour

Crème fraîche

1 bunch chervil

Salt and pepper

1. Prepare a fish bouillon with the chopped onion and shallots sweated in 3/4 oz (20 g) butter, the sole bones cut in pieces, salt, pepper, and the bouquet garni. Moisten with the white wine and 2 glasses of water. Simmer with the lid on.

2. Meanwhile, prepare the turbot. Trim its fins and tail and then sever it from the head and tail as far as the backbone. Slide the knife flat along the backbone. Detach the flesh from the bone. Cut off the head and tail and detach it. To do this, you need to lift the fish from the tail end and slide your fingers underneath the bone.

3. Trim the mushrooms and sweat them in 1 tbsp (20 g) butter and 3 tbsp water. Reserve a few whole mushrooms, chop the rest, and combine with the chopped whiting fillets, 3 tbsp (40 g) softened butter, egg yolks, salt, pepper, and four-spice.

4. If necessary, add some stale breadcrumbs dipped in bouillon, as there must be enough of this stuffing to force the turbot half-open. Push the stuffing well into the fillets to plump them up.

5. Pour the bouillon into a buttered baking pan. Add the turbot and cook in the oven at 430 °F (220 °C) for 40 minutes. Remove the black skin and keep it warm. Bind the juice with butter mixed with flour and crème fraîche. Add the plucked fresh chervil leaves and coat the fish.

Recommended drinks

Dry champagne
Chablis
Meursault

Menu suggestions

1. As turbot is a luxury fish, serve it as a main course, with fried liver pâté with grapes as an appetizer. Follow with praline meringue or chocolate soufflé.

2. For a banquet, serve a caviar taster and the turbot as an appetizer, followed by roast capon and a charlotte with marrons glacés for dessert.

Crab with melon salad

Serves 4
2 melons
1 stalk celery
Meat of 1–2 crabs (or 1 can crabmeat)
Chervil
1 lemon
Oil
Salt and pepper

1. Cut the melons in two. Scoop out the flesh with a small spoon or melon baller.

2. Wash the celery and chop into small sticks 2 in (5 cm) long.

3. Fill the melon halves, arranging the various ingredients attractively. Put a few chervil leaves on top. Prepare a lemon vinaigrette with the juice of 1 lemon, oil, salt, pepper, and chopped chervil. Serve chilled.

Concarneau crêpes

2 generous cups (250 g) flour
4 eggs (2 fresh, 2 hard-boiled)
1 tbsp oil
2 cups (50 cl) milk
1 large dab butter
1 can sardines in oil
1 lemon
A few gherkins
Mayonnaise
Salt

1. Prepare a crepe batter with the flour, fresh eggs, oil, salt, and a little milk. Leave to rest. Fry the crepe and set aside.

2. Prepare the mayonnaise. It should be well seasoned. Clean the sardines and mix their lightly crushed fillets with the mayonnaise. Add the lemon juice and 2–3 gherkins cut into small pieces. Divide the mixture between the crêpes, roll them into horns, and arrange on a serving platter garnished with slices of hard-boiled egg and chopped gherkins.

Anchovy tapas

Serves 4
12 very fresh anchovies
2 lemons
1 tomato
1 small jar olives
1 small jar small pickled onions
Salt

1. Wash and fillet the anchovies. Wipe and put them in a shallow dish with the salt and lemon juice. Roll them in this mixture so they absorb it thoroughly. Leave to macerate overnight.

2. Just before serving, cut the tomato into small pieces. Wrap the olives, tomato pieces, and small onions in the well-drained anchovy fillets. Spear them on skewers, alternating them with fine slices of quartered lemons. These anchovy fillets can be kept for a few days in layers in a jar, topped with a thin layer of olive oil.

Flaked haddock with spinach

4 small haddock fillets
2 lemons
3 bunches young spinach
Wine vinegar
Olive oil
Mustard
2 shallots
4 eggs
Cherry tomatoes
Salt and pepper

1. Flake, then finely slice the haddock fillets. Marinate in the juice of 2 lemons.

2. Sort and wash the spinach, removing the stalks. Drain. Prepare a vinaigrette with the shallots, vinegar, olive oil, and mustard. Place the spinach on plates, season with vinaigrette, and arrange the haddock on top.

3. Poach the eggs for 1 minute and drain. Place 1 hot egg in the middle of each plate and garnish with cherry tomatoes.

Artichokes Roscoff style

Serves 4
8 small artichokes
2 tbsp flour
1 can sardines in oil
1³/₄ oz (50 g) butter
3 hard-boiled eggs
Vinaigrette
Salt and pepper

1. Trim the artichokes. Mix the flour with a little salted water and pour it into a pan with 8 cups (2 liters) boiling, salted water, put in the artichokes, and allow them to boil for 45 minutes. Drain them, points downward. Remove all the leaves and the fibers.

2. Remove the skin and backbone from the sardines. Using a fork, combine the butter and half the sardine flesh.

3. Separate the egg yolks from the whites. Chop separately. Fill the artichokes with the purée, the remaining sardine flesh, and the chopped egg. Add a dash of vinegar.

Capilotade of cod

Serves 4
1 lb 9 oz (700 g) de-salted cod
1 bunch thyme
1 bay leaf
A few peppercorns
1 lb 9 oz (700 g) potatoes
1 glass olive oil
5–6 chopped garlic cloves
1 bunch chopped parsley

1. Cut the cod into pieces and place in a pan with the thyme, bay, and pepper. Cover with cold water and heat. It is cooked as soon as it starts to simmer. Drain, making sure to reserve the bouillon, then remove the skin and bones and flake the flesh.

2. Cook the potatoes, cut into rounds, in the fish bouillon. Place the potatoes and fish in an oiled casserole.

3. Sauté the garlic in a skillet with the oil and add to the casserole. Cook in the oven at 350 °F (180 °C) for 10 minutes. Sprinkle with parsley.

Eggs and cheese

Advice

Freshness plays an important part: a recently laid egg has a very thick consistency and cooks more slowly than an older egg, which will be more liquid. The initial temperature is important too: an egg kept at room temperature cooks more quickly than a very cold egg of the same size—and it is a good idea to put eggs just removed from the refrigerator in a little lukewarm water to warm them up. If suddenly immersed in boiling water they will burst. The cooking water should be simmering gently. If you are cooking several eggs at once, put them in a metal basket to stop them hitting one another and breaking during cooking. As soon as cooking is complete, serve the egg. Too long a wait allows the very hot egg to continue cooking. It will change from soft-boiled to hard-boiled in less than three minutes.

Fingers

Soft-boiled eggs are even more delicious when accompanied by dipping fingers, or "soldiers," of bread, meat, or vegetables. The simplest is a small slice of bread spread with unsalted or semi-salted butter. There are many variants. Bread-based: plain farmhouse bread, buttered, with a slice of smoked local ham, or a bread finger spread with taramasalata. Meat-based: thin sticks of plain or smoked ham. Vegetable-based: green asparagus tips, celery stalks.

Utensils

Soft-boiled eggs are served in eggcups. The top is then sliced off with an egg-cutter or serrated knife. To eat them without dipping fingers, choose a small spoon of stainless steel. Aluminum utensils should not be used as they react chemically with the lipids and proteins in egg yolk, which impairs the flavor.

Cooking

Put some water in a large saucepan and bring to the boil. Put the eggs in a metal basket. Immerse them all together and calculate the cooking time exactly. Remove the eggs as soon as the desired degree of cooking has been reached. Put the eggs in their cups, open the top of each, and serve with a spoon and dipping fingers. A new-laid egg can be eaten soft-boiled until the 9th or 10th day after it was bought. Carefully note the date when it was laid.

Average cooking times.
New-laid eggs at room temperature are plunged into gently simmering water. The cooking time is calculated from the moment of immersion.

	Large eggs	Medium-sized eggs
Soft-boiled	4 min.	3 min.
Well-done	7-8 min.	6 min.
Hard-boiled	10-11 min.	9 min.

A refinement

Serve excellent soft-boiled eggs with a spoon accompanied by blinis and caviar. You can use salmon roe instead of caviar. In both cases, serve the eggs very hot and the fish roe icy cold: the contrast in temperature is the original feature of this recipe, which is found on the à la carte menus of the greatest chefs.

Tip

Eggs can also be soft boiled by plunging them into water that has stopped boiling. In this case, allow about 7 minutes. With this method, the white remains soft and does not become rubbery.

Uses

Hard-boiled eggs are an essential component of good cuisine. They can simply be eaten whole with a little fine salt and pepper, but are also included in numerous recipes: salads, hot and cold stuffed eggs, egg mayonnaise, gratins, sauces, and fried rissoles. Egg mayonnaise is as easy to make as it is delicious to eat. Stuffed eggs make a very good hors d'oeuvre.

Scotch eggs

Hard-boiled eggs with herb sauce

The eggs are cut in two. The white is kept whole while the yolk is mixed with mayonnaise, cream, or a sauce and then used to stuff the white. These dishes are garnished with chopped parsley.

Hard-boiled eggs sliced in two, coated with Mornay sauce, and then put in the oven make a classy gratin.

Rissoles are prepared by mixing chopped, hard-boiled eggs and a thick white sauce. The mixture is shaped into balls the size of a nut and then fried very hot.

Lastly, hard-boiled eggs can be served hot in a sauce.

Make a white sauce with onions and stir in quartered, hard-boiled eggs. The whole is cooked for a few minutes and served immediately.

Eggs Snow-White style

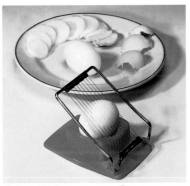

Shelling and cutting

Shell hard-boiled eggs as soon as they are cold by tapping the shell with a knife handle. Take care to remove the membrane at the same time. Do not let eggs dry out for too long, as the shell will stick to the white and become difficult to remove.

Eggs mimosa

Hard-boil some eggs and leave to go really cold. Separate the whites from the yolks. Sieve the yolks. Sprinkle the cooked whites in a mayonnaise with the sieved yolks and some chopped parsley. Garnish with parsley or cress.

Hard-boiled eggs Norman style

Marbled eggs

Marbled eggs

Hard-boil some eggs. Break the shells without removing them, then plunge them into an infusion of tea for 15 minutes. Drain, then allow to cool. The colored liquid marbles the egg whites by penetrating into the cracks.

Pickled eggs

Put the hard-boiled eggs in a bottle. Boil some vinegar for 5 minutes with pepper, thyme, cloves, and four-spice. Pour the preparation over the eggs, allow them to cool, and place in the refrigerator. They will keep for 10 days.

Cooking

Boil a large amount of unsalted water. Plunge the eggs in one by one or all together in a metal basket. Adjust the heat so the water is simmering: cooking too fast risks breaking the shells and making the whites rubbery. Allow 9 minutes from the moment when the eggs enter the water. Cool the cooked eggs in cold water. This prevents them continuing to cook. Drain and shell them.

Tip

Contrary to a generally received idea, hard-boiled eggs do not harm the liver: fresh and cooked without any fat or oil they are easy to digest. Conversely, the yolk is high in cholesterol.

481

Eggs Brazilian style in an avocado nest

Eggs "en cocotte"

Butter some ramekins, then break 1–2 eggs into them, adding 1 tbsp of crème fraîche to each. Put them in a pre-heated bain-marie or baking pan of water, and place in the oven to cook; the white will harden while the yolk remains semi-soft.

Poaching eggs

1 Boil some unsalted water with a little vinegar in a shallow, fairly large pan and keep it simmering. Do not poach more than 4 eggs at a time. Allow 4 cups (1 liter) water to 3 eggs.

2 Carefully break the eggs into the water so that the yolk stays intact. Cover the pan and poach the eggs for 5–6 minutes. When cooked, the whites must be opaque and the yolks transparent and soft to the touch.

3 Remove the eggs from the water and drain on a slightly damp, folded napkin. Trim to shape with a small kitchen knife. Poached eggs can be served hot or cold with a range of sauces.

Advice

Poached eggs can seem difficult to prepare, whereas they are really so simple. The first condition is to use the freshest possible eggs. When plunged into a hot liquid, the white of an egg that is too old will spread into filaments without hardening, whereas the white of a fresher egg will stay together and coagulate immediately around the yolk. No special equipment is necessary: a skillet or shallow pan will be sufficient.

Cooking

It is important to keep the water at an even temperature when poaching. Adding eggs to water tends to cool it. Cook them a few at a time in a large amount of liquid. To keep them whole, break them beforehand in a cup and shake the pan a little so that the surface of the cooking liquid moves. Eggs are traditionally poached in water with a little vinegar added, but they can also be cooked in poultry bouillon or red wine, sometimes bound with flour or a roux to make a sauce to accompany them. To stop the white of a poached egg becoming too hard, make sure the cooking liquid is simmering, but not boiling. Cooking is tested by touch: the white should be firm and the yolk flexible. Allow 3–4 minutes for lightly poached eggs and 5–6 minutes for medium-poached ones.

Eggs in ramekins

1. Butter the ramekins. Pour 2 tbsp crème fraîche into each and break in the eggs without piercing them. Add salt and pepper and grate in a little nutmeg. Add 1 dab butter to each ramekin.

2. Put the ramekins in a shallow pan or skillet of water, to make a bain-marie. Place the pan over low heat so that the water simmers. Cover and cook thus for about 6 minutes. The eggs are ready when they feel just firm to the touch.

Presentation

After cooking, remove the eggs with a slotted spoon and drain on a clean, damp cloth. Then "shave" the egg by cutting off any irregularities with a small knife. Poached eggs are usually served hot in a salad, in sauce, or "au gratin." If you serve them cold, plunge them into very cold water when you remove them from their cooking water and then drain and shave them. Do not keep them like this longer than 48 hours. A variant is "eggs en cocotte."

Soup Lubéron

Advice

With very few exceptions, fried eggs are always cooked in a skillet. The skillet used has a considerable influence on the final result. A non-stick coating prevents the eggs from sticking during cooking and it is not essential to add any oil or fat. The cooked eggs are quite easy to digest, uniformly colored, and usually remain unbroken during cooking. This is a practical solution and is suitable for people on a low-fat diet. Conversely, purists use only a black cast-iron skillet. Here, fat or oil is essential to prevent the eggs from sticking. The taste of the melted, fresh butter is greatly appreciated, but one can also use fine lard and duck or goose fat, with their marked flavors, or peanut or sunflower oil whose neutral taste does not mask the taste of the eggs themselves. Whichever fat or oil is chosen, the quantity must be moderate. It should

Eggs Mexican style

cover the bottom of the skillet and not constitute a deep-frying medium. Similarly, and regardless of which method of cooking is chosen, the eggs must be put in the skillet when the fat is hot, but has not started to smoke. If it is smoking, the flavor will become acrid or bitter.

Vienna Holstein

Fried eggs with tomatoes

Plain fried eggs

Cooking

Put 1 tbsp butter in a skillet over medium heat. When foaming, break in the eggs. Tilt the skillet and moisten the yolks with hot butter. Cover the pan for about a minute. When the whites are firm, remove the skillet from the heat and slide the eggs on to a plate. Do not forget to season each yolk with salt and one turn of the pepper mill, or a dash of vinegar.

Fried eggs with red pimentos

Eggs Lorraine style

Variants

Eggs Lorraine style is prepared as follows: fry thin slices of bacon in some butter. Add the eggs and cook them for 3 minutes. Add salt and pepper, sprinkle with grated gruyère cheese, add 1 tsp cream per egg, and place in the oven at 350 °F (180 °C) for 4 minutes. Another idea—the famous English breakfast of bacon and eggs. The bacon is fried first in a little butter, then the eggs are added and cooked in turn.

Eggs, sausages, and bacon

Mirror eggs with herbs

Mirror eggs

These are cooked in a special ramekin of material similar to Corning Ware. Heat some butter in the ramekin over medium heat. Break in 2 eggs and cook for 1 minute. Cover the whites with crème fraîche. Firm the eggs by putting them in the oven at 350 °F (180 °C) for 4 minutes. Serve in the ramekin.

Tip

The undersides of fried eggs are always more thoroughly cooked than the tops. To correct this, finish cooking them by covering the skillet with a lid. Eggs can also be basted with hot fat using a spoon during cooking. The result will be a nice, golden surface.

Threaded egg

This is an unusual preparation method whose constraints are comparable to those of poached eggs. Here, too, the eggs must be absolutely fresh. Otherwise, they will form inconsistent threads that are too fine and virtually invisible,

so choose eggs in the extra-fresh category or recently laid ones. A few minutes before cooking them, the cold eggs, just out of the refrigerator, are beaten by hand for a moment to combine the whites and yolks. The threads are made directly in the food with which they are to be eaten. Threaded eggs are used in many Chinese and Asian soups, Italian dishes, and French soups such as the "tourin" of south western France, based on bouillon and onions cooked in goose fat.

Prepared plain, they garnish rice or pasta dishes or are served with salads. To make them, bring some water with a dash of vinegar to the boil and keep it simmering. Break and then beat the eggs in a basin for not more than 1 minute. Gently and concentrically swirl the vinegar and water. Progressively pour in the beaten eggs in a steady flow. The threads form instantly through coagulation. Drain after they have cooked for 1 minute.

Threaded eggs for soups

Bring the soup or broth to the boil and keep it simmering. Break and then beat the eggs in a salad bowl for not more than 1 minute. Slowly and concentrically swirl the liquid, and a small vortex will form in the center. Slowly pour the eggs into the soup in a regular flow. The threads will form instantly. Stop boiling and serve.

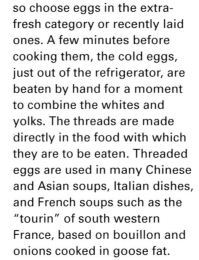

Tip

A fried egg should not touch the sides or bottom of the skillet, but should float and remain in suspension in a bath of oil. This oil must be hot when the eggs are put into it. It is important that they start frying at once.

Fried egg and threaded egg

Fried eggs

1 Heat 2$^{1}/_{2}$ in (6 cm) oil to simmering point in a deep skillet. Break the egg into a cup or glass, then slide it into the oil. Eggs for frying must be extra-fresh and should be cooked individually. The oil should be heated to 350 °F (180 °C) (i.e., smoking). Keep the glass as close as possible to the skillet to avoid being splashed by oil.

2 Use a wooden spatula to baste the surface of the egg and move the white around the yolk. Cook for about 1 minute. Remember that the eggs must be very fresh so that the white will coagulate immediately and coat and protect the yolk. An egg that is too old will spread over the pan and be impossible to serve.

3 Remove the egg with a dry, metal, slotted spoon. Handle carefully so as not to break it. Fry the other eggs in the same way.

Tip

For preference, use only neutral-tasting vegetable oils—peanut, corn, or sunflower oil—so as not to impair the flavor of the egg. Olive oil is sometimes used—it gives an unusual, fruity flavor, but cannot withstand excessive heat. Butter or margarine cannot be used because of the frying temperatures required.

4 Drain on paper towels. Serve at once: fried eggs should be served very hot. Accompany them with onion rings or fried parsley, broiled tomatoes, and slices of bacon fried in butter, or place them on toast, garnished with a few sprigs of parsley or chervil.

Plain scrambled eggs

1 Butter the inside of a thick-bottomed saucepan (diameter 5¹/₂ in/14 cm for 4–8 eggs). Break the eggs into a bowl and beat them vigorously to mix the yolks and whites, then strain them through a fine sieve. If you are planning to serve a garnish with the scrambled eggs, prepare it first—once the eggs are cooked they must not wait.

2 Add salt and pepper and about ³/₄ oz (20 g) butter per egg and 1 tbsp thick crème fraîche. Pour into the saucepan, place this in a skillet of water to form a bain-marie or double boiler, and heat gently. Scrambled eggs need a lot of fat. Choose butter of the best possible quality and new-laid eggs.

3 Stir the mixture constantly, taking care to scrape the bottom and sides of the pan so that the eggs do not stick. As soon as they have acquired the desired consistency, ideally that of a smooth cream, serve at once. Do not leave them in the pan, as they will continue to cook. The cooking time is relatively short (15 minutes for 6 eggs): the result should be creamy and smooth with no large lumps.

Tip
If your scrambled eggs are cooking too quickly and suddenly start to thicken, add 1 tbsp cold milk for 3 eggs and plunge the cooking pan into a basin or sink full of cold water.

Piperade

for 4

1 Finely chop 1 onion and fry it in olive oil in a skillet over medium heat. Add 2 chopped garlic cloves, 2 tomatoes cut into rough cubes, two sliced red pimentos, salt, and pepper. Cover and cook for 20 minutes, stirring with a wooden spoon, until the vegetables have become a purée.

2 Break and beat 6 eggs into a bowl. Pour them into the skillet and incorporate the cooked tomatoes and pimentos. Cook over moderate heat, constantly scraping so as to form small pieces of egg. Flavor the piperade with chopped parsley and a dash of olive oil. Turn it onto a serving platter, garnished with fried slices of Bayonne or Parma ham.

Eggs princess style

Scrambled eggs with gruyère

Scrambled eggs with salmon roe

Advice

The secret of scrambled eggs lies in one word: "patience." It is thanks to slow and gradual cooking that the liquid eggs are transformed into a creamy mass in which the whites and yolks are so closely bound they cannot be distinguished. Choose a thick-bottomed saucepan that will distribute the heat uniformly. Cook directly over a low gas flame or in a bain-marie or double boiler.

Scrambled eggs Provençal style

Scrambled eggs with mussels

Scrambled eggs with cilantro

Cooking and flavors

The exact point at which cooking is complete is not easy to determine. It depends on each person's taste and is measured by consistency: the more thoroughly the mixture is cooked, the harder it will be. The ideal consistency is that of a mixture that can just be picked up with a fork without falling off. The most usual accompaniments are sautéed white mushrooms or asparagus tips, but also tomatoes or even salmon roe and caviar. In season, sliced or chopped raw truffle can be used. To develop its aroma, break the eggs with the truffle and leave them in the refrigerator overnight. Plain scrambled eggs can also be served in a puff pastry crust.

Omelet with langoustines

Monteux omelet

Advice

There are many kinds of omelet, but all are based on beaten, whole eggs. The most usual omelet is folded over itself, with or without a filling. It is made in a black, cast-iron or non-stick skillet. The eggs should never be allowed to stick during cooking, which is done over quite a high heat. The cooking fat used is either oil (sunflower or peanut) or fresh butter, or a mixture of the two.

Tip
The size of the skillet is important: a diameter of 7 in (18 cm) is suitable for 3 eggs, while 10 in (25 cm) is perfect for 5 eggs.

Flat zucchini omelet

Green pimento omelet

Variants

There are many fillings for omelets: from tomatoes to mushrooms, chanterelle and cep, to sorrel with bell pepper. The filling is incorporated during cooking, before the omelet is folded over. It is also possible to make a flat omelet, the thickness of which can be varied to taste. The beaten eggs are poured into a hot skillet and gently spread out with a fork, so that the omelet takes the shape of the pan as it cooks.

Plain omelet

Break the eggs into a bowl and season with salt and pepper. Heat 1 tbsp butter in a skillet and beat the eggs with a fork. Pour the eggs into the skillet all at once, before the butter begins to smoke. Move the back of the fork through the liquid egg, taking care not to scratch the skillet. Continue like this until the omelet reaches the desired consistency. Fold it by bringing the edges to the middle. Seal and cook through for another moment or two, pressing down with the tines of the fork. Turn the omelet onto a serving platter with a single movement and dab with a little butter.

490

Flat omelet with tomatoes and pimentos

for 4

1 Wash one red and one green pimento, remove the stalks, cut them in two, and seed. Cut the flesh into fine strips. Peel 2 medium-sized onions and chop very finely. Wash 2 tomatoes and cut them into fine slices. If you want to add flavor to this omelet, you can add one finely sliced chili.

2 Heat 2 tbsp olive oil in a large skillet. Add the pimentos and onions and sauté them for 10 minutes, stirring with a spatula. Fry the tomatoes rapidly in another oiled skillet and reduce them to a purée. If they give off too much water, remove the surplus liquid with a spoon.

3 Add the puréed tomatoes to the onion and pimento mixture and cook for 10 minutes, season with salt and pepper, and set aside. Break 3 eggs into a basin, add salt, pepper, and 1 tbsp chopped chives, and beat together with a fork. You can use thyme or basil instead of chives.

4 Pour the eggs onto the cooked vegetables. Cook the mixture over medium heat, preventing it from sticking, until it has thickened well. Let the underside color for 30 seconds, then turn the omelet over like a pancake and cook for a further 2 minutes. Serve in a round dish, cut into triangular sections like a tart. Eat hot or cold.

Soufflé parmentier

The art of the soufflé

For long the preserve of the great chefs, soufflés are now cooked in all kitchens. Remember that a cooked soufflé never waits and will lose three quarters of its volume if it is not served as soon as it is removed from the oven. The bigger a soufflé, the gentler and more gradual the cooking should be. Sweet soufflés are based on sugared egg yolks, blanched and floured, or pastry cream (also called confectioner's

Spinach soufflé

Grapefruit soufflés

custard), into which stiffly beaten egg whites have been incorporated. Soufflés can be flavored with vanilla, orange flower water, and rum, as well as fruit: mandarin, pineapple, orange, and lemon. For fruit soufflés, use deep-frozen fruit purées, unless you are using banana purée. Savory soufflés are always prepared according to the same principle: a thick white Béchamel type sauce is mixed with an ingredient (cheese, fish, vegetables) and then stiffly beaten egg whites are added.

Chicken liver soufflé

Chocolate soufflé

Chocolate soufflé

To serve 6, break 7 oz (200 g) dark chocolate into pieces and melt in a bain-marie or double boiler. Break 6 eggs and separate the whites from the yolks. Sieve 2^1/$_2$ tbsp (40 g) cornstarch and mix with a generous ^{1}/$_4$ cup (60 g) sugar. Incorporate the yolks into the melted chocolate, followed by 1 sachet vanilla sugar and the cornstarch-sugar mixture. Beat the egg whites stiffly and add a scant ^{1}/$_4$ cup (50 g) sugar. Incorporate into the yolk mixture and pour into a buttered and sugared soufflé dish. Cook at 430 °F (220 °C) for 30 minutes.

Banana soufflé

**Savory
soufflé**

for 4

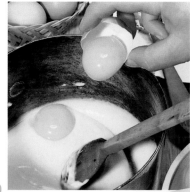

1 Before preparing the soufflé cream, butter the dish in which it is to be cooked and grate or chop the cheese you will need later. Prepare 2 cups (50 cl) basic Béchamel sauce with 1 2/3 cups (40 cl) milk, 2 oz (60 g) butter, and 1/3 cup (40 g) flour. Heat the butter in a saucepan. When it has melted, add the flour and mix vigorously with a wooden spoon. Cook over low heat continually stirring with a beater or spoon for about 2 minutes, to obtain a light colored roux.

2 When the mixture is well blended, pour in the milk and cook, while stirring, for 20 minutes until a smooth consistency is obtained. For soufflés that will always be successful, keep to the following proportions: one-third for the "base," two-thirds for the stiffly beaten egg whites. Also make sure that the consistency of the base is not too firm: it would produce a very uneven result.

3 Add 1 pinch of salt and nutmeg, 5 1/2 oz (150 g) grated gruyère (or chopped Blue Auvergne or even Roquefort cheese) and 4 egg yolks. Beat the egg whites stiffly with 1 pinch salt (not too much, because of the cheese). Fold the whites into the base and pour into a buttered 1 1/2-quart (1.5-liter) soufflé dish.

Tip

To obtain well risen, even soufflés, fill the molds to 3/8 in (1 cm) below the rim. Being lighter, the soufflé will rise more easily. To butter the molds, chill them in the refrigerator for 30 minutes, then swirl them with melted butter. The cream will not stick to the walls when the soufflé is developing.

4 Cook in the oven at 345–350 °F (175–180 °C) for about 35 minutes. If you cook this soufflé in small, individual molds, reduce the time to 15–20 minutes.

Crème caramel

for 6

1 Melt a scant ¹/₂ cup (100g) sugar moistened with a little water in a pan, and heat until it turns brown. Coat the cooking mold with it. If the mold is flameproof, melt the sugar in it directly over medium heat. If not, prepare the caramel in a small saucepan and place the empty mold in a warm oven, so that caramel does not congeal when it is ready. Tilt the mold both ways to coat the bottom and sides evenly.

2 Separately, boil 2 cups (50 cl) milk with 1 vanilla bean cut in two lengthwise, and keep it simmering. Put 2 yolks and 2 whole eggs into a bowl with a scant ¹/₂ cup (100 g) sugar. Beat together with the warm milk. Eggs that are too old will not sufficiently solidify the mixture, which will either remain flaccid in spite of prolonged cooking or result in an unpleasant, gritty texture.

3 Filter the mixture and pour into the caramelized mold. Put the mold in a barely simmering bain-marie or baking pan of water. Cook in the oven at 300 °F (150 °C) for 40 minutes. The crème is done when the blade of a knife plunged into it emerges clean. Leave to cool completely and serve chilled. Take care with the cooking: if overcooked, the crème will be pitted with holes; if undercooked, it will be soft and lack texture.

Eggs in milk

for 6

1 Put 1 scant cup (200 g) superfine sugar and 4 cups (1 liter) milk in a saucepan, mix, bring to the boil, and keep the mixture simmering. Break 8 whole eggs into a bowl and beat for 2 minutes. Pour the warm, sweetened milk over the eggs. Mix well. Filter the mixture through a fine sieve and pour into a buttered mold.

2 Put the mold in a barely simmering bain-marie or baking pan of water. Cover with aluminum foil. Cook in the oven at 350 °F (180 °C) for about 35 minutes. Instead of superfine sugar, you can vary the taste of this dish by using either 1 scant cup (200 g) brown sugar lightly flavored with rum, or 4 tbsp fir- or lime-tree honey.

3 The crème is ready when the blade of a knife inserted into it emerges clean. Leave to cool completely and serve chilled. This dish makes a perfect end to a rather rich meal. You can also flavor it like any other flan with vanilla, a liqueur, or the finely grated zest of a lemon, orange, or grapefruit.

Desserts with eggs

Snowballs

for 6

1 A simple mixture of stiffly beaten egg whites and sugar produces a light, foamy, and refreshing dessert that is always enjoyed. Stiffly beat 8 egg whites using an electric beater. Then add $2/3$ cup (150 g) superfine sugar and continue beating to obtain a stiff mousse. It must adhere firmly to the beater and take on a satiny look.

2 Mold the mousse into patties or balls using a soup spoon or two spatulas, then cook in 4 cups (1 liter) simmering milk. Allow 1 minute each side, then drain. Working quite quickly, you can poach 3 balls at a time. When they are well drained, put them in a large colander, avoiding piling them on top of one another.

3 Leave to cool, then place the snowballs on 4 cups (1 liter) custard and garnish with caramel, black chocolate shavings, or broiled, slivered almonds. You can also place the snowballs on a red fruit sauce with a garnish of blueberries and fresh half strawberries: the contrast between the textures and flavors will be especially successful.

Floating islands

for 6

1 Very similar to simple egg snowballs and often confused with them, floating islands make a very light dessert. Stiffly beat 8 egg whites with a pinch of salt using an electric beater. Then add $2/3$ cup (150 g) superfine sugar and beat vigorously to obtain a fine mousse.

2 Mold the egg whites into six "islands" and place in a buttered soufflé dish. Cook in the oven, in a bain-marie or baking pan of water, at 300 °F (150 °C) for 25 minutes. Leave to cool, then place on 4 cups (1 liter) custard and drizzle with brown caramel. Using the separated yolks, prepare a vanilla custard for final presentation.

495

Club Mornay

There are all sorts of recipes for additions to a croque-monsieur: for example, slices of bread are spread with a thick layer of cheese Béchamel sauce and garnished with cooked ham and tomato slices.

Raclette

Raclette is a traditional recipe from the Valais region of France. To serve 4, cut 1 lb 5 oz (600 g) raclette cheese into small slices 1/16 in (4 mm) thick. Melt the cheese, taking care that the process does not take too long, and pour onto boiled potatoes. Season with pepper and serve with pickled onions and gherkins. Raclette goes well with smoked ham or bacon.

Brewers' croque-monsieur

For an unusual snack, prepare croque-monsieur garnished with small frankfurters, slices of

Beaufort or Comté cheese, and strong mustard. Eat with beer: Pilsener, for example.

Croque-monsieur

For this delicious and easy-to-make recipe, choose the best gruyère and red-seal, white ham. Butter slices of bread.

Cover them with alternating layers of cheese and meat. Brown on each side in a skillet over low heat.

Fondue, raclette, and croque-monsieur

Advice

Hard cheeses cut into pieces and slowly heated in white wine turn into a smooth sauce. The melting temperature is an important factor in the success of this dish: overheating or heating too quickly separates the fats from the proteins, so that the mixture ceases to flow and appears oily and dull. The cooking vessel is a thick-bottomed, enameled steel fondue pot. During the meal it is kept hot by a heater or small spirit lamp. The choice of wine is important: opt for very dry and fruity whites.

Fondue for 4

Tip

There are several varieties of fondue, depending on which cheese is used: Savoy style, Neuchâtel style, and Vaud style. In Wales, we find Welsh rarebit using cheddar and beer, and in Italy the delicious fonduta made with fontina, egg yolks, and white truffles.

1 Cut 1 lb 5 oz (600 g) cheese into thin, regular strips after carefully removing the rind. Mix several varieties (gruyère, comté, and emmental). Rub the walls of a fondue pot with a clove of skinned garlic. Cut about 10½ oz (300 g) slightly stale, farmhouse bread into regular, bite-sized pieces.

2 Pour in 1 generous cup (25 cl) white wine and half the cheese. Heat slowly while stirring. When the mixture has melted, pour in the other half of the cheese and continue heating gently. Cooking must be done over moderate heat while stirring continually with a wooden spoon so that the cheese melts evenly without forming lumps.

3 When a smooth blend is obtained, mix 1 tsp cornstarch in some dry, fruity white wine and bind the fondue. Add pepper and nutmeg to taste. Stir 1–2 tbsp kirsch into the fondue and serve immediately. Keep the fondue pot warm throughout the meal.

Endives au gratin with gruyère

for 6

1 Cut off the roots of 6 nice, well-blanched endives and remove the damaged leaves. Cook for 10 minutes in plenty of water with salt and lemon added. Drain and wipe the endives. If they are not well drained the sauce will be too liquid. Separately, prepare 1¼ cups (30 cl) Béchamel sauce finished with 1 egg yolk.

2 Roll each endive in a slice of ham. Choose top quality white ham that is soft and quite fat, in slices big enough to wrap the endives completely. Trim the ham first, removing the rind. Do not use dry ham. You can, however, use braised ham.

3 Arrange the endives in a baking pan, covered with the sauce. Sprinkle with grated gruyère and cook at 430 °F (220 °C) for about 12 minutes. Instead of gruyère or Beaufort cheese, you can use a mixture of emmental and parmesan. If necessary, scatter a few dabs of butter on top of the gratin before putting it in the oven.

Gratin of onion soup

for 6

1 Sauté 2¼ lb (1 kg) finely chopped onions moistened with 1 scant cup (20 cl) dry white wine, then add 6 cups (1.5 liters) beef bouillon and cook slowly for 1 hour. Season with salt and pepper. Onion soup au gratin is a typically Parisian dish traditionally served in the bistros of Les Halles (the former Parisian wholesale food market) where people ate late. It was said to have the merit of warding off a hangover.

2 Pour the soup into small, individual, ovenproof china soup bowls. Put in thin slices of toast. Sprinkle on a generous layer of grated gruyère. Put under the broiler for 4–5 minutes. Just before pouring the soup into the soup bowls you can add a sauce to it made with 3 egg yolks and ⅓ cup + 1½ tbsp (10 cl) port. Serve piping hot.

Gratin of potatoes Savoy style

for 6

1 Choose Belle de Fontenay or Bintje potatoes. You can also make a mixture of cheeses (comté, emmental, gruyère). Cut 2 lb 11 oz (1.2 kg) potatoes into slices about $1/8$ in (3 mm) thick. Rinse and drain them, then season with salt and pepper. To obtain fine, regular slices, use a special grater or, better still, a mandoline.

2 Butter a gratin dish and rub it with 1 peeled garlic clove cut in two, then place the seasoned potato slices in it. It is the addition of grated cheese that distinguishes the Savoy-style gratin from the Dauphinoise style. You can also sprinkle a few spoonfuls between the layers of potato slices.

3 Beat together 1 scant cup (20 cl) milk, 1 egg, and a few pinches of grated nutmeg. Pour the mixture over the potatoes. You can replace the milk bound with egg with quite strongly flavored chicken or beef bouillon. Pour it over the potatoes to give it time to penetrate to the bottom of the dish. Salt moderately because of the cheese and add pepper according to taste.

4 Sprinkle on $4^1/2$ oz (120 g) finely grated cheese and dab with butter. Bake at 400 °F (200 °C) for about 1 hour and 20 minutes. If the heat is too intense the dish will cook unevenly: the oven must not be hotter than 430 °F (220 °C). This temperature enables the cheeses to melt gradually before browning.

Tip

The greater the area exposed to heat, the more even the color will be. Do not prepare gratins in dishes that are too small, and use finely grated cheese rather than pieces, whichever types of cheese you choose. If you can, use a fan-assisted oven.

Cheese tart with chives

For all tastes

Quiches, tarts, pies, and pizzas are nourishing dishes and can form the main course of a meal. Accompany them with a simple salad or sliced, raw vegetables. They are easy to make. First of all, choose cheeses that are not too mature. Remove the rind of blue cheeses and cooked or pressed cream cheeses.

Goats' cheese tart

Tart with comté cheese and bacon

Retain the rind of goats' cheeses and rinsed cream cheeses. The various forms of tart pastry are best for cheese-based recipes. A distinction is made between tarts in which the cheese comes into direct contact with the heat of the oven and pies in which, conversely, the filling cooks under a pastry cover. Pastry prevents the cheese from running out during cooking. The most commonly used is piecrust, with or without the addition of an egg yolk. It can be found ready-prepared in stores, but the flavor of homemade pastry is inimitable

Cabécou cheese tartlets

Rillette tart Tours style

and it is easy to make. When using a particularly wet cheese filling, it is a good idea to pre-cook the pastry shell in the oven to keep it as dry as possible. Puff pastry is chosen for pies, its texture and appearance being highly prized. Almost all kinds of cheese can be used. Your choice should be guided by the result you are seeking: blue cheeses for strong flavors, cooked cream cheeses for their oiliness, and fromage frais to lighten the texture.

Corsican broccio cheese tart

Tip
For all these recipes, avoid pieces of cheese that are too thick—they will not melt properly during cooking.

Pizzas, quiches, and cheese tarts

Quiches

Quiches can be prepared in numerous ways based on the model of the quiche Lorraine with bacon. People also like serving them with a cooked cream cheese that adds its oiliness and characteristic threads. But they are also delicious with small goats' cheeses such as Cabécou. Blue cheese is wonderful: choose a nice slice of fourme d'Ambert cheese, remove the rind, and mix it with the egg-cream-milk blend: the result is surprising. It is also worth highlighting the compatibilities between fillings and cheeses. A subtle combination is fresh salmon and mozzarella, mushrooms go well with cantal or laguiole cheese, and a quiche with smoked

Mozzarella pizza and egg pizza

Goyère Flanders style

magret of duck or langres cheese is a refined delight. Lastly, there is the "goyère," a specialty of northern France prepared with maroilles, a big slab of cheese with a strong flavor and unique aroma, from which the rind has to be removed.

Cheese pie with thyme

Flamiche

This is a fairly thick tart originating from the Picardy region of France. It is usually prepared with leeks. Flamiches can also be cooked with onions.

Pizzas

These are made with bread dough and vary according to the cheeses and garnishes used. We are familiar with the margherita based on mozzarella, basil, and tomatoes, the four-cheese pizza with comté, goats' cheese, and gouda, and the "four seasons" with sliced vegetables, olives, and cheese. Finely grated blue cheeses are also used. Avoid using only cooked cream cheeses on pizzas. Combine them with lighter cheeses: goat's cheese without too much salt, for example. Try the little-known, but tasty, Italian fondita too.

Tip

If the cheese overhangs the dough during cooking, it becomes impossible to remove it from the mold. Avoid this problem by lining your mold with buttered and floured wax paper.

501

Triangles of fromage frais

White cheese tart with honey

Chester cake

Cooking

Fromage frais lends itself well to cooking. It is the basis of many desserts. The cheese used must have a fairly neutral taste. Its freshness and rich texture is highly prized, and it should be cooked fairly slowly and gently: excessive heat would impair the cheese and its flavor. These dishes must also be allowed to cool before being eaten: this improves both texture and taste to a remarkable degree. Put the fromage frais in the refrigerator overnight, wrapped tightly in plastic film. The most often-used types of fromage frais are cottage cheese (drained in a cheese-draining cloth), mascarpone, cream cheese, and ricotta.

Ricotta tart

Fromage frais tart

To serve 4–6, put 4 egg yolks and 1 lb (450 g) ricotta in a bowl and beat to obtain a smooth mixture. Melt $3^1/_2$ oz (100 g) butter and incorporate it into the cheese, stirring constantly. Then add a scant $1/_2$ cup (55 g) flour, $2/_3$ cup (150 g) superfine sugar, and 3 drops vanilla extract. Beat the egg whites stiffly and mix them with the cheese. Pour it all into a pre-cooked, floured pastry shell. Smooth the surface. Bake in the oven at 320–330 °F (160–165 °C) for 50 minutes. Personalize it by adding finely chopped preserved fruit.

Cheesecake

To serve 5–6, put 13 oz (370 g) Kiri- or Samos-type cheese and 7 oz (200 g) smooth white cheese in a bowl and mix with $3/_4$ cup (175 g) sugar and 4 eggs. Add 4 drops vanilla flavoring, $2^3/_4$ oz (80 g) melted butter, and $7/_8$ cup (100 g) flour. Pour into a pre-cooked, floured pastry shell. Bake at 345 °F (175 °C) for 40 minutes.

Cheese straws and sweet pastries

Advice

Cheese is also useful for making excellent little canapés. They usually combine puff pastry made with butter and a filling of cooked gruyère, emmenthal, etc. Parmesan also gives good results, but is rather dry. Add another "melting" cheese for texture. Cheese straws do not keep well once cooked. The dough can, however, be frozen before cooking and thawed out when required. Make the puff pastry yourself: the result will be outstanding. If you buy ready-made pastry, choose a product made with butter and which has not been rolled out.

Cheese twists

for 4

Tip

When cheese cannot be drained and seems too fluid, add 1 tsp cornstarch per 7 oz (200 g) cheese.

1 Prepare a piecrust with 2 generous cups (250 g) flour, 3^1/$_2$ oz (100 g) butter, and a little fine salt. While mixing, incorporate 2 tbsp thick crème fraîche and 3^1/$_2$ oz (100 g) finely grated soft cheese. Form a ball combining all the ingredients.

2 Press the dough into a container measuring 10–12 in (25–30 cm) square. Cut the slab using a serrated cutter. Make strips 3/8 in (1 cm) wide by 2 in (5 cm) long. Roll them over on themselves to form little twists. Butter a baking sheet.

3 Brush the pastry twists with egg yolk. Bake them in the oven at 430 °F (220 °C) for about 10 minutes. Leave to cool completely on a wire rack before serving. You can keep them for a few days in an airtight container.

503

The parish priest's omelet

In the world of the culinary arts, Jean-Anthelme Brillat-Savarin is an appealing figure. A judge, a chemist, and a member of the Constituent Assembly, he is known today for his contribution to gastronomy. Apart from his articles and works on the subject, he left a series of recipes including the famous "parish priest's omelet." In its original form, this omelet was prepared as follows: obtain some carp's roe. Soak in water and vinegar, then blanch. Slowly fry in butter, shallots, and parsley. Mix with beaten eggs and cook as an omelet (quite a liquid one, it would appear). This is an 18th-century recipe and is therefore a little out of date. Nowadays, gourmets still prepare the parish priest's omelet, but not in exactly the same way. Large and richly filled, it will be the star dish of your menu.

Serves 4
Preparation: 25 minutes
Cooking: 16 minutes

Ingredients

2 dozen snails
1 shallot
1 oz (30 g) fresh or canned truffles
3$^1/_2$ oz (100 g) part-cooked liver pâté
10 eggs
Butter
A few chive sprigs
Salt and pepper

1 Drain the snails. Burgundy snails are the biggest and most highly prized. Preparing snails oneself requires care and patience, which is why snails are canned. They are easy to use because they only need draining and chilling before use and make a good alternative, provided they come from a good source.

2 Peel and finely chop 1 shallot. Cook the snails gently for 10 minutes with the shallot. Watch the heat carefully so this little stew heats gently without really cooking, which would risk toughening the snails and making them rubbery. Peel and chop one or more truffles.

3 Add to the pan and cook for a further 3 minutes. An average-sized truffle weighs 1–2 oz (30–60 g). Fresh truffles (in season) are the most tasty and economical, but canned truffles (labeled "choice"), brushed, raw, and simply salted, can also be highly recommended.

4 Remove the pan from the heat. Add the liver pâté cut into cubes (use duck liver pâté). Mere contact with the other hot ingredients is enough to make its surface melt slightly. Once it is added to the filling, stop heating.

5 Vigorously beat the eggs until they are foamy, and season with salt and pepper. Heat a few dabs of butter in a skillet big enough to contain a 10-egg omelet and all the filling. When the butter foams, tip in the beaten eggs. Cook, making sure they do not stick to the bottom of the skillet.

6 Put the snails, liver pâté, and truffles into the skillet, wait a few seconds, and then fold the omelet over the filling. Keep it moist or cook until fairly firm, according to taste. Transfer to a well-heated platter, sprinkle with chopped chives, and serve immediately.

General points

Butter is a fatty foodstuff obtained by churning the cream of milk. It is mixed and washed cold so as to isolate the buttermilk in it. Butter contains 82 percent fats, the other 18 percent consisting essentially of water and proteins. It includes saturated and unsaturated fatty acids, cholesterol, and liposoluble vitamins A and D, and provides 750 calories per $3^{1}/_{2}$ oz (100 g). Its color varies from straw yellow to broken white, depending on the type of milk used. Its smell should be quite subtle and reminiscent of nuts with no other alien flavor. There are different categories of butter. Raw butter is prepared from cream and milk which has not undergone any other kind of temperature processing other than refrigeration. It is the tastiest, but its conservation time is brief. Extra-fine butter is manufactured with pasteurized milk. It keeps well and is

suitable for all normal purposes. Fine butter is made from pasteurized milk. Some of the cream from which it is derived may have been frozen. This product should be reserved for pastry-making, recipes that require intense cooking. Semi-salted butter contains between 0.5 and 2 percent salt. Salted butter contains much more, up to 4.5 percent, and is made from the three preceding categories. Lastly, there are low-fat butters (41–65 percent) and "special milk products for spreading" (20–40 percent) where the fat is replaced by water (and sometimes mixed with vegetable fats). Butter is kept in the refrigerator, away from light and the ambient air. It should be stored in plastic wrap covered in aluminum foil. If it is left unprotected for a few hours, its surface will oxidize and a rancid flavor will develop.

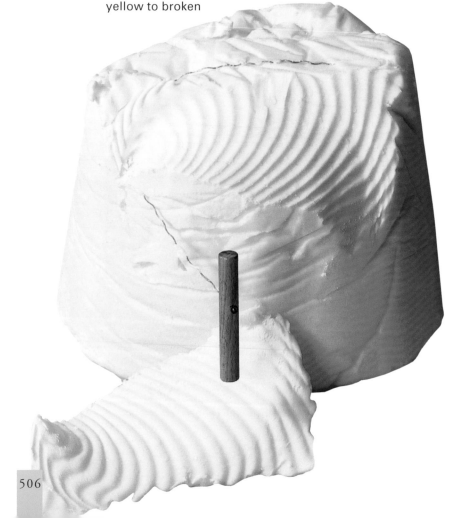

Uses

Uncooked, butter is eaten spread on bread or melted on broiled red meat, fish, and vegetables. It is mixed with various ingredients—anchovies, garlic, or parsley—to produce butters with the same name. Worked, that is to say, mixed with an equal

quantity of flour, butter is a preferred binding agent for white sauces. Incorporated in small pieces, it fills out and softens stuffings and fish mousses. It has countless uses in cooking. Whipped butters can be made with it (white butter) as well as cooked, emulsified sauces (béarnaise, hollandaise). Melted with lemon juice or as "beurre noisette" it accompanies poached fish. Never eat black butter, as it is somewhat indigestible. A dab of butter in a soup or broth enriches the taste. Pastry, especially puff pastry, would not exist without butter: its creamy, melting consistency giving texture to both sweet and savory dishes. All cookie recipes contain butter. It must be allowed to reach room temperature before it is incorporated as it then becomes easier to knead.

Eggs and tradition

According to many traditions, the world was hatched from an egg. The Egyptians exchanged eggs at the spring equinox. A symbol of life and a sign of perfection, the egg features in the most diverse civilizations, which attach rites and beliefs to it. In Europe, the tradition of decorated eggs arose in the fifteenth century. Later, after Easter Mass, the Sun King would distribute painted eggs to his courtiers. Then there were the famous Fabergé eggs, which were real jewels. Nowadays, the use of eggs has continued, taking on new forms, and they always play a leading role at Easter. They are eaten either cooked (poached,

Egg marbled with tea

Multicolored eggs

scrambled, jellied in aspic) or presented in unusual ways. The most remarkable preparations are: Easter pie, colored eggs, and chocolate eggs. Colored eggs are fun to prepare and will give your Easter meal a unique touch. The principle is as follows: boil some water containing natural colorants and let them infuse, then cool. Plunge in the eggs and cook them to your taste. The harder, and therefore more cooked, the egg, the more vividly colored it will be. By wrapping a string round the egg you will create white patterns on its shell. Natural colorants are: beet (purple), onion and saffron (yellow), tea (brown), spinach (green), and bilberry (violet). After cooking and cooling the eggs, wipe and polish them with a cloth soaked in peanut oil.

Easter eggs Sicilian style

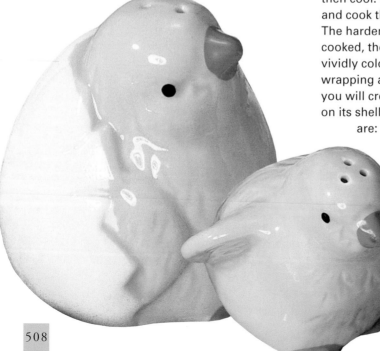

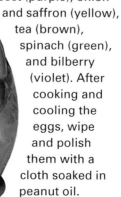

Preparing the pie

Easter pie

This is a pork or veal stuffing, seasoned with salt, pepper, four-spice, and liqueur, into which whole, peeled eggs are incorporated, the whole then being wrapped in a crust and baked in the oven. The puff pastry is often enriched with finely chopped goat's cheese. This pie is served warm or cold. The pastry crust specialty made without a mold used to be a traditional part of the Easter Sunday dinner in the Berry region of France. It was followed by a braised leg or stuffed shoulder of lamb.

Easter pie

Chocolate eggs

They can be molded in the shell. To do this, empty the egg as follows: pierce two holes, one at each end of the egg, insert a stick, stirring, then blow gently so that the contents run out. Melt some chocolate and add 1 tbsp butter. Then fill the empty shells and let them cool. Shell-less chocolate eggs are bigger, and are prepared using molds: melt the chocolate, then coat the inside of the molds, letting the surplus run out. Bring the two half-molds together, then let the chocolate set. Carefully remove the mold and decorate each egg with a colored ribbon. These eggs can be prepared using white, dark, or milk chocolate.

Chocolate eggs

An Easter menu

Easter pie
Jellied eggs with smoked salmon
Roast leg of lamb
Cheese
Snow eggs
Decorated eggs, white and black chocolate eggs.

Cheese ramekins

A party dish

Serves 4
Preparation: 15 minutes
Cooking: 20 minutes

Ingredients

2 cups (50 cl) milk

Nutmeg

3½ oz (100 g) Emmental cheese

4 eggs

1¾ oz (50 g) butter

½ can peeled tomatoes

1 tbsp olive oil

1 bouquet garni: parsley, thyme, bay

2 crushed garlic cloves

2 tsp lemon juice

Salt and pepper

1. Put the milk in a small saucepan with a little salt, pepper, and grated nutmeg. Heat and boil for a few moments.

2. Grate the cheese. Break the eggs into a bowl, beat them as for an omelet with a hand whisk, then pour in the boiling milk in a thin stream, while beating. Add the grated cheese, continuing to beat. Distribute this mixture in small, previously buttered ramekins. Put the ramekins in a baking pan and pour in hot water up to two thirds of their height.

3. Set over medium heat until the first bubbles rise, then put the whole thing in the center of the oven at 330 °F (165°C). Cook for 15–20 minutes. The contents of the ramekins should then be fairly firm to the touch.

4. While the ramekins are heating, put the drained tomatoes in a small casserole with the olive oil, bouquet garni, garlic, salt and pepper. Cook this mixture so as to obtain a good coulis when the ramekins are perfectly cooked: crush the tomatoes with a fork when they start to boil and let them simmer, covered or uncovered depending on how liquid they are.

5. To serve, coat the serving dish (or dinner plates) with a little of the coulis, place the cheese custard from the ramekins over, and garnish with a few sprigs of parsley.

Recommended drinks

Jurançon sec
Bourgogne aligoté
Côtes-du-Jura

Menu suggestions

1. Serve these ramekins as an appetizer, followed by baked sea bream and a gratin of citrus fruits, still with the same wine.

2. You could also follow these ramekins with roast veal and mushrooms and a blackcurrant bavarois for dessert.

Empanadas con huevos (egg turnovers)

An exotic dish

Serves 4
Preparation: 15 minutes
Resting: 2 hours
Cooking: 25 minutes

Ingredients

For the pastry:

1³/₄ cups (300 g) wheat flour
1 tsp sugar
2 tbsp olive oil
1 tsp salt

For the filling:

Olive oil
1 onion
6¹/₂ oz (180 g) small smoked bacon
  slices
1 can red kidney beans
1 tsp chili powder
1 egg per turnover
Salt

1. Prepare the pastry. Crumble the yeast into a bowl and dissolve it in ³/₄ cup (15 cl) of warm water. Let it swell for a few moments. Make a well in the flour and pour the yeast into the middle with the sugar and salt. Gradually incorporate the flour, working quickly with your fingertips until you obtain a smooth, malleable pastry.

2. Knead it for 10 minutes, gather it into a ball, flatten it by pulling, form it back into a ball, and put it in a clean bowl. Cover the bowl with a cloth and let it rest for 2 hours in a warm place.

3. Prepare the filling. Heat a dash of oil in a large skillet, add the peeled and chopped onion, and sweat it for 5 minutes. Incorporate the bacon slices and the drained kidney beans. Let the mixture heat for 5 minutes, adding the chili. Remove from the heat.

4. Heat the oven to 410 °F (210°C). Flatten the pastry with floured hands, pushing it in front of you. Cut it into fairly thin circles 8 in (20 cm) in diameter (using a plate as a guide). Place the circles on an oiled baking sheet.

5. Cover only half the surface of each with the filling. Form a well in the center of the filling and break 1 egg into it. Salt the egg. Moisten the edges of the pastry. Fold the unfilled part over the filled part and pinch the edges, forming a turnover. Brush with oil and cook in the oven for about 15 minutes. Serve with oil flavored with pimento or Tabasco®.

Recommended drinks

Very cold beer
Provençal rosé
Madiran

Menu suggestions

1. If you serve these turnovers as an appetizer, continue the exotic note with a chicken and pimento fricassee and coconut ice cream.

2. These turnovers can also be served hot as hors d'oeuvres with a lime cocktail.

513

Feuilleté of ham and fromage frais

An easy dish

Serves 5
Preparation time: 20 minutes
Rest time: 1 hour

Ingredients

2 tomatoes

Herbs in season

1 lb 2 oz (500 g) fromage frais

10 fine slices cooked ham

Salt and ground pepper

1. Peel and seed the tomatoes, after plunging them briefly in boiling water. Coarsely chop their pulp and the herbs. Mix the well-drained white cheese with this mixture, adding salt and pepper.

2. Remove the rind and much of the fat from the slices of ham. Line the bottom of a rectangular dish with the ham and put a layer of flavored white cheese on top of it. Put in a second layer of ham, and so on, until you have used up all the ingredients (finishing with a layer of ham).

3. Put the dish somewhere cool for at least an hour before cutting the preparation into slices the size of a mille-feuille. Serve these feuilletés accompanied by a green salad and mustard.

The success of this dish depends essentially on choosing the right cheese: the range is relatively large. You can in fact choose either a fromage frais made from cow's milk (for example, Saint-Florentin, Neufchâtel, or carré Gervais), or fromage frais made from goat's or ewe's milk whose taste is stronger and less creamy (Chavroux, Corsican broccio, Banon frais, or even Italian ricotta). You can also use an industrially produced cheese flavored with pepper, herbs, or garlic (of the Boursin, Tartare, or Roulé type). On the other hand, avoid white cheeses that too are watery, or the feuilletés will not "take." Use best-quality ham. It should be soft, not too moist, and of an even pink color. For the accompanying salad, use oak-leaf lettuce, which best complements the combination of flavors.

Recommended drinks

Bandol rosé
Muscadet
Chinon

Menu suggestions

1. Fresh, easy, and quick to prepare, this appetizer can precede lamb chops and green beans with fruits in season for dessert.

2. You can also prepare this feuilleté in the morning to serve in the evening, for a quick dinner with a chicken and sweetcorn salad and crème caramel.

Chanterelles with Beaufort cheese

An easy dish

Serves 4
Preparation: 10 minutes
Cooking: 15 minutes

Ingredients

2¼ lb (1 kg) chanterelles

Vinegar

1 small bacon slice

⅓ cup + 1½ tbsp (10 cl) oil

2 garlic cloves

1 bunch parsley

3½ oz/100 g Beaufort cheese

Salt and pepper

1. Clean and sort the chanterelles, breaking them into two or three pieces depending on their size. Put them one by one into a bowl containing enough water and vinegar to cover them easily. Wash them in this water carefully, rinse them in fresh water and drain them. If the chanterelles you have bought, or gathered yourself, are not very dirty, simply cut off the base which may be muddy and dust them using a pastry brush. Leaving them in water too long risks making them taste insipid.

2. Remove the rind from the bacon and cut it into small lardoons. Heat the oil in a large skillet. Put in the chanterelles and sweat them with the lid on over low heat until they begin to swim in their own juice. Then add the bacon, salt, and pepper, and continue cooking, with the lid off, over high heat. Reduce the heat when the water has almost completely evaporated.

3. Then add the chopped garlic and parsley. Grate the Beaufort cheese over the top. Let it fry for 1 or 2 minutes in the oil, which will have become clear again. Serve on a hot dish or in the skillet itself (in which case, remove some of the cooking oil).

The texture of Beaufort is smooth with no holes. Manufactured in Alpine chalets, it has a fine, fruity flavor. Instead, you can use Comté, Fribourg, or Appenzell. If you like the taste, use smoked pork belly: it goes very well with the flavor of the mushrooms and the cheese. It is important to serve this dish very hot as soon as cooking is complete.

Recommended drinks

Bergerac rouge
Côtes-du-Jura blanc
Roussette de Savoie

Menu suggestions

1. Accompanied by a chicory and walnut salad, these chanterelles can make a dinner, with apple tart for dessert.

2. This chanterelle fricassee can be an accompaniment for trout meunière style. Serve a soup to start with and fromage frais for dessert.

515

Egg gratin with black olives

An economical dish

Serves 6
Preparation: 15 minutes
Cooking: 10 minutes

Ingredients

2 oz (60 g) butter

1/4 cup (30 g) flour

2 cups (50 cl) milk

Nutmeg

6 hard-boiled eggs

3 1/2 oz (100 g) pitted black olives

Salt and pepper

1. Make a fairly dry béchamel sauce with the butter, flour, milk, salt, pepper, and grated nutmeg. Pour it into the bottom of a dish. To produce a successful béchamel, melt the butter and pour in all the flour at once, then beat vigorously with a whisk. Cook over low heat, stirring constantly for 2 minutes. When the mixture is nice and smooth, remove the pan from the heat and gently pour in the milk, continuing to beat regularly. Then return the pan to low heat and cook it, stirring constantly for about 12 minutes until the sauce is creamy. Do not overdo the seasoning, because of the olives that are to be included in this preparation, and do not forget a few pinches of grated nutmeg. You could use powdered Espelette chili or paprika instead of pepper.

2. Shell the eggs, cut them in half, place them on the bed of sauce, only partly coating them, and arrange the olives evenly around them. To peel hard-boiled eggs easily, break the shell by knocking it on the worktop when the egg is cooked, then soak in a casserole of really cold water for about 10 minutes.

3. Heat your oven. Put the dish in the oven just long enough to heat it and let it just start to brown. Watch the dish carefully while it starts to brown, as the sauce tends to burn. You can incorporate 1 tbsp Emmental into the sauce at the same time. Serve with small slices of toast spread with tapenade.

Recommended drinks

Corsican rosé
Côtes-de-Provence rosé
Cassis rosé

Menu suggestions

1. After this unusual appetizer, serve rib steaks in anchovy butter with Provençal style tomatoes and then small goat's cheeses marinated in olive oil.

2. Served after a cabbage and bacon soup, this egg gratin can precede baked apples flavored with honey.

Eggs Dijon style

A regional dish

Serves 4
Preparation: 20 minutes
Cooking: 4 minutes

Ingredients

2 or 3 shallots

1 bunch tarragon

1 glass dry white wine

8 eggs

1 small pot crème fraîche

1³/₄ oz (50 g) butter

Strong mustard

Salt and pepper

1. Peel and chop the shallots and put them in a small saucepan with a few chopped tarragon leaves and the white wine. Simmer until the volume of the liquid has reduced by half.

2. Meanwhile, medium-boil the eggs: put them in a pan of cold water, heat, then keep them just simmering for 4 minutes. Shell and place them in warm water (about 140 °F/60°C).

3. When the wine has reduced, pour 3 or 4 tbsps of crème fraîche into the saucepan and again reduce the volume by half. Then, off the heat, beat this sauce with a hand whisk while gradually incorporating small pieces of butter and 2 tsps of mustard into it. Add salt and pepper to taste.

4. Heat small individual plates, pour some sauce onto them, put 2 eggs on each, and open them carefully. Garnish with tarragon leaves and serve at once.

The shallot is a typically French ingredient that plays a leading part in gastronomy, between garlic and onions: select with care for its delicate flavor, especially in this cream and mustard sauce. Specimens should be firm, dry, and uniform in color—gray or coppery yellow. As for the strong, or white, mustard, a specialty of Dijon, it loses some of its piquancy when combined with cream: increase the proportion of mustard if you like strong flavors.

Recommended drinks

Volnay
Rully
Givry

Menu suggestions

1. For a Burgundian menu, follow these eggs with a larded veal and sorrel stew followed by blackcurrant custard cream.

2. Keeping the local note, follow this dish with calves' kidneys in mustard and then a fruit purée.

517

Eggs Antibes style

A family dish

Serves 4
Preparation: 15 minutes
Cooking: 45 minutes

Ingredients

3 lb 5 oz (1.5 kg) spinach

2 medium-sized onions

1 lb 9 oz (750 g) potatoes

2 garlic cloves

3 tbsps olive oil

Saffron

4 or 8 eggs

Salt and pepper

1. Wash and sort the spinach, then blanch it for 5 minutes in boiling, salted water. Drain and press it, then chop it coarsely. Peel and slice the onions. Peel and wash the potatoes, wipe them, and cut into round slices. Peel and chop the garlic.

2. Heat the oil in a casserole and lightly brown the onions in it, followed by the garlic and potatoes. Add the spinach, season with salt, pepper, and saffron, and moisten with a large glass of water. Cook with the lid on for 40 minutes over low heat.

3. At the end of this cooking time, break the eggs into the casserole. Add a little more salt, pepper, and saffron and continue cooking until the eggs are just right.

4. Watch the progress of the dish to see that the liquid has completely evaporated when cooking is complete. There should be no juice left, but the spinach should be very soft.

Spinach is available all year round, but has two main seasons, spring and fall. Always choose nice, green spinach with thick, shiny leaves and stalks that are firm and fresh when cut. The French city of Antibes has many culinary specialties, such as cold tomatoes stuffed with anchovies or tuna and gratin of scrambled eggs with tomatoes or zucchini. This egg and potato dish with spinach, cooked with garlic and olive oil, is also flavored with saffron: a small amount will suffice, as this spice is particularly concentrated.

Recommended drinks

Côtes-du-Rhône
Beaujolais
Tavel

Menu suggestions

1. Preceded by tomato soup, eggs Antibes style can constitute the main course, followed by sweet pancakes.

2. For a family dinner, serve these eggs with a green salad with bacon lardoons and a chocolate mousse for dessert.

Scrambled eggs Mediterranean style

A regional dish

Serves 4
Preparation: 18 minutes
Cooking: 10–11 minutes

Ingredients

1 onion

1 red pimento

2 small zucchini

1¾ oz (50 g) butter

8 eggs

4 tbsp milk

Cayenne pepper

Parsley and chervil

Salt and pepper

<u>Microwave oven only</u>
The cooking time is calculated for a 600–650 watt oven. In a lower-powered oven, increase the cooking time in proportion: for example, with a 500-watt oven, increase the time by 15–20%.

1. Peel the onion and chop it very coarsely. Heat a non-metallic baking sheet for 4 minutes at full power (100%) and butter it lightly. Sweat the chopped onion gently for 1 minute at full power on the hot sheet.

2. Cook the pimento for 1 minute at full power (100%) so you can peel it easily. Open it and remove the fibers and seeds. Cut its flesh into very small cubes. Peel the zucchini and cut them into very small cubes too. Put them in a dish with 2 tbsps of water, some salt, and a dab of butter. Partially cover the dish with plastic wrap and cook for 4 minutes at full power (100%).

3. Put the rest of the butter in a serving dish and melt it for about 30 seconds at full power (100%).

4. Break the eggs into the dish and add the milk. Beat with a fork to obtain a smooth mixture and add salt and pepper. Cook for about 2 minutes at full power. When the eggs start to solidify round the edge of the dish, bring the cooked parts to the middle. Finish the cooking in 2 or 3 minutes, stirring once or twice. The eggs should then be three-quarters cooked.

5. Add the onion, pimento, and zucchini and allow the dish to rest for 2 to 3 minutes until the eggs are just right, as they will go on cooking during this resting period. Stir one last time, adding a little Cayenne pepper and plenty of chopped parsley and chervil, and serve.

Recommended drinks

Tavel rosé
Côtes-de-Provence
Lirac

Menu suggestions

1. After a bouillabaisse, scrambled eggs accompanied by slices of toast will be welcome. Serve nougat ice cream for dessert.

2. If you serve these scrambled eggs as an appetizer, follow them, for example, with rabbit with olives and a fig tart for dessert.

Recommended drinks

Beaujolais
Chianti
White Bordeaux

Menu suggestions

1. Serve these fried eggs followed by spaghetti carbonara and ice coffee for dessert.

2. With a main dish of roast chicken and green salad, this hot dish makes a well-balanced appetizer, followed by papillottes of fruit for dessert.

Casserole of fried eggs

An economical dish

Serves 4
Preparation: 5 minutes
Cooking: 15 minutes

Ingredients

7 or 8 onions

5 tbsp oil

White wine

2 tbsp vinegar

Juice of $1/2$ lemon

4 very fresh eggs

Parsley

Salt and pepper

1. Peel the onions and chop them into rounds and then separate them into rings. Wipe them while the oil heats in a skillet. Sauté until they start to turn golden. Watch this first cooking operation attentively to prevent the onions burning, which would give the final preparation a bitter taste. The varieties of onion grown in northern France have a quite strong flavor, while those from more southern parts are milder. You can choose between white onions (Languedoc or Aquitaine) and yellow onions (Burgundy, Ardennes), but you can also choose red onions, that are much milder, originating from Italy or Spain.

2. Put them in a saucepan and add enough wine to cover them plus a bit more, and salt and pepper. Add the vinegar and the lemon juice. Bring to the boil, then reduce the liquid until you obtain a fairly smooth sauce. Meanwhile, fry the eggs. To cook fried eggs successfully, heat the oil in a fairly deep skillet. When it is good and hot, break one egg into a cup and slide it into the oil. As soon as it touches the boiling oil, move the white around the yolk with a wooden spatula, then remove the fried egg with a slotted spoon when the white is golden.

3. Pour the onion sauce into a warm dish and put the fried eggs into it one by one as they are cooked. Garnish with parsley and serve hot.

To go with this dish you can serve toast garnished with bacon slices, heated in a skillet without fat until they are crisp.

Mirror eggs with braised endives

A light dish

Serves 2
Preparation: 15 minutes
Cooking: 25 minutes

Ingredients

1 lb 2 oz (500 g) small endives

1³/₄ oz (50 g) butter

1 small pot light cream

2 eggs

Salt and ground pepper

1. Remove the outer endive leaves, empty the core using a small pointed knife, and slice them. This will remove their bitterness. Blanch them for 10 minutes in boiling, salted water. Drain them thoroughly. A good endive should not be longer than about 6 in (15 cm), but for this recipe it is best to choose even smaller ones, 4–4¹/₂ in (10–12 cm) long, quite plump and with ivory colored outer leaves. Really small endives about two weeks old, full of taste and freshness, can be found in northern France and will give this recipe a unique flavor. When you empty the core of an endive, take care not to cut into the base itself or the leaves may come apart. The endive must remain whole. Once the endives are blanched, put them on a plate covered with a folded cloth and wipe them delicately to remove as much water as possible.

2. Melt the butter in a casserole and put in the endives to braise gently, add salt and pepper, and cover. They will be perfectly cooked after about 20 minutes. Divide them between two small ramekins and cover them with the cream, then break 1 egg into the center of each ramekin and pepper it.

3. Heat the oven to 365 °F (185 °C) and put the ramekins in the oven for about 5 minutes. Serve these little dishes as soon as you take them out of the oven after giving one turn of the pepper mill to the top of each yolk.

Recommended drinks

Chinon
Saumur-champigny
Beajolais-villages

Menu suggestions

1. With a romaine lettuce and anchovy butter appetizer and semolina cake for dessert, these mirror eggs make a well balanced dinner.

2. Follow an appetizer of mirror eggs with a pasta dish and serve seasonal fruit for dessert.

Poached eggs Bacchus style

A party dish

Serves 4
Preparation: 20 minutes
Cooking: 5 minutes

Ingredients

2 shallots

3 glasses rather dry, but fruity, white wine

6 cups (1.5) liters chicken or turkey bouillon

2 lemons

2³/₄ oz (75 g) butter

8 nice slices of round white bread

1 pot thick crème fraîche

8 eggs

2 nice firm bunches of grapes

Salt and pepper

1. Peel and chop the shallots, then heat them in a saucepan with half the white wine. Reduce the liquid over low heat until only a third of the wine remains.

2. Heat the bouillon after adding the rest of the wine and the lemon juice. Lightly fry the slices of bread in butter. Season the shallots with salt and pepper, add the crème fraîche, and reduce again over low heat.

3. Poach the eggs in the flavored bouillon, drain them on a cloth, and trim them. To poach eggs more easily, cook them in two phases, four by four, in a large pan. Once they are poached, remove them delicately with a slotted spoon and plunge them into a bowl containing cold water. Drain them again and place them on a folded cloth to remove the threads of white adhering to the egg.

4. Wipe the grapes and poach them in a little simmering bouillon. To serve, coat the plates with sauce, put the croûtons on this bed, the eggs on the croûtons, and garnish with the grapes. Serve the remaining sauce in a warm sauceboat. Choose oval grapes of the Italia variety, which are crunchy and juicy. As their skin is thicker, for a more elegant presentation you can take the time to peel and seed them after wiping them. With a small pointed knife and a large tapestry needle, the operation is a little time-consuming, but worthwhile.

Recommended drinks

Chablis
Meursault
Montrachet

Menu suggestions

1. After this delicate appetizer, you could serve pike with white butter, followed by an almond tart.

2. If you prefer meat, serve a white veal casserole or tarragon chicken after the eggs, followed by choux-pastries with whipped cream.

Poached eggs in aurora sauce

An economical dish

Serves 4
Preparation: 20 minutes
Cooking: 20 minutes

Ingredients

1¹/₂ oz (45 g) butter

3 tbsps flour

2 cups (50 cl) milk

2 tsps tomato paste

Coarse salt

1 lemon

1 glass white wine vinegar

8 eggs

Chives

Salt and pepper

1. Gently heat 1 oz (30 g) butter in a saucepan and wait until it melts (do not really cook it). Add 1 tbsp flour. Stir to mix well. Moisten with milk trickled in slowly while stirring and mix vigorously with a spoon to prevent lumps forming. Let it simmer for about 10 minutes over low heat, stirring from time to time.

2. Add the rest of the butter all at once. Let it melt on the surface of the sauce. Add salt and pepper before mixing vigorously again while incorporating the tomato paste and a dash of lemon juice. Cook for a good 10 minutes, still over low heat and stirring from time to time.

3. Meanwhile, heat 8 cups (2 liters) of water in a skillet and add some coarse salt and the white wine vinegar. Place the skillet so that the source of heat is off-center and it boils only in one part of the edge. Poach the eggs by letting them slide gently into the simmering vinegar and water. You can either break the eggs just above the water or break them beforehand into a small bowl or glass and then slide them into the water.

4. Remove the eggs with a slotted spoon, place them on paper towels, and then trim them carefully. Cover a warm dish with aurora sauce and put the poached eggs on top. Sprinkle each egg with a few chopped chives.

Recommended drinks

Muscat d'Alsace
Savoie
Riesling

Menu suggestions

1. As a star dish to follow these poached eggs, serve guinea fowl with cabbage followed by French toast and jelly.

2. For a lighter meal, serve herring fillets and potato salad followed by apple purée.

523

Recommended drinks

Vouvray
Graves blanc
Jurançon sec

Menu suggestions

1. For a quick, cold meal (prepared beforehand), follow this dish with carpaccio of beef and a vanilla ice cream.

2. After this rolled omelet as an appetizer, follow with a chicken fricassee and then white cheese with herbs.

Rolled omelet with ham

A family dish

Serves 4
Preparation: 10 minutes
Cooking: 10 minutes
Resting: 2 hours

Ingredients

6 eggs

$^1/_4$ cup (6 cl) milk

1 tbsp flour

$2^3/_4$ oz (75 g) butter

15–20 small pickled gherkins

1 tbsp mustard

3 slices lean, cooked ham

Cherry tomatoes

Salt and pepper

1. Beat the eggs in a bowl, then add the milk, flour, salt, and pepper. Heat $1^3/_4$ oz (50 g) butter in a skillet. Put the omelet in to cook. Turn it when it is two-thirds cooked so as to brown it lightly on both sides. Slide it on to a plate and let it cool. Unlike the traditional omelet, which is usually served "foamy," the flat omelet must be a little more thoroughly cooked and should resemble a big, soft pancake. To turn it easily two-thirds of the way through cooking, use a big, round dish placed over the skillet like a lid. Turn the whole omelet in one quick movement and slip it back into the skillet to finish cooking it.

2. Prepare the filling. Chop the gherkins and mix them in a bowl with the mustard and 2 tbsps of butter softened with a fork. Beat the mixture well until it looks creamy, almost foamy, and spread it over the omelet in a fairly thick layer.

3. Distribute the slices of ham on top of the filling, after removing the rind and some of the fat, then delicately roll the omelet on itself, enclosing the filling. Wrap it in plastic wrap and put it in the bottom of the refrigerator for at least 2 hours. To serve, line a dish with lettuce leaves, cut the rolled omelet into broad slices, arrange them on the lettuce, and garnish with gherkins and small cherry tomatoes. You can replace the mustard, butter, and gherkins in the filling with other mixtures: for example, tapenade, a little purée of potatoes and pitted green olives, or the remainder of a ratatouille or piperade.

Gouda bread

A foreign dish

Serves 6
Preparation: 15 minutes
Cooking: 20 minutes

Ingredients

1 complete round loaf,
    diameter 8–9$^{1}/_{2}$ in (20–24 cm)

3 shallots

1 red pimento

1$^{3}/_{4}$ oz (50 g) butter

9 oz (250 g) Gouda cheese

2 eggs

Milk

Worcestershire sauce

Tabasco®

Salt and pepper

1. Slice the top quarter off the loaf and remove almost all the crumb, taking care not to pierce the crust. Break two-thirds of this crumb into a bowl. To make this recipe successfully, it is a good idea to order a special loaf from your baker like the ones used for "pain surprise" (party loaves, cut into fun shapes and filled with mini sandwiches) and let it go stale for a day so it is firm and easy to slice.

2. Peel and coarsely chop the shallots. Sear the pimento over a flame to make it easy to peel, then cut it into small strips. Sauté the pimento and shallots in butter.

3. Grate the Gouda cheese after removing the rind and put it in a bowl with the bread crumbs. Mix well before adding the beaten eggs, a few tbsp milk, the contents of the skillet, a little salt and pepper, and some Worcestershire and Tabasco sauce. Mix well again before pouring it into the hollowed-out crust. Gouda is a Dutch pressed paste cheese that can be soft, firm, or hard depending on its maturity: to grate without crushing it, choose semi-cooked (with a red rind) or cooked (with a yellow rind). Be careful not to add too much salt because cheese, especially when cooked, makes a dish relatively salty.

4. Heat the oven to 435 °F (225 °C). Put the loaf in the center of the oven and cook it for about 20 minutes. Serve hot. The crust should be good and crunchy and the filling creamy.

Recommended drinks

Beer
Dry cider
Sylvaner

Menu suggestions

1. After this hot appetizer, offer a contrast with an assortment of herrings either marinated or in a sauce, followed by a caramel ice cream.

2. This Gouda bread can also be served at the end of a meal. Serve a fish broth with potatoes first and Liège-style coffee for dessert.

Small chicken soufflés

A light dish

Serves 4
Preparation: 15 minutes
Cooking: 20 minutes

Ingredients

10 1/2 oz (300 g) chicken livers
    or cooked poultry meat
2 cups (50 cl) milk
6 eggs
1 3/4 oz (50 g) butter
Salt and pepper

1. Carefully clean the livers (or cooked poultry meat). Grind them finely in a vegetable mill or blender. A very fine paste must be obtained as it is intended to form a purée mixed with milk. The purée must be even and very light. Heat it while beating with a fork, but make sure it does not boil.

2. Separate the eggs, taking care not to touch the whites with your fingers or they will be more difficult to whip stiffly.

3. Heat the oven to 365 °F (185°C), as your soufflé dish must not wait before being put into the oven. Stiffly beat the egg whites and fold them delicately into the chicken preparation: quickly put 1 tbsp of stiff egg white into the well thus obtained and let it drop on to the mixture. Repeat the operation until all the whites are mixed.

4. Butter four small soufflé dishes. Make sure, when filling them, to leave a margin of about 3/4 in (2 cm) at the top. Put them in the oven and cook them for 20 minutes. Be certain not to open the oven while they are cooking and serve as soon as they leave the oven.

If you do not have any individual soufflé dishes, cook this preparation in a large dish with a diameter of 8 1/2 in (22 cm) and allow 30 minutes' cooking time.

Recommended drinks

Anjou-gamay
Brouilly
Chinon

Menu suggestions

1. Start with Batavia salad with strips of apple, and serve strawberry or pear sorbet for dessert.

2. If you serve these soufflés as an appetizer, accompany them with a vinaigrette of celery stalks and fromage frais presented in a cheese strainer.

526

Roast pork Gouda style

A foreign dish

Serves 6
Preparation: 15 minutes
Cooking: 1 hour 30 minutes

Ingredients

1 pork joint weighing 3 lb 5 oz (1.5 kg),
  cut from the ribs or back

Strong mustard

1 small pot crème fraîche

9 oz (250 g) Gouda cheese

1 lb 2 oz (500 g) small potatoes

2$^1/_4$ lb (1 kg) Brussels sprouts

Salt and pepper

1. Put the meat in a roasting pan, coat it generously with mustard, moisten the pan with a glass of water, and roast for 1 hour and 15 minutes in the oven at 400 °F (200 °C). You can use chicken bouillon or white wine instead of water and add a few sprigs of thyme or cumin seeds to the pan.

2. After 30 minutes, when the water has almost evaporated, add the crème fraîche. Complete the cooking, basting with the juice from time to time.

3. Carve the roast into slices up to three-quarters of its height. Insert a slice of Gouda between each slice. Add salt and pepper. Cook in the oven for about 5 minutes. Watch the cooking carefully to check that the cheese is melting steadily without browning. It should start to sizzle at the edges of the slices.

4. Serve with small boiled potatoes and Brussels sprouts steamed while the meat is roasting.

This Dutch-inspired recipe can be interpreted in other ways depending on the cheese you have available: you can follow the same recipe using other pressed paste cheeses (Mimolette, Cantal or Tomme de Savoie), or cooked paste cheeses (Beaufort, Comté, Appenzell, or Fribourg). Whichever cheese you opt for, cut regular slices around 3 in (7–8 cm) long by 1$^1/_2$ in (4 cm) wide and $^3/_{16}$ in (5 mm) thick. As a vegetable, you could also serve sauerkraut sprinkled with juniper berries, or braised fennel.

Recommended drinks

Stout
Gewürztraminer
Côtes-du-Jura

Menu suggestions

1. Maintain the Dutch theme with a platter of smoked fish as an appetizer and serve ginger cookies with the coffee.

2. To introduce this substantial dish, serve, for example, a curried tomato soup, and a floating island with caramel for dessert.

American salad

A light dish

Serves 8
Preparation: 15 minutes
Cooking: 9 minutes

Ingredients

6 eggs
2 small romaine lettuces
    (or 1 big one)
1 grapefruit
2 green pimentos
1 pear
Oil
Vinegar

Paprika
Salt and pepper

130 calories per person with regular oil; 110 with paraffin oil.

1. Boil the eggs for only 9 minutes so they are still a little soft. Plunge them into cold water as soon as you remove them from the pan then shell them.

2. Wash the lettuces and trim them, removing the bases, but do not cut them too short; you need to make little boats once they have been cut into halves or quarters.

3. Peel the grapefruit, divide it into quarters, then cut each quarter into two or three parts. Sear the pimentos over a flame to make them easier to peel and slice them into strips and fine rings.

4. Separate the yolks and whites of 2 eggs and finely chop the whites. Peel the pear and divide it into strips. Put the chopped egg whites into a bowl and add plenty of well-seasoned vinaigrette. To serve 8, allow 8 tbsp oil and 2 tbsp vinegar.

5. Arrange the salad boats on a serving platter then fill them with the sections of grapefruit and strips of pear. Garnish with the strips and rounds of pimento. Pour the contents of the bowl over them. Stand the hard-boiled eggs up on end and sprinkle them with paprika.

Depending on the market and your taste, you can vary the composition of this mixed salad without altering its calorie content. You could replace the grapefruit with orange, the pear with an apple, and the romaine lettuce with endives, which are easy to use as little boats.

Recommended drinks

Grapefruit juice
Tomato juice
Anjou-gamay

Menu suggestions

1. With this tasty mixed salad, serve a carpaccio or fish tartar, followed by white cheeses presented in a cheese strainer.

2. For an elegant dinner, follow this salad with trout "en papillotte," with an orange mousse for dessert.

Quail's egg salad with green mayonnaise

A party dish

Serves 4
Preparation: 15 minutes
Cooking: 5 minutes

Ingredients

1 bunch cress

1 bunch flat parsley

1 bunch fresh mint

Oil

1 small lettuce

1 egg yolk

1 tsp strong mustard

1 small pot crème fraîche

Vinegar

12 cooked prawns

12 quail's eggs

Salt and white pepper

1. Cut off the cress stalks and wash, drain, and chop the leaves. Do the same with the parsley and mint. Heat 2 tbsp oil in a small skillet and sweat (but do not sauté) these chopped herbs over low heat. Meanwhile, prepare the lettuce. Remove the leaves, cutting off the base, discarding the coarse outer leaves, and retaining the tender and delicious inside leaves. Keep the heart for another salad.

2. Prepare the mayonnaise: mix the egg yolk, mustard, 1/2 tsp fine salt, and 1/2 tsp white pepper. Add the oil drop by drop, stirring with a wooden spoon.

3. Once they have cooled, put the herbs in a blender and mix the purée obtained with the mayonnaise. Add a few tbsp crème fraîche. Add a dash of vinegar and adjust seasoning to taste with salt and pepper. Remove the prawns from their shells, or keep half of them in their shells.

4. Hard-boil 8 quail's eggs. Fry the others. Arrange these various components on individual plates, making sure that the fried quail's eggs are still good and hot.

To heighten the flavor of the green mayonnaise, you can use tarragon or dill instead of mint. If you cannot find prawns, use pink shrimp or crawfish and, if you like, garnish the plates with fine slices of tomato.

Recommended drinks

Château-chalon
Gewurztraminer
Vouvray

Menu suggestions

1. After this colorful appetizer, serve duck in orange sauce followed by a cinnamon pear tart.

2. For fish-lovers, serve poached turbot after this salad followed by a Norwegian omelet for dessert.

529

Sambal goreng telur (hard-boiled eggs with chili sauce)

An exotic dish

Serves 4
Preparation: 30 minutes
Cooking: 10 minutes

Ingredients

4 eggs
4 tbsp sambal
3/4 tsp grated fresh ginger
2 or 3 grated Brazil nuts
Coconut milk
1 lemon

For the sambal flavoring

15–20 small dried red chilies
2 or 3 onions
8 garlic cloves
2 tsp trasi (dried shrimp purée)
Scant 1/2 cup (12 cl) peanut oil
1 generous cup (25 cl) tamarind juice (bottle)
Brown sugar
Salt and pepper

1. Hard-boil the eggs, stirring them during the first 3 or 4 minutes of cooking time to center the yolks well. Shell them.

2. Heat the sambal with the grated ginger and Brazil nuts. Pour in a little coconut milk and the lemon juice. Let it simmer until the sauce reaches a good consistency.

3. Cut a small slice off the larger end of the eggs so they can stand upright, and cut a little hat with a bit of yolk in it off the other end. Stand the eggs on a dish coated with sambal sauce. Put a little sauce on top of each egg. Serve hot.

Sambal recipe

1. Soak the chilies in some hot water for 10 minutes. Meanwhile, peel the onions and garlic cloves and chop them coarsely. Put them and the trasi in a blender with enough oil to obtain a paste and mix until smooth.

2. Heat the rest of the oil in a skillet, stirring constantly until it colors and the oil separates from the mass. Pour the tamarind into the blender to recover whatever may remain in it and pour it into the skillet. Add salt, pepper, and 2 tbsp sugar and cook for a few minutes, stirring. Let the mixture cool in a china bowl then put it in a jar. Store in the refrigerator. This sambal is now ready for use to accompany vegetables, prawns, hard-boiled eggs, soy cheese, sautéed fish, and strips of meat. All you need do is heat 1 tbsp sambal per 9 oz (250 g) of the main ingredient, already cooked, and heat it all up rapidly.

Recommended drinks

Tea
Tavel
Côtes-du-Rousillon

Menu suggestions

1. This can be followed by the great Indonesian classic, nasi goreng, rice with chicken and pimentos. Serve fresh pineapple for dessert.

2. You can also include this specialty in a western menu with beef kebabs and a fruit salad.

Truffade with Cantal cheese

A regional dish

Serves 4–5
Preparation: 30 minutes
Cooking: 25–40 minutes

Ingredients

2¹/₄lb (1 kg) potatoes

Oil

9 oz (250 g) young Cantal cheese

Salt

1. 1. Peel, wash, and wipe the potatoes and cut them into fine rounds. Heat 4–5 tbsp oil in a skillet, arrange the potatoes in it, salt them, and cook for 20–30 minutes over low heat. Do not let them brown. Traditionally, the potato rounds in a truffade are cooked in fat bacon cut into lardoons (3¹/₂ oz/100 g for 2¹/₄ lb/1 kg of potatoes). Heat them in the skillet and squash them slightly while stirring to extract as much fat as possible. As soon as they start to color, remove them, then add the potatoes to the melted fat.

2. Cut the Cantal cheese into think slices. Mash the potatoes with a fork, add the Cantal, and mix it all together for 5–10 minutes over medium heat until a smooth, grainy, and flexible paste is obtained. To produce a successful truffade, incorporate the cheese in two stages, breaking the potato rounds regularly with a spatula.

3. Let the mixture turn golden for a few moments, remove the surplus fat, and turn it out onto a hot dish. Serve a green salad with the truffade. This typical dish from the Aubrac hills in France, theoretically prepared with fresh Tomme de Laguiole, was among the recipes shepherds used to prepare in the "burons" in summer, while their Salers cows were grazing the fragrant pastures. They often accompanied it with poached sausages or boiled bacon. Small fried bacon slices or a little chopped garlic can also be added to the truffade.

Recommended drinks

Saint-Pourçain
Côtes-d'Auvergne
Côte-Roannaise

Menu suggestions

1. For a family dinner, follow the truffade with black pudding and apples and a clafoutis for dessert.

2. In a typically regional meal, truffade will be served, for example, before boiled bacon with lentils and a rhubarb tart.

Potato soufflés

N.B.

Usually prepared as a gratin, leftovers can make very good dishes. Keep them only a short time, in closed containers at the top of the refrigerator. The best cheeses for gratin are cooked pastes, such as Emmental and Gruyère. Being wetter, mozzarella does not color as well when cooked, but gives recipes a delightful softness. Parmesan can also be used in small amounts: it will pleasantly heighten the flavor of the dish. Leftover eggs can also be used. Be careful about the freshness of raw eggs: if you're in doubt, it is best to discard them. Cooked eggs present no risks if they have been kept in their shells.

Macaroni and mozzarella gratin

Ingredients for 4
1 lb 2 oz (500 g) cooked
  macaroni
3¹/₂ oz (100 g) crème fraîche
1³/₄ oz (50 g) parmesan
10 oz (280 g) coarsely grated
  mozzarella
1¹/₂ oz (40 g) butter
Salt and pepper

1. Put the cooked macaroni, cream, and parmesan in a salad bowl.

2. Mix them together and season with salt and pepper.

3. Put a layer of macaroni, a layer of mozzarella, and another layer of macaroni in a buttered gratin dish and top with mozzarella.

4. Put the dish in the oven at 410 °F (210 °C) for 35–40 minutes.

Fish gratin

Ingredients for 4
12¹/₂ oz (350 g) cooked fish
14 oz (400 g) cooked potatoes
10¹/₂ oz (300 g) tomato sauce
7 oz (200 g) crème fraîche
Powdered sweet chili
Chives
2 oz (60 g) parmesan
Butter
5¹/₂ oz (150 g) grated gruyère
Salt and pepper

1. Flake the leftover fish and remove the bones. Cut the cooked potatoes into slices.

2. Put the tomato sauce, fresh cream, sweet chilli, chopped chives, flaked fish and parmesan in a salad bowl.

3. Arrange the sliced potatoes in a buttered gratin dish. Pour the fish preparation on top and sprinkle with gruyère.

4. Put the dish in the oven at 410 °F (210 °C) for 35–40 minutes.

Country moussaka with eggplant

Ingredients for 4
1 onion
4 garlic cloves
Olive oil
12$\frac{1}{2}$ oz (350 g) cooked lamb
4 tomatoes
2 tbsp tomato paste
7 oz (200 g) white mushrooms
Parsley
2 tbsp flour
3 eggplants
2$\frac{3}{4}$ oz (80 g) parmesan
Salt and pepper

1. Sweat the chopped onion and garlic in the olive oil. Then add the chopped lamb.

2. Cook over medium heat for 10 minutes.

3. Incorporate the tomatoes, cut into rounds, tomato paste, and chopped mushrooms. Add salt, pepper, and the chopped parsley and cook for 20 minutes.

4. Bind the mixture with the flour mixed with olive oil. Adjust the seasoning and set it aside.

5. Cut the eggplant into slices 3/8 in (1 cm) thick and fry them lightly in a skillet in a little oil.

6. Alternate layers of eggplant and layers of meat mixture in an oiled gratin dish, topping it off with eggplant. Sprinkle with parmesan and a dash of olive oil.

7. Put the dish in the oven at 400 °F (200 °C) for 20–25 minutes.

Cheese pancake with egg

Ingredients for 4
4 pancakes
2$\frac{3}{4}$ oz (80 g) grated gruyère
Butter
4 eggs

1. Fill the pancakes with grated gruyère and roll them.

2. Heat them slowly in a skillet with a little butter.

3. Arrange them on a dish and top each pancake with a fried egg.

4. Serve good and hot.

Tip

A commonplace Oriental dish in Turkey, Greece, and the Balkans, moussaka enables you to use leftover cooked lamb to which eggplant and tomato sauce are added: grated cheese is essential to brown the gratin.

Desserts and candies

Batter for 25–30 crêpes, depending on the diameter of the skillet.

1 Sift 1^1/$_2$ cups (280 g) wheat flour. Mix with 1/4 cup (60 g) sugar and a pinch of salt in a bowl and make a fairly deep well in the middle. Put 2^3/$_4$ oz (80 g) melted butter, 6 beaten eggs, and 1^1/$_2$ cups (35 cl) milk into the well. Stir with a fork or wooden spoon, moving from the center outward so the flour falls in and mixes with the other ingredients bit by bit.

2 When the batter reaches a good consistency, add 1 ^{2}/$_3$ cups (40 cl) cold milk. Strain the batter, cover with a cloth, and let it rest 1–2 hours before cooking: your pancakes will be tastier and better colored. Putting the melted butter in the batter will give you softer pancakes that never stick to the skillet.

3 Wipe an oily cloth over the bottom of the skillet and place it over medium heat. Pour in 1 ladleful of batter when the oil begins to smoke. There must be enough batter to cover the cooking surface and it should start to sizzle at once. Tilt the skillet to spread the batter evenly. Make thin pancakes: pour any surplus batter back into the bowl. Remove any threads of batter that have stuck to the rim of the skillet.

4 Return the skillet to the heat and cook for a few moments. When the edges of the pancake lift slightly, allow 10 seconds, then turn the pancake, using a spatula to pick up one of the edges. Cook the other side in the same way. Place the cooked pancake on a plate of appropriate size.

N.B.

In the past, crêpes were cooked on griddles, very flat skillets of various sizes made of black cast iron that were troublesome to maintain as they had to be heated and oiled regularly. Nowadays, people prefer thick-bottomed, non-stick skillets. The crêpes never stick to them and they can be easily cleaned by wiping with a soft cloth. To keep the crêpes warm as they are cooked, pile them on a plate placed over a saucepan of simmering water. Cover them all with a slightly damp dishtowel. Thus, your crêpes can be served soft and warm.

Crêpes with prunes

Crêpe gateau with orange and rum for 4

1 Put 2 generous cups (250 g) flour in an earthenware bowl and make a well in it. Break 4 eggs into the well, add 1 generous cup (25 cl) milk and then a pinch of salt. Then gradually add 2 cups (50 cl) milk, 1/4 cup (50 g) sugar, 3 1/2 oz (100 g) melted butter, 1 tbsp of oil. Stop adding milk when the batter easily makes a ribbon. Let it rest for 1 hour. Grate the zest of 1 orange. Squeeze 4 oranges and 1 lemon.

2 Melt 3 1/2 oz (100 g) butter in a thick-bottomed skillet. Add the juice then 2/3 cup (150 g) sugar. Allow to simmer while you prepare the pancakes. Pour a ladleful of batter into the hot skillet and brown it on one side. Turn the pancake and brown the other side. Keep the pancakes hot as they are made.

3 Just before serving, add 8 tbsp rum and the orange zest to the simmered juice. Stack the pancakes on a warm plate, spreading each with the sauce. Be sure to arrange them regularly. Pour a little sauce over the stack and let it rest for a few minutes in the hot oven. Serve with the rest of the sauce in a hot sauceboat. Cut like a cake.

Batter for 10 waffles

1 To make 10–12 waffles you need 3 eggs, 1$\frac{1}{2}$ cups (250 g) wheat flour, $\frac{1}{3}$ cup (40 g) confectioner's sugar, 2 pinches salt, 1¾ oz (50 g) butter, and 1 generous cup (25 cl) milk. Separate the yolks from the whites and set them aside. Sift the flour. Mix it with the confectioner's sugar and a pinch of salt in a bowl and make a fairly deep well in the center. Pour the melted butter, egg yolks, and milk into the well.

2 Using a whisk, beat from the center outward so the flour falls in and mixes gradually. When the batter reaches a good consistency and no longer contains any lumps, let it rest for 1–2 hours. According to a different formula, you can mix the egg yolks, sugar, melted butter, and milk first and then incorporate the flour, sifted if necessary.

3 Put the egg whites in another bowl, add the rest of the salt, and beat them very stiffly. Add the beaten egg whites to the first mixture using a wooden spoon. Cook the batter within the next hour. You can use it just as it is or add the flavoring of your choice: vanilla sugar, orange flower water, kirsch, or an orange or other liqueur.

4 Heat the waffle iron and butter it: the fat should melt and sizzle at once. Pour in a good ladleful of batter. Shut the waffle iron at once and turn it over so the liquid batter spreads into the whole mold. Cook for 3–5 minutes, depending on the desired color. Serve the waffles good and hot.

Soft waffles

Chocolate and orange waffles

Domino waffles

Variants

Waffles are traditional sweetmeats dating back to the Middle Ages. They were prepared by traveling merchants and sold at church doors on religious festivals, particularly Easter. There are several kinds. Dutch waffles are quite rich in butter, while Liège waffles, which are relatively thick, contain yeast. In France, the traditional square or rectangular waffle with dimples in it is distinguished from a much finer variant rolled in a tube that originated in southwestern France. Rolled waffles are neither as thick nor as soft as traditional waffles. They are fine, crunchy tubes of batter about 4 in (10 cm) long that break if held too tightly and soften quickly.

Fillings

Waffles are served plain or garnished with whipped cream, confectioner's sugar, vanilla or chocolate sauce, liquid caramel, maple syrup, or various jellies. All sorts of presentations are possible, depending on your taste: whipped cream rosettes alternating with red fruit; sprinkled with cocoa powder; drizzled with melted chocolate; garnished with chopped crystallized fruit or sugared orange peel. But do not forget— just one plain waffle contains about 80 calories!

Equipment

Most modern waffle irons are electric. They consist of two half-molds that close to form a watertight structure to prevent the batter running out during cooking. The hot plates, made of cast aluminum, are deeply scored for fast cooking. Keep these plates in good condition: clean them often and remember to oil them from time to time.

Fruit waffles

Waffles with jam

539

Raised batter for 20 fritters

1 Sift 4¹/₂ cups (500 g) flour, pour it in a heap on the work top, and make a well in it. Warm ¹/₂ cup (13 cl) milk and mix it with 4 tsps (20 g) sugar, 1 pinch fine salt, and 4 tsp (20 g) active dry yeast. Pour the mixture into the middle of the flour, with 6 whole broken eggs. Flatten the mixture with the palm of your hand, making circular movements from the center outward to incorporate all the flour.

2 Knead for about 10 minutes with 5¹/₂ oz (150 g) butter cut into small pieces, until the batter becomes flexible and slightly elastic. Make it into a ball in a container and let it rest overnight in the refrigerator. You can also incorporate the same amount of butter after melting it.

3 Take up the batter, roll it into a long cylinder with a diameter of around 2 in (4–5 cm). Cut it into lengths 1¹/₄ in (3 cm) thick using a knife. Put the pieces on a baking sheet, flour them, and let them rise for 2 hours in a warm place. Pour 12 cups (3 liters) sunflower or peanut oil into a deep-fat fryer or other suitable vessel and set over medium heat for 7 minutes.

4 Check the temperature of the oil by dropping a small piece of batter into it. It should fry at once without coloring too quickly. Take the pieces of batter and plunge them into the fryer. Turn each fritter after 4 or 5 minutes. Cook on the other side for the same length of time. Remove the cooked fritters with a slotted spoon that is completely dry, to avoid splashes.

Churros

Beer and jelly bugnes

Merveilles

Variants

There are two main categories of fritter: salted or sweet, in which an ingredient is inserted into the batter, and then fritters consisting only of batter and cooked by frying. The latter are always sweet and are made of different batters: kneaded, choux, or raised batter. There are many regional specialties, often served at carnival time or at the end of Lent. The best known are the "roussettes" of the Beauce region of France flavored with orange flower water, the triangular "merveilles" of southwestern France, the "tourtisseaux" of Anjou, the "bottereaux" of the Charente region, and the "oreillettes" of Montpellier. "Pets-de-nonnes" are small fritters made with choux batter. In Spain, street vendors sell "churros"—long fritters made with a fairly thick batter.

Garnishes

Fritters are served plain, dipped in confectioner's or superfine sugar. To find new flavor combinations, you can also powder them delicately with a pinch of cinnamon. Another method consists of stuffing them. Make a lengthwise cut into the fritter and, with a glazing nozzle fill it with apple purée, strawberry, raspberry, or apricot jelly or good, bitter orange marmalade. This is the method used to make ring doughnuts. Many garnishes are used. The top can be caramelized or covered with a thin layer of melted chocolate.

N.B.

To achieve tasty, digestible, and uniformly colored fritters, use clean, well-filtered oil. Do not use the same oil more than four or five times. Do not keep it at room temperature, but somewhere cold. Above all, avoid extremes of temperature.

Oreillettes

541

Crème brûlée

for 4

1 Prepare the cream. Preheat the oven to 375 °F (190 °C). Put 2 cups (50 cl) light cream in a saucepan and set over low heat with a vanilla bean split in two, from which you have saved the seeds by scraping with the blade of a knife. Beat to disperse the little black seeds thoroughly and they will release all their flavor into the cream. Cover and allow to infuse for about 15 minutes.

2 Put 5 egg yolks in a bowl with $1/2$ cup (100 g) white superfine or brown sugar, according to your taste. Beat the mixture for about 5 minutes until it whitens and becomes almost foamy. Then pour the warm cream over the yolk-sugar mixture. Beat vigorously, then strain the mixture to remove the vanilla bean and any impurities. Wait a moment for the foam to subside.

3 Pour the preparation into a large gratin dish. Put it in a bain-marie or baking pan of warm water, cover with a sheet of aluminum foil, and put it in the oven. Bake for 15–20 minutes. Remove the cream from the oven, let it cool, cover it, and place in the refrigerator overnight. You can also prepare crème brûlée in individual ramekins.

4 Heat a broiling plate on the stove. Sprinkle the surface of the cream with superfine sugar to a depth of about $1/16$ in (1 mm). When the broiling plate starts to redden, remove it from the heat and bring it to the surface of the cream, which will caramelize at once. Repeat the operation twice and serve.

General points

Caramel crèmes are easy desserts to prepare and have the advantage of pleasing nearly everyone. Egg creams, upside-down creams, and cream pots are family desserts for simple enjoyment. Crème brûlée is a more sophisticated pleasure. Its unique feature is its combination of a hot, crunchy surface with a soft, ice-cold inside. The contrast is striking and goes a long way to explain the popularity of this dessert, so beloved of gourmets.

Delicious crème brûlée

The traditional recipe is flavored with vanilla, but you can choose many other flavorings. Cinnamon gives good results. Orange or lemon zest lightly infused in the cream goes well with the rich texture of this recipe. You can also try coffee or chocolate, always previously infused or dissolved in the cream. Substituting acacia honey for the superfine sugar mixed with eggs will give this recipe yet another aspect.

Crèmes catalanes

Equipment

The most suitable containers are small, glazed, brown earthenware pots around 1¼ in (3 cm) deep. Acquire a suitable broiling plate, which should consist of a thick metal disk, a fairly long stem, and a wooden handle.

1 Soak 15 sugar lumps in a little water in a saucepan. Set the pan over medium heat and shake it from time to time to ensure the caramel cooks evenly. Above all, do not stir it. When it has turned a light mahogany color, pour it into a brioche or charlotte mold, or distribute it between individual ramekins.

2 Pour 2 cups (50 cl) milk into a saucepan, add 1 vanilla bean split in two, and bring to the boil. Add ⅓ cup (75 g) superfine sugar. Let it infuse for 5 minutes. Remove the vanilla bean. Break 3 eggs into a bowl and beat them. Pour the boiling milk on top, beating constantly. Pour this preparation into the caramelized mold and put the mold in a bain-marie or baking pan of water.

Upside-down crème caramel for 6

3 Cook gently in the oven (320 °F/160°C) for 40 minutes. Remove the bowl from the oven and let it cool completely. Loosen the edges of the cream using the blade of a knife. Put the serving plate over the mold, turn it over quickly, and lift off the mold. Pour the caramel over the cream tower. You can only successfully remove the mold if the cream is completely cold. Prepare it the day before.

543

Norwegian omelet for 8–10

1 Start by preparing the syrup you will use to soak the Genoese cake. Pour 1 scant cup (20 cl) water into a small, thick-bottomed pan. Add 1 scant cup (200 g) superfine sugar and mix to make it dissolve, then bring it to the boil slowly and boil for a few seconds. Remove the pan from the heat and let it cool. Then add $^1/_3$ cup + 1 $^1/_2$ tbsp (10 cl) rum, mix, and set it aside.

2 Cut a ready-made Genoese cake to fit your serving dish. This will form the basis of the recipe. You can take a round cake and cut off two sides, for example. You can divide the cake into two equal rolls. Shape them like an omelet. Soak the two halves of cake with the rum syrup using a brush, then put them in the freezer for 2 hours.

3 Prepare a vanilla ice cream. When it has set, chop 3$^1/_2$ oz (100 g) preserved fruit, keeping a few whole, and add to the ice cream. Mix well. Put the ice cream on one half of the chilled cake. Give it an elongated, rounded shape like an omelet. Put the other half of the cake on top. Leave this preparation in the freezer for 24 hours to set.

4 Prepare the meringue needed to cover the dessert—a simple, uncooked French meringue. Put 4 large egg whites in a really clean bowl and beat with an electric whisk at full speed; then gradually add just under 1 $^1/_3$ cups (150 g) confectioner's sugar and continue to beat for 7–8 minutes. The meringue must be very firm and shiny.

5 Place this meringue in a glazing bag with a grooved nozzle. Cover the whole surface of the cake, both the top and the sides, forming loops and rosettes: it must be completely covered. Sprinkle with 1$^3/_4$ oz (50 g) slivered almonds, add the rest of the preserved fruit, and sprinkle with $^1/_4$ cup (30 g) confectioner's sugar using a small sieve.

6 Just before serving, put the omelet in the oven at 410 °F (210 °C) for a few minutes. Take it out when it has turned a nice, blond color. Heat some rum in a saucepan and pour it on to the dessert when it is flaming. Based on this standard recipe, vary the taste by using other flavorings: coffee, caramel, strawberry or raspberry.

Omelet as dessert

Norwegian omelet

True or false omelet

Served only too seldom, the Norwegian omelet is a dessert as spectacular as it is delicious: an iced heart placed inside a soft Genoese cake, all covered in meringue and browned in the oven. The contrast between hot and cold makes this dessert thoroughly original. But the Norwegian omelet is only a "surprise" omelet. Real sweet omelets are also delicious desserts and are easier to make, either flavored simply with fruit purée or a liqueur, or "souffléed" with a high proportion of stiffly beaten egg whites.

Stuffed omelet

Omelet stuffed with purée

A simple sweet omelet can be filled with poached or puréed fruit. At the moment of serving, just make a delicate cut in the top to show the filling. Here is a variant of this dessert that can take all kinds of flavorings: to serve 8, beat 8 whole eggs in a bowl with 1 tbsp sugar, 1 tbsp powdered almonds, and 1 tbsp crème fraîche. Add a small pinch of salt. With this mixture, make two slightly undercooked flat omelets. Put one of them in a round, flameproof dish. Spread 8 tbsp apple purée mixed with 2 tbsp crème fraîche and a few raspberries over. Put the second omelet on top of that, powder it with confectioner's sugar, and turn barely golden in the broiler. Serve very hot.

Gooseberry jelly

Soufflé omelet with jelly

To serve 3–4, separate 5 eggs. Beat the yolks with 3 tbsp superfine sugar and add 1 tbsp flour. Whip the whites very stiffly. Pour the sugared yolks over the whites and mix together quickly with 1 tbsp rum, using a spatula. Set a skillet over medium heat and pour the mixture into $1^1/_2$ oz (40 g) hot butter. Swirl the preparation two or three times, then let it cook for 2 minutes. The omelet will swell up rapidly. Be careful not to overheat it. Spread 5 tbsp strawberry jelly on half the omelet and fold it over on itself using a fork. Serve at once: the omelet will subside before your eyes as soon as it is removed from the skillet. Of course, you can make this dessert with the jelly or liquor of your choice.

Tip

To prevent a Norwegian omelet melting while in the oven, the ice cream must be very hard and should have been kept in the freezer with the cake for at least 24 hours.

General points

Apple charlotte is a dessert that requires lengthy baking. It must be served hot or warm. The mold is lined with slices of bread without the crusts, but to enrich the recipe brioche can be used. Choose flavorful cooking apples—pippins are very suitable. On the same principle, cooked charlottes can be served hot with a mixture of apples and pears or apples and apricots. Charlottes can also be served coated with chocolate sauce, apricot coulis, or vanilla cream.

Chocolate charlotte

Apple charlotte for 6

1 Peel 2^1/$_4$ lb (1 kg) apples and remove the core and seeds. Grease a charlotte mold with 3^1/$_2$ oz (100 g) butter. Remove the crusts from 1 lb 9 oz (700 g) sliced bread using a knife. Cut the slices into triangles to cover the bottom of the mold and into rectangles for the sides. Overlap them slightly so the mold is completely lined.

2 Slice the apples and put them in a saucepan with 1 vanilla bean, 2 pinches of powdered cinnamon, the zest of ^{1}/$_2$ a lemon, 1^3/$_4$ oz (50 g) butter and 1/3 cup + 1^1/$_2$ tbsp (10 cl) water. Bring the mixture to the boil, cover, and cook over moderate heat for 15–20 minutes. Remove from the heat, then add ^{1}/$_2$ cup (100 g) brown sugar. Mix, remove the vanilla bean and the lemon zest, and then sieve.

3 Pour the purée into the mold, being careful not to dislodge the bread lining. Put the charlotte in the oven at 400 °F (200 °C) for 30–40 minutes. When cooked, the bread should be nicely browned. Remove the charlotte from the oven and let it cool in its mold at room temperature for at least 30 minutes. Then turn it from the mold onto a serving platter and sprinkle with confectioner's sugar.

Diplomate with preserved fruit

Banana diplomate

Cherry diplomate

General information

The diplomate is a typically French dessert with two versions: one eaten hot and the other cold. In the first formula, layers of brioche, sometimes moistened with milk, alternate with preserved fruit, the whole being covered with an egg custard cooked in a bain-marie. In the second, soaked ladyfingers alternate with preserved fruit and marmalade or egg custard. The whole preparation is put in the refrigerator. The diplomate can be prepared in a cake mold, a charlotte mold, or a simple gratin dish.

Diplomate with preserved fruit

To serve 6, coarsely chop $5^1/_2$ oz (150 g) mixed preserved fruit with a knife. Combine it with 3 oz (90 g) raisins in a bowl and macerate the mixture in $^1/_3$ cup + $1^1/_2$ tbsp (10 cl) rum. Cut 1 lb 5 oz (600 g) brioche or "pain brioché" into slices $^3/_{16}$ in (5 mm) thick and remove the crusts. Put these slices on a baking sheet and brown them for a few minutes. Set aside. Generously butter a mold with $3^1/_2$ oz (100 g) butter. Put a first layer of brioche in the bottom of the mold and cover it with macerated fruit. Repeat this operation until the mold is completely full. Break and beat 6 eggs in a bowl. Then add 1 scant cup (200 g) superfine sugar, 4 cups (1 liter) milk, 1 sachet vanilla sugar, and the liquor used to macerate the fruit. Beat together, then strain through a fine sieve. Pour this preparation onto the brioche and fruit, making sure the liquid is thoroughly absorbed. Put the mold in a bain-marie or baking pan of water and bake in the oven at 300 °F (150 °C) for between 50 minutes and 1 hour. Remove the diplomate from the oven and let it cool for an hour before removing it from the mold. Decorate it with preserved fruit (angelica, red, and green cherries).

Apple charlotte

Bread pudding for 6

1 Cut a slightly stale 12$\frac{1}{2}$ oz (350 g) loaf of bread into regular slices 3/8 in (1 cm) thick. Butter these slices on both sides and place them end-on on a sheet of aluminum foil. According to your taste, you can use white bread or whole-wheat bread and unsalted or semi-salted butter. Remember to take the butter out of the refrigerator in good time.

2 Generously butter the baking dish. A simple gratin dish will do very well, but you can use a round, spring-form cake pan or a fairly deep pie dish. Arrange the slices of bread in the dish, overlapping them regularly. You can slip a few raisins or preserved fruits between the slices.

3 Break 3 whole eggs into a bowl. Beat them as for an omelet, then add $\frac{1}{8}$ cup (30 g) superfine sugar, 1 sachet of vanilla sugar, and a good pinch of ground nutmeg or cinnamon. Beat the mixture vigorously until it becomes foamy, white, and completely smooth. Pour in 2 generous cups (60 cl) milk and beat thoroughly with a whisk.

4 Pour this very fluid mixture over the slices of bread arranged in the dish, gently so as not to spoil the arrangement. Let it rest for an hour, then bake it in the oven at 400 °F (200 °C) for 45 minutes. Check that the outside is nicely golden. Do not remove it from the mold. Serve it hot or warm, with a spoon, directly onto individual plates at the table.

Roman pudding

General points

Originally, puddings were desserts designed to use up leftover bread. Very popular in England, they are less so in France where they are unjustly little known. Their taste depends on the flavorings used, but also mainly on the type of bread. There are numerous pudding recipes. Some use margarine or even beef or veal fat instead of butter. The most famous, of course, is the English Christmas pudding, prepared far in advance of the great day. But the word "pudding" itself has developed considerably. Nowadays, this name is given to all kinds of desserts, often consisting of or richly garnished with dried or preserved fruit. Roman pudding is made of pain brioché, hazelnut cream, and fresh walnuts. In the West Indies, sweet potatoes or bananas are often included in its preparation.

Christmas pudding

Christmas pudding

The day before, soak 1 lb 2 oz (500 g) raisins in 2 cups (50 cl) water and 1/3 cup + 1 1/2 tbsps (10 cl) rum. Take the zest of a lemon, using just the yellow part. Dip it in boiling water for 1 minute, cool it, and chop finely. Set it aside. On pudding-making day, take 1 1/2 cups (160 g) flour, 1 sachet active dry yeast, 5 oz (140 g) white breadcrumbs, 9 oz (250 g) creamed butter, 2/3 cup (150 g) brown sugar and 3 pinches of salt. Mix together with a wooden spoon for a few minutes. Then add 1 scant cup (20 cl) milk, 4 whole eggs, and 1/4 nutmeg, grated. Mix again for 2 minutes. Finally, add the drained raisins, the chopped lemon peel, 9 oz (250 g) chopped, pitted prunes, 9 oz (250 g) preserved fruit, and 2 pinches of powdered cinnamon. Work the paste for 5 minutes using a wooden spatula then let it rest for 6 hours. Add 2 tbsp brandy, mix again, then pour the mixture into a well-buttered

Sweet potato pudding

pudding basin. Stand the basin in a baking pan of simmering water, cover, and bake in the oven at 300 °F (150 °C) for 8 hours. After cooking, let it cool and put it in the refrigerator until Christmas Eve. Then reheat the pudding in a bain-marie or double boiler for 2 hours, and turn it out onto a round dish. Boil 1/3 cup + 1 1/2 tbsp (10 cl) brandy in a small saucepan, set it alight, and, at the last minute, pour it over the pudding. Cut the Christmas pudding into slices with a fairly fine knife. Serve it hot with brandy butter. To make this, beat 7 oz (200 g) butter until it turns creamy. Add 4 tbsp brandy, 7/8 cup (100 g) confectioner's sugar, the juice of 1 lemon, and a pinch of grated nutmeg.

Baked custard Parisian style for 4

1 Split one vanilla bean. Put it in a saucepan with $1/3$ cup (75 g) white superfine sugar and 2 cups (50 cl) milk. Bring to the boil. Cover, remove it from the heat, and let it infuse. Mix 4 tsp (20 g) cornstarch in a little water. Return the pan to gentle heat and bring it to the boil slowly, stirring constantly with a wooden spoon. Remove the pan from the heat the moment it begins to simmer.

2 Beat 2 eggs as for an omelet and incorporate them into the vanilla-flavored milk when it has cooled a little. This is the moment to enhance your custard by adding the flavoring of your choice: orange flower water, rum, cinnamon. Vanilla alone may suffice, however. Instead of white superfine sugar, you could use brown sugar, the taste of which is more marked.

3 Sprinkle your worktop with flour. Flatten 7 oz (200 g) prepared piecrust using a rolling pin likewise sprinkled with flour. Form it into a round a little bigger than the pie dish. It should be $3/16$ in (5 mm) thick. Butter the pie dish generously and evenly. Roll the pastry round the floured rolling pin and take it to the pie dish. Unroll it.

4 With your fingertips, press the piecrust against the grooves to make it stick to the edges of the pie dish. Pass the rolling pin over the edges to cut off any surplus pastry. Lightly beat the custard one more time and pour it into the pastry shell. It should almost come up to the top. Smooth the surface with the back of a wooden spoon to give it an even finish.

5 Heat the oven to 445 °F (230 °C). Put the pie dish in the center of the oven and bake for 30 minutes. Wait for the custard to cool thoroughly before removing it from its container on to a wire rack. Serve it completely cold. The top should be lightly caramelized. If it is not, put it in the broiler for a short time, powdered with sugar.

Baked custard with grapes

Baked custard with plums
Bourdaloue style

Baked custard with fruit

General points

The expression "baked custard" ("flan" in French and Spanish) is very old, proving that this dessert was fashionable in the Middle Ages: in fact, it comes from the old French word "flado" which means "disk" or "flat object." In principle, it means a sweetened tart filled with an egg cream to which vanilla is often added: this is the famous "Parisian baked custard," which is cut into triangular or rectangular slices and found in every bakery. The cornstarch incorporated into the crème makes it firmer. Baked custard can be enriched with fresh or dried fruit incrusted in the crème. It then becomes virtually a variant of the fruit tart. Conversely, in everyday parlance, baked custard is simply a crème caramel, turned upside-down or not, without any pastry support, or a sort of clafoutis made of fruit cooked in cream on a base of rice or brown sugar.

Baked custard with plums Bourdaloue style

To serve 6, pit $1^3/_4$ lb (800 g) big, red plums, after splitting them in two. Poach them in a light, vanilla-flavored syrup. Drain and wipe them. Spread a layer of partly cooked rice pudding in the bottom of a deep, flameproof dish. Arrange the halved plums on top, cut side uppermost. Beat 2 eggs as for an omelet with 3/8 cup (80 g) superfine sugar and $^1/_3$ cup + $1^1/_2$ tbsps (10 cl) milk, add 1 tsp cornstarch, and beat the mixture well. Pour it directly between and all round the fruit. Bake in the oven at 430 °F (220 °C) for about 15 minutes. Remove the dish, let it cool, and sprinkle the plums with a few flaked almonds. Instead of plums, you can use apricots, peaches, large grapes, or even bananas.

Baked custard with strawberries

Line a tart mold with piecrust and bake it blind. Leave to cool. Spread a layer of confectioner's custard on the bottom and stick some red, but not overripe, strawberries into it. Broil for a few minutes.

Baked custard with strawberries

Sugars and syrups

Sugar is the ingredient shared by all desserts, cakes, confectionery, ice creams, and sorbets. It is used in various forms: confectioner's sugar, superfine sugar, granulated sugar, brown sugar, fondant, and sugar syrup. The viscosity of a cold sugar syrup varies according to the temperature at which it was cooked: the higher the temperature, the more concentrated the syrup and the thicker its consistency. To cook sugar syrups, a few precautions are necessary. Always use a thick-bottomed saucepan with a very strong handle and keep your eye on it.

Precautions

Before you become adept at correctly assessing the degree of cooking, use a candy thermometer whose measurements are more precise and which is, above all, less dangerous. Whatever the end purpose of the sugar, always respect the following few instructions. Weigh the sugar, measure the glucose syrup and water, and mix them in the saucepan. Use a small damp brush to clean the sides of the pan so the little sugar crystals do not burn before the sugar is cooked. Boil the syrup over high heat.

If you are cooking over a flame, make sure it does not extend beyond the bottom of the pan and lick its sides. Temperatures should be checked as soon as boiling point is reached. Before use, the thermometer must be kept in very hot water to avoid the risk of its breaking when suddenly immersed in the hot sugar. Set a basin full of water and ice-cubes to hand so you can stop the cooking when you decide to. You will plunge the pan into it to cool it down.

Smoothing

Cooking temperature: 217 °F (103 °C). Assessment: the minute the syrup boils. The pan is covered in smaller bubbles. Use: sugar syrup for fruit sauces, cake rolls, babas, preserved fruit, almond pastes.

Coating

Cooking temperature: 214 °F (101 °C). Assessment: as soon as the syrup boils. The pan is covered in bubbles. Use: sugar syrup for soaking Genoese cakes, cake rolls, rum babas, fruit syrups in sterilized jars.

Threads

Cooking temperature: 223 °F (106 °C). Assessment: when poured with a spoon, the syrup forms small, tenuous threads because of its viscosity. Use: syrup for cooking certain jellies, syrup for sorbets, butter creams, icings.

Fruit pies

Blowing

Cooking temperature: 230 °F (110 °C). Assessment: plunge a slotted spoon into the syrup and blow into the holes; many sugar bubbles will form. Use: sugar syrup for fruit liqueurs, crystallized chestnuts, sugared fruits.

Small sugar ball

Cooking temperature: 239 °F (115 °C). Assessment: pour some syrup into water; a somewhat sticky ball can be formed between the fingers, but quickly flattens. Use: making soft caramels, jellies and jellos, nougat.

Large sugar ball

Cooking temperature: 257 °F (125 °C). Assessment: pour some syrup into water; a ball can be formed easily between the fingers and keeps its shape without flattening. Use: Italian meringue, sugar decorations.

Crazed sugar

Cooking temperature: 311 °F (155 °C). Assessment: pour some syrup into water and then pull it between your fingers; the sugar breaks like glass and takes on a slightly yellow hue. Use: humbugs, lollipops, hard caramels.

Light caramel

Cooking temperature: 320 °F (160 °C). Assessment: pour some syrup into water, then put the cooled piece on a white plate; the color is golden. Use: caramelized buns, nougatine, caramel crèmes, and ice creams.

Dark caramel

Cooking temperature: 338 °F (170 °C). Assessment: pour some syrup into water, then put the cooled piece on a white plate; the color is dark gold. After that stage, the sugar burns. Use: for coloring sauces.

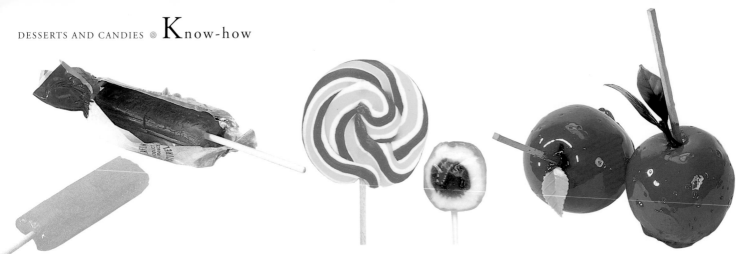

Lollipops
General points

It is fun to prepare your own candies. To make them, you simply need to know how to cook crazing sugar and have a marble slab to cool it on. You can combine flavors and colors using the natural fruit essences and colorings now to be found in the specialist sections of supermarkets. You can also use fruit juices you have squeezed yourself: the candy will taste better, but it will not be so transparent. To prevent your sugar from crystallizing during cooking, use glucose syrup that can be obtained from a local pastrycook. Lollipops made of cooked sugar contain practically no water, which is why they tend to turn sticky quite quickly in damp weather: before starting to make them, listen to the weather forecast.

Ribbon lollipops
Tastes and colors

Lollipops are a recent form of candy as they were invented by a Parisian confectioner who had the brilliant idea of inserting a small wooden stick (nowadays often made of white plastic) into barley sugar to prevent children getting sticky fingers: his patent was registered in April 1924. The range of lollipops is as varied as the range of boiled candies. They can be flavored with fruit, caramel, mint, or licorice. There are also ribbon lollipops combining several colors and flavors.

Tip

The glucose syrup added at the start of cooking prevents the sugar syrup from crystallizing and becoming opaque and grainy. It greatly assists the work of the sugar and does not alter the taste of the confectionery. You can obtain it from a cake shop or drugstore.

Toffee apples
A treat for the children

Toffee apples are traditional candies very popular with children. First, carefully wash and wipe the apples. Separately, cook a crazing sugar and color it bright red. The apples are pierced with big wooden sticks, plunged into the melted sugar, and then simply cooled on a marble slab. The contrast between the soft apple and its crunchy coating is always pleasant. To make them yourself, take care to choose relatively small apples, such as pippins, with a fairly fine skin and slightly tart taste. The sugar coating must be even and quite thick. Do not hesitate to dip them twice, and make sure to let them cool thoroughly.

lollipops

1 Prepare the raspberry juice. Press 7 oz (200 g) raspberries, boil the purée obtained, and filter it through a fine sieve. Set it aside. Combine 1³/₄ cups (400 g) superfine sugar, the raspberry juice, 1¹/₄ cups (30 cl) water, and 1 tbsp glucose syrup in a fairly large, thick-bottomed saucepan. The method is the same for other fruit flavors such as blackcurrant or strawberry.

2 Heat the mixture, stirring constantly so as to dissolve the sugar thoroughly. Brush down the walls of the pan to remove any crystals and impurities. Using brown sugar or a mixture of sugar and honey (especially if the honey is flavored with lavender or thyme) can give homemade lollipops a special flavor of their own.

3 As soon as the mixture starts boiling, insert the candy thermometer and watch the progressive increase in temperature. When the crazed sugar temperature is reached (about 311 °F/155 °C), plunge the pan into a basin full of water and ice cubes. Oil a marble slab. Pour out the cooked sugar in large, fairly flat drops 1–2 in (3–5 cm) in diameter, using a soup spoon.

4 While the sugar is still soft, slip a stick into each drop. Let them cool and harden completely on the marble slab. Unstick the lollipops one by one using a fairly fine metal spatula. Pick them up by the stick and wrap them in little squares of plastic wrap. They can be kept for up to a month in a metal box.

Chocolate caramels (makes about 25)

1 Coarsely grate 7 oz (200 g) dark chocolate and set it aside. Put 1 generous cup (25 cl) light cream in a saucepan, bring it to the boil, and add the chocolate, 1 generous cup (250 g) superfine sugar, and $^1/_2$ cup + $1^1/_2$ tbsp (10 cl) runny honey. Bring it to the boil over medium heat, stirring constantly with a wooden spoon to prevent the syrup sticking to the bottom of the pan. Check the rising temperature with the candy thermometer.

2 When it reaches 239 °F (115 °C), reduce the heat and continue simmering. When the temperature reaches 257 °F (125 °C), plunge the bottom of the pan into a basin of cold water to stop the cooking. Allow about 8–9 minutes' cooking time for the mixture to reach the desired temperature. Then, oil a marble slab and four metal rulers arranged to form a square with sides of about 6 in (15 cm).

3 When the mixture of chocolate, cream, sugar, and honey forms a perfectly even, smooth, and flowing mass, pour the contents of the pan into the square formed by the metal rulers (which you can protect with oiled aluminum foil). Leave to cool for 2 hours until the mass has thoroughly solidified.

4 If the mass is still too soft, you can return it to the heat in a clean pan, let it melt, and then boil it for 2 minutes. Spread it out and let it cool. Remove the rulers forming the square and detach the block of caramel, using the point of a knife if necessary. Cut the hardened caramel into strips 1 in (2.5 cm) wide and then into squares of the same size.

5 To wrap the caramels, cut squares of plastic wrap. Wrap them one by one. They can be kept for about two weeks in an airtight box, preferably in the bottom of the refrigerator. You can also leave the caramel in a single block, again wrapped in plastic wrap, and cut it into squares according to your requirements.

Kalougas

Milk and nut caramels

Fudge

General points

Milk caramel syrup contains a large proportion of fats and lactose. It is therefore important to cook it slowly, to avoid any sudden browning. The color and taste of caramels are the result of a complex chemical reaction between the sugar and the proteins in the milk, so it is wise to choose the best basic ingredients. The honey used here flavors the mixture and prevents crystallization. Once the caramels have cooled and been cut, remember to wrap them quickly so they do not stick to one another. In the same family as caramels are specialties from elsewhere such as taffy, very similar to soft caramels, made with milk or cream and variously flavored; hopjes, the hard Dutch caramels flavored with coffee; and fudge, which has the texture of a fondant and the flavor of caramel.

Milk and nut caramels

To make about 25 pieces, coarsely chop 50 nuts with a knife and roast them for a few moments in the oven. Set them aside. Bring 1 scant cup (20 cl) light cream and 3 1/2 tbsp (5 cl) milk to the boil. Add 1 vanilla bean split in two, 1 generous cup (250 g) superfine sugar, and 1/3 cup + 1 1/2 tbsp (10 cl) runny honey. Cook over medium heat, stirring constantly with a wooden spoon to prevent the syrup sticking to the bottom of the pan. Check the rising temperature with a candy thermometer. When it reaches 239 °F (115 °C), reduce the heat. Meanwhile, oil a marble slab and four metal rulers covered in aluminum foil. Arrange the rulers to form a square with sides of about 6 in (15 cm). When the temperature reaches 257 °F (125 °C), remove the vanilla bean and pour in the roasted nuts and 1 oz (30 g) semi-salted butter. Continue as for the chocolate caramel recipe.

Fudge

Fudge is a British candy with the consistency of a fondant. To make about 25 pieces, put 15 oz (425 g) superfine sugar, 2/3 cup (15 cl) whole milk, and 2 oz (60 g) butter in a saucepan. Bring to the boil, stirring constantly. Cook to 239 °F (115 °C) then plunge the pan into cold water. Stir. When it whitens and thickens, add 1 tsp vanilla essence and 3 1/2 oz (100 g) chopped almonds. Then pour it into a buttered mold. Let it set and cut it into squares. The preparation is ready when a drop of the mixture plunged into a bowl of cold water hardens at once. The use of a big, square mold avoids having to use the slab and metal rulers. In some fudge recipes, flaked almonds or chopped nuts are added.

White nougat (makes 4 bars)

1 Roast 10½ oz (300 g) almonds and 3½ oz (100 g) pistachios in the oven for a few moments. Do this in two stages, spreading the nuts on a baking sheet in a single layer. Set them aside. Put 9 oz (250 g) sugar, ½ cup (12 cl) water, and 1 tbsp glucose syrup in a saucepan, mix, and bring to the boil. Meanwhile, stiffly beat 3 egg whites with an electric whisk.

2 When the temperature of the syrup reaches 284 °F (140 °C), add ⅔ cup (15 cl) runny honey (use either acacia honey, which is naturally runny, or lavender honey melted in a double boiler). Heat again up to 289 °F (143 °C), and plunge the bottom of the pan into cold water. Then fold in the egg whites, constantly stirring the mixture with a wooden spoon.

3 Once the mixture is perfectly even, put it in the top of a double boiler and continue to stir the mixture vigorously over simmering water for about 10 minutes. Then incorporate the roasted nuts, mixing slowly with a wooden spoon.

4 The traditional way of cooling the nougat is to use a frame formed with metal rulers placed on a sheet of rice paper and pour the mixture into it. Place a second sheet on top of it and press the whole block for 24 hours. More simply, you can pour the mixture into a square or rectangular metal mold around 2 in (5 cm) deep.

5 It is essential to wait until the mixture is well firmed and solidified before cutting it into regular strips 2–2½ in (5–6 cm) wide with a large knife. Nougat is not merely a fairground candy. If made with care, it can be served with coffee among other dainties. It can be kept in a cool place in an airtight container for 4 or 5 weeks.

Corsican nougat

Chinese nougat

Black nougat

From nuts to nougat

The word "nougat" comes from the Latin "nux" which means "nuts." It is a very ancient confection based on sugar, honey, dried fruit, and egg whites. The best-known kind comes from the town of Montélimar. There are several kinds of nougat in France: white nougat, whose consistency can be soft or hard, brown nougat, containing honey, which is more caramelized, and Provençal nougat, which contains dried and sometimes crystallized fruit. They should not be confused with ice nougat, which is a vanilla ice cream containing almonds and preserved fruit accompanied by nougat or nougatine, which is an almond caramel garnished with raised pieces of nut. The final texture of this delicacy depends on how much the syrup is cooked: the more it is cooked, the harder and crunchier the nougat will be.

Chinese nougat

Although it is called nougat, this recipe has little connection with the nougats just described. In fact it is made from highly gelled sugarcane syrup to which peeled peanuts are added. The preparation is molded into large squares around $^5/_8$ in (1.5 cm) thick and solidifies gradually. The mass is then cut by machine into small squares that are coated with tiny sesame seeds. Chinese nougat, which is served at dessert, is eaten in many Asian countries. It is sold in exotic food shops and can make an unusual addition to a litchi fruit salad or mango or coconut sorbet. Serve it at teatime too, together with other goodies.

Black nougat

Roast 8 oz (220 g) almonds and $3^1/_2$ oz (100 g) pistachios in the oven for a few moments. Set them aside. Put 9 oz (250 g) sugar, $^1/_2$ cup (12 cl) water, and 1 tsp glucose syrup in a saucepan, mix, and bring to the boil. When the temperature of the syrup reaches 284 °F (140°C), add $^2/_3$ cup (15 cl) runny honey. Heat again to 311 °F (155 °C) then plunge the saucepan into cold water. When the syrup stops boiling, add the nuts, mixing with a wooden spoon. Form a square with metal rulers on a sheet of rice paper and pour in the mixture. Put another sheet on top and press it with a board and weights for 24 hours. Then break up the nougat into pieces of different sizes with a large knife.

General points

Frangipane is a traditional way of using powdered almonds. It is a cooking paste used to enrich all kinds of desserts. Prepare it in advance: it keeps well in the refrigerator for 5 or 6 days and in the freezer for 3 months. Choose peeled almonds to obtain a nice, clear frangipane. It is included in the famous Bourdaloue tart. More simply, you can spread frangipane on slices of brioche, sprinkle them with flaked almonds, and put them in the oven. This will give you delicious sugared toast.

Twelfth Night cake

Frangipane (makes about 4 cups/1 liter of paste)

1 Prepare a confectioner's custard: heat 4 cups (1 liter) milk (you can flavor it with a vanilla bean split in two). Beat 2 whole eggs and 4 yolks with $^2/_3$ cup (150 g) sugar. Incorporate 1 generous cup (125 g) sifted flour then pour in the boiling milk. Transfer to a saucepan and cook for about 20 minutes. Let it go completely cold.

2 Take $12^1/_2$ oz (350 g) confectioner's custard (keeping the rest to fill éclairs or cover a tart). Mix it with 9 oz (250 g) creamed butter, 9 oz (200 g) powdered almonds, 2 $^1/_3$ cups (250 g) confectioner's sugar, 5 tsp (25 g) cornstarch, and 6 tbsp rum. Stir the mixture thoroughly with a wooden spoon, then fold in 3 whole eggs, one by one, continuing to stir.

3 When the cream is nice and smooth, add another tbsp of coarsely chopped flaked almonds, and the frangipane is ready for use. Poured and spread between two layers of puff pastry it lends all its creamy, delicious flavor to a Twelfth Night cake. As it is quite time-consuming to prepare, it is a good idea to make plenty and freeze the surplus.

Issoudun marzipan

Orange filled with praline marzipan

Baklava

Marzipan

Marzipan is an almond-based confectionery supposedly invented by a religious order and enjoyed by aristocrats in the seventeenth century. There are various formulas for marzipan in the Confiturier Royal, published by Claude Prud'homme in 1732. Later, in the nineteenth century, there was a story that Honoré de Balzac personally ran a marzipan factory in Rue Vivienne in Paris. The affair, a cleverly orchestrated tall story, caused a sensation and mystified fashionable Paris at the time. The marzipan we know today is a cooked mixture of almonds, sugar, and egg whites, more or less colored and flavored. To make about 2$\frac{1}{4}$ lb (1 kg), put 1 lb 2 oz (500 g) sugar, $\frac{2}{3}$ cup (15 cl) water, and 1 tbsp glucose syrup in a saucepan. Bring it to the boil, using a candy thermometer to monitor the temperature. When it reaches 237 °F (114 °C), plunge the saucepan into a basin of cold water to stop the cooking process. Mix the syrup for 2 minutes with a wooden spoon, then add 12$\frac{1}{2}$ oz (350 g) powdered almonds and 2 lightly beaten egg whites. Mix to form an even paste. Set the saucepan over low heat and cook the marzipan slowly, stirring it constantly. This operation takes about 8 minutes. The paste thickens and whitens little by little. Powder a marble slab with 1 tsp confectioner's sugar and pour on the marzipan, let it cool for 1 minute, and then pound it vigorously with your hands for 5 minutes: the texture becomes smooth and elastic. At this stage, plain marzipan is ready. Divide it into balls of the desired size. Choose your colorings and flavorings and mix them with the marzipan by hand, kneading it on the marble.

Variants

Colored and flavored in various ways (chocolate, coffee, vanilla, praline), marzipan is formed into dainty mouthfuls. There are striped marzipans (several layers of different colors), spiraled marzipan (two layers combined as for a cake roll), checkerboard marzipan, and marzipan in cylinders and squares. It is used in the preparation of many foreign specialties such as baklava or the Portuguese party "eel."

Portuguese eel

561

Glace Plombières

Inherited from a set of 19th-century recipes, glace Plombières is a truly French specialty that can make a perfect finish for a winter party meal whose menu might include chicken vol-au-vents and duck in orange sauce, to retain the traditional note. You can accompany it with a selection of small cookies (cigarettes russes, almond tiles, and small almond macaroons) and serve it with cold, dry champagne. The origins of glace Plombières are not known for certain, but it is thought to come from Plombières-les-Bains where Napoleon III was taking a cure. It is also said to owe its name to the lead molds in which it was set to cool. It is an ice dessert based on milk, almonds, whipped cream, and preserved fruit that can be made without a sorbet-maker. Allow it to set in the refrigerator for 24–48 hours.

Serves 6
Preparation: 30 minutes
Waiting: 2 hours
Cooking: 15 minutes
Freezing: 24 hours

Ingredients

4¹/₂ oz (120 g) powdered almonds
6¹/₂ oz (180 g) preserved fruit
1 generous cup (25 cl) milk
6 egg yolks
²/₃ cup (140 g) superfine sugar
1 generous cup (25 cl) light cream

1 Assemble all the ingredients for the recipe. Pay particular attention to the powdered almonds, which must be absolutely fresh for a high-quality ice cream with no rancid after-taste. Mix at least two or three different varieties of preserved fruit (bigarreaux cherries, angelica, orange peel, citron, and pineapple, for example).

2 Mix the milk and powdered almonds in a thick-bottomed saucepan. Put the pan over medium heat and bring to the boil gradually, beating constantly with a whisk. Remove from the heat, cover, and allow to infuse for at least 2 hours, then filter the mixture through a sieve, gently crushing any lumps with the back of a wooden spoon.

3 Put the egg yolks in a bowl or casserole. Pour the superfine sugar on top and start to beat with a hand whisk, then use an electric whisk to obtain a puffed-up, foamy cream. Pour the infused milk on top, continuing to stir. Pour the whole mixture into a saucepan and set it over low heat.

4 Cook the mixture as for custard. As soon as it starts to thicken and take on consistency, remove the pan from the heat and beat it at high speed with an electric whisk until it has gone completely cold. Separately, beat the (very cold) light cream stiffly and then fold it delicately into the first mixture.

5 Cut the preserved fruit into small, even cubes and set them aside for the final garnish (particularly slices of angelica, bigarreau cherries, and pieces of citron cut into small stars). Pour a layer of cream into a cake mold, add preserved fruit, another layer of cream, and continue thus to fill the mold, ending with a final layer of cream.

6 Put the mold in the freezer for at least 24 hours. When serving the glace Plombières, remove it from the mold by dipping the bottom in boiling hot water and turning it upside-down on an oval platter. Glace Plombières is cut like a Yule log in fairly thick slices. Serve it on well chilled plates.

General points

Chocolate is a mixture of cocoa, sugar, and cocoa butter. The proportion of these three components determines the different qualities you can find on the market: eating chocolate, dark or bitter chocolate, etc. The more cocoa it contains and the less sugar, the more bitter the chocolate will be, and vice versa. Dark chocolate can contain 50% of cocoa in the whole dry ingredients and "bitter" chocolate, 60%. Milk chocolate also contains powdered milk, while white chocolate is a mixture of cocoa butter, sugar, and milk, stabilized with emulsifiers. "Coating" chocolate is used by professionals. It melts well and is suitable for all covering operations. It is presented in

Chocolate assortment

large blocks weighing 4$\frac{1}{2}$ lb or 6$\frac{3}{4}$ lb (2 or 3 kg). You can obtain it from a confectioner or cake-maker. In the chocolate trade there are special blocks for cooking (confectioner's chocolate) and tablets for eating (with milk, rice, hazel nuts, and almonds). Take care not to confuse them with one another.

Filled chocolates are usually presented in small, wrapped, bite-size pieces. Cocoa powder has many uses: delicious at breakfast in hot

milk, it is also used to garnish cakes, prepare sweet sauces, and flavor mousses. There is one area where the use of chocolate is not so well known: savory cooking. In fact, bitter, dark chocolate is used in certain sauces spiced with red wine so as to improve their taste and color. Two specialties from Aragon in Spain illustrate this practice: crayfish and calf's tongue.

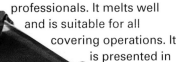

Coating chocolate

Chocolate nun

Chocolate éclair

Florentines

Working with chocolate

When melting chocolate, always work at a low temperature: sudden heat adulterates chocolate and it becomes irremediably dull and grainy. For cakes or desserts, it is advisable to choose chocolate with a high cocoa content (whether in powder or block form), and its flavor can always be heightened by adding unsweetened cocoa powder. For specific confectionery purposes such as coating, garnishing, or glazing, dark chocolate can be used, but the required coating chocolate is used in particular. Grated chocolate is sometimes used, either to embellish a cake or

to garnish a dessert or sweetmeat. If the weather is hot, take care to put the chocolate in the refrigerator for a few moments before grating it, and hold it in aluminum foil to prevent it melting in your hand. To break chocolate, use a board and a cleaver or a long-bladed knife. Do not break it up too small, as this increases the risk of melting.

Little chocolate berets

Saint-Émilion charlotte with macaroons and chocolate

ICE DESSERTS

Although they are often served plain, soufflés, Norwegian omelets, ice creams, and sorbets take on a new look with custard or flaked, broiled almonds. Sorbets go brilliantly with spirits and liqueurs.Blackcurrant liqueur and blackcurrant sorbet, peach cream and peach sorbet, vodka and lemon sorbet, or again Williamine and pear sorbet are reliable combinations.

Bavarois, mirrors, and fruit mousses

These are often accompanied by fresh fruit coulis in a contrasting color. The result looks as good as it tastes. Be sure to serve your coulis very cold: the impression of freshness will be all the stronger.

Black chocolate mousses

These can be served straight onto the plate or in goblets, formed into balls with a spoon, with a rosette of whipped cream or a dash of custard.

Waffles and pancakes

Waffles go well with a dark chocolate, or even caramel, sauce. Crêpes are a favorite with the most varied spirits: rum, Armagnac, brandy, Imperial Mandarin, or Grand Marnier.

Baked charlottes

As these are sometimes quite compact, you can accompany them with caramel or chocolate sauce, or custard.

Success and progress

A red fruit sauce and a garnish of roast dried fruit make excellent accompaniments.

Elderflower fritters

A regional dish

Serves 4
Preparation: 10 minutes
Resting: 1 hour
Cooking: 15 minutes

Ingredients

9 oz (250 g) flour
4 eggs
Salt and pepper
1 small bottle beer
12 elderflower clusters
Oil

1. Put the flour in a large bowl. Separate the eggs. Put the yolks on top of the flour and set the flour aside. Melt the butter, without letting it cook, and pour it hot, but not boiling, over the eggs. Add salt and pepper and start to beat the mixture, gradually pouring in enough beer to obtain a smooth batter. Let it rest for an hour. Trim and clean the elderflower clusters, removing any that are faded.

2. Heat the oil (it should be at 356 °F/180°C when you use it). Beat the egg whites stiffly and fold them into the batter, which should be used at once. Check the temperature of the frying oil by dropping a little bit of fresh bread into it: it should rise bubbling after about 20 seconds. Your oil should be barely colored and not smoking.

3. Dip an elderflower cluster in the batter and turn it over, making sure it is completely covered. Drop it into the frying oil. Wait until the fritters are golden underneath and then turn them over and fry them on the other side. Keep them warm on paper towels. Arrange them on a dish and season with salt and pepper.

4. Do not fry too many fritters at once, as that would reduce the temperature of the frying oil and prevent the fritters from cooking as they should. You can vary the proportions of the batter according to your taste: if it is more liquid it will be clear, crunchy, and light, but will tend to disperse in the frying oil. If it is thicker it will stick to the flowers better, but may not be so crunchy.

Recommended drinks

Monbazillac
Loupiac
Barsac

Menu suggestions

1. Elderflower (or acacia) fritters are popular mainly in southwestern France: include them in a regional menu with a salad of duck magret and confit.

2. You can also serve these fritters for a country supper with rolled waffles and jelly.

Mint candies

A family dish

Makes about 50 candies
Preparation: 15 minutes
Cooking: None

Ingredients

4 cups (450 g) confectioner's sugar
2 tbsp lemon juice
1 egg white
1 tsp mint liqueur
Green coloring
Confectioner's sugar for shaping

1. Put the confectioner's sugar, lemon juice, egg white, and mint liqueur in a bowl. Beat the mixture vigorously until it is smooth. Divide it into halves and color one half with a few drops of green coloring.

2. Turn it out on a board sprinkled with confectioner's sugar and sprinkle the mass itself with confectioner's sugar. Pound and reduce it to a thickness of about $3/8$ in (1 cm). Cut it into various shapes with a pastry cutter. You can also simply cut it into pieces and roll it into little balls.

3. Leave them somewhere cool for 24 hours before packing them in airtight boxes. Take the precaution of putting a sheet of wax paper on top of each layer. Packed like this, these mint candies can be kept in a cool, dark place for a month.

4. Make these mint candies look even nicer by dipping one side of them in dark chocolate melted in a bain-marie or double boiler—the combination of chocolate and mint is a great classic of candy-making, especially in English-speaking countries where they are essential with after-dinner coffee. Prick each candy with the end of a fondue fork and plunge it rapidly into the melted chocolate. Put the candies on a sheet of aluminum foil and let them dry completely. In this case, they should be eaten fairly soon. You can also flatten the mixture a bit more and stick the small pieces together two by two with a little melted chocolate, to obtain mint and chocolate confections.

Recommended drinks

Black coffee
Lemonade
Earl Grey tea

Menu suggestions

1. These mint candies can, of course, be eaten at any time of day, but are delicious with coffee at the end of a meal.

2. For a children's tea party, serve these candies in an assortment with other dainties, or at afternoon tea.

571

Recommended drinks

Banyuls
Maury
Rasteau

Menu suggestions

1. For a winter meal, serve a mixed salad with smoked salmon as an appetizer, followed by a casserole of white veal with mushrooms.

2. This chocolate charlotte also makes a splendid dessert after a duck and orange casserole, itself preceded by jellied eggs.

Charlotte with chocolate

A party dish

Serves 4
Preparation: 25 minutes
Cooking: 10 minutes
Resting time: 3 hours

Ingredients

1 large pot crème fraîche
1 tsp instant coffee
1 small glass brandy, Armagnac, or rum
Ladyfingers
1 block dark chocolate

1. Take 1 tbsp crème fraîche, put it in a small saucepan, and heat: when it starts to simmer, add the coffee, stir until it melts, and then remove it from the burner.

2. Pour the brandy (or spirit of your choice) into a soup dish. Take the ladyfingers one by one and dip just the underside of each in the liquor. Add them one at a time to a charlotte mold, lining the bottom and sides. For the bottom, overlap them in a star shape.

3. Stiffly whip the rest of the crème fraîche and then mix it quickly with the coffee-flavored cream. Set aside a few spoonfuls of this mixture. Take one-third of the chocolate and grate it. Mix this grated chocolate with the coffee cream.

4. Gradually transfer this mixture to the mold with a soup spoon. Arrange a layer of ladyfingers star-wise on top, overlapping one another. Once the mold is full, put a plate on top of the charlotte and a centered weight on top of the plate. Put the charlotte in the refrigerator for at least 3 hours. You can cool it more, for up to 8 hours.

5. Shortly before serving the charlotte, break the rest of the chocolate into a small saucepan, add 2 tbsp water, and melt it in a bain-marie or double boiler, or in a saucepan over very low heat. Delicately remove the charlotte from the mold onto a round serving dish, then pour the chocolate on top and let it run over the sides. Return it to a cool place. Garnish with small rosettes using the reserved crème fraîche mixture.

Raspberry charlotte

A party dish

Serves 6
Preparation: 30 minutes
Cooking: 8–10 minutes
Resting: 7–8 hours

Ingredients

For the frangipane:
1 generous cup (25 cl) milk
1 vanilla bean
3 1/2 tbsps (50 g) granulated sugar
1/4 cup (30 g) flour
1 3/4 oz (50 g) powdered almonds
2 eggs

To finish the charlotte:
14 oz (400 g) raspberries
24 ladyfingers
1 small glass raspberry liqueur

1. Start by preparing the frangipane. Pour the milk into a saucepan and heat gently, adding the vanilla bean split in two, and let it simmer. Then remove it from the heat, cover, and leave to infuse for 10 minutes.

2. During the infusion, mix the sugar, flour, and powdered almonds in a bowl. Stir with a spatula so these three dry components are thoroughly mixed. If necessary you can sieve them together. Make a well and break 1 egg into it, then add 1 yolk. Mix with a spoon then gradually pour in the hot, vanilla-flavored milk.

3. Pour the cream back into the saucepan when it is homogenized, set it over medium heat, and bring to the boil, stirring constantly. When two or three bubbles appear, remove it from the heat and leave to cool.

4. Prepare the raspberries: sort them and remove the stalks, but do not wash them. Cut a dozen ladyfingers to form triangular shapes. Quickly dip the flat side in a mixture of water and raspberry liqueur (or simply syrup).

5. Line the bottom of a charlotte mold with the shaped ladyfingers then place whole ones around the sides, having also quickly dipped them (take care not to let them dry out). Pour a little frangipane in the bottom, arrange almost all the raspberries over, and continue filling with the cream. Shake down well and leave the charlotte somewhere cool for 7–8 hours. Turn the charlotte out of the mold on to a circular serving dish and arrange the rest of the raspberries around it.

Recommended drinks

Cabernet d'Anjou
Bourgueil
Chinon

Menu suggestions

1. Ideal for a summer lunch between friends, this charlotte is perfect with a menu including mushroom salad with herbs and pike with white butter.

2. If you prefer a meat dish, you could follow a vegetable terrine, for example, with a loin of veal or veal sweetbreads with a macedoine of vegetables.

Cookies

A family dish

Makes 50 cookies
Preparation: 20 minutes
Cooking: 10 minutes

Ingredients

$4^1/_2$ oz (125 g) butter
Scant $^1/_2$ cup (90 g) brown sugar
3 oz (90 g) sugar
2 eggs
$^1/_2$ tsp vanilla essence
$^1/_2$ tsp bicarbonate of soda
$^1/_2$ tsp salt
$^3/_4$ cup (90 g) flour

1 glass milk
$1^1/_2$ cups (150 g) oat flakes
$4^1/_2$ oz (125 g) dark cooking chocolate
2 oz (60 g) dried fruit

1. Make sure the butter is at room temperature. Put it in a bowl with the brown and white sugar. Beat with a hand whisk until you obtain a smooth cream. Incorporate the eggs, beaten with a fork, and the vanilla, continuing to beat.

2. Mix the bicarbonate of soda and the flour and sift them together. Add the sifted flour to the contents of the bowl and stir thoroughly with a spoon, also pouring in the milk a little at a time. Add the oat flakes and mix with a wooden spoon to distribute them evenly in the mixture.

3. Coarsely chop the chocolate and dried fruit. Incorporate them into the mixture. Using a level teaspoon each time, put this mixture straight onto a baking sheet; you could cover it first with wax paper. Take care to allow a space of 2 in (5 cm) in all directions between each spoonful. Pressing on each spoonful, use a floured fork to draw little crosses on them without breaking the paste, as your cookies should be fairly thick. The fork should be re-floured for each cookie.

4. Heat the oven to 350 °F (180 °C), then bake and lightly brown the cookies for 10 minutes. Wait a couple of minutes before detaching them with a metal spatula, and place them on a wire rack to cool. These cookies can be easily stored in a tightly closed metal box. If you wish to make some brown chocolate cookies and other, lighter ones, divide the dough in two and add 4 tbsp (30 g) cocoa powder to one half. For the dried fruit, mix almonds and pistachios in equal proportions, or walnuts and hazelnuts.

Recommended drinks

Orangeade
Ice chocolate
Lemon tea

Menu suggestions

1. Popular with children, cookies can be included in a meal devised specially for them: sweetcorn salad and roast chicken or pizza.

2. Cookies are also welcome at teatime, together with other snacks such as mini-sandwiches made with sliced, white bread.

Strawberry meringue

A light dish

Serves 4
Preparation: 10 minutes
Cooking: 1 to 2 minutes

<u>Microwave oven only</u>
The cooking time is calculated for a 600–650-watt oven. In a lower-powered model, increase the cooking time in proportion: for example, for a 500-watt oven, increase the time by 15–20%.

Ingredients

1 egg white
4 cups (450 g) confectioner's sugar
1 lb 11 oz (750 g) strawberries
1 small pot cream

1. Put the egg white in a bowl and beat it with a fork—but not for too long. Gradually add $2^1/_2$ cups (300 g) confectioner's sugar, continuing to beat with the fork. You should obtain a fairly firm paste.

2. Knead the mixture on a board sprinkled with $^1/_2$ cup (50 g) confectioner's sugar. Form the mixture obtained into a ball and then shape it into a fairly long roll. Cut it into slices and form little balls. Group them, six by six, on wax paper and cook for 1–2 minutes on full power (100%).

3. Set aside a few nice strawberries. Put the others in a blender with $^7/_8$ cup (100 g) confectioner's sugar. Whip the cream with an electric mixer until it reaches a firm consistency. There's no point in sweetening the cream, as the meringues and coulis both contain plenty of sugar.

4. Pour the strawberry coulis into dessert bowls. Spread half the meringues with whipped cream and stick them together with the other half. Arrange them over the coulis and garnish with the reserved strawberries. You can also use raspberries or a mixture of red fruits for this recipe.

Recommended drinks

Sparkling water
Strawberry milk shake
Ice tea

Menu suggestions

1. For fish lovers, serve grapefruit filled with shrimp as an appetizer, followed by papillotte of trout.

2. For meat lovers, serve artichoke salad vinaigrette as an appetizer, and then roast chicken in a salt crust.

Crème caramel with saffron

A family dish

Serves 4
Preparation: 25 minutes
Cooking: 25 minutes

Ingredients

3 cups (75 cl) milk
1 generous cup (250 g) superfine sugar
8 eggs
1 large pinch saffron threads

1. Pour the milk into a thick-bottomed saucepan, bring it to the boil, and let it simmer for a few moments. Using a wooden spoon, stir in half the sugar until it is completely dissolved. Remove the pan from the heat and let it rest.

2. Prepare a caramel with the rest of the sugar. Pour it into a small saucepan, moisten it with water, and heat until it reaches the desired color. Take care not to let it burn. Pour it into the saucepan containing the milk and mix thoroughly. Return the saucepan to very low heat to keep the milk warm without letting it boil.

3. Break 3 eggs in a bowl. Break the remaining eggs, separating the whites from the yolks. Set the whites aside (keep them to make meringues, for example) and add the yolks to the bowl. Beat them with the whole eggs until you obtain a foaming, almost white, mixture.

4. Pour the warm, flavored milk over the beaten eggs, little by little, beating gently. Spread the saffron threads on the baking sheet covered with a sheet of wax paper and put it in a barely warm oven with the door half open to dry them thoroughly. Crush half of them between your fingers and add them to the cream. Put the cream back on the heat and warm it gently, without boiling, until it nicely coats the back of a wooden spoon. Pour the cream into a bowl or serving dish and leave it to cool completely. Sprinkle the rest of the saffron threads on top of the cream. Serve cold.

Recommended drinks

Muscat de Rivesaltes
Mousserende Vouvray
Crémant de Loire

Menu suggestions

1. For a family winter meal, serve a good, thick stew after meat broth garnished with a little vermicelli as an appetizer.

2. This baked custard can be served after a mushroom omelet accompanied by a salad of curly endive and bacon lardoons with a selection of cheeses.

Bourdaloue baked custard with apricots

A family dish

Serves 4
Preparation: 20 minutes
Cooking: 30 to 35 minutes

Ingredients

1³/₄ oz (50 g) butter
12¹/₂ oz (350 g) piecrust dough
2 cups (50 cl) milk
¹/₂ vanilla bean
²/₃ cup (150 g) granulated sugar
3 eggs
¹/₃ cup (40 g) flour

2–3 macaroons
1 lb 2 oz (500 g) apricots
10 fresh almonds

1. Butter a pie dish, roll out the dough, and line the dish with it, then cover with a disk of paper and spread dried beans or fruit pits on it. Heat the oven to 350 °F (180 °C) and bake the pastry shell "blind" for 20–25 minutes. Remove the pie dish from the oven, remove the paper and dried beans or pits, and leave the pastry shell in the warm oven.

2. Meanwhile, prepare a confectioner's custard. Heat the milk with the vanilla, remove the pan from the heat as soon as the first bubbles rise, and let it infuse. Stir together ¹/₂ cup (100 g) sugar, 2 whole eggs, and 1 yolk in a thick-bottomed saucepan. Gradually add the flour and then the warm milk.

3. Place over low heat and wait for the first bubbles to rise, stirring the custard constantly with a wooden spoon. With the pan off the heat, add 1 dab of butter and 1 or 2 crushed macaroons. Leave the mixture to cool.

4. Cut the apricots in half. For preference, use apricots that are flavorful, but not too ripe (their best season is July and August). Remove the pits. Fill a saucepan with water, add the rest of the sugar, and bring it to the boil. Add the halved apricots and let them poach gently for 2–3 minutes. Drain them with a slotted spoon and wipe them delicately using a folded cloth.

5. While it is still hot, pour the confectioner's custard onto the pastry, arrange the apricots and blanched almonds over, and sprinkle on the finely crushed macaroons. Heat the oven to 520 °F (270 °C). Drizzle a little melted butter on the custard and brown it a little. Allow to cool before serving.

Recommended drinks

Peach wine
Muscat de Beaumes-de-Venise
Frontignan

Menu suggestions

1. A traditional dessert dating back to the nineteenth century, this baked custard with apricots is perfect for a Sunday dinner after roast beef and potatoes dauphinoise.

2. You can also serve it more simply at dinner, after a macaroni and cheese and a seasonal salad.

577

Semolina cake with prunes

A regional recipe

Serves 4
Preparation: 20 minutes
Cooking: 25 minutes

Ingredients

9 oz (250 g) prunes
1 small glass Armagnac
2 cups (50 cl) milk
1 vanilla bean
$1/2$ cup (100 g) semolina
A few pinches powdered cinnamon
$2/3$ cup (150 g) granulated sugar
2 eggs

$1^3/_4$ oz (50 g) butter
1 oz (35 g) powdered almonds
Orange marmalade

1. The day before, soak the prunes in a little warm water with a small glass of Armagnac added. If you are in a hurry, you can simply moisten the prunes with boiling water and a little Armagnac and let them rest while you prepare the semolina.

2. Pour the milk into a saucepan, add the vanilla bean split in two, and bring to the boil. Leave to infuse for 10 minutes, then remove the vanilla. Drizzle the semolina into the boiling milk and cook for about 10 minutes while stirring. Still stirring, add the cinnamon and then $1/2$ cup (100 g) sugar.

3. Break and separate the eggs. Whip the whites very stiffly. Separately, beat 1 oz (30 g) butter in a bowl with a fork to reduce it to a cream, then add the egg yolks and the powdered almonds. Mix thoroughly and then fold in the stiff egg whites. Add this mixture to the semolina, which by now will have finished cooking.

4. Butter a ring-shaped mold and pour the mixture into it. Heat the oven to 400 °F (205 °C) and place the mold in a bain-marie or baking pan of water for 25 minutes.

5. Cook the prunes in their soaking liquid with $1/4$ cup (50 g) sugar added. Remove them when they have swollen nicely and reduce their cooking liquid to the consistency of light syrup. Turn the mixture out of the mold when cold onto a serving platter. Garnish with prunes moistened with syrup and top with orange marmalade.

Recommended drinks

Cahors
Madiran
Armagnac

Menu suggestions

1. This prune dessert can be served at the end of a meal based on the cuisine of southwestern France: Roquefort cheese in puff pastry and magrets with shallots.

2. For a lighter meal, serve green bean and duck's gizzard salad as an appetizer and slices of lamb broiled in garlic purée as a main dish.

Waffles with citrus zest

A family dish

Serves 4 (i.e., 12 waffles)
Preparation: 15 minutes
Cooking: 20 minutes

Ingredients

10 sugar lumps
1 lemon
1 orange
2 $\frac{1}{3}$ cups (275 g) flour
2 eggs
1 large pinch salt
3$\frac{1}{2}$ oz (100 g) butter
1 glass milk

Oil
$\frac{1}{8}$ cup (30 g) granulated sugar

1. Put the sugar lumps in a thick-bottomed saucepan with 2 tbsp water. Heat, stirring with a wooden spoon, until you obtain a thick syrup (the bubbles that form on the surface are small and tight, like pearls). Let the syrup cool and moisten with the juice of 1 lemon and 1 orange. Retain the peel and keep the syrup warm, without boiling it.

2. Put the flour in a bowl. Make a well in it and put in the egg yolks, salt, and melted butter. Start to work the mixture before gradually adding the warm, but not boiling, milk. Beat the egg whites stiffly and fold them in. The paste should be a little thicker than a pancake batter.

3. Cook the waffles in a lightly oiled, preheated waffle iron. Keep them warm in an open oven and serve with a sprinkling of granulated sugar and the flavored syrup. Garnish some with finely grated orange zest and the others with lemon zest.

4. If your waffle iron is a traditional model, you will have to oil or butter the dimpled compartments lightly before pouring in the batter. If you have a non-stick waffle iron, this precaution is not necessary. In either event, you must heat the waffle iron beforehand so the batter "takes" as soon as it is poured in. You will thus obtain crunchy, well-browned waffles. To remove them once they are cooked, lift one corner with a wooden spatula.

Recommended drinks

Beer
Orange juice
Ice chocolate

Menu suggestions

1. With a vegetable soup to start with, following by roast chicken, this traditional dessert will be popular with young and old alike.

2. You can also prepare these waffles for a birthday tea party for a few children, centered on chocolate cake and a large fruit salad containing mainly bananas.

Chestnut ice cream

A party dish

Serves 4
Preparation: 20 minutes
Setting: 1 hour

Ingredients

4 egg yolks
$1/4$ cup (50 g) superfine sugar
2 cups (50 cl) milk
1 vanilla bean
7 oz (200 g) thick crème fraîche
$10^1/2$ oz (300 g) chestnut purée
$3^1/2$ oz (100 g) bitter cooking chocolate

1. Start by making a custard: put the egg yolks in a bowl and beat them with the sugar until the mixture foams. Boil the milk with the vanilla. Then, off the heat, pour this still boiling milk into the egg and sugar mixture, continuing to beat steadily until it becomes smooth.

2. Return the pan to the heat and beat, stirring, until the cream nicely coats the spoon. You must not let it boil.
Pour the mixture into a bowl and let it cool.

3. Combine this custard, $3^1/2$ oz (100 g) crème fraîche, and the chestnut purée, beating thoroughly until the mixture becomes smooth. Pour it into a sorbet-maker and let it set.

4. Shortly before serving, whip the rest of the cream stiffly, without sugar, and melt the chocolate in 2 tbsp water, without stirring. This operation must be carried out so that the chocolate is still warm when you fill the dessert dishes (previously put in the refrigerator) with the chestnut ice cream.

5. Pour the chocolate sauce over the ice cream. It should solidify at once. Garnish with a few dabs of whipped cream and put it back in the refrigerator until the time comes to serve it. You can also scatter a few pieces of crystallized chestnuts on top of this ice cream.

Recommended drinks

Dry champagne
Pink champagne
Rum

Menu suggestions

1. Perfect for a winter meal, this ice cream can follow chicken vol-au-vents and salmon with dill.

2. You can also serve this ice cream after a crayfish salad and roast partridges with slices of bread fried in butter.

Yogurt and orange ice cream

A light dish

Serves 4
Preparation: 30 minutes
Setting: 2 hours

Ingredients

4 or 5 oranges
5½ oz (150 g) sugar lumps
2 pots plain yogurt
1 small pot crème fraîche

1. Choose unwaxed oranges with smooth, fragrant peel. Wash them. Rub the sugar lumps over the skin of 2 oranges so that they absorb the essence in the peel. Put them in a bowl one by one.

2. Pour the yogurt and cream into the bowl, add a little orange juice and beat vigorously until you obtain a foamy cream.

3. Fill a sorbet-maker with this mixture and freeze it.

4. Fill small molds with the mixture. Return them to the freezer for a few moments before emptying the molds onto a very cold dish. Garnish them with fine strips of orange zest barely poached in syrup, and quarters of fresh orange.

5. Many other citrus fruits can be used in this recipe: grapefruit, mandarins, or clementines. You can also change its presentation by arranging small pineapple cubes or mango slices round the ice cream. Moreover, choose full-milk yogurt whose consistency is creamy enough to set well when freezing.

RECOMMENDED DRINKS

Sparkling water
Freshly squeezed orange juice
Orgeat syrup

Menu suggestions

1. With spinach and chicken breast salad, pilaf rice and mushrooms, and this ice cream for dessert, you will create a light and delicious meal.

2. For a very light meal, serve this dessert after a fish papillotte and a bowl of soup.

Mendiants de Gordes

A Provençal dish

Serves 4
Preparation: 10 minutes
Cooking: 15 minutes
Resting: 1 hour

Ingredients

1 cup (125 g) flour
1 generous cup (125 g) confectioner's sugar
1 large pinch active dry yeast
2 oz (60 g) butter
1 egg
1 pinch salt
3$^{1}/_{2}$ oz (100 g) raisins

8 preserved orange zests
16 almonds
8 green walnuts
12 pre-cooked prunes
1 lemon

1. Put all the flour, $^{1}/_{4}$ cup (30 g) confectioner's sugar, the yeast, and the very cold butter, cut into pieces, in a bowl. Mix with your fingertips, then roll small pieces of paste between your palms to mold it and make it friable.

2. Add the egg and 1 pinch of salt, mix gently, roll into a ball, and put it somewhere cool for about an hour, wrapping the paste in plastic wrap.

3. Meanwhile, fatten the raisins in warm water, cut the orange zest into thin strips, open the almonds and walnuts, and pit the prunes and cut them in two. Roll out the pastry on a floured board and cut it into ovals.

4. Heat the oven to 400 °F (200 °C) and bake the cookies for about 15 minutes (they should not be really golden). Remove the cookies from the oven and put them on a wire rack to cool a little—they should be just warm. Meanwhile, squeeze the lemon juice into a bowl, add the rest of the confectioner's sugar, and mix thoroughly.

5. Finally, arrange the halved prunes, well-drained raisins, almonds, walnuts, and slices of preserved orange on the cookies, sprinkle them with lemon-flavored sugar (or paint them with it using a small brush), and let them cool.

Recommended drinks

Muscat de Beaumes-de-Venise
Rasteau
Mulled wine

Menu suggestions

1. This delicacy is inspired by the famous 13 desserts of Provence served on Christmas Eve, after celery salad, a fish dish, and endives with anchovies.

2. You can also serve these little cookies after a rich and substantial aioli (boiled vegetables, hard-boiled eggs, snails, and poached cod).

Lemon mousse

A Scandinavian dish

Serves 4
Preparation: 20 minutes
Cooling: At least 2 hours

Ingredients

2 eggs
$1/2$ cup (130 g) granulated sugar
1 lemon
4 sheets gelatin
6 oz (175 g) very flexible white cheese
8 tbsps crème fraîche

1. Break and separate the eggs. You must use absolutely fresh eggs, as they are not cooked at all in this recipe. Put the yolks in a bowl, add $6^{1}/2$ tbsp (100 g) granulated sugar, and stir the mixture until it whitens.

2. Wash the lemon, wipe it, and grate its zest very finely. Cut it in half and squeeze the juice of $1/2$ lemon into the egg mixture. Add the zest and beat the mixture at length with a hand whisk to obtain a well-bound and even cream.

3. Plunge the gelatin sheets into cold water for a few minutes, then drain them and put them in a bowl with 2–3 tbsp very hot water: they will dissolve very quickly. Add the melted gelatin to the lemon cream and mix thoroughly.

4. Whip the white cheese to aerate it as much as possible. Separately, beat the egg whites very stiffly. Fold into the lemon cream mixed with gelatin first the white cheese and then the stiffly beaten egg whites.

5. Pour it all into a dessert dish and put it in the refrigerator until the time comes to serve it. Then garnish the center with a nice slice of lemon. Whip the fresh cream with the rest of the sugar and arrange small rosettes all round using a glazing bag.

Recommended drinks

Beer
Aquavit
Lemonade

Menu suggestions

1. This mousse can be the finishing touch of a meal consisting of a salad of herring and beets, followed by salmon marinated in dill with potato vinaigrette.

2. You can also serve this mousse in a Scandinavian buffet, with small raisin brioches garnished with smoked fish on slices of fried bread.

583

Nougatine parfait

A party dish

Serves 5
Preparation: 30 minutes
Freezing: 3–4 hours

Ingredients

1 vanilla bean
2 cups (50 cl) milk
1½ cups (375 g) granulated sugar
6 egg yolks
1 generous cup (25 cl) crème fraîche
4½ oz (125 g) shelled hazelnuts
Oil

Recommended drinks

Sauternes
Loupiac
Barsac

Menu suggestions

1. This flavorsome, ice dessert can give the finishing touch to a fall meal based on mushrooms (wild mushroom croustade as an appetizer) and game (roast pheasant or venison chops).

2. More simply, you can serve it after a marinated leg of lamb or braised shoulder of lamb, preceded by a cold salmon mousse.

1. Split the vanilla bean lengthwise. Put it in the milk with 6½ tbsp (100 g) sugar. Bring it to the boil. Remove the pan from the heat, cover, and let the vanilla infuse for 10 minutes. Put the egg yolks in a bowl and beat them with ½ cup (110 g) sugar until you obtain a foamy, almost white mixture. Remove the vanilla bean from the milk. Heat the milk again and, as soon as it starts to boil, pour a few spoonfuls of boiling milk on to the yolks, beating constantly, then pour the contents of the bowl into the pan with a single movement. Continue to stir the mixture with a wooden spatula over low heat while it slowly thickens. You absolutely must not let it boil. Cooking is finished when the cream nicely coats the spatula (a line drawn with a blunt knife in the cream coating the spatula should remain clearly visible).

2. Remove the pan from the heat and incorporate the crème fraîche, still beating with the spatula. Put the pan in a bowl of cold water and stir at regular intervals. Meanwhile, put the hazelnuts on a baking sheet and let them dry and roast for a few minutes in the oven at 350 °F (180 °C). Rub them between your palms to remove the film that covers them. Make quite a strong, dark caramel with the rest of the sugar and a little water. Put the nuts on a lightly oiled marble slab and pour the thickened caramel on top. Let it cool and set. Break the nougatine thus obtained and crush part of it quite finely.

3. Add this crushed nougatine to the contents of the pan, which by now should be almost completely cold. Put it in a sorbet-maker and place it in the refrigerator to set. Remove it from the mold, garnishing it with pieces of nougatine.

Pavlova

An English dish

Serves 4
Preparation: 15 minutes
Cooking: 15 minutes
Waiting: 1 hour

Ingredients

2 egg whites
1 scant cup (200 g) superfine sugar
1/4 tsp salt
1 1/2 tbsp cornstarch
1 tsp vanilla essence
1 tsp vinegar
1 pot crème fraîche

Scant 1/2 cup (60 g) confectioner's sugar
4 kiwi fruit

1. Beat the eggs very stiffly. Moisten with 4 tbsp cool water and beat again. Gradually add the sugar while beating and make sure each spoonful is thoroughly absorbed before adding the next. Add the salt, cornstarch, vanilla essence, and vinegar on completion, stirring gently.

2. Heat the oven to 345 °F (175 °C). Line a mold with a sheet of buttered wax paper, soaked in water so a few drops remain on it. Pour the meringue into the mold. Put it into the oven at once for 15 minutes and leave it in for 1 hour with the oven turned off. Leave it to go completely cold away from draughts.

3. Vigorously beat the very cold crème fraîche with an electric whisk for 2 minutes, add the confectioner's sugar, and continue to whip the cream until it is very firm and shiny. Peel the kiwi fruit. Cut two of them into small cubes and the others into thin, round slices. Mix the whipped cream with the kiwi fruit cubes and garnish the meringue with the mixture. Arrange the kiwi slices on top.

4. This meringue has a particularly soft texture, obtained by adding vinegar and cornstarch to the mixture of egg whites and sugar. For preference, choose a fine vinegar with a fairly subtle flavor, such as raspberry, sherry, or champagne vinegar. As the cooking time is relatively short, the meringue remains rather flexible.

Recommended drinks

Ice pear liqueur
Gewurztraminer
Eiswein

Menu suggestions

1. This famous English dessert was created in New Zealand. Serve it after a roast leg of lamb, preceded by avocadoes stuffed with crab.

2. You can also include it in a meal of crustaceans and seafood: oysters and grilled lobster.

Redcurrant pudding

A family dish

Serves 5
Preparation: 15 minutes
Cooking: 2 hours

Ingredients

$6^1/_2$ oz (180 g) calf's kidney suet
2 cups (250 g) flour
2 tsp (10 g) baking powder
1 large pinch salt
$4^1/_2$ oz (125 g) stale bread
6 cups (1.5 liters) milk
9 oz (250 g) redcurrants
1 small slice fresh ginger
1 generous cup (250 g) granulated sugar

1 oz (25 g) butter
1 vanilla bean
5 egg yolks

1. Chop the suet into small pieces. This is easier if the suet is very cold. Remove it from the refrigerator only at the last moment. Put the pieces into a bowl and add the previously sifted flour with the raising agent and the salt. Mix thoroughly. Break the stale bread into small pieces (the crust can remain on). Mix again, then pour in enough milk to obtain a fairly flexible paste (about 2 glasses).

2. Top and tail the redcurrants, wash them quickly, and wipe them. Peel and finely grate the ginger (you can also use finely chopped dried ginger). Add the ginger and the redcurrants to the previously made paste (keeping a few for the final garnish), followed by $^1/_3$–$^1/_2$ cup (80–100 g) granulated sugar. Mix thoroughly.

3. Butter a pudding mold and pour in the mixture. Cover and cook in the oven at 400 °F (200 °C) in a bain-marie or baking pan of water, for about 2 hours. Remove the mold from the bain-marie and let the pudding go completely cold.

4. Prepare a custard: heat the rest of the milk with a vanilla bean split in two, cover the pan, and leave to infuse. Put the egg yolks in a bowl, add the rest of the sugar, and beat the mixture until it foams. Remove the vanilla bean, gently pour the hot milk on to the egg and sugar mixture, and mix. Pour the cream into the saucepan and cook it until it coats the back of a spoon. Let it go completely cold. Remove the pudding from the mold onto the serving dish, surround it with custard, and garnish with the remaining redcurrants.

Recommended drinks

Grenadine
Flavored milk
Lemonade

Menu suggestions

1. Serve this sharp-flavored pudding in summer, after a meal of barbecued kebabs and vegetables papillottes.

2. You can also serve it for a family dinner after a plate of cold cuts and a good green salad.

Rice pudding Angers style

A Loire valley dish
Serves 8
Preparation: 15 minutes
Cooking: 25 minutes
Waiting: 12 hours

Ingredients

1 generous cup (250 g) granulated
sugar
4 nice pears
1 sachet vanilla sugar
1¼ cups (250 g) rice
4 cups (1 liter) milk
1 vanilla bean
1 tbsp butter
1 pinch salt

1 tbsp finely grated orange zest
6 egg yolks
1 tbsp crème fraîche
3½ oz (100 g) preserved fruit
1 pot apricot jelly

1. Put ½ cup (125 g) sugar and 1 large glass of water in a saucepan, heat gently, and then boil, for 5 minutes. Meanwhile, peel the pears evenly, leaving the tail on. Choose Hardy or Louise-Bonne pears, for example. Poach them gently in the syrup with 1 sachet of vanilla sugar and enough water to cover them. Cook without boiling in the simmering syrup. The pears are cooked when they can be easily speared with a skewer. Let them cool in the syrup.

2. Wash the rice, drain it, and put it in another saucepan with the boiling milk, the rest of the sugar, the vanilla, butter, salt, and 1 tbsp finely grated orange zest. Heat gently. Watch the pan return to the boil and allow just 20 minutes' cooking time over very low heat in the barely simmering liquid.

3. Beat the egg yolks with the crème fraîche. Pour this mixture into the hot rice, off the heat, and stir for a few moments with a wooden spatula. Cut the pears in two and set them aside. Reduce the cooking syrup considerably. Pour the rice into a mold, adding the coarsely chopped preserved fruit. Leave to cool overnight.

4. Turn the mold out on to a dish. Arrange the halved pears around it in a ring. Coat with a little apricot jelly heated for a few moments in the reduced syrup. Preserved fruit are a specialty of the Loire valley. You can add a few lengths of preserved angelica.

Recommended drinks

Dry Saumur
Quarts-de-chaume
Bonnezeaux

Menu suggestions

1. The cuisine of the Loire valley can give you a menu for fall: fillets of pike-perch with mushrooms and chicken breasts with walnuts.

2. More simply, but keeping the regional tone, start with a potted meat salad followed by rabbit casserole.

Rhubarb trifle

An English dish

Serves 6
Preparation: 20 minutes
Cooking: 20 minutes

Ingredients

1 lb 2 oz (500 g) rhubarb stalks
$^2/_3$ cup (150 g) sugar
6$^1/_2$ oz (180 g) ginger cake or
gingerbread
4 tbsp ginger wine or ginger beer
2 tbsp sifted flour
1 generous cup (25 cl) milk
1 pot plain yogurt
12 preserved cherries

3 sticks angelica
A few slices preserved ginger
1 scant cup (20 cl) crème fraîche

1. Wash the rhubarb stalks, string them, and cut into small pieces. Put them in a saucepan with 3$^1/_2$ tbsp (5 cl) water. Bring to the boil gently, adding $^1/_2$ cup (125 g) sugar, until the rhubarb is tender (allow about 10 minutes).

2. Cut the ginger cake (or gingerbread) into regular slices and line the bottom of a dessert dish with them, overlapping them slightly. Moisten with ginger wine or ginger beer. Drain the rhubarb pieces, reserving a few for the garnish.

3. Mix the flour with 1 tbsp sugar and 1 tbsp milk. Heat the rest of the milk and, when it starts to boil, pour a little of it over the flour and sugar mixture. Stir well and put this mixture back into the saucepan. Then let it boil for 1 minute. Let it cool after lightly sprinkling it with sugar to prevent a skin forming.

4. Put some of the pieces of rhubarb on the slices of gingerbread. Mix the yogurt with the previously described mixture and pour it all on top of the rhubarb. Garnish with the rhubarb you have set aside, the cherries, angelica, ginger, and whipped crème fraîche. The principle of a trifle is similar to a zuppa inglese: you can replace the ginger cake not only with gingerbread, but also simply with some Genoese cake. Ginger and rhubarb are two flavors that go well together, but you can also use small pieces of preserved pineapple.

Recommended drinks

Ginger beer
Sherry
Lemonade

Menu suggestions

1. Naturally included in an English menu, this trifle could follow roast beef and Yorkshire pudding.

2. This dessert is also perfect for a meal based on fish and seafood: moules marinières, followed by haddock poached in milk served with potatoes.

Vacherin with red fruit

A party dish

Serves 8–10
Preparation: 25 minutes
Freezing: 1 hour

Ingredients

4 cups (1 liter) strawberry ice cream
4 cups (1 liter) vanilla ice cream
1 lb 2 oz (500 g) raspberries
2 scant cups (200 g) confectioner's sugar
1 orange or 1 lemon
1 large pot crème fraîche

¹/₃ cup + 1¹/₂ tbsps (10 cl) milk
8–10 large meringues
7 oz (200 g) mixed red fruit

1. Line the bottom and sides of a non-stick charlotte mold with the strawberry ice cream. Use an ice cream, not a sorbet, with small pieces of strawberry in it. Scoop out tablespoonfuls of the vanilla ice cream and fill the well made in the middle of the strawberry ice cream. Shake down well and smooth the top with the back of a spoon. Put the filled mold in the freezer for about an hour.

2. Meanwhile, prepare the raspberry coulis: sort the raspberries, removing their stalks, and put them in a blender with a few spoonfuls of confectioner's sugar. Purée, adding a dash of orange or lemon juice.

3. Whip the crème fraîche very stiffly with a few spoonfuls of milk. Add a little sugar half way through the beating. Put all the utensils you are going to use to whip the cream in the refrigerator a little while beforehand. You will achieve a better result and your cream will stiffen more easily. Carve the meringues into roughly triangular shapes. Remove the two flavors of ice cream onto a serving dish.

4. Garnish the ice cream with the meringues, spreading them with the whipped cream one by one. See that they slightly exceed the height of the ice cream. Embellish this center with the red fruit and cover them with a little coulis. Depending on the market, your red fruit can comprise a mixture of wild strawberries and small raspberries or redcurrants and even bilberries. Using a glazing bag, garnish the dish with the rest of the whipped cream and serve as soon as possible. Serve the rest of the coulis in a sauceboat.

Recommended drinks

Dry champagne
Bourgueil
Pink champagne

Menu suggestions

1. The perfect end to a spring or summer meal, this sumptuous vacherin could be served after asparagus in a cream sauce and veal fricassee with green peas.

2. If you are a fish-lover, serve the vacherin as a dessert after a creamed cress soup and paupiettes of sole.

589

Coupe panachée

N.B.

You can devote a whole morning to making a delicious dessert, but sometimes there just is not time. You have to be able to adapt. With very simple ingredients and the leftovers of a previous meal, a minimum of equipment, and a bit of imagination, you can confront last-minute invitations with zest. Here are a few simple ideas you can use, or adapt to your culinary preferences.

White dessert

White dessert

Ingredients for 6
Pear sorbet
Lime sorbet
Coconut sorbet
Preserved angelica
Small white meringues
Silver balls

1. Remove the sorbet containers from the freezer about 15 minutes before serving so you can mold the sorbet into balls quickly at the last moment. Use a special ice-cream spoon.

2. Cut some angelica into small sticks. Shape the sorbet into balls and arrange them on very cold plates. Decorate them with angelica, little meringues (two or three per person), and the silver balls.

3. Along the same lines, you can make other colored iced desserts: a pink dessert (raspberry, strawberry, and blackcurrant sorbets with preserved cherries and Rheims cookies) or a brown dessert (chocolate, coffee, and crystallized chestnut ice creams, with coffee beans and chocolate macaroons).

Dried fruit creams

Dried fruit cream

Ingredients for 4
12$\frac{1}{2}$ oz (350 g) white cheese
1 egg yolk
Scant $\frac{1}{2}$ cup (95 g) superfine sugar
1 tbsp flour
1 glass milk
1 sachet vanilla sugar
2$\frac{3}{4}$ oz (75 g) powdered almonds
3$\frac{1}{2}$ oz (100 g) raisins
1 lemon

1. Drain the white cheese thoroughly in a colander. Beat the egg yolk with 5 tsps (25 g) sugar in a bowl, then add the flour, taking care that there are no lumps. Boil the milk with the vanilla sugar and then gradually pour it into the mixture while beating. Continue to beat until the custard is very smooth. Let it cool. Put it on the heat and wait until the first bubbles rise, stirring constantly with a wooden spoon. Let it cool again.

2. Stir the powdered almonds with the rest of the sugar and mix it with the white cheese, custard, raisins, and a little grated lemon zest.

3. Pour the mixture into dessert dishes and keep cool until required.

Chestnut mousse

Chestnut mousse

2 cups (50 cl) canned chestnut purée
4 tbsp Armagnac
1¼ cups (30 cl) light cream
⅞ cup (100 g) confectioner's sugar
3 crystallized chestnuts
Dark chocolate (optional)

1. Open the can of chestnut purée, empty the contents into a bowl, add the Armagnac, and stir with a wooden spoon to give it a more flexible consistency. Set aside.

2. Put the really cold cream and confectioner's sugar in another bowl and whip it stiffly. Mix the chestnut purée with the whipped cream, not over-stirring the mixture so as to retain its foamy texture. Put it in the refrigerator.

3. Put the resulting mousse into individual dessert dishes. Smooth the surface with a metal spatula. Garnish with half a crystallized chestnut placed in the center of each dish.

For a richer embellishment, at the last moment you can make shavings of dark chocolate and arrange them in little bundles all around.

Baked custard with French toast

Baked custard with French toast

Ingredients for 4
1 vanilla bean
2 cups (50 cl) milk
3 eggs½ cup (125 g) superfine sugar
1¾ oz (50 g) butter
9 oz (250 g) stale brioche
3½ oz (100 g) raisins
Preserved orange peel

1. Split the vanilla bean, put it in the milk, and heat until it starts to simmer. Beat the whole eggs with the superfine sugar. Gradually pour the hot, but not boiling, milk over the sugared eggs, still beating gently with a whisk.

2. Butter a dish. Pour the mixture of vanilla, sugar, and eggs into it. Place the pieces of brioche on top, pressing down slightly and overlapping them. Put some dabs of butter on top. Sprinkle on the raisins and the fragments of preserved orange peel. Heat the oven to 430 °F (220 °C).

3. Put the dish in a bain-marie or baking pan of water in the center of the oven for 30 minutes.

Apricots aumonière style

Apricots aumonière style

IIngredients for 4
9 oz (250 g) puff pastry
2¼ lb (1 kg) apricots
A few flaked almonds
Sugar lumps
1 jar apricot jelly
1 egg yolk
1 tbsp flour

1. Roll the pastry and cut it into rectangles, forming the "aumonières." Wash the apricots, split them, and pit with a small knife. Heat the almonds in a skillet to dry.

2. Put one apricot on each small rectangle of pastry. Put a sugar lump inside and a little apricot jelly mixed with the heated, flaked almonds. Close the pastry over the apricots, sealing the four corners after moistening them. Brush with lightly beaten egg yolk. Arrange the "aumonières" on a sparsely floured baking sheet.

3. Heat the oven to 350 °F (180 °C) and cook for 30 minutes. Serve hot or warm. You can use plums or cherries (three per pastry) instead of apricots.

Fruit

Quails with grapes

for 4

1 Peel 4 very large, firm potatoes. Wash and wipe them. Remove a strip along the whole of one side so they can lie flat. Cut a wide lid from the other side. Make a hollow in the potatoes so you can put the quails into them. Use a small, sharp-edged spoon or a special spoon used for making potato balls, known as a Parisian spoon.

2 Gently melt 3^1/$_2$ oz (100 g) butter in a saucepan. Put the potatoes in a gratin dish just big enough to hold them close together. Brush generously with melted butter. Gut, clean, and trim 4 quails. Roll them in a mixture of crushed salt and pepper. Fill each one with two or three white or black grapes.

3 Fold the quails' legs back against their bodies and tie them with a single loop of string. Then roll each quail in half a slice of cooked ham from which you will previously have removed the rind. (You can also use little slices of raw ham. In that case, don't use too much salt). Put the quails in the emptied potatoes.

4 Hold the potatoes and quails together with a cocktail stick pushed through them. Moisten with a dash of olive oil. Cook in the oven at 350 °F (180 °C) for 30 minutes. Add 14 oz (400 g) grapes and put them back in the oven for 15 minutes. Remove the quails in their potatoes and keep them warm. Skim the sauce, adding 1^3/$_4$ oz (50 g) butter. Season to taste with salt and pepper, and pour the sauce over the quails.

Paupiettes of pork with prunes

Rabbit with prunes

Pork chops with grapes

General points

Grapes and prunes are often used in cooking where they enhance meat with their succulent flavor and soften the sauces that go with them. Prunes go well with various roasting or braising meats (rabbit, shoulder of pork, goose, and turkey). While cooking, they fill with juice and are served as an accompaniment. As hors d'oeuvres, prunes wrapped in bacon and baked in the oven are always a great success. The flavor of fresh grapes is delicious with quails or fried white pudding. Grapes also make a refined garnish for hot liver pâté. Their sweet, sharp juice forms a sauce popular with connoisseurs. White grapes are generally used because of their lovely, light color. Choose varieties with firm seeds that will not break even when cooked: Italia grapes are perfect. If you do not care for the seeds, choose a seedless variety. You can also remove the seeds from your favorite grapes. The operation is somewhat time-consuming, but

the result is exquisite. Skin the grapes first. Grasp the skin of each grape between the blade of a small knife and your thumb and then remove the skins by pulling slowly. Cut the peeled grapes in two and remove the seeds in the central cavity of the grape using a small needle. Do not squeeze the grapes too hard during the process, to avoid crushing them.

Tip

German cuisine contains many recipes combining meat and dried fruit, such as smoked meat or poultry served with a purée of prunes and apricots or potato cakes stuffed with prunes. There is also Blindhuhn, a pork stew with dried fruit in a spicy sauce, green bean casserole, and green vegetables with dried fruit.

Rabbit with prunes

To serve 4, cut 5$^1/_2$ oz (50 g) smoked bacon into lardoons and blanch for 1 minute. Drain and set aside. Pit 10$^1/_2$ oz (300 g) prunes and cut them in two. Cut a rabbit into 8 or 10 pieces and season with salt and pepper. Heat 3 tbsp peanut oil in a casserole. Fry the seasoned pieces of rabbit on all sides for about 10 minutes. Drain the pieces and discard the oil. Put the rabbit back into the casserole and add 2 chopped onions, the blanched lardoons, and the prunes. Cook for 10 minutes. Add 1 scant cup (20 cl) white wine, boil for 3 minutes, add 1 $^3/_4$ cups (40 cl) chicken bouillon, and cook with the lid on, simmering gently, for 30 minutes. Skim the sauce with a slotted spoon and adjust the seasoning.

Fillets of sole with citrus fruit

Chicken with figs

Parma ham with figs

General points

Figs and oranges are popular in cooking because of the unusual and pleasant taste they bring to the dish. Oranges produce a delicious juice and the tasty zest cooked with leg of veal, calf's liver, and duck. It also seasons endive and beet salads, giving them a pleasant freshness. You can use blood oranges for cooking, too. Figs lend their delicately flavored red pulp to hot recipes. They are a favorite accompaniment for fresh liver pâté or raw ham.

Chicken with figs

The day before, to serve 6, cut a large chicken into about 10 pieces. Put them in a bowl, adding salt and pepper. Add 3 pinches of powdered cinnamon, 1 chopped onion, 2 tbsp runny honey, and $4/3$ cup (15 cl) sweet white wine. Mix, cover, and allow to marinate in the refrigerator overnight. On the day of the meal, drain the chicken pieces and keep the marinade. Wash $10^1/_2$ oz (300 g) figs, remove their purple skin, sprinkle them with lemon juice, and cut them in four. Brown the chicken pieces on all sides in a casserole with a dash of oil. Discard the oil, then add 4

chopped shallots. Simmer over medium heat, stirring from time to time, then add $3/_4$ cup (15 cl) Muscat wine and the marinade. Boil for 3 minutes, then add $1^1/_4$ cups (30 cl) chicken bouillon. Cook with the lid on for 25 minutes. Remove the chicken pieces and keep them warm. Skim the sauce and boil it for 5 minutes. Season with salt and pepper then add the fig quarters and cook over low heat for 5 minutes. Add the chicken pieces and simmer for 5 minutes. Take the mixture off the boil and stir in $1^3/_4$ oz (50 g) butter. Adjust the seasoning and serve hot with fresh steamed vegetables (zucchini, carrots, or new turnips). Another delicious recipe consists of stuffing a roasting partridge with dried figs previously soaked in port.

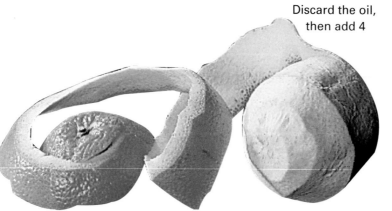

Figs and oranges in savory dishes

1 Gut a duck weighing about 3 lb 5 oz (1.5 kg) (or have your butcher do it for you). Lightly season the inside of the bird with a few pinches of salt. You can add a trace of four-spice or nutmeg. Wash 2 oranges and peel them. Remove the zest with a sharp knife, then peel the oranges, open them, and separate them into quarters, removing the fine skin that covers them. Lightly pepper the quarters.

2 Slip the orange quarters thus prepared inside the duck. (According to another recipe, the duck is not roasted whole, but cut into pieces that are marinated overnight with a few pinches of cinnamon, 1 scant cup/20 cl orange juice, a little superfine sugar, and a chopped onion. The pieces are then browned in butter and finished with an orange sauce sprinkled with zest).

3 Truss the bird and butter it lightly. Put it in a roasting pan in which you have placed a small gridiron so that it does not lie directly on the bottom of the pan. Roast the duck in a hot oven (350 °F/180°C) for an hour, so it is well cooked and not bloody. Turn it from time to time, taking care not to prick the skin. (The duck can be braised instead of roasted).

4 Finely peel 3 oranges. Cut the zest into very narrow strips. Peel and finely chop an onion. Melt 1 oz (30 g) butter, add the onion, sweat it gently without browning, then add $1/4$ cup (30 g) flour. When this roux is brown, moisten it with 2 cups (50 cl) chicken bouillon. Scald the zest, add it to the sauce, and set the sauce aside.

5 For the garnish, peel 3 more oranges, remove the skin between the segments, and detach the pulp. For preference choose oranges of the bigarade variety (or bitter oranges) which give the dish a special flavor. Reheat the sauce, bringing it just to the boil. Add salt and pepper. Add a small glass of Curaçao to the liquid. Mix well.

6 Heat the dinner plates and a flameproof serving platter. Remove the duck from the oven and salt it. Carve the duck, put the carcass on the platter, and reform the bird, arranging the pieces on it. Cover it with the orange zest sauce and arrange the orange segments round it. Return the dish to the over for 3 minutes to heat the oranges.

Grilled red mullet with peaches for 4

1 Fruit is frequently included in meat or poultry recipes, but it also gives delicious and surprising results with fish, as this recipe demonstrates. Scrape 8 mullet. Clean them. Gut them, or leave them ungutted (according to your taste), but do not remove the liver from these "sea woodcock," as it is the liver that gives them their flavor.

2 Pour $1/2$ cup olive oil into a dish. Add the juice of 1 lemon (keeping the peel), a few fine onion rings, a little rosemary, and a large pinch of salt. Beat with a fork. Place the mullet in this marinade and leave to soak for at least 2 hours, but not more than 4, basting and turning them from time to time.

3 Peel $2 1/4$ lb (1 kg) peaches either just as they are or after plunging them into boiling water for a few moments if they are a little reluctant to part with their skins. Divide them in two and pit. Yellow peaches are better for this type of cooking than white ones and their flavor is more lasting, but you can also use nectarines or even bush peaches—peaches grown in a vineyard alongside the vines.

4 Heat the barbecue. Line it with a thick sheet of aluminum foil. Put the well-drained mullet on it and the slightly oiled half peaches. Allow 3–4 minutes and turn the fish. Put them on a hot serving dish, decorated with sprigs of rosemary. Drizzle the peaches with a dash of lemon, salt, and pepper. Serve at once.

Apples and peaches in savory dishes

General points

The apple is one of the best fruits for accompanying meat, as its flesh has the advantage of always remaining firm. It goes well with pork offal, such as black pudding and broiled andouillettes (small chitterling sausages), and game birds like pheasant. In Germany, it is found in "Himmel und Erde" (heaven and earth), where there is a recipe with potato purée to accompany white and black puddings and grilled sausages. The peach is also delicious in savory recipes. Raw, it goes well with a crab salad; when cooked, it makes a refined accompaniment to liver pâté, calf's liver, and duck.

Choose well ripened, but reasonably firm, white peaches. Yellow peaches can also be used, but are often less flavorful than white ones. Cook only fresh peaches in season and avoid canned fruit, which is sometimes too sweet and flavorless. Goose and duck have the reputation of sometimes being heavy, as they release a lot of fat during cooking. Cooking them with fruit provides sharp, flavorsome sauces that ameliorate the situation. Moreover, when cooked in the meat juice, the fruit becomes tender.

Black pudding with apples

Goose and apples for 8

1 Gut a good, free-range goose. Peel 2^1/$_4$ lb (1 kg) pippins, core, and cut them into quarters. Sprinkle with 1⁄2 cup (100 g) superfine sugar and moisten them with ^{1}/$_3$ cup + 1^1/$_2$ tbsp (10 cl) calvados. Peel and core 8 cooking apples, sprinkle them with lemon juice, and put them in a skillet in which you have melted a little butter. Add a cinnamon stick. Allow to brown.

2 Marinate the apple quarters for 30 minutes. Season the inside of the goose with salt and pepper and stuff it with the apples. Truss the bird, oil it lightly on all sides, and add a little more salt and pepper. You can also slip 1 or 2 peeled and finely chopped onions inside the goose, with a small bunch of chopped fresh sage leaves.

3 Preheat the oven to 350 °F (180 °C). Cook the goose on a gridiron in a roasting pan, basting frequently, for about 2 hours. Remove the goose from the oven, let it rest for a few minutes, and then carve it. Serve the pieces with the cooked apple quarters. Accompany this dish with browned, whole apples and a lamb's lettuce salad.

599

General points

In Creole cuisine, fruit is very widely used in savory dishes. Pork with pineapple, or chicken with banana, are the best known examples. But many other dishes, which are all delicious, use mango, papaya, coconut, passion fruit, guava, or breadfruit. Bananas are sometimes used in "classic" recipes. Some great chefs reduce bananas to a purée and create sauces to accompany fish, in particular sole. Bananas can also be successfully cooked with fresh or slightly salted belly of pork: the dish has a very pleasant, slightly sweet

Chopped pork with pineapple

Grilled chicken with pineapple

flavor. With exotic cuisine, you need to select plantain bananas, which are larger and firmer than their European counterparts. With their delicate fragrance, they're ideal for cooking. Pineapple goes very well with duck: its slightly acid taste flavors the meat, and makes it very easy to digest. Roast pork with pineapple can almost be called a "classic" recipe. Pineapple-glazed ham is a traditional West Indian dish served at Christmas and New Year celebrations. This recipe is prepared for special occasions, which cater for 20–25 people. Pineapple is a great favorite because, when cooked, it is transformed into a fine purée and then a sauce, but never loses its flavor. Always select very ripe pineapples, which are cut down at the right moment, transported by air, and marketed a few days after harvesting.

Creole cuisine

Medallions of veal with pineapple for 4

1 Peel 1 moderately ripe pineapple and remove any small traces of skin remaining in its cavities. Cut into slices approximately $3/8$ in (1 cm) thick. Prepare on a dish so that the juice is recovered. Gently brown the slices in butter in a skillet and set aside. Cut up 8 medallions of veal to almost the same size as the pineapple slices.

2 Sauté the medallions of veal in a skillet in 1 tbsp butter and 1 tbsp oil, over high heat, for 2 minutes on each side. Sprinkle with dark rum, and flambé. Rapidly brown 4 slices of smoked back bacon, together with the medallions of veal. Thread them onto wooden skewers. Place the medallions of veal on a hot dish and each time insert 1 slice of pineapple between 2 medallions of veal.

3 When you have threaded all the ingredients onto the skewers, keep them warm just inside the oven. Blend the cooking juices at the bottom of the pan with the pineapple juice you collected in a dish; add salt and pepper—cayenne pepper for a spicier flavor—and boil rapidly for a few moments. Top the dish with sauce and thread 1 tomato quarter onto the tip of each skewer. Serve either with or without cherry tomatoes.

Chicken sauté with bananas

To serve 6, first peel 3 plantain bananas. Halve and place them in a saucepan of cold water. Cook for approximately 1 minute. Drain and then cut into $3/4$ in (2 cm) slices. Cut $5^1/2$ oz (150 g) bacon streaked with fat into lardoons and set aside. Cut 1 large chicken into about 10 pieces; add salt and pepper. Heat 2 tbsp peanut oil in a pan and then fry the strips of bacon and chicken, making sure that all the pieces turn golden brown. Add 4 chopped shallots, cover, and braise for 5 minutes. Next add 1 generous cup (25 cl) coconut milk, 4 pinches ground cumin, 1 scant cup (20 cl)

water, and the banana slices. Cook over a gentle heat for 30 minutes, stirring occasionally. Finally, add 1 bunch chopped cilantro and adjust the seasoning.

Tip

To prepare a pineapple, cut its base and top. Remove the skin from top to bottom with a serrated knife. Remove the brown pieces embedded in the flesh. Cut the fruit into $3/8$ in (1 cm) slices. Remove the center of each slice with a pastry cutter. Cut the slices into the desired shape.

601

Peach compote

General points

Good compotes are prepared with fresh fruits cut into pieces. They are cooked over medium heat with a small amount of water and superfine sugar. The version most commonly used is prepared with apples, but try more unusual, tasty combinations, such as apple-raspberry; peach-apple-blackcurrant; or mango-apricot-apple. Try adding cinnamon, vanilla, or citrus fruit peel to "plain" compote. Compote can either be served on its own or with Chantilly cream or soft white cheese as an accompaniment.

Compote of dried fruit for 4

1 Put $^1/_2$ cup (125 g) superfine sugar into a saucepan and mix with 1 glass of water. Gently heat and then boil slowly while turning until the superfine sugar has completely melted. Let it cool almost completely before adding 1 stick of cinnamon and 1 large glass of dry white wine. Heat until it starts to simmer.

2 Put 6 prunes, 1 soft apple, 7 oz (200 g) raisins (preferably golden raisins), 9 oz (250 g) small dried figs, and 7 oz (200 g) dried apricot halves in a gratin dish and pour the boiling syrup over them. Add the peel of 2 lemons and some cloves, when the syrup is still very warm. Steep for a few hours. Pour the juice of 1 lemon over the fruits.

3 Garnish the perimeter of a serving bowl with very thin slices of lemon or orange and, when the compote of dried fruits is ready, pour it in. Serve cold or at room temperature. Pastry desserts can be made from this compote—a tart, for example, or turnovers. This is a fresh product that should be kept in the refrigerator.

compotes and baked apples

1 This quick and easy recipe is one of the best ways of serving whole, cooked apples. Select the "Belle van Boskoop" variety, or pippins from Le Mans or Canada. Wash 6 apples thoroughly without peeling them. Hollow them out with an apple corer. Heat the oven to 350 °F (180 °C). Lightly butter 7 slices of bread, $2^3/_4$–3 in (7–8 cm) in diameter.

2 Blend $5^1/_2$ oz (150 g) butter with 1 level tsp ground cinnamon, 1 level tsp flour, 8 tbsp rum, and $^1/_3$ cup (80 g) superfine sugar. Spread this mixture in and over the apples with a small spoon. Put the slices of buttered bread into a baking dish and arrange the apples over. Add 1 small glass of water and cook for approximately 1 hour 15 minutes.

3 Sprinkle $1^3/_4$ oz (50 g) of split almonds over the apples 15 minutes before they are cooked and add a little more water to the bottom of the dish if necessary. Serve very hot with 1 bowl of thick, very cold, crème fraîche. You can make this apple dessert, which is often referred to as "bonne-femme," by leaving out the buttered bread or using gingerbread slices lightly spread with honey instead.

Rhubarb compote

To serve 6, first peel 1 lb 11 oz (750 g) rhubarb stalks and dice them finely. Put them into a saucepan, cover with water, and add the juice of 1 lemon, 1 scant cup (200 g) superfine sugar, and 1 vanilla bean split lengthwise. Bring to the boil, cover, and cook over gentle heat for 30–35 minutes, stirring all the while. When the pieces of rhubarb are cooked, leave to cool and then remove the vanilla bean. Place in a blender and reduce the mixture to a fine purée. The compote is now ready; leave to cool.

603

Apple crumble for 4

1 Peel 2^1/$_4$ lb (1 kg) apples, cut into quarters, and remove the core and seeds. Put the apples into a saucepan and sprinkle with the juice of 1 lemon. Stir until all the quarters are soaked with juice. Cook over gentle heat and partially cover, until the apples are tender. Select apples with firm flesh so that they do not fall apart during cooking.

2 When the apples are cooked, crush them gently with a fork until you obtain a rough compote; some of the quarters should remain almost whole. Add 4^1/$_2$ oz (125 g) superfine sugar and ground cinnamon, stirring all the while. You can also add flavor to your apple compote by using vanilla sugar instead of superfine sugar or by adding some lemon peel to it.

3 Put 4^1/$_2$ oz (130 g) butter into a basin and soften with a fork. Add ^{2}/$_3$ cup (150 g) brown sugar, a pinch of salt, and 1 ^{1}/$_3$ cups (150 g) flour. Using your fingertips, blend while crumbling until you obtain a rough sugar crust pastry. The success of the crumble depends on the blending of this mixture. Do not try to obtain fine breadcrumbs. It does not matter even if large dabs of butter remain.

Tip

Adapt the basic crumble mixture according to taste: you could, for example, add walnuts, pecans, hazelnuts, or raisins. The secret of success lies in the dryness of the mixture: do not inadvertently add water, either with your hands or via a utensil.

4 Butter a gratin dish and pour in the compote. Add a handful of raisins and a few split almonds, making sure you spread them evenly. You could steep the raisins in a little rum first, while you are preparing the compote and the crumble mixture; drain them thoroughly before using.

5 Cover the mixture with the sugar crust pastry. Heat the oven to 350 °F (180 ° C). The crumble will be ready in about 30 minutes, or when a golden-brown crust is formed. You can either serve the crumble hot, as is customary in America, or lukewarm with custard, as in Europe.

6 The contrast in the consistency of the fruits and the crust gives this traditional recipe its interest: mellow fruits, which melt in the mouth, versus crunchy crust. Crumbles do not keep long after cooking, because the juice from the fruits seeps out and soaks the topping. They do, however, freeze very well and can easily be warmed up in the microwave.

crumbles and pies

General points

In Britain, fruits from the garden are much in evidence in a large number of pastry recipes. A crumble is a kind of upside-down cake. The fruit, which is either cooked or raw, according to variety, is placed at the bottom of the baking dish first, and then covered with a delicious, crumbly crust. The pie is another delicious specialty of Anglo-Saxon cuisine. The term covers both sweet and savory dishes, e.g., fruit, meat, and fish, which are prepared with plain, piecrust, or puff pastry. Pies can be either round or rectangular and are more deep-filled than traditional tarts.

Tip

A pie is a pastry rich in filling and therefore very delicate: serve it from the dish it was baked in, as there is a risk of it breaking if it is turned out.

Pie with apricots

Redcurrant pie for 4

1 Wash 2¹/₄ lb (1 kg) redcurrants. Drain them thoroughly. Put 9 oz (250 g) superfine sugar into a saucepan. Add 2 liqueur glasses of water. Leave the water to soak up the sugar. Bring slowly to the boil while stirring continuously with a wooden spatula. Boil for a few minutes. Pour the boiling syrup over the redcurrants.

2 Roll out 7 oz (200 g) prepared puff pastry dough and make a circle slightly larger than the diameter of the pie dish. Cut out a circlet ¹/₂–1 in (2–3 cm) wide and place it around the edge of the dish after moistening it well. Press it slightly so that it thoroughly encompasses the edge. Moisten the circlet and then place the rolled-out pastry over the top of the dish.

3 Trim the pastry around the edge of the dish with a very sharp, small knife. Carefully make a small hollow in the center. Set the oven at 445 °F (230 °C). Beat 1 egg yolk with a little water and brush the mixture over the top of the pastry, making sure you avoid the edge. Cook for 25 minutes. Allow to cool, and serve with crème fraîche.

Far with prunes for 6

1 Far is a cake that looks like a tart. It is made with dried fruits, prunes, or raisins, and can be eaten cold or lukewarm. It is made in a similar way to the clafoutis, which is a type of fruit cake. Put 14 oz (400 g) pitted prunes into a bowl and sprinkle them with 3^1/$_2$ tbsp (5 cl) tea and 3^1/$_2$ tbsp (5 cl) Armagnac. Steep for a good hour.

2 Pour 1 ^{1}/$_3$ cups (150 g) flour and ^{1}/$_4$ cup (50 g) superfine sugar into a bowl. Mix and then add 4 eggs and ^{2}/$_3$ cup (15 cl) milk. Mix again, then add 1^1/$_4$ cups (30 cl) milk with the marinated prunes and juice. Stir with a spatula. Butter a circular mold and drizzle with superfine sugar. Pour the mixture into the mold and distribute the prunes with a spoon.

3 Make sure that the far is no more than 1^1/$_2$ in (4 cm) in depth. Cook in the oven at 400 °F (200 °C) for 1 hour. The surface of the cake should be golden brown. The far is a typical Breton pastry, and was originally a kind of buckwheat flour to which prunes or raisins were added; it was poached in bouillon encased in a cloth pocket, and served with butter.

Cherry clafoutis for 6

1 Select 1 lb (450 g) very ripe cherries, remove their stalks, and pit them. Put them in a bowl with 1 small glass of kirsch. Boil 1^1/$_4$ cups (30 cl) milk with 1 vanilla bean cut in half lengthways then remove from the heat. Add ^{1}/$_2$ cup (12 cl) crème fraîche. Allow to cool and then filter. Break 4 eggs into a bowl.

2 Add 1 scant cup (200 g) superfine sugar to the eggs and beat for 2 minutes with a hand whisk. Add 2 tbsp flour and 1 pinch salt. Mix again then gradually pour in the milk while beating. Butter a baking dish and pour in the cherries and their juice. Distribute them evenly in the dish then pour in the cake mixture. Cook in the oven at 400 °F (200 °C) for 20–25 minutes.

3 Allow to cool and sprinkle the clafoutis with confectioner's sugar before serving. Authentic clafoutis originates from Limousin (a former province in central France): its name is derived from a provincial dialect word: "clafi" which means "filled," the implication being "with cherries." Of course, clafoutis can also be made along the same lines with grapes, small yellow plums, plums, or even apples and pears cut into pieces.

clafoutis and fars

Clafoutis with yellow plums for 6

1 Clafoutis is a dish that can be made with almost any fruit, even if the original recipe was prepared with unpitted black cherries. Cooked in the oven in a rich, egg-based mixture, yellow plums remain firm and juicy. To give extra flavor to this family dessert, try marinating them in brandy or your favorite spirit.

2 After steeping 1 lb 2 oz (500 g) small, very ripe, yellow plums for 2 hours in a bowl with a small glass of plum brandy, measure out approximately 6^1/$_2$ oz (180 g) flour and sieve it into another bowl. Make a hollow in the center and add a good pinch of salt. Break 3 large eggs into a basin and beat them with a fork to form an omelet batter.

3 Pour the beaten eggs into the hollow made in the all-purpose flour, and then add 1 tbsp peanut oil and at least 1 glass of whole milk. Combine these ingredients thoroughly with a wooden spoon. The mixture should have the consistency of a fairly thick pancake batter, but nevertheless quite fluid. Do not be tempted to add more flour; if you do, the clafoutis will be too dense.

4 When the batter is smooth, stand it in a cool place. Meanwhile, prepare the baking dish for the clafoutis by buttering it quite generously. Drain the yellow plums, reserving the liquor. Arrange the fruits compactly in the dish in a single layer. Sprinkle them with a spoonful of the brandy they were steeped in.

5 Ladle the clafoutis batter over the plums, without displacing them. Dab with butter and cook in the oven at 410 °F (210 ° C) for approximately 30 minutes. Take the dish out of the oven and sprinkle the clafoutis with superfine sugar before serving.

Banana fritters

Orange fritters

Plum dalken

General points

Encased in a thin egg batter and seared in boiling hot oil, fruits are transformed into delicious fritters. You can make them with pineapples, apples, apricots, bananas, and even pitted prunes, as in the Viennese Zwetschgenknödel (plum dumpling). To make your fritters even more exquisite, steep the fruits in various spirits: rum, calvados (apple brandy distilled in Normandy), Armagnac, and Grand Marnier are the most commonly used. To make good fritters, use fresh or thoroughly filtered peanut oil. Fritters are calorific as they tend to absorb the oil: do not forget to drain them on paper towels before serving. You can also insert a tasty coating between the fruit and the batter: frangipane, crushed macaroons or other cookies, or ground dried fruits.

Fritter batter

Consider preparing this batter 2 hours in advance: the fritters will brown more evenly. To make approximately 30 fritters, sieve 2 cups (250 g) flour into a bowl and make a hollow in the center. Add 3 eggs, 2 tbsp superfine sugar, and 1 pinch salt. Mix with a spatula while adding 2 tbsp oil. Gradually pour 1^1/$_2$ cups (35 cl) whole milk and work the batter vigorously. Filter it through a fine sieve to remove any lumps then let it stand until you need to use it. To make a lighter batter, you can use a mixture of water and light beer with a mild flavor, instead of milk.

N.B.

For the batter to stick well to the fruits, they should not be too moist: if you must wash them first (or if you use dried fruits that have been soaked or fruits that have been steeped), do not forget to remove any excess liquid before immersing them in the batter. Heat some plain vegetable oil to 375 °F (190 °C); test the temperature by dropping a globule of batter into the oil: if it starts sizzling, then the oil is hot.

Apple fritters steeped in calvados for 6

1 Peel 4 apples and squeeze some lemon juice over them, to prevent discoloration. Hollow them out with a corer and then cut into $^3/_{16}$ in (5 mm) slices. For preference, select pippins or the "Belle van Boskoop" variety, whose flesh softens and melts gently during cooking, but without falling apart; the flesh also acquires a very pleasant, smooth texture and flavor.

2 Arrange these slices on a plate and then sprinkle with superfine sugar and 8 tbsp calvados. Steep for 2 hours while turning occasionally. If you steep them for any less than 2 hours, the alcohol will not flavor the flesh of the fruits sufficiently. Leave them to stand at room temperature and cover the dish with plastic wrap.

3 Then sieve 2 cups (250 g) flour into a bowl, making a hollow in the center. Add 3 yolks, 2 tbsp superfine sugar, and 1 pinch salt. Mix with a spatula while adding 2 tbsp oil. Gradually pour in $1^1/_2$ cups (35 cl) whole milk and work the batter vigorously. Filter it through a fine sieve to remove any lumps and to obtain a smooth texture.

4 Beat 3 egg whites until stiff and then add to the mixture. Heat some peanut oil in a saucepan. Test the temperature is right by dropping a small spoonful of batter into the hot oil: it should fry immediately and swell. The temperature is too high if the batter browns too quickly: if this happens, reduce the heat.

5 Drop 6 steeped slices of apple into the batter. They should be only just covered with batter: turn them over rapidly, remove them with a fork, and lightly drain them. Immerse them immediately in the hot oil, without putting too many in at once. Turn them over after approximately 20 seconds.

6 Drain them on paper towels and serve immediately, as hot as possible. There is no better accompaniment to an apple-based dessert than a drink that has also been prepared with apples: serve a bottle of good farmer's cider with this hot dessert, preferably a sweet one that will complement the sweet flavor of the fritters.

Pear rabotes

General points

As their flesh is firm, apples and pears can be cooked whole in the oven, without becoming too soft. They're also more delicious when encased in puff or piecrust pastry. The pastry protects the fruit from the heat of the oven, while preserving their flavor and fragrance. Select varieties of firm fruits that are not too juicy; that way the pastry turns crispy and the flesh does not get squashed. Comice and dessert pears, as well as pippins from Le Mans and Canada, are very suitable. Puff pastry provides a very crispy case, but piecrust, which is simpler and quick to make, is also excellent. Lightly knead your pastry dough in advance, as this makes it easier to roll out. The pastry must be cut up into circles for the apples, and into squares for the pears. As a general rule, the fruits you use should be peeled and hollowed out to ensure a more consistent and faster cooking time. You can sprinkle the fruits with a brandy or a spirit before you encase them in pastry: this will give them a stronger flavor. These fruits encased in pastry are known as "douillons" or "rabotes:" a baked specialty of Normandy.

Pear rabotes for 6

1 To prepare piecrust pastry: sieve 2 2/3 cups (300 g) flour onto the worktop, make a hollow in the center, and add 5 1/2 oz (150 g) butter, cut into pieces, 1 pinch salt, and 2 tbsp superfine sugar. Combine these ingredients while crumbling the butter into the flour, then fold in 2 egg yolks and knead the mixture while adding 4 tbsp cold water. Form into a ball and leave to stand for 1 hour in a cool place.

2 Wash 4 unblemished dessert pears of the same size. Remove the fibrous center with an apple corer and peel, leaving the stalk intact. Squeeze a little lemon juice over them. Pre-heat the oven to 400 °F (200 °C). Roll out the pastry onto the floured worktop to a depth of 3/16 in (5 mm). Cut out 4 large squares of the same size. Put 1 pear in the center of each square.

3 Roll up the pastry over the sides while encasing the pears and seal the edges. Shape the corners into thin, decorative strips. Butter a baking sheet and place the rabotes on it. Cook for 50–60 minutes, or until the pastry is golden brown and crispy. Serve hot with crème fraîche.

apples and pears in pastry

1 Prepare the piecrust pastry. Sieve 3 cups (350 g) flour onto the worktop and make a hollow in the center. Add 7 oz (200 g) softened butter, 2 tbsp milk, 1 scant tsp (3 g) salt, 1 tbsp (15 g) superfine sugar, and 1 egg. Mix these ingredients. Depending on the consistency you obtain, it might be advisable to add a small amount of cold water, just to combine the ingredients properly.

2 When the pastry is made, knead it into the shape of a ball. Wrap in a damp dishtowel and put in the refrigerator for 30 minutes. Prepare the flavored butter. Put 5^1/$_2$ oz (150 g) softened, but not melted, butter into a bowl. Add 4 pinches ground cinnamon; ^{3}/$_8$ cup (80 g) superfine sugar, and 2 tbsp rum. Beat.

3 Prepare the douillons. Peel 6 apples with a paring knife and then hollow them out with an apple corer. Rub the flesh with ^{1}/$_2$ lemon, so that it does not go black. Set aside. Select either the "Belle van Boskoop" with its fairly firm flesh and slightly acid flavor, or the clochard pippin with its fragrant aroma and slightly sweet taste, for this recipe; these varieties are perfect for cooking.

4 Spread the pastry over a floured worktop and roll out until it is approximately 1^1/$_2$ in (4 cm) in diameter. Cut out even circles, 4^1/$_2$ in (12 cm) in diameter, with the help of a small plate. Check whether they are large enough to encase the fruits adequately. Roll out the rest of the pastry to the same thickness and cut out tops of 1–1^1/$_2$ in (3–4 cm) in diameter, which will be used as a "hat" for each douillon.

5 Fill each apple with flavored butter, using a small spoon. Push the butter well into the center of the fruit with your finger. Using both hands, encase each fruit in a pastry circle. Fold the pastry toward the base of the fruits, making sure that it sticks thoroughly to them. Beat 1 egg in a bowl and brush it over the pastry lids. Finish covering the fruits.

6 Using a brush, glaze the douillons with the rest of the beaten egg. Pierce the pastry lids with a cocktail stick so that the steam released during cooking can escape. Put the douillons on a baking sheet and cook in the oven at 400 °F (200 °C) for 30-40 minutes. When cooked, they should be golden brown and crispy. Serve hot with custard.

Pear jam

General points

You can find all kinds of jam in the stores, but none of them can compare to the flavor of homemade jams. You need to know that jams should be made at the peak of the season and very ripe fruits selected. Essentially, success is linked to the quality of the fruits used. The consistency of jams depends on the acidity of the fruits and their pectin content. That is why some fruits (cherries, blackcurrants, peaches) remain fairly liquid and need a gelling agent mixture to give them more substance. Cooking must be fairly consistent; it is important to thoroughly remove the scum that forms on the surface. The jam must be poured into perfectly clean jars while it is still extremely hot. To preserve it well, the jam is covered with circles of wax paper or plastic wrap after it has cooled; the mouth and neck of the jar is then covered with a circle of thick paper or plastic wrap that is hermetically sealed with a rubber band. The most common recipes are for simple jams, which are prepared with strawberries, apricots, or redcurrants. You can add a personal touch to your recipes by combining different fruits and spices: peach and redcurrant jam with lemon peel; orange and plum jam with walnuts and raisins; fig and grape jam with vanilla.

Tricks and tips

If the jam remains liquid several days after cooking, it means that it is not sufficiently cooked. Empty the jars into a preserving pan and boil all the jam again with 1 tbsp "special jam" sugar. If the jam has crystallized, then it contains too much sugar. Empty the jars into a preserving pan, add 1 tbsp water per jar, and boil for 10 seconds. If the surface of the jam is moldy, scrape off the whitish layer and remove 3/16 in (5 mm) of the jam; eat the rest quickly. If the jam ferments, it means that the jars were dirty or there was an insufficient amount of sugar. Do not eat it. All or part of the sugar can be replaced with honey: the result is interesting with redcurrants or raspberries.

Peach jam

Raspberry jam

Peach and raspberry jam

jams

Apricot jam (makes 6 jars)

1 Measure out 3 lb 5 oz (1.5 kg) fruits. Wash the apricots quickly and dry them in a dishtowel; pit by opening them in two then cut into four. Put them into a large bowl. You can break a few of the pits with a hammer, recover the kernels, remove the husks, and set aside to add to the jam at the end of cooking.

2 Add 2 lb 11 oz (1.2 kg) sugar to the apricots, mix rapidly with a wooden spoon, then cover and steep for 24 hours in the refrigerator. After the apricots have been steeped, drain them and place them to one side. Pour the syrup obtained into a preserving pan and add the juice of 2 lemons. Mix thoroughly and bring to the boil.

3 Cook for 4-5 minutes, and then add the apricots. Next, boil rapidly for approximately 10 minutes while stirring frequently to avoid the jam sticking to the bottom of the pan. Carefully skim the surface with a small ladle. If you wish, add the pits. Remove from the heat and fill the jars; allow to cool, and hermetically seal.

Strawberry jam (makes 4 jars)

1 Gently wash 2¹/₄ lb (1 kg) ripe strawberries, but do not overdo it; pat dry with paper towels and then remove the stalks. Keep them whole, unless they are very large, and set aside. Pour 1 lb 11 oz (750 g) sugar into a preserving pan and add ¹/₃ cup + 1¹/₂ tbsp (10 cl) water. Mix and cook this syrup over low heat (240 °F/116 °C). Skim.

2 Add the strawberries to the pan and cook for a few moments until their juice is drawn out. Remove them with a skimming ladle and place them to one side in a bowl. Cook the syrup over low heat again, then put the strawberries back into the preserving pan and cook for 5 minutes.

3 The temperature of the syrup should by now have exceeded 212 °F (100 °C) (it is cooked very slowly to allow it to thicken and to obtain a smooth consistency); the strawberries will have become practically translucent. Put the jam into the jars. Cover immediately or allow to cool first. Once you have opened a jar of jam, it is always better to store it in the refrigerator.

Preserving pan

General points

When referring to jams, the term "marmalade" implies the use of citrus fruits: lemons, limes, grapefruit, and oranges. Their delicious flavor comes from the skin and peel that are cooked with the pulp. These marmalades, which were originally a Scottish specialty, are a great favorite in Britain. You can make simple orange marmalades, but also combine different citrus fruits: a mixture of pink grapefruit and lime, or blood orange and lemon, produces delicious marmalades. To spice up marmalades, fresh ground ginger is often used, which gives them a light, original flavor. Also, whisky is commonly used: you need to add it during the last 5 minutes of cooking, on the basis of $1/3$ cup + $1 1/2$ tbsp (10 cl) per $2 1/4$ lb (1 kg) marmalade. In some recipes, cinnamon or tea is used. Marmalades can keep for more than 6 months under the right conditions: i.e., in a cool, dark place. According to legend, orange marmalade was introduced to Scotland by the French cook of Mary Stuart, though it seems it was only generally made much later. Originally, marmalades were in fact made with quinces: the term "marmalade" is in fact derived from the Portugese word "marmelo," meaning "quince." James Keiller & Son, of Dundee, Scotland, was the first company to produce a genuine, authentic orange marmalade, toward the end of the eighteenth century. It has been part of the British breakfast ever since.

Orange marmalade (makes 6 jars)

1 Wash 3 lb 5 oz (1.5 kg) oranges. Put them into a saucepan of cold water and bring to the boil. Cook for 15 minutes and drain the oranges. Allow to cool and then cut into approximately $3/8$ in (1 cm) slices. Discard the pips. Remove half the slices and finely dice them. Collect the juice in a bowl and set aside.

2 Combine 2 lb 11 oz (1.2 kg) sugar, the juice of 1 orange, and 1 generous cup (25 cl) water in a preserving pan. Bring to the boil and cook for 5 minutes. Add the orange slices and small cubes, and cook over medium heat for approximately 25 minutes (the temperature should reach 221 °F/105 °C). Fill the jars with the boiling hot marmalade and then allow to cool.

Quince jam

Marmalades

By extension, marmalades are mixtures that combine fruits, sugar, and water. These jams are the easiest to make. Here is a recipe for apricot and kumquat marmalade: measure out the same weight of fruits and sugar. Pit the apricots and cut the kumquats in two; combine in a preserving pan, add the sugar, mix, and steep for 4–5 hours; add $1/3$ cup + $1^{1}/_{2}$ tbsp (10 cl) water and boil rapidly for $1/2$ hour over high heat, while stirring often.

Lemon and grapefruit marmalade (makes 6 jars)

1 Thoroughly wash 1 lb 11oz (750 g) pink or yellow grapefruit and 1 lb 11 oz (750 g) lemons. Put them into a saucepan of cold water and bring to the boil. Cook for 15 minutes then drain the fruits. Allow to cool for a few minutes and then cut into approximately $3/8$ in (1 cm) slices. Discard the pips and reserve the juice.

2 Peel $3^{1}/_{2}$ oz (100 g) fresh ginger and pass through the fine plate of a vegetable mill. Set aside. Remove half the citrus fruit slices and dice them finely with a knife. Combine 2 lb 11 oz (1.2 kg) sugar, the juice from the fruits, and 1 scant cup (20 cl) water in a preserving pan, bring to the boil, and cook for 5 minutes.

3 If you use a candy thermometer, the temperature must reach 230 °F (110 °C). Next add the chopped ginger and the sliced and cubed fruits. Cook over medium heat for approximately 25 minutes (the temperature should reach 221 °F/105 °C). Fill the jars with the boiling hot marmalade and allow to cool.

Redcurrant jelly

Quince and lemon jelly

Blackcurrant jelly

General points

As their name suggests, jellies have a more solid, gelled consistency. This aspect is attributable to one of the constituents of fruits: pectin. The effect of this substance is produced after cooking and when there is a sufficient amount of acidity present. It is the reason why only fruits rich in pectin and fairly acid produce firm jellies. Select fruits which are "just ready," as fruits that are too ripe lose their pectin and their ability to gel. Fruits that have passed their best or have become too soft are more suitable for jams. In contrast to jams or marmalades, jellies, which are prepared with juice and not pulp, do not contain pieces of fruit. That is why they have a translucent, clear, appearance and are free from impurities. In addition to apples, the fruits that are most suitable for jellies are quince, blackcurrants, redcurrants, bilberries, raspberries, and blackberries.

Flavors

Especially if apple jelly is made with good pippins, it is delicious plain, but it also lends itself very well to a complementary flavor that can be added when the apple juice is boiled with the sugar: for example, you can choose between 1 tbsp good rum; the juice and zest of 2 oranges; 2 Earl Grey teabags; or a handful of fragrant, unwaxed, red rose petals.

Preservation

Blanch the jars and then wipe them thoroughly for a few minutes before filling them. Pour the jelly into the jars when it is nearly boiling; never let it cool down or leave it in the preserving pan. If you use jars with lids, fill and seal them immediately. Turn the jars over and then leave them to cool.

Blackcurrant jelly

To make 5 or 6 jars, take approximately 4$\frac{1}{2}$ lb (2 kg) blackcurrants and discard the stalks. Put the blackcurrants into a saucepan, add $\frac{1}{3}$ cup + 1$\frac{1}{2}$ tbsp (10 cl) water per 2$\frac{1}{4}$ lb (1 kg) fruit, and bring to the boil. Then reduce the heat immediately and simmer. Stir the blackcurrants while crushing them with a wooden spoon for approximately 10 minutes. When the blackcurrants have softened, pour them into a sieve and squeeze them over a bowl. Reserve the juice and discard the skins and pips. Pour this juice into a preserving pan and add 3 lb 5 oz (1.5 kg) sugar. Place over low heat and boil while stirring continuously. Cook for 8 minutes, while skimming off the purple froth that continuously forms on the surface. Quickly fill the jars with the boiling hot jelly and allow them to cool completely before hermetically sealing.

Quince jelly (makes 6 jars)

1 Select 3 lb 5 oz (1.5 kg) very ripe quinces with bright yellow skins: they release an enchanting fragrance. Rub them vigorously under the cold tap to clean them, but also to remove the fine down that covers the skin. Do not peel them. Cut them into quarters, then remove the cores and set them aside. Wash the quince quarters. There is no need to add lemon juice.

2 Put the fruit quarters into a preserving pan with just enough water to cover them. Cook over low heat; wrap the quince cores in a muslin square and put this "knot" into the preserving pan while the fruits gently cook. After 30 minutes, check whether it is cooked.

3 Remove a slice of quince, put it on a plate, and press it: if it flexes, it is cooked. If it does not flex, then boil for a further 5 minutes. Empty the contents of the preserving pan into a sieve lined with a clean dishtowel. Leave the juice to seep through overnight. Fasten the dishtowel to recover the maximum amount of juice. Measure the juice collected.

4 Pour the juice into the preserving pan and add sugar in proportion: allow $3^1/_2$ oz (100 g) sugar to $^1/_3$ cup + $1^1/_2$ tbsp (10 cl) juice. Bring to the boil, then remove from the heat. Mix to dissolve the sugar. Pour into jars. Quince jelly has a delectable flavor: it should be as transparent as apple jelly, but with a russet tint.

Chutneys

General points

Chutney is an Indian condiment adopted by the British. It accompanies curry dishes, cold meats, and vegetables, and features in a very large number of recipes. Some chutney is very spicy and consumed in small quantities; on the other hand, other varieties are mild and slightly acid. Chutney is made with a very wide variety of ingredients. The most commonly used are mangoes, green tomatoes, apples, grapes, garlic, pineapples, and onions. In some recipes, such as mango chutney, only one variety of fruit is used; in others, there is a mixture of fruits. These fruits and vegetables are cut into small pieces and cooked in a syrupy sauce with varying amounts of spice, which is made up of brown sugar, vinegar, and fruit juice in addition to various spices (cinnamon, chili, pepper, cardomom, and coriander). You can find chutneys in the stores. Most commercially produced chutney is made with mangoes, but you can make different types yourself. As it keeps for at least 6 months, you can cook chutney in large quantities. The word "chutney" is typically British, but is derived from a Hindustani term, "chatni," which means "strong spices."

Fruit chutney (makes 5 jars)

1. Peel 3 apples, 2 pears that are just ripe, and 1 small pineapple. Cut the flesh diagonally into cubes of around 1 in (2 cm). Peel 3 garlic cloves and chop them roughly. Put the garlic and cubes of fruit into a pan. Cover and "sweat" for 15 minutes over very gentle heat. Stir occasionally so that the mixture does not stick to the bottom of the pan. The ingredients should slowly blend and hardly brown at all.

2. Add 1³/4 cups (400 g) brown sugar, 1 tsp salt, 1 tsp ground cumin, 1 large pinch ground ginger, 1 pinch cayenne pepper, and 1³/4 oz (50 g) golden raisins rinsed in tepid water and sprinkled with 1 glass of wine vinegar. Cook for 30 minutes, uncovered so that you can see when it boils. Stir occasionally.

3. Allow to cool before filling the jars. Seal in the same way as you would for jams; chutney will keep for just as long unopened. Once a jar has been opened, store it in the refrigerator. You can vary the seasoning while cooking, according to taste: for a spicy flavor, add chili powder and increase the proportion of ginger and garlic.

Chutneys

1 Wash 3 lemons, wipe dry, slice while removing the pips, and then chop roughly. Put them into a bowl and sprinkle with 1 tbsp salt. Steep for approximately 10 hours. Peel 3 small onions and dice. Select very ripe lemons, which are full of juice and have a delicate skin. You can use gray shallots instead of small onions.

2 Put them into an enamel saucepan with the steeped lemon. Mix, then add 1¼ cups (30 cl) cider vinegar and 1 tsp allspice. Allspice is a mixture that can be bought ready-made and combines the flavor of ground pepper, grated nutmeg, ground cloves, and ground cinnamon. Sometimes ginger is added too.

3 Add 2 tbsp rounded mustard seeds, 1 cup (225 g) brown sugar and 1¾ oz (50 g) raisins. Bring rapidly to the boil over a high heat. Reduce the heat and leave to simmer for approximately 50 minutes, or until the lemons are very tender. You can use either blond or brown mustard seeds, or a mixture of both.

4 Sterilize the jars with boiling water and drain on a clean cloth or paper towels, and then fill them while they're still warm. Seal and label. This chutney goes very well with grills, particularly fish and kebabs. It will keep for a long time in a cool, dry, dark place.

Peach Melba

Peach Melba is a one-hundred-year-old dessert created by the great chef and cook Georges Auguste Escoffier in honor of Dame Nelly Melba, a very famous, Australian operatic soprano (1861–1931). These famous desserts did not disappear during the decades that followed. The very opposite was true: they continued to be appreciated, though they have reached us in a slightly simplified form. In fact, when Nelly Melba sang "Lohengrin" in London, Escoffier served her peaches placed on a bed of vanilla ice cream, mounted between the wings of a swan sculpted in ice. He was born in 1846. His brilliant career unfolded in Britain, where he supervised notably the opening of the Savoy. He died in 1935, at the age of 89. He left behind a certain number of famous recipes, but above all many theoretical texts, which, despite the passage of time and culinary trends, are still useful references today.

Serves 6
Preparation: 30 minutes
Resting: 2 days
Cooking: 20 minutes
Freezing: 1 hour

Ingredients

6 white peaches
$4^1/_2$ lb (2 kg) superfine sugar
2 vanilla beans
2 cups (50 cl) milk
8 egg yolks
2 cups (50 cl) light cream
1 lb 2 oz (500 g) raspberries
$^1/_3$ cup + $1^1/_2$ tbsp (10 cl) mineral water
1 lemon
Almond cookies

1 Prepare the fruits and syrup. Immerse the white peaches in a large quantity of boiling water and then immediately allow to cool in a bowl of ice water; peel them. When buying them, always select packaged fruits rather than loose ones. Select ripe, fragrant peaches, i.e., picked when they have matured.

2 Combine 8 cups (2 liters) water, 3 lb 5 oz (1.5 kg) superfine sugar, and 1 vanilla bean split lengthwise in a saucepan. Bring to the boil and then simmer. Immerse the peaches in this bubbling syrup and cook for approximately 20 minutes. When poaching the peaches, the syrup should not be allowed to boil fiercely: fruits should crystallize slowly. The vanilla bean is not essential.

3 Remove the peaches, one by one, from the syrup using a skimmer. Arrange them in a large glass salad bowl as you go along. Allow the syrup to completely cool down and then pour it gently over the fruits (after removing the vanilla bean). Cover the salad bowl and steep the peaches in the syrup in a cool place or in the refrigerator for at least 48 hours.

4 Prepare the vanilla ice cream. Boil the milk in a pan, add 1 vanilla bean, and leave to infuse. Combine the egg yolks with 1 1/3 cups (300 g) superfine sugar and beat the mixture to blanch it. Pour the filtered milk over it, add the cream, still beating, and then cook in the same way as a custard. Filter and allow to cool. Put the cream into an ice-cream maker.

5 Let the ice cream set. Then put it into the freezer. Prepare the raspberry sauce. Combine the raspberries, mineral water, 1 scant cup (200 g) superfine sugar, and the juice of 1 lemon in a mixing bowl. Blend the mixture to a fine purée, filter the sauce, and set aside. Ensure all pips are removed so that the sauce is smooth and clear.

6 Just before serving, put 1 scoop of vanilla ice cream from the freezer compartment into bowls. Place a cold, poached peach in each. Garnish with fresh raspberries and top with raspberry sauce. Serve with almond cookies. You can also keep the syrup in the refrigerator, which you can use to poach other delicate fruits.

Vruchtjes

Sugar

Sugar is a sweet-flavored substance, which is found in plants in various forms. It is extracted from the juice of sugar beet and sugar cane, but also from sorghum, grapes, and from maple sap. When talking about "sugar" in the singular, "sucrose" is implied. It is the only chemically "pure" element in foods. Sugar beet and sugar cane are crushed and leached. The juice obtained is treated to remove any impurities. Then it is concentrated by using various

Sugar table overview

Types of sugar	Appearance	Type	Uses
Superfine sugar	White powder	Dry, refined sugar	Pastries, Cooking, Desserts, Confectionery
Sugar syrup	Transparent liquid	Sugar in solution	Sauces, Sorbets, Pastries, Confectionery
Soft brown sugar	Fragrant brown powder	Crystallized sugar, not much refined	Pastries, Chutneys, Confectionery
Vanilla sugar	Light brown powder	Flavored sugar	Pastries
Confectioner's sugar	Fine, white powder	Ground sugar mixed with starch	Pastries, Confectionery
Granulated sugar	White powder with large crystals	Cystallized from refined syrup	Jams, Jellies, Chutneys, Confectionery, Marmalade
Jam sugar	Fine white powder	Sugar mixed with pectin and citric acid	Jams, Jellies, Chutneys, Marmalade

Fruit pastes

given concentration, it slows down or prevents bacteria multiplying. It is a high-calorie food and is not balanced: for 1/2 cup (100 g), 400 kcal, 0 protein, 0 lipids. In the form of white cube sugar or finely ground white sugar (superfine sugar), it enhances the flavor of drinks; sweetens dairy products, yogurts, and fromage frais; and enhances fruit salads and compotes. While sugar is used to make jams and jellies, pastries and desserts, ice creams and sorbets, it is also cooked to make syrup or caramel and plays an essential part in preparing crystallized flowers, crystallized and glacé fruits, and fruit pastes. In cooking, it is used to bring out the flavors of other foods, such as onions or glazed carrots; in bittersweet condiments; when cooking peas; in tomato sauces; and in the caramelization of certain brown sauces. Finally, did you know that, if you add a few pinches of sugar to the water when cooking shellfish

physical methods until sugar as such is obtained. Sugar is essential in pastry making and especially confectionery. It is also used a lot in cooking to sweeten recipes that are too strong or acidic. Just like salt, sugar is an excellent preservative: on the basis of a

Cherries and crystallized orange skins

(in the same proportion as salt), it enhances their flavor and color?

Crystallized orange peel

Cane sugar

623

Florentines

Duck with cranberry sauce

Florentines

These are delicious, round candies made of nougatine, mixed dried fruits, and crystallized fruits. The success of this recipe depends on the quality of fruits used, which should be perfect in quality. Florentines are coated on one side with dark chocolate.

Cranberry sauce

This is one of the best accompaniments when serving game animals or game birds. First you prepare a crushed peppercorn sauce base, from the meat marinated in red wine; then the sauce is reduced, allowed to settle, and finally slowly thickened. Just before serving, add the cranberry jam or whole cranberries and a dab of butter to the sauce. The sauce then has a very pleasant, bittersweet flavor.

General points

There are numerous ways to cook fruits, which are the basis of a great variety of sweet and savory recipes. They are to be found in every cuisine, with sometimes very welcome results.

Pears Belle-Hélène

This recipe is a great classic of French cuisine. Firstly, the pears are peeled, poached, and cooled in vanilla sugar syrup. Then you arrange pretty balls of vanilla ice cream in bowls and next add the poached half-pears; finally, the dish is topped with a hot chocolate sauce.Pears Belle Hélène, which is quite simple to make, is a superb dessert with few ingredients; you can savor its different flavors and the contrast between the hot sauce, the cool pears, and the cold ice-cream.

Verjuice Chicken

Verjuice chicken

This is a recipe from the southwest of France, and is a legacy of the time when verjuice (green, acidic juice extracted from green grapes) replaced vinegar. The sauce obtained is quite acid and very fragrant. Pieces of chicken are browned in oil with seasoning, and then simmered with bouillon and verjuice.

Mendiants

These sweetmeats are a mixture of figs, almonds, hazelnuts, and raisins. Typically, they are served at Christmas in Provence, and can be found in confectionery and pastries such as mendiants de Gordes in Provence, which are enriched with crystallized orange peel.

Apple sauce

In Britain, apple sauce

Mendiants de Gordes

accompanies roast meats. It is cooked like a compote, and seasoned with salt, pepper, cloves, and cinnamon.

Banana split

This is an easy recipe to make, with an original presentation: the bananas are split into two halves and presented over vanilla ice cream, supplemented with strawberries and Chantilly

Pork chops with apple sauce

Banana split

cream. You can use chocolate sauce instead of strawberries, garnished with almonds.

Pecan tart

This tart is a typical North American dish: pour a mixture of butter, flour, superfine sugar, and cane syrup into a plain pastry shell then cover with whole pecans. Bake for 45 minutes at 400 °F (200 °C).

Pecan tart

Recommended drinks

Farmer's rum
Pineapple juice
Mango juice

Menu suggestions

1. This light dessert can conclude a somewhat hearty menu, consisting of crab quiche followed by roast pork with eggplant gratin.

2. You can take your inspiration from West Indian cuisine when serving this dessert, with cod acras and barbecued spare rib of pork.

Pineapple filled with fruits

An easy dish

Serves 4
Preparation: 15 minutes
Cooking: none

Ingredients

2 nectarines

2 kiwi fruits

1 mango

5^1/$_2$ oz (150 g) strawberries

Cane sugar

White rum

1 lemon

1 fairly ripe, very fresh pineapple

1. Prepare a fruit salad by dicing the nectarines, cutting the kiwi fruits into thin slices, the mango into cubes, and the strawberries into slivers. Spice it up with 2 tbsp cane sugar and 1 liqueur glass of white rum, and the juice of 1 lemon. Mix well so that all the fruits soak up the sauce. Steep in a cool place while you prepare the pineapple.

2. Lay the pineapple on a board and cut it approximately 1–1^1/$_2$ in (3–4 cm) below the plume using a very sharp, large knife. Stand the pineapple upright and plunge the knife into the pineapple approximately 3/8 in (1 cm) from the skin, making sure you tilt it toward the base. Take it all around the pineapple being very careful not to pierce the skin. Drive the knife into the pineapple from the base and cut, without widening the fissure, by turning the blade from right to left first. Twist the knife and cut from left to right.

3. Remove the main part of the pineapple. Cut it into slices then into cubes; mix them into the fruit salad, which will be used to fill the main part of the pineapple.

This recipe is easy to make, but its success depends on attention to detail: take the trouble to peel the kiwi fruits very carefully, before cutting them into thin slices; select strawberries that are not too large, with a regular shape easy to cut into slivers. Pit the nectarines, but do not peel them. It is advisable to peel and cut the mango in two, remove the pit, and cut the fruit into regular cubes, as far as is possible, and not too large.

Pork kebabs with pineapple

An economical dish

Serves 4
Preparation: 20 minutes
Cooking: 10 minutes
Marinade: 30 minutes

Ingredients

14 oz–1 lb 2 oz (400–500 g) pork (preferably loin)

7 oz/200 g smoked bacon streaked with fat

1 fairly ripe, small pineapple

Olive oil

Tabasco® sauce

Salt

1. Cut the pork meat into $1/2$–1 in (2–3 cm) cubes cut sideways; remove the rind from the bacon and cut it into 3/8 in (1 cm) cubes; remove the pineapple skin, cut the pineapple into 2 or 3 $1/2$ in (2 cm) slices, and cut into small triangles.

2. Put 2 tbsp olive oil into a bowl and season generously with Tabasco. Add salt to the pieces of pork and steep for 30 minutes in the flavored oil.

3. Thread the kebab skewers by alternating pineapple, bacon, and pork, so that each piece of pork is flanked by a piece of pineapple and a cube of bacon.

4. Cook for 8–10 minutes over a pre-heated, oiled grill, set over charcoal that is moderately hot.

5. You can supplement these pork kebabs with pineapple with a variation inspired by Chinese cuisine, which often uses sesame seeds to add a distinctive, crunchy texture to meat or game recipes. Mix 2 tbsp sesame seeds and 2 tbsp breadcrumbs in a hollow dish; add 1 tsp ground cumin, a pinch of chili powder, and salt and pepper to taste. Once the kebabs have marinated and the charcoal is ready, dip the kebabs in this mixture and turn them over so that they are thoroughly coated on all sides. Then start cooking them. Just before serving, try sprinkling them with a few drops of sesame oil and at the same time serve a soy bean sprout salad with mint as a fresh garnish.

Recommended drinks

Rosé de Provence
Côtes-du-Rhône
Côtes-du-Lubéron

Menu suggestions

1. You can serve these kebabs after tomatoes with mozzarella as an appetizer. As an accompaniment, try potato chips, with apricot tart for dessert.

2. You can also include kebabs in a Mediterranean menu, with Greek appetizers and an orange and cinnamon salad for dessert.

Duck with apples

A regional dish

Serves 4
Preparation: 20 minutes
Cooking: 1 hour

Ingredients

1 duck
3 slices cooked ham
4$^{1}/_{2}$ oz (125 g) butter
3 lb 5 oz (1.5 kg) apples
Breadcrumbs
1 glass bouillon
1 small pot crème fraîche

1 lemon or a little cider vinegar
Salt and pepper

1. Trim the duck ready for roasting. Before trussing it, stuff it with a slice of roughly chopped ham, and then sauté it in butter mixed with 1–2 peeled and diced, seeded apples, 3–4 tbsp breadcrumbs, salt, and pepper.

2. Heat the oven to 435 °F (225 °C) and put the duck in a roasting pan; rub it with softened butter, put it in the oven, and roast for 1 hour. Meanwhile, prepare a rough compote with the 4 best apples you set aside. Peel these apples, hollow them out, and butter them thoroughly before cooking in the oven. Cut two slices of ham into long triangles and sauté them in butter.

3. Once the duck is cooked, keep it warm, skim the fat from the roasting pan, and then add the bouillon to the cooking juices to make a sauce. Reduce it a little and then beat with 5 tbsp crème fraîche, which has already been whipped with a little lemon juice or cider vinegar; adjust the seasoning according to taste.

4. Arrange the duck on a bed of apple compote and surround with the oven-cooked apples; garnish with the triangles of ham and serve the sauce separately.

5. Select very fragrant, crispy apples that are not too sweet, but especially apples with firm flesh that will not fall apart during cooking: for example, the "Belle van Boskoop" variety or pippins. Use cooked ham, preferably on the bone. You can also add a few roughly chopped, fresh sage leaves to the stuffing.

Recommended drinks

Farmhouse cider
Bergerac Rouge
Muscadet Sur Lie

Menu suggestions

1. This duck with apples is a classic recipe from Normandy. It can be preceded by mussels cooked in wine and followed, after salad and camembert cheese, by a dessert of pancakes with Benedictine liqueur.

2. You can also try a lighter menu, with sorrel soup as an appetizer and jam brioche for dessert.

Fig chutney

A foreign dish

Makes 4 jars
Preparation: 15 minutes
Cooking: 1 hour

Ingredients

1 ginger root
2¼ lb (1 kg) fresh figs
1 apple
2 or 3 onions
5½ oz (150 g) raisins
10 oz (275 g) superfine sugar
2 glasses white vinegar

Salt
Four-spice

1. Peel the ginger and grate it until you obtain 2 heaped tsp. Remove the fig stalks and cut the figs into four. Peel the apple then seed, core, and dice it. Peel the onions and chop them very roughly.

2. Put the mixture into an enamel bowl with the raisins, superfine sugar, white vinegar, 1 level tsp salt, and a pinch of four-spice. Cook over medium heat and simmer for 1 hour (the juice should cover the spatula comfortably). Allow to cool while stirring occasionally.

3. After scalding and draining the jars upside down on a cloth or paper towels, pour the mixture into them. Wait until they have completely cooled before covering them. This chutney is a wonderful accompaniment to cold meats, particularly leftover boiled beef, and will even transform plain white rice into a really delicious dish.

Chutneys are sometimes disregarded in French cookery, but you can make use of all kinds of fruits (not necessarily exotic) in a delicious, original way. The natural sugar content of figs, reinforced by the added sugar and the vinegar, generally ensures good preservation. It is also worth knowing that brown sugar and malt vinegar enhance both the color and the flavor of chutney.

Menu suggestions

1. If this chutney is served as a condiment with rice, it can accompany lamb curry; try serving prawn fritters as an appetizer and mango sorbet for dessert.

2. If it accompanies leftover cold meat, for a quick meal try potato salad with cider vinegar as a side dish, and fromage frais with mixed herbs for dessert.

Clafoutis meringue

A family dish

Serves 4
Preparation: 20 minutes
Cooking: 35 + 5 minutes

Ingredients

1 lb 11 oz (750 g) cherries

1 tbsp kirsch or maraschino

$^7/_8$ cup (100 g) flour

1 pinch salt

$^1/_2$ cup (125 g) superfine sugar

6 eggs

1 generous cup (25 cl) milk

Butter

1. Set aside a few of the best cherries. Pit the rest, put them into a basin, and sprinkle with 1 tbsp kirsch or maraschino. Steep while preparing the recipe.

2. Pour the flour into a basin. Add the salt and mix, as you should avoid putting the salt in direct contact with the egg. Make a hole in the center and add $^1/_2$ cup (100 g) superfine sugar and 4 eggs; then 2 egg yolks (setting aside the whites), one by one, gradually folding them into the mixture. To do this, first blend the sugar with the eggs, then the flour, gently working the batter with a spatula.

3. Do not work the batter for too long, as this would remove much of its light texture and give it too much elasticity. When it really begins to thicken, gradually dilute it with the milk. The exact quantity is difficult to specify: it depends on the quality of the flour and the size of the eggs; the batter should simply be fluid, and not liquid.

4. Butter a gratin dish quite generously, ensuring even coverage. Arrange the pitted cherries at the bottom of the dish, so that they completely cover it, but are not packed too tightly together. Pour in the batter. The cherries should be almost level with the batter. Dab with butter. Pre-heat the oven to 400 °F (200 °C) and cook for 30–35 minutes.

5. Stiffly beat 2 egg whites with a little superfine sugar. Pour it over the slightly cooled clafoutis. Push the reserved cherries into the meringue and return to the oven for a few minutes to allow the meringue to brown very lightly. Serve cold or slightly warm.

Recommended drinks

Cabernet
Armagnac
Maraschino

Menu suggestions

1. This classic, but sophisticated, dessert is suitable for a traditional family menu. Serve a green salad and broiled goat's cheese as an appetizer and blanquette of veal for the main course.

2. If you want to prepare a simple, quick meal, serve onion soup au gratin as an appetizer, and chicken sauté with mushrooms as the main course.

Dog-rose jam

A family dish

Makes 4 jars
Preparation: 1 hour 15 minutes
Cooking: 45 minutes

Ingredients

4$^1/_2$ lb (2 kg) dog-rose berries
1 lb 11 oz (750 g) pippins
4$^1/_2$ lb (2 kg) sugar

1. Wash the dog-rose berries (otherwise known as rose hips) in a large colander and immerse several times in cold water. Put them into a large saucepan. Peel the apples, cut into quarters, and remove the stalks and cores. Put them into the saucepan too. Fill with just enough water to cover them. Bring to the boil and simmer gently for 30 minutes.

2. Prepare the jars: scald them in boiling water then turn them upside-down to drain on paper towels. Weigh a bowl and make a note of its weight. Place the colander over the bowl and pour the cooked fruits into it. Keep the juice in the bowl and put the fruits back into the saucepan. Fill with just enough water to cover them and cook over very low heat for a further 30 minutes. Put a vegetable mill over the bowl. Pour the contents of the saucepan into it and grind carefully, particularly at the end—the vegetable mill must retain the pits and hairs of the berries. Weigh the bowl when full, and deduct its weight when empty to work out the weight of the fruit purée; weigh out the same amount of sugar.

3. Pour the purée and sugar into a preserving pan. Mix well and cook over low heat, turning the mixture until the sugar has melted. Next, increase the heat to bring it rapidly to the boil, and then set the temperature so that it cooks gently and evenly.

4. The jam is ready when the thermometer has reached 220 °F (104.5 °C) or 31° on the Baumé scale, or when a few drops of syrup are sprinkled over a cold plate: if ready, they will turn into jelly and form round pearls, without spreading. Skim the jam, put it into jars, then cover.

Menu suggestions

1. The original flavor of this jam that grandma used to make can complement a warm brioche for dessert, following a main course of roast chicken with salad. Try a small rabbit pâté as an appetizer.

2. Like all jams, this one would be wonderful as a pancake filling for a children's meal. Try grated carrots as an appetizer, and fish croquettes for the main course.

633

Melon jam

A family dish

Makes 5 jars
Preparation: 30 minutes
Cooking: approximately 45 minutes

Ingredients

6³/₄ lb (3 kg) melons
2 lemons
2¹/₄ lb (1 kg) sugar

1. Put the melons by turns on a board, cut them in two, and then into 6 or 8 slices. Remove the fiber and seeds, and then the skin of each slice by taking it off very gently. Cut the pulp into 1 in (2 cm) cubes. Toss them into a bowl as you go along, having first weighed it when it was empty. Remove the lemon peel and cut into thin strips. To make a delicious jam, select melons that are just ripe, but not past that point.

2. Weigh the full bowl to calculate the weight of the melon pulp. Weigh out ³/₄ of this amount in sugar. Pour 1 glass of water per 1 lb 2 oz (500 g) sugar into a preserving pan. Add the sugar, stir the mixture well over low heat, and increase the temperature as soon as all the sugar has melted. Cook this syrup until it forms "pearly drops" (the surface of the syrup is covered in small round, dense bubbles that look like pearls).

3. Put the melon pieces and lemon peel into the preserving pan, mix gently, and bring to the boil again. Set the temperature so that it cooks slowly and, above all, very evenly. Turn occasionally. Meanwhile, prepare the jars: scald them and turn them upside-down to drain on a cloth.

4. When the melon has become translucent and resembles crystallized melon, check whether the jam is cooked: a few drops of syrup sprinkled over a cold plate should transform into jelly by forming round pearls, and not spreading. Take the preserving pan off the heat, remove the lemon peel, and fill the jars while evenly distributing the fruits and syrup. Seal with plastic wrap when warm.

Menu suggestions

1. Delicious at breakfast with very lightly broiled toast, this melon jam is a perfect accompaniment to brioches with crystallized fruits and lemon or orange pound cakes.

2. As an original dessert in a menu from Charente (a department in southwestern France) try cruchades (cornmeal fritters) accompanied by this melon jam; with mouclade (mussels in white wine); and duckling with small turnips.

Hare cutlets with blueberries

A regional dish

Serves 4
Preparation: 30 minutes
Waiting: several hours
Cooking: 25–30 minutes

Ingredients

Thighs and legs of 1 hare

White wine

1 bouquet garni

Peppercorns

Cooking salt

Olive oil

Butter

Breadcrumbs

Bouillon

Oregano or marjoram

9 oz (250 g) blueberries

Cornstarch

1. Carefully clean and skin the hare meat. Marinate for several hours in a medium dry white wine with 1 bouquet garni, peppercorns, cooking salt, and a dash of olive oil. Drain. Chop the meat with $1/4$ of its weight in butter and the same weight of breadcrumbs soaked in bouillon and drained. Adjust seasoning with salt and pepper according to taste. Make cutlet-shaped croquettes and embed a bone in each from the hare's flank.

2. Put the croquettes on oiled sheets of wax paper. Flavor with oregano or marjoram leaves. Carefully seal and grill for 15–20 minutes over attenuated heat. Turn over two-thirds of the way through cooking.

3. Meanwhile, poach the blueberries and reduce the marinade after straining it; thicken with a little cornstarch and color it with some blueberry juice. Serve the hare cutlets on warm plates and garnish with the blueberries poached in sauce. The sauce as such is served separately in a warm sauceboat. Make sure you seal the oiled wax paper properly, as the croquettes are delicate and moist. Their cooking juice must not be allowed to escape after they have been turned over. To maintain the "cutlet" appearance of these croquettes, embellish each bone with a small frill.

Recommended drinks

Riesling
Pinot Noir
Tokay

Menu suggestions

1. To complete this recipe from Alsace, serve foie gras escalopes as an appetizer for a celebratory meal, followed by cinnamon tart with raspberry sorbet for dessert.

2. For a more family-oriented meal, try a selection of cooked pork meats as an appetizer and rhubarb tart for dessert.

Recommended drinks

Grapefruit juice
Sparkling mineral water

Menu suggestions

1. This light, original, sophisticated appetizer can be followed by fish and mushroom parcels as a main course, with a lemon sorbet served in its skin to follow.

2. You can also try a seasonal vegetable fricassee to follow this fruity appetizer, and an exotic fruit salad for dessert.

Crab with peaches

A light dish

Serves 2
Preparation: 30 minutes
Cooking: 15 minutes

Ingredients

1 carrot

1 onion

1 large bouquet garni
(parsley, thyme, bay leaf)

1 glass dry white wine

1 fine edible crab

2 fine yellow peaches

Tabasco® sauce

Paprika

1 small pot crème fraîche

Salt and pepper

1. Grate the carrot; cut it into slices and put them into a stewpot containing enough water to cover the crab comfortably; add the peeled, sliced onion, the bouquet garni, salt, pepper, and the white wine.

2. Put the crab into this cold court-bouillon; bring it rapidly to the boil; cook it slowly and evenly for 5–10 minutes; allow to cool in the court-bouillon. Open the crab without damaging it; remove all its meat, not forgetting the thorax meat and the brown-colored meat it contains.

3. Peel the peaches; set aside a few unblemished quarters: crush the rest with a fork and blend the crabmeat with the peach purée. Distribute a first layer of meat in the crab shell, from the dark-colored meat of the thorax blended with the peach purée and spiced with salt and Tabasco. Cover with the white crabmeat and peach purée and add salt, pepper, paprika, and crème fraîche. Sprinkle with paprika, add the reserved peach quarters, and serve cold.

It is, of course, possible to find pre-cooked crab in the store. When you buy it, check its weight and the condition of the shell. The edible crab, or crab, in principle contains the highest proportion of edible meat. As you will use the shell for presentation purposes, make sure you open the crab by sliding the blade of a knife between the shell and the thorax. The brown meat of the thorax (mainly composed of the liver) and the yellow, creamy meat of the shell blend pleasantly with the white flaky meat of the legs and pincers.

Pork tenderloin "à la limousine"

A regional dish

Serves 4
Preparation: 25 minutes
Waiting: 1 hour
Cooking: 45 minutes + 20 minutes

Ingredients

2 x 14 oz (400 g) pork tenderloin fillets

1 lemon

Oil

1 small bunch fresh sage

$2^1/_4$ lb (1 kg) sweet chestnuts

Bouillon

1 or 2 shallots

$1^3/_4$ oz (50 g) butter

Dry white wine

2 or 3 apples

1 small pot crème fraîche

Chervil

1 egg yolk (optional)

Mustard (optional)

Salt and pepper

1. Carefully trim the pork fillets. Absorb any excess liquid with paper towels. Place them on a dish, sprinkle with lemon juice, and drizzle with oil. Add salt and pepper, flavor with sage, and leave to stand for at least 1 hour. Meanwhile, cook the sweet chestnuts: strip off their brown outer skin and cover them with cold water, bring to the boil, and then peel off their pale inner skin. Finally, cook them for 40–50 minutes in a small amount of good bouillon over very gentle heat, and cover.

2. Start preparing the sauce: peel and finely chop the shallot. Brown it in butter over medium heat and then braise it for a moment over low heat while stirring. Moisten with 1 glass of dry white wine and reduce over gentle heat.

3. Heat a skillet containing the very minimum of oil and brown the fillets. Turn them over so that they color evenly on both sides. Reduce the temperature and cook for about a further 15 minutes. Keep them warm. Add a little water to the cooking juices and reduce the white wine; add salt and pepper, and reduce a little more.

4. Peel the apples and cut them into quarters. Rapidly sauté and brown them in butter in another skillet. Finish the sauce by thickening it with the crème fraîche, and add a substantial amount of salt and pepper. Flavor it with chopped chervil at the last moment. Arrange on warm plates. To make the sauce more delicious and subtle while you are keeping the meat warm, instead of just thickening it with crème fraîche, you could add a finishing touch by whipping the crème fraîche with 1 egg yolk and a little mustard.

Recommended drinks

Saint-Pourçain Rouge
Côtes-d'Auvergne Rouge
Côte-Roannaise Rouge

Menu suggestions

1. This is a typical dish from Limousin, which may be preceded by a green salad with gizzards as an appetizer and followed by clafoutis with black cherries for dessert.

2. For a lighter menu, you can try hard-boiled eggs stuffed with Roquefort cheese as an appetizer, and fruit compote for dessert.

Apple and lemon jelly

A family dish

Makes 4 jars
Preparation and initial cooking: 45 minutes
Cooking: 40 minutes

Ingredients

9 lb (4 kg) apples
2 lemons
5 lb 9 oz (2.5 kg) white cube sugar

1. You can use two methods: you can either peel the apples or leave their skins on. If you peel them, you will obtain a perfectly transparent jelly; on the other hand, if you do not peel them, you will obtain a jelly that is not so clear, but is much more delicious. So having either peeled or scrubbed them, washed, wiped dry, and cut them into quarters, put them into a large preserving pan of water with the juice of 1 lemon, without removing their cores. The apples should be able to float easily in the preserving pan.

2. Heat the preserving pan on the stove and then cook very evenly. When the apples start dissolving, pour them into a fine sieve placed over a large basin. Let all the juice drain without pressing the fruit.

3. Clean the preserving pan and pour the collected juice into it; add the same weight in white cube sugar and cook slowly until it almost immediately turns into drops, if you pour a little jelly onto a cold plate. Then add the peel of 1 whole lemon, removed very delicately; cook for just 2 minutes, collect with a skimmer, and set aside.

4. Fill the jars with jelly and put a piece of lemon peel into each. Cover.

5. Select very firm apples, which are juicy and slightly acidic: the "Granny Smith" variety predominates in this case, but you can also mix several other types—pippins, "Starking Delicious," and "Belles van Boskoop". Above all, do not be tempted to press cooked fruits to extract the juice, as you could easily cloud the translucency of the jelly.

Menu suggestions

1. For the dessert, you can use this delicious jelly to top an apple tart in the Normandy tradition, after chicken and mushrooms with cream for the main course.

2. In the Basque tradition, apple jelly accompanies ewe's milk cheese: this is an original way to combine cheese with the dessert.

Fig and white grape gratin

A party dish

Serves 4
Preparation: 15 minutes
Waiting: 1 hour
Cooking: 5–6 minutes

Ingredients

1 lb 2 oz (500 g) white grapes

1 glass spicy white wine
or sweet wine

Butter10 fairly ripe figs

White pepper

Brown sugar to taste

1 small jar crème fraîche

Confectioner's sugar

1. Peel the grapes and steep for at least one hour in the wine.

2. Butter 4 small, individual gratin dishes. Remove the fig stalks, halve or quarter the figs according to preference, and put them into the dishes; add a very small amount of white pepper, and sprinkle them with brown sugar; add a few of the steeped grapes and sprinkle them with a little of the wine they were soaked in.

3. Brown in the oven at 545 °F (285 ° C) for 5–6 minutes, the time it takes to whip the crème fraîche, lightly sweetening it with confectioner's sugar at the same time. Take the dishes straight from the oven to the table and serve the hot figs and cold crème fraîche together.

Take some muscat grapes, either black or white (or a mixture), which are large and firm enough to be able to hold them with one hand; split them with a light cut using a very sharp knife, and remove the pips and skin. The procedure is a little tedious but gives a more sophisticated finish. For the wine to steep the grapes in, select a spicy white wine, a Muscat, or a sweet wine, the same as you will serve as an accompaniment: Frontignan, Rasteau, Rivesaltes, Beaumes-de-Venise, or even a Greek Samos. In preference, select purple figs that do not fall apart so easily when cooking, and preserve a honey flavor; white figs are too delicate. Instead of crème fraîche as an accompaniment, you can make a zabaglione, and still use the same wine: 5 egg yolks briskly worked with 3⁄4 cup (180 g) superfine sugar until a frothy consistency is obtained, to which is added 11⁄4 cups (30 cl) wine and a pinch of grated lemon peel, while whipping in a bain-marie or double boiler.

Recommended drinks

Frontignan
Rasteau
Rivesaltes

Menu suggestions

1. This fruit gratin will come into its own as part of a Mediterranean menu: stuffed squid or broiled Mediterranean shrimp as an appetizer, and Catalan tuna as the main course.

2. You can serve a Provençal menu, with stuffed zucchini flowers as an appetizer and bass with basil as the main course.

Recommended drinks

Rosé wine
Muscat

Menu suggestions

1. For the summer, plan a menu with a harmony of flavors: salade niçoise as an appetizer and, for the main course, roast chicken with lemon and basil, accompanied by green beans Provence style.

2. This dessert could conclude a sophisticated menu comprising mullet "en papillote" as an appetizer and broiled lamb's kidneys with small stuffed vegetables for the main course.

Melon with seasonal fruits

An easy dish

Serves 4
Preparation: 15 minutes
Cooking: none

Ingredients

1 peach

2 apricots

9 oz (250 g) grapes

9 oz (250 g) redcurrants

9 oz (250 g) strawberries

1 large melon

1 lemon

 Superfine sugar

1. Sort, wipe, and remove the stalks from the fruit; cut the peach and apricots into quarters and seed the grapes. Reserve a few of the best redcurrants for the garnish. Set aside in a cool place.

2. Open the melon up to one-third of its length and cut the top out zigzag fashion, into "wolf's teeth." Hollow out the melon and cut its pulp either into small balls or small cubes. Arrange with the other fruits in the melon skin.

3. Add a few drops of lemon juice, garnish with the reserved redcurrant bunches, and keep in a cool place—but not too cold—until you serve the dish. Serve the superfine sugar separately, which can be added according to taste.

To present a melon decoratively, either in the form of a zigzag or a serrated shape, is quite straightforward. You just need a little precision. Take a sharp knife and mark out a line in the form of a zigzag on the skin approximately up to two-thirds of its length, where the melon is still quite bulbous. Then cut through the skin, following this line: make sure you push the blade well into the core of the fruit. The top will come off easily. Then all you need to do is scoop out the pulp and discard the fibers and seeds.Whether you use a cantaloupe or other type of muskmelon, select a very ripe fruit that yields near the stalk when lightly pressed with the finger. If you are entertaining a large number of people, use a watermelon instead.

Sweet and sour venison noisettes

A regional dish

Serves 4
Preparation: 15 minutes
Marinating: 48 hours
Cooking: 5–7 minutes

Ingredients

1 bottle red wine

1 bouquet garni
(parsley, thyme, celeriac)

9 oz (250 g) fat trimmings

Oil

12 noisettes of venison

Butter

5 juniper berries

1 clove

3 garlic cloves

1 bunch Muscat grapes

1 scant cup (20 cl) fond de veau

1 scant cup (20 cl) port wine

1 tsp coarse-ground pepper

Salt and pepper

1. Bring half the bottle of red wine to the boil with the bouquet garni and allow to cool. Add the trimmings and steep them for 48 hours in the refrigerator prior to using. Add oil and pepper to the noisettes of venison and leave to marinate in the refrigerator for 24 hours.

2. Brown the marinated trimmings in butter. Bring the filtered marinade to the boil, skim, and pour over the trimmings. Add the crushed juniper berries, clove, and garlic. Simmer for a few moments and then add the crushed Muscat grapes and fond de veau. Add a little salt and cook gently until the sauce has reduced by half.

3. Cook the port wine until you obtain a syrupy liquid; add the rest of the red wine and thicken again. Pass the marinade through a small, conical strainer and pour over the reduced port wine. Add the coarse-ground pepper, and mix in a large dab of butter for a smooth sauce.

4. Fry the noisettes for a few minutes on each side. Serve with the sauce and a small blini pancake.

As an extra side dish, serve fresh pasta, or a wild mushroom fricassee. Another delicious idea is to make "spätzle," which are small balls of pasta poached in boiling water: mix together 4$\frac{1}{3}$ cups (500 g) flour, 4 eggs, 2 tbsp heavy cream and 1 tsp table salt; add pepper and nutmeg. Scoop the dough with a small spoon and immerse the balls thus formed in a large saucepan of boiling water. Poach, drain, and drizzle a little melted butter over the pasta before serving.

Recommended drinks

Chambertin
Volnay
Pommard

Menu suggestions

1. This sophisticated dish can be served at a fall dinner, with foie gras pâté as an appetizer and blueberry vacherin for dessert.

2. These noisettes of venison can also form part of a simpler meal, preceded by smoked salmon as an appetizer and followed by green apple sorbet for dessert.

Christmas bread with dried fruit

A foreign dish

Serves 4
Preparation: 15 minutes
Cooking: 1 hour 15 minutes

Ingredients

3 eggs
$^1/_2$ cup (125 g) superfine sugar
Salt
$3^1/_2$ oz (100 g) butter
1 1/3 cups (150 g) flour
1 tsp ground cinnamon
1 tbsp (15 g) baking powder
2 oz (60 g) ground almonds

$4^1/_2$ oz (125 g) ground hazelnuts
$4^1/_2$ oz (125 g) currants
$4^1/_2$ oz (125 g) golden raisins
$4^1/_2$ oz (125 g) dried apple slices
$4^1/_2$ oz (125 g) crystallized orange peel

1. Put the egg yolks, superfine sugar, and a pinch of salt into a bowl. Work the mixture vigorously until it becomes frothy and whitish. Then add $2^3/_4$ oz (75 g) butter, first softened with a fork, the flour, cinnamon, and baking powder.

2. Continue working the mixture while adding the almonds, hazelnuts, currants, and golden raisins, and the finely chopped apple and orange peel. Reserve a few currants and golden raisins to garnish the top of the bread.

3. Line a rectangular loaf pan with buttered wax paper. Fill the pan to just three-quarters of its capacity as the bread rises during cooking. Heat the oven to 345 °F (175 °C). Pour the mixture into the pan. Cook for 1 hour 15 minutes. Wait until the bread has completely cooled before turning it out of the pan.

This pastry, which is German in origin, belongs to a very rich variety of breads filled with dried fruits and nuts. In particular, apples, walnuts, and almonds are considered symbolic Christmas fare: according to tradition, the apple represents the tree of knowledge, whereas walnuts and almonds, with their very hard shells, represent the mysteries and trials of life. According to taste and availability, however, you can use dried figs or dried apricots instead of the dried apple slices.

Recommended drinks

Mulled wine
Cinnamon tea
Hot punch

Menu suggestions

1. This Christmas bread served with a scoop of cinnamon ice cream is a traditional Christmas and New Year dessert; start with vol-au-vents, and serve roast beef with boletus mushrooms for the main course.

2. This dried fruit bread can be served with jelly and candies at a children's party. Fruit juice would be a suitable beverage.

Grape and sesame pudding

A foreign dish

Serves 4
Preparation: 15 minutes
Resting: 1 hour

Ingredients

1 glass flour

7 glasses fresh grape juice

1 large handful sesame seeds

Ground cinnamon

1. Sieve the flour as you pour it into a bowl. Add 2 glasses of cold grape juice and mix, stirring to break down the lumps. Meanwhile, pour the rest of the grape juice into a saucepan and bring slowly to the boil. Gradually add the flour while stirring continuously over low heat. Let it gradually thicken while continuing to stir, until the mixture easily covers the back of the spoon.

2. Check the cooking progress by removing a small quantity with a spoon and dropping it onto a cold plate: it should immediately form a flexible ball. Take the saucepan off the heat and pour the mixture into a large, flameproof dish.

3. Mix the sesame seeds with the ground cinnamon on a plate. Spread immediately over the surface of the grape pudding, with the sesame seeds lightly embedded. Allow it to cool down completely. To serve, cut the pudding into small squares.

This Greek pudding is called "moustalevria" ("grape wine pudding") and is easy to make: you just need to pass sufficient grapes through a juicer to obtain the required amount of juice. It is not unlike a French specialty from Burgundy called "le raisiné" ("grape jelly,") which is made by slowly cooking pressed grapes: a concentrated must is obtained to which peeled, seeded or pitted, and thinly sliced fruits are added.

Recommended drinks

Samos
Muscat de Frontignan
Rasteau

Menu suggestions

1. This Mediterranean delicacy would be a welcome dessert after a main course of broiled fish with vegetable salad. Accompany it with small, crispy, almond cookies.

2. You can also include it in a typically Greek menu: after the "meze," (small appetizers served with drinks) serve moussaka with lamb kebabs for the main course.

643

Cold coconut soup

An exotic dish

Serves 4
Preparation: 10 minutes
Cooking: 30 minutes
Standing: 1–2 hours

Ingredients

2 cloves garlic

2 medium-sized onions

$1^3/_4$ oz (50 g) butter

$10^1/_2$ oz (300 g) floury potatoes

3 cups (75 cl) chicken bouillon

1 pot crème fraîche

1 bunch chives

Salt and pepper

2 coconuts

1 mango

2 kiwis

1. Peel and finely chop the garlic and onions. Melt the butter in a thick-bottomed saucepan and cook the chopped garlic and onions gently until transparent. Do not allow them to brown.

2. Peel and roughly chop the potatoes. Pour the chicken bouillon over the chopped garlic and onions; add the chopped potatoes. Simmer gently until the potatoes are easily crushed (approximately 20 minutes). Pass the soup through a blender with the crème fraîche and add the chopped chives. Add salt and pepper and stand in a cool place.

3. Cut the coconuts in two. Serve the soup in the coconut halves, after scraping off the flesh to add to the soup, according to taste. Garnish with small pieces of fresh mango and kiwi fruit, and top with the rest of the chives.

When coconuts become available in Western markets, they are ripe: the skin is brown, the flesh is dense, and the liquid inside is milky. To select a coconut, shake it: if it is too old, you will not hear the sound of any liquid inside. To open a coconut easily, start by making three small holes at the top using a gimlet. Let the liquid run out of the holes. Keep the milk so that you can enjoy it when it is very fresh (but filter it first). Put the coconut on a dishtowel and then hit it with a hammer, at a point around one-third up its length. A light cracking sound will reveal the natural fault in the coconut. Continue hitting it until the coconut easily splits in two.

Recommended drinks

Coconut milk
Light beer
Rosé de Provence

Menu suggestions

1. This is an original soup that can introduce an exotic menu: serve fish fillets marinated in lemon juice with a green papaya salad for the main course and mango sorbet for dessert.

2. It can also be included in a traditional menu: serve veal escalope with eggplant gratin for the main course and an orange salad for dessert.

Chicken with pineapple and peanuts

An exotic dish

Serves 4
Preparation: 20 minutes
Cooking: 20 minutes

Ingredients

4 chicken fillets
Oil
1 onion
2 cloves garlic
4 or 5 tomatoes
1 small pineapple
1 tbsp curry paste

1 lb 2 oz (500 g) peanuts
Salt

1. Cut the chicken fillets into cubes. Heat 2 tbsp oil in a skillet. Sauté the thinly sliced onion and chopped garlic and then add a peeled tomato cut into very small pieces. Simmer for a few minutes.

2. Meanwhile, peel the pineapple. Cut it into slices and then cubes, making sure you keep the juice. Chop all the pineapple scraps and fry them with the tomato. When the mixture has almost reduced to a purée, crush it completely with a fork.

3. Add the chicken and pineapple cubes, and simmer until the chicken is tender. Add the curry paste and 1 large handful of shelled peanuts.

4. Keep the chicken pieces and pineapple warm; pour the pineapple juice into the skillet and cook for a few moments. Serve the chicken and pineapple (possibly reheated) with the fresh tomato cubes and sauce, after adding the remaining, roughly chopped peanuts.

Above all, make sure you select natural peanuts rather than smoked or salted ones. As a side dish, serve a spicy sweet potato gratin. To serve 4, steam 1³/₄ lb (800 g) washed and scrubbed sweet potatoes for 20 minutes; drain, peel, and crush them with a fork; then combine this purée with 4 eggs beaten to the consistency of an omelet, 2 pinches Cayenne pepper, a dash of chili powder, and 1 tsp ground cumin. Butter a gratin dish, pour in the purée, dab with butter, and cook in the oven at 350 °F (180 °C) for 20 minutes.

Recommended drinks

Light beer
Tea
Côtes-du-Rhône

Menu suggestions

1. This chicken and pineapple dish is inspired by African cuisine, which is often spicy; you could serve Parma ham with melon as an appetizer and apricot tart for dessert.

2. If you wish to continue the exotic theme, serve curried zucchini fritters as an appetizer and banana flambé for dessert.

Sicilian sardines

A foreign dish

Serves 4
Preparation: 15 minutes
Cooking: 15 minutes

Ingredients

5½ oz (150 g) golden raisins

2¼ lb (1 kg) very fresh, small sardines

Olive oil or butter

3 oranges

Fresh breadcrumbs

5½ oz (150 g) pine nuts

Salt and pepper

1. While the golden raisins are expanding in a little warm water, open up the sardines into two halves; remove the heads and bones and separate them into two fillets. Arrange them in an oiled or buttered gratin dish as you go along.

2. Grate the peel of one orange. Fry 3 handfuls of freshly prepared breadcrumbs in a generous quantity of olive oil. Drain on paper towels before mixing them with the grated peel and golden raisins, which will have thoroughly swelled. Add the pine nuts.

3. Add salt and pepper to the sardines then squeeze the juice of 1 orange and pour it over them. Drizzle a fair amount of olive oil over them and set thin slices of orange halves along the edges of the dish. Sprinkle over the breadcrumb mixture.

4. Heat the oven to 350–400 °F (180–200 °C) and cook for about 15 minutes, making sure it browns only lightly. Garnish with fresh orange slices.

Lemon and fish is a traditional combination, whereas orange is more unusual in this context. Nevertheless, in many Mediterranean cuisines, orange also serves as a slightly acid, yet fruity condiment. In Sicilian cuisine, the presence of golden raisins, pine nuts, and oranges is a reminder of the Arab influence in this part of the Mediterranean. You can use almonds instead of pine nuts. As a side dish, serve spaghetti with a simple seasoning of olive oil, garlic, and a dash of chili powder, or semolina supplemented with diced tomato.

Recommended drinks

White wine and blackcurrant liqueur
Vin de Corse blanc
Costières du Gard

Menu suggestions

1. As an appetizer, serve a zucchini salad with small artichokes marinated in oil; for dessert, Sicilian cassata.

2. Serve these sardines as an appetizer; for the main course, roast pork with bay leaves and sage, accompanied by fresh fava beans; and strawberries spiced with balsamic vinegar for dessert.

Soles in escabèche

A foreign dish

Serves 4
Preparation: 25 minutes
Marinating: 8 hours
Cooking: 25 minutes

Ingredients

2 soles x 10$^1/_2$ oz (300 g)

Peanut oil

4 tsp pine nuts

4 tsp golden raisins

A few currants

4 sweet red onions

2 bay leaves

Ground cinnamon

1 glass dry white wine

4 tsp white wine vinegar

Salt and pepper

1. Ask your fish seller to gut, clean, and skin the fillets of sole. Lightly seal them in a very small amount of oil in a non-stick skillet for 2 minutes on each side before marinating. Do not allow them to brown.

2. Drain on paper towels. Add salt and pepper, but not an excessive amount, and transfer the fish to a dish. Sprinkle over the pine nuts, golden raisins, and currants.

3. Peel the onions, slice them into 3/16 in (5 mm) strips, and put them in a skillet with 2 tbsp oil and the bay leaves. Fry them gently without browning for a maximum of 15 minutes, turning frequently; the onion should be almost transparent. Sprinkle with salt, pepper, and cinnamon, and drizzle over the wine and vinegar. Boil for 10 seconds and pour the mixture over the fish.

4. Marinate for at least 8 hours before serving chilled.

This marinade is a cooking method that originated in Spain: it is very spicy and, as it is poured over food when still boiling, it acts as a preservative for a while. This dish has become popular throughout the whole of the Mediterranean basin and varies from country to country: in North Africa, for example, dried fruits and hot spices are added. In the main, small fish such as sardines, mackerel, whiting, and mullet are used, but it is also used for cooking diced chicken, and even partridge.

Recommended drinks

Chablis
Sancerre
Jurançon sec

Menu suggestions

1. When served as a cold appetizer, this dish can be followed by a main course of roast chicken with lemon and a green salad, and almond tarts for dessert.

2. For a quick lunch, serve tabouleh, eggplant dip, and Lebanese-style flat bread with this marinated sole, and a lemon tart for dessert.

Apples "à la mascotte"

Avocadoes with shrimp

Herring fillet salad

Delicious ideas

Small quantities of European or exotic fruits can be used to garnish meat, game, chicken, or fish in original recipes. It is the ideal solution if you do not have quite enough fruit to make a dessert or pastry. As a complementary side dish, you can always serve rice or semolina with diced bell peppers or tomatoes.

Avocadoes with shrimp

Ingredients for 6
3 avocadoes
1 lemon
7 oz (200 g) canned shrimp tails
Olive oil
Mustard
Salt and pepper
Chervil

1. Cut the avocadoes in two and pit. Add a generous amount of lemon juice.

2. Drain the shrimp tails. Cut the lemon into quarters and finely dice the pulp.

3. Prepare a vinaigrette by mixing 5 tbsp lemon juice, 10 tbsp olive oil, 1 tsp mustard, salt, and pepper.

4. Arrange the shrimp tails, lemon, and vinaigrette in a salad bowl. Add salt and pepper. Fill the avocado halves with this mixture. Garnish with a few sprigs of chervil.

Apple and herring salad

Ingredients for 6
2 Granny Smith apples
1 lemon
2 beets
6 mild herring fillets
5 tbsp sherry vinegar
10 tbsp olive oil
Mustard
Salt and pepper

1. Peel the apples, core them, and slice very thinly. Then cut the slices into short, thin strips. Add lemon juice to prevent them from turning brown.

2. Cut up the beets in the same way. Finely dice the herrings. Prepare a vinaigrette by combining the sherry vinegar, olive oil, mustard, salt, and pepper.

3. Arrange the herrings, apples, beets, and vinaigrette in a salad bowl. Add salt and pepper, and serve. You could arrange a few thin slices of sweet orange and a handful of black olives on the plate as an additional garnish.

Citrus fruit sole

Orange salad

Roast beef with mango

Citrus fruit sole

Ingredients for 4
2 tomatoes
2 peeled garlic cloves
8 tbsp olive oil
3 oranges
1 grapefruit
Flour
4 sole fillets
2³/₄ oz (80 g) parsley butter
Salt and pepper

1. Blanch, peel, and seed the tomatoes. Dice then mix them with the sliced garlic cloves. Cook with 1 tbsp olive oil in a saucepan.

2. Peel the citrus fruits. Cut them into quarters and collect the juice expressed. Sprinkle salt and pepper over a little flour sifted onto a plate. Cover both sides of the trimmed, gutted, and cleaned fillets with the flour.

3. Heat the olive oil in a skillet and brown the fillets. Serve them on a bed of chopped tomatoes, surrounded by citrus fruit quarters. Add the juice to the skillet to make a sauce. Drizzle the sauce over the fillets and garnish with parsley butter.

Mixed fruit compote

Ingredients for 6
2 apples
4 pears
6 apricots
5¹/₂ oz (150 g) raisins
¹/₃ cup + 1¹/₂ tbsp (10 cl) rum
1 scant cup (200 g) superfine sugar
A few strawberries
1 vanilla bean

1. Peel the apples and pears; core them, and cut into quarters. Pit the apricots. Put the raisins into a salad bowl with the rum, and leave them to swell for 1 hour.

2. Combine all the fruits in the salad bowl then add the superfine sugar and the vanilla bean, split lengthwise. Steep for 4 hours, and then pour the fruits and the syrup into a saucepan. Bring to the boil, cover, and cook slowly for approximately 1 hour, stirring occasionally. Remove the vanilla bean.

3. Put the cooked fruits into a blender and reduce them to a fine purée. Allow to cool before serving.

Roast beef with mango

Ingredients for 6
2 lb 14 oz (1.3 kg) fillet steak
Peanut oil
2 mangoes
Salt and pepper
Avocadoes
Bananas
Lemons

1. Sprinkle pepper over the steak and coat it with oil. Roast in a very hot oven for 15 minutes so that the juices run. Take it out of the oven and let it stand for 10 minutes, then slice it.

2. While the fillet is roasting, cut the mangoes into halves. Serve the roast beef with the mango halves seasoned with pepper. Complete the dish with cubed avocado and banana halves with a dash of lemon juice.

Mixed fruit compote

Pastries

Sugar crust pastry, piecrust pastry, and puff pastry are ideal bases for a wide variety of tarts and pies. The fruit juices, which percolate through the tart during cooking, mix with the sugar content of the pastry and often form a caramel, thus causing it to stick to the mold. That is why the plate or mold must be prepared before lining it with pastry. Aluminum tart pans are cheap, but easily lose their shape, whereas earthenware or Pyrex plates and molds are flameproof, tough, yet attractive enough to be used as oven-to-table ware.

Preparation of a tart mold

1 Put the tart mold into the freezer for a good hour. Heat some butter gently in a pan. Take the mold out of the freezer and brush it with the melted butter. The butter will congeal instantly on the ice-cold mold and stick perfectly to the inside surfaces, including the fluted edge. Allow the mold to warm up again for a few minutes and then pour 1 tbsp flour into it.

2 Turn the mold over and tilt it in different directions until the flour conceals and covers the entire buttered surface. Brush off the excess flour and tap the mold to remove any lumps. If a mold is prepared like this, the food will never stick. This technique works not only for tarts and pies, but also for sponge cakes, cookies, pound cakes, and batters.

3 You can also line the mold with wax paper. Cut out a circle of wax paper with a slightly larger diameter than that of the mold, using a sharp knife. Press this sheet down so that it is firmly wedged at the bottom of the mold, with particular emphasis on the vertical inside surfaces and fluted edges. You do not need to butter the wax paper.

"White" cooking

"White" cooking of a pastry shell is necessary when you want it to be impermeable to liquid. In fact, when pastry is cooked with very juicy fruits (apricots, strawberries, raspberries) or when served with Chantilly or pastry cream, there is a risk of it becoming saturated and soft. That is why it is helpful to pre-cook it "white", which means cooking it slowly and without browning it. Put the tart mold into the freezer for 1 hour. Melt some butter. Take the mold out of the freezer and butter it with a brush and then pour 1 tbsp flour into the mold. Turn it

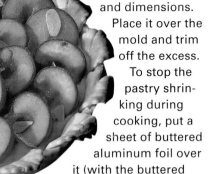

over and tilt the mold in different directions until the flour conceals and covers the entire buttered surface. Brush off the excess flour and tap the mold to remove any lumps.

Roll out the pastry to the required thickness and dimensions. Place it over the mold and trim off the excess. To stop the pastry shrinking during cooking, put a sheet of buttered aluminum foil over it (with the buttered side covering the pastry), including the base and edges of the mold. Cover this sheet with uncooked rice or dried navy beans. Heat the oven to 350 °F (180 °C) and bake the pastry shell for 15 minutes. Take it out of the oven, remove the beans (keep them for another time), and carefully lift off the sheet of foil. Allow the pastry to cool and then fill with your favorite fruits before putting it back in the oven. Using this method, you can make smooth, sweet fruit tarts with a crispy pastry. This creates a delicious contrast and is the sign of a very successful tart.

Tip

Pastry shells can be prepared in advance. Prepare your molds with wax paper or butter. Line them with pastry and wrap them in aluminum foil. When frozen, they will keep for 3 months. Defrost them for a few minutes and then use them as freshly prepared pastry shells.

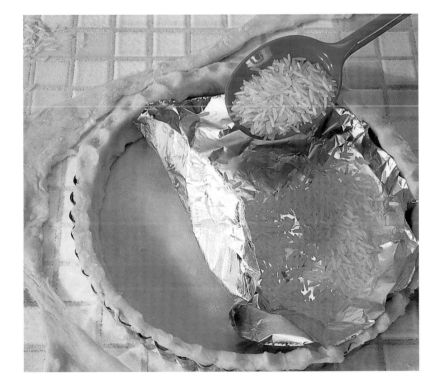

Confectioner's custard

1 Boil 2 cups (50 cl) milk with ¹/₂ vanilla bean split lengthwise in a saucepan. Take the saucepan off the heat and let the vanilla infuse for a few minutes. Put 4 egg yolks and ¹/₂ cup (110 g) superfine sugar into a mixing bowl.

2 Beat the mixture for 2 minutes so that it turns white. Stir in 3 tbsp (45 g) cornstarch. Remove the vanilla bean and pour the boiling milk over the eggs, cornstarch, and superfine sugar mixture. Stir well, then pour the mixture into the saucepan.

3 Bring the confectioner's custard gently to the boil. Boil for 10 seconds while stirring continuously, paying particular attention to the base of the pan to prevent sticking. Pour the custard into a dish and dab lightly with butter so that a skin does not form on the surface. Leave to cool completely.

Confectioner's custard

Confectioner's custard is frequently used in pastry making; it can be plain, or flavored with vanilla, coffee, chocolate, or praline. When finished with egg whites, it is called Chiboust cream. Due to its thick, smooth consistency, confectioner's custard is used to fill éclairs, pastry shells, chou pastry balls, "puits d'amour" (heart-shaped pastries), polkas, and round eclairs. It is made with egg yolks, superfine sugar, cornstarch, and milk. You can use flour instead of cornstarch, but the cream may be too liquid and difficult to use. Confectioner's custard is a delicate product and will keep for a limited period: consume it within 48 hours of making it.

Lemon curd

Lemon curd is a typically British specialty used to fill tarts; it can also be served like jelly and spread on bread, buns, or muffins at breakfast. It can also be used to fill cookies and sponge cakes, and makes an original jelly roll. It is very easy to make and only takes a few minutes. Lemon curd contains egg yolk and must therefore be kept in the refrigerator. Select juicy lemons with a very delicate skin: they should be heavy for their size.

Lemon curd for 6

1 Put 7 oz (200 g) chilled butter in a saucepan and cook very gently while mixing with a wooden spoon until you obtain a creamy consistency. Gradually add 1 cup (220 g) superfine sugar while mixing continuously (but without allowing the butter to melt completely).

2 Meanwhile, wash and dry 2 lemons and grate the peel finely. Squeeze and filter the lemon juice while removing all the pips. Add this juice slowly to the mixture of egg yolks and superfine sugar while stirring continuously and cook over low heat for a further 3–4 minutes.

3 Add 4 egg yolks one by one and cook them for approximately 5 minutes until the cream easily covers the top of the spoon (like custard). Take the lemon curd off the heat and add the lemon peel. Stir well then pour the mixture into a bowl. Leave to cool and then put it in the refrigerator.

Sponge cake for 8

1 Put a large piece of wax paper over a jelly-roll pan or baking sheet. Melt 1 oz (30 g) butter in a saucepan and brush the wax paper with it. Combine 3 egg yolks and 1/3 cup (75 g) superfine sugar in a bowl. Beat for 3 minutes so that the mixture turns white.

2 Add 2/3 cup (75 g) flour and mix for another minute. Put 4 egg whites and 1 pinch of salt into a mixing bowl. Beat the egg whites very stiffly. Slowly fold the egg whites into the first mixture. Make sure that the bowl in which you beat the egg whites is scrupulously clean.

3 Spread the mixture over the buttered wax paper using a fairly long spatula. Work quickly without pressing down too hard. Spread it over the entire surface evenly to a depth of approximately 9/16 in (1.5 cm). Make sure you do not leave any holes or areas with too thin a layer of the mixture. Carefully continue right up to the edges.

Jelly roll

To serve 8, combine 9 oz (250 g) raspberry jelly and 4 tbsp rum in a saucepan. Cook them slowly while mixing to obtain a consistent texture. Leave to cool for 20 minutes. Place the sponge cake, on the dishtowel and with the wax paper removed, in front of you. Spread the jelly evenly over the sponge cake with a spatula. Start rolling up the sponge cake inside the dishtowel; try to hold it firmly when you first roll it, so that it maintains a regular shape. Continue rolling with both your hands. When it is completely rolled up, top it with jelly and garnish with 4 1/2 oz (120 g) roasted split almonds. Cut the two ends at a slight angle. Transfer the jelly roll onto a serving dish and serve cold.

4 Bake in the oven at 445 °F (230 °C) for 7–8 minutes. Take the pan out of the oven. Put a clean, moist dishtowel over the worktop. Slide the paper with the sponge cake onto the dishtowel and turn the paper over. Use a brush to moisten the entire surface of the wax paper with water. Leave it to stand for 5 minutes and then gradually remove the paper from the sponge cake, by taking hold of one of its corners. Allow the sponge cake to cool for 15 minutes.

**Chocolate
Yule log
for 8**

1 Make 14 oz (400 g) chocolate-flavored butter cream and 7 oz (200 g) sugar syrup flavored with 3 tbsp rum. To make the required quantity of cream, allow 8 egg yolks and 1 pinch of salt; 9 oz (250 g) cubed sugar and the same proportion of butter; and 2 tbsp unsweetened cocoa powder. It will keep for 2 days in the refrigerator.

2 Place the sponge cake in front of you, on a clean, damp dishtowel and with the wax paper removed. Moisten the entire surface of the sponge cake with the syrup, using a brush, and then spread the butter cream evenly over it with a spatula. Brush over the surface several times to obtain an even layer.

3 Start rolling up the sponge cake inside the dishtowel; hold it firmly when you first roll it, so that it maintains a regular shape. When the sponge cake is rolled up, cut off the ends at an angle. Stick these two ends to the cake with a little cream, to resemble the branches of a tree.

4 Put some butter cream into a glazing bag with a flat, grooved nozzle. Cover the sponge roll with the cream, imitating the irregularities of bark. Also cover the ends. Garnish the Yule log with meringue mushrooms, ivy leaves, and sugared almonds. Put the Yule log in the refrigerator and serve cold. Use a serrated knife to slice it.

Gingerbread

Gingerbread

Gingerbread is a cake with a very long history. It was first made when the only known sweetening agent was honey and is said to have been introduced to Europe by an Armenian bishop who took refuge in Pithiviers in the eleventh century. Its success was rapid and it became popular throughout Europe. "Gingerbread maker" guilds were formed and in 1596 the Rheims guild was even officially recognized by Henri IV of France. Then the tradition became established in Dijon, which is still the gingerbread capital today. Gingerbread is called "Pfefferkuchen" ("pepper cake") in Germany and "pain d'épice" ("spice bread") in France. There are many gingerbread recipes, but it is usually prepared with honey, flour, milk, and spices (aniseed, citrus fruit peel, cinnamon, clove, ginger). Gingerbread can be cooked

Gingerbread Avesnois style

in a rectangular loaf pan or in different shapes on a cookie sheet: balls, hearts, animals, people, etc.

Gingerbread for 6–8

1 Heat and then boil 14 oz (400 g) honey in a saucepan. Skim it with a small ladle to remove the impurities. Weigh out 4 $\frac{1}{3}$ cups (500 g) flour and blend with 1 sachet of baking powder; 1 tbsp (15 g) ground cinnamon; 2 pinches grated nutmeg; 4 pinches ground ginger; 2 pinches ground cloves; 4 tsp (20 g) aniseed; and the chopped peel of half a lemon.

2 Pour the hot honey over the flour with 1 tsp (5 cl) warm milk and 2 egg yolks. Mix well with your hands, with the help of a wooden spoon, or with an electric mixer for a good 5 minutes to obtain a consistent texture. Leave to stand in the mixing bowl at room temperature for 30 minutes. Meanwhile, butter and flour a loaf pan.

3 Pour the mixture into the buttered pan and smooth out the surface with your hands, so that it looks even. Glaze with a little honey, using a brush, and then bake in the oven at 350 °F (180 °C) for approximately 30–35 minutes. Remove the cooked gingerbread by turning the loaf pan upside down. Leave to cool for 2 hours and then wrap it in aluminum foil.

Lebkuchen (makes 30 pieces)

1 Lebkuchen are small fingers of spicy bread glazed with sugar or fondant, which are traditionally served in Alsace at Christmas. Mix and boil 3^1/$_2$ oz (100 g) honey and ^{1}/$_2$ cup (100 g) superfine sugar in a saucepan for 10 seconds. Skim the mixture while it is heating.

2 Pour the liquid into a bowl and add 2 cups (250 g) flour, 3^1/$_2$ oz (100 g) chopped almonds, 2 tsp (10 g) ground cinnamon, ^{1}/$_2$ sachet baking powder, 2 egg yolks, and 2^3/$_4$ oz (80 g) chopped, crystallized orange peel. Combine the different ingredients by kneading them for 4–5 minutes. Then leave the mixture to stand for 2 hours.

3 Spread the mixture into a fairly thin layer and cut into pieces the size of an eclair. Put the Lebkuchen on a floured cookie sheet and bake them in the oven at 350 °F (180 °C) for 30 minutes. Leave to cool. Warm 7 oz (200 g) confectioner's fondant and 4 tbsp kirsch in a bain-marie or double boiler. Mix well with a spoon.

4 Still using a spoon, glaze the cookie fingers with the fondant: their surface should be finely, but completely, covered, and white. Allow the Lebkuchen to dry for 1 hour and then store them in an airtight cookie tin. You can cook the mixture in one piece and cover it with fondant before cutting it into fingers. Lebkuchen are often dusted with confectioner's sugar too.

Fruit cake for 6

1 Cut up a sheet of wax paper and butter it. Line a loaf pan with the paper, so that it extends over the edges. Soften 4 oz (110 g) butter in a bowl using a wooden spoon. Add ¹/₂ cup (125 g) superfine sugar and beat the mixture with a whisk for 5 minutes.

2 Add 3 eggs, one after the other, while continuing to beat. Each egg must be thoroughly combined before breaking the next one into the mixture. If the mass should start to fragment, put it in a fairly hot bain-marie or double boiler and beat it to obtain a smooth consistency once more. Meanwhile, mix 1¹/₂ cups (170 g) flour, 1 sachet baking powder, and 9 oz (250 g) chopped crystallized fruits in a bowl.

3 Knead these ingredients gently with your fingers, so that all the pieces of crystallized fruits are thoroughly coated. Then fold this mixture into the mass of eggs, superfine sugar, and butter. Work the mixture together with a spatula for 1 minute. Do not overwork it.

4 Using a rubber spatula or wooden spoon, scrape the mixture into the lined pan. Bake in the oven at 445 °F (230 °C) for 8 minutes and at 345 °F (175 °C) for 35–40 minutes. To check whether the cake is cooked, run a metal skewer into the center. Leave it for approximately 10 seconds and then remove it: if it comes out clean and dry, the cake is done. Take the cake out of the oven and put it on the worktop.

5 Turn the cake out of the pan, carefully remove the wax paper, and leave to cool. Put the cake on a cutting board and cut into ¹/₂ in (1 cm) slices with a serrated knife. Do not press too hard, to avoid squashing it. If the cake is wrapped in a sheet of aluminium foil and stored in an airtight container, it will keep for over a week at room temperature. It also freezes very well.

1 Line a rectangular mold with buttered, wax paper. Soften 4 oz (110 g) butter in a bowl. Add ½ cup (125 g) superfine sugar and beat for 5 minutes. Add 3 eggs, one after the other, while continuing to beat. (Each egg must be thoroughly combined before breaking the next one into the mixture.)

2 Soak 12 figs and 1 handful of raisins for 1 hour in tea. Drain then mix with 1½ cups (170 g) flour and 1 sachet baking powder in a bowl. Knead gently using your fingers. Then fold this mixture into the mass of eggs, sugar, and butter.

3 Mix well and work the mixture with a spatula for 1 minute. Pour it into the lined mold. Bake in the oven at 445 °F (230 °C) for 8 minutes, then at 345 °F (175 °C) for 35–40 minutes. Garnish the top of this fig cake with walnut halves.

General points

The English term "cake" corresponds to "gâteau" in French, and English pastry making includes a wide variety of cakes. The one that is actually known as "cake" in France, however, is the fruit cake: very distinctive, filled with crystallized fruits and raisins, rectangular in shape, and with a fairly dense consistency. This is the most commonly used basic recipe, but you can also add a personal touch to it with the ingredients of your choice. You can flavor the fruit cake with ground almonds, aniseed, or citrus fruit peel. Fruit cake goes very well with a cup of tea

Tip

People passionate about fruit cake never eat it the day it is baked; on the contrary, they leave it 1 or 2 days, as then it is at its best.

Pound cake and gâteau manqué

Pound cake for 6

1 Butter a round or rectangular mold, or line it with buttered wax paper. Combine 3½ oz (100 g) slightly salted butter, 3½ oz (100 g) unsalted butter, and 1 scant cup (200 g) superfine sugar in a bowl. Beat the mixture, first with a wooden spoon and then with a hand or electric whisk, until the superfine sugar is completely absorbed; the mixture will then have a clear and creamy consistency.

2 Scrape the inside surface of the bowl clean to obtain a thoroughly consistent texture. Gradually add 7 oz (200 g) eggs (that is, approximately 4 eggs), making sure that you combine them thoroughly, beating all the while. Fold in 1¾ cups (200 g) flour and 1 sachet baking powder. Work the mixture for 2 minutes with a wooden spoon.

3 Using a spoon, fill the mold with the mixture. Bake in the oven at 350 °F (180 °C) for approximately 1 hour 15 minutes. Check whether the cake is cooked by running a metal skewer into the center. If it comes out clean and dry, the cake is done. Turn it out of the mold and, if you used wax paper, carefully remove it.

Gâteau manqué

The type of sponge cake known as gâteau manqué looks like Genoa cake, but is prepared in a different way. It is smooth and mellow and can be served plain as a dessert. Melt 4 oz (110 g) unsalted butter in a saucepan without browning it. Separate the whites and the yolks of 6 eggs. Combine the 6 yolks with 1 generous cup (250 g) superfine sugar. Beat these ingredients

for 5 minutes until the mixture turns white. Add 1⅔ cups (190 g) sieved flour and continue mixing for 30 seconds. Then pour the melted butter over the mixture and stir in 2½ tbsp (4 cl) rum. Put the egg whites in a bowl with 1 pinch salt. Beat them very stiffly with an electric whisk. Gently fold them into the mixture with a spatula. Butter and flour a cake pan. Pour the mixture into the pan and level it out with the back of a tablespoon. Bake in the oven at 375 °F (190 °C) for 40–45 minutes. Turn the cake out of the mold onto a gridiron, and leave to cool for 1 hour before serving with custard.

Pound cake

Pound cake derives its name from the proportions of its ingredients. This delicious cake, which is very easy to make, is ideal for breakfast and a great favorite of children. At one time, it was made purely with salted butter. It can be baked in a round or rectangular mold.

Tip

You can make this recipe with slightly salted butter. Similarly, you can cut out the baking powder, provided that you stiffly beat the egg whites and add them last. Pound cakes can be flavored with chopped lemon peel, vanilla, or even rum.

Marble cake

Marble cake

This recipe combines two batters before the marble cake is baked (one mixture is vanilla or plain, and the other is chocolate).They must be very lightly combined in order to retain the distinct color contrast.

Apple pound cake

1 The light batter
Melt 2 oz (60 g) butter without browning it. Separate the whites and yolks of 4 eggs. Combine the 4 yolks with 1/2 cup (120 g) superfine sugar. Beat together for 5 minutes so that the mixture turns white. Then add 3/4 cup (85 g) sieved flour. Continue mixing for 30 seconds.

3 The dark batter
Melt 2 oz (60 g) butter. Separate the whites and the yolks of 4 eggs. Combine the 4 yolks with 1/2 cup (120 g) superfine sugar. Beat together for 5 minutes. Then add 5/8 cup (70 g) sieved flour and 1 oz (25 g) cocoa powder. Continue to mix for 30 seconds. Pour the melted butter over the mixture and stir. Put the egg whites and 1 pinch salt into a large bowl. Beat them very stiffly.

2 Pour the melted butter over the mixture and combine thoroughly with a few drops of vanilla extract. Put the egg whites and 1 pinch salt into a large bowl. Beat them very stiffly with an electric whisk. Gently fold in the whites and work up the mass with a spatula.

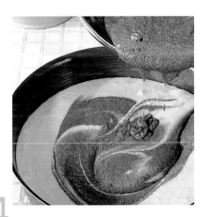

4 Gently fold in the egg whites and work up the mass with a spatula. Butter and flour a cake mold. Pour the dark batter into the light batter and stir gently with two turns of a wooden spoon. Pour the batter into the mold and level it out with a tablespoon. Bake in the oven at 375 °F (190 °C) for 40–45 minutes. Turn the marble cake out of the mold onto a gridiron and leave to cool for 1 hour before serving.

Rum baba for 10

1 Warm ⅓ cup + 1½ tbsp (10 cl) whole milk in a saucepan. Mix it with 1 tbsp (15 g) active dry yeast, 2 tsp (10 g) superfine sugar, and 1 tsp (5 g) table salt, by working it with your fingertips. Do not over-heat the milk. Sieve 2 ⅓ cups (270 g) flour into a mixing bowl. Make a well in the center. Break 3 eggs and beat them with a whisk for 10 seconds. Pour the eggs, milk, superfine sugar, salt, and yeast mixture into the well.

2 Using your hands, combine these ingredients to form a smooth dough. Knead and mold it into the shape of a ball. Continue like this for 5 minutes until you obtain a smooth, elastic texture. Sprinkle 2¾ oz (80 g) butter, cut into small pieces, over the surface of the dough wit-hout incorporating them. Cover the dough with a moist, clean dishtowel, and leave it to rise in a warm place for 35 minutes.

3 Meanwhile, soak 2 oz (60 g) raisins in ⅓ cup + 1½ tbsp (10 cl) rum. When the dough has expanded by one-third of its volume, drain and then add the soaked raisins.Knead the dough again for 3–4 minutes, until the butter and raisins have been completely assimilated. For preference, choose small currants or golden raisins, which are pale and smoother.

4 Lightly butter and flour a large baba mold. Put the mixture into the mold with the help of a rubber spatula (the dough should only fill two-thirds of the mold). Put the filled mold in a warm place and leave the dough to rise for 40 minutes. Bake the baba in the oven at 375 °F (190 °C) for 12–15 minutes.

5 Meanwhile, prepare the syrup by bringing 1½ cups (350 g) superfine sugar and 2 cups (50 cl) water to the boil for 20 seconds. When the mixture is cold, add 3 tbsp rum and mix it in. Take the baba out of the oven and turn it out of the mold while it is still warm; leave it on a gridiron to cool comple-tely. Next, pour some syrup over the baba, using a small ladle.

6 Put the baba onto a clean gridiron and heat 7 oz (200 g) apricot jelly with 1 tsp (5 cl) water to obtain a smooth paste. Brush a fine layer of this mixture over the surface of the baba. Garnish the baba with crystal-lized cherries and, using a glazing bag with a grooved nozzle, embel-lish the center of the cherries with stiffly whipped Chantilly cream.

Baba and savarin

Baba and savarin are prepared with leavened dough, supplemented with raisins. Their very simple consistency distinguishes them from other cakes. After cooking, they are soaked in a sugar syrup flavored with rum and then topped with Chantilly cream, confectioner's custard, or diced fruits in syrup.

1 Gently heat $1/3$ cup + $1^1/2$ tbsp (10 cl) whole milk in a saucepan. Mix with 1 tbsp (15 g) active dry yeast, 2 tsp (10 g) superfine sugar, and 1 tsp (5 g) table salt, by working it with your fingertips. Be careful not to overheat the milk, because a temperature in excess of 158 °F (70 °C) would destroy the yeast. Sieve 2 $1/3$ cups (270 g) flour onto the worktop. Make a well in the center. Meanwhile, break 3 eggs and beat them with a whisk for 10 seconds.

2 Pour the eggs, milk, superfine sugar, salt, and yeast mixture into the well. Using your hands, work all these ingredients together to obtain a smooth dough. Knead and mold it into the shape of a ball. Continue like this for 5 minutes until you obtain a smooth, elastic texture. Add 2¾ oz (80 g) butter, cut into small pieces. Cover the dough with a damp, clean, dishtowel and leave to rise in a warm place for 35 minutes.

3 When the dough has expanded by one-third of its volume, break it up and leave it to rise for a further 15 minutes. Lightly butter and then flour a savarin mold. Put the dough into the mold. Put the filled mold in a warm place and leave the dough to rise for 40 minutes. Bake the savarin in the oven at 375 °F (190 °C) for 12–15 minutes.

4 Meanwhile, prepare the syrup by bringing $1^1/2$ cups (350 g) superfine sugar and 2 cups (50 cl) water to the boil for 20 seconds. When the mixture is cold, add 3 tbsp kirsch and stir. Take the savarin out of the oven and turn it out of the mold while it is still warm. Put it on a gridiron to cool completely. Pour syrup over the savarin so it is completely soaked.

5 Place a dish under the savarin when soaking it, in order to conserve the drips of syrup. Transfer the savarin to a clean gridiron. Prepare 12½ oz (350 g fresh fruit salad with strawberries, raspberries, pears, and pineapples in syrup. Flavor with kirsch and arrange in the center of the savarin. Garnish with a few crystallized cherries and serve cold.

Tarte Tatin for 6

1 Roll out 9 oz (250 g) of your preferred dough mixture onto a floured worktop. Roll it out to $1/8$ in (3 mm) in thickness and around 10 in (26 cm) in diameter. Prick the dough with a fork so that it does not blister during cooking, and place in the refrigerator. Meanwhile, peel 2¼ lb (1 kg) slightly acidic apples. Core and halve them, checking that all the seeds have been removed.

2 Melt 5½ oz (150 g) butter in a 9-in (24-cm) diameter flameproof mold and add 1 generous cup (250 g) dark brown sugar. With the inside of the apples uppermost and without burning yourself, arrange the apples uniformly in concentric circles from the middle toward the edges. The apples should be quite tightly packed, keeping each other in place. The quantity of apples may exceed the dimensions of the mold, but they will shrink during cooking.

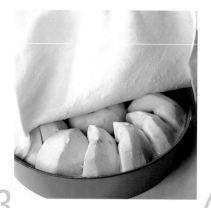

3 Set the mold over medium–high heat and caramelize the apples (without burning them) in the butter-sugar mixture. Cook for approximately 15 minutes and then bake in the oven at 430 °F (220 °C) for 20 minutes. Take the mold out of the oven and check progress: the apples should be nearly cooked—golden brown, but slightly firm. Take the dough out of the refrigerator and cover the apples with it.

4 Bake in the oven at 375 °F (190 °C) for approximately 35 minutes. Before you turn the tart over, allow it to cool for about 10 minutes. Then put a dish or a plate with a suitable diameter over the tart. With one hand, keep this lid firmly pressed against the pastry, and, with the other hand, turn the mold over. Serve the Tarte Tatin hot, either on its own or with crème fraîche.

tarte Tatin and upside-down tarts

General points

For a successful upside-down tart, first of all you need to pre-cook and caramelize fruit with firm flesh (apples, pears, pineapples, or peaches), cover them with rolled-out pastry, and then cook the dish, finally turning the piping-hot tart over onto the serving dish. Every type of pastry is suitable (puff pastry, piecrust pastry, or sugar crust pastry). The interesting feature of upside-down tarts is the contrast between the mellow cooked fruits and the thin pastry, which should always be crispy. Cooking times are divided as follows: two-thirds just to cook the fruits and the remaining third for the pastry. It is essential that the fruits

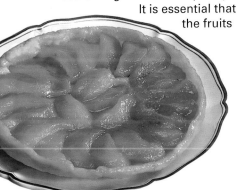

Plum tart

are cooked before they are covered with pastry, and their cooking time can vary according to type, level of ripeness, and juice content. You therefore need to appraise each type of fruit and adjust the cooking time by tasting them before covering them with pastry: they should look cooked, but remain slightly firm.

1 Roll out 9 oz (250 g) sugar crust pastry onto a floured worktop. Roll it out to 1/8 in (3 mm) in thickness and around 11 in (27 cm) in diameter. Prick the dough with a fork and put it in the refrigerator. Meanwhile, peel 1 very ripe pineapple. Cut it into four pieces lengthwise and remove the core. Check that there are no indigestible pieces of skin remaining. Cut the pineapple quarters into 3/8 in (1 cm) pieces.

2 Melt 5 1/2 oz (150 g) butter in an 11-in (24-cm) diameter flameproof mold and add 1 generous cup (250 g) dark brown sugar, 5 pinches ground cinnamon, and the pineapple. Place the mold on a baking sheet and sauté over moderately high heat to brown the pineapple pieces thoroughly. They should be caramelized (but not burned). Cook them for approximately 10 minutes and then bake in the oven at 430 °F (220 °C) for 20 minutes.

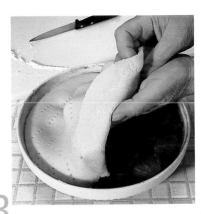

3 Remove the mold from the oven and check progress: the pineapple pieces should be nearly cooked with a good, golden-brown color, but still slightly firm. Take the dough out of the refrigerator, and, taking care not to burn yourself, cover the pineapple pieces with it. Bake in the oven at 375 °F (190 °C) for about 35 minutes.

4 To turn the tart over, first allow it to cool for about ten minutes. Then put a dish or a plate with a suitable diameter over the tart. With one hand, keep this "lid" firmly pressed against the tart, and turn the mold over with the other. Serve hot. If you wish, you can serve the tart with crème fraîche.

Chocolate slab cake for 6

1 Melt 1 tbsp butter and then butter and flour a cake pan, 1–1¹/₂ in (3–4 cm) deep and 10 in (25 cm) square. Cut 7 oz (200 g) dark chocolate into small pieces with a large knife. Put the chopped up chocolate into a bowl and stand the bowl in a skillet containing lukewarm or tepid water. (If the water is too hot, the chocolate may form a sticky mass). Stir the chocolate until it has completely melted.

2 It should be smooth, lump-free, and very glossy. Meanwhile, melt 5¹/₂ oz (150 g) butter over very low heat; do not let it boil or brown. Then put it in a warm place, so that it does not solidify. In another bowl, beat 4 whole eggs with a scant ²/₃ cup (150 g) superfine sugar for 2 minutes, and then add ⁷/₈ cup (100 g) flour and mix until you obtain a smooth, and lump-free mass.

3 Pre-heat the oven to 320 °F (160 °C). Pour the melted butter into the melted chocolate and mix rapidly; then pour the liquid over the eggs, flour, and sugar mixture. Work all these ingredients for 1 minute with a wooden spoon to combine thoroughly. The mixture should be a lovely dark brown color and perfectly smooth. Pour the mixture into the buttered, floured mold.

4 Tilt the filled mold gently from side to side, so that the mixture is evenly distributed. Bake in the oven at 320 °F (160 °C) for approximately 30 minutes. Then take the cake out of the oven. Allow to cool for 10 minutes and then turn it out of the mold onto a moist dishtowel. Allow to cool again for 1 hour and then cut it up into 2–2¹/₂ in (5–6 cm) squares with a knife.

General points

Melted chocolate gives cakes and pastries a unique, smooth texture as well as a delicate flavor, which is a favorite with adults and children alike. There are two main types of chocolate cake. The first contains stiffly beaten egg whites and baking powder. The soft crumb that forms during cooking is thus very light and airy, and the cake rounded and fluffy. This type of gateau is sometimes cut and filled with cream or chocolate-cream. The second type does not contain baking powder or beaten egg whites. A cake prepared in this way is flatter; its crumb is denser and sometimes resembles chocolate truffle. It melts in the mouth and has a very smooth consistency. This type of chocolate cake is often cut into squares and can be eaten plain. The quality of the chocolate is the determining factor. For the glazing, choose chocolate that contains at least 50 % cocoa.

Chocolate gâteau

Chocolate gâteau for 6

1 Melt 1 tbsp butter and then butter and flour a round cake pan, 1–1^1/$_2$ in (3–4 cm) deep and 8 in (20 cm) in diameter. Place 7 oz (200 g) dark chocolate on the worktop and cut it into very small pieces with a large knife. Put 4^1/$_2$ (120 g) chocolate pieces into a bowl. Boil a scant ^{3}/$_4$ cup (18 cl) crème fraîche then pour it over the chocolate.

2 Stir these ingredients together until you obtain a smooth, glossy mixture. Keep it in a warm place, while stirring it occasionally to prevent it from solidifying. Meanwhile, melt 6 oz/175 g butter. Combine 1 cup (220 g) soft brown sugar and 4 egg yolks in a bowl and beat with a whisk for 1 minute. Then add 2^1/$_2$ cups (280 g) flour, 1 sachet baking powder, and the melted butter.

3 Blend the mixture thoroughly with a wooden spoon until you obtain a uniform, lump-free mass. Put 4 egg whites and 1 pinch table salt in a mixing bowl and then beat it very stiffly. Pour the chocolate over the egg white mixture and stir until you obtain a smooth consistency. Add to the flour mixture and stir very gently.

4 Pour the cake mix into the mold. Spread very evenly using the back of a spoon. Bake in the oven at 365 °F (185 °C) for 30 minutes. Check whether the cake is cooked by running a metal skewer into the center: it should come out clean and dry.

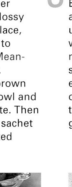

5

Tip

The flavor of almonds goes very well with chocolate. To give your cake an even more delicate flavor, add 1^3/$_4$ oz (50 g) ground almonds at the same time as the flour.

Take the cake out of the oven and leave it to cool for 10 minutes, and then gently turn it out of the mold onto a serving dish. Melt the remaining chocolate in a bain-marie or double boiler, and use it to glaze the cake. You can embellish it with crystallized fruits or marzipan.

Twelfth Night cake for 6

1 The day before, prepare a puff pastry base with butter and keep it in the refrigerator. Prepare 6³/₄ oz (190 g) confectioner's custard and allow it to cool. Combine the cold confectioner's custard, 2 eggs, 1 tbsp (15 g) corn-starch, 1 tbsp rum, 1 generous cup (120 g) confectioner's sugar, and 4¹/₂ oz (130 g) ground almonds in a bowl. Blend together with a wooden spoon, so that you obtain a fairly thick, smooth mixture.

2 Put half the very cold dough onto a floured worktop and roll it out lightly into a 10-in (25-cm) square and to a thickness of ¹/₈–³/₁₆ in (4–5 mm). Using a plate, cut a circle 9 in (23 cm) in diameter out of the rolled-out pastry. Put the circle of dough in the refrigerator. Then roll out the other half of the flaky pastry dough on the floured worktop.

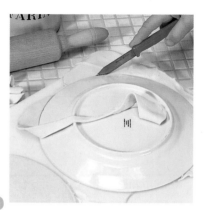

3 Cut out a larger circle, 10 in (25 cm) in diameter, as this will be placed over the filling. Put it in the refrigerator. Put the smaller circle of dough onto a buttered, floured baking sheet. Prick the entire surface of the dough with a fork. Put the almond paste into the center of the dough and spread it evenly with a small spatula, to a thickness of around ³/₈ in (1 cm).

4 Only the outer edge of the circle should be free of almond paste. Beat 1 egg and glaze this band of dough. Choose your bean or lucky charm and bury it in the almond paste. Take the other circle of dough (the larger one) out of the refrigerator. Prick it with a fork. Put this circle on top of the almond paste. Stick the two circles firmly together. Fold them over each other to form a continuous roll.

5 Gently press the join down with the point of a knife to ensure that the two circles hold together well. Make a grid pattern on the surface of the pastry using a small wire brush without pier-cing the dough; first draw ¹/₂-in (1-cm) parallel lines, and then squares with other perpendicular lines. Make sure you do not press too hard.

6 Brush the entire surface and join of the cake with beaten egg. Put 1 tbsp confectioner's sugar into a small, fine sieve and shake it over, covering the pastry evenly. Bake in the oven at 410 °F (210 °C) for approximately 35 minutes. If it browns too quickly, reduce the temperature and cover with aluminum foil.

Twelfth Night cake and jelly dartois

1 Roll out half the pastry dough on a floured worktop and shape it into the form of a rectangle, 12 in (30 cm) long and 4½ in (12 cm) wide, and ⅛–³⁄₁₆ in (4–5 mm) thick. Roll out and then cut up another rectangle, 8½ in (22 cm) long and 6 in (15 cm) wide. Put the smaller rectangle of flaky pastry dough on a buttered, floured baking sheet. Do not forget to prick the entire surface of the dough with a fork.

2 Put your favorite jelly (strawberry, apricot, blueberry) into the center of the dough and spread it evenly to a thickness of at least ⅜ in (1 cm) with a spatula. Leave ¾ in (2 cm) of the outer edge free of jam. Brush this bare band of dough with beaten egg. Glazing with egg yolk serves two purposes: it not only browns the pastry and makes it glisten, but it is also very useful when sticking two pieces of rolled-out dough together.

3 Take the other rectangle of dough (the larger one). Prick it with a fork and put it over the jelly. The first rectangle of dough should be completely invisible. Stick the two rectangles together by pressing down gently with your fingertips. Firmly seal the two layers of pastry. You can also garnish them with compote or confectioner's custard.

4 Cut ½-in (1-cm) wide strips from the remaining dough. Brush beaten egg over the entire surface and the join of the cake. Then use the strips of dough to make a grid pattern on the dartois. Trim off any excess dough. Lightly dust the cake with confectioner's sugar. Bake in the oven at 400 °F (200 °C) for approximately 35 minutes or until the top is golden brown.

tulipes and tuiles

Almond tuiles (makes about 25)

1 Prepare the recipe for tulipe pastry and leave it in the refrigerator for 24 hours. Butter a baking sheet and spread out small circles of pastry, 2–2³/₄ in (5–7 cm) in diameter, using a metal spatula. Sprinkle some flaked almonds generously over he pastry and then shake the baking sheet to remove the excess. Cook in the oven at 400 °F (200 °C) for approximately 10 minutes.

2 Lift the tuiles with a metal spatula and place them on rolling pins with the almonds uppermost. Leave to cool for 5 minutes. Serve them immediately or keep for 2–3 days in an airtight cookie tin. You can also leave them to cool lying flat on a clean worktop.

Tulipe pastry (makes about 15 pieces)

The day before, put 1¹/₂ oz (40 g) butter in a saucepan and melt it slowly, without allowing it to boil or brown. Remove from the heat and allow to cool. Carefully separate the whites and yolks of 4 eggs. Keep the yolks for another time and weigh out 4 oz (115 g) egg whites. Combine the egg whites and ³/₄ cup (185 g) superfine sugar in a bowl. Mix well and then add 1 oz (30 g) flour and the melted butter. Put the dough into a bowl, cover, and leave in the refrigerator for 24 hours.

Cooking tulipes

1 Put a baking sheet in a cool place and butter it lightly. Take 1 tbsp of the tulipe pastry and put it on the baking sheet. Knead and spread it out very thinly in the form of a circle, using a small spatula. It should be so thin that you can almost see the baking sheet through it. You can choose the diameter, but 4–4¹/₂ in (10–12 cm) is suitable.

2 Equip yourself with two or three small bowls or fluted molds to help you shape the pastry when it is cooked. Bake in the oven at 350 °F (180 °C) for 8 minutes. The disks should be very light golden, but never brown. Open the oven and lift off the first disk with a metal spatula. Take it out of the oven quickly. When it is hot, it is still soft. Push it down gently into a mold.

3 Hold it down for a few moments and leave to cool for 5 minutes. Repeat this procedure with the other disks. Then take them out of the molds: tulipes keep the shape they acquire while cooling. They are very delicate, so should be handled carefully. Tulipes do not keep for long, as they soften very quickly: use them as soon as possible.

Cigarettes (makes about 25 pieces)

Prepare the tulipe pastry dough and leave it in the refrigerator for 24 hours. Butter a baking sheet and spread out small circles of pastry, approximately 2³/₄ in (7 cm) in diameter, using a metal spatula. Bake in the oven at 400 °F (200 °C) for approximately 10 minutes, making sure that the disks do not over-brown, as it would then be difficult to roll. Lift off the disks of cooked pastry, one by one, using a metal spatula. Using your fingers, quickly roll them around the handle of a clean wooden spoon and allow them to cool like this. They will keep the cylindrical, "cigarette" shape they acquire while cooling.

Tuiles and disks

The pastry for tuiles and tulipes is very malleable when hot. You can mold it straight from the oven into various forms, including receptacles for ice cream or fruit salads. If you add flaked almonds, you can make slabs; if you add raisins, you can make disks from the same pastry.

Tip

Using this recipe and method, you can easily add a personal touch to your tuiles. Instead of sprinkling them with flaked almonds, try ground coconut, crushed hazelnuts, or even sesame seeds. You can also create an original assortment, and combine a variety of different tuiles.

1 Soften 9 oz (250 g) butter in a bowl. Add 3¹/₂ cups (400 g) confectioner's sugar. Beat this mixture thoroughly, and then add 9 egg whites, one after the other.

2 Finally, fold in 3¹/₂ cups (400 g) sieved flour and a few drops of vanilla extract. Butter a baking sheet. Spoon the mixture into glazing bag with a plain, round nozzle.

Langues-de-chat (makes about 50 pieces)

3 Make fingers of approximately 2³/₄ in (7 cm) in length. Bake in the oven at 400 °F (200 °C) for approximately 7 minutes. Lift the langues-de-chat off the baking sheet, leave to cool, and store them in an airtight cookie tin.

"Dry" macaroons (makes about 20 pieces)

1 Mix together 9 oz (250 g) ground almonds and 1 generous cup (250 g) superfine sugar in a bowl, using a wooden spoon. Gradually add 5 egg whites, one after the other. Work for 2–3 minutes to consolidate the mixture and thoroughly combine the different ingredients. Leave to cool for 1 hour.

2 Melt 1 tbsp butter in a saucepan. Brush a baking sheet with the melted butter then flour it. Spoon the almond paste into a glazing bag with a plain nozzle. Squeeze the mixture into small heaps, the size of a walnut, at least 3/4 in (2 cm) apart, and leave them to stand for 1 hour, so that their surface hardens slightly and is covered with a thin crust. Bake the macaroons in the oven at 265 °F (130 °C) for 1 hour.

3 Take them out of the oven, lift them off the baking sheet, and put them on a gridiron to cool. Dry macaroons can be kept for a few days in an airtight cookie tin. The macaroon mixture can be prepared in advance and kept for 1 week in an airtight container in the refrigerator. Take it out of the refrigerator 2 hours before cooking, so that it can soften and will be easier to squeeze from the glazing bag.

General points

These small, round pastries can be either smooth and mellow or dry and brittle. They are made from egg whites, almonds, and sugar, and can be flavored in different ways.

Smooth and mellow chocolate macaroons

Melt 5½ oz (150 g) dark chocolate in a bain-marie or double boiler over gentle heat until you obtain a smooth, glossy mixture. Stiffly beat 4 egg whites and then add 5½ oz (250 g) ground almonds, 2⅓ cups (250 g) confectioner's sugar, and then the melted chocolate. Blend for as short a time as possible to avoid the mass collapsing. Using a tablespoon, shape the mixture into balls, 2–2½ in (5–6 cm) in diameter, on a sheet of wax paper placed over a baking sheet. Bake in the oven at 265 °F (135 °C) for 1 hour. Allow the macaroons to cool, lift them off the baking sheet, and put them on a gridiron.

Tip

You can easily vary this recipe by using ground hazelnuts instead of almonds. The macaroons will have a slightly darker color, but they will taste delicious. You can also try a mixture of almonds and hazelnuts.

(the part that has been in contact with the baking sheet) and then stick another macaroon to it. Gently press them together to make sure they are completely joined. You can also make double macaroons with a chocolate cream filling, ice cream, or sorbet.

Preparation of cream macaroons

Soften 7 oz (200 g) butter cream using the flavor of your choice. Put a small quantity of cream on the flat part of the macaroon

N.B.

You can use 3 tbsp (45 g) cocoa powder instead of melted chocolate, which is sometimes difficult to blend; the result will be equally delicious. To make macaroons with coffee, cut out the chocolate and add about 15 drops of coffee extract.

Plain and "mellow" macaroons (makes about 20)

1 Combine 10¹/₂ oz (300 g) ground almonds and 2¹/₂ cups (300 g) confectioner's sugar in a mixing bowl, using a wooden spoon. Add 6 egg whites, one after the other, and continue to mix. Then add 4¹/₂ oz (120 g) thick crème fraîche. You should obtain a smooth, light mixture.

2 Separate 4 egg whites into another bowl; add 1 pinch salt and beat them very stiffly. When the egg whites have risen sufficiently, add ¹/₃ cup (40 g) confectioner's sugar. Add the egg whites to the first mixture, while working the mass up thoroughly.

3 Cover a baking sheet with wax paper. Make the macaroons using a glazing bag fitted with a nozzle ³/₈ in (1 cm) in diameter. Shape into small balls, the size of a walnut. Bake in the oven at 275 °F (135 °C) for 50 minutes. Leave to cool and then remove the macaroons very gently from the baking sheet.

675

Madeleines (makes about 30)

1 Finely grate the peel of ¹/₂ unwaxed lemon. Place the madeleine molds in the refrigerator for 1 hour, and then butter and flour them. Madeleine batter sticks significantly, so take great care over the preparation of the molds. Sieve and combine 3¹/₂ cups (400 g) flour and 1 sachet baking powder. Break 6 whole eggs into a mixing bowl and add 1¹/₃ cups (300 g) superfine sugar.

2 Beat the mixture with a whisk for 1 minute and then fold in the flour and baking powder, using a wooden spoon. Thoroughly blend these ingredients and finally add 7 oz (200 g) melted butter and the grated lemon peel. Work the mixture thoroughly, so that you obtain an entirely consistent texture. Put it into a glazing bag and fill the madeleine mold segments to three-quarters of their capacity.

3 Be careful when you are doing this, as this batter is very fluid and can easily seep out. You could also use a tablespoon to transfer it to the molds. Pre-heat the oven to 400 °F (200 °C) and bake the madeleines for approximately 5 minutes. Take the molds out of the oven. Loosen the madeleines gently with the point of a knife and turn them out.

General points

Madeleines are small pastries that take on the shape of the special mold they are cooked in. You can find these madeleine molds in most specialist stores. If you buy non-stick molds, it wil be a great deal easier to turn the pastries out.

N.B.

Madeleines will be tastier and smoother if they are very slightly "undercooked:" bake them rapidly at a fairly high temperature and on no account let them brown for too long in the oven.

Variants

If you would like to try different flavors, below are three lists of ingredients, allowing for 30 madeleines, and using the same method as the previous one.

Coconut madeleines
3 eggs; 1 scant cup (200 g) superfine sugar; 2 cups (250 g) flour; 1 sachet baking powder; 5¹/2 oz (150 g) butter; ¹/₃ cup + 1¹/₂ tbsp (10 cl) milk.
Almond madeleines
3 eggs; 1 scant cup (200 g) superfine sugar; 1 ¹/₃ cups (150 g) flour; 5¹/₂ oz (150 g) ground almonds; 1 sachet baking powder; 5¹/₂ oz (150 g) butter; ¹/₃ cup + 1¹/₂ tbsp (10 cl) milk.
Orange madeleines
3 eggs; ³/₄ cup (160 g) superfine sugar; 1³/₄ oz (50 g) honey; 2 cups (250 g) flour; 1 sachet baking powder; 5¹/₂ oz (150 g) butter; ¹/₃ cup + 1¹/₂ tbsp (10 cl) milk; 1 oz (30 g) chopped orange peel.

madeleines and financiers

General points

Financiers are pastries that are generally baked in small, rectangular molds. They are quite flat, with their distinctive quality deriving from the butter and ground almonds they contain. This batter should be prepared in advance and left to stand in the refrigerator for 1 or 2 days before it is baked. Financiers are also very rich in sugar, and can be kept in the refrigerator for at least 2 weeks.

Tip

Financiers owe their delicious flavor not only to the almonds, but also to the taste of the "hazelnut" butter. You need to be careful not to overcook this butter. To really appreciate the difference, pour a little melted butter onto a white plate and then the hazelnut butter next to it: compared with the color of the melted butter, the hazelnut butter should be very light brown, but not yellow.

Financiers (makes about 30 pieces)

1 Put 5¹/₂ oz (150 g) butter in a saucepan and bring to the boil over medium heat. Cook for approximately 5 minutes, until you obtain a slightly golden color: at this point, it turns into "hazelnut" butter. Immerse the bottom of the saucepan into cold water to stop it cooking, and allow it to cool.

2 Blend 2¹/₃ cups (250 g) confectioner's sugar, ¹/₂ cup (60 g) sieved flour, and 5³⁄4 oz (135 g) ground almonds in a mixing bowl. Then add 5 egg whites (5¹/₂ oz/155 g) all at the same time. Work the mixture with a wooden spoon, and then gradually add the hazelnut butter. When the mixture is a consistent texture, put it into the refrigerator for 24 hours in a covered container.

3 Butter and flour the financier molds. Spoon the mixture into a glazing bag and fill the molds to three-quarters of their capacity. Bake the financiers in the oven at 400 °F (200 °C) for approximately 12 minutes. As soon as they are cooked, turn them out of their molds. Financiers will keep for 1 week in an airtight container.

Gâteau opéra

Gâteau opéra consists of several layers of ground almond sponge, which is traditionally known as "Mona Lisa" sponge. Coffee-cream filling is spread between each layer, and the gateau is topped with very smooth chocolate icing. There are several variations on the theme, one of which alternates coffee butter cream and chocolate cream filling between the sponge layers. This famous gateau is in fact Parisian in origin, and was created in the 1950s, as were other less well-known pastry-making specialties, such as the "longchamp," the "poincaré," and the "clichy." When Gaston Lenôtre settled in the capital, he revived this recipe and made his own version, which is regarded as a model nowadays. After you have glazed this gateau, it is important to trim the edges neatly using a knife with a wide blade. Keep it in a cool place.

Serves 8
Preparation: 45 minutes
Cooking: 35 minutes

Ingredients

5¹/₂ oz (150 g) unsalted butter
⁷/₈ cup (100 g) flour
5 eggs
1 cup (220 g) superfine sugar
3¹/₂ oz (100 g) cornstarch
3¹/₂ oz (100 g) ground almonds
14 oz (400 g) dark cooking chocolate
1 scant cup (25 cl) light cream
2 tsp (1 cl) coffee extract
Syrup
12¹/₂ oz (350 g) chocolate-flavored icing
3¹/₂ oz (100 g) butter cream

1 Butter and flour a rectangular cake mold, approximately 10 in (25 cm) long and 8 in (20 cm) wide. Combine 5 egg yolks and the superfine sugar in a mixing bowl. Blanch by beating the mixture for 2 minutes. Then add the flour, the cornstarch, and the ground almonds. Mix these ingredients with a wooden spoon and then pour in 1³/₄ oz (50 g) melted butter.

2 Meanwhile, stiffly beat 4 egg whites and add them to the first mixture. Quickly empty the mixture into the mold and level it out. Bake in the oven at 350 °F (180 °C) for approximately 35 minutes. Check that the cake is cooked by running a metal skewer into the center: it should come out clean and dry. Turn the cake out onto a gridiron and leave to cool. Wash the cake mold, which will be used to "build up" the gâteau opéra.

3 Coffee cream filling. Put thin shavings of dark cooking chocolate into a bowl. Boil the cream and pour it over the chocolate, while it is still piping hot. Stir with a wooden spatula and add the rest of the butter and the coffee extract, until you obtain a smooth and shiny mixture. Store at room temperature.

4 Preparation of the gâteau opera. Line the cake mold with one or two layers of plastic wrap. Cut the cake into three with a serrated knife across the depth, to obtain 3 layers of the same thickness. Put a first layer into the base of the mold (the smoothest layer). Lightly brush over the entire surface of the cake with syrup.

5 Pour half the coffee-cream filling over it, spreading it evenly. Then put another layer on top and brush over it with syrup. Pour over the rest of the coffee-cream filling, spreading it out evenly. Finish with the last layer of cake. Gently press the three layers flat together with your hands, and then put in the refrigerator for 6–8 hours. Take the nicely cooled gâteau opéra out of the refrigerator and turn it out of its mold onto a gridiron, set over a baking sheet. Remove the layers of plastic wrap.

6 Heat 12¹/₂ oz (350 g) chocolate-flavored glazing in a bain-marie or double boiler over very gentle heat. As soon as you obtain a very runny, shiny liquid, pour it into the center of the gateau. Tilt the gateau at different angles, so that it is completely covered. Allow to cool for 30 minutes and then put it in the refrigerator for 2 hours. Write the word "Opéra" in the center of the gateau, using a small glazing bag filled with butter cream, and serve it just as it is.

Tea varieties

Tea comes in an endless variety of flavors, which give this beverage its appeal. There are black teas fermented with whole leaves (orange pekoe, flowery orange pekoe, pekoe, pekoe souchong, and souchong); teas fermented with "broken" leaves (broken orange pekoe, broken pekoe, broken tea, fannings, and the dusts). Green teas are not fermented, but they undergo a heating process that preserves the color of the leaves. Hayswen is a Chinese green tea, which is very popular; there is also gunpowder, hyson, and twankay. Oolong is semi-fermented tea, which is grown in Taiwan. There are different qualities of teas: choicest, choice, finest, fine, superior, good, fair, and common. Flavored teas are also very popular. Black teas are frequently used, and are supplemented by petals from other plants: jasmine, camellia, lotus, aniseed, or even passion fruit, mango, blackberry, and raspberry. Tea rapidly absorbs external odors and must be stored in an airtight container.

Japanese tea

Indian tea

Ceylon tea

Preparation

Even though tea making can sometimes adhere to a very elaborate ritual (kaseiki tea or Japanese green tea, for example), it is still quite a simple operation. Always make sure you thoroughly warm the teapot. To serve 6, allow 6 tsp per person of your favorite tea. Pour 4 cups (1 liter) freshly boiled water directly over the tea. Cover and leave the tea to stand for 5–8 minutes, according to variety

Afghanistan tea

and the strength required.
A samovar is used in Russia.
The basic idea is to make a very
concentrated infusion and dilute
it with water kept at the right
temperature in the samovar,
just as you are about to serve it.
In Morocco, tea is flavored with
a large quantity of mint leaves
and sugar. Then the infusion is
poured into suitable small
glasses, which are constantly
refilled as and when they are
emptied. Due to the richness
of its constituents (tannins,
polyphenolic derivatives,
flavonoids), tea is a healthy
beverage, and is often regarded
as a medicine in Asian countries.

Iced tea

Tea Moroccan style

681

Sweetmeats à la carte

Each region and each country has its own specialty, gateau, or pastry recipe. The variety of shapes, fillings, and flavorings is infinite.

Fouace

Fouace has distant origins and looks like a fairly thin, plain, flat loaf. It was made at the time of Rabelais, with flour, eggs, and fat, and cooked directly on the hearth. This specialty was such a success that fouace makers formed themselves into an important guild. Though now forgotten, it gave rise to the fougasse, a flat loaf embellished with openwork that is still made in Provence.

Stollen

This popular Germany delicacy is a kind of brioche with the addition of crystallized fruits, almonds, and dried fruits. Stollen is molded into the shape of a large loaf, about 12 in (30 cm) long. It has a dusting of confectioner's sugar and is traditionally eaten at Christmas.

Baklava

Baklava is very popular throughout the Middle East. There are quite a number of recipes, but it is always made with a very thin, puff pastry base. It is filled with walnuts, cinnamon, pistachios, and almonds. The pastry is baked in the oven in a square mold. After it has cooled, it is soaked with sugar syrup flavored with lemon and honey. It is then cut into portions.

Fouace

Vatrouchka

This is a Russian pastry made with soft white cheese, eggs, flour, and butter. It is flavored with grated lemon peel and raisins. It looks like a round, thick pie, and the top is often crisscrossed with piecrust pastry.

Stollen

Baklava

Vatrouchka

Panettone

Trois-frères

Swiss wine tart

This tart has a raised pastry base and a creamy filling made from sugar, egg yolks, and dry white wine. Dusted with confectioner's sugar and dabbed with butter, it is transferred to the oven to caramelize.

Panettone

Panettone is a large-size bread similar to brioche. An Italian delicacy, it is rich in egg yolks and traditionally served at Christmas. It is molded into a cylindrical shape and filled with raisins, crystallized lemon, and orange peel. Panettone is served for dessert with a syrupy wine, but also at breakfast with coffee.

Angel food cake

This American specialty is often flavored with vanilla. It is very light and frothy, due to the considerable quantity of beaten eggs it contains. The method used to prepare angel food cake is similar to that of Genoese cake.

Trois-frères

This pastry takes the form of a large, twisted crown and was created by the three Julien brothers, who were very famous 19th-century pastry-makers. The mixture is rich in eggs and superfine sugar and contains chopped sweet almonds, crystallized angelica, and maraschino. After baking, the trois-frères is topped with apricot marmalade and encrusted with chopped almonds.

Swiss wine tart

Baba with exotic fruit

A party dish

Serves 5
Preparation: 10 minutes
Cooking: 25 minutes
Standing: 1 hour 30 minutes

Ingredients

1 1/3 cups (150 g) flour

Salt

$^1/_4$ cup (60 g) superfine sugar

2 eggs

1 tbsp (15 g) active dry yeast

$^1/_2$ glass milk

2$^1/_2$ oz (70 g) butter

1 small glass white rum

1 pot crème fraîche

$^1/_8$ cup (30 g) confectioner's sugar

A few crystallized fruits

1 small can pineapples in syrup

1 lb 2 oz (500 g) kumquats

1. Combine the flour, 1 pinch salt, $^1/_8$ cup (30 g) superfine sugar, the beaten eggs, and the yeast, blended with the warm milk, in a bowl. Mix, and then gradually add 2 oz (60 g) melted, but not boiling, butter. You should obtain a fairly soft mixture.

2. Work this mixture, without beating it, for about 10 minutes. Cover with a cloth and leave it to rise at room temperature until the mixture has doubled in size (just over 1 hour).

3. Gently work the mixture again for a few moments and transfer it to a buttered, crown-shaped mold, very lightly dusted with flour. Leave it to stand for another 30 minutes. Pre-heat the oven to 400 °F (200 °C). Wait until it is very warm before you put in the mold, and bake for 25 minutes.

4. Meanwhile, prepare the syrup with rum, the rest of the superfine sugar, and a few tablespoons of water. Allow this syrup, which should not be thick, to cool.

5. Whip the crème fraîche and add the confectioner's sugar. Wait until the baba is tepid before you turn it out of the mold. Allow to cool while generously sprinkling it with syrup, until it is thoroughly soaked.

6. Fill the baba with the crème Chantilly. Garnish the center with crystallized fruits, pineapple pieces, and halved kumquats.

Recommended drinks

Farmer's rum
Grand Marnier
Champagne

Menu suggestions

1. As an appetizer, serve a seafood salad, for example; then duck with olives or quail with grapes for the main course.

2. You can also continue the West Indian theme with cod croquettes as an appetizer, followed by ham with pineapple for the main course.

Lucerne biscôme

A foreign dish

Serves 10
Preparation: 15 minutes
Cooking: 50–60 minutes

Ingredients

1 scant cup (20 cl) milk

1³/₄ oz (50 g) crystallized lemon and orange peel

1 scant cup (20 cl) crème fraîche

9 oz (250 g) molasses

Ground aniseed

Ground cinnamon

Grated nutmeg

Ground clove

1 pinch salt

1¹/₃ cups (150 g) superfine sugar

³/₄ oz (20 g) ground yeast

3 cups (500 g) whole-wheat flour

1 tbsp butter

1. Warm the milk. Cut up the crystallized fruits into small cubes. Whip the crème fraîche and combine it with 2³/₄ oz (80 g) molasses, 1 pinch of each spice, the salt, and the superfine sugar.

2. Then add the yeast, the flour and the milk, and mix until you obtain a very smooth texture. Next, add the fruit peel.

3. Cover a buttered pie plate with wax paper and pour this mixture into it. Bake in a pre-heated oven at 350 °F (180 °C) for 50–60 minutes.

4. When you have taken it out of the oven, spread a thin layer of molasses over the top of your biscôme to make it glisten.

N.B: of course you can use any crystallized citrus fruit peel you like to fill this bread, which is Swiss in origin. Citrus fruit and grapefruit peel are especially fragrant. To crystallize orange peel yourself: blanch, drain, and simmer the peel for 2 hours in sugar syrup; remove from the heat and steep the mixture for 12 hours. This biscôme keeps for a few days as long as it is well wrapped up in aluminum foil: in this case, do not coat it with molasses, but wrap it up dry, once it has thoroughly cooled down. You can give it a shiny appearance when you serve it, either with molasses as in this recipe, or with well-sieved apricot marmalade gently heated in a small saucepan.

Recommended drinks

Riesling
Crémant d'Alsace
Arbois

Menu suggestions

1. For a winter menu, serve fillets of smoked trout with horseradish sauce as an appetizer, followed by roast venison with celery purée for the main course.

2. For a summer menu, serve frogs' legs with parsley and garlic as an appetizer, followed by trout au bleu or perch meunière for the main course.

687

Gypsy's arm with strawberries

A family dish

Serves 6
Preparation: 15 minutes
Cooking: 7 minutes

Ingredients

4 eggs
$3/8$ cup (85 g) superfine sugar
$2/3$ cup (75 g) flour
$13/4$ oz (50 g) butter
1 lb 2 oz (500 g) strawberries
Confectioner's sugar

1. Break the eggs, and separate the whites from the yolks. Using a whisk, gently beat the yolks with $1/3$ cup (75 g) superfine sugar for a good 5 minutes. The mixture must turn white. Fold in the flour without working it. Stiffly beat 3 egg whites, adding 1 tsp superfine sugar halfway through.

2. Melt the butter, without boiling it. Pour the melted butter and stiffly beaten egg whites into a mixing bowl containing the beaten yolks, superfine sugar, and flour. Carefully stir these ingredients without working the mixture too much.

3. Cover a baking sheet with a buttered sheet of wax paper. Pre-heat the oven to 465 °F (240 °C). Spread out the mixture evenly to a thickness of $9/16$ in (1.5 cm). Bake in the oven for 7 minutes.

4. Take the cake out of the oven and turn it over onto a damp dishtowel. Using a brush, moisten the wax paper with water and remove it. Spread the cake with strawberry sauce, prepared by putting the fruit through a blender and then saturating the purée with confectioner's sugar.

5. Roll up the gypsy's arm using the dishtowel. Dust with confectioner's sugar and allow to cool. Trim at each end before serving.

N.B: you can also fill the gypsy's arm—otherwise known as "arm of Venus" – with confectioner's custard flavored with Grand Marnier. This specialty originates from Roussillon.

Recommended drinks

Jurançon doux
Blanquette de Limoux
Crémant de Bourgogne

Menu suggestions

1. Serve tomato salad with mozzarella as an appetizer; a tasty dish of fresh pasta with pesto for the main course; and individual goat's milk cheeses to finish.

2. If you like meat, serve rib of beef and Provençale tomatoes for the main course, followed by this delicious fruit roll for dessert.

Bûche cévenole

A party dish

Serves 6
Preparation: 30 minutes
Cooking: 15 minutes

Ingredients

11 eggs
1¹/₃ cups (300 g) superfine sugar
2 cups (225 g) flour
14 oz (400 g) butter
2 cups (50 cl) milk
¹/₂ vanilla bean

4¹/₂ oz (125 g) ground praline
3¹/₂ oz (100 g) green almond paste
12¹/₂ oz (350 g) walnut halves
A few meringues in the shape
of mushrooms

1. Break 5 eggs in a bowl and add ²/₃ cup (150 g) superfine sugar. Beat briskly until you obtain a frothy mixture. Transfer to a bain-marie or double boiler, which should be hot but not boiling, and let the mixture thicken for 5 minutes, while beating. Take it off the heat, and sprinkle 1¹/₃ cups (150 g) flour into it.

2. Pre-heat the oven to 350 °F (180 °C). Place a sheet of buttered wax paper on a jelly roll pan or baking sheet and pour the mixture over it, spreading it to a thickness of ³/₁₆ in (5 mm). Bake for 15 minutes.

3. Boil the milk with the vanilla bean. Break the 6 remaining eggs and separate the yolks from the whites. Beat the yolks with ²/₃ cup (150 g) superfine sugar and ²/₃ cup (75 g) flour. Pour the boiling milk into the mixture, while still beating. Allow to almost completely cool down before adding the butter, praline, and roughly chopped walnut halves, after setting some aside.

4. Turn the cake out of the pan onto a damp dishtowel, cover it with a second dishtowel, and allow to cool. Remove the top cloth, spread the cake with the cream mixture, and roll it up with the aid of the dishtowel underneath. Lift it into a pie dish and set aside in a cool place.

5. Just before serving, gently heat the almond paste and brush it over the log. Garnish with mushroom meringues and walnut halves.

Recommended drinks

Champagne
Vin jaune du Jura
Xérès

Menu suggestions

1. For a Christmas Eve or New Year's menu, serve scallop salad as an appetizer and roast pheasant served with mushrooms for the main course.

2. Another suggestion is foie gras poached "au torchon," served with a lamb's lettuce salad as an appetizer, followed by filet of beef in pastry and artichoke hearts as a side-dish for the main course.

689

Cookies

An easy dish

Makes 50 cookies
Preparation: 20 minutes
Cooking: 10 minutes

Ingredients

$4^1/_2$ oz (125 g) butter
$3/_8$ cup (90 g) soft brown sugar
$3/_8$ cup (90 g) white sugar
2 eggs
$1/_2$ tsp vanilla extract
$1/_2$ tsp bicarbonate of soda
$1/_2$ tsp salt
$3/_4$ cup (90 g) flour

1 glass milk
1 scant cup (150 g) oatmeal
$4^1/_2$ oz (125 g) dark cooking chocolate
2 oz (60 g) nuts:
almonds, pistachios

1. Make sure that the butter is at room temperature. Put it into a bowl with the soft brown sugar and the white sugar. Beat these ingredients with a hand whisk until the cream has thickened well. Beat the eggs with a fork and add to the sugar mixture with the vanilla, while continuing to beat.

2. Combine the bicarbonate of soda, salt, and flour. Sieve. Add to the egg and sugar and stir the mixture thoroughly with a spoon, while gradually adding the milk. Add the oatmeal.

3. Roughly chop up the chocolate and nuts. Add these to the mixture. Transfer level teaspoonfuls of the mixture to a cookie sheet (neither buttered nor lined with wax paper). Leave a 2-in (5-cm) gap between each spoonful.

4. Use a floured fork to draw a crisscross pattern in each, without squashing the mixture, as the cookies should remain fairly thick. You need to re-flour the fork for each cookie.

5. Heat the oven to 350 °F (180 °C) then bake and brown the cookies in 10 minutes. Wait 1–2 minutes before lifting them off the cookie sheet with a metal spatula and putting them on a gridiron to cool.

N.B: if these cookies are stored in an airtight tin, they will keep well. If you want to make both brown chocolate-flavored cookies and paler cookies, divide the mixture into two and add 2 tbsp (30 g) cocoa powder to one of the halves.

Recommended drinks

Coffee
Milkshake
Ice chocolate

Menu suggestions

1. These cookies can be included in a children's buffet, with canapés and small sandwiches with various fillings, fruit salad, and chocolate-filled pastries.

2. You can also serve them at teatime, alongside various delicacies, marshmallows, and multicolored sweetmeats.

Danish crown

A foreign dish

Serves 4
Preparation: 20 minutes
Standing: 1 hour 30 minutes
Cooking: 30 minutes

Ingredients

3½ oz (100 g) butter

1¾ oz (50 g) ground almonds

¼ cup (50 g) superfine sugar

12½ oz (350 g) prepared
puff pastry dough

3½ oz (100 g) raisins

Confectioner's sugar

1. Work the butter, ground almonds, and superfine sugar until you obtain
a softened, smooth, and well-thickened cream.

2. Roll out the pastry dough to a thickness of ⅛ in (3 mm), forming
a rectangle at least twice as long as it is wide. Spread the softened cream
over the pastry with a spatula. Leave a 1 in (2.5 cm) border around the
edges. Scatter the raisins over the softened cream as evenly as possible.

3. Roll up the pastry very tightly so that you obtain a regular cylinder-shape.
Curve it round to form a crown. Moisten the joins and seal the ends.

4. Put the crown on a buttered baking sheet. Cut into the crown with scissors,
every 1 in (2.5 cm), and to within ⅜ in (1 cm) of the center. Make sure you
obtain an even number of sections. Push every other section toward the
center, while holding down the adjoining sections with two fingers, so that
they are not dragged along and the crown keeps its shape. Cover with a deep
bowl and leave to rise for 1 hour 30 minutes.

5. Approximately 15 minutes before it has fully risen, heat the oven to 510 °F
(265 °C). Put the crown in the oven, and reduce the temperature to 375 °F
(190 °C) after just 2 minutes. Bake for a total of 30 minutes. Turn it onto
a gridiron and allow to cool a little. Dust with confectioner's sugar shortly
before serving.

N.B: take the butter out of the refrigerator a fairly long time in advance.
If it is cold, you will find it really difficult to make your cream.

Recommended drinks

Ice tea
Liqueur wine
Pinot noir d'Alsace

Menu suggestions

1. You can serve a selection of flavored herrings
as an appetizer, followed by meat croquettes with
a red cabbage salad for the main course.

2. For a more classic menu, serve smoked
salmon as an appetizer, and roast beef with
a dill and fennel potato salad for the main course.

Sofia's delight

A family dish

Serves 4
Preparation: 20 minutes
Cooking: 35 minutes

Ingredients

4 pots natural yogurt
5 tbsp (75 g) bitter cocoa powder
1 scant cup (200 g) superfine sugar
4 eggs
5 tbsp (75 g) cornstarch
1 orange
1 tbsp rum

1 pinch salt
1 tbsp butter
Confectioner's sugar

1. Pour the yogurt into a piece of muslin and drain, but without compressing it. Put in a bowl, add the cocoa, and beat for a few moments.

2. Then add the superfine sugar and vigorously beat the mixture until you obtain a light cream. Add the egg yolks, one after the other, while continuing to beat. Sprinkle with cornstarch and mix well.

3. Wash the orange, wipe dry, and grate the peel over the mixture. Flavor with the rum and mix one last time.

4. Beat the egg whites stiffly with the salt and fold gently into the yogurt cream, working from bottom to top.

5. Butter a round cake pan and pour in the mixture. Bake in a pre-heated oven at 435 °F (225 °C) for 35 minutes. Allow to cool almost completely before turning it out of the mold onto a gridiron. Dust with a little confectioner's sugar.

N.B: cocoa and orange is a particularly delicious combination, but variations of this simple-to-make pastry are easy to imagine. For example, you could use vanilla sugar or cinnamon-flavored sugar instead of cocoa; lemon or grapefruit instead of orange. Whatever you decide, select citrus fruits with a very thin skin and always wash them before removing the peel. You can also enhance the flavor of the orange by using Cointreau or Grand Marnier instead of rum. Above all, make sure you use traditional whole milk yogurts.

Recommended drinks

Sauternes
Banyuls
Xeres

Menu suggestions

1. Serve artichoke hearts and tartare sauce as an appetizer, followed by grilled rib steaks and navy beans for the main course.

2. For a winter menu, serve pumpkin soup as an appetizer, followed by stewed veal shank for the main course.

Feuilletés with poppy seeds

An exotic dish

Serves 4
Preparation: the day before–20 minutes;
the following day–20 minutes
Cooking: 40 minutes

Ingredients

1 pinch salt

2 eggs

4 $^1/_3$ cups (500 g) flour

Oil

2$^3/_4$ oz (75 g) butter

$^1/_2$ cup (125 g) superfine sugar

9 oz (250 g) apples

4$^1/_2$ oz (125 g) poppy seeds

Cognac or armagnac

or fruit brandy

1. Put 1 pinch salt, the eggs, and 1 generous cup (25 cl) water in a bowl. Beat vigorously with a fork, and then gradually fold in the flour. Knead this mixture with your hands for 30 minutes, by squashing it with your fist and frequently hitting it against a board. Coat it generously with oil and leave it to stand until the following day, covered with a damp cloth.

2. Cover a large table with a cloth and gently roll out the dough as thinly as possible. With a little patience, you should obtain a large sheet of pastry, which is tissue-thin.

3. Melt 1$^3/_4$ oz (50 g) butter in a little oil; brush over the entire surface of the pastry, and then sprinkle it with superfine sugar. Leave it to dry. Lightly butter some small, shallow molds. Cut the dough into equal pieces and cover the molds with three or four layers, alternating with the very thinly sliced apples, sprinkled with poppy seeds. Dust with the rest of the superfine sugar and sprinkle with armagnac, or cognac, or fruit brandy, mixed with 1 generous cup (25 cl) water.

4. Heat the oven to 365 °F (185 °C) and bake for 10 minutes. Take the molds out of the oven. Make pastry lids from sheets of dough rolled into cones, and place these on top of the puff pastry layers. Sprinkle with poppy seeds again. Heat the oven to 300 °F (150 °C) and bake for 30 minutes. Serve warm.

N.B: if you do not have time to prepare the layers of puff pastry, use filo pastry instead.

Recommended drinks

Turkish coffee
Steamed tea
Barley water

Menu suggestions

1. Serve a selection of appetizers (stuffed grape leaves, eggplant dip, stuffed olives, etc.), followed by lamb and sweet bell pepper kebabs for the main course.

2. You can also serve tabbouleh as an appetizer, followed by eggplant stuffed with lamb for the main course.

Walnut gâteau

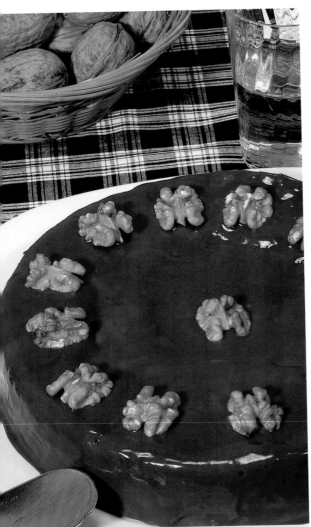

A regional dish

Serves 4–5
Preparation: 25 minutes
Cooking: 50 minutes

Ingredients

1³/₄ oz (50 g) butter

10¹/₂ oz (300 g) walnut halves

3 eggs

¹/₂ cup (125 g) superfine sugar

3¹/₂ tbsp (50 g) cornstarch

2 tbsp rum

1 pinch salt

3¹/₂ oz (100 g) dark chocolate

1 tsp instant coffee

2 tbsp milk

Confectioner's sugar

1. Butter a round cake pan, 7³/₄ in (20 cm) in diameter. Butter a sheet of wax paper and place at the bottom of the cake pan. Set aside 12 good walnut halves and grate the others with a cylindrical vegetable mill, fine grater, or electric mixer. Pre-heat the oven to 320 °F (160 °C).

2. Break the eggs, separating the whites from the yolks. Beat the yolks and the superfine sugar with a hand whisk in a bowl, until the mixture turns white. Then add the cornstarch, followed by the rum. Beat the egg whites very stiffly with 1 pinch salt. Add them to the mixture in two stages, while working it up with a spatula. Finally, add the grated walnut halves, still proceeding very carefully so as not to allow the mixture to collapse.

3. Pour into the cake pan and bake in the oven for 50 minutes. If the surface of the cake browns too much during cooking, cover it with a sheet of aluminum foil. Turn the cake out onto a gridiron and remove the wax paper. Allow to cool completely.

4. Break up the chocolate into pieces. Put them into a double boiler or bowl in a baking pan of water with the instant coffee, the rest of the butter, the milk, and the confectioner's sugar. Heat gently. When the chocolate has melted, mix and pour this "glazing" over the gâteau (set the grid over a dish, in order to collect the excess). Level out the surface with a spatula. Embellish with walnut halves. Keep cool until it is served.

N.B: if you use a mixer to chop the walnut halves, turn it on intermittently, so that the nuts do not heat up in the apparatus.

Recommended drinks

Monbazillac
Barsac
Black coffee

Menu suggestions

1. For a typical menu from the Périgord district, serve foie gras pâté with walnut oil salad as an appetizer, followed by magret of duck with pommes sarladaises for the main course.

2. If you prefer a lighter menu, serve a small dish of whitebait as an appetizer, followed by boletus mushroom omelet for the main course.

Millas with cherries

A light dish

Serves 4
Preparation: 35 minutes
Standing: 30 minutes
Cooking: 1 hour

Ingredients

3$^1/_2$ oz (100 g) butter

2 cups (225 g) flour

1 scant cup (200 g) superfine sugar

1 pinch salt

1$^1/_2$ glasses milk

1 lb 9 oz (700 g) black cherries

4$^1/_2$ oz (125 g) ground almonds

2 eggs

1. Start by making a piecrust pastry, which is not too sweet: cut the butter into small pieces over 1$^3/_4$ cups (200 g) flour, with a well in its center and combine rapidly with your fingertips. Make another well and add $^1/_4$ cup (50 g) superfine sugar, 1 pinch salt, and just enough milk to knead into a smooth mixture that does not stick. Leave to stand for 30 minutes.

2. It is up to you whether you pit the cherries or not. If they are pitted, the tart will be easier to eat; if you leave the pits, it will have more flavor.

3. Prepare the cream: mix the ground almonds and $^1/_4$ cup (25 g) flour in a bowl. Break the eggs over the mixture, add $^1/_2$ cup (125 g) superfine sugar, and dilute with 1 glass milk, while continuing to beat.

4. Heat the oven at 375 °F (190 °C). Roll out the pastry; line a buttered pie dish with it; prick the base with a fork; arrange the cherries on the pastry; and pour the cream over it all. Put in the center of the oven and bake for 1 hour. Take it out of the oven and dust with superfine sugar. Serve hot or cold, according to taste.

N.B: on the same model as the famous clafoutis, you can make this millas with other seasonal fruits. It is also delicious with small yellow plums or nectarine quarters. If you use cherries, select fairly large, very ripe, and juicy ones. Out of season, you can also make this millas with dried fruits, such as raisins or prunes.

Recommended drinks

Grape juice
Apple juice
Brouilly

Menu suggestions

1. Serve cucumber salad with light whipping cream as an appetizer, followed by fish parcels with small slices of zucchini in olive oil for the main course.

2. Another suggestion for a fairly light menu: gazpacho garnished with finely diced vegetables as an appetizer, followed by chicken breast steamed in fennel for the main course.

Dijon spice buns

A regional dish

Makes approximately 25 buns
Preparation: 10 + 10 minutes
Standing: 2 hours
Cooking: 30-40 minutes

Ingredients

14 oz (400 g) runny honey

1 scant cup (200 g) superfine sugar

5$^1/_2$ oz (150 g) butter

4$^1/_3$ cups (500 g) flour

2 tbsp (30 g) baking powder

1 tsp (5 g) bicarbonate of soda

Ground cinnamon

2 tsp (10 g) aniseed seeds

1 lemon

7 oz (200 g) crystallized orange
or lemon peel

Orange marmalade

2 eggs

Confectioner's sugar

1. Heat 1$^2/_3$ cups (40 cl) water in a saucepan. Add the honey, superfine sugar, and 3$^1/_2$ oz (100 g) butter and bring to the boil. Take the saucepan off the heat, skim, and finish mixing.

2. Pour the flour into a bowl. Make a well in the center. Add the baking powder, bicarbonate of soda, cinnamon, and aniseed. Combine with the flour. Pour the warm honey into the well and mix thoroughly with a wooden spoon. Amass it into the shape of a ball, wrap in a cloth, and leave to stand for 1 hour at room temperature away from drafts.

3. After rolling it in the flour, sprinkle either grated lemon peel, or very finely chopped crystallized citron or orange peel, or a combination of both, over the dough. Work in rapidly.

4. Butter and flour some small cylindrical molds. Pour in the mixture and put 1 small tsp orange marmalade into the center of each bun. Leave it to "expand" for approximately 1 hour. Heat the oven at 400 °F (200 °C). Bake for 30–40 minutes. As soon as they are cooked, brush some egg white saturated with confectioner's sugar over the surface of the buns. Leave them to dry just inside the oven, with the door open, for a few moments.

N.B: these buns will keep very well in a dark place away from drafts. If stored in an airtight container, they will taste even better after 1 or 2 days.

Recommended drinks

Black coffee
Freshly squeezed orange juice
Hot chocolate

Menu suggestions

1. To pick up the Burgundy theme again, serve a snail omelet appetizer, followed by calf's kidneys with mustard for the main course.

2. For a spring menu, you could also serve eggs "en meurette," followed by andouillettes in white wine with a green salad for the main course, and white cheeses with mixed herbs for dessert.

Picanchâgne

A regional dish

Serves 4
Preparation: 20 minutes
Cooking: 50 minutes

Ingredients

1 lb 2 oz (500 g) prepared
puff pastry dough

$2\frac{1}{4}$ lb (1 kg) pears

1 lemon

$5\frac{1}{2}$ oz (150 g) crème fraîche

$\frac{1}{2}$ cup (100 g) superfine sugar

1 pinch pepper

1 egg

1. Divide the dough into two roughly even pieces. Roll one piece out on a floured worktop. Butter a mold and then place this layer over it. Push the dough down along the edges.

2. Peel the pears and cut them into quarters. Seed them and slice the quarters. Squeeze lemon juice over them. Put them in a bowl and add the crème fraîche followed by the superfine sugar. Mix thoroughly.

3. Add 1 pinch pepper, and then pour the contents of the bowl into the dough. If the dough is slightly thin, bake your picanchâgne pastry shell "blind" for 10 minutes in a moderate oven without browning it before pouring the pears in.

4. Roll out the second piece of dough. Put this layer over the mold. Brush over the underside edge with egg white, so that it thoroughly sticks to the layer of dough at the bottom. Pinch the two edges together and trim the circumference with a small, sharp knife. This will enable the pastry to rise.

5. Trim off a strip of dough to create a circular shape, and stick it down in the centre of the piecrust (still using egg white); prick to make a small well. Brush egg yolk diluted with a little water over the entire surface and embellish with dough trimmings.

6. Bake in a pre-heated oven at 400 °F (200 °C) for 50 minutes. Keep an eye on the cooking and put a sheet of wax paper over the pie if it browns too quickly. Wait until it cools before serving.

Recommended drinks

Coteaux-du-layon
Jurançon doux
Vouvray

Menu suggestions

1. This pie from the Bourbonnais makes a delicious fall dessert; you could serve duck terrine as an appetizer, and roast quails garnished with chanterelle mushrooms for the main course.

2. You could also start with a light cheese tart as an appetizer and follow with sweet and sour noisettes of venison with fried, small cep mushrooms for the main course.

Scania with apples

An economical dish

Serves 6
Preparation: 15 minutes
Cooking: 40 minutes

Ingredients

5³/₄ oz (165 g) butter
9 oz (250 g) breadcrumbs
2¹/₄ lb (1 kg) apples
(half red, half green)
1 lemon
1 scant cup (200 g) sugar
1 tsp ground cinnamon

Confectioner's sugar
To serve: custard or crème fraîche

1. Melt 3¹/₂ oz (100 g) butter in a skillet and brown the breadcrumbs.

2. Set aside 2 apple quarters (1 green and 1 red); immediately put them in lemon juice, to prevent them from turning brown. Peel and core the apples, cut them into quarters, and then thinly slice them.

3. Generously butter an earthenware or Pyrex dish. Sprinkle the browned breadcrumbs over the pastry shell, and arrange a first layer of thin apple slices over the breadcrumbs; sprinkle with white sugar, and add a few dabs of butter.

4. Finish filling the dish, alternating layers of breadcrumbs and sweetened, buttered apple. Add a final layer of breadcrumbs, flavored with ground cinnamon.

5. Heat the oven to 400 °F (200 °C) and bake the tart for 30–40 minutes. Your scania should be thoroughly browned on the outside and sweet and pulpy on the inside. Serve hot or cold.

6. Garnish the scania with the thinly sliced apple quarters you set aside and dust with confectioner's sugar. This tart can be served with either a plain or cinnamon-flavored custard; it can be served cold to enhance the contrast in temperature between the tart and the hot sauce, or just with a bowl of very cold crème fraîche. Another delicious suggestion: arrange slices of scania on individual plates served with 1 scoop of vanilla or cinnamon ice cream.

Recommended drinks

Pear milkshake
Jurançon
Grapefruit juice

Menu suggestions

1. Serve a selection of raw vegetables as an appetizer, followed by pork loin roast with ratatouille for the main course.

2. You could also serve eggs in aspic with ham as an appetizer, followed by chicken liver kebabs for the main course.

Apple strudel

A regional dish

Serves 6
Preparation: 30 minutes
Cooking: 55 minutes

Ingredients

To make the dough:
2 cups (250 g) flour
4¹/₂ oz (125 g) butter
1 egg
1 pinch salt

To make the filling:
2¹/₄ lb (1 kg) firm,
slightly acidic apples

To make the custard:
1 generous cup (25 cl)
runny crème fraîche

1 large egg
¹/₄ cup (50 g) superfine sugar
1 tbsp (15 g) vanilla sugar

To make the strudel:
4¹/₂ oz (125 g) butter
1 generous cup (125 g) flour
¹/₂ cup (125 g) superfine sugar
4¹/₂ oz (125 g) ground almonds
Ground cinnamon
Confectioner's sugar

1. The dough: put the flour, softened butter, yolk of 1 egg, and salt into a bowl. Mix with enough water to obtain a smooth consistency. Knead the dough into the shape of a ball, cover, and leave to stand for 30 minutes at the bottom of the refrigerator.

2. The filling: peel and finely dice the apples. Heat the oven at 400 °F (205 °C). Butter a moderate-size mold, so that your strudel will be thick enough. Roll out the dough and place it in the mold, forming an edge.

3. Pierce the bottom with a fork. Fill with the diced apples and bake in the oven for 20 minutes; the fruit should be three-quarters cooked.

4. The custard: beat the crème fraîche with the egg, superfine sugar, and vanilla sugar. Pour it slowly over the apples and bake for a further 15 minutes.

5. The strudel: combine pieces of softened butter, the flour, superfine sugar, ground almonds, and ¹/₂ tsp ground cinnamon. Knead these ingredients until you obtain a fairly granular mixture.

6. Pour this mixture over the tart. Put the tart back in the oven, set at 435 °F (225 °C) this time. The surface should turn golden brown and crispy in about 20 minutes. Allow to cool and then dust with confectioner's sugar.

Recommended drinks

Crémant d'Alsace
Bonnezeaux
Farmer's cider

Menu suggestions

1. Serve pike-perch quenelles as an appetizer, followed by sauerkraut with a selection of smoked meats and pork meats for the main course.

2. For a lighter menu, serve soup prepared with frogs' legs and mixed herbs as an appetizer, followed by trout au bleu or meunière for the main course.

Orange tart

An economical dish

Serves 4
Preparation: 20 minutes
Cooking: 30 minutes

Ingredients

1 glass milk

$1/2$ vanilla bean

2 eggs

$1/3$ cup (70 g) superfine sugar

4 tsp (20 g) cornstarch

5 cups (140 g) butter

$4^1/2$ oz (125 g) ground almonds

$1/2$ cup (125 g) confectioner's sugar

2 or 3 oranges with thin peel

7 oz (200 g) prepared piecrust dough

1. Boil the milk with the $1/2$ vanilla bean split into two. Beat 1 egg yolk with $1/8$ cup (35 g) superfine sugar until the mixture turns white and frothy; add 2 tsp (10 g) cornstarch without mixing too much. Pour the boiling milk into the bowl while beating continuously for a few minutes until you obtain a smooth, consistent texture.

2. Decant the mixture into a saucepan with a solid base and warm over low heat until it starts to simmer, continuing to beat. Make sure you thoroughly scrape the bottom of the saucepan. Take the saucepan off the heat and allow to cool, uncovered.

3. Soften $4^1/2$ oz (125 g) butter with a fork, to obtain a creamy consistency. Add the ground almonds, confectioner's sugar, and 1 egg yolk, briskly working the mixture; add the rest of the cornstarch. Blend the vanilla cream into the mixture, one spoonful at a time.

4. Wash the oranges and thoroughly wipe them dry. Hold the oranges down firmly on a cutting board and, using a good, sharp knife, halve them, one at a time. Then slice the half-oranges as finely as possibly. Remove the pips from the slices.

5. Heat the oven to 410 °F (210 °C). Roll out the pastry dough and place it in a buttered mold; top with the rest of the superfine sugar. Fill it with the almond cream, and then top with the thin orange slices. Bake for 30 minutes then turn it out of the mold while it is still warm.

Recommended drinks

Rivesaltes
Muscat de Beaumes-de-Venise
Cérons

Menu suggestions

1. Serve country pâté with green salad as an appetizer, followed by beef casserole with olives and carrots for the main course.

2. You could also serve a lamb's lettuce salad with pickled gizzards as an appetizer, followed by roast chicken with lemon and small potatoes for the main course.

Date tart

A family dish

Serves 5
Preparation: 30 minutes
Cooking: 40 minutes

Ingredients

1¹/₃ cups (150 g) flour
2³/₄ oz (75 g) butter
1 generous cup (25 cl) milk
1 vanilla bean
3 eggs
¹/₄ cup (50 g) superfine sugar
2³/₄ oz (75 g) walnut halves

7 oz (200 g) dates
3 bananas
¹/₂ cup (50 g) confectioner's sugar
Salt

1. Quickly mix together the flour and butter, cut into small pieces. Add enough salted water to obtain a granular mixture. Leave to stand for 15 minutes before rolling the dough out. Place in a buttered pie plate, and pierce the pastry shell with a fork.

2. Line the pastry shell with a circle of waxed paper and cover with rice or dried beans, as is usually done when pastry needs to be cooked slowly and without browning. Pre-heat the oven to 400 °F (200 °C) and bake for about 15 minutes.

3. Meanwhile, heat the milk. Split the vanilla bean in two lengthways and place in the milk to infuse. Beat 1 whole egg and 2 yolks with the superfine sugar. Break the walnut halves into small pieces, crush the dates, and finely dice the bananas; add them to the mixture. Mix well then pour the boiling milk over.

4. Pour this mixture over the cooked pastry. Put it back in the oven for a further 20 minutes or so.

5. Meanwhile, prepare the meringue by beating the 2 remaining egg whites with the confectioner's sugar. Spread the meringue over the tart, and put it back in the oven for a further 5 minutes or so (until the meringue has just started to brown). Garnish with pitted dates and serve cold.

N.B: you could also serve a small selection of dried fruits, such as raisins, figs, almonds, and hazelnuts with this winter tart.

Recommended drinks

Quincy
Condrieu
Hermitage

Menu suggestions

1. Serve broiled sweet bell pepper salad as an appetizer, followed by sauté of lamb with eggplants for the main course.

2. Another suggestion for an even more summery menu would be seafood salad as an appetizer, followed by bream with fennel for the main course.

701

Yogurt tart

An economical dish

Serves 4–6
Preparation time: 15 minutes
Leave to stand: 1 hour
Cooking time: 50 minutes

Ingredients

To make the dough:
1¹/₃ cups (150 g) flour
¹/₃ cup (75 g) superfine sugar
1 sachet vanilla sugar
1 pinch salt
3¹/₂ oz (100 g) butter
To make the filling:
1³/₄ oz (50 g) raisins
Tea

1 pot natural yogurt
1 oz (30 g) butter
2 eggs
²/₃ cup (150 g) superfine sugar
1 sachet vanilla sugar
1 level tbsp cornstarch
2 cups (50 cl) milk
1³/₄ oz (50 g) crushed walnuts

1. Steep the raisins in a little tea. Pour the yoghurt into a cloth and strain for at least 1 hour.

2. The dough: mix the flour, superfine sugar, vanilla sugar, and salt in a bowl, and then combine this mixture with the butter, cut in pieces. Form into the shape of a ball, then roll it out and line the bottom and sides of a pie plate with it. Leave to stand.

3. Meanwhile, prepare the filling: mix together the butter, egg yolks, superfine sugar, and vanilla sugar. Stir the cornstarch into the milk and add to the mixture with the drained raisins, crushed walnuts, and yogurt. Thoroughly work all these ingredients together until you obtain a smooth consistent texture. Heat the oven to 400–435 °F (205–225 °C).

4. Beat the egg whites stiffly and add them carefully to the yogurt-based mixture. Pour the mixture into the pastry shell. Level out the surface with a spatula and put it immediately into the oven.

5. Bake the tart for approximately 50 minutes. Turn the oven off and allow to cool in the oven; do not turn it out of the pie plate until it is quite cold.

N.B: it is important to pre-heat the oven, as there should be no delay between adding the stiffly beaten egg whites to the filling and baking the tart in the oven. For the filling, select small, seedless raisins (currants or golden raisins).

Recommended drinks

Vouvray
Crémant de Bourgogne
Orange juice

Menu suggestions

1. Serve celeriac in remoulade dressing as an appetizer, followed by stuffed tomatoes "à la charcutière" with potato purée for the main course.

2. Another quicker menu suggestion: radishes with a sprinkling of salt as an appetizer, followed by spaghetti bolognaise, or tagliatelle with thin strips of ham, for the main course.

Tarte Belle-Hélène

An easy dish

Serves 6
Preparation: 20 minutes
Standing: 1 hour
Cooking: 25 minutes

Ingredients

1³/₄ cups (200 g) flour

6 oz (175 g) butter

1 pinch salt

Superfine sugar

6 pears

4¹/₂ oz (125 g) dark chocolate

1 small pot crème fraîche

Flaked almonds

1. Start with the piecrust pastry: make a well in the center of the flour, and work in 3¹/₂ oz (100 g) butter cut into small pieces, 1 pinch of salt, 1 tsp superfine sugar, and just enough water to obtain a soft dough, which does not stick to your fingers. Leave to stand in a cool place.

2. Peel the pears, halve them, and hollow them out removing the cores and pips. Put these half-pears into a bowl and pour a little superfine sugar over them. Leave them to steep.

3. Meanwhile, roll out the pastry to a thickness of ¹/₈ in (4 mm). Butter a mold, line it with the pastry, and cover with a sheet of wax paper. Place rice or dried beans on top of the wax paper, in order to bake the pastry slowly and without browning. Bake in a hot oven at 435 °F (225 °C) for 15 minutes.

4. Remove the weights and the wax paper. Substitute the half-pears and finish baking the tart at 400 °F (200 °C) for 10 minutes. Allow to cool and then turn it out of the mold.

5. Break up the chocolate into a saucepan with a solid base; put it into a bain-marie or double boiler and let it melt without stirring. Take it out of the bain-marie, add 1 tbsp hot water, and mix with 1³/₄ oz (50 g) butter. Whip the crème fraîche without working it up into a Chantilly cream consistency, and add the chocolate. Pour this chocolate cream over the cooled tart and garnish with lightly baked flaked almonds.

Recommended drinks

Sauternes
Loupiac
Madère

Menu suggestions

1. Serve grapefruit filled with crab and shrimp meat as an appetizer, followed by medallions of veal with chanterelle mushrooms for the main course.

2. You could also serve smoked salmon soufflé as an appetizer, followed by leg of lamb with fresh flageolets for the main course.

703

Fall tart with nectarines

A simple dish

Serves 4
Preparation: 20 minutes
Cooking: 30 minutes

Ingredients

1 glass milk

1/2 vanilla bean

2 eggs

1/3 cup (70 g) superfine sugar

4 tsp (20 g) cornstarch

5 oz (140 g) butter

4 1/2 oz (125 g) ground almonds

1 1/3 cups (150 g) confectioner's sugar

7 oz (200 g) prepared
piecrust dough

2 or 3 nectarines

5 1/2 oz (150 g) hazelnuts

1. Boil the milk with 1/2 vanilla bean split into two. Beat 1 egg yolk with 1/8 cup (35 g) superfine sugar in a bowl until the mixture turns white and frothy; add 2 tsp (10 g) cornstarch without mixing it in too much. Pour the boiling milk into the bowl while beating continuously.

2. Decant the mixture into a saucepan with a solid base and warm over low heat until it starts to simmer, while continuing to beat. Make sure you thoroughly scrape the bottom of the saucepan. Allow to cool.

3. Work 4 1/2 oz (125 g) butter using a fork to obtain a creamy consistency. Add the ground almonds, 1 generous cup (125 g) confectioner's sugar, and 1 egg yolk, while briskly working the mixture; add the rest of the cornstarch. Blend the vanilla cream into this mixture, one spoonful at a time.

4. Heat the oven to 410 °F (210 °C). Roll out the dough, place it in a buttered pie dish, and top with the rest of the superfine sugar. Fill it with the almond cream, and top with the finely sliced nectarine quarters and thinly sliced hazelnuts. Dust generously with confectioner's sugar. Bake for 30 minutes; turn it out of the pie dish while it's still warm.

N.B: using the same method as this nectarine tart, you could make a fresh fig tart, and garnish it with crushed pecans.

Recommended drinks

Coteaux-du-Layon
Montlouis
Barsac

Menu suggestions

1. Serve artichoke hearts filled with taramasalata as an appetizer, followed by slices of broiled lamb with navy beans for the main course.

2. You could also serve salade niçoise as an appetizer, followed by fresh pasta filled with basil and parmesan for the main course.

Fruit valentine

A party dish

Serves 4
Preparation: 5 minutes
Cooking: 25 minutes

Ingredients

Prepared puff pastry dough

3½ oz (100 g) butter

1 glass milk

2 small eggs

1 tbsp (15 g) superfine sugar

½ sachet vanilla sugar

1 tbsp (15 g) cornstarch

1 orange

Crème fraîche

1 pear or 1 large yellow peach

2 or 3 clementines

3 kiwis

2 or 3 pineapple slices

A few fresh cherries

Apple jelly

Confectioner's sugar

Salt

1. Bake the dough "à blanc": roll it out, put it into a buttered, heart-shaped tart mold, and line the pastry shell with wax paper and dried navy beans; bake in the oven at 445 °F (230 °C) for 25 minutes. Make sure you fold the dough over on itself toward the interior of the tart all around the edge, so that the thickness of the edge is doubled. If you do not have a heart-shaped mold, use a round one.

2. Prepare the cream while the pastry shell is cooling: combine 1 glass of milk, the egg yolks, superfine sugar, vanilla sugar, and cornstarch in a saucepan. Beat the mixture with a whisk and heat, while stirring.

3. As soon as it has boiled, take it off the heat. While it is still hot, add 2 or 3 tbsp orange juice and a little finely grated orange peel; next, when the milk is cold, add a few spoonfuls of crème fraîche.

4. Peel the pear and halve it, and remove the core and pips. Poach it very lightly in a small amount of highly sweetened water. Peel the clementines and remove the pith from each quarter; peel the kiwis and finely slice them. Cut up the pineapple slices into pieces. You can use a large, yellow peach instead of a pear.

5. Spread the cream over the pastry shell then garnish with the fruits you have prepared. Dilute the apple jelly in a minute trickle of warm water and generously brush the fruits with it. Brush the edge of the tart with apple jelly and sprinkle some confectioner's sugar over.

Recommended drinks

Champagne rosé
Sauternes
Bellet

Menu suggestions

1. For a very festive menu, serve caviar as an appetizer, followed by roast rack of lamb and soufflé potatoes for the main course.

2. You could also start the meal with a scallop salad, followed by tournedos Rossini for the main course.

Index

PHOTOGRAPHIC CREDITS

All the photos in this book are taken by Michel Barberousse, except for:Front cover:
STOCKFOOD France/Studio X/Köb Ulrike (bottom); from left to right: GETTY-IMAGES/FoodPix/Brian Hagiwara;
SUCRÉ SALÉ/P. Gaurier; TOP/J.F. Riviere; SUCRÉ-SALÉ/A.Caste; MARIE-CLAIRE/design Jacqueline Saulnier, photo André Martin.
Back cover: SUCRÉ SALÉ/A.Caste (bottom); Photo Alto/SUCRÉ SALÉ (top)Outside back cover, from left to right: Jean-Blaise Hall/PhotoAlto;
SUCRÉ SALÉ/Bananastock: STOCKFOOD France/StudioX/ChrisMeier;SUCRÉ SALÉ/Bananastock; Jean-Blaise Hall/PhotoAlto